COLLINS LONDON & GLASGOW in association with THE CONDE NAST PUBLICATIONS LTD

HOUSE & GARDEN DICTIONARY OF DESIGN & DECORATION

Published by COLLINS LONDON & GLASGOW
in association with THE CONDE NAST PUBLICATIONS LTD 1973

The material which originally appeared in *House & Garden*
© 1962-71 The Condé Nast Publications Ltd. This revised and enlarged edition
© 1973 The Condé Nast Publications Ltd

ISBN 0 00 435092 8

Printed in Great Britain by William Collins Sons & Co Ltd

DICTIONARY OF DESIGN & DECORATION

HIS DICTIONARY was essentially a journalistic enterprise, sponsored by the growing post-war popular interest in subjects, which, pre-war, had been considered the preserve of specialists and dilettantes.

Architecture, for example, had mainly been a subject for historians and archaeologists – even, occasionally, for architects – but rarely a subject for school study, radio and television entertainment or a hobby for civil servants, soldiers, sailors or tourists.

Furniture and decoration, whether period or modern, were also somewhat esoteric pleasures, usually reserved for the rich and their favourite decorators and furnishing houses. Hence the somewhat doleful appearance of such characters in theatrical revues and cinematic comedies.

Now all is changed. Far more people than footnote-specialists are interested in the influence of Hawksmoor upon Vanbrugh at Castle Howard and Blenheim; the impact of Neo-classicism notions upon furniture design; the ingenuities of Thomas Jefferson at Monticello. And a guest genuinely interested in the fact that he is seated at a table designed by Duncan Phyfe or Thomas Hope or on a chair designed by Eames and not Breuer would not now be regarded as an outlandish eccentric creature.

So it seemed a reasonable, even logical procedure to publish monthly sections dealing with aspects of design and decoration which would prove of interest to a widespread and ever-widening public. The alphabetical approach had an invincible appeal. Each of us has a pet fantasy or hobby on which he or she would like to compile a dictionary, however rudimentary. Trial entries were prepared and a pair of young researchers began to sort out relevant illustrative material, with but one editorial proviso or injunction: conventional photographs and frequently-seen drawings were to be eschewed from the beginning.

Reginald Williams, then the chairman of *Vogue, House & Garden* and other Condé Nast publications, and possessed of a paradoxically sceptical yet encouraging attitude towards the projects, proposals and general poppycock of his editorial staffs, said 'Why not? You'll probably get as far as E and then lose interest. But I suppose we can always say the editor's had a stroke.'

Yet here is the *Dictionary of Design and Decoration*, A – Z, vastly revised and extended in response to all those many enquirers – particularly school-teachers and other instructive numeros, who, through the years, were always wanting to know when the sections would be published in book form.

Here, too, I would like to thank the scores of designers and decorators who provided us with data concerning their careers; the curators and archivists who did the same for those long dead; the dealers and owners who provided pieces to photograph or photographs to reproduce – and, above all, my editorial associates listed below. Their numerical paucity is some indication of their prodigious labours.

Editor: **Robert Harling**
Art Editor: **Alex Kroll**
Editorial associates: **Ann Barr, Nick Harris, Leonie Higton, Rosemary Lamont**

Alvar Aalto

Aalto, Alvar (*b* 1898). One of the world's most eminent architects. Aalto was born at Alajarvi in North Central Finland and studied at the School of Architecture of the Helsinki Polytechnic. He worked for a short period in the drawing office of Gunnar Asplund (qv), a famous Swedish architect who designed much of the 1930 Stockholm Exhibition. In 1924 Aalto married Aino Marsio, who had studied with him, and they worked together until her death in 1949.

Much of Aalto's early work was commissioned as a result of competitions. One such commission was the tuberculosis sanatorium at Paimio (1929–33), which, through its advanced planning and use of new materials – plate glass and reinforced concrete – had a profound influence on the evolution of modern architecture.

Between the completion of Paimio and World War II, Aalto's industrial buildings included the cellulose factory at Sumila (1936–9) on the shores of the eastern Baltic, with staff housing among the surrounding pine forests. Another of his brilliant innovations was the ceiling of the lecture hall at

Viipuri, which was constructed of narrow strips of wood, rising from behind the lecturer to flow in undulating curves over the length of the auditorium. Aalto achieved similar effects in the Finnish Pavilion at the New York World Fair of 1939, using a serpentine wall which towered dramatically above the exhibits. He has also designed a number of houses, including the Villa Mairea, built on a lavish scale for the head of a timber firm. The delicate textures of waxed timber, whitewashed brick, and tiles are exploited in this building, which is planned as a coherent unit around a garden court, containing a swimming pool and sauna.

Aalto designed all the furniture for the Paimio clinic, and has since designed many mass-produced pieces in plywood. In these, sheets and strips of ply are moulded to the curves of the human body. Aalto's technique involves using thin strips of wood glued together, which he terms 'wood macaroni', since the wood is bent to form the arms and legs of chairs.

At the end of World War II, Aalto was visiting professor at the Massachusetts Institute of Technology (where he designed a student dormitory block), but he has always felt that his rightful place is in Finland. In recent years he has been chiefly concerned with the planning of new communities, often in collaboration with other architects. He redeveloped Rovaniemi, the war-scarred capital of Lapland, and the northern industrial centre Oulu, which he replanned on a group of islands in a river estuary. At Otaniemi, on another island site overlooking the archipelago, he designed a new group of buildings for the University of Helsinki.

The Villa Mairea, Noormarkku, by Aalto, 1939

A house at Bazoches, France: typical of Aalto's interiors

Chairs and stool designed by Aalto for Artek

Adam. *The decoration of the entrance hall of Harewood House, Yorkshire, with dark red porphyry-marble ceiling and pilasters, 1758–71*

Cane stools designed by Eero Aarnio

Abacus on a temple

Aarnio, Eero (*b* 1932). Finnish industrial and interior designer. Aarnio studied at the Helsinki Institute of Industrial Art, then in 1962 opened his own office at Niittykumpu, Tontunmäki. He has designed a wide range of products, notably steel and fibreglass furniture. He held a one-man exhibition of fibreglass furniture in Helsinki and Stockholm in 1968. He has contributed to exhibitions throughout Europe and has won a number of awards including first prizes at the Scandinavian Park Furniture Competition, Stockholm (1964), and the International Furniture Competition at Cantù, Italy (1965); he also received an award from the American Institute of Decorators. His best known design is probably his low Pastilli chair (1968), which won the American Interior Design International Award.

Abacus. The architectural term for the flat slab on top of the capital of a column; the abacus carries the architrave. In the Greek Doric capital, the abacus is a straightforward rectangular section with no moulding, but in the Roman Doric the abacus is more decorative, carrying a moulding round the upper edge. In other orders the rectangular or square working is replaced by a curving section.

The working of the abacus is often the only means of determining the date of the capital.

Abbotsford furniture. Early Victorian mock-medieval furniture in a very heavy and extravagant Gothic-ecclesiastical style. Its vogue has been attributed to the historical novels of Sir Walter Scott, who had a mock-medieval library at his home, Abbotsford.

Abercrombie, Sir Patrick (Leslie) (1879–1957). Abercrombie was without doubt the foremost British town-planner of this century. He was responsible for a creative reconsideration of urban and rural planning, although it is arguable that many of the lessons he taught have still not been properly absorbed. He first made his mark as professor of civic design at Liverpool University (1915–35), during the university's most fruitful period of intellectual activity. He was afterwards professor of town planning at London University (1935–46). He is chiefly known for his comprehensive *County of London Plan* (prepared with J H Forshaw and published in 1943) and the *Greater London Plan*, published under his general direction in the following year. But he also prepared similar, though less ambitious, reports on the planning problems of Plymouth, Edinburgh, Hull, Clydeside, and Bournemouth. These reports were notable for Abercrombie's insistence upon the necessity for seeing the problem as a whole. He contended that transport was indivisibly linked with housing, and that population and industry could not be discussed in isolation from the problems of land use.

Abutment. Any solid structure, part of a wall or pier, placed to resist the lateral thrust of an arch or vault.

Acacia-wood. *Robinia pseudoacacia.* A native of North America, but also found in Britain and elsewhere. Although it has been dismissed as 'suitable for gateposts', the decorative qualities of this yellowish wood appear to effect in much excellent British and Continental furniture. It is often used for inlay work and banding in the less sophisticated pieces of Georgian cabinet-work. Acacia is an outstandingly strong wood and rivals oak for durability.

Acanthus. An architectural motif used in ancient times as the decorative motif on capitals of the Corinthian and Composite orders. It derived from a simplification of the leaves of *Acanthus spinosus.* The acanthus leaf has since been the basis for quantities of carvings, mouldings, and stampings in architecture and cabinetmaking, particularly of the Regency era, when it became a standard item in the mock-antique repertoire. Extensive use inevitably debased the motif, and within a few years of the Regency period any apprentice carver could cut a rough-and-ready acanthus frieze around a heavy bookcase. Soon, wood-working machines could do mechanically perfect and aesthetically doleful acanthus strips by the yard. The fact remains that in many of its earlier Regency variants the motif had considerable charm, particularly when executed in brass and ormolu.

Achievement of arms. The heraldic term for a complete display of armorial bearings.

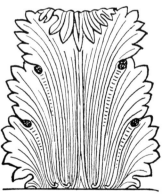

Acanthus (Greek)

Acanthus (Roman)

Moulded fibre-glass chair by Eero Aarnio

Ackermann aquatint of the Horse Guards

Ackermann, Rudolph (1764–1834). A German who settled in England and in 1795 established a fine art publishing business in London. Ackermann's Repository was a combined print shop, factory, and drawing-school in the Strand. In the next few decades the majority of British aquatints were Ackermann prints, produced and sold at his Repository. They were coloured by hand by an army of skilled watercolourists, trained by Ackermann himself. Prout, Alken, Rowlandson, Cooper Henderson, and T H Shepherd were among the well-known artists who provided the originals.

Lithography was still scarcely known as a fine art. In 1817 Ackermann set up a lithographic press, the first of its kind in England, and printed a topical series of military prints of Wellington's campaigns with it.

Two years later he published *A Complete Course of Lithography* by its inventor, J A Senefelder. Ackermann was thus a pioneer of the process that was to supersede the aquatint.

Ackermann initiated the English fashion annuals, beginning in 1825 with *Forget-me-not*. Until 1828 he brought out a monthly *Repository of Arts, Literature and Fashions*; Rowlandson was a regular contributor. Other books (all illustrated in aquatint) include *The Microcosm of London* (1808–11), *Westminster Abbey* (1812), *The University of Oxford* (1814), *The University of Cambridge* (1815), *The Rhine* (1820), and *The World in Miniature* (1821–6).

Acropolis (Greek, *akros* 'high', *polis* 'city'). The Acropolis is usually thought of as a single place – the citadel of Athens – but in fact the word is a general term, and other examples of these hill forts, palaces, and/or temples existed in ancient Greece. The Acropolis of Athens, with its complex of buildings, has had an impact upon the architecture of the western world which has persisted for over 2,500 years. Here were to be found all the elements of what we now think of as institutional and monumental architecture: the vast and impressive portico with majestic, towering columns, the pointed pediment, the unbroken classical gable lines, the sculptures of ancient deities – elements which have been endlessly duplicated from Moscow to Minneapolis. In their modern form they derive not from Greece but from the architecture of Palladio.

Acroterion. Pedestal for a statue, urn, or other ornament placed at the apex and lower angles of a pediment. Used loosely for the ornament itself.

Act of Parliament clock. A mural clock made in Britain from the early eighteenth and throughout the nineteenth century. It owes its name to Pitt's Act of 1797 taxing clocks and watches. The Act was repealed the following year, but in the meantime gave an impetus to the popularity of Act of Parliament clocks, which generally hung in public places such as taverns, inns and coffee-houses.

This kind of clock has a large unglazed dial and a weight-driven movement encased in a small trunk.

Robert Adam

Adam family. William Adam (1688–1748), the most important Scottish architect of his time, had four sons, of whom the most gifted was Robert Adam (1728–92). The rise of the Adam family is one of the most romantic in the history of architecture, and the influence of the father on his sons should not be overlooked, for William Adam was an energetic tycoon as well as an architect of considerable achievement.

Yet the works of Robert Adam are those we seek out and return to again and again, for his were among the most graceful, decorative, and revolutionary designs in the whole history of British architecture and interior decoration.

Like many other men of genius, Robert Adam trained himself by a prodigious amount of study and hard work. He used his patrimony to visit Italy in 1754 to study ancient and Renaissance art. During his four-year residence and travels abroad he carried out a survey of Diocletian's palace at Spalato (now Split) in Dalmatia (1757), and on these studies based his famous folio.

Adam was an intensely ambitious, single-minded man, and on his return to England quickly established himself as the leading architect-decorator of his time. He contended that the architect should be responsible for the building, furnishing, and decoration of his houses, and that only in this way could a coherent decorative scheme be achieved.

Within a few years he numbered several aristocrats among his patrons, including Lord Coventry at Croome Court (from 1760), Lord Shelbourne at Bowood (1761–4), Sir Nathaniel Curzon at Kedleston (from 1759), and the Duke of Northumber-

The Acropolis, Athens

Mid-eighteenth-century Act of Parliament clock. Over 5 ft high

The north front of Osterley Park designed by Robert Adam

The south front of Kedleston Hall, Derbyshire

The library, Osterley Park, Middlesex

Veined alabaster columns and stuccoed ceiling at Kedleston

land at Syon. Other patrons were Robert Child at Osterley (1761–80) and Edwin Lascelles, later Lord Harewood, at Harewood (1758–71). Many of Adam's commissions were for the remodelling of existing houses, which made great demands upon his ingenuity and versatility. His ill-fated Adelphi project (1768–72, now demolished), for twenty-four impressive houses on the Embankment, ran into endless

difficulties; financial disaster was only averted by disposing of the property by lottery.

Adam was a prolific designer of great originality and wide-ranging distinction, for he designed commodes and ceilings, chimney-pieces and chairs. His mastery of the classical manner enabled him to evolve a highly personal Neo-classic style which dominated English decoration in the last quarter of the eighteenth

century, and even as late as 1812 Sir John Soane spoke admiringly of 'the electric power of this revolution in Art.'

Apart from his gay, elegant, and wholly assured interiors, Adam is chiefly renowned today for the superb furniture he designed for Harewood, Osterley, and other houses. He employed several of the leading cabinet-makers of his day, including Thomas Chippendale (junior),

and commissioned artists such as Angelica Kauffmann and her husband Antonio Zucchi for the painted ceilings and furniture.

His work deeply influenced London cabinetmakers, and a great many pieces were made in the Adam manner.

In 1773, in association with his younger brother and partner, James, Adam began to publish, in parts, his *Works in Architecture*.

Santa Fé's Palace of the Governors, built of adobe in 1610

Adams, William (1745–1805). British potter who lived at Greengates in Staffordshire. He was a friend, pupil, and imitator of Josiah Wedgwood, and one of a large and famous Staffordshire potting family.

He made black basalt, jasper and stoneware, and also cream-coloured earthenware and blue transfer printed ware, all very much in the style of Wedgwood. His ware was sometimes marked 'Adams & Co' or just 'Adams', but was often unmarked.

Adobe. A method of building known to antedate the Aztec civilization. Adobe dwellings were made of unbaked bricks of clay and water, without straw, each layer of bricks having to dry before the next could be added.

Early Spanish missions were made with adobe bricks, for though adobe was used for the most humble dwellings it was also employed where stone was in short supply. Some of the most notable examples of adobe architecture are to be found in the south-west of the United States, particularly in New Mexico.

Aedicule. An opening framed by columns and a pediment. Although the term was originally limited to such openings in shrines, it now has a general application.

Aerostyle. Vitruvius used this term to describe columns spaced at distances of four or more diameters. This is very wide spacing.

Affleck, Thomas (1740–95). American cabinetmaker. Affleck was born in Scotland and emigrated to Philadelphia in 1763. He became a member of the Philadelphia school of cabinetmakers, working primarily in the Queen Anne and early Chippendale styles. He was known for his highboys, lowboys, and chairs; and in 1794 made a number of pieces for Congress Hall.

Afrormosia. *Afrormosia elata.* A West African hardwood which in many ways resembles teak, though it is less expensive. It has been used widely, both in solid and veneer forms, by furniture manufacturers.

Agate ware. A marbled or mottled earthenware, made by blending different coloured clays. The 'bats' of clay were pressed together, cut with a wire, pressed together and cut again until the colours were intermingled, giving an effect that resembled agate. The markings went through the whole body of the ware, which was then finished with a lead glaze. A kind of agate ware was made in England as early as the late seventeenth century by John Dwight of Fulham, and later by Dr Thomas Wedgwood (c 1730). It was also copied by other potters.

Air twist stems. These were an English innovation, made from c 1740 to c 1770, and sometimes advertised as 'wormed' or 'wrought' glasses. They probably developed from the accidental trapping of an air bubble in the

Staffordshire teapot in agate ware, c 1745. White with red markings

base or stem of a glass, the bubble becoming drawn out into an elongated 'tear.' It was discovered that several of these tears could be introduced by pricking the base of the bowl with a blunt instrument before covering it with a further gathering of glass, and that air spirals could be formed by giving the stem a twist as it was being drawn out.

Aisles. Lateral divisions parallel to the nave of a church, and usually divided from it by piers or columns.

Alberti, Leone Battista (1404–72). Italian architect, scholar, mathematician, philosopher, theorist, poet, and genius of the Italian Renaissance. More surely than any other man, Alberti embodied the Renaissance ideal of the 'universal man.' He was probably born in Genoa, the illegitimate son of a Florentine exile, Lorenzo Alberti. At an early age he was sent to Barizizza in Padua, where he received a humanist education, after which

Lowboy made by Thomas Affleck

Eighteenth-century air twist stems showing a variety of spirals

S Andrea Mantua, designed by Alberti, 1470

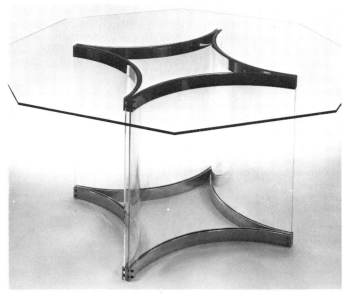

Octagonal glass and chrome dining table by Albrizzi

he studied law at Bologna University. Then, on the completion of his formal education, he took up a prolonged study of mathematics, literature, philosophy and allied subjects. He became a fine athlete, a polished conversationalist, and an authority in most fields of human knowledge.

He took service with the Papacy and travelled extensively with various ecclesiastics, perhaps as far as Germany and Burgundy. The next years he spent in Rome, the northern Italian cities, and especially Florence, where he was in contact with leading figures of the early Renaissance. In Florence the published his *Della Pittura* (1436), a treatise on painting dedicated to (among others) Brunelleschi.

From 1447 to 1455 he was an inspector of monuments for the Papacy, an appointment which provided him with opportunities for practical engineering, and

reconstruction and restoration (S Stefano Rotondo). He designed the Palazzo Rucellai, Florence (1445–51), and the recasing of S Francesco, Rimini (1450), beginning its transformation into a monument to Sigismondo Malatesta. During this period Alberti published his major architectural treatise, *De Re Aedificatoria* (1452).

Although Alberti was forty before he began to practise architecture – and even then his work involved only design and not construction – his few buildings represented a great contribution to the early Renaissance. Academic but not dogmatic, they Seated the scholarly foundations for the Renaissance style. His major works were the façade of S Maria Novella (1456–70), the Shrine of the Holy Sepulchre (1467), and Rucellai chapel (1467) in Florence, and S Sebastiano (1460) and S Andrea (1470) in Mantua.

Albrizzi, Baron Alexander R de C (*b* 1934). Italian furniture designer. Born in Venice, Albrizzi studied in Italy and Switzerland, and took a law degree at the University of Florence. He worked as a journalist in Paris before taking up interior decoration and furniture design as a full-time occupation.

He decorated a number of houses and apartments in London for private clients before opening his own shop. Trestle tables with heavy glass tops and metal stands are among his most successful designs.

Alcove. A recess in the wall of a room, primarily used for decoration. In France a bed was sometimes enclosed within this space, which could be partitioned off by drawing curtains across the opening.

Alder-wood. *Alnus.* Found in American, North African and European temperate zones. It is often used for cottage furniture, but only rarely for more sophisticated pieces. It is fairly pale wood which can be polished to a richly textured surface – somewhat like maple. Among cabinetmakers, alder is sometimes called 'Scottish mahogany.'

Aleijadinho, António Francisco Lisboa (1738–1814). Brazilian architect and sculptor. Aleijadinho was a mulatto, the illegitimate son of a Portuguese architect and a native woman. He gained his greatest renown as a sculptor, although his design for the church of São Francisco in Ouro Preto, which occupied his energies for twenty-eight years (1766–94), has been called 'a completely evolved design', for he designed and decorated

Alcove by William Kent

Modern alcove in a converted mill

Monticello, Charlottesville, Virginia, designed by Thomas Jefferson, 1769

Sao Francisco, Sao Joao d'El Rey, Minas Gerais, Brazil

American architecture. Architectural initiative in the thirteen American colonies came from England, with a time lag of anything up to half a century. Around 1670 the designer of Bacon's Castle, Surrey County, Virginia, built a brick house in a style that had been popular in England around 1610. Sixty years later the builder of Westover, Charles City County, executed a palatial country house design in a style that in England could be mistaken for c 1680. Detailing was often much more up-to-date, since much of it was shipped complete from England.

This time lag was only short-ened by the appearance of architectural treatises (Campbell's *Vitruvius Brittanicus* from 1715; Gibbs's *Book of Architecture* in 1728), themselves a product of architectural controversy. The ideological serious-mindedness of the Burlington group made no impression on colonial architects, whose aesthetic was based upon 'fancy'; so it was from Gibbs rather than Campbell that they took their ideas. Gibbs's elegant but rational late Baroque was translated into the local material, wood. Hence colonial architecture of the mid-century tends to be up-to-date; Dr Kearsley's Christ Church, Phila-

The Mission House, Stockbridge, Massachusetts, 1739

the entire building. He virtually repeated this design at São Pedro at Mariana (1771–3). Aleijadinho's work was the first step towards a Brazilian architecture independent of that of Portugal; this was partly due to his genius and partly to the softer materials in which his structures were built. Aleijadinho's other major works are São Joao d'El Rey (1774–1804) and the sculptures and staircases for Bom Jesus de Matozinhos, Congonhas do Campo (1800–5).

Alkanet. A red dye made from the root of the anchusa plant and used chiefly for the staining of woods. Sheraton gives a recipe for it in his *Cabinet Dictionary* 1803).

Amboyna. *Pterospermum incum.* A West Indian wood which found favour with cabinetmakers in the eighteenth century and the Regency period. Its richly figured, multi-knotted, curly grain, and warm honey-gold colour, made amboyna a splendid foil for the straighter grain of rosewood and mahogany, and it was much used both as a veneer and in solid form. It was widely employed for banding of large circular dining tables, and for bureaux, bookcases, and cabinets.

Ambulatory (Latin *ambulare*, 'to walk'). An aisle around the East end of a church. It was used for processional purposes and so is particularly characteristic of pilgrimage churches.

Mount Vernon, Virginia: home of George Washington, completed 1759

Independence Hall, Philadelphia

delphia, was begun in 1727, only one year after the completion of Gibbs's St Martin-in-the-Fields, on which it is clearly based. This architecture is also pretty and sometimes very clever, especially in the hands of Peter Harrison (1716–75).

This tradition was continued in the Federalist period by Charles Bulfinch (1763–1844), who, with a characteristic blend of visual felicity and intellectual vacuity, managed to absorb the rival programmes of both Adam and Chambers, the latter notably in Bulfinch's Boston State House of 1793.

After the Revolution, American architecture underwent a process similar to that which English architecture went

through after the Glorious Revolution (1688), the intellectual master-of-ceremonies being, in both cases, John Locke. Thomas Jefferson (1743–1826) sought in 'natural law' the ultimate sanction in matters both social and architectural; but when in 1786 he visited England, where 'nature' had supplanted 'fancy' as a critical canon half a century earlier, he found contemporary architecture 'wretched.' In France, however, he saw the work of antiquity at first hand (Maison Carrée, Nîmes), and a contemporary architecture that was clearly its equal (in particular, Rousseau's Hôtel de Salm). Whereas his own house, Monticello, begun in 1769, was derived from English textbooks (Robert

Morris and Gibbs), the Virginia State Capitol, begun to his design before his return from France in 1789, is a contemporary version of the Maison Carrée, ie a temple put to modern use.

Jefferson's part-intellectual, part-archeological approach was overshadowed by the mature Neo-classicism of Benjamin Latrobe (1764–1820). Latrobe was a pupil of S P Cockerell, and fully acquainted with the latest European work. His Bank of Philadelphia (1798) incorporates a domed rotunda within an Ionic temple with an ease that makes the correctness of the Virginia State Capitol look irrational; while the monumental scale and awe-inspiring bareness of his Baltimore Catholic Cathedral

(1805–18), despite its obviously European pedigree, reveals an originality which Jefferson could not equal. From 1803 to 1817 Latrobe was federal surveyor of public buildings; his pupil, Robert Mills (1781–1855), was government architect and engineer from 1836 to 1851; another pupil, William Strickland (1788–1854), established himself in Philadelphia, the cultural capital during the Federalist period, and in 1818 acquired a national (if not international) reputation with a Doric edifice, the Branch Bank of the United States. Furthermore, all three were engineers as well as architects. Their influential positions and their omnicompetence established Neo-classicism as the characteristic mode of a newly expanding country that already needed banks, factories and engineering works as well as state capitols and court houses. Strickland's Philadelphia Merchants' Exchange (1832–4), in a highly accomplished linear style, is reminiscent of C R Cockerell or Hittorff. Alexander Parris (1780–1852) provided Boston, hitherto under the retrograde influence of Bulfinch, with a market hall (Quincy Market, 1823) and granite warehouses of flat, grid-like design, equal to the best English commercial work of the time. Town and Davis provided state capitols for Connecticut (1827–31), Indiana (1831–5), and North Carolina (1833), and equipped New York City with Neo-classical housing. Isaiah Rogers (1800–69) built Neo-classical hotels of an un-

Tryon Palace, New Bern, North Carolina, completed 1770

precedented size and efficiency all over the country. Mills's obelisks and government offices contrive to make Washington one of the most striking Neo-classical cities in the world. At another level, local builders' guides provided the designs for countless Greek mansions for private citizens.

With greater architectural awareness, Americans were unable to ignore developments in England during the 1840s and 50s. The new ideas of these decades came to America by way of English periodicals such as *The Builder* or *Building News*. But by contrast with the 1720s, British influence was confined to general principles. For instance, in the 1840s the Picturesque aesthetic made its appearance, but in a variety of strange guises. The books of A J Downing (1815–52) made a very real contribution to small house design, but treated questions of style with a cavalier eclecticism that embraced everything from Italian farmhouse to Tudor cottage. Downing's friend, A J Davis, employed Grecian for public buildings (Colonnade Row, New York City, 1832), Italianate for villas (Munn House, Utica, New York, 1854), and the fake castle for Hudson Valley magnates (Ericstan, Tarrytown, New York, 1854). He also popularized the gabled, veranda-ed, and elaborately barge-boarded cottage advocated by Downing (William J

Rotch House, New Bedford, Massachusetts, 1845), and despite his eclecticism, displayed the same regard as contemporary English architects for stylistic appropriateness. The same is true of the slightly older Richard Upjohn (1802–78), who used Pugin's interpretation of Gothic for Trinity Church, New York City (1839–46), the round-arched style of Schinkel or Persius for the Congregational Church of the Pilgrims, Brooklyn (1844–6), and Italianate for Edward King's villa at Newport, Rhode Island (1845–7). But of greater significance than Upjohn's stylistic virtuosity is the vertical board-and-batten construction of his small wooden churches in New England, which parallels English developments such as Pugin's direct expression of construction and Street's interest in vernacular architecture.

Stylistic appropriateness may also have prompted the adoption of the French Second Empire style to express the extravagant, opulent period of the Grant administration (1868–76), culminating in Mullet and Gilman's State, War and Navy Department at Washington (1871–5). The opulence and plasticity of Gilman's Boston City Hall (1862–5), with its densely arcaded treatment of the wall surface, is closer to British models than to the flatter, more linear taste of contemporary France. But fidelity to a prototype, whether French or English, was not the major concern of American architects, who were more interested in using this style as a vehicle for ingenious planning and stylistic originality. This is as true for such public buildings as Renwick's Vassar College Hall, Poughkeepsie, New York (where the plan is French, but the details are not, 1860), as for Gilman's mansarded town houses in the Back Bay area of Boston.

The Anglo-American relationship is most clearly illustrated by the American reaction to Ruskin. *The Seven Lamps of Architecture* (1849) and *The Stones of Venice* (1851–3), together with Street's *Brick and Marble Architecture* (1855), were received in America with even greater enthusiasm than in England. Yet only a few buildings reveal a specific visual indebtedness to these books. The best example is Ware and van Brunt's Memorial Hall at Harvard College (1870–8), the polychrome brickwork of which is reminiscent of Butterfield. At Yale College, New Haven, the Second Empire protagonist Richard M

Georgian church at Litchfield, Connecticut

Old Swedes church at Wilmington, Delaware, built in 1698

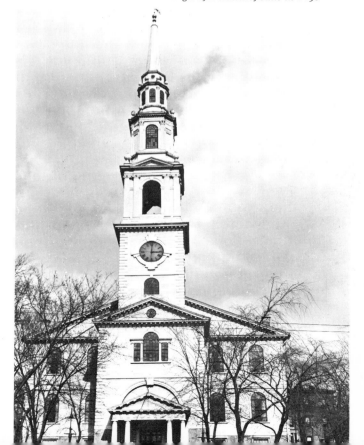

The Raleigh Tavern, Williamsburg

First Baptist Meeting House, Providence, Rhode Island, 1774–5

Quincy Market (Faneuil Hall), Boston, by Alexander Parris, 1823

Carpenters' Hall, Philadelphia, by Robert Smith, 1770–5

Hunt (1827–95) provided an echo of Toulon with his Divinity School of 1869; and Russell Sturgis' (1836–1909) Farnham Hall, also 1869, echoes Waterhouse or even Webb. On the other hand, a major Gothic monument in New York City, Renwick's St Patrick's Cathedral (1859), shows no evident trace of Ruskin's influence. Nearly all these architects built in other styles as well; and in domestic house design there appear to be no visual echoes of Ruskin at all.

It seems that Americans read Ruskin for his aesthetics rather than for his architectural theory.

Out of the mid-century period of gestation an unmistakably indigenous architecture emerged around 1870 – one characterized by honest expression of materials, an original (or interpretative) approach to style, and a rigidly functionalist planning. The powerful buildings in Philadelphia by Frank Furness (1839–1902) are the first indications of the new approach, and demon-

strate the link between High Victorian Gothic and the proto-modernism of Richardson, Louis H Sullivan, and Frank Lloyd Wright.

It was from Ruskinian Gothic that H H Richardson (1838–86) acquired an interest in the quality of his buildings' masonry, which led him away from Gothic (Grace Episcopal Church, Medford, Massachusetts, 1867–8) towards Romanesque (Trinity Church, Boston, 1872–7), and ultimately towards Armenian or

Syrian (Crane Library, Quincy, Massachusetts, 1880–3), a style which became known through the French archæologist De Vogüé after 1865. The sense of mountainous stoniness which Richardson developed was assisted by dramatically rusticated granite blocks of Piranesian scale. This alone would have established his reputation (as similar preoccupations had established Furness's), but the implications of his work were still more far-reaching. Although his decor-

Virginia State Capitol, designed by Jefferson, begun 1789

Andalusia near Philadelphia by Nicholas Biddle and T V Walters, 1833

ation was eclectic, the originality of its treatment make its stylistic origins irrelevant. Richardson's most monumental work, the Marshall Field Wholesale Store in Chicago (1885–7), seemed so obviously derived from the Renaissance Palazzo Strozzi that he capped it with a cornice of thirteenth-century crockets, culled from the most abstract period of medieval sculpture. On the other hand, Richardson's composition was rarely derivative, except in his ecclesiastical work; it was determined by a combination of functional and picturesque considerations. The dramatic asymmetry of the functionally planned Allegheny County Gaol, Pittsburgh (1884–8), links Richardson to both the 1840s and the 1890s.

The new approach had shown itself in domestic architecture around 1850. The 'stick style' (as in Newton's Sturtevant House, Middletown, Rhode Island, 1872), represented a development from Downing's 'bracketted' style in two ways. In the first place, the casual eclecticism of the bracketted cottages was gradually modified to an almost astylar (or at least stylistically inscrutable) treatment, owing an only just discernible allegiance to Gothic or Second Empire. Second, the adoption of board-and-batten construction led to a clear expression of the wooden structure within (and frequently without); in the mid-West this was usually of the new lightweight 'balloon frame' type, a product of industrialisation popularized by William E Bell's *Carpentry Made Easy* (1858).

By the time the building trade got going again after the panic

The Capitol, Washington, central block: W Thornton and others, 1792–1828; wings and dome: T U Walter, 1851–65

of 1873, the influence of Norman Shaw had begun to modify the stick style. As Shaw had pointed out the virtues of the Queen Anne vernacular in England, so Arthur Little (1852–1925) publicized the Colonial style in *Early New England Interiors* (1878). Specifically Shavian details such as Sussex tile-hanging were translated into a more American idiom and applied to American exteriors in the form of shingles. Interiors, especially those of McKim, Mead and White's

houses, began to reflect the European interest in Japanese decoration. This eclecticism represented a move away from the more astylar approach of the mid-century stick style; nor was it qualified by the sense of stylistic appropriateness that had distinguished the Picturesque. Queen Anne, Colonial, Sussex vernacular, and Japanese all played a part in the shingle style. Whereas the board-and-batten construction of the stick style revealed the structure, shingles

concealed it; and an attitude of 'art for art's sake' tended to prevail. The new developments in English planning were also made available through Shaw. This led to a still greater emphasis upon functionalism, irrespective of whether it created a picturesque disparate effect dependent upon subtly interpenetrating spaces and volumes (as in McKim, Mead and White's Isaac Bell House at Newport, Rhode Island, 1881–2), or whether it created a more compact and

House in Rhinebeck, New York, by A J Davis, 1844

Belle Grove, Louisiana, by Henry Howard, 1857, destroyed 1952

Jefferson Memorial, Washington: John Russell Pope, 1943

Lincoln Memorial, Washington: Henry Bacon, completed 1917

often symmetrical effect (as in the same architects' W G Low House, Bristol, Rhode Island, 1887). There was in any case a functionalist tradition in American small house architecture, inherited from the Picturesque and the stick style. E C Gardner (1836–1915), for instance, illustrated such practical designs as a one-roomed house for a spinster client in *Illustrated Homes, Describing Real Houses and Real People* (1875).

The move away from mid-century modernism towards fin-de-siècle self-indulgence reached its climax in the houses built by Frank Lloyd Wright around Chicago in the 1890s. The eclecticism of Shaw and the English Arts and Crafts movement finds its most extreme expression in Wright's preoccu-pation with the memorable decoration at his houses; he utilized styles ranging from Japanese to pre-Columbian, but – like Richardson, and Wright's own master, Sullivan – applied them with great originality. More specifically Shavian are the long horizontal window bands of River Forest Golf Club, Illinois (1888), although in Wright's Prairie houses Shavian tendencies towards horizontality are taken to a mannered extreme. Both aspects of shingle style planning can be seen in the symmetrical Winslow House, River Forest (1893), and the spreading Willits House, Highland Park (1902), both in Illinois; and the interpenetrating volumes of McKim, Mead and White's Bell House are handled even more cleverly in the Robie House, Chicago (1909). None-theless, Wright's relationship to mid-century functionalism is most clearly expressed in the Coonley House, Riverside, Illinois (1908), where the different volumes are 'zoned' according to their function.

A concurrent but independent development was that American architects began to take the lead in advanced industrial and commercial architecture. The development of a practicable form of elevator by Elisha Otis after 1857 made it possible to build considerably higher warehouses and offices than those of the advanced English architecture of the previous half-century, though these remained the stylistic models. Hunt's 1873 Tribune Building in New York City is the first building which can properly be called a sky-scraper; its nine storeys (260 ft) were nearly twice the height of any existing offices. Other advances were to follow, often in buildings that were not sky-scrapers at all. The 1871 fire in the Chicago Loop prompted a demand for new methods of construction that were fireproof: cast-iron buildings of the type developed around 1850 by James Bogardus (1800–74) had shown that unprotected metal buckled in great heat. Metal skeletons were then developed which could be sheathed in masonry piers. William Le Baron Jenney (1832–1907) invented by accident the principle of 'skyscraper construction', placing the masonry outer walls of his Home Insurance Company Office (1883–5) on an internal metal skeleton. In 1888–9 Bradford Lee Gilbert (1853–1911) applied this principle throughout to his Tower Building in New York City (a mere 119 ft). Daniel H Burnham (1846–1912) and John Wellborn Root (1850–91) overcame the problem of heavy construction on a soft base by spreading the foundations of their 1882–3 Montauk Block in Chicago.

With these technical innovations, skyscraper architecture became a reality, but a significant skyscraper style was not fully developed until *c* 1890. Several different modes of expression emerged. The Wainwright Building in St Louis (1890–1), by Dankmar Adler (1844–1900) and Louis Sullivan (1856–1924), emphasises the vertical structural components by running un-broken brick piers from the first floor to the cornice, with windows in recessed panels in between. This solution was taken

Harvard Memorial Hall

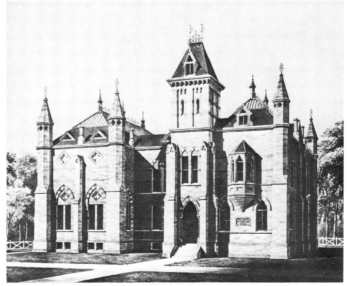

Street Hall, Yale University, by Peter D Wight, 1864

Cincinnati Music Hall, Ohio, 1878

State Capitol, Springfield, Illinois, finished 1888

still further by the same architects' Guaranty Building at Buffalo, New York (1894–5), where the piers are isolated at ground floor level in the manner of twentieth-century *pilotis*. By contrast, some architects attempted to minimize the number of storeys by subsuming two or more in a single arcade: this practice was followed by Richardson in the Marshall Field Store

The Schiller Building in Chicago Louis Sullivan, 1892

of 1885, the very high architectural quality of which blinded contemporaries to its essentially retrogressive character. It was followed by Adler and Sullivan's Auditorium Building, Chicago, in which the basement was filled out with mezzanines and yet another storey subsumed in the arcade. Indeterminacy, with identical windows set in a completely unarticulated façade, was a more 'honest' solution, perhaps more suited to the load-bearing walls of Burnham and Root's Monadnock Building (1891) than to Sullivan's Carson Pirie Scott Store, Chicago (1899–1901). In the Reliance Building (1890–1), Burnham and Root evolved a solution which later seemed of great significance: a glazed box with the structural skeleton reduced to a minimum, vertical integrity maintained by continuous oriels from first floor to roof, and the predominant horizontals expressed by the spandrels dividing window strip from window strip. It is worth speculating to what extent the formation of a skyscraper style was influenced by the French scholar and restorer Viollet-le-Duc (1814 –79), whose *Entretiens sur l'Architecture* were translated at Boston in 1875 and again in 1881. The great height and skeletal structure of the early skyscrapers were clearly analogous to Viollet-le-Duc's skeletal theory of Gothic buildings and to their height, unsurpassed until the 1880s. Certainly the linkage between the storeys of Jenney's Sears Roebuck Store (1889–90) is closer to Amiens Cathedral than to the Marshall Field Store.

The new architecture of the

period 1870–90 was not followed up but was succeeded by diametrically different styles. One was the internationally popular Neo-Baroque of the fin-de-siècle, represented in the USA by John H Duncan's Soldiers' and Sailors' Memorial Arch, Grand Army Plaza, Brooklyn (1892). Neo-Baroque in the USA eventually found a historical justification in the form of a Spanish colonial revival, popularized at the San Diego Exhibition of 1915 by Bertram G Goodhue (1869–1924). Irving Gill (1870–1936) built houses in California in a less Baroque variant of Spanish colonial that possesses an abstract simplicity reminiscent of Loos.

There was also a curious revival of the flattened linear style whose source was the Parisian Ecole des Beaux Arts of the 1830s and 1840s. The New York firm of McKim, Mead and White led the field in designing libraries in the manner of Labrouste (Boston Public Library, 1888–92) and Italianate palaces (Villard Houses, New York City, 1883–5). Buildings of this kind, which would not have been out of place in von Klenze's Munich, were still being put up in New York a century later (Racquet and Tennis Club, 1918). This development has no parallel in European architecture, although in painting its counterpart is the dream-like classicism of Puvis de Chavannes, who actually decorated the interior of Boston Public Library. Dream-like also was the 1893 World's Columbian Exposition, held at Chicago in a setting of lagoons and parkland by the

landscape architect F L Olmsted (1822–1903). At its most abstract, the severe Beaux Arts mode is reminiscent of Ledoux or Boullée, as in Reed, Stem, Warren, and Wetmore's Grand Central Station in New York City (1903–13). Other severe and linear styles were also favoured, such as Schinkelesque classicism (Henry Bacon's Lincoln Memorial, 1917) and a rather

Laboratory, Racine, Wisconsin: Frank Lloyd Wright, 1950

Kaufman House, Bear Run, Pennsylvania by Wright, 1936, cantilevered over a natural waterfall

French Palladianism (McKim, Mead and White's Hall of Fame in the Bronx, 1896–1900). The Anglo-Palladianism of Lord Burlington also made a belated appearance on the New York streets. In this atmosphere of heady eclecticism, Cass Gilbert (1859–1934) interpreted his Woolworth Building in New York City (1913) as a vertiginous Flemish cloth hall.

Modernism had survived in California in the form of a late variant of the shingle style, maintained largely by John Gaylen Howard (1864–1931), a pupil of Richardson who was dean of the school of architecture at California University. Charles S Green (1868–1957) and Henry M Greene (1870–1954) developed along similar lines to the early Wright, experimenting with space and mass by means of projecting roofs and huge verandas. Like Wright, they were influenced by Japanese architecture, for example, in their Gamble House in Pasadena, California (1908–9).

Wright continued to build in his earlier manner down to the mid-1920s, becoming more original in both decoration and planning. After a ten-year hiatus,

1934 marked the beginning of a new phase, in which he continued to develop themes that he had used in his Prairie houses; his planning, for example, became more and more open, culminating in the first 'Usonian' house for Herbert Jacobs at Westmoreland in Winsconsin (1937). Wright's utilization of new materials, apparent as early as the Millard House, Pasadena (1923), became increasingly bold. In the Kaufmann House, Falling Water, at Bear Run, Pennsylvania (1936), he cantilevered huge concrete slabs over a waterfall; but, by contrast with the Millard House, the concrete is completely plain. Wright's belief in the organic nature of materials led him to juxtapose concrete with rough-hewn stone (at Falling Water), or to mix the two and call it 'desert concrete' for the house he built for himself at Taliesin West, outside Phoenix, Arizona, in 1938. He despised the International Style but nonetheless used its elements in a more picturesque way. Because its limited canon of form held no appeal fot him, he experimented with new forms: spirals at the Guggenheim Museum, New York City (1956–

9); lotus pads at the Johnson Wax Company Building at Racine, Wisconsin, (1936–9); 45° angles at Taliesin West. It was as if the forms he had originally used as decoration in the Prairie houses now provided him with entire designs.

Modernism, declining in the USA by 1900, remained an active tendency in Europe, partly as a result of European interest in the early work of Wright, published in Berlin in 1910. This tendency played its part in the formation of the International Style, which did not reach the USA until the late 1920s. The flight of refugees from Europe in the 1930s had a profound effect on American architecture, since it included the key figures of classical modernism. The Austrian Richard Neutra (1892–1970) settled in the USA as early as 1923, but only developed as an International Style designer by 1927, when he began the Lovell House in Los Angeles. The slender supports and combination of glazed areas with balconies make it an International Style building, although the massing is reminiscent of Loos and the picturesque composition of its components is almost

Wrightian. In 1930 Raymond M Hood (1881–1934), a native-born architect whose Chicago Tribune Building of 1923 had been Neo-Gothic, built the Daily News Building in New York City, a slightly Futurist and completely astylar structure. In 1932 George Howe (1886–1955) and the Swissborn William Lescaze (b 1896) built the first International Style skyscraper, the Philadelphia Savings Fund Building in Philadelphia. In the best traditions of the Chicago School, the vertical members are expressed on the sides and the horizontal cantilevers expressed at the end, but the ` idiom is European, an astylar glazed box.

In 1937 Walter Gropius (1883–1969) arrived, to be followed by Marcel Breuer (b 1902) later that year, by Mies van der Rohe (1886–1969) in 1938, and by Erich Mendelsohn (1887–1953) in 1941. Gropius became professor of architecture at Harvard, with Breuer as one of his assistants; Mies went to teach at the Illinois Institute of Technology in Chicago. The arrival of the Europeans coincided with a renewal of Wright's creativity; his work was very different from that of the Europeans but from this time was undoubtedly influenced by them.

Gropius and Breuer continued to build in the style of the 1920s. The Graduate Center at Harvard, built by Gropius and The Architects' Collaborative (TAC) in 1949–50, is a group of smooth, regular, astylar blocks on *pilotis*, although brick has replaced stucco and there are a few tentative curves. By the 1960s, however, Gropius's work had grown more dramatic (US Embassy, Athens, 1961) without departing from his characteristic regularity. Breuer moved to New York City in 1946, and his work also became more expressionistic, the sweeping curves of his Litchfield High School Gymnasium (1954–6) being reminiscent of Saarinen. Mendelsohn introduced undulating forms in a synagogue at Cleveland, Ohio (1946–52).

Mies, on the other hand, remained true to the principles of classical order that had characterized his Barcelona Pavilion (1936). The Illinois Institute of Technology, which he designed between 1939 and 1945, consists of low steel-skeleton buildings grouped in a rectangular area, the light brick walls of which are divided into a regular grid by the black-painted skeletal components. His Farnsworth House, Plano, Illinois (1950), is reduced

Robert Wiley house in New Canaan, Connecticut: Johnson, 1953

Seagram Building, New York: Mies van der Rohe, 1957

giving a cage-like impression. With Philip Johnson (*b* 1906), Mies built a comparable skyscraper, the Seagram Building in New York City (1956–8), a crystal box of inscrutable elegance and absolute regularity–which many consider the most beautiful skyscraper in America.

Mies's work around 1950 represents a classical moment in American, and indeed in world, architecture. Two of his distinguished followers were Philip Johnson (Johnson House, New Canaan, Connecticut, 1947–9) and Gordon Bunshaft (*b* 1909) of the Skidmore, Owings and Merrill firm (Lever Building, New York City). Since 1950, American architects have moved away from the Miesian aesthetic in various directions. A reaction against the all-over glazed cage is evident in Harrison and Abramowitz's Alcoa Building, Pittsburgh (1953), in which the curtain wall consists of aluminium panels each incorporating a smaller window; however, this solution does not involve abandoning the cage-like frame. An objection to Mies's formal geometry as untrue to the functional criteria of early modernism is implicit in the planning of Louis Kahn's (*b* 1901) Richards Medical Research Center, University of Pennsylvania (1958–60). This is mid-nineteenth century in the sense that its picturesque appearance is dictated by functional needs. A similar feeling is evoked by Paul Rudolph's (*b* 1918) Yale University Art and Architecture Building, New Haven, Connecticut (1962), the brutalism of which is somewhat reminiscent of Richardson. The expressionist reaction appears in the sweeping curves of Eero Saarinen's Yale Hockey Rink, New Haven, Connecticut (1958). Rudolph, a pupil of Gropius, appears to have reversed the master's dictum 'function precedes form' in his Jewett Art Centre for Wellesley College, Massachusetts (1959). Here the predominant formal articulation acts like a screen around a building whose interior it does not reflect at all, although it does echo the nineteenth-century Gothic building opposite. Minoru Yamasaki (*b* 1912) seeks purely decorative effects derived from styles of the past (McGregor Memorial Community Conference Center, Detroit, Michigan, 1959). This post-classical phase coincides with the geographical expansion of American architectural influence, for in the 1950s and 1960s American architects were accepting commissions all over the world.

to a white steel skeleton, glazed almost all round, within which the services are grouped in a central core; its simplicity and elegance make the strongest possible contrast with the spatial drama and organic forms of a Wright house. Mies's Lake Shore Drive flats in Chicago (1949–51) are enclosed in a regular grid of black-painted I-bars, completely free-standing at ground level,

Richards Medical Research Building: Louis Kahn, 1957–61

Yale Hockey Rink, New Haven, Connecticut: Eero Saarinen, 1958

The main concourse of St Louis Airport: Yamasaki, 1949

A school in Florida: Paul Rudolph, late 1950s

American furniture.

American furniture design started as a compromise between backwoods necessity and old world sophistication. The earliest immigrant designers wanted to make the kind of furniture they had had at home but, hampered at first by inadequate tools and unable to find wealthy patrons, they built simple and functional furniture with native woods. It was not until the end of the seventeenth century that more sophisticated work was done.

Early Colonial furniture could almost be described as 'English Provincial.' During the seventeenth century most American furniture was copied from Jacobean and Restoration work. But the copies were crude in proportion and detail because the designers lacked the necessary skills and the buyers had no need for beautiful drawing-room pieces in their unpretentious homes. So for nearly a century after the landing of the first settlers in Virginia in 1607, American furniture was functional and primitive.

Many craftsmen, such as Thomas Dennis, were born and trained in England, and then emigrated to America. Not surprisingly, their designs were reproductions of remembered English pieces, or of pieces other colonists had brought with them. Gradually some of these designs were adapted to local needs. For instance, the butterfly table, an American version of the English dropleaf table, was made with broad, wing-like brackets to support the leaf. Two other adaptations of English designs were the Connecticut and Hadley chests, which were Americanized versions of Jacobean chests. The Hadley chest stood on four legs and had one, two or three drawers. It was decorated with simple incised carving and then stained. The Connecticut chest also had four short legs. This chest was often gaily painted and decorated with split spindles or carved panels. It might have one or two drawers.

The chest was, in fact, the most important piece of furniture in early America because of its versatility. The colonists used chests for both storage and seating in their sparsely furnished homes. At first, all chests were squat, with hinged lids, and often with one or two drawers at the bottom. Later, taller chests of drawers were made. Chests on small legs became desks; on higher legs they were known as cupboards.

Dropleaf, stretcher, and trestle tables appeared. Chairs of this period were built on straight lines; wainscot, Carver, Brewster and slat-back chairs were popular. In the second half of the seventeenth century upholstered chairs were introduced.

In 1683 German and Swiss Mennonites began to arrive in eastern Pennsylvania, forming one of the first groups of non-English colonists. They quickly established a close-knit community which has continued to this day. The Mennonites spoke German and called themselves Deutsch (anglicized to Dutch). Simple and industrious, they made plain furniture on the sturdy Germanic model. Their utilitarian pieces were well made, of such local woods as cherry and pine. Unlike English furniture, their pieces were either painted or left unfinished. Brightly painted tulips, trees-of-life, hearts, birds, leaves, or geometric designs were used as decoration instead of the carvings and turnings that English craftsmen favoured. Typical furniture pieces were bride's chests, dough-tables, sawbuck tables, spice boxes, hanging wall cabinets, and wardrobes. The rustic look of Pennsylvania Dutch furniture still appeals to many Americans.

Towards the century's end, English Restoration influences became noticeable with the introduction of the scroll as an ornament. At the turn of the century cabinetmakers began to copy the Dutch-influenced William and Mary style. It was not until then that veneering appeared in America. This was a time when Americans were beginning to think of themselves as a separate civilized people and started to demand better workmanship and more elaborate designs. A new wave of immigration in the early eighteenth century brought many talented English cabinetmakers to the Colonies, where their skills were soon put to use. Pattern books by Chippendale and other designers and architects were widely available in the Colonies, and the Americans who read them quickly sought to copy English furniture styles. Design became as important as function.

From 1720 to 1790, American craftsmen were producing furniture that we now call American Eighteenth Century. Queen Anne and Chippendale designs were the basis of this more mature furniture. Furniture imports from the mother country became more regular, and there was a greater variety of pieces for American cabinetmakers to use

Seventeenth century: **1** *Late seventeenth-century pine bed with trundle bed fitting underneath* **2** *Simplified version of Charles II chair, with cane seat and back* **3** *Joint stool of cedar with turned legs* **4** *Sturdy wainscot chair with low stretchers* **5** *Cedar bench with straight legs and turned stretchers* **6** *New England Colonial rectangular post chair of medieval derivation* **7** *Connecticut Valley oak chest with carved panels and split spindle ornament* **8** *Butterfly table with wing-like supports* **9** *William and Mary style highboy with shaped stretchers and turned feet* **10** *New England chest of oak and pine with geometric moulding and painted designs* **11** *Early maple desk on a stand*

Eighteenth century: **1** *Classic Martha Washington chair with turned arms and legs* **2** *Queen Anne style side chair with cabriole legs* **3** *Chippendale's rococo style and* **4** *Hepplewhite shield back side chairs were both produced in Philadelphia* **5** *Sofa in the Chippendale style* **6** *New England chest on chest of block front construction and scrolled pediment* **7** *Queen Anne highboy with a flat top*

8 *Chippendale style slant top desk with drawers and pigeon holes* **9** *Swell fronted Hepplewhite chest of drawers* **10** *Characteristic Newport block fronting with shell decoration on a chest* **11** *Elaborate Chippendale style highboy with scrolled 'bonnet' top and carving* **12** *Blockfronted secretary bookcase with a slant top, scrolled pediment, and finials* **13** *Large Dutch Kas with painted decoration*

as models. Many pieces were copied exactly, but individual cabinetmakers, such as the Dunlaps and Thomas Elfe, put their own imprint on the English styles.

Because of the size of America, regional differences in furniture-making were much more important than in England or France. Along the eastern seaboard a number of cities – including Boston, Newport, New York, Philadelphia and Charleston – became major independent centres for design adaptation.

Philadelphia was particularly important. The 'Philadelphia school of cabinetmakers', which included Thomas Affleck and William Savery, did its finest work between 1742 and 1796. It was famous for mahogany chairs, highboys and lowboys in the Queen Anne and Chippendale styles. Philadelphia is especially known for Queen Anne chairs. A number of details of these pieces differed from the original English design: scrolled splats; concave arm supports; web, pad and trifid feet; and horseshoe-shaped seats.

From about 1760, chiefly in Rhode Island, Massachusetts and Connecticut, furniture-makers like the Townsend-Goddard families produced cabinets, desks and chests in a unique block-front style.

Several American chairs that have remained popular to this day were first made in this period. The Queen Anne splat-back chair was and still is very widely

used as a dining-room chair.

The making of Windsor chairs was well established in America by about 1740. By 1760 practically every home had at least one. The American versions of this chair differed in many ways from the English original. They were lighter, more graceful, and without a wide back-splat. Instead of cabriole legs, American Windsor chairs had slender turned legs. These legs were set at a slant and were attached to the seat slightly towards the centre instead of at the corners.

A perennial favourite, the rocking chair, first appeared in America about 1750 and quickly became a household standard. It was originally made by adding rockers, or 'bends', to an ordinary chair. Windsor rocking chairs were very common, but nearly every other chair style was used as well.

Other popular pieces in this period were secretaries and desks with slant lids, knee-hole desks and tables, swivel chairs, and tilt-top piecrust tables. Sofas with loose cushions or upholstered covers were common. And, for the first time, furniture suites were available.

Soon after the American Revolution a religious sect known as the Shakers settled in upstate New York, Kentucky, and New England. During the late eighteenth and early nineteenth centuries Shaker furniture achieved national prominence. Like the Pennsylvania Dutch, the Shakers believed in functional furniture,

but for religious reasons no decoration was allowed. Light varnish was about the only finish they used, although some communities preferred coloured stains. The Shakers favoured pine, but also used maple and fruitwoods. They liked large built-in cupboards and chests, but their chairs were light; many had slat backs and woven rush or tape seats. The Shakers were excellent craftsmen and their furniture was well made. With their use of clean lines and plain surfaces, they were forerunners of modern furniture design.

The national antagonisms of the Revolutionary period affected even furniture design. English influence persisted, but American designers began to take a lead more from their wartime ally, France. The work of the postwar period (1790–1820) was called Federal.

Charles Honoré Lannuier was a Frenchman who emigrated to New York and opened a shop there in 1805. He introduced a number of Louis XVI and Empire designs, which are said to have influenced the work of Duncan Phyfe. Phyfe was unquestionably the finest American cabinetmaker of the Federal period. His early work was strongly influenced by Chippendale and Hepplewhite. But Phyfe's early designs were easily identifiable because of their grace and simplicity. Before 1810 Phyfe chair legs were usually straight, reeded and fluted. Tables often had vase pedestals

on curved legs. Waterleaf carving and cloverleaf table tops are outstanding characteristics of Phyfe's work. From about 1810 he became more heavily influenced by the Directoire and Empire styles. The lyre motif appeared frequently in chair backs, sofa arms and table pedestals. Chairs had curved legs that recalled the Greek *klismos* chair.

Several other craftsmen whose work is prized today were working during this period. Samuel McIntyre was an architect and carver in Salem, Massachusetts. His ornamental carving appeared frequently on chests, chairs and mirrors made by other cabinetmakers.

Lambert Hitchcock was also active in the early nineteenth century. He was particularly known for the 'Hitchcock chair', based on a Sheraton design. This chair had a rush seat, straight turned legs, and a wide top rail. It was almost always painted black and decorated with gold-stencilled motifs. It is still popular today.

After about 1820, French influence on American furniture styles was paramount. This period is known variously as Greek Revival, American Empire, American Restoration, Gothic Revival, and Victorian. In 1833 Joseph Meeks & Sons published a colour lithograph advertizing 44 items of furniture available on order. The style was basically Empire, with large, undecorated surfaces, scroll sup-

Nineteenth century: **1** *Shaker food cupboard with perforated tin panels* **2** *Simple drop leaf table and* **3** *Sewing cabinet also made by the Shaker sect* **4** *Federal period cabinet with open shelves and storage space* **5** *Southern dining-room sugar chest* **6** *Empire pedestal table with heavy base* **7** *Classic Federal period card table on a pedestal base* **8** *Ornate French rococo style table by John Belter* **9** *Extremely simple chest of drawers of Shaker design* **10** *Late American Empire sofa with scrolled arms* **11** *Chest of drawers of early Federal period* **12** *American Empire version of Greek Klismos chair* **13** *Late nineteenth-century English Morris chair produced in America* **14** *Hitchcock chair of 1820s and 30s with stencilled decoration* **15** *Elaborately draped American Empire bed with paw feet* **16** *Boston rocker popular throughout the century* **17** *Upholstered armchair with floral carving*

ports and use of columns.

In the late 1840s very ornate adaptations of the French Rococo style began to appear. Chairs had curved, heavily carved frames, usually of rosewood, oak, or black walnut. John Henry Belter, a German craftsman who set up a shop in New York City in 1844, was influential in developing this style. One of the first furniture-makers to use laminated wood, Belter was very popular in the 1850s, especially with the very wealthy.

However, in the early 1860s his work lost favour as inexpensive, mass-produced furniture became widely available. In fact, mass production brought furniture design to a near-standstill.

One new style that appeared as the nineteenth century moved to a close was Mission furniture. During the eighteenth and early nineteenth centuries, Spanish culture gradually moved north from Mexico into the southwestern part of the United States, and Spanish priests founded missions throughout the area to help the local Indians. Furniture for the missions was sturdy but crudely made. This was copied in heavily proportioned chairs, tables and chests of darkly stained oak, and sometimes trimmed with nail-heads. Cushions were usually covered in leather.

Late in the 1870s, the British artist William Morris denounced mass-produced furniture, arguing that good design was incompatible with the economics of the assembly line. American architects and designers were moving in the opposite direction. By the beginning of the twentieth century they were developing the idea that form follows function, and trying to prove that it was possible to turn out well-designed furniture on an assembly line. They began designing specifically for mass production, using metal, plastics, and plywood, which are particularly suitable for machine processes.

The major influence on twentieth-century American furniture design was the German Bauhaus.

Walter Gropius, founder of the Bauhaus, arrived in the USA in the late 1930s. After World War II he founded The Architects' Collaborative. This organization brought together American architects and designers interested in pursuing the Bauhaus design philosophy – technical command as the key to creative design. By this time America was beginning to rival Scandinavia and Italy as a world leader in modern design.

The first important twentieth-century American furniture designers were also architects: Eero Saarinen and Charles Eames. In 1941 they jointly won first prize in a Functional Furniture Competition sponsored by the Museum of Modern Art. Saarinen worked only with man-made materials – and designed the pedestal chair and the 'womb chair' before his early death in 1961. Eames worked primarily in moulded plywood and metal. His lounge chair with ottoman is considered one of the greatest chair designs of this century.

During the 1950s other American designers gained recognition for their work. Among them were George Nelson, Ward Bennett, Florence Knoll, and Edward Wormley. Much of their work gained acceptance initially in offices, where functional pieces with simple, clean lines and little ornamentation were appreciated.

Early in the twentieth century, interior design as a profession began to flourish in America. One of the first successful interior decorators was Elsie de Wolfe, who left a career in the theatre to become a decorator; she opened an office in New York in 1904.

Other talented interior designers later in the century include William Baldwin, Dorothy Draper, Marion Hall, Dorothy Liebes, William Pahlmann, Mrs Henry Parish II, T H Robsjohn-Gibbings, and Dianne Tate.

Architects continued to be influential in designing interiors. A case in point is New York's Seagram Building, for which Mies van der Rohe and Philip Johnson designed the interior furnishings.

Glass decanter with blown mould decoration, early 19th century

Stiegel blue sugar bowl and cover

Stiegel amethyst panelled vase

American glass. Glassmaking was introduced into America by the early English settlers at Jamestown, Virginia, in about 1608. The glass produced was rather coarse and bubbly, and was mainly used for windows and bottles. During the next hundred years there were several attempts to produce glass in other parts of the country, but none seems to have been very successful until 1739, when a German, Casper Wistar, brought over some trained craftsmen from the Continent and opened a glasshouse at Salem County in New Jersey. Although mainly employed in producing windows and utilitarian vessels, they also made clear, opaque white and a range of coloured glass in greens, blues, and ambers. Simple jugs, bowls, and richer pieces, made by the workers in their spare time (usually of pale green window glass), became known as South Jersey wares and were soon copied by other factories.

Another German, Henry

Press-moulded glass dish, c 1830

William Stiegel, also imported foreign-trained workers for the three glasshouses which he ran in Pennsylvania from 1763 to 1774, before he was imprisoned for debt. His glass was fairly sophisticated, and included wheel engraving, coloured enamelled decoration, and a soft pattern-moulded decoration known as 'Diamond Daisy' which became a favourite form of decoration for pocket bottles.

An extremely high standard was achieved by the New Bremen Glassmanufactory in Maryland. It was established by John Frederick Amelung in 1784, but owing to financial difficulties only operated for 11 years. Besides the staple window and bottle glass, Amelung produced some fine covered goblets and presentation glasses, engraved with heraldic devices and Rococo scrollwork by skilled German craftsmen.

From 1825 patents were granted for the new and rapid

process of mechanical pressing, which made possible the mass production of elaborate designs, sometimes with stippled backgrounds resembling embroidery or lace; hence the term 'lacy' glass. The New England Glass Company (1818–88) and the Boston and Sandwich Glass Company (1825–88) produced vast quantities of this 'lacy' glass, but they also made free-blown glass, some of which was cut in the Anglo-Irish tradition, and from about 1850 to 1880 they made a variety of paperweights.

In 1878 the Louis C Tiffany and Associated Artists Company was formed, and two years later Tiffany (qv) took out a patent for his famous iridescent glass, which he called *Favrile*.

The Steuben Glassworks at Corning, New York, was established in 1903 by an English glassmaker, Frederick Carder. In 1918 the Steuben works was acquired by the Corning Glass Company, but most of the work they produced was over-elaborate and reactionary in design. In 1933 Arthur Amory Houghton, Junior, great-grandson of the Founder of the Corning Glass Works, took over the Steuben division and decided to aim for a flawless crystal glass of good workmanship and design. He also took the then unusual step of employing and commissioning famous architects, sculptors, and painters (Eric Gill, Sidney Waugh and others) to design the glass, which resulted in originality of both form and subject.

Tiffany Studios lamp

American pottery and porcelain. The early American settlers found it cheaper and easier to import pottery and porcelain from Europe and the Far East than to make it themselves. It was not until the nineteenth century that a ceramic industry was established on any kind of commercial scale.

Exactly when the first European colonists started making pottery in America is unknown, but several potteries were at work in Virginia by 1650, turning out domestic wares of the crudest kind.

The Dutch settlers in New Jersey were making pottery near Burlington in 1684. A fine cream burning clay, which was suitable for the manufacture of a fine stoneware, had been discovered in the area. Later, 'Yellow ware' and a Rockingham glazed ware

Pennsylvania Dutch pie plate with sgraffito decoration, 1786

Pennsylvania Dutch flower vase with sgraffito decoration, 1849

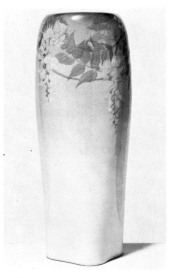

Earthenware, Rockwood, 1900

Castleton china designed by Eva Zeisel, 1947

were made at Burlington. There were also potteries in the Boston area in the 1660s.

John Remmey was making pottery in New York as early as 1735, and the Crolius family was active from 1698, though its first known marked piece is dated 1775. Both made salt-glazed stoneware.

During the eighteenth century, quite elaborately decorated incised slipware pieces were made in Pennsylvania, and some of the makers' names are of German origin. At Weston, Massachusetts, a factory was started for pottery making in 1765. Pottery was also made at Litchfield, Connecticut, where there were three potters at work in 1735.

The four chief kinds of pottery made in America during this period were common red ware with a lead glaze and little or no decoration; grey stoneware, sometimes decorated with incised decoration and occasionally by the addition of blue colouring; imitations of English salt-glazed ware; and Pennsylvania slip-decorated ware, which carried incised designs of quite an intri-

cate character and sometimes polychrome decoration. Later in the nineteenth century, cream-coloured earthenware, tortoise-shell ware, and whiteware were also made.

At Bennington (qv) in Vermont, John Norton made red ware, then salt-glazed ware, and then an imitation Queensware and Whieldon ware – all of good quality. East Liverpool, Ohio, early became an important pottery-making centre, and by the 1880s was said to have nearly seventy kilns in operation.

In 1769 the first American porcelain factory was started at Southwark in Philadelphia by Bonnin and Morris. They advertized that they could make porcelain just as good as that from the Bow factory in London, England; and they had undoubtedly engaged some workmen from Bow. However, the competition

from imported wares from Europe and the Far East put them out of business, and in 1774 the factory was sold up.

In Philadelphia, William Ellis Tucker was making porcelain rather like a hard-paste oriental porcelain. Pattern books have survived from this factory (1825–38) from which some of the ware can be identified; sometimes the pieces are marked. Tableware, jugs, and pitchers were a speciality.

American silver. The best and most important period of American silver was probably from 1650 until 1810. The majority of good-quality pieces were made in Boston, New York, and Philadelphia, the largest and wealthiest cities. There were fewer types of American than European silver, the objects produced tended to be smaller, and

the Puritan tradition promoted a preference for plain and simple styles, particularly in Boston.

It is not possible to give an exact date for most pieces of early American silver, because federal, colonial and state governments did not regulate silversmithing in any way, although Boston and New York had societies or guilds of smiths, and a very strict apprenticeship was observed. In the absence of any definite system of marking, the only guides to the dating of early American silver are the presentation dates on commemorative silver, the use of a silversmith's mark, and contemporary documents. The English standard of silver was used and the smiths' marks were similar to contemporary English ones.

Seventeenth-century American silversmiths used the initials of their first name and surname,

White House service made by Lenox for President Truman, 1952

Early American sugar-box by John Coney, Boston, c 1700

Punch bowl by Jacob Boelen, New York, c 1700

Punch bowl with crest of Riddell Family by Coney, Boston Mass, c 1720

but in the eighteenth century the full surname sometimes appeared. In nineteenth-century Philadelphia and New York there was some use of pseudo-English hallmarks, and after 1860 American silver is usually marked Sterling. The first American assay office on the British pattern was established in Baltimore in 1814.

The style of American silver was strongly influenced by imported engravings from Europe and from imported English plate in particular. There was some Dutch influence, particularly in New York, as well as influence from immigrant Huguenot smiths and from the trade between Boston and Portugal. By the eighteenth century most of the large towns had good local silversmiths. The styles of American silver have the same period names as in England, although they were often used at a slightly later date.

In the early settlements there was little call for ostentatious plate, so (with the exception of fine pieces of church plate, which were made from a very early date) only ordinary utilitarian pieces were produced. A silversmith called Thomas Howard is known to have been in Jamestown in 1620, the year of the *Mayflower*'s voyage; and John Hull (1624–83), who came from Market Harborough about 1634, became master of the first mint in America, established at

Miniature cup by Caleb Shields, Baltimore, 1700

Boston in 1652. The silversmith was an important member of the community in the seventeenth century. There were no banks, and the influx of coin from trade encouraged the craft. The Puritan influence in Boston encouraged simple, plain shapes, and silver from excess coinage was converted into plate; the style was closely allied to that of seventeenth-century English silver, especially that of the Commonwealth period. The most important American silversmith of this early period was John Coney (1656–1722).

In the so-called Queen Anne period, the first half of the eighteenth century, American silver was closely modelled on that of early eighteenth-century England. The popularity of tea gave rise to a far greater variety of silver objects, containers and kettles. Pieter van Dyck (1684–1751), working in New York, produced some of the finest pieces of this period, as did Jacob Hurd (1702–58) in Boston.

From 1750 until 1785, the Rococo era, America had very close links with Europe – especially, during the French and Indian wars, with Britain. Quantities of English Rococo silver were imported, and this had a profound influence upon American silversmiths. Highly decorative and ornamental silver was made, especially in Boston, which was the centre of American trade and the home of many wealthy patrons, until the American Revolution in 1775.

At the end of the eighteenth century, American silver, like that of contemporary Europe, returned to simplicity of form and to a sparing use of decoration. This was inspired by the study of classical shapes, which particularly appealed to the new republic with its strong classical ideals. There was still a strong influence from the shapes of English silver, and in 1797 George and Robert Armitage

from Sheffield began to manufacture Sheffield plate in Philadelphia. After the Revolution the new freedom of American trade greatly encouraged the use of ceramic shapes for silver, Liverpool jugs being typical.

The greatest and best known of American smiths, Paul Revere (qv) (1735–1818), worked in this classical style of the late eighteenth century.

In the nineteenth century, American silver, like that of Europe, began to proliferate, to become eclectic, and manifest the results of machine mass production. All types, shapes, and sizes of silver objects were produced, and design trends were much the same as in Europe.

The finest pieces of early American silver were made in New England, and particularly in Boston, with its close trade links with Europe; and because of the social stability of Boston, much of its silver has survived.

Amorino (Italian, 'little love'). A small cupid or winged *putto*, common in Italian painting and sculpture, and found also on picture frames, etc.

Amphi-prostyle. A temple with a portico to the rear as well as in front. There are no columns along the sides.

Ancone. An alternative name for a console (qv); it is used to support a cornice.

Andirons. Fire-dogs, horizontal bars placed at either side of a fireplace to support logs. They are normally found in pairs, but are occasionally joined by a rail which partly encloses the fire. At the back of each bar is a low plain foot and at the front a 'guard' or 'standard' which can be decorated.

Many illuminated manuscripts illustrate examples, most of which have 'guards' ending in cup or crozier motifs. The great

variety of the decoration is shown by early inventories, such as that of Cardinal Wolsey (1523–5), in which some andirons are described as displaying 'my Lordes armes and Cardinall hattes on the toppes.' In another, taken at the death of Henry VIII, there were 'andyrons of yron, eche of them with a roose', in the Privy Chamber at Hampton Court. Andirons provide a catalogue of decorative motifs for at least five centuries.

In some countries the use of the coal fire, and the diminishing size of houses towards the end of the eighteenth century, led to the gradual obsolescence of andirons. In countries well stocked with timber, notably the United States, wood fires are still common and andirons are extensively used.

Angel bed. A canopied bed without bedposts. The canopy or half-tester extended over only part of the bed, and was supported either by chains suspended from the ceiling or by brackets.

Anglo-Saxon architecture. The native English architecture of the period between the Roman evacuation of the fifth century AD and the eleventh-century Norman conquest. Pre-conquest Romanesque also describes this architecture. Only a few ecclesiastical buildings have survived, since the abundance of timber made construction in stone exceptional. The first were single-celled halls, but these gradually increased in size with the addition of other small chambers or the lower storey of a tower. At Barton-upon-Humber the base of the tower forms the principal chamber.

Two basic forms of church plan were devised in the Anglo-Saxon period. One, found mainly in the North, has a long, high, rectangular nave and a straight-ended chancel; the plan of

St Peter's Church, Barton-upon-Humber, Lincolnshire

Characteristic terracotta antifixae in the Plaka, Athens

southern churches – of which no examples have survived intact – has a rectangular nave divided from its eastern apse by a triple-pierced screen. Both forms were elaborated and augmented by additional chambers. Long and short work (qv) is a typical treatment of Anglo-Saxon towers. Bradwell-juxta-Mare, Essex (654), Reculver, Kent (c 669), Brixworth, Northamptonshire (c 670), Earls Barton, Lincolnshire (ninth century), and Bradford-on-Avon, Wiltshire (tenth century), are some of the best preserved.

Angular capital. A variation on the classical Ionic capital. The invention is attributed to Scamozzi and has four similar faces, whereas on the antique capital adjacent views are different.

Annulet. In architecture, a small flat band or ring around the top of the shaft of a column.

Anta. A square pilaster, or one in which the capital and base differ from the usual order appearing elsewhere. They are frequently found flanking a doorway or on the corner of a building.

Antefix. An ornamental block placed on the eaves and cornices to hide the ends of roof tiles. It is a feature of Greek and Greek Revival architecture.

Anthemion. The stylized Greek honeysuckle, a motif often used in late eighteenth-century design. Its symmetrical scrolls were frequently cast in iron for balconies, punched in gilded

Chancel of St Laurence, Bradford-on-Avon, Wiltshire, tenth century

Anthemion motif in iron and plaster: Adam brothers, 1768

Anthemion back chair, 1770

metal, or hewn in marble for chimney-pieces and the bases of statues and urns.

Antis, in. A portico described as being *in antis* is recessed into the fabric of the building so that the columns are on the same plane as the surrounding wall. It was used extensively in the Italian Renaissance, and also in Palladian buildings.

Apothecary jars. Like many other objects which were originally utilitarian, apothecary jars are now rare collectors' pieces and are apt to command high prices in the saleroom.

The earliest known jars were medieval, made of green, glazed pottery. In England this was replaced by enamelled earthenware, made in blue and white by the Delft potteries on the south bank of the Thames: the jars were then known as Lambeth jars. From the middle of the seventeenth century there are three periods of design, each with its characteristic appearance. The first is known as the Commonwealth period; during this the jars usually carried a representation of a man smoking a pipe on either side of the cartouche enclosing the name of the preparation. The second period

is known as the Angel because an angel with outspread wings appeared over the name of the preparation; it lasted until the end of the seventeenth century. In the third period, which lasted until the end of the eighteenth century, the jars were decorated with bird motifs, and were also made in Bristol and Liverpool potteries.

The jars used for decoration in apothecary shops were larger (about 16 in high) and more elaborate than those containing drugs (usually about 7 or 8 in high). The most decorative and colourful of these jars were those made on the Continent, particularly in Italy and Spain.

Apple-wood. *Malus.* A timber known to the ancients and much used in England for seventeenth-century furniture, including many long-case clocks. Applewood has been more widely, ingeniously and decoratively employed in France, especially in the making of chairs, some of which have a most pleasing warmth of colour and fine grain. Even the coarser grain of the wild apple has been imaginatively exploited in France, particularly in small dining and elbow chairs.

Applied decorations. Decorations fixed upon the flat surfaces of furniture, doors and chimney-pieces. Small geometric facets in triangular and lozenge shapes were used on the framework of furniture and chimney-pieces of the late sixteenth and early seventeenth centuries. Then, during the first half of the eighteenth century, mouldings, which were used extensively upon cabinets and chests, were also applied to walls and doors to simulate panelling.

Appliqué or **applied work.** In needlework this is the application of decorative material shapes to a contrasting ground

material. The pieces are usually attached by ornate stitching or cording. The work is known to have been practised in ancient Egypt. Much fine work was done during the Middle Ages and in later centuries, and appliqué is enjoying a great revival today.

Apron or **apron piece.** In furniture, as in sartorial and nautical usage, a protective covering. The apron is to be found, usually in a decorative form, immediately below the seat rail of a chair or below the main body of a cabinet, bookcase, commode or table.

Apron piece on chest of drawers

Apse. A semi-circular or polygonal recess, vaulted or domed, which is found at the end of a chancel. Its ecclesiastical use may derive from the structure of Roman basilicas converted into Christian churches.

Aqueduct. An invention of the ancient world for carrying water in an artificial channel. Remains of systems in Syria, Cyprus and Greece are extant, some having long underground tunnels; an example is the Hadrian Aqueduct at Athens (AD 134–40), with over fifteen miles of tunnel that have again been brought into use. The most splendid were the aqueduct bridges built by the Romans, the first of which was constructed by the praetor Marcius in 145 BC.

Arabesque

A number were built in Rome and elsewhere under the empire. The aqueduct at Nîmes in southern France is probably the most impressive still in existence.

Arabesque. A decorative pattern much used by the Arabs, the Saracens, and the Moors in Spain, for enriching painted surfaces, mosaics and carvings. Because their religion frowned on the representation of animals, Muslim artists evolved these complex patterns based upon flower, fruit and plant motifs. Stalks, tendrils and stems provided the basis for a variety of slender forms. The term is now applied to almost all repetitive and intricate patterns, and is as often employed to describe a typographical border as an architectural frieze.

Apothecary jars of the Angel period, 1660–1700

The Pont du Gard, Nîmes, fourth century

Paradise dinner set, designed by Wärtsilä for Arabia

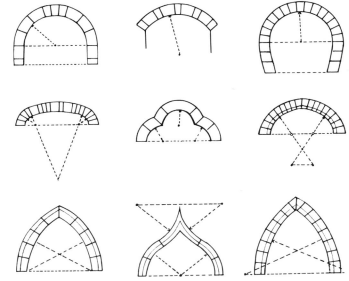

A selection of arches. From left to right: top, stilted, segmental, horseshoe; centre, depressed or basket, round trefoil, four centred Tudor arch; bottom, equilateral, ogee, lancet

Arabia. A/B Arabia, on the outskirts of Helsinki, is the chief ceramic factory in Finland, and one of the largest in the world. Arabia has a high reputation for simple domestic pottery and ovenware in contemporary designs.

Scientists and technicians from all over the world have studied in the ultra-modern laboratories of Arabia, and designers and artist potters vie with one another for the chance to study there. The firm's group of industrial designers and artists, each with his or her own atelier, produces not only prototypes for Arabia's mass-produced domestic wares, but also more ambitious original decorative pieces. Among the artists who work or have worked at Arabia are Rut Bryk, Kaj Franck, Liisa Hallamaa, Birger Kaipaainen, Francesca and Richard Lindh, Ulla Procope and Aune Siimes.

Arcade. Properly speaking, a series of arches upon columns or piers. The term is used by extension to describe a covered promenade, partly open on one side, which consists of a series of arched openings. The arcade is one of the most useful and decorative of all urban architectural devices, as any visitor to Paris, Venice or Turin will readily agree. In England a notable example is London's Burlington Arcade.

Arch. The structure and function of all arches are basically the same. By means of the self-supporting arch, the super-imposed load is carried over an opening whether the load consists of three extra courses of bricks for a garden wall or several hundred tons of masonry above a cathedral door. The same principles of stress and strain apply when the architect substitutes an arched window for the conventional rectangular piercing of a wall.

As with most of man's architectural inventions, the arch was soon used for decorative as well as functional purposes. The early Egyptians knew of the arch and its structural possibilities; so did the Greeks. But the Romans were the first to exploit its practical potential to the full, and many of their simple semicircular arches, in buildings as different as temples and aqueducts, are still standing after 2,000 years. This kind of arch was then used for the Romanesque architecture of western Europe and the Byzantine styles of eastern Europe.

Most people are more familiar with the pointed Gothic arch, although the rounded arch again came into favour during the Renaissance, especially for domestic and institutional architecture. Another variant is the Muslim horseshoe arch.

The decorative possibilities of the arch have led to experiments with many types, ranging from the ogee arch, which (in company with cusped and lancet arches) has entranced all visitors to Venice, to the flattened segmental arch which has given many vast Victorian warehouses an impressive if utilitarian grandeur. Lancet and ogee arches have exercised considerable influence over architectural dilettantes, mainly because they combine the possibility of highly personal interpretation with more or less serious ecclesiastical associations. This fanciful approach dates back as far as the eighteenth century, with its taste for 'gothick' forms.

In modern architecture the arch is seldom used, although it could be an effective decorative element in the simpler forms of modern building.

Arcade of Maison de Victor Hugo in the Place des Vosges, Paris

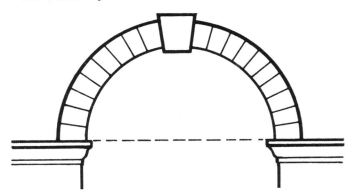

The inside face of the arch is called the intrados; the outside, the extrados. The wedge-shaped blocks are the voussoirs, the centre one is the keystone, and the two end voussoirs are the springers of the arch. The top of the wall or pier is the impost from which the arch springs, the springing line. The masonry surrounding the arch is the abutment

St John's church, Westminster, by Thomas Archer, 1714–28

Archer, Thomas (1668–1743). British architect. Archer was among the few native designers with a true understanding of Baroque, that most difficult and elusive of architectural styles. It used to be said that Archer gained his knowledge and mastery of the Baroque manner from Sir John Vanbrugh, but it is now thought that he derived them from studying Borromini's works. Archer was at Eton and Oxford, then studied abroad before returning to practise in London. He was one of the commissioners

for building the Fifty New Churches in 1711. His most famous works are the north front of Chatsworth and the churches of St Philip in Birmingham (now Birmingham Cathedral), St John, Westminster, and St Paul, Deptford, the last three introducing an extraordinary Baroque emphasis into British ecclesiastical architecture.

Architects' co-partnership. British architectural partnership formed in 1939. Six of the present seven partners were founder-

members and trained together at the Architectural Association. Their first notable commissions were the rubber factory at Brynmawr in South Wales (1949) and part of the 1951 Festival of Britain Exhibition. The firm's practice is diverse and has included work in industry, housing, and defence, and a large number of educational buildings – schools from Tunisia and Tobago to Derbyshire and Dorset, as well as university buildings in Oxford and Cambridge, Carmarthen, Leicester and London. The master plan and the greater part of the new University of Essex was the work of the partnership.

Architrave. The architectural term for the lowest of the divisions of the entablature, the division below the frieze. It is also the general name for mouldings around doors and windows. In this sense a shouldered architrave is one in which the moulding forms a shoulder around the corner of the opening.

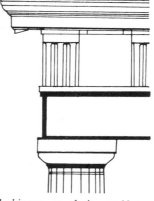

Architrave on doric entablature

Archivolt. The undercurve of an arch and the mouldings with which it is ornamented.

Armchair. The Egyptians designed formal armchairs which are somewhat too reminiscent of throne seats for modern taste, although Thomas Hope successfully revived several of the ancient shapes in his *Household*

Elizabethan oak armchair with linenfold panelling

Wing armchair upholstered in gros point

Furniture and Interior Decoration (1807). Nevertheless, until the mid-Victorian period the so-called armchair remained basically what the name suggests – a chair for resting the arms. (The wing chair (qv) was an exception.) We are now inclined to call such chairs elbow chairs, for they have little in common with the deep-buttoned leather armchair of Victorian clubland. Since then the armchair has been a large, comfortable chair in which to relax.

Dunelm House, University of Durham: Architects' Co-partnership, 1967

The Ateljee chair, designed by Yrjö Kukkapuro

Armillary sphere used as a garden ornament

Armillary sphere. An astronomical instrument of great antiquity, rather like a skeleton celestial globe. The name is derived from the Latin for a hoop, *armilla*, for the sphere consists of a number of rings revolving around each other with the earth (Ptolemaic) or, later, the sun (Copernican) in the centre. Each ring represents one of the important circles of the celestial sphere.

The origins of this instrument are uncertain, but the earliest known forms appeared in China and, by 300 BC, in Greece. It is possible that they were invented independently.

In their more complex forms, armillary spheres closely resembled astrolabes (qv) but were widely different in size and appearance and more used for instruction than for practical astronomy. They were introduced to Europe by the great astronomer Tycho Brahe (1546–1601), and although many examples were made, few have survived.

Armoire. The French term for a cupboard or wardrobe. It seems to have been anglicized to aumbry, armory and almery but never to have become part of English terminology. In France, early armoires were of massive proportions; so too were their English equivalents, for in his translation of the Aeneid in 1582 Richard Stonyhurst likens the Trojan Horse to an 'od hudge ambry' in which 'they ram'd a number of hardye Tough Knights.'

The earliest armoires were painted with religious subjects both inside and out. Notable examples are in the cathedrals of Bayeux and Noyon. By the end of the fourteenth century, painting had given way to carving and even insets of semi-precious stones. New kinds of carved decoration were introduced during the Renaissance, and there was a change in the general appearance of armoires: from huge static Gothic cabinets they became taller, lighter, and narrower objects.

André Charles Boulle, cabinetmaker to Louis XIV, used his inlaid tortoiseshell and brass techniques to create armoires which surpass all others in elegance of design and richness of decoration.

The armoire illustrated is typical of the later eighteenth-century provincial wood carver's work. Such pieces are almost invariably constructed with slotted sections held by wooden pins, so that they can be easily taken down, moved, and re-assembled.

Arris. The sharp edge formed at the point where two surfaces meet.

Arsedine. Gold-coloured alloy of copper and zinc, commonly used for imitation gold leaf in the sixteenth century.

Art Deco. Architectural and decorative style which flourished in Europe and America c 1905–c 1930. The term gained wide currency in the late 1960s, and is often used to mean all the decorative arts and most of the low-brow architecture of the 1919–39 period.

The origins of the style can be traced to 1900, when the Scottish architect Charles Rennie Mackintosh was invited to design a room for the Secession Exhibition in Vienna. Mackintosh's spare rectangular shapes were adopted by the Austrians Josef Hoffman and Adolf Loos, and the work of these three c 1905–7 displays all the characteristics of Art Deco.

The first true Art Deco design was Hoffmann's Palais Stoclet, Brussels (1905), followed in 1907 by Loos's interior of the Kärtner Bar, Vienna, and Mackintosh's exterior of the Glasgow School of Art library. Mackintosh's Bassett-Lowke House, Northampton (1916), is a fully-fledged Art Deco design.

The most immediately apparent feature of these four designs is their rectangularity. This was already a characteristic of works by the American architect Frank Lloyd Wright, and European acquaintance with his designs after 1910 accelerated Art Deco tendencies.

The materials used in the four early examples already mentioned include polished or lacquered wood, marble, tiles, aluminium, steel, leather, and glass. Their common denominator is that they are all shiny: where roughness is the predominant tactile quality of mid-Victorian design, and brittleness that of Art Nouveau, glossiness is the hallmark of Art Deco. In the 1920s an increasing number of glossy materials was employed: jade, onyx, obsidian, crystal, polished brass, chrome, new materials like Bakelite or Vitrolite, an astounding range of obscure woods, and blackened glass. To some extent the use of austere, shining

Eighteenth-century French provincial armoire in oak

Art Deco hand-beaten silver tea set, 1935

Daily Express Building, Fleet Street, London: Ellis and Clarke, 1931

Staircase in the Maison Tassel, Brussels, designed by Horta, 1892–3

materials was a symbolic acknowledgement of the machine age; but it was at best only symbolic, for despite the brave talk of reconciling art and industry, most Art Deco objects are glaringly and expensively handmade.

Not even symbolic acknowledgement is reserved for the structure, concealment of which is a feature that distinguishes Art Deco from avant-garde styles both before and since. All the interiors are sheathed, the Palais Stoclet with marble, the Kärtner Bar with glass, the Bassett-Lowke House with wood. Nor is any attempt made to hide the fact; in later buildings the bolts which hold the sheathing in place are even assertively displayed. Exteriors are also sheathed, the most noticeable example in London being Ellis and Clarke's Daily Express Building in Fleet Street (1931), clad in black glass. In Art Deco furniture too, the structure is often blatantly ignored, veneers and lacquers playing a part comparable to that of sheathing on buildings. In their heady enthusiasm for modernism, Art Deco designers overlooked the rational basis of modern design. Like the Expressionists they

had a taste for the 'primitive' colours and forms. This was partly satisfied by the use of motifs derived from ancient or supposedly barbaric cultures. The first of these was Russia, as interpreted by the Russian Ballet of Sergei Diaghilev, which opened in Paris in May 1909. The use of African masks in Cubist paintings appeared to complement the vogue of jazz; while interest in the pre-Columbian civilizations of North and South America resulted in the incorporation of Mayan, Aztec and Zapotec features into Frank Lloyd Wright's most characteristically Art Deco work, the Imperial Hotel, Tokyo (1915–22). Finally, the opening of Tutankhamun's tomb in 1925 gave Egyptian motifs a new range and popularity.

The Paris International Exhibition of 1925 showed off the opulent and decorative character of French Art Deco, and is often regarded as the climax of the style. The Americans, who had been developing an Art Deco style of their own, absorbed French ideas very quickly. The British were slower, and Art Deco began to appear in Britain only c 1928, when it was already declining elsewhere.

Art Nouveau. Architectural and decorative style which flourished in Europe and America from c 1890 to the early years of the twentieth century. Its theoretical beginnings are clearly rooted in the Victorian tradition of originality in ornament, exemplified in E W Goodwin's spindly 'art' furniture, and later in the Palacio Güell (1885–9), by the Spanish architect Antoni Gaudí, and Louis Sullivan's decoration of the Auditorium Building in Chicago (1887–8).

The hallmark of full-blown Art Nouveau was a sinuous and interlacing line, derived from natural (usually vegetable) forms which, as Voysey put it, 'have to be reduced to mere symbols.' In England there was already an avant-garde tradition of painting which was at least in part decorative, and in which extensive use was made of this motif (Blake, Rossetti, Burne-Jones). In the 1880s William Morris and his circle carried this tendency into the design of craft products, notably wallpapers, textiles and

book illustration, all two-dimensional media into which sinuous lines could easily be introduced.

This aspect of British art was hardly known on the Continent. The Belgian designer Henri van de Velde said that when he first saw designs by C F A Voysey and Arthur Mackmurdo, 'It was as if spring had come all of a sudden.' In France painters

Art Nouveau candlestick

Trefoil shaped bowl and bottle by Gallé

Exotic inlay and marquetry on commode by Emile Gallé, Paris, 1889

began to turn away from realism during the 1880s, and led by Gauguin, sought to produce a more decorative art; here too the sinuous line made its appearance. Both British designers and French painters were influenced by Japanese graphics, in which flat unmodelled areas of colour and decorative line were used to superb effect.

These developments were brought together in Belgium by Les Vingt, an avant-garde artists' club which exhibited Gauguin in 1889, and Voysey and Mackmurdo in 1892. Also in 1892, Victor Horta designed no 6 rue Paul-Emile Janson,

Moser glass ewer with raised enamel decoration

Brussels, in which all the architectural elements assume the sinuous, tendril-like forms of Art Nouveau graphics. They are executed in a variety of materials, iron for columns and balconies, mosaic for the floors, and paint for walls and ceilings.

Horta's use of these forms brought Art Nouveau into the three-dimensional field of architecture. Such a transformation would not have been possible using traditional materials, which is why Horta used a malleable metal, iron, in his first Art Nouveau building and in his more ambitious Maison du Peuple, Brussels (1896). A still better known use of iron occurs in Hector Guimard's Paris *Métro* entrances, built between 1899 and 1904. The employment of iron in the service of new forms is significant: both High Victorian and modern architects have insisted that form should be determined by the materials; in adopting the opposite approach, Art Nouveau represents a curious and interesting side-turning in the development of modern design theory.

By this criterion, Gaudí is not really an Art Nouveau architect: his forms are usually too spiky and angular, and he was passionately interested in utilizing the qualities of his materials. Nonetheless, two of his houses in Barcelona, begun in 1905, the Casa Milá and the Casa Battló, share an affinity with Art Nouveau. Here, like Horta, Gaudí fused sinuous forms in three dimensions and used new materials (in this case concrete) in the service of his forms.

Other avant-garde architects of the 1890s, although not strictly Art Nouveau in the same sense as Horta, used Art Nouveau motifs for decoration. August Endell's Elvira studio (1896) has swirly, seaweed-like

forms that are applied to a completely flat exterior surface. The architecture of Charles Rennie Mackintosh in Glasgow is not Art Nouveau at all, but his decorative ironwork for his Glasgow School of Art (1897–9), his graphics, and his low-relief metalwork (especially when done in conjunction with his wife, Mary Macdonald), employ the stylized vegetable forms of advanced Belgian taste. The decorative ironwork which Louis Sullivan applied to the ground floor exterior of the Carson Pirie Scott Store (1899) in Chicago is denser and still more vegetable-like, though the building itself has no connection with the style.

French display cabinet with metal mounts

Arts and Crafts Movement.

English movement of the second half of the nineteenth century. It was essentially a response to the medieval enthusiasms and anti-machine ideas of Ruskin and the pre-Raphaelites, and later provided the basis for Art Nouveau (qv) and movements such as the Deutscher Werkbund (qv). The year 1861 may be taken as its beginning. It was then that William Morris (qv) founded his firm of artists and craftsmen – Morris, Marshall, Faulkner & Co – dedicated to raising standards of craftsmanship; ironically, in view of Morris' admiration for the everyday objects once produced by medieval workmen, the firm's products were so expensive that only the really rich could afford them.

The movement inspired by Morris was a revolt against the ugly mass-produced objects turned out after the Industrial Revolution. Craftsmanship was to be revived and pride and satisfaction brought back into work. The whole scheme was impregnated with a romantic socialist idealism and, more dangerously, with the anti-machine attitudes of Morris and Walter Crane (1845–1915). C R Ashbee (1863–1942), himself a prominent figure in the Arts and Crafts Movement, described this aspect of it as 'intellectual Ludditism.' Ashbee recognized the inevitable and necessary place of the machine in modern society, while retaining a belief in the importance of good craftsmanship and design. He was one of the founders of the Guild and School of Handicraft (1888), which later moved to the Cotswolds; and he was responsible for the Arts and Crafts Exhibition of 1888, regarded by many as the culmination of the movement.

Stockholm City Library, by Asplund

Pulpit at Freising, Bavaria, by the Asam Brothers, 1723

Asam, Cosmas Damian (1686–1739), and Egid Quirin (1692–1750). Bavarian architects and decorators, the sons of Hans Georg Asam (1649-1711), a painter. The Asam brothers studied under Carlo Fontana at Rome and evolved a dramatic and extravagant Baroque style in which illusionism is carried to its limit. They decorated many churches in south Germany; of the four that they built, St Johann Nepomuk (begun 1733) is their masterpiece.

Ash. *Fraxinus excelsior.* A strong, flexible hardwood that has always been used for furniture-making. However, although ash can be used for the same purposes as oak, it is rarer. The paler variety is generally used for lumber. Ash is usually employed for the framework and curved elements in furniture design. With its creamy colour and brownish or grey markings (or, in the case of black-hearted ash, strong black markings), this wood provides richly-coloured veneers.

Ashlar. Squared and worked-on stone used in facing the walls of buildings. These thus present smooth and often beautiful sur-

faces, in sharp contrast to stone used in its rough quarried state.

Aslin, Charles Herbert (1893–1959). English architect. As county architect of Hertfordshire, Aslin gained an international reputation for his original and ingenious solutions to the problem of designing sound, economical and visually satisfying school buildings. His Hertfordshire Schools Programme was widely admired outside Britain and led to the construction of many fine primary and

Charles Aslin

secondary school buildings. He has received many awards for his work.

Asplund, Gunnar (1885–1940). A Swedish architect who was one of the masters of the modern movement. He was born in Stockholm and attended the city's technical high school and academy of art. Most of his early commissions were gained as the result of competitions, including two schools (Karlshamn in southern Sweden and Hedemora in Dalecarlia). He also designed a number of villas. Asplund's first major work was his design for the Stockholm City Library, a monumental building with a domeless rotunda and an interesting interior. He first gained international renown with his designs for the Stockholm Exhibition of 1930, in which his fountains and restaurant showed that functionalism could be combined with gaiety and beauty. The Stockholm Exhibition has exerted a profound influence upon all succeeding exhibitions, including the British South Bank Exhibition of 1951. Asplund's most impressive achievement was his last, an austerely beautiful

Gunnar Asplund

design for the woodland crematorium in the Stockholm South Cemetery (1935–40). Here a majestic portico overlooks a magnificent landscaped park with a background of pine woods. This crematorium has been called by one eminent critic 'an architectural landmark in our century.'

Asplund was not a notable theorist or innovator, but his work contributed significantly to the history of modern architecture, proving that it could be graceful as well as useful.

School at Stevenage, Hertfordshire, by Aslin

Musicians made by Astbury in pottery, 1730

Astbury, John (1688–1743). Staffordshire potter. Astbury made fine red earthenware with stamped white clay decoration and lead glazes. In addition to bowls, teapots, etc, he made a number of small pottery figures, notably of musicians. These too were made with different coloured çlays for colour contrast, and lead-glazed. It was John Astbury who first added ground calcined flints to the body of earthenware to produce a whiter clay.

Astragal. Originally a small semi-circular moulding. The term is now almost exclusively (albeit erroneously) applied to decorative wooden mouldings on the glazed doors of cabinets and bureaux. This is an interesting example of a word which is incorrectly used but of general currency; it is to be found in books and catalogues issued by auctioneers of the highest repute.

Astrolabe. An astronomical and surveying instrument of remarkable ingenuity and usefulness. The earliest known dated example is Persian, of the tenth century AD; but astrolabes were used long before by the Arabs, the Persians, and probably the Greeks. Their invention has been attributed to Hipparchus (second century BC), though on little evidence. The first unquestionable description occurs *c* AD 500 in the works of Philoponus of Alexandria.

Basically, the astrolabe consists of the *safiha*, a circular plate engraved with the celestial sphere; another plate, the *rete*, also of the celestial sphere but bounded by the tropic of Capricorn and largely cut away to show the major fixed stars; and the *mater*, a thicker plate on which the *safiha* and *rete* are fitted. It is engraved with a circular scale of hours and

Modern use of attic space

Astragal mouldings on door

Persian spherical astrolabe, 1480–1

degrees from which altitudes can be read. The astrolabe was of primary interest to astrologers, who in early centuries played an important role in public life. Astrolabes were also used for a large number of astronomical and navigational purposes. Much has been written about them since the first century BC; Chaucer, for example, wrote a *Treatise on Astrolabes* for the instruction of his son.

By the end of the seventeenth century astrolabes were superseded by instruments capable of greater precision, and the 'mathematical jewel' was consigned to museums and collectors' cabinets.

Astylar (Greek, *a + stulos*, 'without columns'). An architectural term used to describe a façade without columns or pilasters, or one in which they are incidental to the main design.

Atlantes. Carved figures or half figures of men used as columns to support an entablature (qv). They were particularly common in German Baroque architecture.

Atrium. The term for the central room or court of a Roman house, leading off into the main rooms. The early atrium had a hearth in the middle of the floor and an opening in the roof above. It gradually developed into an inner court, still roofed, but with a central opening to the sky and sometimes colonnaded. In ecclesiastical architecture of the early Christian and medieval periods the atrium was the open, quadrangular, colonnaded forecourt in front of the church.

Attic. Originally the term applied to a low storey above an entablature or cornice of a building. It is now used to describe any room under the rooftop of any building, whether house or warehouse, in which storage space or domestic quarters can be incorporated. Changes in economics and taste have promoted attics from servants' quarters to habitations much sought-after by the young; the interesting and unexpected wall and ceiling planes offer exciting challenges to the would-be interior designer.

Aubusson. A French town, some 50 miles east of Limoges, celebrated for its tapestry weaving. When, in 1664, Colbert asked the citizens of the town for the history of the industry,

Louis XV Aubusson tapestry depicting a fête champêtre

Military Barracks at Parramatta, New South Wales, 1820

Australian architecture. All forms of early building in Australia derived from English prototypes. New buildings were erected by settlers without any apparent awareness of differences of climate, in much the same way that the English had once imitated Palladio's buildings, designed for the *campagna* and climate of the Veneto. In Australia the only concession was to

they replied 'that the establishment had been from time immemorial, no person knowing the first institution of it.'

Its legendary beginnings date from 732, when the Moors were defeated by Charles Martel between Tours and Poitiers. Moorish prisoners are said to have settled in the neighbourhood, and earned a living by practising and teaching the art of tapestry weaving.

Louis XIV ordered an inquiry into the state of the industry at Aubusson; from which it emerged that in 1664 the town had only 1,600 weavers. As an encouragement, in July 1665, the king authorised the use of the title 'Royal Manufactory of Aubusson.' But despite promises of financial support, little or nothing was done to help the industry, and it was not until the beginning of the eighteenth century that it recovered from a long depression.

Examples of the charming rustic tapestries of this period can be found in the royal inventory of 1715, such as 'Landscapes and Views', 'Verdures', and 'Elements of Earth.'

Aubusson is best known today for its carpets, most of which were produced during the nineteenth century. Large numbers of these were exported to England and America.

Auger flame. American term for the spiral decoration sometimes found on long-case clocks

Auger flame from a secretary by Townsend-Goddard

and tallboys. The name is derived from the screw point of the carpenter's auger.

Aumbry, ambry or **almery.** A term widely used with general as well as specialized meanings. The aumbry can be described as an enclosed place for storage; it might be an early form of freestanding cupboard (for 'cupboard' did not have its modern meaning until after 1500), an enclosed recess in a wall, or the small compartment of a press. In ecclesiastical terminology it describes both built-in and movable cupboards for holding vestments, books, and sacramental vessels.

St Matthew's Church, New South Wales: Francis Greenway, 1817

AUSTRALIAN ARCHITECTURE

Old Government House at Parramatta, New South Wales, 1815–16

Parliament House, Melbourne, designed by Peter Kerr in 1856

The Australian Academy of Science in Canberra, 1959

The Myer Music Bowl, Melbourne, for open air concerts, 1959

the powerful sunlight; even so, widespread use of canopies and verandas echoed Cheltenham by way of India rather than implying any new approach to the problem of 'solar penetration.' Many of these buildings now have considerable period charm, and Australians are at pains to preserve at least a few of their old villas, houses, shopping arcades and churches. Francis Greenway, sponsored by the inspired and far-sighted Governor Macquarie, was responsible for many of the fine buildings erected in the early nineteenth century.

The early 1900s witnessed a growing revolt against the traditional European forms, and Australian architects are now deeply concerned with designing buildings suitable for Australian conditions. Although much of their practice is based upon European or American prototypes (and European architects are also commissioned), determined efforts are being made to evolve an indigenous manner. In the process, some remarkable buildings have been designed, including several unusual churches; the vast noise-deflecting aluminium canopy of the Melbourne Myer Music Bowl,

Marist Brothers' Chapel at Kogarah: Kevin J Curtin

Ithaca Gardens apartment building, Sydney: Harry Seidler

Left: Sydney Opera House, Bennelong Point, by Jorn Utson

House at Vermon, Victoria: Kenneth McDonald

designed by Barry Patten; AMP's curved skyscraper by Peddle, Thorpe, & Walker; the Sydney Opera House, one of the most remarkable buildings anywhere in the world, designed by the Danish architect Jørn Utzon; and the domed Australian Academy of Science designed by Grounds, Romberg, & Boyd.

Much post-war domestic architecture in Australia has been of a highly experimental nature and equal to any designed elsewhere. Blocks of flats, such as the Ithaca Gardens development in Sydney, owe much to the teachings and example of Le Cor-busier. In much the same way, several vast new office blocks in Melbourne and Sydney owe a good deal to Mies van der Rohe's work in New York and Chicago. But a number of smaller houses are highly individual in design, and take full advantage of the abundance of unusually attractive sites on Australia's endless coastline. Among the most enterprising architects in this sphere have been Maurice Morrison, Kenneth McDonald, Harry Seidler, Sydney Archer, Peter Muller, and Bill Lucas.

Aventurine. Name given to the gold wire used in japanning. It was powdered and scattered over the surface to give a gold-spangled effect similar to that found on the glass and quartz that is properly called aventurine.

Axminster. In 1755 Thomas Chitty founded a carpet manu-factory at Axminster in Devon. He worked in the court house near the church, though he later built a large shed to accommodate a carpet for the Empress of Russia in 1791. Here also were probably woven the huge carpets supplied to the Royal Pavilion at Brighton.

Chitty was helped by grants from the Royal Society of Arts. He appears to have opened the works at Axminster with the intention of supplying carpets in the Turkey style. Samuel Curwen, an American refugee who described a visit to Ax-minster in 1775, noted that a carpet in the Turkey style 36 ft square was being made for the Countess of Salisbury. By 1790, however, Axminster had en-larged both its range and quan-tity of production; in his *Tour through the South of England*, E J Clarke mentions that forty women were employed in weav-ing a carpet for Lord Harewood.

Probably the most interesting reference to Axminster occurs in the correspondence of Sir Edward Knatchbull with Chippendale, Haig, & Co. Chippendale was engaged in furnishing the draw-ing-room of Mersham Hatch in Kent, and on 23rd June 1778 the firm writes, '. . . a design for an Axminster Carpet to correspond with your ceiling and at equal distance from the plinth all round the room, the Expense of it will be according to their best price about £100.'

Carpets continued to be made at Axminster till 1835, when the looms were transferred to Wilton. It is now very difficult to ascribe carpets to the manufactory unless the original bills survive.

Axonometric projection. Geometrical drawings which give a three-dimensional but incom-pletely realistic picture of a build-ing. They are developed from the actual plan, and all measure-ments on the horizontal planes (flat roofs and floors), and all vertical dimensions (walls), are accurate. Only the curves and diagonals on vertical planes are inaccurate.

House by Harry Seidler near Sydney

House at Roseville, New South Wales: Maurice Morrison

An early nineteenth-century Axminster carpet

Baccarat paperweight containing a millefiori mushroom, c 1845

Baccarat, Cristalleries de. Originally founded in 1765 as the Verrerie de Sainte-Anne at Baccarat, near Nancy in Lorraine, France. It was renamed the Cristalleries de Baccarat in 1822 and is still flourishing today.

By the second half of the nineteenth century, Baccarat had become world-famous for fine crystal. Its clientele included kings, emperors, sultans, presi-

Baccarat wineglass with copper wheel engraving, 1910

dents, and maharajas, one of whom ordered a love temple and a set of furniture made of clear Baccarat crystal. In addition to a wide range of tableware and chandeliers, Baccarat, like St Louis and Clichy, is famous for its ornamental paperweights, which were first marketed in 1846. Many Baccarat millefiori (qv) paperweights include silhouettes of animals and stylized flowers among the colourful canes, and some of those made between 1846 and 1849 contain the letter B, followed by the date.

Apart from millefiori, Baccarat produced a number of weights with other subjects, such as a single flower, bouquets of flowers, snakes, butterflies and caterpillars. Overlay weights are in great demand by collectors; in these, windows are cut at the top and the sides, usually exposing a thin layer of opaque white glass that shows off the internal design to great advantage. Occasionally gilding is also used.

Most paperweights averaged about 3 in in diameter. Larger ones of 4 in or more were known as magnums, and miniature weights, measuring only 1½ to 2 in, have been called 'hand coolers.'

Bachelor's chest. Small, early eighteenth-century chest of drawers with a hinged top that could be raised and so used as a table. Any small chest of drawers now tends to be called a bachelor's chest.

Back stool. A crude stool with a triangular seat and three vertical legs, one of which was extended upwards to form a rough back.

From about 1600 until the 1750s the name referred to the kind of stools with backs, or

Lijnbaan shopping area, Rotterdam: J B Bakema and J H van den Broek

chairs without arms, that gradually came to be known as single chairs.

Bacon cupboard. A useful piece of farmhouse furniture that is probably of medieval origin. It is both a settle and a cupboard, for the sitter could rest his back upon the cupboard doors.

Bailey. The courtyard, or ward, of a castle; or a court enclosed by a circuit of walls. The name survives in London's Old Bailey, which lay within the city wall running between Lud Gate and New Gate.

Bakema, J B (b 1914). This architect and his associate, J H van den Broek (b 1886), have done more than any others to win international recognition for Dutch architecture since World War II. They are most closely associated with the rebuilding of Rotterdam, the birthplace of the famous De Stijl (qv) movement of the twenties. Their work is a direct development of the De Stijl style. Their architecture is vigorous and spare, but the materials are handled with sympathy and sensitivity.

During the war the inner town of Rotterdam was completely devastated by bombing. When

the great rebuilding started in 1948, the opportunity was taken to incorporate into the city's new form, advanced and imaginative town-planning ideas. Bakema and van den Broek were responsible for the celebrated and delightful Lijnbaan, a shopping area which provides a pedestrian way from the station to the city centre. It is 700 yds long, with some 85 shops interspersed with cafés, green spaces, and free-standing window displays. Covered ways and overhead bridges link the two sides at convenient intervals. Vehicular access is confined to the rear of the shops.

Baker, Sir Herbert (1862–1946). British architect. Baker was apprenticed to Sir Ernest George (1839–1922), architect of the brick and gabled houses of Collingham Square, in South Kensington, London. Any favourable assessment of Baker's work rests on his buildings in South Africa, for he was responsible for some unfortunate work in London. His reputation in Britain is correspondingly low, largely owing to his unsympathetic and even disastrous alterations to Soane's Bank of England (1921–37), and his design for South Africa House (1935).

In South Africa, his best

Baroque. *The star-like interior of Guarino Guarini's dome on the church of S Lorenzo in Turin, 1668–87*

Groote Schuur, the Prime Minister's residence, Capetown: Baker, 1890

Regency balcony in Brighton

Modern balcony

known buildings are Groote Schuur (1890), a traditional colonial-style house designed for Cecil Rhodes and now the official residence of the South African Prime Minister, and the Government House and the Union Buildings (1910–13) in Pretoria.

Baker later went with Lutyens (qv) to India, where he designed the Secretarial and Legislation Buildings in New Delhi, both of which are generally compared unfavourably with Lutyens' work.

Balcony. Despite its domestic associations, the balcony is mili-tary in origin. The earliest balconies were no more than protective battlements, built out from the walls of fortified buildings. From them, the defenders could cast down stones, boiling liquids, and other missiles upon their assailants.

The balcony as we know it, a platform enclosed by a railing, seems to combine features of the oriel window and the balustraded superstructure of the porch. It began to appear in domestic architecture of the late fifteenth century. It became common in Italian, Spanish, and other Mediterranean architecture, and in England and America its heyday was undoubtedly the nineteenth century. Improved building methods, combined with the wider use of cast-iron and wrought iron, helped to popular-ize this agreeable and usually decorative addition to the house. Modern architects seem to have rediscovered its merits – perhaps because outdoor life is so popular – and houses now have dramatic and even picturesque balconies.

Baldacchino. A canopy above an altar. It may be suspended, projected from the wall, or, as in the most celebrated example, Bernini's *Baldacchino* in St Peter's, Rome, rest on columns.

Baldwin, William. American interior designer and decorator. Baldwin is particularly known for his ability to re-create a room, overcoming the limitations imposed by the original propor-tions. He is also extremely in-genious in his treatment of small apartments, and his success in this sphere has contributed much to his present international repu-tation.

William Baldwin

The baldacchino in St Peter's, Rome, by Bernini, 1624

New York apartment, decorated in brown and white, by William Baldwin

Gothic ball flower decoration on a window of Gloucester Cathedral

Elegant roof balustrade, c 1725

Ball flower. Ornamental motif suggesting a ball within a circular flower, the three petals of which form a cup round it. The motif is found in the decorated style of the thirteenth and fourteenth centuries, for example on the west front of Salisbury Cathedral.

Ball foot. A spherical foot used mainly on heavy oak and walnut case furniture from the late seventeenth century until 1715.

Ball turning. A common form of turning of ancient origin. It consists of a succession of small balls of similar size, and was most popular as a furniture decoration in the second half of the seventeenth and the early eighteenth century.

Balloon clock. A late eighteenth- and early nineteenth-century clock with a circular face and a curving case. The trunk was high and waisted, and rested on a rectangular base, so that the whole had a balloon-like shape.

Baluchistan rugs. Baluchistan lies in the north-west of Pakistan, between Persia, the Arabian Sea, and Afghanistan. Inhabited for centuries by nomadic tribesmen, the Baluchis, it has provided Europe with a limited number of distinctive rugs. Most of these are relatively modern and were not made for export until the beginning of this century. Early Baluchistan rugs were woven for use in the tents and on the pack animals of the weaver's family.

All Baluchistan rugs are dark blue, red, or brown in colouring, sometimes with a purple tinge as well. The unmistakable feature is the use of white hooks or flowerheads in the borders: the contrast is remarkably effective. The design of the field also includes a limited use of white on patterns of geometrical floral groups. This distinguishes Baluchistan rugs from two other types which belong to the same class, Afghanistan and Bokhara rugs, both of which are decorated with field patterns of octagons.

Baluster Banister or or ballaster. A small shaft up to about 3 ft 6 in high, usually made in stone for use in a balustrade (*ie* a series of balusters supporting a cornice or coping) or in wood or metal for use in staircases to support a handrail. Stone balusters are normally circular in section with a graduated swelling towards the base, but when used for stairs, in wood or metal, their forms are apt to be more diverse, ranging from simple square sections to spirals, from complex 'gothick' patterns to chinoiserie trellis infilling between th balustrades.

Baluster and bobbin. Ornamental turning presenting a sequence of balusters and alternating bobbins and rings. Also called baluster and ring.

Bamboo furniture. Sheraton called the bamboo (*bambusa*) 'an Indian reed', which is a reasonable description, although it fails to convey the extraordinary strength and resilience of the bamboo stem. This jointed wood made a considerable appeal, and British cabinetmakers set about imitating its exotic appearance in beech, the wood they normally used for making chairs, chests, and sofa-frames. Pieces were usually painted in a dull ochre colour to simulate the colour of bamboo, but were sometimes also painted in extravagant colours. These mock-bamboo pieces had much charm, and were popular until the beginning of the Victorian era. The Victorians, however, took to the true bamboo, with dubious results. Recently, with the return to favour of Victoriana,

Balloon clock with an inlaid mahogany case, c 1810

Wine glass with baluster stem, early nineteenth century

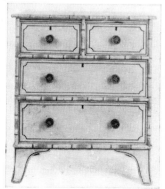

Mock-bamboo chest of drawers, early nineteenth century

Cane-seated bamboo chair, late nineteenth century

Banding on mahogany serpentine fluted sideboard

Early 19th-century banjo clock possibly by the Willard family

these wash-stands and umbrella-racks are reappearing, but their charms are somewhat lack-lustre when compared with the painted examples of the previous century.

Banded column. A column with bands of rustication evenly spaced upon its shaft.

Banding. The cabinetmaker's term for a border or edging to a piece of furniture, usually on the top surface of a chest or table, or a drawer front. Banding is most frequently seen on eighteenth-century furniture, although it was known as a decorative practice even before the Age of Walnut. Exotic woods such as zebrawood, rosewood, and amboyna were used for banding. Strips of veneer were sometimes simulated by painting the banding. Cross-banding, in which the veneer is cut across the grain, gives a diagonal emphasis to the border and is frequently seen in mahogany furniture, where the banding itself was often thinly bordered with satinwood or tulipwood.

Banister or **bar back.** A chair with vertical bars or banisters between the top rail and cross bars. They first appeared in England c 1685, and in America in the early years of the eighteenth century. Their backs were framed by two vertical uprights, and they frequently had rush seats. The most famous bar back designs belong to the late eighteenth century. Many of Hepplewhite's and Sheraton's chairs and settees had slender banisters between the curving yoke rail and the base, which was just above the seat. The frames of these backs were frequently shield-shaped.

Banjo clock. The descriptive modern name for an American clock shaped like the musical instrument. It was invented by Simon Willard (1753–1848), a clockmaker from Roxbury, Massachusetts, who patented it in 1802. The clock had a circular face and an elongated trunk, with flaring concave sides resting on a rectangular base. The trunk was decorated with an *églomisé* (Verre églomisé, qv) panel, and the whole was often crowned with a cone or a spread eagle.

Bannenberg, Jon (*b* 1929). Australian-born interior designer who has been based in England since 1952, forming his own company in 1966. He has built up an international business with a reputation for good design in many fields. As well as private houses and apartments in Britain, America, Greece, France, and Switzerland, he has designed hotels, shops, aircraft, cars, boats, and jewellery.

Jon Bannenberg

Banded columns on the gate of the Botanic Gardens, Oxford

Jon Bannenberg's design for the bedroom of a modern yacht

Baptistry at Pisa Cathedral, Tuscany

He was responsible for the Double Room on the Queen Elizabeth II, which has been described as the largest room afloat, as well as a swimming pool, a card room, and the first-class cabins. He also designed one of the largest and fastest private yachts ever built.

Bannenberg's work includes carpets, wallpapers, and furniture, and his interiors successfully combine the ultra-modern with the antique.

Banquette. This word is now most frequently used to describe a long cushioned seat, with or without a cushioned back, which is usually placed against a wall. The word derives from the Italian *banchetta*, which is the diminutive form of *banca*, a bench.

Bantam work. Incised lacquer. This kind of work dates from the late seventeenth century and is named after the Java province of Bantam, with which England had close commercial ties. Also called cut work.

Baptistery. The area in which baptism is administered. Until about the tenth century, the baptistery was separate from the church and circular or polygonal in plan.

Bar back. See Banister.

Barberry or **berbery.** Shrub of the *Berberidaceae* genus. A hard, close-grained wood from which a yellow dye can be obtained. The wood has been used for inlay work since the seventeenth century.

Barber's chair. See Shaving chair.

Barbican (French, *barbacane*, 'outer defence of a city'). The general term for the outer walls of a city, of which medieval and Roman examples still exist. It is also applied to the outworks of a city gate, which made it possible to control entry into the city.

London's Barbican area, severely damaged in the bombing raids of World War II, has been redesigned by the architects Chamberlin, Powell, and Bon, in consultation with the various groups for whom new houses are being provided. The Royal Shakespeare Company, Guildhall Schools, the London Philharmonic, offices, and flats, are all proposed for the site in an endeavour to inject new life into the city centre.

Barcelona chair, 1929

Barcelona chair. The memorable steel and leather chair designed by Mies van der Rohe for the Barcelona Exhibition of 1929. The chair caused an immediate sensation amongst designers and critics, for, despite much theorising concerning the beauty of functionalism, designers themselves had hitherto produced few examples. This prewar chair has remained one of the few true modern classics, and is still in production.

A barge-board

Barge-board. A board applied to the gable ends of houses and other buildings; usually no more than a simple board to cover rafters, but often used to decorative and even dramatic effect. The decorated barge-board was most common in the fifteenth century, when embellishments of feathering, panelling, and foliage were cut deeply into the timber boards.

Barley sugar twist. The modern name for an English ornamental spiral turning, similar to the traditional stick of barley sugar. It is also known as double rope or double twist, and was used chiefly on the legs and underframing of chairs, tables, and cabinet stands from the late seventeenth century.

Barn. The barn was designed in answer to practical requirements – storing grain and housing cattle – but has come to be admired and examined for its decorative merits alone. Earlier barns were built of local materials

Double barley sugar turning on a late seventeenth-century walnut table

A barn at Bradford-on-Avon, Wiltshire

A barn in Eastern, Pennsylvania, painted with hex signs

A George I barometer in an ebony case with silver gilt mounts, c 1720
Right: Torricellian barometer, with acanthus scrolls, c1770

such as wood and stone, and this, with the splendour of their proportions and the logical sturdiness of their construction, has given them much of their charm. Their construction exemplifies the early building methods employed for both farm buildings and dwelling-houses.

Nowadays, few traditional barns are built; they gave way to buildings with curved, corrugated iron roof units. These have more recently been replaced by the prefabricated concrete units of the large agricultural firms.

Barometer. The barometer, or baroscope, records variations in atmospheric pressure. The way of forecasting weather intrigued scientists from early times, but no accurate instrument existed until the behaviour of mercury in a vacuum tube was analysed. This was the work of Evangelista Torricelli (1608–47), a pupil of Galileo.

Torricelli's discovery was introduced to England by Dr Hooke, the celebrated scientist, at the time of the restoration of Charles II in 1660. Hooke influenced the greatest of English clockmakers, Thomas Tompion, and other craftsmen. As a result,

at the end of the seventeenth century, England produced some of the finest barometers ever made.

The design of the instrument allowed much scope for decoration, and before 1700 various forms of barometers had evolved. Tompion provided the royal palaces with some superb examples, usually in walnut enriched with gilt metal and based on the design of the hoods of grandfather clocks.

At about the same time, Daniel Quare was making both hanging and portable standing barometers with japanned, ivory, or even ebony cases, spirally moulded like the chair legs of the period and often enriched with silver mounts.

At the beginning of the eighteenth century, the shapes of barometers changed, and in much the same way as those of clock cases. Classical pediments and columns became common features. By 1750 the influence of Chippendale's Rococo carving was widely felt. It lasted until Sheraton's drawings gave the barometer its best known form, that of a banjo, which remained standard throughout the last century.

Baroque. Few aspects of architecture are more elusive of definition than Baroque. Although we are apt to think of it as a known category of seventeenth- and eighteenth-century building, the word does not

seem to have been in general use until 1818. It derives from the Portuguese *barocco*, a term applied by the jewellers of that country to pearls of irregular shape. No word could more appositely describe the elements

Façade of San Carlo alle Quattro Fontane, Rome, by Borromini, 1667

The dome of the Karlskirche, Vienna, by Fischer von Erlach

S Agnese in Agone, Rome. Façade by Borromini, 1652–7

of Baroque, for the style arose as a result of a fierce aesthetic reaction against the severe classicism of Palladio and his followers.

Some critics have seen the origins of Baroque in the exuberant architectural designs of Michelangelo, who brought to building much of the imaginative scope and *bravura* of a great artist. But the break with the past is more clearly seen in the buildings of Bernini (1598–1680) and Borromini (1599–1667). The inventiveness and assurance of both men have left us with many remarkable buildings and established Baroque as one of the most notable and representative expressions of seventeenth-century art.

Baroque can most simply be defined as a powerful imaginative exuberance translated into graphic forms, a piling up of decorative motifs into unashamedly theatrical composition on canvas or in brick and stone. To this end, almost any visual device or even trick was employed. Symmetry, with its attendant qualities of balance and serenity, is avoided. A strong sense of movement is introduced which, allied to richness of

ornament and decoration, gives vitality to the whole composition – a vitality that to the purists seemed to border on vulgarity.

We can see this exuberance in architecture in its most obvious forms in Bernini's Roman fountains (the *Four Rivers* and the *Triton*). It is at its most flamboyant (giving great offence to Ruskin) in the *Baldacchino* (qv) under the dome of St Peter's, and at its most distinguished in the great curving colonnades which flank the forecourt of St Peter's.

Borromini had an even greater influence than Bernini in freeing architectural design from late Palladian classicism, and in transforming Rome into a Baroque city. Many of Borromini's churches and secular buildings have survived.

The success of these masters of Baroque inevitably influenced architecture abroad, although Bernini's designs for the Louvre were never carried out. The impact of Baroque was felt in France and Spain, and a magnificent Baroque architecture was produced in Austria and south Germany. From Spain the style was taken to Central and South

The Triton fountain, Rome, by Bernini

The north front, Blenheim Palace, Oxfordshire, by Vanburgh

The marble hall pavilion of the convent of St Florian, Austria

St Paul's Cathedral, London

America, where churches of an amazing decorative complexity were built. Wren met Bernini briefly in Paris. The lessons of Baroque were not lost upon the mathematician-turned-architect; they are apparent in St Paul's, although Wren never practised the full-blooded Italian Baroque.

More emphatically, Baroque styles were developed by three other English architects: Nicholas Hawksmoor, Sir John Vanbrugh, and Thomas Archer. Each pro-

The nave of the church of St Florian, Austria

The town tower and Helbling house, Innsbruck

Christ Church, Spitalfields, London: Hawksmoor, 1723–9

The south front of Castle Howard, Yorkshire, by Vanburgh, 1699–1726

Seaton Delaval in Northumberland, by Vanbrugh, c 1720–8

The Traveller's Club, Pall Mall, London, designed by Barry, 1829

duced remarkable designs, the best of which hold their own for originality and vitality with any Roman Baroque building. Hawksmoor's churches (St George in the East and Christ Church, Spitalfields), and his work with Vanbrugh in the designing of Blenheim Palace, place him in the foremost ranks of masters of Baroque. Vanbrugh's masterful, theatrical designs for Blenheim and Seaton Delaval remain unsurpassed in England as examples of the splendours of the style. Archer's Baroque works are his churches, notably St John's, Smith Square, Westminster, and St Paul's, Deptford.

The same ebullience is also to be found in furniture, silver, and glass of the period, although it became even more marked later.

Barrel-back chair. A nineteenth-century American upholstered chair. It had a circular seat and a high, concave, barrel-like back, the sides of which curved down to give a semblance of sloping arms. See also **Tub chair.**

Barry, Sir Charles (1795–1860). Barry is chiefly remembered as the architect of the Houses of Parliament in London. In fact, he was by no means in sympathy with the Gothic style which was decided upon for the building, and employed Pugin to design most of the mock-medieval detail, himself retaining responsibility for the planning and supervision of the whole.

Following a prolonged series of travels in Italy, Greece, and the Near East as a young man, Barry quickly showed unusual talent as an adaptor of the Italian palazzo-form for public buildings, and his design for the Travellers' Club, Pall Mall (1829), has been called the last Neo-classical building in England. He built churches in London, the King Edward Grammar School in Birmingham, parts of Dulwich College and a considerable number of mansions throughout England, notably Cliveden.

Bartizan. The proper name for the small turrets of which Scottish builders and architects have been so fond. They are usually seen on the angles of towers and parapets.

Base. An architectural term which generally refers to the lowest part of a pillar, on which the shaft is placed; it is also occasionally used to describe the lowest course of brickwork or masonry on which a wall or building rests. In the classical orders, the forms and proportions of bases followed certain rules, and the base was divided into plinth and mouldings. In other styles, however, the design followed no such rules. An extra-ordinary variety of shapes resulted, ranging from a solid square slab to something very much higher and more decorative, sometimes almost a podium or pedestal.

Basement. The basement was originally the lowest storey of a

Portuguese bartizans, 19th-century

Houghton Hall, Norfolk, 1722–32, showing the basement storey

large house, forming the base for the principal floor or *piano nobile*. It was not necessarily below ground: in fact, it was more frequently above it.

Basevi, George (1794–1845). A British architect of Italian descent, Basevi was the most accomplished and successful of Sir John Soane's pupils. On the expiry of his articles he travelled widely in Italy and Greece. Between 1825 and 1840 he designed most of the houses in Belgrave Square and much of the area of South Kensington that includes Pelham Crescent, Sydney Place, Alexander Square, and Thurloe Square. Basevi's well-designed terraces and squares (particularly the lesser scale of his South Kensington work) are the last achievements of the Georgian

urban tradition before the advent of Victorian laissez-faire building. Basevi was killed by falling from the tower of Ely Cathedral while surveying the bell tower.

Basilica. In Roman architecture, an oblong hall used as a court of justice; it had double colonnades and a semi-circular apse at one end. Under Constantine some basilicas were converted into Christian churches, and both form and name were thus carried over into church design.

Basin or **bason stand.** An eighteenth-century term used to describe a great variety of wash stands, from the surviving medieval tripod to the many contemporary types. Some of these were tripods with a

Mahogany basin stand, c 1760

moulded ring for the basin, two fitted drawers in the otherwise open stand, and a second ring at the base for the ewer or pitcher. Others were of a pillar, corner, or four-legged construction. The last, belonging to the second half of the eighteenth century, were usually elaborately fitted with drawers, cupboards, and a small rising mirror, and were also known as wash-hand tables.

Basket arch. An arch curved like the handle of a basket. It is usually constructed from three centres, one of which is below the springing line.

Bas-relief. An English adaptation of the more melodious Italian original, *basso-relievo*. The term is applied to a work of sculpture which is carved and projects from a wall, plaque, tablet, medallion, or other surface, whether flat or rounded. Originally, the exact degree of the projection from the surface governed the definition: *mezzo-relievo* for carvings in which half of the figure or figures projected; *alto-relievo* for more than half. These Italian terms are no longer deemed necessary, and all such sculptures are called bas-reliefs. The most widely known bas-reliefs are the Elgin Marbles in the British Museum. Josiah Wedgwood commissioned many bas-reliefs from sculptors to use on his ware.

Bateman, Hester (1709–94). When Hester Bateman was widowed in 1760, she took out her own mark and struggled to keep on her husband's silver business. She was one of the most successful English silversmiths at a time when many contemporary smiths were turn-

Alexander Square, Kensington, by Basevi

Belgrave Square, by Basevi, 1825–40

Bas-relief figures on Wedgwood's copy of the Portland Vase, 1790

Boat-shaped sugar basket by Hester Bateman, 1786

ing away from silver and using the cheaper Sheffield plate. By 1790, when she retired, she had established a sound reputation for the firm, which carried on under the direction of her children.

Mrs Bateman's elegant silverware is in the Neo-classical taste popularised by the architect-designer Robert Adam. She used the classical urn-shape for many of her pieces, and also drew on antiquity for her ornament: swags or festoons of cornhusks, or ribbons, laurel wreaths, classical medallions, etc. She employed fine piercing and used beading and fluting frequently; her speciality appears to have been bright-cut engraving (see **Silver, decoration techniques**). Her delicate ware appeals to a wide public today and is particularly highly prized in the USA.

Plate by Richard Freeman

Bath Pottery. The Bath Pottery was started in 1950 by John Shelly, who had worked with Raymond Finch at the Winchcombe Pottery. The Bath Pottery's early output was useful ware, including ovenware, much of it decorated with slip. Marks were a monogram JS for the pieces actually made by Mr Shelly, while the rest of the pottery's productions were stamped with an impressed BATH POTTERY. In 1955 Richard Freeman bought the pottery and John Shelly left. Freeman now makes most of the pieces himself, still essentially useful ware.

Batik. A Malayan term which originally described a process and now more generally describes a type of pattern. The process was used by the natives of the East Indies for dyeing parts of their fabrics. By covering parts of their designs with melted wax, dyeing the remaining areas, and then discarding the wax in boiling water, they produced vivid and frequently complex patterns. The method was brought to Europe by the Dutch and was used on expensive coverings such as velvets and velours. Later, batik patterns, in the vegetable colourings of the Orient, were produced on cotton by industrial methods.

Batten. A carpenter's term, derived from boat-building which is used to describe narrow strips of wood. In the timber trade the word is used more specifically to mean square-sawn softwood within the range 2 to 4 in thick and 5 to 8 in wide.

Batter. Walls rising with an inward inclination are said to be battered; the object is usually to strengthen the structure.

Battersea enamel. An enamel works was set up at York House, Battersea, London, in about 1750. So far as is known, it closed in 1756, but despite the very short duration of the works, its fame has been considerable. The founder was Stephen Theodore Janssen, who had a stationer's business in St Paul's Churchyard. In 1754 he was elected Lord Mayor of London, but two years later he became bankrupt and the enamel works was sold at auction.

From the catalogue of this sale, one can get an idea of the products made at Battersea. There were 'Beautiful, enamell'd pictures, snuff-boxes, watchcases, bottle tickets . . .' – for the main output was devoted to small objects such as are mentioned by Horace Walpole in *Strawberry Hill*. In the Green Closet, says Walpole, there was 'A Kingfisher and Ducks of the Battersea enamel.'

Battersea enamel is now rare and is often very difficult to identify, for it had many imitators and rivals, especially at Bilston in Staffordshire. It exemplifies that decorative skill in miniature in which many eighteenth-century craftsmen excelled.

Battlements. Medieval notched parapets whose function was to protect the defenders of fortified buildings. During the eighteenth century they enjoyed a

Battersea oblong snuff box with transfer printing on the lid

great revival through the buildings of architectural amateurs, who were prepared to borrow any device, however anachronistic, to satisfy their craze for the medieval and 'gothick.'

Bauhaus. The Bauhaus in Germany was perhaps the most powerful single influence in the development and eventual public acceptance of modern architecture. The original Bauhaus was founded by Professor Walter Gropius as an extension of the Weimar School of Arts and Crafts in the spring of 1919, under the name of *Das Staatliche Bauhaus, Weimar.* There, Gropius attempted to solve what he has termed 'the ticklish problem of combining imaginative design and technical proficiency.' To this end he converted the Bauhaus drawing-offices and workshops into what were virtually industrial design laboratories, deliberately directed towards creating well-designed articles for mass-production.

Teaching at the Bauhaus effected a revolution in art education. By arrangement with manufacturers, promising pupils worked for short periods in factories. Many talented but

Battlements on Saltwood Castle, Kent

Bauhaus models of metal lamps

China service designed by O Lindig

Wall decoration of Bawden designs

impecunious students were also enrolled, and, to help with their fees, were paid for work which proved saleable. Above all, every student was involved in what Gropius regarded as the 'umbrella' for all their work: the development of a new and rational architecture. In this he was echoing the beliefs of earlier designer-architects, such as Robert Adam and Soane, who held that the architect should be responsible not only for the design of the house but for all its appurtenances, from textiles to cutlery.

In 1925 the Bauhaus (now with 24 instructors and 180 to 200 students) moved to Dessau. Gropius returned to private practice in Berlin in 1928, handing over control to his successor, the great architect Mies van der

Rohe.

The teaching methods established by Gropius were responsible for the design of many objects which became prototypes for mass-produced ceramics, lighting fitments, rugs, and textiles of a high order of design. It is also now apparent that many of the theories underlying the International Style in architecture were worked out in the Bauhaus.

The modernism and international character of the Bauhaus teachings were at variance with the Nazi outlook; and its principals and principles moved to the USA where a new Bauhaus was founded in Chicago.

Bawden, Edward (*b* 1903). British artist-designer whose prolific output has included oil- and

water-colour painting, lithography, wood engraving, etching, and lino-cutting. His interests have ranged from recording the World War II campaign in Abyssinia as a war artist, to designing murals for the Lion and Unicorn Pavilion at the 1951 Festival of Britain; from illustrating limited editions for American publishers to designing and decorating china for Wedgwood. He has also designed wallpapers, rugs, textiles, and murals for ships.

Bay. Bays are the areas in a building, whether interior or exterior, that are marked off by units of vaulting, columns, windows, etc.

Bay leaf. Ornamental motif used in wreaths or swags, or

applied to convex mouldings.

Bay window. An early form of window which, by projecting outwards from the wall of a building provided a well-lit recess in a room. Bay windows are to be found in Perpendicular buildings and in the halls of aristocratic houses and colleges. Later the 'bay' became the 'bow' window, which was regarded as a corrupt form. Then, in reaction against the solid Victorian bay, the bow window came to be preferred. Nowadays both curved bow and angular bay windows are to be seen in many small houses, and modern methods of construction ensure that the main

The Bauhaus, Dessau, designed by Gropius, 1925–6

Early bay windows

object of both features – to let in as much light as possible – is achieved.

Bead. A small convex moulding that is also called an astragal or a roundel. It is frequently found on flush panelling. 'Bead and butt' is the name for a way of decorating framed panelling. The bead moulding runs vertically between the panel and the stiles, but not horizontally between panel and rails.

Bead and reel or **reel and bead.** A classical moulding of alternating beads (near-oval convex mouldings) and narrow coupled reels. Another moulding, found on furniture of the early sixteenth century, has occasionally been called bead and reel; this consists of small circular mouldings and spiralled cylinders placed horizontally.

Beadwork. The use of coloured glass beads instead of, or in conjunction with, silk and wool needlework is found at an early date. Coptic examples are known, and others from thirteenth-century Germany. Italian gloves were enriched with beadwork in the 1500s, and in late Elizabethan England beads were an accepted feature in a large variety of domestic objects, including jewel-caskets, bottles, snuff-boxes, stockings, and the frames of looking-glasses.

English beadwork had its greatest vogue in late Stuart times and in the Victorian period, when it was also popular in America. It was used on Victorian chair and stool covers, on needlework pictures, on fire-screens, and on almost all purses.

Beadwork is a traditional craft of the American Indians, who continue to use it in the ornamentation of clothing.

The great advantage of beads

Beamed medieval hall

is that they can neither fade nor wear. No other decorative medium has been less subject to the effect of age, and few retain such bold colouring or freshness.

Beakhead. This is characteristic Norman ornamental motif consisting of a bird's head and tongue used in a series as a moulding enrichment. Sometimes it is shown biting into a roll moulding.

Beam. From Old English, *beam* 'a tree.' The beam has been one of the basic elements in building since early times. Stone beams were used by the Egyptians, but probably the finest examples of stone beam construction are the temples of the Aegean.

The word has come to be associated mainly with wood because in masonry the stone beam was soon replaced by the arch. In wood construction, the timber cruck type of dwelling in which two inclined beams supported a ridge beam, developed into the fine half-timbered constructions of the fourteenth and fifteenth centuries. The old form of frame structure was replaced by solid walls, and the timber beams remained only in the floor joists and the roof.

Recent developments in architecture have led to a revival of

Modern use of exposed beams

frame building. The architect, less concerned than his forerunners to hide either the structure of his buildings or the materials in which he builds, now often exposes the structural beams to obtain dramatic effects. Thus they become a decorative part of the interior.

The tall, multi-storey buildings of today have been made possible by the use of steel and reinforced concrete beams and columns, and beams spanning 60 to 100 ft present no problems to modern architects and engineers.

Bearer. The general and cabinetmakers' term for a horizontal member that gives support to another member.

Beau Brummell table. A gentleman's toilet table made in England and America in the later

eighteenth century. This kind of table was in vogue before Beau Brummell (1789–1840) was born, but the name is not inappropriate, for the table was fitted with one or more rising mirrors, with facilities for washing and shaving, and with other prerequisites of dandyism.

Beauvais. A town in France where the art of tapestry weaving has been practised intermittently for at least a thousand years. The modern foundation of this industry was the work of Louis XIV, who in 1664 issued letters patent to Louis Hinart, a weaver of Paris. Hinart, at great financial profit to himself, organized the workshops till 1684, when he was replaced by the great weaver Philippe Behagle. The work of this period reflects the mood of the age, and series of tapestries

Norman beakhead carvings

A Louis XV Beauvais tapestry from 'The Loves of the Gods' by Boucher

Elizabethan carved oak bed with inlaid decoration, c 1590

Modern Italian bed which converts into a sofa

Beauvais has carried on with varying fortunes until the present day. The last designer of note in the eighteenth century was Francesco Casanova (1727–1802), brother of the great adventurer.

Bed. The most important piece of furniture man possesses. In bed occur the vital events of life and the greatest pleasures; and a third of most people's lives is spent there. It seems strange that modern beds are less ostentatious than in previous ages, but this is probably because the bedroom is more private than ever before, rendering conspicuous opulence unnecessary.

From ancient Egyptian times to the fall of the Roman Empire, beds were either rectangular wooden constructions, like those on show at Herculaneum, or richly decorated throne-beds in gold, ivory, silver, and ebony, often so high that they could only be mounted by ladder.

There were few beds of interest in the Dark Ages, but illuminated manuscripts provide evidence of a revival of the craft of bed construction from the twelfth century. Beds usually had enclosed wooden headboards, and this eventually gave rise to the four-poster so common until the last century.

The finest beds were made in Britain and France. In France the apogee of the art was reached in the eighteenth century. The massive four-poster became a small, intimate, feminine bed, often let into the wall, gilded, carved with flowers, oval or circular, hidden in a profusion of silk draperies or partly enclosed by curtains falling from the ceiling or wall. The names of such beds (*lit clos, lit de glaces, lit d'alcove, lit bâteau*) indicate the variousness of their designs.

The best English beds were made in Stuart times. The magnificence of the giant four-poster, with its sumptuous embroideries rising to lambrequined canopies carrying ostrich plumes under immense ceilings has perhaps never been surpassed.

Eccentric and unusual beds are innumerable: the bed of nails of the fakir, the *lit de justice* of the French kings, the Chippendale chinoiserie bed from Badminton. A remarkable Celestial Bed was installed by the charlatan Dr James Graham in 'The Temple of Health and of Hymen' in Pall Mall, London. Supported by 'forty pillars of brilliant glass', which incorporated musical instruments, it was let for as much as £500 a night as a cure for sterility. Alas, it no longer exists.

Bed mould. Moulding beneath a projection; in classical architecture, the mouldings immediately under the corona of the cornice.

Beech. *Fagus sylvatica.* A soft, pale wood much used in seventeenth- and eighteenth-century furniture-making. In both England and France it was widely employed on pieces to be painted, lacquered, or gilded. Its silver flecking appears to advantage in chairs with polished frames made in the reigns of Louis XV and XVI. In Stuart England it was used as a substitute for walnut or oak. It is liable to woodworm attacks, which prompted Evelyn to write in *Sylva* (1664), 'I wish the use of it were by law prohibited.'

Behrens, Peter (1868–1914). German artist, designer, and architect. Behrens trained to

were woven entitled 'Victories of the Swedes over the Danes,' 'Conquests of Louis the Great', 'The History of Achilles', and a remarkable set in the manner of Jean Berain, 'Grotesque Chinois.'

Behagle died in 1704 and Beauvais's fortunes immediately began to decline under less competent leadership. In 1726 it was saved from disaster by the appointment of the gifted organizer J B Oudry. Beauvais carried on with only fair success until the painter François Boucher

began his great series of tapestries in 1736. These, produced until 1755, established Beauvais at the pinnacle of its fame and gave the world some of the gayest, loveliest, and most sophisticated tapestries ever created. The subjects Boucher chose reflect the taste of the period for frivolous but enchanting scenes, and include 'Loves of the Gods', 'Fêtes Italiennes', and a 'History of Psyche.'

Oudry died in 1755 and Boucher moved to Gobelins, but

A factory in Berlin, designed by Peter Behrens, built in 1909

become an artist at the art school in Karlsruhe, and then at Düsseldorf. He was a founder-member of the Munich Secession in 1893, but after travelling in Italy began to take an interest in designing for industry. In 1899 he was asked by the grand duke of Hesse to join a group of artists and architects in Darmstadt known as *Die Sieben* (The Seven). Here he first began the serious study and practice of architecture which was to make him one of the most important figures of the early modern movement.

In 1909 Behrens became designer and architect to AEG, the large electrical organisation in Berlin. In this capacity he designed his earliest major work, the Turbine Factory (1908–9), which was Germany's first steel and glass industrial building. This was followed by a factory for small motors (1910–11) and a large machine assembly hall (1911–12). Despite his logical approach to industrial building, Behrens sometimes gave in to pressure from conservative clients, and several of his later buildings have Neo-classical or similarly traditional façades superimposed upon tough and rigorous structures. Examples are the offices he designed for the Mannesmann Steel Company at Düsseldorf (1913–23) and the Continental Rubber Company at Hanover (1911–12). During the 1920s he was greatly influenced by the International Style which he had earlier helped to create.

Behrens was not only the leading architect of his generation in Germany, but also a graphic and typographical designer of considerable achievement. In his office at AEG, three great figures of the modern

Wine glass painted in white enamel by Beilby family c 1770

movement (Gropius, Mies van der Rohe, and Le Corbusier) received their early training.

Beilby, William (1740–1819), and his sister Mary (1749–97). Famous glass enamellers who practised in Newcastle from c 1762–78, when they moved to Fife and apparently ceased working.

The majority of their decorations were done on goblets and wine glasses with compound opaque twist stems, and on decanters or bowls, some of which show traces of gilded rims. Their decorative repertory ranged from butterflies to pastoral scenes, from heraldic devices to Rococo scrolls. Their brushwork is remarkable, whether in colours or in white sometimes faintly tinged with pink or blue.

Belanger, François-Joseph (1774–1818). French architect and designer who played a leading part in forming the Neo-classical style in late eighteenth-century Paris. Like Robert Adam in England, he not only designed buildings but also the furniture and fittings for each room.

His influence on contemporaries stems from his reconstruction and furnishing of the remarkable Château Bagatelle in the Bois de Boulogne executed for the Comte d'Artois in 1777. Artois wagered Marie Antoinette 100,000 livres that Bagatelle could be completely reconstructed during the Queen's late summer visit to Fontainebleau. Belanger's plans were approved within two days, and 64 days later, on the 26th November, Artois won his bet. The cost was about 1,200,000 livres, the livre being worth something like a modern pound sterling.

Belfast truss. A roof truss that has a curved principal rafter and a horizontal tiebeam or string that is joined to the upper beam by a lattice of smaller members. The Belfast truss is also known as a bowstring.

Belfry. A bell-tower. The term was first used to describe a watch-tower containing a bell used to give warning of approaching enemies. Later the term was used to describe an ecclesiastical bell-tower or campanile; it was usually part of a church, but was occasionally detached. The room in the tower in which the bells are hung is also called a belfry. Belfries have sometimes been incorporated into domestic architecture, particularly in Victorian and Edwardian mansions.

Belfry

Belgian architecture. See **Dutch and Belgian architecture.**

Bell and baluster. An ornamental form of turning in which each unit is a narrow baluster with a bell on top. It was chiefly used for the legs of tables and stands in the late seventeenth and early eighteenth centuries.

Bellflower. An American decorative motif of the late eighteenth century, resembling the contemporary English husk motif (qv). The standard bell-flower is a stylised flower of bell shape with only three petals. Variations are blunted petals and an elongated centre petal with a circle added beneath.

Belter, John Henry (1804–63). Furniture maker. Belter was born in Germany, where he was apprenticed as a wood carver and cabinetmaker at Württemberg. By 1844, however, he had settled in New York and established a flourishing furniture business.

The Château Bagatelle, built by Belanger in the Bois de Boulogne, 1777

Ornate sofa made by John Belter

Belvederes from an old book 'L'Art de Composer et Décorer les Jardins'

His furniture was in a neo-Rococo style akin to the ornate carving of his native Black Forest. It is usually made of laminated rosewood by a process that Belter patented in 1856. Panels of laminae of rosewood were made, that enabled him to shape and carve this heavily grained wood in a way that would not otherwise have been possible.

Although Belter was the foremost furniture manufacturer of the mid-nineteenth century, the steady flow of French imports and the Civil War hindered his success. Within four years of his death his firm was bankrupt.

Belvedere (Italian, *bel* 'beautiful', and *vedere* 'sight') has come to mean almost any structure, or

Silver bowl made by Gerald Benney

addition to a larger structure, from which the surrounding countryside may be viewed. The belvedere seems to have originated in Renaissance Italy, but really came into its own in the age of the Picturesque, when any *ferme ornée* was incomplete without its belvedere and/or gazebo. The illustration gives some idea of the structures which were recommended to French landowners with aesthetic inclinations by the editors of *L'Art de Composer et Décorer les Jardins*.

Bench. A long plank of wood or stone on trestles or similar supports. Once the commonest form of seat furniture in Europe, it is now more often found in the schoolroom, public house, or

gymnasium than in a private house.

The gregarious household habits of medieval times led to 'benching about.' The hall or refectory of all large houses was lined with benches fixed to the floor or walls.

The movable bench, early examples of which are now very rare, developed on similar lines to the stool and was decorated with often rich and surprising Gothic motifs. The addition of a panelled back similar to the walls against which it stood, transformed the bench into a settle or church pew.

Bended back. A single or elbow chair with a baluster-shaped back splat in a tall frame, and with cabriole legs. The whole back had a slight concave curve to afford extra comfort. Early eighteenth century. See also **Hogarth chair.**

Benney, Gerald (*b* 1930). British silversmith. Benney received his early training in Brighton before going to the London Royal College of Art in 1951. In 1954 he opened his own silver workshop.

Benney works in the classical tradition of simple forms but makes much use of contrasting surface textures. His output covers the entire range of silverware from ecclesiastical and ceremonial plate to domestic table silver, for which he receives

the greater part of his commissions.

The cutlery he has designed for Viners, the biggest Sheffield cutlers, has had enormous commercial success throughout the world. More recently his work has included a gold decanter presented to President Pompidou, a silver bowl for Herr Willy Brandt, a mace for Glasgow University, a pair of candelabra for Croydon Corporation, and all the table silver for the new Institute of Chartered Accountants.

Benney held a one-man exhibition at the Rutland Gallery, London (1968), and has contributed to many others in Europe, America, Australia, and Japan.

Bennington pottery. The earliest kiln at Bennington, Vermont, USA, began operations in 1793. It was founded by Captain John Norton and manufactured red earthenware, bricks, and later stoneware. Julius Norton, grandson of the founder, became a partner of Christopher Webber Fenton *c* 1845, and together they established the principal Bennington Pottery, which flourished until 1858. In 1853 it became the United States Pottery, with Fenton as a founder-member, Norton having earlier withdrawn from the business.

A large variety of ware was produced, including many utility articles such as door knobs and platters, as well as the tableware and figures for which Bennington is best known. Mottled Rockingham and Bennington Parian were manufactured, both adapted from English ware.

Typical products were recumbent cows and deer in flint enamelware, blue and white porcelain vases and pitchers, toby jugs of contemporary figures, and hound-handled pitchers. These pitchers were most distinctive, with a mottled Rockingham glaze, a hound for the handle, and boar and stag hunting scenes on the body of the jug. Daniel Greatbach, a Staffordshire potter, joined the factory in 1851 and was probably responsible for the better animal pieces in Rockingham ware.

'Bennington' is used generally to describe all Rockingham ware that was manufactured during the lifetime of the pottery and down to 1900; the most noteworthy was made in the Ohio valley.

Bennington is still made in Vermont where traditional designs are copied (along with contemporary and modern tableware).

Westminster Cathedral: Bentley

Bentley, J F (1839–1902). One of the best late-Victorian, Gothic architects, though mainly remembered for a building in the Byzantine style. He built several fine churches in the London area, notably the Sacred Heart Convent at Hammersmith.

At the age of 56 he was commissioned by Cardinal Vaughan to design Westminster Cathedral.

Bentley went to Italy and Istanbul to study the Byzantine style, returning to start work in 1894. Unfortunately his plans for lining the building with marble and mosaic were not completed (the decoration inside is only nów being finished). The gigantic cathedral, with its red-and-white striped brick outside, its high tower and row of green domes may not be in the purest Byzantine tradition, but it is none the less impressive.

Bentley's last work was the planning of a Gothic cathedral for Brooklyn, for which he went to New York. However, he died before finishing the designs.

Apart from his work as an architect, Bentley designed a number of stained glass windows, furniture, and fabrics.

Bentwood furniture. The type of bentwood furniture shown here was originally developed by Michael Thonet, who lived and worked in Bohemia (now part of Czechoslovakia) during the last part of the nineteenth century. He was responsible for some of the earliest successful experiments in wood laminate furniture. Later he created his famous bentwood chairs, devising a method of mass production which enabled the chairs to be made really cheaply. These later became popular throughout Europe and America and were used as all-purpose school, café, and public building chairs. Their main characteristics are their lightness and strength. Seats on bentwood chairs were either wood laminate or, on the more elaborate pieces, cane.

Berain, Jean (1637–1711). Interior decorator and architect to Louis XIV, Berain exercised a major influence on French (and therefore European) decoration. He was born into a family of gunsmiths in Lorraine, moved to Paris, and, attracting the notice of Charles Le Brun, became *Dessinateur de la Chambre et du Cabinet du Roi* in 1674.

His work for the Crown included designing theatrical performances, ballet costumes, and firework and other displays; but he is remembered above all as an interior designer. He brought an element of personal fantasy to the fashionable arabesque motif, which continued to be used after Berain's death and was a forerunner of the Rococo style of the mid-eighteenth century. Most typical of Berain's fantasy were the *singeries* – groups of monkeys and other animals imitating men, taunting grotesque beasts, or acting ludicrous scenes from the Italian *Commedia*. Few decorators have impressed upon their age such an idiosyncratic genius.

Decorative composition by Berain

Bergère. A comfortable French upholstered armchair that became fashionable c 1725. It was an informal, movable piece of furniture, not used as an element in the formal arrangement of most French drawing-rooms. The bergère was larger than a fauteuil (qv) with a higher back and wider seat. The area below the arm pads was upholstered, and the seat was fitted with a loose cushion. There are variations on the basic form, notably the *bergère en confessional, bergère à joues,* a chair with wings; and the *bergère en gondole,* which had back, wings, and arms joined in a single sweep. See also **Birgair.**

A Louis XV bergère

Bentwood rocking chair in a modern interior

The colonnade of the Piazza of St Peter's in Rome by Bernini, 1656 onwards

Bernini, Giovanni (1598–1680). Italian architect and sculptor. Bernini was born in Naples, the son of Pietro Bernini, a sculptor. In about 1605 the family moved to Rome, where Bernini was to spend the rest of his life. His only long visit abroad was to Paris in 1665, when Louis XIV solicited his help in enlarging and improving the Louvre. Bernini's designs were eventually rejected, and his sojourn was neither rewarding nor pleasant.

Bernini's genius found its fullest expression in sculpture. However, he was also a great architect, his finest achievement being the great curving colonnades which encompass the forecourt of St Peter's. The remodelling of the Cornaro Chapel in S Maria del la Vittoria, with the intensely dramatic marble group *Ecstasy of St Teresa* placed above the altar, is probably his most famous work. The Barbarini family were his patrons for many years, and he designed the façade of their palazzo. Other major works of architecture by

Bernini include churches at Castelgandolfo and Ariccia, and S Andrea al Quirinale in Rome.

Bertoia, Harry (*b* 1915). Italian-born American sculptor, furniture designer, and architect. Bertoia left for the United States in 1930 and began his career by studying sculpture, mechanical drawing, and metalcraft at the Detroit School of Arts and Crafts, then at Cranbrook Art Academy, where he later taught. After World War II he did extensive research into Human Engineering at the American Navy Electronics Laboratory.

In 1950 he was persuaded by Hans and Florence Knoll (later Form International) to set up his studio next to their factory. They encouraged him to develop his own ideas, and the following year he began to produce a series of wire shell chairs. These have chromium-plated, steel-wire mesh seats suspended by triangular braces over a cradle of steel rods; the angle of the seats can be adjusted automatically.

These chairs have won awards from the Architectural League, the American Institute of Architects (1953), the Institute of Decorators (1955), and the Graham Foundation for Advanced Study in Fine Arts (1957). Bertoia has chosen to remain primarily a sculptor, and turned down several teaching positions. His commissions have included work for the chapel at the Massachusetts Institute of Technology, Dallas Public Library, and St Louis and Dallas Airports. He has exhibited on both sides of the Atlantic.

Betty lamp. An oil lamp used in Britain and America from the seventeenth to the early nineteenth century. Similar to the Scottish crusie, it was a shallow open dish, made of tin or iron, with a floating wick. Some betty lamps were fixed to vertical stands; others were hung from ratchets on the ceiling.

Bevel. A bevel is a sloped or canted surface. It is generally used in architecture to describe the sloping edge formed when the corner of a beam or other member is cut off at an angle.

A bevel is often employed because the bevelled edge is not as prone to damage as a sharp corner. The word is used especially when the sloped surface is relatively small, 'splay' being used of larger surfaces.

Bibelots. A word we have annexed from French and use to describe any small *objets de vertu*, usually made of some precious material and of superior craftsmanship. Snuff-boxes, seals, miniature boxes, small vases, and objects made by Fabergé or Cartier in gold, semi-precious stone, crystal, or enamel can all be described as bibelots.

Bible box. A term used to describe many kinds of oak boxes, especially those with sloping lids dating from the late sixteenth and the seventeenth century. Many have held Bibles but most were for general storage or for use as reading stands or desks.

Biedermeier. The name applied to a type of furniture made in Germany, Austria, and to a lesser degree, Scandinavia. It derived indirectly from the

Welded lattice wire shell chairs, designed by Bertoia

Carved oak Bible box, first half seventeenth century

A bedroom in Biedermeier style

Billiard table with turned legs, seventeenth century

French Directoire and Empire styles, and perhaps more directly from English sources: in many respects Biedermeier forms resemble Adam furniture stripped of its Neo-classical decoration. Furniture designed in this manner has a curiously 'modern' appearance, for much of the elaborate decoration and almost all the brass and ormolu of the Empire period are omitted, and the pieces are made in the lighter walnut and fruitwood instead of the darker mahogany. Decorative effects are achieved by the use of pilasters and columns, usually in ebony, which provide strong contrasts with maple, pear, cherry, and applewood.

Biedermeier, by the way, was not a decorator-innovator or cabinetmaker, but a character, 'Papa' Biedermeier, in a series of cartoons which appeared in the German periodical *Fliegende Blätter*. This character personified the German and Austrian bourgeoisie of the period 1815 to 1840. The solid and popular Biedermeier furniture was long used as a symbol of homely, uninspired bourgeois taste. Today, however, authentic Biedermeier furniture is greatly sought-after, and high prices are paid for it in the saleroom.

The term Biedermeier is also applied to china and glass ware of this period, which has much

Biedermeier chest, c 1825

in common with late Regency and early Victorian products.

Billet. From the French *billette*, diminutive of *bille* 'tree-trunk.' This is a form of ornamental moulding found in Norman and Early English (qv) architecture. It consists of a sunk moulding within which small projecting blocks, resembling small billets of wood, are arranged at regular intervals. The billets can be arranged in a variety of ways and are used either in single or multiple rows. Their shape is usually but not always cylindrical.

Billet moulding on a Norman arch

Billiard table. The game of billiards is of remote and uncertain origin. Cotton, in his *Compleat Gamester* (1674), calls it a 'most gentile, cleanly and ingenious game,' while Shakespeare, in 'Let us to billiards: come, Charmian,' represents it as a suitable diversion for Cleopatra in the absence of her lover. Louis XIV, who installed a table covered in gold-fringed red velvet at Versailles, played on the advice of a physician. Even Oliver Cromwell possessed a small table, and Pepys found it an agreeable occupation for himself and his ladies.

Early tables, such as the charming example in the Adam

style at Alnwick Castle in Northumberland, are now exceedingly rare. Most towns and many private houses in Europe certainly contained them from the sixteenth century onwards. They were made of oak, with cottonwaste cushions, and were difficult to play on. The beginning of the game in its modern form dates from 1836, when rubber cushions and the heavy slate top (which dictates the massive build of the table) were introduced.

Birch. *Betula alba.* This streaked, brownish wood, although called by Evelyn (*Sylva*, 1664) the 'worst of Timber', was used quite extensively throughout the eighteenth century. The North American variety of birch was popular for upholstery interiors in America and was imported to Britain after 1750. The invention of the cutting lathe at the end of the nineteenth century extended the use of birch to the manufacture of plywood.

Birdcage. The practice of keeping birds for the brilliance of their plumage, the sweetness of their song, or their succulence, is of considerable antiquity. The Chinese emperor with his pet nightingales and the English gourmet ordering 'a hondred quayles' both required cages. Collecting birds was popular in Europe from the end of the Middle Ages, if not before. Sir Thomas More was the most notable bird-fancier of his age, and Charles II had a huge collection in Birdcage Walk.

The design of cages allowed considerable scope for invention. Simple circular metal or wicker constructions with domed tops, gave way to cages designed like lanterns, clock cases, and even houses. The majority were made in Holland and France, where at the end of the sixteenth century, the bird-catchers were incorporated and permitted to make their own cages. Superb examples

were made in eighteenth-century Britain.

Birdcage support. The small, cage-like device on which the hinged top of a pedestal table rests when it is in a horizontal position; it can be released when it is to be tipped up.

Birdsbeak moulding. A moulding on which the downward curving beak of a bird appears in profile. It was originally used in Greek architecture, where it occurs beneath the abacus of a capital.

Birgair or **burjair.** Originally the upholstered French armchair called a bergère (qv). The word was anglicized and applied both to chairs with very long seats and to armchairs which had caned backs and arms, and were filled with loose cushions. This last type was illustrated by Sheraton in *The Cabinet Dictionary* (1803).

Black, Sir Misha (*b* 1910). Professor of industrial design (Engineering) at the Royal College of Art, senior partner of the Design Research Unit, and one of the few industrial designers in England whose range and achievements rival those of designers in the United States.

Black's designs range from

Sir Misha Black

BLACKAMOORS

Post office design: joint architect Misha Black

Blackamoor, eighteenth century

Gothic double blind arcade

dust-wrappers and kitchen utensils to shops and exhibitions. He is design consultant to London Transport. His commissions have included work as co-ordinating architect for the South Bank Exhibition in 1951 and the design of the Small Mammals House at London Zoo. He has also played a great part in the Civic Trust programme to bring back to life the centres of old towns. He has written and edited several books on the problems of industrial design, including *Public Interiors* (1959) and *Exhibition Design* (1950).

Blackamoors. The immobile, barbaric splendour of the blackamoor figure, often carved in life-size; virile, and brilliantly coloured, has once again attracted the attention of collectors.

Blackamoor figures are of two distinct types. The charming negro slave with a bunch of tobacco leaves in one hand and perhaps a pipe in the other, appears on the signboards of early tobacconists. The second type is based on the Moorish servants of seventeenth-century Venice: a pair of figures, each with a raised hand to support

candlesticks, flowers, or vases of pot-pourri. ·

The finest ones came from Venice though others were made in Paris in the eighteenth century. The vogue for such blackamoors seems to have been mostly confined to Italy until the early 1800s. From the end of the Napoleonic wars to the middle of the century, blackamoors were made in ever-increasing numbers.

Black basalt ware was perfected by Josiah Wedgwood in 1766, though an 'Egyptian black' of a coarser kind was made earlier, possibly by the Elers. In this hard, fine, black stoneware, Wedgwood made vases, medallions, and busts, as well as teapots and other useful ware. Black basalt ware was copied by other potters, and ware of a fairly good quality was produced at the Cambrian pottery at Swansea at the end of the eighteenth century. It is still made by Wedgwoods at Barlaston.

Blanc de Chine. White porcelain with a milky glaze. See **Chinese porcelain.**

Blanket chest. A deep storage chest with a hinged lid and one or more drawers in the base. For a more detailed account see mule chest, which is an alternative name.

Blind arcade. A series of arches applied to the surface of a wall as decoration; used in Romanesque and some later architecture. It is also called a wall arcade. A similar device was imitation window tracery or blind tracery (qv).

Blinds. The origin of blinds is uncertain. The Egyptians and Chinese may have used reed window blinds, but there is no record of them in Europe until 1250, when Marco Polo brought the idea of a louvred window-cover from Cathay to Venice; hence 'Venetian blinds.' Spring blinds and roller blinds, made of calico, leather etc, reached England in the eighteenth century. The sturdy wood of Victorian blinds has now given way to aluminium and plastic.

Black basalt vases made by Wedgwood: left, 1769; right, modern

Venetian blinds screening a french window

Connecticut blockfront-and-shell chest of drawers, 1770–90

Blockfront or **blocking.** An American treatment of case furniture that is especially characteristic of eighteenth-century New England. The blocking is in three vertical panels of three flattened curves, the outer two convex and the inner concave. These are frequently crowned with shell motifs.

Blocking course. The architectural term now used for the projecting course of stone or brick at the base of a building. In classical architecture it was the plain course of stone over the cornice.

Blow-up chair. See **Plastic furniture.**

Blue John or **fluospar.** A good many legends have grown up about Blue John. It is a blue or purple fluospar rock, sometimes banded with white or yellow. It was exported from Britain to France where the name was corrupted to '*bleu et jaune.*' There are considerable collections of late eighteenth-century Blue John in the Louvre and other French museums.

Blue John is found only in Derbyshire, at three mines near Castleton. The story of its discovery by the Romans is probably apocryphal. The earliest references to it say that it was discovered in the early 1700s. Robert Adam used it as an inlay to decorate fireplaces at Kedleston Hall. Solid, turned ornaments were made from this curiously beautiful stone until

about 1780; then it was used for hollowed out ornaments, vases, cups etc, and a multitude of obelisks and other decorative pieces. By the early nineteenth century, delicate thin-walled hollow pieces were being made. Large pieces are very rare, though small ones are fairly common.

Blunt arrow. American term for the turned decoration resembling blunted arrows. It is found on the legs of Windsor chairs made in Philadelphia in the mid-eighteenth century.

Board. The medieval 'bord' was a plank or board of wood which when placed upon trestles could be used as a table. The word 'table' replaced 'board', though the older usage persists in such phrases as 'board and lodging' and 'board of directors.' See Table.

Boarded chest. A storage chest of a simple plank construction without uprights. In some instances only six boards were pegged together. Although boarded chests are medieval in origin, most existing examples are the work of provincial cabinetmakers or carpenters in the seventeenth and eighteenth centuries.

Bobbin turning. An ornamental turning of the later seventeenth century. It consists of a series of small bobbins or bulbs, and is found on the underframing of chairs and tables.

Bocage. A background of foliage, flowers, or trees, especially on pottery and porcelain.

Boffrand, Gabriel Germain (1667–1754). French architect and decorator, one of the great masters of the French Rococo. Boffrand was born at Nantes and followed his father's profession

of sculptor and architect. He went to Paris in 1681 to work under the sculptor Girardon. He soon transferred his allegiance to the architect Jules Hardouin Mansart (qv), with whom he was later to collaborate. He was admitted to the Academy of Architecture in 1709.

Boffrand indulged in the speculative building of Paris *hôtels*: the Hôtel Montmorency (1712), the Hôtel de Seiguelay (1713), and the Hôtel de Torcy (1714). He made a great deal of money but then lost most of it in the Mississippi Bubble financial panic (1720).

The exteriors of Boffrand's buildings were usually quiet and simple, in marked contrast with the interiors, which were the epitome of Rococo luxury. Other works of interest by Boffrand are the Hôtel Amelot (1701), built around an oval court; decorations and a pavilion added to the Hôtel Soubise (1737–40); and châteaux at Nancy and Lunéville, France, and at Bouchefort in the Netherlands. He published his *Livre d'Architecture* in 1745.

Bog or **black oak.** A wood similar to ebony in colour; it is obtained from timber that has been submerged in a peat bog. It was used for sixteenth- and seventeenth-century furniture, and occasionally for the finer applied or inlay work, in imitation of ebony.

Bohemian glass. See **German and Bohemian glass.**

Bois durci. A wood-based plastic made of blood and the fine sawdust of rosewood, ebony, and other woods. It looked like ebony and was very hard and capable of taking fine moulding; hence its use for medallions, plaques, and other ornaments. It was invented in the mid-nineteenth century.

Early 19th-century Blue John urn

Palais de la Malgrange, near Nancy, by Boffrand

Boiserie in a house in Paris, early eighteenth century

Dutch marquetry bureau with bombé outline

Boiserie. The word used in France for carved wooden panelling that included the doors, overdoors, frames, cupboards, and shelves. During the eighteenth century, *boiserie* was designed and painted as part of a comprehensive decorative scheme.

Bokhara. The largest town in the central Turkoman area. The term Bokhara has been applied to carpets woven in the area bounded by the Caspian Sea in the west, Afghanistan in the south, China and the Pamirs in the east. For two centuries the carpets and rugs of the nomadic tribes – the Tekkes, the Salors, the Yomuds, and others – have been gathered for export at Bokhara. The only rugs made in the area itself are those of Beshir, which are curiously unlike all other rugs of Turkestan.

The dominant features of Bokhara weaving are the rich red or brown overall colouring, the use of rows of octagons or 'elephants' feet' in the field, and the panelled geometric borders of motifs like sunbursts.

The nomadic existence of the weavers restricted its production to rugs and small carpets. The traditional designs have scarcely altered since the eighteenth century.

Bolection. A form of projecting moulding, frequently found in the framework of a door or of panelling. It was used to span the angle between two different surface levels.

Bombé. A French word meaning 'bulged', used of furniture to describe a commode, chest, or bureau whose shape featured pronounced convex curves. Dutch bombé chests frequently have a more pronounced bombé shape than their French counterparts. English cabinetmakers adopted and adapted the form in the middle of the eighteenth century to produce magnificent pieces of furniture.

Bone china. The hard-paste porcelain body discovered by William Cookworthy at Plymouth in the late eighteenth century was modified by the addition of bone-ash in about 1800, and became the standard English porcelain. It is translucent, very white, and much stronger than earthenware. However, the very perfection of this material, free from any impurities, gives it a glassy lifeless appearance, less satisfying than that of eighteenth-century porcelain.

French bonheur du jour

Bonheur du jour. The French term for a lady's writing table. Although such pieces vary considerably in shape, the basic design is that of a small rectangular table, with a drawer often fitted with writing slides, tray, and inkwells, and with a superstructure set at the back of the table. This upper section, with small drawers and cupboards, gave cabinetmakers a broad vertical space on which to display their decorative ability; types of decoration include basketwork, marquetry, panels of trellis, sprays of flowers, conversation pieces, views of palaces, and porcelain groups.

The *bonheur du jour* is a rational creation designed to suit the needs of small and intimate late eighteenth-century rooms; as such it has no immediate forerunner. It was made *c* 1760 in France, but did not come into vogue until 1770.

Bokhara saddlebag rug

Bonnet scrolls on an eighteenth-century library bookcase

Built-in bookshelves in a modern interior

Bonnet scroll. The American name for a scrolled or swan-neck pediment found on cabinets, bookcases, etc.

Bonnet tile. A curved tile used over the hip of a hipped roof.

Bookcase. The high cost of early books placed them out of reach of all but the richest. It was not until the reign of Charles II that they became common enough to need movable accommodation. The bookcase, at first scarcely differing from the fixed shelf and panelling of seventeenth-century rooms, was slow to evolve. Pepys had a set of 12 bookcases made for his library, and others of the period exist, though most have been either destroyed or remade into smaller pieces of furniture.

Walnut was sometimes used, but even with the vogue for the cheaper mahogany, the size of bookcases made the cost extraordinarily high. For this reason large bookcases were often carved in deal or pine and then painted and gilded. Glass fronts were uniform until the advent of brass trelliswork in the late eighteenth century.

From about 1740, massive libraries, which became popular throughout Europe, contained architectural bookcases, breakfronted, crowned by a pediment, and carved with flowers, fruit, and busts. Chippendale and Hepplewhite designed large bookcases that were simpler and were made in mahogany; they became popular in America. It was not until the early nineteenth century that small bookcases in rosewood, yew, or satinwood, inlaid with marquetry or cut brass, began to replace the giants of previous times.

Bookshelves. Instead of bookcases, most people now make do with some kind of arrangement of shelves. 'Bookshelves' is a term that conveniently covers hanging, fixed, built-in, or free-standing sets of shelves.

Borromini, Francesco (1599–1667). Italian architect, genius of Roman Baroque. Borromini was born at Bissone on Lake Lugano, the son of a stone cutter, and at first followed his father's trade. In 1611 he went to Rome, which was thenceforth his home. He worked for Bernini as a stone cutter and draughtsman, and finally became Bernini's assistant, by which time the antagonism between the two men was firmly established and they parted company. Both were great artists of the Baroque, Bernini successful, rich, popular, and assured, whereas Borromini was lonely, embittered, and neurotic. He received no formal training as an architect and was mainly self-taught; he amassed a large collection of books.

The Monastery of S Carlo alle Quattro Fontane was his first commission. It was erected on an irregular site between 1638 and 1641. The façade was probably his last work, and dates from 1665-7.

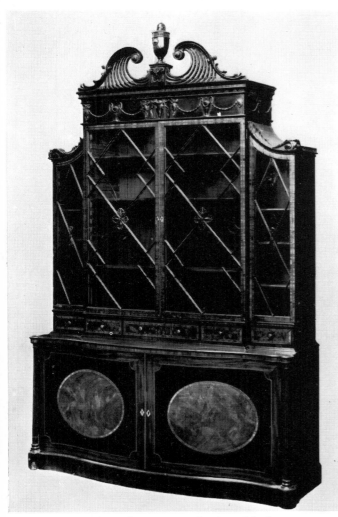

An Adam mahogany serpentine-fronted bookcase

Courtyard view of S Ivo della Sapienza, Rome, by Borromini, 1642-50

The Oratory of St Philip Neri, Rome, by Borromini, 1637-50

Borromini used geometry rather than the classical module as the basis for his designs, and his undulating diamond plan for S Carlo is a preparation for the complexities of his masterpiece, S Ivo della Sapienza (1642–60).

A number of his other works were unfinished, including S Agnese in Piazza Navona (1663–7), on which he took over from Carlo Rainaldi. Borromini's designs for the Pamphili, Spada, and Falconieri palaces are imag-inative and impressive, though his ecclesiastical work is more dynamic and original. His last complete work, the Collegio di Propaganda Fide (*c* 1660), is remarkable for its unorthodoxy of design and disregard for the usual canons of architecture.

Borromini committed suicide in 1667 and was buried anonymously, according to his wish, in the tomb of his relative Carlo Maderno, for whose work he had a great regard.

Boss. A projecting ornament or decoration placed at the inter-section of the ribs of ceilings, whether flat or vaulted, or at the inter-section of mouldings in furniture. The term is most frequently applied to carvings on ecclesiastical architecture. They are little seen in Norman work, but are more common in Decorated and Perpendicular.

Boston rocker. A nineteenth-century, American rocking chair, with a seat that has a downward curve at the front and an upward curve at the back. The chair back is full of vertical spindles and the scrolled top rail has a tablet in the centre.

Bouillotte table. *Bouillotte*, a word used in French for a small tea-kettle, and a game of cards, was the name given to a table suitable for both. It was developed at the end of Louis XVI's reign, and was a circular, marble-topped object, supported on four tapering legs. The marble top was for the tea or coffee pot, and as the table was small (about $2\frac{1}{2}$ ft in diameter) it could be moved about. For cards a reversible baize-covered panel was inserted.

The *table à bouillotte* survived the Revolution and was in use throughout the nineteenth century.

Boulle or **buhl.** The technique of inlaying brass in tortoiseshell, invented by André Charles Boulle (1642–1732).

Thin layers of the material were laid together and the design cut out with a fret-saw. Usually furniture of this type was made in pairs, the first piece having a design of brass inset in tortoise-shell, and the second carrying the reverse, called *contra-boulle*.

Boulle furniture was common in France throughout the eighteenth century, and was always very highly prized. It did not become popular elsewhere until the early 1800s, under the influence of Regency cut brass.

Technically excellent, English boulle in no way compares

Boss in a thirteenth-century church

Boston rocker of about 1835

A typical bouillotte table

A Louis XIV boulle table

Trompe-l'oeil arcade at Palazzo Spada, Rome, by Borromini

A Louis XIV boulle writing-table, probably by A C Boulle himself

Pair of Bow figures of musicians, painted in enamel and gilded, 1765

artistically with the work of French *ébénistes* under Louis XIV and XV.

Boultine. A small rounded moulding, also known as a quarter round or quadrant bend, or in medieval architecture as a boltel.

Boulton, Matthew (1728–1809.) British engineer and manufacturer of metal *objets de vertu*, toys, coins, and reproductions of oil paintings by a mechanical process.

In 1775 Boulton entered into partnership with James Watt, and it was Boulton's capital and engineering genius which ensured the success of Watt's steam-engine. He worked at Soho, Birmingham, and it was largely due to his influence that Sheffield and Birmingham were granted assay offices in 1773.

Boulton is remembered today for his influence on the design of mid- and late eighteenth-century metalwork and for the superb objects he manufactured.

Gilt bronze and Blue John candelabrum by Boulton

The finest of these, based on the influence of Robert Adam's style, rivalled if not surpassed the work of the French *fondeurs ciseleurs*, and Boulton in fact sold much of his output to France.

Most of Boulton's pattern books survive. Their publication would provide invaluable information on a subject still little explored by experts on eighteenth-century art.

Bow. Soft-paste porcelain was made at the factory at Bow, England, from about 1750, though a patent for a porcelain body was taken out in 1744 by Thomas Frye and Edward Heylyn. Nothing appears to have survived from the experimental days of the factory, but we know that by 1755 they were selling £18,000 worth of porcelain annually – an enormous sum for the time. The Bow works closed down in 1776, so that all Bow china was produced within a period of 30 years.

Like other porcelain factories, Bow was largely inspired by the work being done at Meissen. Bow craftsmen also copied Chinese porcelain, and underglaze blue was made from the earliest days, both transfer-printed and hand-painted. The figures copied from Meissen are generally cruder and less sophisticated than the originals; the earlier ones had plain bases and the later ones Rococo bases which became more elaborate as time went on. The bocage was much used as a background to the figures, though the treatment was clumsier than that of the Chelsea factory.

Bow figures are generally very heavy for their size. A great variety of marks was used. The crown and dagger frequently seen on Bow porcelain is now

known to be the mark of James Giles, a decorator of porcelain with his own works at Kentish Town. The Worcester crescent, many pseudo-Chinese characters, and various workmen's marks were also used.

Bow back. In British joinery the bow is the horseshoe-curved frame used in several types of Windsor chair, for example, wheel back (qv) and smoker's bow (qv). In America, bow back or hoop back describes the particular variety of Windsor chair that is known in Britain as the double bow back. This is a chair in which an ordinary horizontal bow has another bow

placed vertically across the centre of its back, giving the chair a high back. Both bows are filled with spindles.

Bowfront. The convex shape commonly found in furniture at the end of the eighteenth century. Chests of drawers and sideboards lent themselves most readily to this type of design, but it is also found on such unlikely objects as knife-boxes and dressing mirrors.

Bowl turning. A variation of a cup turning in which the turning resembles an inverted bowl rather than an inverted cup. It was one of the turnings used in

A mahogany china table by Ince and Mayhew with an open bowfront

Chippendale giltwood wall bracket

America on chair and table legs during the late seventeenth and early eighteenth centuries.

Bowstring. See **Belfast truss.**

Box-wood. *Buxus sempervirens.* A pale yellow, close-grained wood which sinks in water. It was much used in Europe for carving, especially in churches, and in marquetry inlay in the sixteenth and seventeenth centuries. In the eighteenth century it was employed for the narrow bandings, or 'stringing', common on English furniture of the period.

Brace. In framed construction, particularly of roofs, the brace is a diagonal stiffener. Arched braces are those used in hammerbeam construction.

Bracket. In architecture, a small projecting support frequently made in the shape of a scroll or volute. The wall·bracket was a small decorative shelf used for the display of porcelain

Ebony bracket clock, 1690, by Joseph Knibb

clocks and other ornamental objects. Its form accordingly followed design fashions. The earliest existing examples are from the late seventeenth century and reflect the ideas of Daniel Marot. Throughout the eighteenth century, great care was lavished upon their design. The early brackets were probably used for displaying porcelain and Delft. Heavy brackets were later needed to support marble busts and bronzes, and as a result, baroque forms were given full play. The most graceful brackets are those in the light, delicate Rococo style.

Bracket clock. This term is now commonly used to describe any clock that sits.upon a shelf, a mantel, or even a table. It was, however, the name given to a spring-driven clock that sat upon its own bracket fixed to the wall.

Bracket foot. In its unadorned angular form, this is one of the most common of all feet on case furniture. It was used from the seventeenth to the nineteenth century and was sometimes ornamented; the cabriole bracket, for example, consisted of a squat cabriole, usually decorated with gadrooning or acanthus leaves.

The American goddard foot, named after the Newport cabinetmaker John Goddard (1748–83), is a curved bracket foot that protrudes beyond the width of the carcase. It was frequently used in conjunction with blocking (qv).

Bramante, Donato (Donato di Pascuccio d'Antonio, 1444–1514). Italian architect. Bramante was born at Monte Asdruvaldo, outside Urbino, and he probably worked on the construction of the ducal palace during his early years. In any event his hand is discernible in the illusionistic treatment of the *studiolo* (c 1475–6), the small wood-panelled study of Duke Federigo da Montefeltro.

In 1477 Bramante was in Bergamo, where he painted perspective decorations at the Palazzo del Podestà. Two years later he was employed in Milan by the Sforzas, with whom he stayed until the French invasion of 1499. During his stay he executed a large number of decorative paintings (now lost) and several architectural works. The most important of these were S Maria presso S Satiro (begun 1482), which involved recasing the tiny chapel and rebuilding the church, and the Canons' Cloister of S Ambrogio (1492).

Bramante's Tempietto in the cloisters of S Pietro in Montorio, 1502

From Milan, Bramante fled to Rome, where his first work was a cloister at S Maria delle Pace (1500). After this he designed what is probably the greatest monument to the High Renaissance, the Tempietto at S Pietro in Montorio (1502). This is a small but monumental circular chapel, built on the alleged site of St Peter's martyrdom.

In 1505, commissioned by Pope Julius II, Bramante began work on the courtyard of the Cortile del Belvedere, and on St Peter's. His reputation as a structural engineer and mathematician, well-versed in the new principles of vaulting, was second to none. He devised a large Greek cross plan for St Peter's, with a smaller Greek cross at each corner; the whole edifice was to be roofed by one huge dome and four smaller domes. By 1512 the arches for the great dome were ready but the Pope died the following year, Bramante became gravely ill, and work was halted. His position at St Peter's was later filled by Raphael, whose appointment he had recommended.

Brass. An alloy of copper and zinc. When burnished it closely resembles gold, and it has often

Regency brass curtain tie-back

A mahogany breakfast table, about 1760

Cesca chairs, with and without arms, designed by Breuer, 1928

been used as a substitute for it. From earliest times, brass was employed in the manufacture of scientific instruments, weapons, and coins. In the last 300 years it has been used in much the same way as bronze, especially for chimney furniture. Brass is particularly effective for decorative work, and has been widely used for ornamental mounts, door fittings, and inlay. See also **Boulle.**

Brattishing. Late Gothic cresting used on screens. It was made up of Tudor flowers (qv), by which name it is sometimes known, leaves and miniature battlements.

Brazil-wood. *Caesalpinia brasilensis.* A red wood, first known as a native of China and Japan, and named *Caesalpinia japonica* after Andreas Caesalpini, a famous sixteenth-century Italian botanist. Later explorers discovered the wood in Brazil. It was occasionally used for

decorative purposes and inlay work, especially at the beginning of the nineteenth century.

Breakfast table. A small table with two hinged flaps, below which is a drawer, enclosed shelf, or cupboard. Breakfast tables made their appearance in the mid-eighteenth century and were illustrated by Chippendale in his *Director* (1762) where there is a much-quoted example whose shelf is enclosed with Chinese fret.

Breakfront. A device used especially in the design of large pieces of furniture whereby the centre of the piece projects some few inches from the sides. This made the centre deeper, and thus able to accommodate more books, bottles, or clothes, and it effectively avoided the dullness which threatens all large pieces of furniture with straight fronts.

Breuer, Marcel (*b* 1902). American architect and furniture

designer. Breuer was born in Pécs in Hungary. After early training as an artist at the Vienna Academy, he decided upon a practical apprenticeship and joined the Bauhaus at Weimar as one of its youngest pupils. He designed the furniture for the new Bauhaus when it moved to Dessau, and took charge of the furniture department. He designed some famous tubular steel chairs, the *Wassily* in 1925 and the *cesca* (still a perennial favourite) in 1928; these and his other furniture were among the most important influences in modern furniture design.

Breuer left the Bauhaus in 1928 and embarked on an architectural career, at first in Berlin and then (1935) in England, where he worked with F R S Yorke (qv). In 1937 he went to America with his one-time teacher, Walter Gropius, who had a professorship at Harvard. The two formed a partnership at Cambridge, Massachusetts, which lasted from 1937 to 1941. Breuer then established his own office in New York, and has been responsible for a number of fine buildings, chiefly in Massachusetts and Connecticut. But the buildings which assured him international success were the UNESCO buildings in Paris, which he designed with others (1952–8).

Among Breuer's other works, for which he has received a great many awards, are the United States Embassy at The Hague (1954–8); the IBM-France Research Centre, La Gaude (1960–1); Whitney Museum of American Art, New York (1963–6); Satellite Town at Bayonne, France (1963–9); and the University of Massachusetts Campus Centre (1970).

Marcel Breuer

Brewster chair. A New England armchair of turned 'stick' construction. It was named after Elder Brewster of the Massachusetts Bay Colony, and is one of the more elaborate of the 'stick' types. It has distinctive vertical spindles below the arm and seat rails, and frequently includes a rush seat. It is contemporary with the seventeenth-century Carver chair (qv).

New England Brewster chair

A Louis XVI boulle vitrine with breakfront, by Levasseur

The Rialto bridge in Venice

Brick. This word probably derives from the Anglo-Saxon *brice*, a fragment, which has the same origin as the French *brique*.

Early handmade bricks were made of clay, moulded into blocks and baked. They were prepared by mixing the clay with sand or ashes (to keep the brick from cracking) and then grinding the mixture until it was soft. After this the mixture was moulded into the required shape in a small box with a loose base, so that when the sides were removed the brick was left on the base ready for baking in a large kiln. Baking by this method frequently took up to two weeks.

Handmade bricks were usually 2 in thick, 4 in wide, and 8 in long. The modern brick is usually about 8¾ by 4¼ by 3 in, but bricks have been and are made in a wide variety of sizes.

They have been used in building from ancient times. The Chinese made bricks with a surface akin to porcelain. The walls of Babylon were built of brick in 4000 BC. The Egyptians, Greeks, and Romans also made excellent bricks. The sun-dried mud bricks with which Californian and Mexican houses have been built for centuries are called adobe bricks (qv).

In Europe the industry developed on traditional lines, utilizing, for the most part, handmaking processes. The first English patent for a clay-working machine was granted in the year 1619, but mechanisation did not begin to replace manual methods until the middle of the nineteenth century. The moulded products were fired in relatively inefficient, intermittent kilns until about 1858, when Hoffman introduced a continuous kiln, which enabled all the processes connected with the firing to be carried out concurrently and continuously. Since the introduction of clay-working machinery and the Hoffman kiln, the industry has made great progress.

No systematic nomenclature for bricks has so far been evolved, and the designations used today are based on different and unrelated modes of classification – place of origin, raw material, method of manufacture, and so on. However, it is usual to distinguish three main classes of bricks: common, facing, and engineering.

Common bricks. The term 'common' is applied to the multifarious varieties of brick which constitute the major output of many brickyards, and which are used externally and internally for general construction, usually above damp-proof course level.

Facing bricks. Any type of brick which combines attractive appearance and colour with good resistance to exposure, falls into the category of facing bricks. They are generally specially made or used to provide an architectural feature.

Engineering bricks. This category is probably the best example of rational brick classification, involving as it does the possession of definite and ascertainable properties. With the advent of the machine age, the civil engineer needed structural material of immense load-bearing capacity. This was forthcoming in the form of semi-vitrified bricks such as the reds, blues, and brindles which are so well known today. Clay engineering bricks have very low porosity, very high crushing strength (up to as much as 16,000 lb per square inch), and a vitreous acid-resisting character which has made it possible to employ them in sewers, engine pits, and power houses. Because their maintenance costs are nil, engineering bricks have largely replaced alternative materials which, owing either to their moisture movement or sensitivity to corrosion or chemical attack, have failed to stand the test of time. Properly laid in suitable mortar, engineering bricks constitute an ideal damp-proof course of great durability.

In domestic architecture, bricks have been more commonly used in Europe than the United States, where the frame house became popular as a result of America's vast natural resources of wood. However, beautiful old red brick houses exist in New England and the South, designed along similar lines to English eighteenth- and nineteenth-century houses.

Bridge. The Chinese built bridges at a very early date, but the Romans were probably the first people to construct bridges similar to those still in use today. The Emperor Augustus built one near Narnia on the Via Flaminia, about 60 miles from Rome, with arches over 100 ft high and spans of 150 ft, but Trajan's 60 ft wide bridge over the Danube was the

The Palladian bridge at Wilton House, near Salisbury

Chequered brickwork on a mid-nineteenth-century house

Covered bridge in Pennsylvania

Golden Gate Bridge at San Francisco, California

greatest of all the Roman bridges, resting on 20 piers, 130 ft in height from their foundations, and 170 ft apart. Some idea of the skill involved can be gained by recalling that London Bridge had spans of only 25 ft, and that even in the eighteenth century, few English bridges had more than 75 ft spans. The Romans were also skilled in building aqueducts (bridges for the transportation of water).

After the fall of the Roman Empire, little bridge-building was done in Europe until the twelfth century, when the great bridge of Avignon (3,000 ft long) was constructed. A bridge built over the Allier in 1454 had an arch with a span of 184 ft, a figure comparable with those of many modern bridges. The most famous bridge in the world, the arcaded Rialto in Venice, has a deceptively wide span of nearly 100 ft.

But the great era of bridge-building began with the Railway Age. As the leading railway nation, Britain was responsible for many still-famous railway bridges, including the wrought-iron bridge over the Menai Straits (1826), in which the main span is 580 ft wide, the Forth Bridge (1882–89), and scores of others. A vast number were built in the United States, where the rugged nature of the terrain and the swift industrialization of the continent prompted tremendous bridging achievements. New York is famous for its Manhattan, Queensboro, and George Washington bridges, and San Francisco for the Golden Gate; its overall length of 9,266 ft making it one of the longest suspension bridges in the world.

Although the bridge is basically a utilitarian structure, its decorative possibilities have proved a challenge to many architects and engineers. Aesthetically satisfying structures range from bridges in the parklands of eighteenth-century

Brise-soleil at the High Court, Chandigarh, with its parasol-like roof

noblemen to the magnificent bridges over the Seine; from Rennie's masterpiece, the earlier Waterloo Bridge (completed in 1817, demolished in 1936), which had nine arches of 120 ft span, to the simple and breathtaking structures of the Swiss engineer Robert Maillart.

Bright-cut engraving. See **Silver, decorative techniques.**

Brise-soleil. A screen, generally louvred, sometimes horizontal and sometimes vertical, used to protect the windows and surface of tropical buildings from the glare of the sun. The brise-soleil, which was popularized by Le Corbusier in many of his earlier designs, has become almost an architectural cliché in much modern architecture, although in tropical climates its use is undoubtedly advantageous to office workers and apartment-dwellers.

Bristol earthenware. Cream-coloured earthenware was made at Bristol in England from about 1786, superseding

Traditional Jali screen: new form

the Delft ware that had been made there before then. The colour of the body is of a deeper cream than that of the Staffordshire ware.

William Fifield and his son William were decorators of earthenware who are known to have worked at Bristol. On their pieces they painted bouquets of flowers (notably roses), and landscapes with buildings. The initials WF for the full name appear on marked pieces.

Saliginatobel bridge in Switzerland, designed by Robert Maillart, 1929–30

Bristol porcelain figures of Summer and Autumn in enamel colours, 1772

Interior of the Corn Exchange, Leeds, designed by Brodrick, 1858

Bristol glass. A generic term used to describe the deeply coloured glass and painted opaque white glass which became popular in Britain during the second half of the eighteenth century. The deep colours included Bristol blue (the best known), green, and purple. In 1805, Isaac Jacobs, one of the West Country glassmakers, presented Queen Charlotte with a dessert set of burnished gold upon royal purple coloured glass.

Bristol porcelain. Porcelain made of a soft paste was produced at Bristol in England as early as 1750. Only a few pieces survive, such as sauceboats decorated with flowers, and copies of Chinese figures. They are sometimes marked with the word Bristol and the date 1750. The factory was amalgamated with the Worcester factory in 1752.

Porcelain made of a hard paste was produced at Bristol for a short time (1770–81), first by William Cookworthy and afterwards by Richard Champion. Useful ware was made as well as vases and decorative figures. The marks used by the factory were a cross, or a letter B with a cross, or crossed swords with a cross in various ⋅forms.

Britannia metal. An alloy of tin, antimony, and other metals that was manufactured in Sheffield in the mid-eighteenth century. It was silver-coloured and used for teapots, spoons etc.

Britannia Standard. Both the coinage and wrought plate contained the same silver content up to 1697. The great demand for plate in the late seventeenth century led to coin-clipping, which was damaging to the economy, and in 1697 the Britannia Standard was therefore imposed by law. Wrought silver now had a lighter silver content than the coinage – 958 parts in 1,000 – and the marks were also changed. Instead of the leopard's head and the lion *passant* (walking), silver was stamped with the seated figure of Britannia and the lion's head

Broach spire

erased (with a jagged neck). The maker's mark now became the first two letters of his surname. In 1720 the Britannia Standard ceased to be obligatory and the old Standard was revived, although several smiths – such as Paul de Lamerie – clung to the Britannia Standard for a few years longer.

Broach spire. A spire that rises directly from a tower without an intervening parapet. The four broaches of pyramid form are placed in the corners left empty when an octagonal spire is placed upon a square tower.

Broadcloth. As the word implies, a wide, plain, woven, durable stuff much used for interior hangings.

In Britain broadcloth is a woollen cloth; in America it is usually an all-cotton fabric. The term was often used of clerical dress.

Brocade. Any textile fabric with an embossed or raised design. Brocade, usually patterned with repeating floral motifs on a silk ground, is found at least as early as the sixteenth century. It was used extensively throughout Europe in the eighteenth century, when it was also imported into America.

Brocatelle. A term applied to fabrics simulating brocade.

Brodrick, Cuthbert (1822–1908). British architect. Brodrick was essentially a Yorkshire architect, closely associated with Leeds. He was born in Hull, where he acquired a local reputation before winning the 1852 competition for Leeds Town Hall. The Town Hall, a classic High Victorian building, is situated prominently on a main thoroughfare. The immense height of the tower, domed and colonnaded upon a high podium, is as striking a feature as the imposing façade.

The design of Brodrick's Leeds Corn Exchange (1861) is based on an oval plan with an elliptical dome, and was much influenced by French classicism. Brodrick's third major work, the opulent, portentous, and luxurious Grand Hotel at Scarborough, was also influenced by French models, with balconies, mock machicolations, small pointed domes on each corner, and semicircular bays at either end extending the whole height of the building. Brodrick's other works in Leeds include the Mechanics' Institute (1865) and the Oriental Baths (1866; now demolished).

Broken pediment. An ingenious but not always beautiful

The broken pediment of a George II mahogany bookcase

Gilt bronze lion on 18th-century clock by Miller of Augsburg

Landscape garden at Nuneham Park, Oxfordshire, by 'Capability' Brown

corruption of the classical pediment; it was first used by the Romans at Petra. The motif was revived and used extensively in Baroque architecture. It is commonly found as the cresting to large pieces of furniture, grandfather clocks, and barometers of the early eighteenth century. It allowed space for the display of porcelain or a heraldic cartouche.

Bronze. An alloy of copper and tin. It has usually been found the most satisfactory material for casting statues in metal, and with age acquires a beautiful patina; this is often of golden brown but is capable of assimilating other colours such as red and green, as in many bronzes by Renoir and Degas.

The term 'bronzes' is used by collectors and dealers of the metal mounts on furniture, which are normally of bronze, lacquered or gilded.

Brown, Lancelot (1715–83). British landscape gardener, known as 'Capability Brown' owing to his habit of asserting,

when shown a park or garden, that it possessed great capabilities. This optimism and enthusiasm, allied to skill and taste, raised him from kitchen-gardener to superintendent of the royal gardens at Hampton Court and Windsor.

Capability Brown was consulted by a great many owners of country seats, and was the high priest of the Romantic style. He created the English park as we know it today, but he was ruthless in sweeping away the magnificent formal gardens of previous generations – many of which must have been in full and splendid maturity when their 'capabilities' were assessed and their doom pronounced. Even the slight differentiation between garden and park provided by the ha-ha or sunk fence (invented by Bridgeman *c* 1720) was frowned on by Brown, who decreed that the park must sweep up to the very walls of the house.

Had Brown been less rigid in

his condemnation of formality, and more able to combine the best of terraces, topiary, and fountains of previous generations with his admittedly inspired conception of the English park, he would have been one of the greatest of all garden-architects. As it is, he is remembered as much for what he destroyed – the great formal garden at Uppark, for instance – as for what he created, at Blenheim, Croome Court, Kew, and elsewhere.

Brownstone. A stone much used in the construction of nineteenth-century New York city houses; hence the use of the term 'brownstone front' to describe a particular type of high, narrow Manhattan house, with a long narrow hall, narrow rooms, and tall windows. These brownstone fronts are gradually disappearing, giving rise among many New Yorkers to a nostalgia similar to that of Londoners for Georgian terraced houses.

Lancelot 'Capability' Brown

Bruce, Sir William (*d* 1710). Scottish architect. The younger son of a Scottish baron, Bruce was as much a courtier as an architect, and he undoubtedly intrigued for the Royalist cause. His activities were rewarded at the Restoration with the lucrative Clerkship to the Bills. In 1671, after he had drawn up revised plans for Holyroodhouse, Bruce

A row of brownstone fronts in West 127th Street, New York

Kinross House, Kinross-shire, 1685, by Sir William Bruce

Clifton Suspension Bridge by Isambard Kingdom Brunel, 1829

The Great Eastern on her first voyage to America in 1860

became King's Surveyor and Master of the Works. Despite the fact that he seems to have had little formal instruction in architecture, Bruce's design was of unusual (and unfashionable) classical symmetry and sophistication. He is thus the Scottish counterpart of Inigo Jones in England, being the first architect to introduce the architecture of the Renaissance into his country. He also built for himself Kinross House (1698–1702), a remarkable and well-documented building which proves that he was uncommonly well versed in the tenets of classicism, and unusually well equipped to supervise their translation into stone.

Sir Mark Brunel

Isambard Kingdom Brunel

Brunel, Sir Marc Isambard (1769–1849), and Isambard Kingdom (1806–59). British engineers. Sir Marc Brunel and his son were involved in some of the most momentous developments of the Industrial Revolution in Britain, although it is the achievements of the son that are now chiefly remembered.

Sir Marc was born at Hacqueville in Normandy, but because of the Revolution abandoned his naval career in France and went to the USA. He worked as an inventor and engineer in New York, becoming the city's chief engineer, but his most productive period began after his emigration to England in 1799. He was variously and successfully employed by the Admiralty and other authorities, but his reputation rests mainly on the tunnel he constructed under the Thames, despite numerous setbacks, between 1824 and 1843. He was knighted in 1841.

Sir Marc's son, Isambard Kingdom Brunel, is more widely known, thanks to the spectacular success of two feats of engineering: the Clifton Suspension Bridge, designed in 1829, and the *Great Eastern*, the first steamer to make regular transatlantic crossings. Brunel died only a week after the *Great Eastern* started on her maiden voyage in 1859. As chief engineer (1833–46) of the Great Western Railway, he was responsible for much important railway engineering and architecture.

Brunelleschi, Filippo (1377–1446). The first important architect of the Italian Renaissance, and one of the greatest. Brunelleschi was born in Florence and trained as a sculptor and goldsmith, visiting Rome on several occasions before turning to architecture. His feeling for classical Roman architecture was one of preference and not dogma, and he drew upon it for inspiration rather than rules.

Brunelleschi's dome to Florence Cathedral (c 1436) is generally considered to be the first important Renaissance construction. It is Gothic in outline, but the structural engineering is entirely Renaissance, as is the crowning marble octagon. He then proceeded with the building of Ospedale degli Innocenti (1421–44), which has a very simple façade with wide arches upon slender Corinthian columns. All of Brunelleschi's buildings are of airy proportions, with very light detailing. This is especially noticeable in his large churches of S Lorenzo (1425) and S Spirito (begun 1436), and the Pazzi Chapel (begun 1429), built in the cloister of S Croce.

The Pazzi Chapel at S Croce, Florence, by Brunelleschi, 1429

Brunelleschi's dome to the Gothic Florence Cathedral, 1436

Chapel at Turku, Finland, by Erik Bryggman, 1940

Brussels. Possibly the earliest and certainly the largest centre of tapestry weaving. Lace has also been a household industry in Brussels for several centuries, and at one time carpets were made there.

Brussels tapestries, usually signed by the initials or monogram of the weaver, and bearing the 'town mark', a red shield between B's, are among the commonest surviving tapestries. Seventeenth-century subjects – battles, mythological and religious scenes – are found in many English houses. The figures tend to be large and somewhat naïve, but the colouring is cheerful. Eighteenth-century Brussels tapestries are as elegant as all but the finest work of Beauvais and Gobelins, with which they are often confused.

Those who have visited the Musée Cinquantenaire in Brussels will be familiar with the finest achievements of the city's late Gothic tapestries, often enriched with gold and silver thread, which rank among the greatest creations of their kind.

Brutalism. Architectural style. See **Smithson.**

Bryggman, Erik William (1891 –1955). Finnish architect. Bryggman was born at Turku in southwest Finland, where he spent the greater part of his life and did most of his important work. Between 1906 and 1909 he studied at the design school in Turku, going on to Helsinki to continue his architectural studies. His first work was the war memorial in Helsinki, which he designed with the sculptor Ilkka. In 1923 Bryggman set up his own office in Turku, to which Alvar Aalto also came for a short time. The two architects collaborated to produce the celebrated 1929 exhibition in honour of the 700th anniversary of Turku.

Bryggman designed two hotels in Turku, the Seurahoune (1928) and the Hospitz Hotel (1927–9), as well as Kinopalatsi cinema, the library at the Academy (1935), and offices (1938). The Resurrection Chapel (1938–41) is his most famous work, a serene building on an asymmetrical plan with only one aisle. The side wall of glass gives directly on to the grass and trees outside.

Buchanan, Professor Sir Colin (*b* 1907). British town planner. Buchanan went to Imperial College, London, and took up his first official appointment in the Sudan in 1930. He returned to England in 1932 and devoted the next few years to regional planning studies and work for the Ministry of Transport (1935–9). After the war, during which he was in the Royal Engineers, Buchanan joined the Ministry of Town and Country Planning (1946–61). He was much involved with the problems of Greater London, and participated in numerous public planning inquiries throughout the country. Then, again with the Ministry of Transport, he headed the team of experts who produced the *Traffic in Towns* report, published in 1963. The same year he was appointed first professor of transport at Imperial College.

Buchanan has a large consultancy practice which has carried out major studies on the future development of Bath, Cardiff,

A late seventeenth-century Brussels tapestry

Sir Colin Buchanan

and Canterbury, the feasibility of large-scale urban growth in the areas of Portsmouth and Southampton, the expansion of Ashford in connection with a Channel tunnel, the conservation of Bath, and various subjects proposed by the Greater London Council. He was a member of the Roskill Commission on the third London Airport, and personally favoured Foulness, the site eventually chosen by the Government.

Buchanan's work overseas has included a development study of Kuwait, a study of Arras in France, and studies in Nairobi.

In 1965 he received the Sir Patrick Abercrombie award of the International Union of Architects; and in 1967 he was awarded the gold medal of the Town Planning Institute.

Bucranium. A curiously macabre decoration resembling the skull of an ox, frequently garlanded. It occurs most often in the metopes (qv) of a Doric frieze.

Buffet. A French term of unknown origin that has been adopted internationally; also spelled beaufet and buffette. It is used to describe certain side or serving tables and units intended to display silver etc. The court cupboard, three-tiered and open-shelved, is one example, and the sideboard is another. A peculiarly eighteenth-century application of the word was to a panelled and shelved alcove in which plate was displayed. Today a cupboard with a superstructure of shelves – a form of dresser – is occasionally called a buffet; this is an extension of Sheraton's use of the term to describe an ornamental but useful china cupboard-cum-side-table.

Bulb. The turned bulbous swelling that occurs on table legs, bed posts, and the vertical supports of frames. Bulbs were frequently carved, and their appearance has led to their being called melon bulbs.

Bulfinch, Charles (1763–1844). American architect, essentially a late Baroque practitioner in a rationalist environment. He introduced a plausible version of the European Grand Manner into the newly-formed USA, and particularly Boston where he practised until summoned to work on the US Capitol at Washington.

His Massachusetts State House, Boston (1795–8), on Beacon Hill, exemplifies his preference for dignified Baroque public buildings.

Bulfinch's later work in Boston showed the increasing influence of Neo-classicism. This was partly a response to the intractable local granite, which largely determined the character of Bulfinch's Boston Court House (1810). The influence of a younger generation also played a part, as in the design of Massachusetts General Hospital (1819–27); while maintaining an Adamish elegance characteristic of Bulfinch, it exhibits a severity and rationalism reminiscent of works by Strickland and Parris.

Bun foot. The name given to a foot in the form of a flattened sphere. It was introduced *c* 1660 and is found especially on oak and walnut case furniture. Like the ball foot (qv), it was out of fashion by 1715.

Bungalow. The term now applied to almost any one-storey house. The word was adapted by British residents in India from the Hindustani *bangla*, belonging to Bengal. These Indian structures were invariably constructed with verandas, as were early British copies.

Owing to the popularity of the bungalow (which was picturesque and comparatively cheap to build), the word

Bun foot on 17th-century oak table

gradually fell into disfavour amongst the *cognoscenti*; town planning reports, for example, refer slightingly to 'bungaloid' growths. Like so many words in the English language, bungalow has acquired class associations, and architects now prefer to speak of 'one-storey' or 'single-storey' houses.

Bunshaft, Gordon (*b* 1909). American architect, since 1946 a partner in the firm of Skidmore, Owings, & Merrill. In 1952 Bunshaft crystallized the development of the SOM firm and convincingly established its architectural leadership with his design for Lever House, at 390 Park Avenue, New York City. Lever House, a tall glazed box

The Harrison Gray Otis House, Boston, by Charles Bulfinch, 1807

A Louis XVI bureau à cylindre: the roll front reveals small drawers

with the thinnest possible supports, is a perfect expression of the classical position arrived at *c* 1950 by Mies van der Rohe. It has found countless imitators all over the world – a fact in some part due to its evident 'tastefulness' and costliness, qualities which seemed valuable to commercial patrons. Since 1952 the SOM firm, like most other American architects, has moved away from Bunshaft's Miesian purism.

Bureau. This term defies any accurate and comprehensive definition, having been in constant use since the eighteenth century, and employed to describe many pieces which might equally well have been called *escritoires*, secretaries, *scrutoires*, or scriptors. To make the term more accurate and useful, it is now generally applied only to pieces that contain a writing compartment behind a sloping fall.

On this definition the first bureau is a small desk of the late seventeenth century, with a fall front upon a turned and (later) carved stand; even this contravenes Sheraton's well-known dictum that the term has 'generally been applied to common desks with drawers under them, such as are made very frequently in country towns' (*The Cabinet Dictionary*, 1803).

The desk on a stand gave way to the type with the familiar drawer-filled base and superstructure. The earliest version was a compartmented cabinet

Lever House, New York, designed by Bunshaft, 1952

top with a bevelled mirror or panelled doors. This imposing and very desirable object was usually crowned with a triangular, swan-necked, or segmental, broken pediment.

The American bureau is a piece of nineteenth-century bedroom furniture, a large chest of drawers with a mirror attached at the back. The mirror was heavily framed, and at either side of it were small shelves for bric-à-brac.

Bureau bookcase. A term introduced in the mid-eighteenth century to describe a particular variety of bureau in two stages. It differs from the late seventeenth-century bureau cabinet in having bookshelves rather than compartments and pigeonholes in its superstructure. These shelves were sometimes behind solid panelled doors, but on good-quality furniture it was more usual to insert glazed doors or a web of carved lattice work.

Burlington, Lord (1694–1753). Richard Boyle, 3rd Earl of Burlington and 4th Earl of Cork, played the most dynamic role in establishing Palladian architecture in England after 1715. He led a movement aimed at the reform of taste by reference to the work of Inigo Jones, Palladio, and classical antiquity.

On coming into his inheritance

in 1715, Burlington set out to indulge the passion for architecture which he had acquired on the Grand Tour. On a second tour, in 1719, he met his lifelong associate William Kent. From 1720 he assembled a circle at Burlington House, including Campbell (architect), Kent (painter), and Bridgeman (gardener), which virtually constituted a proto-Academy.

Although not the originator of the movement, he was its leader after 1720 – a position which he was able to maintain through his enormous wealth and his role within the governing Whig oligarchy. Thus he suc-

ceeded, where Campbell could not, in establishing Palladianism as the Whig style in architecture.

But Burlington was by no means solely a patron. His closest associate, William Kent, was a professional and a self-made man, but he was not Burlington's master; Burlington had some eight or nine buildings to his credit before Kent even started his career as an architect.

Burlington's executed designs fall into three groups. The first is most clearly derived from Palladio, ranging from Palladio's Mannerism (in General Wade's house, Old Burlington Street, 1723) to the Palladio of the Venetian churches (as in the rectangular temple in the grounds of Chiswick House, probably before 1729). The presence of Colen Campbell's influence can be assumed in these works.

The second group shows a tendency towards the Picturesque, as in the garden front of Burlington's villa at Chiswick (1727–36), where overarched Venetian windows are set in an otherwise plain wall. In the conversion of his Jacobean manor at Chiswick, and of another at Northwick Park, Worcestershire (1728–30), Burlington retains the picturesque Jacobean silhouette and augments it with two cubic blocks breaking forward either side of the entrance. His habit of dividing a design into a series of geometrically ordered, three-dimensional compartments is clearly the source of much Neoclassical work of *c* 1780. With Kent also it became part of the Picturesque tradition.

The third group is 'archaeological.' The design for Lord Lincoln's villa at Weybridge is one-storeyed, as Burlington supposed Roman houses to be. The circular temple in the grounds

A Queen Anne bureau bookcase

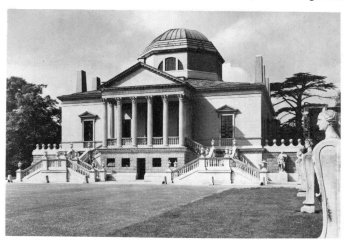

Chiswick House, Middlesex, designed by Burlington, 1727–36

Colonnaded Assembly Rooms at York designed by Burlington, 1730–2

of Chiswick House is based on a Palladian drawing of the Pantheon, and the Chiswick villa itself incorporates a number of Roman features. At York the Assembly Rooms (1730–2) follow Vitruvius as closely as possible. Burlington's unprecedented use of circular and polygonal rooms and apsidal recesses, and the coving of Roman type, was taken up by Robert Adam, through whom it was transmitted to France in the years before 1789. Burlington's influence on the Continent was a result of the eighteenth-century French vogue for all things English.

Burnham and Root. David H Burnham (1846–1912) and John Wellborn Root (1850–91). A Chicago architectural partnership, specializing in commercial buildings, and responsible for some of the innovations which helped to put Chicago on the architectural map. Their Montauk Block (1882–3) solved one of the problems of skyscraper development by spreading the foundations. It also went some way towards solving the problem of what a building which was indeterminately extensible should look like; Burnham and Root's answer was rigorously astylar.

Two buildings from their office rising in 1891 posed the alternative aesthetic possibilities for commercial architecture. In the Monadnock Building, with its walls of load-bearing brick, the astylar windows are expressed as holes cut out of an indeterminate organic shape. The Reliance Building, in which Jenney's 'skyscraper construction' was employed, had the external appearance of a skeleton with glass and terracotta infilling. Neither building was technically very significant; the Monadnock was a development of Holabird and Roche's Tacoma Building (1887–9).

Both of them, however, were very beautiful. The Monadnock was a slab, only two bays deep, which tapered inwards then curved outwards like a tree; the Reliance had continuous vertical oriels which broke up the surface and created the impression of a glittering glass box. Both produced an aesthetic solution that was at once visually compelling and structurally honest, and they are more admired today than they were in 1891.

Flat Iron Building, New York, designed by Burnham, 1902

Columbine, from Bustelli's model

Burr. When cut diagonally, the burr – a growth on the base of a tree – occasionally produced beautifully figured, mottled, or speckled patterns that were employed for inlay work. The burr elm, walnut, and yew were the particular favourites of craftsmen.

Burton, Decimus (1800–81). British architect, a leading exponent of the Classical Revival long after that style had been superseded by the Gothic Revival. He was the tenth son of James Burton, the builder largely responsible for the early development of St Leonard's-on-Sea. After an early architectural training at the Royal Academy Schools, Decimus Burton was befriended by John Nash. His Regent's Park Colosseum, a Greek version of the Pantheon, quickly established him as a successful architect. He is chiefly remembered by Londoners for the Hyde Park Screen and the arch on Constitution Hill, which was originally intended to be the grand northern entrance to Buckingham Palace. But Burton also

Hyde Park Corner Screen, designed by Decimus Burton in 1825

had a very large practice, his commissions ranging from houses in Glasgow to the headmaster's house at Harrow.

Bustelli, Franz Anton (1723–63) was born in Italy, where he received his early training. Later he worked in Germany at the porcelain factory at Nymphenburg, where he was the *Modellmeister* from 1754–63. He was the most important modeller of his time, and his style is the very essence of the Rococo. It is no exaggeration to say that the fame of the Nymphenburg factory rests largely on his work.

Bustelli had a strong theatrical sense, and many of his most famous models are of theatrical subjects. A series of sixteen figures from the Italian Comedy are among his best known works.

Butler's table. A rectangular mahogany tray, with carrying slots at each side, which stands on a simple trestle joined at the top by canvas strips. It became popular at the end of the eighteenth century and was used as an occasional or wine table.

Butterfield, William (1814–1900). British architect; leader of the Gothic Revival, and one

All Saints' Church: Butterfield

Flying buttress over the side aisle of a Gothic church

of the most original and influential architects of his time, although his views on building design would find few adherents today. His fame rests mainly on his designs for churches and his somewhat austere approach to decoration in ecclesiastical architecture.

Butterfield designed St Augustine's Missionary College in Canterbury at the age of 31, but his reputation was established by All Saints' in Margaret Street (1847–59) near Broadcasting House, London. In his book *English Parish Churches,* John Betjeman called it 'the pioneer church of the phase of the Gothic Revival which ceased to copy medieval but went on with new materials like cast-iron and stock brick.' Butterfield did much other work in St Albans, and in Oxford, where he was responsible for the designs of Keble College, the chapel for Balliol, and the extensions to Merton.

Butterfly table. A drop-leaf table claimed to be an American invention of the early eighteenth century. It is a development of the more familiar gate-leg table, but instead of the gate it had a hinged support that was shaped gracefully outwards, giving rise to the name butterfly. The legs of such a table were usually canted outwards, giving it a far lighter appearance than the gate-leg.

Buttress. A mass projecting from a wall to create extra strength and support, as necessary in the construction of a long garden wall as in a cathedral wall. In classical architecture, buttresses are usually disguised as pilasters. Norman buttresses are also fairly unobtrusive, but Early English buttresses are unashamed demonstrations of strength and purpose, sometimes continuing

to the full height without diminution, but often reduced by broken stages with sharply-angled slopes.

The flying or arch buttress separates the buttress from the object to be supported, transferring the thrust via an arch. It seems to have been an innovation in the Early English style, but was not widely used until much later. Although highly decorative in the hands of skilled stonemasons, it did not have the strength of the solid buttress, but was useful in providing a brace for superstructures added to roofs.

Byzantine architecture. The style of building, chiefly ecclesiastical, developed after the Emperor Constantine transferred his capital from Rome to Byzantium (Istanbul) in AD 324. Inevitably the fusing of Greek and Eastern elements resulted in an exotic mixture; for most west Europeans and Africans, its forms and decorative opulence are more evocative of the Near East than Rome. In fact, Greek and Roman influences can easily be detected in the use of a plan based on the Greek cross, and in the large cupola arising from the centre of the building.

The Byzantine style can be divided into three periods: (1) From the time of Constantine to the middle of the sixth century. (2) From the time of Justinian to the eleventh century, the period during which most surviving Byzantine buildings were erected. (3) From the eleventh century to the conquest of Greece by the Turks. Many buildings from this period display Venetian influences, including the pointed arch and fresco painting instead of mosaics.

Although many Byzantine churches are to be seen through-

The mosaics of the Basilica di San Vitale in Ravenna, sixteenth century

out Europe from Ochrida in Yugoslavia to Bonn in Germany, from Palermo in Sicily to Périgueux in France, the Byzantine style is epitomized by the incomparable church of Santa Sophia at Istanbul. Here we see the semi-circular arches, the cupola, and the curious capitals

of the mid-Byzantine era, with their tapering block-form and foliated decoration.

The Byzantine style is also renowned for its decoration. Walls were richly ornamented with carvings and mosaics, of which the mosaic decorations at Ravenna are superb examples.

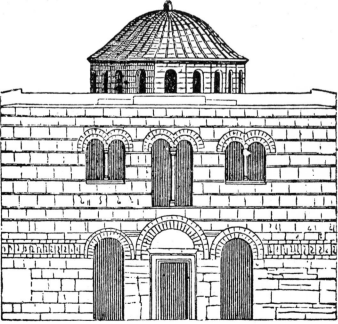

The Byzantine church of St Nicodemus, Athens

Lacquered cabinet with brass mounts on a carved stand, 1660–85

Cabinet. The name given to a piece of furniture with drawers or shelves in which important possessions could be stored or displayed. They were seldom made after the late eighteenth century. Cabinets were already popular in Italy, France, and the Low Countries when the first native English pieces were produced early in the seventeenth century; some found their way to America.

Cabinets were characteristically small and either had their own stands or rested upon another piece of furniture. Towards the end of the seventeenth century they were in great demand as extremely ornamental pieces of furniture with inlay and floral marquetry. This mode of decoration gave way to the japanned (imitation lacquer) cabinets of the early eighteenth century. Most of these pieces were of similar construction. The upper part was enclosed by two doors which opened to reveal a symmetrical arrangement of drawers around a small central cupboard; the whole rested upon a stand that might or might not contain drawers.

In the mid-eighteenth century, shelves and glazed doors were common. Some cabinets now resembled glazed cupboards on stands, while the most notable piece to emerge was an article sometimes indistinguishable from a bureau bookcase. Stands resembling chests of drawers had a long history; this form of cabinet was used primarily for the display of china and was not made after the end of the eighteenth century. Hanging cabinets with drawers, or glazed and with shelves, are not unknown.

Cabinetmaker. The cabinet-maker – maker of fine furniture – is now distinguished from the joiner. This was not always so: the only real distinction at the end of the seventeenth century was between cabinetmakers as makers of case and joiners as makers of seat furniture.

Fine furniture with veneers and inlays had its heyday in the eighteenth century on both sides of the Atlantic. In England, the Society of Upholders and Cabinet Makers was formed to protect the manufacturers' interests and to promote trade through catalogues. The first of these, *Household Furniture in Genteel Taste*, came out in 1760.

Cable moulding. A Norman convex moulding that may be likened to a cable or rope. The motif was revived in the eighteenth century and used to enliven columns: a very narrow cable moulding lay in the grooves between the flutes of the shaft.

Cabochon. A convex and oval ornamental motif which probably owes its origin to the cutting of precious stones before being copied by furniture-makers. The cabochon is most frequently seen on the outjutting cabriole knees of eighteenth-century tables and chairs.

Cabriole. Derived from the Italian capriola, 'a goat's leap', and French, *cabriole,* the dancing term for a leap.

The cabriole leg is double curving and resembles the leg of an animal. It was used in ancient Greece in an extremely stylised form. Its reintroduction at the very end of the seventeenth century was the start of a half-century of popularity. It finally went out of fashion as a result of the great emphasis on linear design in the second half of the century.

Early examples of chairs and stands with cabriole legs have stretchers, but a wider knee obviated the need for them and left a larger surface for decoration. The knees were plain, or

A cabochon

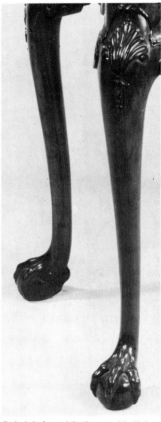

Cabriole leg with claw and ball foot

Castle. *Massive fortified walls at the fifteenth-century Castle of Coca in the province of Segovia, Spain*

Agate Pavilion, Pushkino (Tsarskoe Seloe): Cameron, 1783–5

Oak cabinet veneered with calamander, stamped 'E Levasseur'

Blue drawing room in the Catherine Palace, Pushkino, by Cameron

ornamented variously with acanthus leaves, scallops, honeysuckles, masks, rough animal hair, or even feathers. The foot of such a leg did lend itself to naturalistic treatment. Paw feet abound, although claw and ball are probably the most common.

The broken cabriole occurs when the upper convex curve is continued beyond the usual point and ends sharply, broken off, above the lower part of the leg. In these cases the lower portion is usually more straight than curving.

A cabriole chair is described by Hepplewhite, in his 1788 *Household Guide,* as an armchair with a stuffed back, and by Sheraton in *The Cabinet Dictionary* (1803) as 'stuffed all over.'

Caisson. A recessed panel, usually square or octagonal, in a vaulted ceiling. When this recessed coffering was used in domes, the sizes of the caissons were occasionally graduated to increase the illusion of height; this was especially common in the Baroque era.

Caisson is also used in bridge construction, describing a box or chamber which enables foundations of masonry to be positioned under water.

Calamander. *Diospyros quaesita,* also called coromandel. This wood comes from the East Indies – the Coromandel Coast has been suggested as the origin of the name – and from the same family as the ebony tree. Calamander-wood is most easily described as looking like rosewood striped with ebony. The highly decorative, even dramatic qualities of calamander ensured its employment by cabinet-makers, and it was quite frequently used for card tables and other table tops.

Camber. To bend or cause a slight convex curve to be created in a beam or other horizontal member.

Came. A grooved metal strip used for framing the lights of latticed windows.

Cameron, Charles (*c* 1740–1814). Scottish architect. Of Cameron's early life and training scarcely anything is known except that he studied in Rome in 1768. He returned to England and published *The Baths of the Romans* in 1772. On the strength of this book, the Empress Catherine the Great summoned Cameron to Russia in 1774. The

Campanile of the Duomo at Pisa

Empress had a passion for building, and Cameron soon became her favourite architect.

Cameron's designs were generally somewhat austerely Palladian in external appearance. His interiors were much influenced by the work of his compatriot Robert Adam (qv), although Cameron's decorative themes are executed with a magnificently individual flair. As chief architect to the Empress, Cameron decorated apartments for Tsarskoe Seloe, near St Petersburg, and added to it the Agate Pavilion (1783–5). He designed the palace at Pavlovsk (1781–96) for Catherine's son, the Grand Duke Paul.

Cameron seems to have returned to Britain only once after settling in Russia. On the death of the Empress in 1796, he was dismissed and seems to have set up in some form of private practice. In this private capacity he designed the Batourin Palace in the Ukraine. He was reinstated in royal favour after the death of Paul I, and as official architect to the Russian admiralty designed a naval hospital and barracks at Kronstadt.

Campanile. Italian for 'bell tower.' These are seen throughout Italy, standing beside the churches. The Leaning Tower at Pisa, built between 1174 and 1350, is the campanile of the cathedral. Its lean began during construction and is now more than 16 ft.

Campbell, Colen or Colin (*d* 1729). British architect. He was a Scot of obscure origins, although he later claimed high social connections. He quickly rose to fame with the first volume of *Vitruvius Brittanicus,* published in 1715; further volumes were added in 1717 and 1725. Campbell also published an

Design for Wanstead House, Essex: Campbell

The Mauritshuis at The Hague, by Jacob van Campen, 1633–5

edition of Palladio's *Five Orders of Architecture* in 1729. He became an influential member of Lord Burlington's coterie, which was responsible for the spread of Palladianism in England.

Wanstead House (1715, demolished 1824) was probably Campbell's most influential building. Each of the three alternative plans provided inspiration for later architects such as James Paine (qv) at Nostell Priory, and Henry Flitcroft (qv) at Wentworth Woodhouse, both in Yorkshire. Wanstead was a synthesis of late seventeenth-century trends, the architecture of Palladio, and that of Inigo Jones, Campbell's acknowledged master.

Campbell was undoubtedly the leading spirit in planting the Palladian villa of the Veneto in the English countryside. His own exercises in villa architecture ranged from the minuscule Ebberston Lodge in Yorkshire (1718) to his unashamed copy and skilful adaptation of Palladio's design for the Villa Rotunda. His project for Mereworth in Kent (*c* 1722–5) ranks with Chiswick House as the most exquisite of all Anglicized interpretations of the Italian villa.

Stourhead in Wiltshire (1722) and Newby (now Baldersby) in Yorkshire (1720–1) are other examples of Campbell's skilful and imaginative plagiarism of Palladio.

Campbell was patronized by Lord Burlington and carried out extensive alterations on Burlington House, Piccadilly (now the Royal Academy). He also built Houghton Hall, Norfolk (1721), for Sir Robert Walpole.

Campen, Jacob van (1595–1657). Dutch architect. Campen gained a reputation as a painter before turning to architecture. He was the inaugurator of Dutch classicism or Dutch Palladianism, a style introduced with the Mauritshuis in 1633, and prevailing until about 1670.

Despite the influences from the Italian Renaissance which colour his designs, Campen's steep roofs and prominent chimneys, giant orders and pilasters, retain a distinctly Northern European character. His major works were the Mauritshuis (1633–5), the Nieuwekerk in Haarlem (1645), and Amsterdam Town Hall, now the Royal Palace (1648–55). This last is an impressive building, skilfully incorporating two internal courtyards for lighting the magnificently decorated Hall of Judgement and the central hall.

Candela, Felix (*b* 1910). One of the world's foremost architect-engineers. Candela was born and educated in Madrid, but fled to France after the Civil War, in which he fought against Franco. With Quaker help he was enabled to emigrate to Mexico, where he set up as an architect and also founded his own construction company.

Candela's reputation was established with his remarkable curved shell design for the Cosmic Ray Pavilion (1950–1) for Mexico's University City. He has since used this hyperbolic paraboloid (which has been likened to the Western saddle) in numerous other buildings, from bandstands and restaurants to schools and churches. Although not the inventor of the hyperbolic paraboloid (qv), Candela has probably used the form more widely, ingeniously, and

Felix Candela

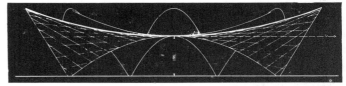

Ebberston Lodge, Yorkshire, designed by Campbell, 1718

A restaurant at Xochimilco, Mexico, designed by Candela, and above, a sectional elevation of it, showing his famous hyperbolic paraboloid

A Louis XIV ormolu and bronze candelabrum

One of a pair of Louis XV ormolu candlesticks

practically than any other architect. With its double curve, the form has great strength and is applicable to timber, metals, and reinforced concrete. To some architectural critics this shell form seems to offer an alternative to (and possible escape from) the rectilinear monotony of the International Style (qv).

Candela has also used other forms of construction. Among the notable buildings designed by him are the churches of San Antonio de Huertas in Loyoaian (1957) and La Virgin Milagrosa in Mexico City (1953).

Candelabrum. A group of candle branches supported on a single stem. It was earlier known – somewhat misleadingly – as a chandelier. Candelabra are usually found in pairs from the Middle Ages until the nineteenth century. Early forms were used to light the naves and altars of churches. The later domestic forms became highly ornate objects of art, worked in silver, ormolu, or gold.

Candlebeam. An early form of chandelier made up of two or more crossed pieces of wood. Candles were fixed to the spikes or sockets at the end of each arm.

Candle-slide. A square, circular, or rectangular flat support for candlesticks, incorporated in furniture such as desks and card tables.

Candlestand. See **Torchère.**

Candlestick. A holder for a single candle. Candlesticks are usually made in pairs, but sometimes in large sets. The medieval candlestick had a spike or picket on which the candle was secured, and it was not until the late sixteenth century that the stick with a socket became the standard type. Candlesticks have been made of base and precious metals, wood, glass, porcelain, and other materials.

Cane was brought to England by the East India Company from about 1660. It came from the type of palms known as rattans, and proved suitable for the backs and seats of chairs. It was even on rare occasions used for table tops.

The mesh of late seventeenth-century caning was extraordinarily fine and has seldom been equalled. The practice had been abandoned by 1700 but was resuscitated briefly in cheaper French seat furniture during Louis XV's reign.

Early Victorians used elegant cane furniture in the drawing-room, and all through the nineteenth century and beyond, cane-seated or cane-backed chairs were perfectly acceptable inside the most decorous homes. By 1900, all-cane chairs for the gentry had become essentially outdoor furniture, used on the terrace or – at a pinch – in the conservatory.

Times and fashions continue

Silver candelabrum designed and made by Keith Tyssen

Modern 'butterfly chair' made of cane

A Regency canopy

to change, and now an ever-increasing number of people buy all-cane chairs, tables, bedheads, and so on, for indoors. The use of cane for chair-backs and seats only has diminished.

Canephora. Sculptured figure bearing a basket upon his or her head.

Canopy. An ornamental projection employed in architecture and also in furniture, for example the canopy over a pulpit, imposing chair, or bed. In this last instance it is known as a tester (qv). In Gothic architecture the canopy was frequently employed as an ornamented projection over doors and windows, and as a protective covering for niches containing effigies. But the canopy was probably most widely used during the Regency period, when almost every small villa had a canopy over its upper-floor windows.

Canteen. A case partitioned for flasks, bottles or cutlery.

A Regency Canterbury

Canterbury. This is a term applied to a type of music stand, and also to a supper trolley; both are said to have been ordered by the Archbishop of Canterbury.

The music stand is the better known. It is a low wooden (usually mahogany) stand with slatted partitions for music books and one or two small drawers below. The legs are short and tapered, with small brass castors that allowed the Canterbury to be

Cantilevered rooms in a modern house

rolled beneath the piano. The other is a 'supper tray, made to stand by the table at supper, with a circular end, forks, and plates, at that end, which is made circular on purpose' (Sheraton in *The Cabinet Dictionary*, 1803).

Cantilever. A projecting beam or bracket used to support eaves, cornices, and balconies. Modern structural development has caused the use of cantilever to be greatly enlarged, and projecting members without apparent support are now referred to as being cantilevered.

Canton. After 1757 the only port in China that was used to export Chinese goods to the west. The largest trading company at Canton was the British East India Company, whose ships carried a profusion of Chinese products for nearly a hundred years.

The rise of Canton as an exporter of art attracted many fine Chinese craftsmen, especially those skilled in carving ivory for chessmen, card cases, openwork fans, and fantastic hollow concentric balls, sometimes as many as fifteen one inside the other. At Canton in the Ch'ien Lung period (1736–95) white porcelain from Kiangsi was decorated before being exported. In Canton in 1768 William Hickey watched this work being done by old men and 'children which were so young as six or seven years.' Blue and white Canton ware, once inexpensive,

is highly prized today. This is particularly so in America, into which Canton ware was originally imported in clipper ships, which used it more as extra ballast than as valuable cargo.

Wallpaper painting reached its zenith in the first quarter of the nineteenth century.

Perhaps the loveliest work done at Canton was enamelling. A simple process on copper was employed, the result resembling porcelain. Its heyday was the early eighteenth century, and it has seldom been surpassed for delicacy of execution and charm of design.

In the enamelling studios of Canton, dinner services decorated with armorial bearings were painted for export to royal or wealthy patrons who had commissioned them. For a long time this porcelain was wrongly supposed to have been made at Lowestoft.

Cape Cod. A cottage style developed primarily on Cape Cod, Massachusetts, during the eighteenth and early nineteenth centuries. This type of cottage is a one-storey building made of wood, with a partial basement. Also characteristic is the large central chimney and gable roof made of shingles.

Capital. The head or top section of a column above the shaft. The capital is the most distinctive feature of the various classical orders, whether it be the carved scrolls of the Ionic or the

acanthus leaves of the Corinthian. Similarly, in Gothic architecture, capitals received equally varied treatment as in crocket (qv) and cushion (qv) capitals.

Capo di Monte. This porcelain factory was founded close to Naples in 1743 by Charles, King of Naples. All the china produced there before 1759, when the factory closed, was of a soft-paste body with a greenish or yellowish colour. In 1771 the factory opened again at Portici, and in 1773 moved to Naples, where both hard and soft paste was made until about 1805, when only hard paste was made. The factory closed in 1821.

Early Capo di Monte is extremely rare. Its main characteristic is the relief moulding, which is unique. There are many copies of this porcelain, notably from a factory at Doccia which acquired many of the original moulds in 1821. However, all the Doccia products are of a hard-paste body, and readily distinguishable. Figures of a quite outstanding quality were made at the Capo di Monte factory, but they are rarely seen outside a museum.

Capping. The moulding between the top of wall panelling and the frieze, or, in architecture, the coping (qv).

Caquetoire, caqueteuse (French, *chaqueter* 'to chatter'). The French term for a light, low-seated conversation chair. The word was also applied to an armchair with a tall, narrow, panelled

A beaker-shaped Capo di Monte vase, made c 1750

Oak caquetoire, sixteenth century

back and out-spreading arms. The sides of the seat followed the curve of the arms, so that it was much wider at the front.

Carcase. The body of a piece of furniture upon which the veneer, marquetry, or lacquer is placed.

Card table. Card games have existed in one form or another for many centuries; the earliest were probably played upon marked wooden boards. Special tables, baize-lined and folding when not in use, did not appear until the reign of Charles II. Among the finest and most desirable of such pieces are the rare walnut tables on cabriole legs with circular tops, produced in the time of Queen Anne. These have money cellars and candlestand corners, set at the edge of needlework panels show-

A Queen Anne walnut card table with needlework top

ing playing cards or other symbols of gambling.

The eighteenth century saw a great vogue for card games and specialized tables were made for quadrille, loo, piquet, etc.

Stoneware cider jar: Cardew, 1950

Cardew, Michael (b 1900). A British potter who was for a time at the Leach Pottery before taking over the Winchcombe Pottery in Gloucestershire. Here his remarkable energy and drive enabled him to fill the enormous kiln – holding about 3,000 pieces – every two or three months. He mainly produced useful slip-decorated earthenware in the English tradition. In 1949, having moved to Wenford Bridge in Cornwall, he began to make stoneware, but a year later settled in Africa, where he had been during the war. Recently he has returned to his pottery in Cornwall, where he continues to work in his bold and pleasing style.

Carlton House table. A distinctive writing table with a

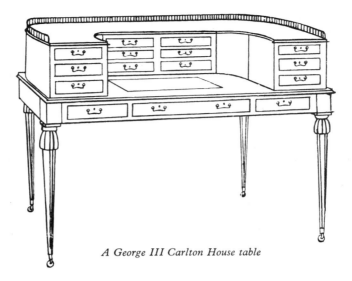

A George III Carlton House table

U-shaped superstructure. It first appeared about 1780, but is not referred to under its present name till 1796, in Gillow's Cost Book. Sheraton designed one in the *Drawing-Book* of 1793 but called it a 'Lady's Drawing and Writing Table.' The Prince Regent is supposed to have had the first of these tables at Carlton House, whence the name; but there is no definite evidence of this.

The design is more or less standard. The width is some $5\frac{1}{2}$ ft and the legs of early examples are usually round, tapered, and capped with panels of gadrooning. The superstructures contain numerous small drawers, which usually curve down at each side and sometimes have slits for letterboxes.

Carolean. Furniture made during the reign of Charles II (1660–85), and characterised by heavy scrolled decoration and

Carolean beechwood armchair

spiral turning. The term is most frequently applied to ornately carved, high-backed chairs somewhat reminiscent of Dutch furniture. They had very elaborate cresting and downward sloping arms, either with or without cane back panels.

Carpet. A thick fabric covering. Methods of manufacturing carpets are remarkably similar throughout the East. Materials such as wool, silk, cotton, hair (usually goat's hair), and vegetable dyes were used everywhere. During the late nineteenth century, synthetic aniline dyes from Europe were introduced, but their brilliance faded and they were seen to be a poor substitute for the original dyes.

There are three techniques of knotting hand-made carpets. In the *Ghiordes* (Turkish) knot, the pile thread is knotted around two adjacent warp threads so that the ends are drawn up between them. The *Sehna* (Persian) knot involves winding the pile around one warp thread and tying it

Ghiordes carnation prayer rug, Turkish, seventeenth century

Kirman carpet, Persian

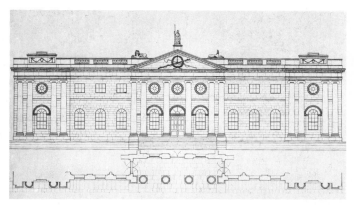

The Assize Courts, York, designed by Carr in 1777

around the next. Finally, in the rare Spanish knot, every alternate warp thread is knotted.

Oriental carpets – runners, small prayer rugs, and large carpets – were all exported to Europe from the late Middle Ages, frequently through Venetian traders. Many were felt to be too precious to be walked on, and were used as table covers and wall hangings; they can be seen in the interiors of paintings by Holbein and the Flemish masters of the sixteenth and seventeenth centuries. Most of those represented are Turkish. Broadly speaking, Turkish, Turcoman, and Caucasian carpets are geometric, whereas Persian carpets have flowing lines and representations of birds, beasts, and even men. Persian carpets are the most highly prized because they are generally of better quality than the others.

One reason is the high number of *Sehna* knots to the square inch, which allows greater detail in the pattern.

Tapestry carpets known as Khelims and Soumaks are made in the Orient. They are light, and the majority are prayer rugs. Khelims have an identical pattern on both sides, and are often referred to as 'double faced.' In eighteenth-century France, tapestry-weavers produced superb decorative carpets in imitation of Khelims and Soumaks; Aubusson, Gobelins, Beauvais, and Felletin are the most famous. (Savonnerie produced pile carpets.) Tournai was the centre of the Belgian tapestry-carpet industry, and in England they were made at Moorfields and Mortlake, near London. Centres of English pile-carpet manufacture were Axminster, Wilton, and Kidderminster.

Most carpets are now machine-made. As a general rule, one of three methods is used, resulting in a Wilton, an Axminster, or a tufted carpet. Whereas the pile threads are woven into the backing to make a Wilton carpet, in an Axminster the pile yarn is inserted into the backing, thereby simulating the technique of hand weaving. Tufted carpet manufacture has been largely developed in America. This is the fastest and cheapest method devised so far. A machine stitches the pile yarn into pre-woven jute backing, and the tufts are anchored with a rubber latex compound.

Man-made carpet materials, such as rayon, acrylic fibre, protein fibre, and acetate have steadily increased in popularity. Whereas a carpet was once primarily a work of art, carpeting, bought by the yard, is nowadays mainly popular because it provides comfort and insulation.

Carr, John (1723–1807). British architect. Carr was born at Horbury, near Wakefield, the son of a stonemason and quarry-owner for whom he worked after leaving the village school. His first independent surveyorship was *c* 1750, when he built Kirby Hall to the designs of Lord Burlington and Roger Morris.

His career as a Palladian (and occasionally Gothic) architect began in 1754, when he won the competition for the grandstand at York Race Course, defeating Sir Thomas Robinson and James Paine (qv). This led to numerous commissions, most of them in Yorkshire. The most notable of Carr's houses were Constable Burton (*c* 1762–8), Farnley Hall (*c* 1786), Denton Park (1778), and Harewood House (1759–71), on which he collaborated with Robert Adam.

Carr worked for the West Riding as surveyor of bridges – unofficially, on behalf of his father, from 1752, and on his own behalf from 1760 until 1770. In 1772 he was awarded a similar surveyorship by the North Riding, which he held until 1803/5. These offices, and his success in competitions, enabled Carr to become one of the most prolific bridge builders of the eighteenth century.

His work in York (where he was twice Lord Mayor) earned him the title 'Carr of York.' For that city he built the County Lunatic Asylum (1772–7), the Assize Courts (1773–7), and the Female Debtors' Prison (1780; now the Castle Museum), as well as a number of private houses. He was a versatile architect, capable of designing stables (those at Wentworth Woodhouse are probably the best known), churches, hospitals (as far apart as Lincoln and Oporto in Portugal), and mansions.

Cartel clock. A wall clock of mid-eighteenth-century origin. It had an ornate frame of gilded bronze, cast brass, or gilt wood.

Modern Axminster carpet

Geometrically-patterned carpet

Ormolu cartel clock by Amy Denten, Louis XV

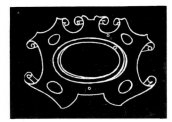

A cartouche

A Carver chair with rush seat

Caryatid on Erechtheum, Athens

The Casino, Marino, Dublin, designed by Chambers, 1765–71

Sir Hugh Casson

Cartouche. A decorative tablet, usually oval, but occasionally rectangular. It is used in a variety of manners and media, from engraved forms in typography and silverware to carved forms in architecture and furniture.

Carver chair. An American armchair, commonly made of maple or ash, with a rush seat and turned uprights. It is called after John Carver (1571–1621), governor of Plymouth and one of the original Pilgrim Fathers, who is said to have owned such a chair. Like the Brewster chair (qv), it is of stick construction.

Caryatid. A carved female figure employed as a column or support; it usually comprises head and torso, but is sometimes a full-length figure. Caryatids are usually employed in pairs or groups. They seem to have been first used in Greek architecture, and the most famous are those on the Erechtheum in Athens. Inevitably such esoteric Greek forms appealed to architects and cabinetmakers of the Directoire and Regency periods; they are used as side supports, on marble chimneypieces and, in wood or metal, on tables and cabinets.

Case furniture. Term for articles of furniture which provide space for storage, as opposed to seat furniture.

Casement. The wide concave moulding between compound columns and in the jambs of doors and windows. The casement window was in general use until the introduction of the sash window in the seventeenth century. It was hinged down one side and so could be opened inwards or outwards.

Casino. An ornamental pavilion or temple, usually within a park. During the eighteenth century the term was also used for a dancing saloon or other public assembly rooms, whereas today it is most often associated with gambling establishments.

Casson, Sir Hugh (*b* 1910). One of the leading contemporary British architects, knighted for his work as director of architecture for the Festival of Britain in 1951. He studied architecture at Cambridge and in 1937 he went into private partnership with Christopher Nicholson. During the war he was camouflage officer in the Air Ministry and then, from 1944 to 1946, technical officer in the Ministry of Town and Country Planning.

After the war he resumed private practice. In 1952 he was consultant for the Coronation decorations. He has designed several displays for exhibitions both in Britain and abroad. In 1951 he became professor of interior design at the Royal College of Art.

Sir Hugh, together with his partners, has designed interiors for shops, offices, and banks, hotels and restaurants, railway coaches and ships. He has also done theatrical decor for Covent Garden and Glyndebourne. His buildings include the new elephant house and foot-bridge for London Zoo; universities including Oxford, Cambridge, Birmingham, and London, the HQ of the General Dental Council in Wimpole Street, the King George VI Memorial Youth Hostel in Holland Park, regional headquarters for the National Westminster Bank in Manchester, the Swindon Arts Centre, the new civic centre at Derby, the county offices, Exeter, and a new information centre in Hampshire country park.

He is the author of several books, including *New Sights of London* (1937), *Bombed Churches* (1946), *Homes by the Millions* (1947), and *Inscape* (1968).

Lady Casson is also an architect and specialises in interior design.

The Elephant House at the London Zoo, Regent's Park, designed by Sir Hugh Casson

Elaborate cassone from Florence known as the Nerli Cassone

Cast-iron supports in Labrouste's Bibliothèque Nationale, 1843–50

Cassone. An Italian chest with a hinged lid, similar to the blanket or vestment chest. Cassones were chiefly made between 1400 and 1700, and enjoyed great popularity. Early examples are relatively simple and unpretentious, but during the Renaissance, elaborate paintings were done on the front panel and inside lid. These are often of great value, as they were com-monly painted by artists who specialised in the work. Cassones became very elaborate and were sometimes gilded. Many, though by no means the majority, were dower chests; another variety, the *cassone nuziale,* a marriage chest bearing the coats of arms of the two families, was fairly common. During the course of the sixteenth century they declined in popularity with the increasing use of the travelling chest and *cassapanca* (a chest with back and arms).

Cast-iron. Decoration in cast-iron first became important in the second half of the eighteenth century, when the Adam brothers introduced cast-iron fireplaces and irons, railings, and standards, into their interiors.

Cast-iron was known in ancient China and had been used in the Middle Ages for firebacks, fire irons, and other objects. But its decorative possibilities were limited, largely because the casting process never produced really finely finished work and the product was rigid and breakable.

Nineteenth century techniques of mass-production made cast-iron cheap and easy to produce —advantages that were exploited to the full. Victorian garden seats and tables and balustrades are all familiar enough, typically florid in design and over-abundant in ornament.

Castellated. Fortified or decorated with battlements.

Castle (Latin, *castellum,* from *castrum* 'a fort'). A term originally meaning a fort or fortified building, but later applied to buildings of a more pacific order which affected some of the outward signs of fortification. Castles in Europe were essentially the creation of the Romans, who needed these strategic strongpoints for the protection of their long lines of communication.

In Britain the medieval history of castle architecture begins with the Norman Conquest (1066)

A castellated deanery in Suffolk dating from the late fifteenth century

A cast-iron garden seat made about 1850 at Cold Spring, New York

and culminates with the concentric Welsh border castles of Edward I (1239–1307). Most of the first Norman castles were of the motte and bailey variety, and very few were made of stone. The motte was usually an artificial mound of earth with a wooden palisade on top; it was unable to support a stone structure. The bailey was an outer courtyard which was enclosed by a stone wall.

The Norman castles of England and France are similar. Two of the best French castles are the Château Gaillard, Normandy (1196), and Carcassone (11th–13th century) in southern France. The experiences of the Crusaders did much to improve the defensive features of castles, and they were directly responsible for introducing machicolations (qv) into western Europe.

Castles are usually classified by the type of keep, the donjon,

Caernarvon Castle in Wales built between 1283 and 1322

Hurstmonceaux Castle in Sussex, founded c 1440

Castillo de la Mota in Medino del Campo, Spain, 1440

Aerial view of Windsor Castle

Kronberg Castle in Elsinore, outside Copenhagen, 1574–85

Castle of Neuschwanstein built by Ludwig of Bavaria

Castleford white unglazed stoneware teapot, eighteenth century

A cauliflower teapot, probably made by Wedgwood, c 1765

which was the living quarters of the lord as well as the last stronghold in any fight to the finish. Types included the simple shell keep with a bailey adapted from the immediate surroundings, and the circular, rectangular, and polygonal keeps. An important improvement was the concentric plan adopted under Edward I. Concentric plans are found at Caerphilly, Beaumaris, and Conway, one bailey being entirely enclosed by another, so that the castle could only be taken by a protracted siege, which was often impossible by the very nature of feudal military organization. The fortress-castle had ceased to be important by the late Middle Ages, and most later so-called castle building involved fortified or quasi-fortified manor houses.

Castle Hedingham. A small pottery was working at this village in Essex, England, during

the second half of the nineteenth century. Edward Bingham made many ornamental pieces decorated with modelling in relief and with various coloured tortoiseshell glazes. The pieces are always marked with a castle on the base.

Castleford. The Castleford pottery was started about 1790 by David Dunderdale, who had worked at the Leeds pottery. Although Castleford made cream-coloured earthenware and Egyptian black ware, its most characteristic products were fine white, unglazed stoneware teapots and other useful objects, with relief mouldings sometimes with blue decoration. They were sometimes, though not always, marked: DD & Co, Castleford Pottery.

Castleford ceased production in 1820 but was re-opened later by Asquith Wood & Co; it then continued under various names

throughout the nineteenth century.

Castor. A small wheel for movable pieces of furniture. The early varieties were wooden (mainly boxwood). Leather castors were introduced c 1750, and brass castors, which were to become standard, c 1770. Pattern books list the different types that were available.

Detail from a Caucasian rug

Caucasian rugs. The Caucasus lies to the north of Persia. Until recently it was largely inhabited by nomadic tribes famous for their rug-weaving. Like all nomadic work, these rugs are small, geometric in design, feature hook and diamond motifs, and are bold in colouring. They particularly suit contemporary styles of interior decoration and rooms containing modern pictures. The chief types of Caucasian rug are the Shirvan, the Hila, the Karabagh, the Kazak, the Daghestan, the Kabistan, and the superb antique rugs from Derbend and Kouba.

Caughley. See **Coalport.**

Caulicole. Literally, a stalk. One of eight small stems which spring from the upper row of acanthus leaves on a Corinthian

capital. They support the scrolls or volutes.

Cauliflower ware. This ware seems to have been made first by Thomas Whieldon in Staffordshire, about the middle of the eighteenth century. Later, when Josiah Wedgwood went into partnership with him, they both made this kind of pottery, and Wedgwood is said to have improved the green glaze that was used on the leaves of the cauliflowers. Certainly the rich dark green contrasts beautifully with the creamy colour of the flower. This kind of ware was imitated by many other potters. Not only teapots, but bowls, jugs, and plates were made, and as well as cauliflowers, pineapples and maize were modelled.

Cavetto. A concave moulding of one quarter of a circle, originally used in Greek architecture and later adapted for other styles. A large cavetto is normally termed a cove.

Cavity wall. See **Hollow wall.**

Cedar. *Juniperus virginia* (North American) and *Cedrela odorata* (West Indian). Pale yellow-brown wood of a smooth, tight grain, much used for furniture fittings such as nests of drawers in bureaux. Even after 200 years, the wood retains an attractive and characteristic smell.

Ceiling (Italian, *cielo,* French, *ciel* 'sky'). The undercovering of the roof of the topmost storey in a building and the floors of lower storeys. In earlier times the timbers of the floor above formed beamed ceilings which are now, when exposed, greatly admired. By the sixteenth century, these ceilings had been boarded or plastered over, and plaster ceilings were increasingly enriched with medallions, rosettes, and other motifs. In England, Hampton Court, Longleat, and Hardwick Hall contain ceilings dating from this period. Throughout the seventeenth

A jug, urn, and pots of Castle Hedingham ware, 1880-1900

Painted wooden ceiling at Crathes Castle

The centrepiece of a ceiling at Syon House, by Angelica Kauffman

century, plasterers were enriching the ceilings of aristocratic houses; but it was the architect-designers of the eighteenth century who created the most highly decorative and imaginative ceilings which have come down to us. Those designed by Robert Adam for Syon, Kedleston, Chandos House, and a score of other mansions are of great beauty and ingenuity. In America the stucco decoration on the hall ceiling in Thomas Jefferson's house, Monticello, and the more elaborate stucco-duro ceiling in the Great Room at Kenmore in Fredricksburg, Virginia, are among the most famous. Today, most architects seem to prefer plain plastered ceilings, although some have experimented with timber strips in houses and acoustic tiles and other decorative materials in public buildings.

See the articles on **Plasterwork** and **Trompe l'oeil.**

Celadon. The name given to a certain kind of Chinese porcelain, first made during the T'ang

Plaster ceiling at St Mary's Church, Hartwell: Keene 1753–5

Breakfast room ceiling at Harewood House, Yorkshire, by Robert Adam

George III mahogany oval cellaret

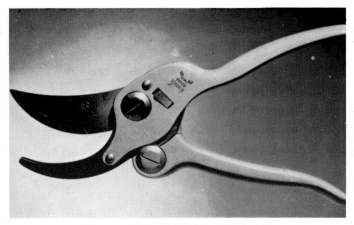

Secateurs designed by Hulme Chadwick

A rococo Louis XV chair with painted and gilt frame

period (AD 618–960). It ranged in colour from a muddy putty, through various greens, to a beautiful soft jade. The colour was due to ferrous oxides in the glaze.

The word 'Celadon' is said to be a corruption of Saladin, the Sultan of Egypt who sent a present of this ware to the Sultan of Damascus in 1171. Celadon ware was greatly esteemed in China, Japan, and the Near East, partly because of its resemblance to jade and partly because of the belief that it could be used to detect the presence of poison in food. It was supposed to change colour or break.

Celadon was also made in Korea, and even in France in the late nineteenth century. A celadon glaze is often used by studio potters today.

Cell. See **Web.**

Cella. The Latin term for the main body of a classical temple, exclusive of colonnades and porticoes.

Cellaret. The general term used from *c* 1750 to describe wine coolers, cisterns, gardes du vin, and the deep drawers in a sideboard – all objects designed expressly to contain bottles. It is

Hulme Chadwick

now used more specifically to describe the free-standing containers positioned below early Georgian side tables, or flanking Georgian fitted sideboards, to provide extra bottle space. They were of various designs, oval, octagonal, circular, or square; towards the end of the eighteenth century they were even shaped like sarcophagi. The cellaret was lined with lead and partitioned for bottles and decanters.

Celure. This term, spelled in several different ways (selour, ceilor, ceeler, etc), has been used loosely to describe the canopy, vertical board, and hangings of a bed. However, when it appears in conjunction with a tester it is usually understood to mean the vertical behind the bed and the tester.

Cenotaph. Monument erected in honour of a person buried elsewhere.

Chadwick, Hulme (*b* 1910). British architect and general consultant designer. He was born in Manchester and gained an industrial art exhibition to the Manchester College of Art. Then he gained a national scholarship to the Royal College of Art, where he was awarded the travelling scholarship in architecture.

In 1945 Chadwick Hulme set up in private practice to work in exhibition, interior, and industrial design. He has gained many awards for industrial design, having been responsible for product designs ranging from razors to garden shears.

Chair. A twelfth-century carving in Chartres Cathedral shows a chair of great distinction, and decorations in manuscript books make it clear that three- and four-legged chairs, turned and

often painted, were in use in Europe throughout the Middle Ages. These chairs were probably made of oak, beech, or elm. Upholstered chairs were little known. Chairs were more common in the sixteenth century; the oldest surviving chair in England is probably the Erasmus chair at Queen's College, Cambridge, which dates from about 1500.

Greater sophistication became evident during the latter half of the seventeenth century (the cabriole leg was probably introduced about 1680), when upholstery also became part of the cabinetmaker's craft. Beech chairs of this period were also painted and lacquered. By the eighteenth century the cabinetmaker had become a most important figure in the furnishing of houses, especially under the direction of such architect-designers as Kent and Adam. The leading cabinetmakers – Chippendale, Hepplewhite, and Sheraton published guides and pattern books which popularized well-designed chairs.

All this was changed by the Industrial Revolution, but chair design benefited from the twentieth-century design revolu-

Mahogany chair by Chippendale

tion associated with the Bauhaus in particular, and Mies van der Rohe, Marcel Breuer, and others have designed superb modern chairs. The variety of well-designed chairs now available to the buyer is probably greater than at any time since the eighteenth century.

Oak chair, mid-17th century

Tubular steel chair by Breuer

Chairback settee of carved and inlaid walnut, early eighteenth century

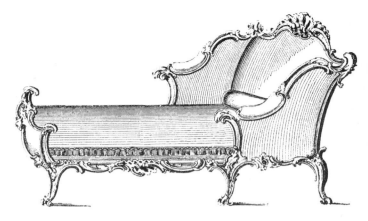

Chaise longue from Chippendale's 'Director', 1772

Chair back settee. A settee with an upholstered seat and a back made up of a series of two or more open chair backs. Examples date from the late seventeenth century. See also **Banister** or **Bar back**.

Chair-table. A sturdy piece of furniture that served as both a chair and a table. It was first made in the late fifteenth century but achieved its greatest popularity in the seventeenth.

The chair-table was usually made of oak. It was an armchair with a circular or rectangular back that was secured with a hinge at the back of each arm. When it was to be used as a table, the back could be pulled down into a horizontal position, resting on the two arms.

Chaise longue. A French term that has been, and still is, loosely used to describe all couches and daybeds. However, it is best applied to the type conforming to the literal meaning of the term, 'long seat.' This was popular in the late eighteenth century, though earlier examples exist, and is very like an elongated chair, having a back, two arms, and a very long seat. An upholstered version of this lounging chair continued to be made in the nineteenth century.

Chalet. A small, picturesque wooden house native to Switzerland but since copied in other parts of Europe and in America. The word has by extension been applied to all sorts of holiday houses. The original Swiss chalet has changed little over the centuries; it is a wooden construction consisting of timber framework with infilling of boards, bricks, or beams laid one upon the other after the fashion of the log cabin. In the mountains the roofs are broad and low to hold the snow for winter warmth. The eaves are wide, and brackets, chimneys, and dormer windows are all exaggerated for decorative effect, their picturesque quality being further enhanced by painted carvings.

Chalkware. American chalkware figures were immensely popular, inexpensive nineteenth-century ornaments. They were made of plaster of Paris and were imported from Europe until works were started in America, notably in New York, and in the Pennsylvania Dutch country. Chalkware figures were chiefly small animals and birds. The plaster was coloured by hand and was never glazed.

Chalkware deer, Pennsylvania 1883

Chamber horse or **horse exercising machine.** This device, made in the form of either a stool or a chair, was used for exercise by the fat and short-winded. The seat is shaped like a concertina, and its leather upholstery hides a series of wooden boards and coiled springs. It was made during the eighteenth and early nineteenth century; and one is illustrated in the 1802 edition of Sheraton's *Cabinet Maker's and Upholsterer's Drawing Book*.

Chamber horse

American oak chair table, 1650–75

Bousfield School, Kensington: Chamberlin, Powell, and Bon, 1965

Chamberlin, Powell, and Bon. British architectural partnership. Peter Chamberlin, Geoffrey Powell, and Christof Bon formed this partnership and won the 1952 competition for the high density housing estate at Golden Lane (1953–7) in the City of London. It was the first of many designs by the firm that have attracted attention. Bousfield School, a low Miesian structure in the heart of Kensington (1952–6), was awarded a London Bronze Medal for Architecture, and others that may be mentioned are a warehouse at Witham in Essex (1953–5); New Hall, Cambridge (1962–9); a sports centre at Birmingham University; the very large-scale expansion of Leeds University (halls of residence, new faculty buildings, lecture theatres, etc), extending down into the town; and the development of the Barbican area in the City of London. The Barbican complex, situated in the commercial nerve-centre of London, will provide a large number of apartments, and schools, a theatre, a concert hall, shops, a restaurant, and an art gallery. It was begun in 1958 and is now nearing completion.

Sir William Chambers

Chambers, Sir William (1723–96). One of the most assured and successful of official architects

in the mid- and late-Georgian period. He is now mainly known as the architect of Somerset House and the designer of the gardens, orangery, temples, and pagoda at Kew. Chambers is too often regarded as an over-academic master of the architectural orders: he could be imaginative and fanciful too, as his pagoda demonstrates.

His early career was unusual. He was born of Scottish parents in Göteborg in Sweden, where his father was a merchant. He was then sent to school at Ripon in Yorkshire, returned to Sweden, and served as a seagoing cadet in one of the Swedish East India Company's ships sailing to the Far East. He left the service when he was 26 and began to study architecture in Paris under J F Blondel. A year later he went to Italy, where he studied for five years.

Chambers returned to England in 1755, and within five years had developed a highly successful practice. His position was further strengthened by the numerous official appointments that he held. He was, jointly with Robert Adam, architect to the king (1760), comptroller of the works (1769), and surveyor general (1782). He was a founder-member of the Royal Academy, and was given a knighthood in 1770.

Chambers was responsible for many buildings, ranging from the Marino Casino and Trinity College, Dublin, to houses in Berners Street, London; from the reconstruction of the complete village of Milton Abbas in Dorset, to the Queen's Lodge at Windsor.

His most influential writing, the *Treatise on Civil Architecture*, was first published in 1759, a further two editions appearing during Chambers's lifetime; it became the standard exposition of Architectural Orders. He is buried at Westminster Abbey.

Somerset House, London: Sir William Chambers, 1776–80

Chamfer. The sloping surface formed when a corner is planed away or cut down. It is a term usually used of stone or woodwork. The most common variations are chamfers sunk below the surrounding surface, concave or moulded. The latter is also known as a beaded chamfer.

Chamfers that exist along only part of the corner or arris and are terminated by an ornamental or splayed stop are called stopped chamfers.

Champlevé. See **Enamel.**

17th-century brass chandelier and a cut glass and silvered one, 19th century

Chancel. The part of the east end of a church in which the altar is placed and which is reserved for clergy and choir. It is commonly used of all of the building east of the nave, from which it is usually separated by a screen or railings.

Chancel screen. See **Rood.**

Chandelier. Although this word is of medieval origin, it only gained currency in the late seventeenth century. It describes the elaborate hanging lights that

A Regency glass 'waterfall' chandelier

Château de Langeais, Loire, c 1570

succeeded the coronas and candlebeams of the Middle Ages. Chandeliers were made of gold and silver in the sixteenth century. Then, as their use became more general, brass and later bronze, rock crystal, and carved gilt-wood were added. Finally glass, a material that made the chandelier sparkle and shimmer, was used from the mid-eighteenth century.

Chantilly. This French porcelain factory was started *c* 1725 by Ciquaire Cirou; the financial backing was provided by the duc de Condé, Louis-Henri Bourbon. The earliest Chantilly porcelain has a tin oxide glaze (similar to that used on Delft pottery) which is easily distinguishable from the ordinary glasslike porcelain glaze. Most of the early work is decorated in the asymmetrical oriental Kakiemon style, the colouring being similar to the originals from which it was copied. In addition to dishes and other tableware, a few rather grotesque figures were made, based on oriental originals. The adaptations from oriental porcelain became freer, and flowers from western gardens (particularly pansies) appeared in the decoration.

Cirou died in 1751 and the factory passed through various hands. After the Revolution it was under the control of an Englishman, aptly named Potter, until 1800.

After 1760 a more conventional porcelain glaze was adopted by the factory, and originals from Meissen were very freely copied. The famous 'Chantilly sprig' was one of the most popular designs used on later ware; the flower is usually blue or mauve, and looks rather like a cornflower. It was copied at Derby and by other English factories.

The commonest mark used at Chantilly was a pencilled hunting horn in either blue or red.

Chantry chapel. A small chapel, in or adjoining a church, endowed for the saying of masses for the soul of the founder or a person of his choice.

Chaplet. A term used in architectural decoration for a moulding carved to resemble a string of small round beads. In painted or carved ornament it refers to a garland.

Chapter house. The building in which the chapter of a cathedral or monastery meet to discuss business. In England many are polygonal in plan, whereas on the Continent they are all rectangular.

Charger. A large plate or flat dish that was used for serving meats.

Chasing. Embossing or engraving in relief on a metal surface.

Château (Latin, *castellum* 'castle'). In the comparatively peaceful period which succeeded the Hundred Years' War (1338–1453), the kings and nobles of France began building residences rather than fortresses. Inevitably the impulse for de-

A pair of Chantilly 'Magot' figures

Château de Blois

signing such buildings came from the buildings of the Italian Renaissance. By the early sixteenth century, châteaux were being built in the Loire Valley. This area comprised the ancient provinces of Orleanais, Touraine, Maine, and Anjou, and already held a number of earlier fortresses; it was favoured because its forests made it ideal for the royal and aristocratic passion for the hunt. Charles VIII (1470–98), Louis XII (1462–1515), and Francis I (1494–1547) provided the main impulse for this vast building effort, which produced two hundred châteaux in a century.

The earlier buildings are a curious mixture of Gothic and Renaissance features. Famous châteaux are those at Amboise, Angers, Azay le Rideau, Chenonceaux, Cheverny, Craon, Langeais, Loche, Saumar, and Valençay. But the most famous of all are probably Blois, which was built between the thirteenth and seventeenth centuries, and Chambord.

Blois shows the involved transitional features already referred to, with Corinthian pilasters, external Gothic-type stairways, and Gothic gargoyles. Chambord, largest of the châteaux, was built between 1519 and 1533 with massive towers reminiscent of the many fortresses it had supplanted. Yet the trend to-

Château de Chenonceaux, over the river Cher

Aerial view of Château du Plessis-Bourré

wards comfort prevailed and even the towers were pierced with windows. Chambord has nearly 400 rooms, some quite magnificent in their furnishings. Like Blois, Chambord is also covered with exuberant decoration of Gothic origin, mingled with Renaissance pilasters and cornices; the rooftop, with massed chimneys and pinnacles, presents a majestic and magical silhouette. Several smaller châteaux are exclusively eighteenth-century structures combining classical architectural motifs with medieval moats, as at Craon.

Most of the châteaux of the Loire country have now become national monuments. They are amongst the foremost tourist attractions of France, especially since the introduction of *Son et Lumière* spectacles.

Cheeks. The protruding wings that occur at head level on easy chairs, first introduced in the late seventeenth century. See also **Saddle cheek.**

In architecture the word is used (rarely) to indicate the flanking uprights or jambs of an opening.

Chelsea porcelain. This porcelain factory (1743–85) was founded by Thomas Briand, a chemist, Nicholas Spimont, a silversmith, and Charles Gouyn, a jeweller. In 1770 it was purchased by William Duesbury of Derby, and from that time the products of the factory are known as Chelsea-Derby.

The Chelsea factory made ware copied from Chinese and Meissen originals. Many figures of very good quality were produced, as well as sauce-boats, tureens, plates, dishes, small toys, and patch-boxes.

The earliest mark is an incised triangle; from about 1750 a raised anchor on a small medallion, or a crown intersected by a trident in underglaze blue, was used. In 1752 a small red anchor marked the pieces, and from 1755 a gold anchor. When the Chelsea factory was taken over by the Derby factory, the mark changed to a capital D enclosing an anchor.

Chelsea's best period was that of the raised and the red anchor, when the work produced compares favourably with any done in Europe. Chelsea-Derby pro-

ducts were inspired by the porcelain of Sèvres and Tournai.

Chelsea pottery. This pottery was founded in Chelsea by

Chelsea pottery fruit dish

Châteaux de Chambord (above) and Valençay

Chelsea porcelain reaper, c 1760

Chermayeff's house at Halland, Sussex, built in 1938

David Rawnsley in 1952. He and his small team of potters produce decorative ware of a high quality both in craftsmanship and design. They specialize particularly in figures (human and animal) and in bowls and tiles. The pottery is unique in that it is also a club where members can meet and make their own pots for a modest annual subscription and small fees to cover the running cost.

Chequer work. The ornamental arrangement of a wall facing so that it resembles a chess board. It was produced by using contrasting materials such as brick and flints, or split flints and limestone. On furniture the chequer motif, created with small squares of light and dark woods, was used for inlaid decoration, particularly in the sixteenth and seventeenth centuries.

Chermayeff, Serge (*b* 1900). An internationally-minded architect with an international background. He was born in Russia and educated in Britain, where he practised before moving to the United States.

During his years in Britain, Chermayeff designed Gilbey House in Camden Town, studios for the BBC, and laboratories for ICI. After leaving Britain he became president and director of the University of Design in Chicago, and was also in practice in Cambridge, Massachusetts. In 1961 he was appointed professor of architecture in the

Serge Chermayeff

Graduate School of Design at Harvard.

When he lived in England, Chermayeff designed for himself one of the first – and still one of the finest – modern houses ever built there (1938). Unlike many 'modern' buildings, Chermayeff's house at Halland in Sussex shows no sign of dating. Chermayeff laid out the garden too, in co-operation with the landscape architect Christopher Tunnard. He also designed a range of unit-furniture which was among the first attempts to make a complete range of interchangeable pieces.

Cherry. *Prunus.* The American cherry is a light, hard wood generally used for cabinet work. It is auburn in colour, well grained, and with an extremely glossy finish when polished. Colonial furniture was frequently made of wild cherry. Cherry has also been used for objects of 'treen' (qv) such as snuff boxes.

Cherub. A winged child akin to Cupid but descended from representations of angels. It was a favourite motif in both painting and wood-carving of the seventeenth-century European Baroque. Among the finest surviving examples are gilded German infants suspended in impossible flight.

Chest or **coffer.** One of the earliest forms of domestic furniture, which survived until the late eighteenth century, when it was finally superseded by pieces with drawers or cupboards.

The chest, an oblong box with a hinged lid, was essentially for storage or travelling. In the Middle Ages it also served as a seat or table. Another important early use was as a large, static, collecting box in a church; Henry II collected money for Crusades in this way. Late medieval chests were frequently carved or painted, for example the tilting chest (qv).

The first chests are described as dugout, being crude, hollowed-out logs with a lid. These were

Painted chest, Pennsylvania Dutch

succeeded by boarded (qv) and joined (qv) chests, and then by the elegant seventeenth-century chests decorated with either marquetry or lacquer, and often resting upon feet or a stand. Drawers were introduced into the base in the late sixteenth century.

In the last period of their production, chests tended to be made by regional cabinetmakers, so that the decoration is sometimes rather old-fashioned. Those covered with leather and used for travelling were usually called coffers.

Chest of drawers. This first appeared at the end of the seventeenth century. It developed from lidded chests with drawers in the bases, such as the mule chest (qv). The chest of drawers soon appeared in its standard form – three or more long drawers and a top drawer that was often slightly shallower or divided into two smaller drawers. In the second half of the eighteenth century, a shallow top drawer was sometimes fitted for toilet preparations.

Chests of drawers might rest upon a stand (up to about 1700) or directly upon feet (bun, ball, or bracket). The chest of drawers on a stand developed into the tallboy. Low chests developed

into commodes in France, while in Britain and (to a lesser extent) America they gave rise to a great variety of serpentine-fronted, bow-fronted, carved, and gilded chests of drawers, frequently seen in museums, salerooms, and furniture collections.

In the United States the chest of drawers is frequently called a bureau.

Chest-on-chest. The general American term for a double piece of case furniture. The most common is probably the highboy (qv), but any number of variations exist.

Chesterfield. A deep-buttoned sofa in which arms and back form one continuous, upholstered, rounded line. The origin of the name is unknown.

The Chesterfield was popular in clubs and smoking-rooms in the Victorian era, but then suffered a decline. During recent years it has again come to be admired and manufactured.

Chestnut, Sweet, *Castanea sativa*; **Horse,** *Aesculus hippocastanum*. The sweet chestnut is a much-prized wood of open grain and broad markings. Age and patina turn it from near white to a pale golden brown. It was a popular choice for

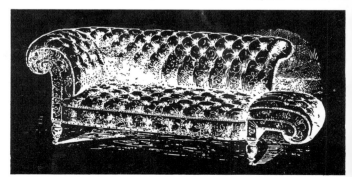

A Chesterfield with one end let down

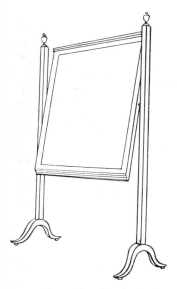

A 'horse dressing-glass'

Small Regency rosewood chiffonier

Chippendale design for a chimneypiece from the 'Director' of 1762

tables and desks at the beginning of the eighteenth century.

Horse chestnut is yellower in tone, and is a softer wood that is not as durable as the sweet chestnut. It was occasionally used for decorative work; it is sometimes used for veneering.

Cheval mirror. The 'horse dressing-glass' or cheval mirror, so called because of its four-legged frame or horse, is a tall, often full-length glass for the bedroom. It is not always an elegant piece of furniture, but it is a useful one, and large numbers were made in the late eighteenth and early nineteenth century. The advantages of the cheval glass are that it can be wheeled to any part of the room to reach the best light, and, being hinged to the supports, can be tilted to any angle.

Norman stone chevron

Chevron. A moulding found in Norman architecture; more usually and understandably known as a 'zigzag.' The term continues to be used, as every soldier knows, for the marks of non-commissioned officers.

Chiffonier. A term that cannot be strictly defined in English. It is now used to describe low Regency cases of shelves, usually for books, sometimes with a cupboard below. In French, a *chiffonier* is a tall narrow chest of drawers made under Louis XV and Louis XVI, while the term

chiffonière means a small four-drawer writing table on tall legs. An Anglicized version of such a piece was supplied to Merstram Hatch by Chippendale, who was the first Englishman to use the term; however, he spelled it 'shiffener.'

Chimney. Chimney-shafts seem to have been first built in England during the twelfth century. Examples are to be seen at Rochester Castle and Castle Hedingham, although the flues were confined for only a few feet before being turned out through rear walls. The device of continuing the flue through the height of the building was of later date. The chimneys of castles and great houses soon became the object of decorative attention from masons and builders, so that square, circular, and octagonal chimneys occur at quite an early date, and by the fifteenth century chimneys were terminating in mock-capitals, spires, and pinnacles. Clustered chimney-shafts were introduced in the late fifteenth century, when the chimney became far

more widely used; it was frequently introduced into halls, which had hitherto been subject to the vagaries of an open hearth in the centre of the room, the smoke escaping through an opening in the roof.

The use of brick for the construction of chimneys also dates

Sixty-three different chimneys on a house designed by Pugin

from about the end of the fifteenth century, and resulted in many highly ornamented shafts. This tradition continued, although exponents of the more austere eighteenth-century style saw beauty in proportion rather than over-elaborate external decoration. Nineteenth-century architects returned to the ornamentation of earlier days. In modern times architects at first sought to hide the chimney, but eventually came to realize that a chimney-shaft can provide an emphatic vertical foil to the mainly horizontal lines of many designs. The chimney has thus reappeared as an important element in the elevations of smaller houses.

Chimneypiece. The term given to the usually decorative framework around the utilitarian opening of the fireplace. The

Gothick mahogany china cabinet dating from c 1760

The Tung Chow pagoda, China

with a gallery usually made of fretwork. Such tables were used to display china, and also served as tea tables.

Chinese architecture. Architecture was practised in China many centuries before it began to be studied in Europe; Chinese builders were building in brick and stone 1,500 years before the birth of Christ. Early Chinese temples and palaces were remarkable for structural as well as decorative qualities. Their foundations and bases were frequently of stone and brick, and, even more surprising, their roofs were supported not by walls but by their wooden framework, a method of building discovered in Europe only several centuries later.

The Chinese were just as advanced in other subjects. The town-planning of the ancient city of Peking (capital of the northernmost state of Yen as early as the sixth century BC) makes the majority of modern cities seem anachronistic and chaotic.

The arch was known to the Chinese builders, and arches and walls were frequently decorated with (and even constructed of) porcelain and ceramics of great beauty. Examples of such arches can be seen in the Temple of a Thousand Buddhas in the Summer Palace of Peking.

To western eyes, Chinese architecture is chiefly characterized by wide-spreading roofs with vast overhanging eaves, curiously and dramatically upturned at the corner soffits. These are seen in palace buildings and in a highly decorative, repetitive form in pagodas. They are familiar through pictures of the Emperor's Summer Palace in Peking and the reproduction of Chinese pavilions in Western textiles and ceramics from the eighteenth century onwards (see **Chinoiserie**). This surface exoticism should not be allowed to obscure the many advanced structural and technical skills of the Chinese, revealed in archaeological discoveries at Anyang, capital of the Shang dynasty (c 1500-108 BC).

Today, most new Chinese buildings are mildly oriental versions of the International style, albeit somewhat heavier in manner than those to be seen in Europe and the USA.

Chinese carpets. Chinese rugs and carpets are easily distinguished from those of the Middle East and central Asia because they carry motifs and

symbols used only in Chinese art. They are tied with the *Sehna* knot and have a long pile which is often cut around the edge of a motif, giving greater emphasis to the pattern. Yellow, blue, and

Pagoda Summer Palace, Peking

chimneypiece has always provided craftsmen with splendid opportunities for displays of decorative skill. The challenge has also proved tempting to modern architects, who have used a wide variety of materials to emphasize the importance of the chimneypiece, which, despite the development of other forms of heating, remains the focal point of most living-rooms.

China. The term 'china' is often used in a general and imprecise way to cover any kind of decorative or tableware pottery. 'China' should be synonymous with porcelain; that is, a hard,

translucent ware made by the addition of bone-ash to the body of the clay. Pottery, on the other hand, is never translucent, and is much more easily chipped and broken.

China cabinet. This was introduced at the end of the seventeenth century, when there was a vogue for oriental ceramics. The china cabinet was simply a cabinet suitable for holding china; some were made with glazed doors so that the china could be displayed.

China table. The eighteenth-century term for a small table

Ming blue-and-white pouring bowl made in the fourteenth century

white are the predominant colours.

The famous pillar carpets are found only in China. They were made to be tied around a pillar, so that the pattern is continuous, in most cases including a long coiling dragon. Chinese carpet designs changed so little that it is exceedingly difficult to date them.

Chinese porcelain. As far as the manufacture of porcelain is concerned, the most important dynasties are T'ang (618–906), Sung (960–1279), Yuan (1280–1367), Ming (1368–1644), and Ch'ing (1645–1911).

T'ang porcelain. This is very much rarer than T'ang pottery. The earliest translucent porcelain known in China was made during the early part of the T'ang dynasty. White T'ang porcelain has a flat base and the glaze often runs, forming irregular 'teardrops.'

Sung porcelain. It was during the Sung period that porcelain makers made their very finest pieces. The beauty of Sung ware depends largely on perfection of shape and form, and on the exquisite colours of the glazes; decoration is less important.

Yuan porcelain. During this period, porcelain was much more elaborately decorated. Underglaze blue was introduced. The shapes were often influenced by

K'ang Hsi famille verte dish made in the early eighteenth century

Near Eastern metalwork, and are less restrained than earlier forms.

Ming porcelain. The earliest Ming porcelain was decorated in underglaze blue. In the early fifteenth century bowls were made of an eggshell thinness. The porcelain made for export at this time was coarser and thicker, and of a generally poorer quality than that which the Chinese kept for themselves. As well as blue and white, porcelain was also coloured with an underglaze copper red, and yellow, red, and green enamels

Ch'ien Lung famille rose crane dating from 1750

were also used. Relief and pierced decoration was carried out.

The porcelain known as *blanc de chine* was made in the later years of the Ming dynasty, in Fukien province. This white porcelain, with a glaze that has been described as 'like milk jelly', was crisply and delicately modelled into small figures. The Buddhist goddess Kuan Yin is frequently represented. As well as figures, small dishes, cups, and other items were made in *blanc de chine* ware.

Ch'ing porcelain. During this period the output of Chinese porcelain factories was enormous and amazingly varied. Blue and white was still made; but it was

now that the various polychrome wares usually known in Europe by the French designations *famille verte, famille noire, famille rose*, etc, were made. They were so called after the predominating colour in the design. The *sang de boeuf* red glaze was used at this period.

Black, brown, yellow, pink, turquoise, lavender, and several different greens were used both as self-coloured glazes and in enamel decoration. It was also during this period that 'armorial' export porcelain (ie with specially commissioned European coats of arms) was made, decorated at Canton, and shipped to Europe and America. During the nineteenth century a great deal of over-decorated porcelain was produced, much of it inferior copies of earlier types.

Chinese pottery. The earliest Chinese pottery was made sometime between 3000 and 1700 BC. It is found in burial places for the dead, who were accompanied by vessels of food and drink. (In early times their wives and servants were sacrificed and also buried with them.)

Many of the Neolithic urns that have been recovered are surprisingly large, and appear to have been wheel-thrown. Sometimes they are painted with bold patterns in red, white, black, or purplish brown.

The first use of glazing can be dated to the Han dynasty (206 BC to AD 220); many wine jars with a reddish brown body, both glazed and unglazed, have been found. The glaze was usually of a greenish colour deriving from copper oxide. By the time of the Han dynasty, the barbarous custom referred to above had been abandoned, and instead of people, images were made in clay – models of the dead man's family, animals, furniture, and even cooking stoves – and were buried with him. Sometimes these figures are dark grey and painted with unfired pigments; sometimes they are covered with a green glaze. The T'ang dynasty (618–906) was a period of great activity and prosperity, and much pottery survives. This is surprising, for it was very lightly fired and is therefore easily breakable and absorbent of moisture. It varies in colour from reddish to pinkish fawn. The colours used in glazing were green, blue, brown, and yellow. The glaze was sponged on, producing a mottled effect.

Many tomb figures were made, cast from splendidly modelled moulds; figures of horses and

T'ang straw-glazed pottery camel dating from the ninth century

camels were sometimes quite large. Bowls, jugs, vases, and other useful receptacles were also made. During the Ming dynasty a reddish brown stoneware with a streaky *flambé* glaze was made, sometimes red streaked with blue and sometimes blue streaked with red.

Red stoneware tea and wine pots – exported in tea chests to Europe during the seventeenth century – were first made during the sixteenth century. It was this ware that the Elers brothers copied in Staffordshire, and which they called 'red porcelain', though in fact it was a fine stoneware. During the Ming dynasty good quality figures were made and there was a revival of pottery decorated with coloured glazes in the T'ang style.

Under the Ch'ing dynasty porcelain was preferred, and pottery of the period is of poor quality.

Chinoiserie. A cult of Chinese and pseudo-Chinese decoration that spread throughout Europe in the eighteenth century, largely thanks to the idealized conception of Chinese life current at the time. This was fostered by the stories – some realistic, some fanciful – told by missionaries, traders, and functionaries, and given substance by the silks and porcelains they brought back. Thus Chinese civilization, so ancient and so productive of beautiful things, became the occasion for one of the forms of escapism so characteristic of the Age of Reason.

The cult of chinoiserie, or 'China-mania', as more dyspeptic observers termed it, spread rapidly across Europe in the mid-eighteenth century and even made some impact in North America. But it was probably taken up most fervently in England, so that James Cauthorn could write in 1756:

Designs for chinoiserie pavilions from an early nineteenth century French book

Chintz designs, late 18th century

Of late, 'tis true, quite sick of
Rome and Greece,
We fetch our models from the
wise Chinese;
European artists are too cool
and chaste,
For Mand'rin is the only man
of taste.

Chinese motifs appear on English silver, porcelain, textiles, and furniture of the period.

Two names are particularly associated with the development of chinoiserie, one frivolous, the other serious. William Halfpenny

Chinese Chippendale chairs are a particularly famous example, always assured of high prices in the saleroom. Buildings in oriental style and the Anglo-Chinese garden were two manifestations of this craze.

published *New Designs for Chinese Temples* and *Chinese and Gothic Architecture properly ornamented* in 1752. These books, backed by those of imitators, gave rise to large numbers of oriental pavilions and alcoves.

In 1757 William Chambers (qv) published *Designs of Chinese Buildings,* which was a somewhat more sober appraisal of Chinese architecture, which he deprecated for use in northern lands. Yet Chambers's own chinoiserie pagoda at Kew has proved one of the most durable and popular of his buildings.

Chinoiserie eventually gave way to a new cult, that of the Gothick (qv).

Chintz (Hindu, *chint*). The origin of printing on cotton cloth is lost in legend. From the time when the East India Company was granted an import licence in 1631, Indian chintzes, as they were called, appealed to English taste. In bedrooms, writing-rooms, and boudoirs, these delicately patterned fabrics were used for wall-linings, curtains, and upholstery.

In 1663 Samuel Pepys visited Cornhill, where, after a good deal of trouble, he managed to buy his wife 'a chintz, that is, painted Indian calico, for to line her new study which is very pretty.' Evelyn mentions dining out in a room hung with Pintado, another name for chintz.

These were imported cloths, but home production flourished, and the export of printed cottons

Chinese Chippendale chimney glass in giltwood frame

to America and other parts of the world accounted for a large part of British trade.

The inventions of Arkwright, Crompton, Cartwright, and others made possible the mass production of fine cotton cloth and the consequent European pre-eminence of English chintz. The men who designed and engraved its printed patterns were for the most part anonymous, for in the eighteenth and early nineteenth centuries fine design was common enough to pass unremarked.

There have always been special chintz patterns for different purposes: medallions and centre-pieces for bed-quilts, carefully centred patterns for chair backs and seats, borders for curtains. Borders are seldom made in England now, but are still fairly common in France and America.

The exotic flowers, fruits, and winding stems of the eighteenth-century patterns derived from the old Indian chintzes and from Chinese hand-painted wallpapers. These are still typical chintz motifs, although changing printing techniques have often sadly altered their character, as is also the case with the parrot and lyre-bird of the Regency and the peacock of the pre-Edwardian era. Pictorial subts, similar to the French *e-de-jouy*, have always been pular. Small floral sprigs, first de in the eighteenth century, still turned out, and have ome synonymous with the n 'English chintz.' However, ny firms now employ artists that the range of subjects has ome much wider.

ip carving. A medieval thod of decorating wooden sts by chipping geometric terns out of the wood. This m of carving continued until early seventeenth century.

hippendale, Thomas (1718– . The most celebrated British niture designer and cabinet- ker. He came from a family of ers and carpenters in Otley, rkshire, moved to London ore he was 30, but was not ablished at St Martin's Lane, ere he built up his great iness, until 1753. He was cted a member of the Society Arts in 1760. He died of sumption. Chippendale's fame derives m the publication of his niture designs in the *Gentle- n and Cabinet-Maker's Director* 754, 1755, and 1762. In these ee editions are to be found finest and most original ideas the Chinese, Gothick, and coco tastes prevalent in the d-eighteenth century. The list subscribers to these editions ws that Chippendale attracted notice of many of the althiest art patrons. It is ious that he was never com- ssioned to supply furniture the royal family.

Despite the success of the *Directors*, and the considerable amount of furniture made from their plates, the tastes they advertise were superseded soon after the last edition by the Adam style. It was, in fact, in co-operation with Robert Adam on four houses – Nostell Priory, Mersham Hatch, Harewood House, and David Garrick's house in the Adelphi – that Chippendale's greatest furniture was produced. The extent to which the craftsman and the architect collaborated is not known, but they certainly met on equal terms.

A study of the accounts supplied by Chippendale reveals the diverse nature of his business. One finds such items, for Mersham Hatch, as '60 yds Lace–£1', and for the Adelphi, '72 yds Canvas to hang the room–£2 8s', while for Harewood House he supplied 'A fine cotton counterpane–£1 4s' and 'A fine Downe Pillow–13s.' Chippendale acted as interior decorator, carrier, and repairer as well as cabinetmaker, and would advise on schemes of decoration and arrange for carpets to be specially woven.

The popularity of Chippendale furniture extended to America, where the term describes the whole period from 1755 to 1790. The designs are simpler than the English, and decorations of Gothick, chinoiserie, and Rococo inspiration were restrained and less plentiful. Several earlier features such as the pad foot, scrolled pediments, and round-headed arches persisted, shell carving abounded, and other elements such as the

block-front gave American Chippendale a character of its own.

Choir. The eastern end of the church where divine service is sung; almost synonymous with chancel.

Ciborium. A canopy over a high altar. See also **Baldacchino.**

Circus. The first circuses were Roman structures, long oblong buildings with apsidal ends and tiered seating. They were used for racing and processions. One of the first and largest was the Circus Maximus, which held as many as 150,000 people.

Eighteenth-century circuses, round or oval ranges of houses that were used in conjunction with crescents, are among the most memorable of all town-planning ventures. Bath is the outstanding example.

Claw-and-Ball-Foot. A foot carved to represent a claw grasping a ball; most probably of Chinese origin. This device was adopted sporadically during the sixteenth and seventeenth centuries but enjoyed its greatest popularity between 1710 and 1750. After 1750 it was still employed by provincial cabinetmakers and in America.

Claw table. The eighteenth-century name for a small table on a single pillar and with three or sometimes four scroll or claw feet at its base.

Clendinning, Max (*b* 1924). British interior designer and

Presumed portrait of Chippendale

architect. Born in Northern Ireland, Clendinning took up a scholarship at the Architectural Association in London. This early training was reinforced by his work with the architects

Max Clendinning

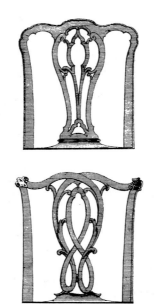

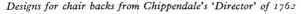

Designs for chair backs from Chippendale's 'Director' of 1762

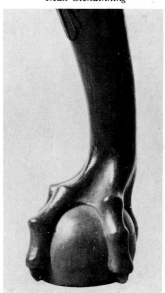

Philadelphia claw and ball, 1760

All white interior by Max Clendinning

Maxwell Fry, Jane Drew, and Denys Lasdun.

However, Clendinning is chiefly known for his many and varied interior designs. His popular reputation derives from his involvement with the Crawley Civic Centre and the range of furniture that he designed for Liberty's in 1965. His interiors are simple, and his preference for a minimal amount of furniture often makes the result amusing, as in the white living-room with 30-foot-long sack seating and *papier mâché* tulip in his own house.

Clerestory or **clear-storey, -story** (Italian, *chiaro piano*, French, *claire étage, cleristère*). The upper part of a building, with walls pierced by windows to provide extra light. Clerestory windows were built by the Romans in their palaces and by early church architects in their naves and towers. In medieval college buildings the clerestory was frequently used in libraries and refectories. Too often the purpose of the clerestory window was vitiated by the heaviness of the stone window-frames and the over-elaboration of the glazing bars and motifs.

In more recent times the clerestory window has come back into use, for it is a device which can invest a simple elevation with a dramatic change of plane and emphasis. Yet, considering its potential usefulness in the design of lecture and assembly halls, it is still strangely under-employed.

Clock. The clock first appeared about the end of the thirteenth century. Previously, time had been measured by sun-dials, sand glasses, water clocks, and burning lamps. The problem facing the earliest clockmakers was how to regulate the speed of revolution of a train of connected wheels. The largest wheel was attached to the motive power, a falling weight; another wheel drove the hand; the last and smallest wheel, the escape wheel, drove the controller – at first a 'verge and foliot', later a pendulum which controlled the speed at which this hand moved. The foliot was an oscillating horizontal bar or ring, the verge a small, crown-like connecting wheel, the pendulum a vertical, swinging, weighted rod.

The Salisbury Cathedral clock, made in 1386, illustrates the general form of simple early clocks, which lasted with only minor changes till the seventeenth century. Smaller portable clocks, similar in mechanism, exist from perhaps the fourteenth century in Italy and Germany. A few were found in England, and one can be seen in Holbein's drawing of Sir Thomas More and his family.

The seventeenth century witnessed remarkable horological advances. In the last quarter of the fifteenth century, springs had been successfully applied to drive the mechanism in place of a falling weight. In the 1600s this was refined, adapted, and improved until many types of spring-driven clocks were evolved.

The earliest form was the table clock in rich pierced and engraved cases of silver or gilt metal. Such clocks are found in many shapes: square, domed, tower, octagonal, pillar, crucifix, and so on.

A later form was the bracket clock, designed to stand on a wall bracket. This is probably the commonest surviving form of small antique clock.

In about 1657 the pendulum was first used; an invention attributed to the Dutchman Huygens. This was an important step forward in the accurate

A long-case clock by Cragg in a Sheraton 'lyre' case

Swiss box watch movement, 18

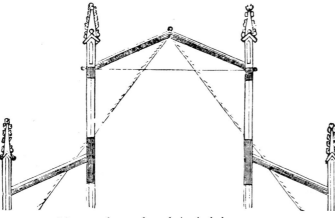

Diagram of an early ecclesiastical clear-storey

A Louis XIV clock and cartonnier in boulle technique

American mantel clock made of iron, c 1850

-day marine chronometer, c 1860

Swiss 2-year battery clock

easurement of time. The pen-
lum was used in all early
acket clocks, and also in long-
se, or grandfather clocks,
which first appeared c 1660. They
were basically wall clocks whose
weights were cased down to the
ground. The development of this
type coincided both in France
and England with the spirit of
scientific inquiry for which the
age is remarkable, and in England
with its greatest clockmakers,
Thomas Tompion, Daniel Quare,
Edward East, and Joseph Knibb.

More great advances occurred
in the eighteenth century. The
bracket clock, in domed walnut
or ebonized cases, underwent
many refinements. The cases
began to be made in mahogany,
in line with fashions in furniture.
Long-case clocks rose to some
8 ft in height, and then became
smaller; by 1800 they were about
6 ft high. By this time they were
superbly accurate regulators. In
France, mantel clocks were made
in marble, ormolu, and bronze,
and all over Europe clocks,
following French designs, were
made in carved and gilded wood
and in painted tin and other
metal cases.

The nineteenth and twentieth
centuries have seen similar advances in technology and variations in design. English clocks
became over-ornate, French
clocks went under glass domes.
American clocks for the most
part followed, often to charming
effect, naïve English designs. In
modern times, mass production
and advances in industrial design
have revolutionised the appearance of clocks.

Cloisonné. A technique of
enamelling first found in common
use at Byzantium in the fifth
century AD. It reached China by

Early Ming cloisonné ritual disc

Wren's cloister, Lincoln Cathedral

the early Ming dynasty (1368–1644), and much superb work in cloisonné was done there.

The ritual disc in the illustration shows how cloisonné was executed. The enamel was poured between copper wires soldered to the back plate, and was then fired. The six-character mark of Hsuan-te at the bottom of the disc is in champlevé enamel. This was made by pouring the enamel into spaces gouged out of the copper back plate.

Cloister (French *cloître*, Italian *chiostro*). A covered ambulatory

Elaborate close-stool, c 1750

forming part of a monastic or collegiate establishment. The cloister normally comprised three or four sides of a quadrangle adjacent to a church or chapel. It was usually colonnaded and the openings were sometimes glazed. Cloisters were occasionally built with cells along one side. The quadrangular area enclosed by the cloister was known as the cloister-garth, and was frequently made into a garden.

Close-stool. Close-stools were introduced in the late fifteenth century and tended to resemble boxes or trunks. At first covered with fabric, they were later left in plain wood. Inside was a pewter or earthenware pan for defecation.

In the eighteenth century close-stools were succeeded by night tables and close-stool chairs – ostensibly fashionable chairs but with a deep apron piece to hide the pan.

Clothes press or **wardrobe.** A piece of eighteenth-century furniture that came into use because clothes had become much finer and less bulky, so that they could now be easily stowed in drawers or shelves.

A clothes press was in two parts. The upper appeared to be a cupboard, although in fact it

contained sliding shelves; the lower part contained two or more drawers. In the *Director* of 1714, Chippendale called this a 'Commode Clothes-Press.'

Cloven foot. A decorative device of Roman origin that was revived in the early eighteenth century. It was an animal's cloven foot, and is usually found in conjunction with a cabriole leg. Also called *pied de biche*.

Club chair. An open-sided Victorian armchair designed primarily for comfort. It had a deep seat and slightly sloping back, and both these and the arm pads were upholstered and buttoned, usually in leather.

The American designer Charles Eames's modern version of the club chair, with seat and back in a continuous curve, enjoys great popularity. It combines comfort with simplicity of design.

Club foot or **pad foot.** A plain foot, in use for most of the eighteenth century on furniture with cabriole or turned legs. The club itself was of a stubby, outward-curving form, rather similar to a golf club. In America it is also called a Dutch foot.

A Chinese Chippendale chair with cluster-column legs

Cluster column. A Gothic architectural motif sometimes known as a compound pier. It is often found in mid-eighteenth-century English furniture and sometimes in Chippendale's *Director*, where it consists of several (usually four) slender columns, joined at top and bottom to form a chair leg or similar support.

Coade stone. A durable artificial stone used for ornamental purposes, chiefly externally for

Caughley porcelain jug, c 17

dressings, friezes, and sculptur[al] ornament; occasionally it w[as] employed for medallions [in] cabinetmaking. It was invent[ed] by Mrs Eleanor Coade, w[ho] manufactured it from *c* 1769 a[nd] closely guarded the details [of] how it was manufactured. Wh[en] production ceased in the 183[0s] the secret was lost.

Coalport. An English porc[e]lain factory was established [in] this village in Coalbrookdale, [on] the river Severn, by John Ro[se] & Co between 1780 and 179[0.] John Rose also had a factory [at] Jackfield, and later purchas[ed] others: Caughley in 1799, Swa[n]sea in 1820, Nantgarw in 182[.]

The factory at Caughley [in] Shropshire had been started [in] 1751 to make earthenware, a[nd] began to make porcelain in 17[72.] Caughley ware is also call[ed] Salopian. At this period Caug[h]ley blue and white products a[re] hard to distinguish from tho[se] of Worcester, and the mark th[en] in use at Caughley was a [C] drawn to resemble the Worces[ter] crescent.

Elaborate services of tabl[e]ware were made at Coalport [in] the styles of Chelsea, Sèvres, a[nd] Meissen. Much gilding was use[d.] Also typical of this factory we[re] vases and other ornament[al] pieces encrusted with flower[s] modelled in relief. The Coalp[ort] factory changed hands sever[al] times in the nineteenth centur[y] and eventually moved to t[he] Potteries. Nowadays, the war[e is] made at the Crescent Works [in] Stoke-on-Trent, and much fi[ne] china is made for export. Coa[l]port is still known for the quali[ty] of its painted decoration.

Coalport is often referred [to] as Coalbrookdale, and a commo[n] mark is the initials CD.

Coaster. A small rimmed tra[y] used for passing food and bottl[es] around the dining table. Ma[de] mostly of japanned or pla[ted]

Mahogany commode with marquetry of other woods by Cobb, c 1773

wood, silver, plate, or *papier mâché*, they were either fitted with small wheels or had baize-covered bases. They are sometimes called sliders. Today the term coaster applies to small mats used under drinking glasses to protect table surfaces.

Coat of arms. The coat of arms, or tabard, embroidered with the armorial device of the wearer, was among the most brilliant decorative garments ever devised. It was commonly worn over suits of armour in the Middle Ages, enabling the wearer to be recognized in the confusion of battle. Coats of arms were used in peacetime as a decoration carved on houses, gates, and tombs, painted on family portraits, in domestic and ecclesiastical stained glass windows, and so on – a practice which has not completely died out. A crest is not the same as a coat of arms, but may be incorporated in it.

Cob wall. A wall built of a mixture of rude clay and straw, supposedly the basis of construction of early European huts. Cob walls are still used in the remoter parts of Cornwall and Ireland.

Cobb, John (*d* 1778). A fine cabinetmaker who, in partnership with William Vile from about 1750 to 1765, worked in St. Martin's Lane, a few doors from Chippendale. He did much work for George III, was employed by Horace Walpole in 1770, and supplied some very fine commodes and vase stands for Paul Methuen at Corsham in 1772. Unfortunately, bills for his work are rare, and few pieces can now be identified.

Cobb is remembered for his haughty demeanour and bearing. J T Smith in *Nollekins and his Times* (the 1829 edition) called him 'one of the proudest men in England.' He even refused to hand a book to George III when requested, and the King, who 'smiled at his pomposity', received it from Cobb's foreman Jenkins.

Cock bead. The simple moulding in semi-circular section, applied to the edges of drawers from 1730. Dating of walnut furniture is often made possible by a study of such mouldings. Before 1730, the drawers were unmoulded; the cock beads, broader and often in double lines, ran on the boards between the drawers.

Cockerell, Samuel Pepys (*c* 1754–1827), and Charles Robert (1788–1863). A remarkable father-son architectural practice which spanned almost a century. After training under Sir Robert Taylor, S P Cockerell became clerk of the works at the Tower of London in 1775, and his son C R Cockerell was working on Basevi's designs for the Fitzwilliam Museum, Cambridge, in the year of his death, 1863.

Both architects achieved considerable success, frequently with buildings of some originality. S P Cockerell's abilities were shown in St Anne's Church, Soho, and his plans for the layout of the Foundling Estate in Bloomsbury.

C R Cockerell is known mainly for his work on the Ashmolean Museum and Taylorian Institute at Oxford. Although he was no Gothic enthusiast, he was a master of the style in revival, as he showed in his designs for St David's College, Lampeter, Cardiganshire (1822–7), and Seckford Almshouses in Woodbridge (1840).

Cockfighting chair. The popular name for a form of the walnut reading chair produced *c* 1725–50. The back had a flat, U-shaped top rail which acted as an arm rest and was centred by a sloping book support. The occupant sat back to front for reading or writing and in the ordinary position for relaxing.

Cocobolo. *Dalbergia retusa.* A wood native to Bengal and Burma. It is a hard, dense wood that is similar to rosewood, being a rich reddish brown in colour. Cocobolo is used mostly for tableware (cutlery handles, salad bowls, etc). Brush backs,

St Anne's, Soho, by S P Cockerell

musical instruments, and door knobs are sometimes made from this wood, and it is also used to inlay large pieces of furniture.

Coffee table. It has been said that the only piece of furniture invented in the twentieth century is the coffee table – a low table designed to stand in front of the low sofas and armchairs of today.

It is strange that there should not have been a special table for coffee in England before this century, since the beverage was introduced in the early seventeenth century. Though Sheraton's 'quartetto' tables are now called coffee tables, there is no justification for this usage. In France the *table à café* had appeared by 1760, and, with its

The Ashmolean Museum, Oxford, by C R Cockerell

A cockfighting chair

Glass coffee table designed by Albrizzi

porcelain or marble top, ormolu mounts, and slender cabriole legs, it remains one of the most beautiful small tables ever made. Coffee tables today range from simple moulded plastic or wood examples to grander glass- or marble-topped versions, and few homes are without them.

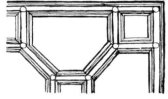

Plan of a coffered ceiling

Coffer. A deep panel set into a ceiling, vault, or dome. See also **Chest.**

Coles. An internationally-known firm of hand-made wallpaper manufacturers. The firm was founded by Edward Crace, coach mantler to George II, who became a printer of wallpapers for the royal establishment. The firm has a long and distinguished history, and since the end of World War II has commissioned many contemporary artists to design wallpaper.

19th-century pattern by Coles

Collarbeam. In roof construction, a small tiebeam that is found high up in the roof, usually connecting a pair of facing principal rafters. This type of construction is not as strong as constructions with a tiebeam at wall-plate level.

Cologne stoneware. A grey stoneware with a brown glaze was made at Cologne in the Rhineland from the early sixteenth century. Tankards and jugs were made, and flagons for holding wines and spirits. The flagons were decorated on the neck with a bearded head in relief. These 'greybeard' flasks or 'Bellarmines' as they also came to be called, were imported into England in some quantity, and were later copied by John Dwight of Fulham and other English stoneware makers. The name 'Bellarmine' derived from Cardinal Roberto Francisco Bellarmine (1542–1621), who was probably unpopular with Protestants because he attacked James I's penal legislation against Catholics. Bellarmines are also sometimes known as 'witch bottles', because it was believed that a witch could harm her enemies by placing their hair clippings or nail parings in a bottle, which was then buried under an enemy's hearth. Witch bottles are sometimes still found under the hearths of old houses.

Colombo, Joe (1930–71). Italian designer and architect of international reputation. Colombo came to industrial design through the traditional arts, first studying drawing at the Brera Academy, Milan, and then architecture at the Milan Polytechnic. In 1961 he established his own office in Milan after practising as an architect (his first building

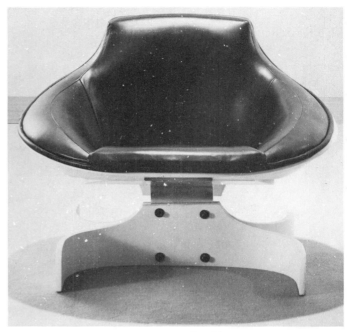

Armchair on a bent plywood frame and rocking spring by Joe Colombo

was constructed in 1953) and as a painter.

One of Colombo's first awards for design was from the National Institute of Architects. This was for the interior of the Hotel Pontinental, Sardinia (1963). From this time, however, he became increasingly involved with the design of individual seating and lighting. In this work he always put functional efficiency above abstract aesthetic considerations.

Among Colombo's numerous design innovations were the first completely plastic chair to be made by injection moulding, and a system of comprehensive living units that combined a variety of domestic services into one dynamic assembly.

Colombo held his own exhibition at Design Research, New

Joe Colombo

York, in 1966, and participated in numerous others on both sides of the Atlantic.

Colonial architecture. A style of building usually adopted from English sources (though deriving from Italian Renaissance

King's House, Spanish Town, Jamaica

The Colonial Secretary's Office, St John's, Antigua

prototypes), which is found in sometime British dependencies, from the Eastern States of the USA to India, from the West Indies to Australia. This style employed the high portico and canopied balconies and galleries of Palladian originals. It was in many respects better suited to the warm climates in which the British set up their trading and military stations than it was to the dales of Yorkshire or the wolds of Lincolnshire. Colonial architecture is undoubtedly seen at its best in Monticello, the home of Thomas Jefferson in Charlottesville, Virginia, which derived from designs in Robert Morris's *Select Architecture* (1757). But Monticello is only one of a superb group of buildings, many in existence still, which demonstrate the adaptability of the Georgian tradition. The Deep South is particularly rich in Colonial architecture. Other examples, less impressive but still handsome, are to be seen in Jamaica and Antigua.

The Palladian manner, established in brick and stone, was adapted to clapboard with con-

siderable success. Later, in the nineteenth century, settlers in Australia showed that the manner could also be adapted to cast-iron techniques, and many Australian houses of this period are now scheduled for preservation.

Colonnade. Any range or series of ranges of columns, whether free-standing or supporting a superstructure. A colonnade may be an integral part of the design of a building, an approach, or a decorative appendage. Perhaps the most famous examples, Bernini's colonnaded wings to St Peter's in Rome, were a late addition but are now regarded as an essential element in the whole complex. Colonnades are a notable feature in Italian architecture, especially in the northern cities. The colonnade and its architectural relation, the arcade, offer many practical as well as decorative advantages.

Colonnette. A small column.

Colour combing. A patterning device used on the paintwork

of cupboards and chests of drawers of the 1920s and 1930s. Broad bands and parallel ridges were created in the paint with a comb of the type usually employed for imitation woodgrain.

Column. The cylindrical load-bearing shaft is one of the most important and persistent features in the history of architecture, and even in an age of cantilevering, remains a significant element in innumerable buildings.

A column is traditionally composed of three parts: capital, shaft, and base. We owe most of our traditional nomenclature and somewhat arbitrary rules concerning columnar dimensions and proportions to the Roman architectural historian Vitruvius, whose *obiter dicta* were accepted as the orders of architecture by his contemporaries, by Renaissance architects, and even by architects of our own time.

The three basic types of column employed in these classical orders of architecture were the Doric (mainly used by Greek builders and, in its earlier version, without a base), the Ionic, and the Corinthian (favoured by the Romans) (qqv); but all three were subject to the whims of architects and carvers and the Romans evolved a mixture, the Composite order (qv). The Tuscan (qv) was developed in Italy in the second century BC.

Most columns are either of uniform section throughout or tapered towards the capital, but many Greek and Roman builders favoured the entasis, a slight swelling in the middle section of a column. Columns were most often fluted throughout their length.

Columns have played an immensely practical and decorative part in the history of architecture, particularly in Roman buildings, in which the column was widely used for the arched, or arcuated, forms which Roman builders developed. The most famous adaptations of the column are still to be seen in the colonnaded cloisters and arcades of Rome, Florence, Venice, and other Italian cities.

Modern columns usually have no decoration, capitals, or bases.

Columna rostrata or **rostral column.** An ornamental column adorned with the beaks of galleys and usually celebrating a naval victory.

Comb back. A type of chair back using many vertical slender bars joined by a broad top rail, known as a comb. The effect is similar to that of a Spanish tortoiseshell comb. It is commonly found on eighteenth- and nineteenth-century Windsor chairs.

Commode. A French word of early eighteenth-century origin, used to describe a low chest with drawers. The term seems to have been fairly loosely applied to any piece of superior craftsmanship. The commode as we know it today dates from the time of Louis XIV. French *ébénistes* excelled all the cabinetmakers of Europe in the construction of these pieces, splendidly proportioned and sumptuously decorated with lavish inlays and a proliferation of floral, ornithological, and martial motifs. The bombé (qv) or convex shape also became fashionable.

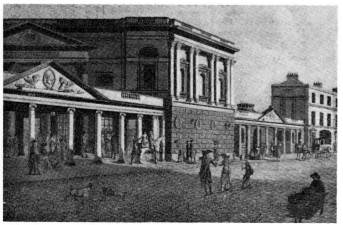

Colonnade at the Pump Room, Bath

A Régence commode. The design shows beginning of rococo

Louis XV ormolu mounted commode with tulipwood marquetry

English cabinetmakers copied the commode, making pieces with a robust simplicity that now has a period charm but is lacking in elegance. The commode 'in the French taste' gradually began to acquire an unmistakably indigenous character, and those made by the great cabinetmakers of the mid-eighteenth century are pieces of supreme assurance and splendour, with bold carving and wrought brass handles. Among the most sumptuous are splendidly baroque examples attributed to William Vile and made about 1740.

English commodes were first made in mahogany, but later examples, in a variety of shapes (bowed, serpentine- and concave-fronted), were frequently lacquered and painted.

Composite order

Common rafter. An ordinary sloping member of a roof truss.

Companion chair. An ingenious if unwieldy piece of Victorian furniture that accommodated six people. It had three double semi-circular seats that all joined at the centre. It was also known as a confidante (qv).

Compass roof. An alternative term, now archaic, for the open timber roof known as a span roof, ie a roof with a centre ridge as distinct from a lean-to roof.

Compass window. An alternative term for an oriel window.

Composite order. The Ionic order fused with the Corinthian order. This adaptation was evolved by the Romans and is often called the Roman order. The first known instance of its use was on the Arch of Titus, Rome (AD 82).

The capital has the double row of acanthus leaves from the Corinthian order and a concave abacus from the same source; but between, immediately above the leaves, is an echinus enlivened with mouldings of egg and dart pattern, and Ionic volutes. The capital was occasionally simplified or even elaborated as at the Baths of Caracalla, Rome (third century AD), where small sculpted figures are interpolated between the volutes. See **Orders.**

Composition. A substance that was used extensively for late eighteenth-century mouldings, notably those struck upon carved fireplaces. It was a mixture of whiting, size, and glue that could be squeezed into moulds com-

paratively easily, after which it set firmly.

Concertina movement. Some eighteenth-century card tables, especially those of the first half of the century, had this type of folded and hinged device instead of a gate-leg.

One pair of legs could be moved into the extended position because the side of the front opened like a concertina. Once in position, the folded top flap could be opened so that the baize table-top was exposed.

Concrete is a mixture, generally in proportions of approximately 1:2:4, of cement, sand, gravel or crushed stone, and water. The water causes the cement to harden by chemical action, binding the other materials together into a monolithic whole. (Cement itself is made from a mixture of chalk or limestone with clay, burned together to a clinker at a high temperature, and ground to a fine powder with the addition of certain chemicals to control the

Exhibition Hall, Turin, designed by Pier Luigi Nervi: the roof is made up of precast concrete units

setting time.)

Concrete – of a kind – has been used since early times. It was in common use by the Romans: the domed roof of the Pantheon (with a 142 ft 6 in span) is of concrete. It did not, however, become a uniformly reliable building material until the invention of 'Portland' cement by an Englishman, Joseph Aspdin, in the early nineteenth century.

The Commonwealth Institute, Kensington, London, designed by Robert Matthew, Johnson-Marshall: concrete frame and curved concrete roof

The College of Education, Wayne State University, USA, by Minoru Yamasaki: the façades are made up of 40 ft high precast concrete 'trees'

The President's palace and private chapel at Brasilia, by Oscar Niemeyer: concrete pilotis arcade, roof and chapel

US pavilion at World Agricultural Fair, New Delhi: concrete domes

The next stage was the invention of reinforced concrete, which took place in France about the middle of the last century. Concrete, while able to withstand great weights (compression), is weak in tension (stretching). Steel bars (the reinforcement) are therefore introduced into the concrete where tension is likely to occur. The development of reinforced concrete brought about a revolution in building and civil engineering, opening up possibilities never before envisaged.

A further extension of the reinforcement principle has been the development of pre-stressed concrete, invented in the late 1920s by a French engineer, Eugène Freyssinet. This entails giving the concrete an initial compression by means of wires or rods passed through it, stretched, and anchored while still extended. Their pull towards contracting to their original length compresses the concrete and counteracts in advance the effect of load. Thus even greater spans can be achieved with thinner members – a great advantage in the design of slim, elegant bridges.

Concrete can be cast on the site, or sections can be pre-cast in factories and later assembled on the site. Among the many forms is 'shell concrete' – very thin, curved concrete sheets used

to form roofs. They gain their strength from their curvature, as an eggshell does; they may be either singly or doubly curved.

Concrete, once regarded as a workaday material that needed to be covered up, is nowadays often exposed on the surface of buildings and other structures. The surface may be patterned by the mould in which the concrete is placed (from rough timber boards to smoothly patterned shapes). Alternatively, the stone in the concrete may be exposed by removing the outer skin of cement, leaving a surface which has colour as well as texture interest. (The stone is made in different colours and sizes, and can be set in coloured cement.)

Besides its use in large-scale building, concrete is much used today in domestic work: concrete paving slabs of different colours, concrete screen walls, pergolas, and the like, are appearing in gardens and patios.

Conder, Neville (*b* 1900). British architect. In association with Sir Hugh Casson (qv), Conder has been a major contributor to the designing of new university buildings, chiefly at Cambridge and Birmingham. He worked with Casson on the general co-ordination of the architectural designs for the Festival of Britain in 1951. He has also carried out a considerable amount of industrial design work.

Confidante. The intriguing name given to a large sofa with separate seats at either end facing diagonally outwards. It is of French origin, but designs were made by Adam and Hepplewhite, who in his *Guide* of 1788 opined that an 'elegant drawing-room, with modern furniture, is scarce complete without a confidante.' He recommended a length of 9 ft.

During the nineteenth century the same word covered all pieces of furniture designed for two or

more couples. See **Companion chair.**

Conran, Terence (*b* 1931). British designer and manufacturer of furniture and textiles. Conran was educated at Bryanston, and then studied textile design at the Central School. He established a furniture and textile business that has made him one of the leaders in modern design. The products of this company – furniture and fabrics, kitchen equipment, and household accessories – are marketed through the Habitat chain of shops. The first Habitat opened in 1964, presenting a range of well-designed goods in gay colours that played a major part in the household design revolution of the 1960s.

Conservatory. A word used since 1164 to describe a house or room, built largely of glass, in which plants are kept and grown. Sir William Chambers designed the great conservatory

Terence Conran

at Kew. There are still conservatories all over Britain, relics of the spacious Victorian period. 'Conservative walls' (walls protected with glass) are also occasionally found. Today greenhouse (qv) and conservatory are differentiated by their status, the greenhouse being a utilitarian plant house and the conservatory an extension of living quarters.

The Great Conservatory at Syon Park

A George III confidante painted white and partly gilded

Modern conservatory by Felix Harbord

A Régence console table in the late Cressent style

Console. An architectural term taken from the French and normally used of a scroll-shaped bracket. Its wider meaning is that of a side table supported by only a pair of brackets or consoles. Such tables probably originated in France; they were in use *c* 1725 in Europe and soon afterwards in America. Both English and American consoles continued to be in fashion until the early 1800s. Examples include the heavy designs of Chippendale, all gilt with marble tops, as well as light Rococo or Neo-classical creations. Architects designed console tables, regarding them as integral to the decoration of a room. These were frequently made *en suite* with pier glasses. See **Pier table.**

Constitution mirror. An American mirror of the late eighteenth century. It was a tall object in the Chippendale style crowned by a scrolled pediment with a phoenix rising in the centre. It was made of mahogany or walnut, with much gilding on the scrolls, birds, and small leaf and flower decorations around the frame. It has also been known as a Martha Washington mirror.

Constructivism developed almost parallel with Suprematism (qv) in Moscow from 1917. It was first defined by two sculptors, the brothers Naum Gabo and Antoine Pevsner, in a manifesto of 1920. Constructivism was described by its innovators as answering a modern need. 'In order to interpret the reality of life,' they affirmed, 'art must be based upon two fundamental elements: space and time. Volume is not the only concept of space. Kinetic and dynamic elements must be used to express the true nature of time.'

As far as architecture is concerned, Constructivism is in effect a variant of Functionalism, stressing the constructional rather than the aesthetic aspect of a building. The use of materials such as metal, glass, and plastic, in constructions underlines the significance of the machine in modern life, and constructionists claimed that its role should also be clearly evident in the structural elements of architecture. An example of Constructivism in action, so to speak, is Vladimir Tatlin's design for a memorial to the Third International (1919). This steel-

Fluted blue-on-white, c two centuries old, still in production

and-wire spiral was planned to be very high; and to contain large buildings placed one on top of another within the framework. Whether Constructivism exercized any lasting influence on modern architecture is debatable, but it may be said to have heralded Le Corbusier's emphasis on the aesthetic elements in structural work.

Conversation chair. A chair for lounging, described by Sheraton as being 'peculiarly adapted for this kind of idle position' (*Cabinet Dictionary*, 1803). The seat was shaped so that the occupant could sit back to front and rest his arms on the padded top rail. In America the term is occasionally used to describe an S-shaped seat that allows two people to converse easily because they face in opposite directions.

Copeland. See **Spode.**

Copenhagen. Franz Heinrich Müller, a pharmacist, introduced hard-paste porcelain to Denmark in 1772. The Danish Porcelain Factory was founded in 1775, and four years later it was taken under royal control. The trade-

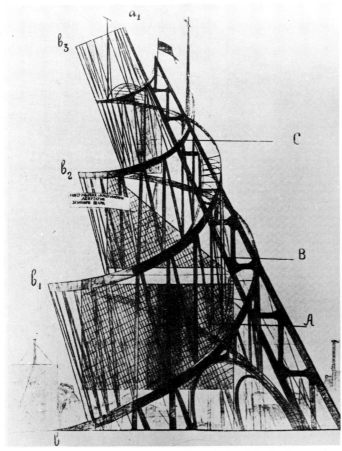

Design for the Monument to the Third International by Tatlin, 1919–20

'Flora Danica' tureen, Royal Copenhagen, made between 1788 and 1803

A new Royal Copenhagen design in white: 'Wheat', by Torkild Olsen

mark – three blue wavy lines symbolizing the Sound and the Great and Little Belt – is said to have been the Queen Mother's idea. Müller's research provided a valuable basis for the present-day work of the Royal Copenhagen manufactory: many of his glazes and pigments are still used, and the popularity of his blue underglaze dinner service, the 'blue fluted' service, has never diminished. The Danish royal family sold the manufactory in 1867. In 1882 Philip Schon took it over and moved it to the outskirts of Copenhagen, close to the earthenware factory of Alumnia, of which he was the manager. The two businesses merged.

Schon's art director, Arnold Krog, created Danish underglaze painting, using intermediate tones of a single colour. Originally this was blue, but then red and pale green were introduced. The production of underglaze painted figures began at about this time.

There were experiments with stoneware in the early twentieth century, and developments in the technique of overglaze colouring and ceramic figure sculpture. Crackled porcelain was produced in large quantities during the 1920s and 1930s.

When Christian Christiansen took over in 1930 he expanded the plant enormously and increased the production of porcelain and earthenware in both traditional and new designs. Experiment is still encouraged.

Coping. The topmost course of a wall, added for the purpose of throwing off rain-water. This course, normally of stone, usually overlaps the penultimate course and frequently has a sloping upper surface. Coping is sometimes also known as capping.

Copper. A metal of dull reddish colour which, when burnished, resembles dark gold. It is malleable and has therefore been used since late Neolithic times for jewellery, domestic utensils, etc. Cooking containers in well-to-do houses were once always made of copper, and were very handsome objects. The reconstructed Regency kitchen at the Royal Pavilion in Brighton, England, has a magnificent collection.

Housewives no longer use copper for pots and pans, but old ones are popular as a decoration and are often hung on kitchen walls or used as containers for indoor plants. Few gourmets are without a display of copper, which has become a sort of status symbol in the modern kitchen.

Coquillage. (French, *coquille* 'shellfish'). The shape of the common shellfish, which, because of its distinctive form, is often found as the centre of an ornament, especially in Rococo decoration.

Corbel or **corbel-stone.** A projection from an interior or exterior wall, used to support a beam or moulding. This projection was first used in Gothic building and was inevitably popular during the Gothic revival. Early corbels were carved or moulded in fanciful shapes and were frequently given the form of heads and gargoyles.

Corbel-table. A row of corbels supporting a cornice or parapet.

Corbie steps at Cologne

Corbie steps. The Scottish term for the stepped gables which were introduced into Scottish domestic architecture from the Continent; they were used in northern France, Germany, and the Low Countries.

Corinthian order. The third order invented by the Greeks. It is a variant of the Ionic, probably dating from the Hellenistic period; the earliest known example is the Temple of Apollo Epicurius at Bassae (c 420 BC). Rather sparing use was made of the order by the Greeks, but the richness of the capital proved so popular among the Romans that it is mainly associated with their architecture. Only in Roman times was it given a standard form. Roman Corinthian became even more slender than earlier versions (themselves thinner than the Ionic), and the outline of the capital was more sharply defined.

The Corinthian column was originally fluted, becoming smooth only in Roman times. Its base was moulded in a very similar way to the Ionic Attic base. The capital is deeper than any other, and above the astragal moulding are two rows of overlapping acanthus leaves between which spring small, stalk-like

motifs called cauliculi. Each of these has two leafy tops, one small and one large, the large ones curling over at the corners in the form of a small scroll. The abacus, which is moulded and has concave sides, projects out over these scrolled corners.

In Greek times the entablature is not distinguishable from the Ionic. The Romans divided the lowest member, the architrave, by three horizontal bands of small mouldings, and added tiny consoles called modillions to the cornice. Modillions only became common towards the end of the Republic, but despite Vitruvius's adverse criticism they became standard features of the Renaissance Corinthian order. See **Orders.**

Cork. The outer layer of the bark of an evergreen oak (*Quercus suber* and *Quercus suber occidentalis*, a sub-species). The thick soft outer bark is first stripped off when a tree is between 15 and 20 years old. At this stage, it is rough 'virgin cork' – low quality cork, used for insulation or ground up for composition cork products. Subsequent strippings occur every eight or ten years, and the quality of the cork improves up to the fifth or sixth stripping. A tree normally produces cork for about 150 years.

The cellular structure of cork gives it its characteristic flexibility, buoyancy, and compressibility, and makes it more or less resistant to penetration by air and water. The Romans discovered this and soled their shoes with cork. Later, by the fifteenth century, Europeans were making

Copper kitchen utensils at the Royal Pavilion, Brighton

Corinthian Order

French marquetry corner cupboard by Gilles Joubert (1689–1775)

Southern American corner cupboard in the Queen Anne style

Victorian glass cornucopias

cork stoppers and bungs for their bottles, jars, and jugs.

At the end of the nineteenth century there were new developments. Experiments were carried out with low-quality cork and by-product scrap from better-quality cork. These were ground up and fused under heat and pressure to make pipe covering, insulating cork-board, and similar items. An improved form of this process continues, particularly in the hard floor-coverings industry. Ground cork is used for linoleum, cork tiles, and cork brick; or it is combined with synthetic rubber and plastic products. Cork is a warm, quiet floor-covering with considerable resistance to stains.

Corner cabinet. The corner cabinet introduced in the late seventeenth century not only filled awkward spaces but was ideal for the display of porcelain, glass, and *objets de vertu*. Early examples were in walnut and tended to be plain, but by 1750 ornate mahogany cabinets were also being made. Both hanging cabinets, with a single glazed door, and tall standing cabinets were popular. Standing cabinets had glazed doors above wooden cupboard doors or a stand.

The corner cabinet continued to be popular throughout the nineteenth century.

Corner cupboard. This is similar in shape to the corner cabinet, but has solid doors and was intended for storage rather than display. Hanging cupboards were in general use by the end of the seventeenth century, often with japanned decoration and shelves of a serpentine curve. Early eighteenth-century examples were in two stages, with a cupboard above and a cupboard or stand below. Others were built into the corners or alcoves of a room to match the panelling.

Corner cupboards were largely superseded by glazed cabinets in the later eighteenth century, though they continued to be made provincially into the nineteenth century. The only fashionable corner cupboard of the mid- or late eighteenth century was the 'coin' (from the French *encoignure*), the upper part of which contained a series of graduated open shelves. It was illustrated by Ince and Mayhew in their *Universal System* (1759–63).

Corner cupboards of simpler design have been popular in America since the time of William and Mary, the earliest separate pieces being recorded in inventories of the 1720s. These cupboards were made by local cabinetmakers along the Eastern seaboard, who used native woods such as walnut, maple, and pine. Cupboards with panelled doors were popular in the South, while in the early homes of New England glazed doors were more common.

Cornice. The term generally applied to a moulded projection from an interior or exterior wall. More specifically, the section which crowns the entablature of one of the architectural orders, each order having its own form of cornice.

Cornucopia (from the Latin, *cornu* 'horn' and *copia* 'plenty'). The horn of plenty, usually held in the hand of the boy Plutus, Ceres the goddess of harvest, or some other mythological deity; it is shown pouring forth an abundance of fruit, flowers, and sweetmeats. The cornucopia became a recognized symbol of prosperity in the West, and was widely used in architecture and painting. In the eighteenth and nineteenth centuries it became a popular decorative feature. It was made in glass and mounted on hands, rams' heads, or winged angels, in brass or ormolu; the engraved or cut-glass horn or holder acted as a flower vase. Curiously enough, despite its popularity the cornucopia receives little attention in most histories of glass manufacture.

Coromandel. See **Calamander.**

Corona. An early form of hanging light or chandelier, used mainly in churches. It was made of a metal crown or series of hoops with a number of sockets for candles or even occasionally cups for oil.

In architecture the corona is the lowest segment, or drip, of the projecting part of a classical cornice. Its horizontal under-

Cortile of the Palazzo Medici, Florence: Michelozzi, 1444-60

surface is called the soffit. The term corona is also sometimes used for the apse or semi-circular termination of a choir.

Corrugation. Corrugating iron (usually galvanized or zinc-plated iron), copper, asbestos, Perspex, and other structural materials, greatly increases their resistance to buckling. Processes vary with materials, but generally involve passing the material through pairs of ridged rollers. In areas lacking in timber and brick supplies, corrugated iron has been widely used for building; this is especially true of roofs, although the exteriors of houses in cities as far apart as Reykjavik and Brisbane have been wholly constructed in corrugated iron. It has been unjustly denigrated as a building material, or when painted in bright colours, as in Iceland, the corrugated surfaces can add substantially to the surface interest of small houses.

Corrugated asbestos is now widely employed in farm buildings, and its unpainted surfaces have done much to disfigure twentieth-century rural landscapes. Corrugated transparent sheets of plastic have been extensively used as roofing for bringing light into industrial and farm buildings.

Cortile. The Italian word for courtyard, most commonly internal and surrounded by arcades, as in Renaissance palaces. Here the architects were able to give the elevations a lighter and less formal treatment than was permissible on the more solemn exterior. For sheer elegance and beauty the cortile of Laurana's Ducal Palace, Urbino, is unsurpassed.

Cortona, Pietro da (Pietro Berrettini) (1596-1669). Italian painter and architect, born at Cortona into a family of stone masons. He became one of the masters of Roman Baroque, both as a painter (Palazzo Barbarini, Palazzo Pitti) and as an architect – despite the fact that he once referred to architecture as only a pastime. As an architect he was largely self-taught, for he studied only under uninspired Florentine masters.

Cortona was patronized by the Sachetti family, joining their household and designing the Villa del Pigneto outside Rome for them shortly before 1630. This no longer exists, and is known only through engravings, though the design was immensely influential in the development of villa architecture. The villa stood above an elaborate arrangement of ornamental staircases and gardens. It had a three-storeyed centre dominated by a tall niche, similar to that in a belvedere, and two low lateral wings that curved forwards to meet the terrace.

SS Martina e Luca (1635-50) was rebuilt after the body of S Martina was discovered in the crypt during excavations for Cortona's own tomb. He was promptly commissioned by Pope Urban VIII to design a new church. SS Martina e Luca and Borromini's contemporary S Carlo alle Quattro Fontane are the first thoroughly Roman Baroque churches.

Cortona created a small piazza in front of S Maria delle Pace, making the first bay and semi-circular porch of the church obtrude into the very centre of the new piazza. He enlarged the façade to either side, thereby hiding a neighbouring monastery

SS Martina e Luca designed by Cortona, 1635-50

and a passageway into the piazza, and making the building appear to be a three-aisled church though it in fact has only one aisle.

Few of Cortona's major projects were executed. Some of his plans for the Louvre can still be seen there. The decoration of his own buildings, and others such as the Palazzo Pitti in Florence, exemplify his dense, vigorous style; the fusion of Florentine Mannerist and Roman Baroque traits on such buildings represents an extension of Cortona's own architectural style.

Costa, Lucio (b 1902). Brazilian architect, one of the leaders of the modern movement in South America and now chiefly renowned as the author of the pilot plan for Brasilia. Costa was born in Toulon in France, and studied in England and France and at the Escola Nacional de Belas Artes in Rio de Janeiro. His earliest work was mainly concerned with the design of apartment houses and government buildings. He began to be known outside South America after working with Le Corbusier and a group of Brazilian architects on Brazil's new Ministry of Education and Public Health, planned in 1936. In collaboration with Oscar Niemeyer, Costa designed the Brazilian pavilion at the New York World's Fair of 1939, which firmly established his international reputation. His plans for Brasilia won the international competition for the commission in 1957.

Lucio Costa

Thatched and half-timbered cottage that once belonged to Anne Hathaway

Cot (Hindu, *khat* 'bedstead'). In the nineteenth century, babies began to have their own small beds instead of sleeping in baskets, cradles (qv), or their elders' beds. These were called cots, a word first used in this sense in English in 1818. Well-known types include the swing cot and the traditional, rather cage-like cot with tall legs and sides.

Cottage. Until the early years of the fifteenth century, most of our ancestors lived in one-roomed huts, built of mud and thatched with reeds or straw. Smoke escaped out of the un-glazed window openings, and the earth floor was strewn with rushes. These huts were too frail to survive, and are known only through documents and pictures. Then came the cottages, of the simplest possible construction, built by local craftsmen from materials readily at hand. Their designs, which give us so much pleasure, were not dictated by aesthetic considerations: the builders were simply attempting to solve the problems of shelter and storage in the simplest possible way.

These early cottages were small buildings of one or two storeys. Living-room, wash-house, and store were on the ground floor, with bedrooms on the upper floor, taking up part of the roof space. Long, low proportions, and the use of local materials, combine to give the impression that these old cottages are an integral part of the landscape.

Roofs were of thatch, slate, stone, and later tile (and in America wood shingle), steeply pitched to shed rain quickly and efficiently. In Europe thatch was the earliest roof covering for cottages and it still has much to recommend it. It is warmer in winter and cooler in summer than slate or tiles. Reed thatch is best, as it will last for 30 years without needing to be repaired, and does not burn quickly.

The expense of glass limited both the number and size of windows in early cottages, and not many were made to open. An open door and large fire opening provided the necessary ventilation. Diamond panes evolved from the practice of filling the window opening with a diagonal lattice of twigs to keep out the rain. When glass came into more general use, this practice was copied in lead; but diamond-shaped panes were gradually superseded by rectangular ones, which were cheaper.

Ground-floor rooms had floors of clay, stone, or brick, and wide boards were laid across joists to form the first floor. A single wood fire sufficed for cooking and heating.

In Britain the first cottage-building period occurred before timber became scarce at the beginning of the seventeenth century. After this, house timbers became smaller and more refined, and in-filling panels larger. Alternative building materials began to be used, depending on the resources of a particular region.

In timber-framed cottages a substantial oak sill was set on a dwarf wall of stone, brick, or flint. Vertical posts were tenoned into this, and supported horizontal headpieces. In the fifteenth and sixteenth centuries, cottages were frequently built with the upper floor projecting beyond the wall of the ground floor. Why this was done is not known for certain; perhaps it was just a way of gaining extra space without encroaching on the highway. Alternatively, it may have been just a survival from the projecting defensive galleries of fortified castles. It certainly halved the amount of water running down the face of the building and into the foundations, and gave added structural stability.

Panels between the framing were filled with a variety of materials. Early builders used a lattice of hazel sticks, rather like a wattle hurdle, daubed on both sides with clay. Later, brick nogging came in. The bricks were laid diagonally, not for effect but because this arrangement ensured that all the joints were kept tight by the weight of the bricks themselves. Tiles and weatherboarding were used to protect the outer face of timber-framed cottages, or of those built of porous under-burnt bricks.

In America and other countries with a plentiful supply of timber, the frame dwelling (such as the Cape Cod cottage) remained common; whereas the increasing shortage of timber in Britain and elsewhere encouraged the use of stone. In the Middle Ages this had been discouraged by the poor foundations of buildings, which frequently collapsed; therefore, when stone was used for walls, it was often only a skin with a separate timber frame to carry the roof and first floor. The stone used was that which was easily available; it was seldom worked, and at best roughly shaped up. Not until the Renaissance is fine ashlar work found. The exteriors of these rough stone cottages were often thickly plastered for extra protection against the weather.

Modern methods of heating, insulation, and construction have so revolutionized building that a light and flimsy-looking structure may well be warmer and more watertight than a more substantial-looking one. And to-day it is often more expensive to use a local material than one from some distance. On the other hand, appropriateness to setting and a sense of solidity and protection are important considerations; and here there are many lessons to be learned from the cottages of the past.

Cottage orné. Ornamental pseudo-rustic cottages were built to meet the demand for the Picturesque in the late eighteenth and early nineteenth centuries. The builders usually put quaintness of effect above formal correctness, often incorporating Gothick windows into these cottages, which were nearly all thatched.

Cottage orné, Blaise Hamlet, Gloucestershire, by Nash

Cottage pot made in Staffordshire about 1850

Cottage pots. A wide range of British pottery figures made throughout the nineteenth century are often referred to as 'cottage pots' because they were produced for a large and unsophisticated market. They were made of a very white clay and were usually decorated with bright enamel colours, a rich, striking dark blue being very characteristic. Cottage pots frequently were simply though ingeniously modelled, and were often portraits of celebrities, famous or infamous – musicians, murderers, boxers, royalty, etc. Sometimes the base of the figure is marked with the celebrity's name.

Cottage pots were made in Staffordshire and Sunderland and also at the Portobello factory in Scotland where they were particularly well modelled and carefully finished. Dogs, horses, cottages, castles, and churches were also made.

Couch. The words couch and day-bed are often interchangeable; here only the pieces described solely as couches are discussed. These belong to the late eighteenth and early nineteenth centuries and are long upholstered seats for reclining.

(See also **Récamier.**) One end is a high back rest, while the other is scrolled or plain. There is frequently an upholstered arm extending part of the way down one side.

Confusingly, a duchesse (qv) is described as a couch, and Chippendale designed canopied couch-beds intended to fit into alcoves.

Coupled columns. A term used to describe the architectural device of placing two columns close together or joining them under the same entablature.

Coupled roof. A form of roof construction suitable for a small span. Pairs of sloping rafters rest upon a ridge at the top without tie or collar beams being used.

Cour d'honneur. The French name for the main or forecourt that gives access to the principal rooms. It is commonly the courtyard in front of a mansion and enclosed by gates through which only important visitors were allowed to pass.

Court cupboard. In modern English usage this is not a cupboard at all, but a three-tiered open sideboard; the name perpetuates the original (medieval) meaning of cupboard – a board upon which cups could be placed.

The court cupboard dates from the very end of the sixteenth century and continued to be made during the first half of the seventeenth in rural areas down to the early 1700s. It was rarely more than 4 ft high, was often elaborately carved, and was used primarily for the display of plate.

In America this open form of court cupboard was not known. However, the characteristic American Jacobean cupboard, with an open shelf either above or below the closed compartment, was probably called a court cupboard as numerous references in inventories suggest.

Cour d'honneur at the Château de Versailles

This kind of cupboard combined storage space for utensils with a shelf for display.

Courting chair. The modern name for chairs with wide deep seats on which a couple could sit close together. They were introduced at the time of the Restoration. See **Love-seat.**

Cove. A hollowed moulding usually less than the quarter of a circumference (or quadrant) which acts as a link between two opposed surfaces (eg wall and ceiling or wall and soffit). Coving was common in seventeenth-century and earlier timber-framed houses, and was also popular in the eighteenth century.

Crackle. A crackle glaze on porcelain was an effect introduced by the Chinese as a form of

Carved and gilded wood couch by Gillow of London, 1805

Carved oak court cupboard, early seventeenth century

Traditional Scandinavian cradle

Royal Crescent, Bath, built by John Wood the Younger, 1761–5

decoration. It consisted of a network of tiny cracks over the surface of lead-glazed softpaste china. The surface of glass can also be crackled. See **Crazing**.

Cradle. A cot on rockers which has changed surprisingly little in design over the last 500 years. Early cradles were made from hollowed-out tree-trunks, but from the fifteenth to the seventeenth centuries they consisted of rectangular boxes of wood mounted on end rockers. Medieval babies of royal and noble birth were provided with 'best' cradles of remarkable sumptuousness, in gold, silver, and precious stones. Such a cradle was called the 'cradell of estate.'

The mid-eighteenth and nineteenth-century cradle was made of wicker and had wooden rockers. The principal innovation was the slinging of the cradle between the end supports which raised it far higher from the ground. Sheraton's 'Swinging Crib Bed' in the *Cabinet Dictionary* of 1803 is a good example of this.

Crazing is the name given to thousands of tiny cracks on the surface of a glaze, due to the uneven shrinkage of the body of the clay and the glaze. This renders the ware porous and thus

unsuitable for use. The effect can be produced intentionally as decoration, in which case it is called crackle (qv).

Creamware. See **Queensware.**

Credence. A term used during the late sixteenth and early seventeenth centuries to describe a small side or serving table – a cupboard on legs or uprights that was used during meals. Nowadays credence is a general term for oak splay-fronted cupboards of the early seventeenth century. It is also the name of the table in the chancel on which the reserved sacrament is kept.

Credenza. After the cassone, the credenza was perhaps the commonest piece of early Italian furniture. It was a long cupboard the height of a dining-room table and with canted corners. The front has two, or sometimes three, doors and there were drawers in the frieze. It served as a dining-room sideboard or serving table. Both style and decoration varied from town to town and from

century to century. The cupboard doors were usually panelled, often with lozenges and diamonds, and the frieze was commonly decorated with lion or satyr masks typical of the Italian taste for the grotesque. During the sixteenth century the credenza gained an upper storey in the form of a recessed cupboard, and corresponded fairly closely to the dresser (qv).

Crenellation, crenelle. Terms for the battlements (qv) of a fortress or castle, and in particular for the embrasures or openings of the medieval pierced parapet through which missiles could be discharged against a besieging enemy. In England a royal licence (kernellare) was required in medieval times before a subject could build a castle or crenellate an existing house. The law was forgotten when fortified buildings became obsolete, and crenellation was gradually adopted as a decorative device for lodges, cottages, and larger houses. This culminated in the eighteenth-century craze for mock-fortification indulged in

by Horace Walpole, Vanbrugh, and scores of other enthusiastic builders.

Crepidoma. The steps forming the base of a Greek temple.

Crescent (Latin, *crescere* 'to grow'). A term used of the waxing and waning moon in its first and last quarters, and adopted by property developers of the eighteenth century to describe curved terraces. These were occasionally introduced into the more usual squares and streets to give variety and interest to the layout. Crescent houses also have a slightly wider frontage than equivalent houses in terraces. Many town and city developments between 1750 and 1850 now provide welcome relief in the urban scene. The Royal Crescent in Bath, perhaps the most famous of all Britain's crescents, was built by John Wood the Younger as part of the Woods' development of that city.

Cressent, Charles (1685–1768). The greatest French *ébéniste* of the Régence period, cabinet-

Crenellations on a seventeenth-century building

Pelham Crescent, Kensington, by Basevi

Cabinet clock perhaps by Cressent

maker to the Regent, sculptor to Louis XV, and a notable collector of works of art. He learned sculpture from his father, but in 1719 married the daughter of the *ébéniste* Joseph Poitou, after which he concentrated increasingly on furniture-making. His productions, few of which are signed, exemplify the flamboyance of the early Régence Rococo style and are remarkable for the contrast between their plain veneers and their magnificent ormolu mounts. Cressent made many of these mounts himself, thus infringing the law, and he was often engaged in legal battles with the bronze-workers' guild and the gilders.

Crest or **cresting**. The decorative finish to the upper edge of a screen, canopy, panel, or any other subsidiary structure or feature in a building, its enrichment being vaguely suggestive of a miniature battlement. The finials of gables and pinnacles are sometimes referred to as crests. The crest, or cresting, was sometimes moulded, sometimes carved and very occasionally made in lead. In more recent times cresting has frequently been employed as the decorative finish to gilded pelmet boards.

In furniture, especially furniture with seats, the cresting is the elaborately carved top rail (found, for example, on chairs of the late eighteenth century). The term is also applied to the decoration on the tops of tall cabinets and mirrors.

Crest tile. An ornamental ridge tile.

Crewel-work. A popular type of embroidery executed in the late seventeenth and early eighteenth century. In crewel-work worsted was worked on a white or beige linen ground. It was commonly used for bed-hangings and curtains, the coarseness of the work making it unsuitable for small items. The designs were based on the printed cottons from Madras imported by the East India Company: tall blossoming trees grow from mounds of earth, brightly coloured birds sit in the branches, and rabbits, deer and hounds run between the trees. In recent years there has been a great revival of interest in this and other forms of embroidery.

Cricket table. The present-day name for a small three-legged table made in the seventeenth century.

Crochet. Working yarn with a hooked needle; its origins are probably very ancient. Extremely fine and elaborate work was pro-

Crochet bed cover with a deep fringe

duced, but in the nineteenth century the craft declined as a result of competition from the machine-made lace of Nottingham and Switzerland. It benefited from the general revival of hand crafts towards the end of the century, reviving again in the 1960s.

Crocket (French, *croc* 'a hook'). The projecting flowers or foliage employed in Gothic architecture to decorate the angles of spires, pinnacles, and canopies, or carved at intervals on the edge of vertical mouldings. In England, crockets are most frequently seen in fourteenth-century ecclesiastical architecture. Their forms are extremely diverse; broad leaves are the most common elements, but animals and figures are sometimes used as, or in place of, crockets.

Crocket capital. A Norman capital encircled by two bands consisting of a simplified leaf motif that bends over at the top into a curl of bunched foliage.

Cross. From earliest times a cross, in its simplest right-angled and diagonal intersecting forms, has been used as a symbol, ornament, and motif in design and decoration. Its widest use has of course been in Christian art. In ecclesiastical architecture it is employed both as a plan form (see **Crossing**) and as a symbol on gable end, nave, and sepulchre.

Cross-banding. In cabinet-making, a banding (qv) of veneer in which the grain runs across the border. It was introduced in the 1660s and was employed throughout the eighteenth century.

Crossing. An architectural term denoting the intersection of nave and transept. The plan forms of Christian churches are usually based on the Latin cross with three short arms and one longer arm which forms the nave. The most common variant is the Greek cross with all four arms the same length; it was favoured during the Renaissance, when the centrally-planned church assumed symbolic significance.

Cross-vault. Used in Roman buildings, and formed by the intersection of two semi-circular vaults of equal span; the pressure was taken by the four angles. The lines of intersection are known as groins.

Crouch-ware. The name given to the earliest Staffordshire salt-glazed stoneware (early eighteenth century). The word probably comes from Crich, which was a kind of clay found in Derbyshire. Crouch-ware was a greyish or buff colour. It was made into teapots and useful ware, which was often decorated with sprigged designs of white pipeclay after the manner of John Astbury and the Elers (qv).

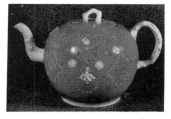

Crouch-ware teapot, c 1720

Crewel-work curtain, 17th century

Crockets on an ogee arch

Fourteenth-century crown steeple

Later salt-glazed stoneware was much lighter in colour because potters discovered how to incorporate ground calcined flints into the clay.

Crown. The highest, and usually therefore, the central, point of an arch or vault. It is frequently ornamented with a boss.

Crown steeple. An ornamental late Gothic flourish on church towers. It is an attractive openwork structure arranged to support its crowning slender spire. The device was occasionally repeated in eighteenth-century ecclesiastical architecture, especially in Scotland.

Cruck. A method of supporting the roofs of early houses and barns. Two heavy timber members (usually suitably carved tree-trunks or heavy branches) were joined at the top, spread apart at the base, and braced on or against stones. Cruck construction supported quite heavy roofs and was employed in remoter areas until well into the fifteenth century.

Crunden, John (1740–c 1828). A remarkably little-known architect to whom London owes one of its most charming and originally designed buildings, Boodle's Club in St James' Street. John Crunden was born in Sussex, and is reputed to have been either a pupil or an assistant of Henry Holland the elder. Apart from his designs for Boodle's (1775), his modest fame rests mainly upon his publications, the chief of which is *Convenient and Ornamental Architecture, consisting of original designs for plans, elevations, and sections from the farm*

The crypt of Canterbury Cathedral

house to the most grand and magnificent villa, published in 1768. Crunden was also district surveyor for Paddington, St Pancras, and St Luke, Chelsea.

Crypt (Greek, *krypto* 'I bury' and *kryptos* 'hidden place'). A vaulted chamber beneath a building, either wholly or partly underground. The term is usually employed only in connection with churches. Crypts are usually of smaller dimensions than the church, and in the past were used as chapels and furnished with altars and other liturgical fittings.

Crystal. A term used today to describe a particularly brilliant and colourless glass, such as prized examples of Baccarat and Steuben.

Crystal Palace. An architectural structure which showed the way towards acceptance and appreciation of unadorned building materials. It was designed by Joseph Paxton (later knighted) for the Great Exhibition of 1851, re-erected at Sydenham in 1852–4, and destroyed by fire in 1936.

This construction – virtually a giant conservatory – was a colossal project of prefabrication: 408 ft wide and 1,848 ft long, rising in three tiers. The 'aisles' and 'nave' were divided by tiered open galleries 24 ft wide, and the roof was supported by openwork horizontal girders carrying ridge-and-furrow glazing. As a last minute modification, a transept was introduced to allow for the enclosure of a growing tree. After the Palace was re-erected in south London, the nave was given a barrel-roof like the transept.

Cubitt, Thomas (1788–1855), William (1791–1863), and Lewis (1799–1883). The three remarkable sons of Jonathan Cubitt, a Norfolk farmer. Of the trio Thomas is by far the most important, for he was the driving

Boodle's Club in St James's Street, designed by John Crunden

Inside of the Crystal Palace at the Great Exhibition

Thomas Cubitt

William Cubitt

King's Cross station designed by Lewis Cubitt

Polesden Lacey, Surrey, built by Thomas Cubitt

force in establishing what has been called 'the first modern building firm.' In order to keep his workers employed he bought land in north London, where he built houses in Highbury and elsewhere. He also helped to develop parts of Bloomsbury, notably Tavistock Square, Woburn Place, and Gordon Square (including the present Courtauld House in Bying Place). But Cubitt's fame and fortune were made by his development of Belgravia (Belgrave Square and Eaton Square), Pimlico, Clapham Park, and Brighton (Kemp Town). In these places he built large stuccoed mansions with imposing porticos. They were designed by his architects, among them George Basevi (qv), John Young, Thomas Cundy, and Cubitt's brother Lewis, the only one of the brothers to have received any architectural training. Thomas Cubitt was also a guarantor of the Great Exhibition of 1851, and a leading authority on the problems of London sewage disposal and the provision of parks.

By a nineteenth-century merger the family firm became Holland & Hannen & Cubitts, and has continued to change the face of London during this century. It built the County Hall, the Senate House of London University, the Royal Festival Hall, and New Zealand House, and took a leading part in the Hyde Park improvement scheme.

Cubitt, Sir William (1785–1861). British civil engineer, a contemporary of Thomas, William and Lewis Cubitt, and also from Norfolk, but not related to them. His works include the Oxford canal, waterworks at Berlin, docks in South Wales and Middlesborough, and a sluice at Boston. He was also chief engineer for the South Eastern Railway.

Cup (Old English *cuppe*, late Latin *cuppa*). The word cup was for centuries a general term for a drinking vessel, until recently, embracing glasses, tankards, chalices, mugs, and drinking bowls.

Endsleigh Place, St Pancras, built by Thomas Cubitt

The basic shapes of cups made today were probably all in use during the Bronze Age. Bronze Age trumpet shapes, hour-glass shapes, bowls on a high stem, two-handled cups, one-handled cups, beakers and cups shaped like eighteenth-century coffee cups have all been excavated.

Though modern cup shapes are only refinements of these early shapes, a great many extremely fanciful cups have been made over the intervening centuries. The Saxons had a glass 'tumbler' with a rounded base, which could not be set down until it was empty. The fifteenth and sixteenth centuries were particularly inventive: there were ostrich eggs and coconuts elaborately mounted in silver; horns – either actual horns, mounted, or horn shapes; silver animals with removable heads; globes, terrestrial or celestial, the top of which formed the lid of the cup; carved wooden peasants carrying a grape-basket (the cup) on their backs; the 'yard of ale', a long glass tube shaped like a coaching horn; leather flagons called blackjacks, and leather cups shaped like a woman's shoe. In the seventeenth and eighteenth centuries, pottery was the material for several idiosyncratic cups; tygs (mugs with several handles), puzzle jugs (with several spouts, only one of which

reached the liquid); fuddling cups (several cups which were interconnected, so that one could not be emptied without all the others); cuckold cups (with a picture of a man with horns, holding a cup); loving-cups; and frog mugs (with a frog modelled in the bottom). The Victorians had their moustache cups, which had a china screen across them.

The modern, narrow sense of the term cup dates from the end of the seventeenth century, and coincides with the rise of the tea- and coffee-drinking habit. By the middle of the eighteenth century, inspired by the cups without handles imported from

The Richmond Cup, 1777

Leeds pottery loving-cup, c *1777*

China, English porcelain factories produced a great variety of imitations. There were soon cups being made with handles for greater convenience; Worcester produced cups with handles by 1775.

In general, modern, poor-quality teacups are straight-sided, whereas better-quality ones curve outwards; coffee cups are seldom rounded. But there are exceptions. Teacups and coffee cups can be plain or patterned, decorated by the silk-screen method or lithographic transfer or hand-painted. Sometimes the design is traditional, featuring, eg flowers; sometimes it is 'contemporary' and abstract.

Fine bone china is no longer necessarily preferred at tea and coffee tables; a reaction against 'refinement' has given coarser earthenware and stoneware something of a vogue.

Rough pottery is even more frequently found on the breakfast table; large breakfast cups, while not new, have become very popular in the last few years. And hard-wearing, easy-to-stack plastic cups, which have proved themselves in the kitchen, are now reaching the dining-room too.

American designs largely followed English styles, though some independent designs such as the mid-eighteenth-century Bennington hound-handled pitchers emerged. The handles for these were elongated hounds with their front paws upon the upper rim.

Modern Wedgwood cup

A late Elizabethan food cupboard in fruitwood

Cupboard. In the Middle Ages this term meant a shelf for the display of cups and other objects. It was literally a board for cups, and was the chief piece of display furniture. From the sixteenth century the term became confused with the aumbry, a piece of furniture with doors that was used chiefly for storage; and gradually the word cupboard took on its present meaning.

Various types of cupboard evolved separately. The only one to which the medieval meaning of the word is still appropriate is the court cupboard, a piece of furniture consisting of three thick shelves supported on columns. Food cupboards of the fifteenth to seventeenth centuries had railed doors and fronts, with patterns pierced in the wood for ventilation. The Victorian larder is a food cupboard at its largest: often it was a whole room. But now that living- and storage-space has contracted and packaged foods are popular, cupboards for fresh food are smaller: the larder has been replaced by the refrigerator. Cupboards for kitchen equipment are more compact; dressers have been replaced by adaptable kitchen units. America led the way in this, and today modern kitchen planning and cupboard units have become international.

Clothes cupboards changed with fashions in furniture design, the substantial late medieval and Tudor wardrobes and presses gave way to built-in cupboards. But massive hanging cupboards became popular again in the nineteenth century.

Modern hanging cupboards have many new refinements: adjustable shelves, shoe rails, and hat shelves, mirrors on an inner door, a light which goes on as the cupboard opens. But demand for free-standing clothes cupboards is diminishing. Built-in wardrobes are more convenient, as their present-day popularity proves.

The common sixteenth- and seventeenth-century oak cupboard with a recessed upper tier, a projecting canopy, columns, and a series of small doors was an essential item in all households for 400 years, though early examples are seldom found today.

Modern units for the living-room generally consist of open shelves and enclosed storage-space adaptable to individual needs. Sometimes an insulated drinks cupboard is included.

Cupola (Italian). A dome-shaped structure set upon a roof, acting either as a lantern for letting light into the interior or as a decorative element. In the latter case it is introduced to give interest and movement to an elevation or to provide a vertical emphasis to counteract an over-long horizontal elevation.

Curricle chair. In his *Cabinet Dictionary* of 1803, Sheraton gave this name to an upholstered chair with a tub-shaped back.

Currier and Ives. What Ackermann prints are to the British collector and interior decorator, the lithographs of Nathaniel Currier (1813–88) and James Merritt Ives (1824–95) are to the American. Currier of Roxbury, Massachusetts, was apprenticed to a lithographer and then started up on his own, first in Philadelphia, then in New York. In 1835 there was a big fire in New York and four days later Currier brought out a lithograph called 'Ruins of the Merchant's Exchange' which sold in large numbers. A few years later the steamship *Lexington* burned in Long Island Sound, and Currier produced a lithograph and report within three days. In the days before newspaper photographs, such a service was hugely popular. Ives was an artist whom Currier employed as a book-keeper and then made a partner.

For many years Currier & Ives turned out best-selling lithographs of topical events, disasters, deathbeds, Wild West

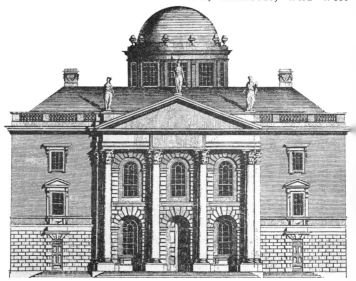

Cupola on the Theatre in Trinity College, Dublin, by Chambers

A Currier and Ives print of a fire at Pittsburgh on April 10th, 1845

Typically ornate, fringed and draped curtains, early 19th century

Plain light floor-to-ceiling curtains in a modern room

scenes, Biblical scenes, and so on. It was newspaper photography which eclipsed these prints, but they have always remained collectors' items and decorate countless American homes.

Curtain. Curtains as we know them today, used mainly for windows, date from the eighteenth century, when printed calicoes and chintzes became common. Previously, curtains had also served as partitions, wall decorations, and aids to the retention of heat – even as substitutes for window glass. The rich used curtains of tapestry, called arras, until Stuart times, after which they became wall decorations. Simpler homes were lined with stained linen and other stuffs. Such painted curtains were called counterfeit arras, but few examples have survived.

Old curtains still in use or in collections are seldom of earlier date than the late seventeenth century, when crewel-work (qv) and Indian cottons, and heavy silk damask became popular.

Eighteenth-century curtains were made in a large variety of materials. Rooms from 1780 were often completely festooned, a practice which lasted well into Victorian times.

With modern heating, larger windows and simpler living, heavy drapery and swagged pelmets have gone out of fashion. The simple pleated heading, long used by the French, and the extended curtain, which at night becomes virtually a draped wall, are very much *de rigueur* in modern interiors. Developments in nylon, Terylene and sheer nets and marquisettes have made light, sheer curtains a practical possibility. But even with these new materials, the cotton muslin curtain, offspring of the Victorian lace curtain, has never lost its appeal. As nets can be woven to a width of 80 ft or so, the possibilities for the designer are infinite. For the architect and decorator, nets and muslins, and other sheer curtains, are even more promising than the solid curtain or drapery.

Curtain wall. The large windows between piers of Gothic cathedrals, and the paper and wood walls of Japanese architecture, represent what might be termed early forms of the curtain wall. Yet it was the development of a window wall, eg at Paxton's Crystal Palace (1851; qv), that demonstrated the need for a structural unit that would provide maximum light within a form that served the functional requirements of a wall. Between the two World Wars the idea was realized by the employment of grids as structural frames, which provided a wall unit that was both aesthetically satisfying and functional. Theories about curtain walls were developed at the Bauhaus, and the projected design by Gropius and Meyer for the *Chicago Tribune* competition of 1922 was typical. Since 1947 the curtain wall has been internationally employed to such an extent that, although it is a constantly evolving structural form, some architects regard it as a cliché, a useful means to a technical end, but one which allows of little originality.

Curtain box at Harewood House, designed by Robert Adam

Curtain wall

Needlepoint and patchwork cushions

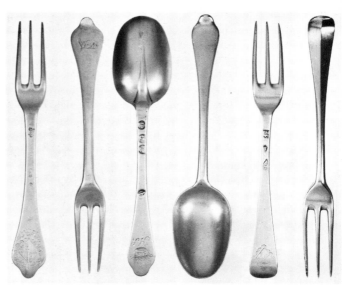

Forks and rat-tailed spoons, Queen Anne and, on the right, George I

Silver knife and fork from the early nineteenth century

Curule (Latin, *currus* 'chariot'). A chair or stool based upon the ancient Roman stools that were used by the higher magistrates. These stools could be folded up like camp-stools and were probably placed in the magistrates' chariots. They had distinctive curving legs, were without backs, and were inlaid with ivory. The design of the curving legs was used again in medieval Italy, although it did not become widely popular until the late eighteenth-century classical revival when it was taken up by chairmakers in France, Britain, and America.

Cushion. There can be little doubt that the cushion, in its crudest form, dates from early Neolithic times. It was already an important item of household property by the dynastic Egyptian era. Hardly anything remains of early examples and few surviving cushions are of earlier date than the sixteenth century, when they were stuffed with wool. A profusion of cushions was used then, on chairs, stools, benches, and on the floor, and they were an important item in the somewhat limited list of domestic possessions. The covers of Tudor cushions were in needlework, leather, fabric (such as damask), or tapestry.

Needlework, done by the ladies of the household, was probably the commonest form of cushion cover from the sixteenth to the eighteenth centuries, and many examples are found today framed as pictures. Beads were used in Victorian times, and throughout that period woven fabrics, matching the curtains and room hangings, were used in the houses of the great.

The modern cushion differs little from its predecessors. Two striking innovations have been the exceptional depth of down stuffing first used in eighteenth-century France, and the contemporary use of foam rubber. The odd cushion which can be used wherever a softener or prop is needed is much less common today than cushions made to fit a particular chair or sofa. Cushioning thus conforms to the twentieth-century trend of built-in furniture.

Cushion capital. A Romanesque capital, of approximately cubical form, in which the lower corners are rounded off and tapered to fit the shaft. Sometimes the flat areas are carved.

Cusp (Latin, *cuspis* 'spear'). Cusps are the projecting points which form the featherings or foliations in Gothic tracery, arches, and panels, and which add to the richness of the pattern of the Early English style. When first introduced, the cusp was independent of the arch or window mouldings, but it later became more ornamented and an integral part of the moulding, often terminating in a splayed leaf or trefoil motif.

Cut-card work. See **Silver, decorative techniques.**

Cutlery. Properly speaking this term describes the whole range of cutting instruments. Today, however, it is used in Britain to describe table implements such as spoons and forks as well as table knives; in America these are known as tableware. The first knives were made of flint and obsidian, which were replaced over a long period of time by bronze, iron, and finally steel. In England, cutlery has been made chiefly at Sheffield since it began to be manufactured, and Sheffield cutlery is still world-famous. Chaucer wrote of the miller of Trumpington, 'a Sheffield thwitel (knife) baar he in his hose.'

Until early Victorian times, only the fairly prosperous used implements solely for eating. Forks, little known until *c* 1700, were made with three prongs until about 1760, after which the four-prong design became the norm. Knives had curved (rats-tail) handles until the Neo-classical movement of the late

Cusps on an aisle compartment

Modern silver cutlery with stainless steel blades

Amalienburg Pavilion at Nymphenburg by Cuvilliés, 1734–9

Satinwood bureau with a cylinder fall, c *1780*

eighteenth century made clean, straight lines fashionable in design. Jacobean spoons were rounded, eighteenth-century ones longer and slimmer; after 1780, the ends of handles turned downwards instead of upwards. Although the finest English table cutlery was gold and silver, much was made in cheap metals, often plated with silver or sometimes gold. Handles were of metal, wood, bone, ivory, or mother-of-pearl. Also made, especially in France, were beautiful porcelain handles in coloured soft pastes from such factories as St Cloud and Chantilly. Bow and Chelsea

in England also produced such pieces.

Heavily adorned implements are rarely produced now; modern cutlery has become increasingly simple, sometimes slender, sometimes almost stubby. Stainless steel has become widely popular through the achievements of Scandinavian design. Georg Jensen, for instance, began working in stainless steel in Denmark at the beginning of World War II when supplies of silver were uncertain; now cutlery of both types is produced. Silver still has great prestige value, but stainless steel has the great advantage that it

does not require cleaning.

Tea knives and forks with decorative porcelain handles are still made, but no longer in large quantities. Wooden handles are still produced, but bone and ivory ones are being replaced by plastic.

Cuvilliés, François de (1698–1768). Flemish architect. Cuvilliés's early career was bizarre, for at the age of 11 he was recruited as court dwarf to Max Emanuel of Bavaria, then Stadtholder in the Netherlands. In his early twenties he was transferred to an orthodox architectural apprenticeship under Effner, the famous Munich architect, and then trained for five years under Blondel in Paris. On his return to Munich he was appointed court architect, an office he shared with Effner.

Cuvilliés's work mainly consisted of decorating the interiors of existing palaces and designing small pleasure houses. The supreme example of the latter is the Amalienberg Pavilion (1734–9) in the Nymphenburg complex. This is an elegant, single-storey building with light and restrained Rococo ornament and a rich profusion of decoration within. Cuvilliés's other major work was the charming little Residenztheater in Munich

(1751–3), which was handsomely restored in 1958.

Cylinder fall. A desk fall front shaped like a quarter of a circle when seen from the side; late eighteenth century.

Cyma (Greek). A double curve or undulating moulding which occurs in two forms: cyma recta, which is hollow in the upper part, convex in the lower; and cyma reversal, also called the ogee curve, which is hollow in the lower part and round in the upper.

Cymatium. The crowning or capping moulding of the upper part of a cornice. The term is also used of the moulding between the corona and cyma (qqv) of a cornice.

Cypress. *Cupressus semperviviens.* The longlasting and distinctive aroma of this Mediterranean wood made it a particular favourite of the ancients. The mummy cases of the Egyptians, the receptacles of the Greeks and Romans, and the chests of Tudor England were all made of cypress wood. The scented cypress, an effective moth repellent, has always been a particular favourite for clothes chests.

The Residenztheater in Munich by Cuvilliés, 1751–3, restored 1958

Dado. A term first used of the solid block or cube forming the pedestal in classical architecture. It is now more generally applied to the lower part of a wall, usually to a height of between 2 and 3 ft above the floor. The dado is usually defined by a continuous moulding, and the dado's height has become standardized to the height of a chair back; hence in domestic architecture and interior design it is often referred to as the chair rail.

Dais. The term used today to describe a raised platform on which the principals at a meeting are seated, or the high table at dinner. In medieval times it was the raised platform on which the family table was placed. The high table at a feast was itself called the dais till the seventeenth century, and the term has also been used since Victorian times for the canopy over a throne.

Damascening or **damaskeening.** An inlay of steel and bronze surfaces with gold or silver wires, usually in arabesque forms. It takes its name from Damascus, where it was invented.

Damask. A figured silk, linen, or woollen material; the name is taken from Damascus in Syria, where silk damask was made in the twelfth century. The patterns on damask are part of the weave and are self-coloured.

Damask was popular for upholstery and curtain hangings from the Middle Ages. Until late in the seventeenth century it was made chiefly in Italy, but before the end of the century it was coming from Spitalfields and other English centres, where it was often called 'of French make' on account of the popularity of Continental fabrics. In his ac-

Guy's Hospital (above) and Newgate Prison, now demolished, (below), both designed by George Dance, the Younger

George Dance, the Younger

count for October 1772, Chippendale charged Sir Edward Knatchbull of Mersham Hatch £52 for 150 yds of blue damask; and similar accounts are found in English houses from the 1660s.

Damask is still used for tablecloths, napkins, and curtains, and although the same weaving principle has often been used to produce cheap imitations, beautiful pure silk, linen, or woollen damask curtain fabrics are being made in Italy, France, and in England.

Dance, George (c 1700–68). English architect. The son of a mason, and himself a stone-cutter who, in the eighteenth-century tradition, graduated to architecture. By 1735 he was appointed to the clerkship of the City works, which guaranteed its holder a considerable influence on building operations in the City. Indeed, because of his position his designs for the Mansion House were accepted in preference to designs by

Danish Architecture. *Osterlars church on the island of Bornholm, built at the end of the eleventh century*

The Mansion House, London, designed by George Dance, the Elder

Gibbs, Leoni, and others. He relinquished his clerkship in favour of his fifth and youngest son George **Dance**, the younger (1741–1825), also an architect. Thanks to his father's success he was able to travel and study in Italy, and afterwards succeeded his father as clerk of the works. As such he was responsible for designing the remarkable, monumental, and forbidding Newgate Prison (demolished in 1902). He also designed All Hallows Church in London Wall and St Luke's Hospital in Old Street, which is now the Bank of England printing works.

As a town planner, Dance was far in advance of his time, and was responsible for projects for the Port of London which came to nothing, and for the layout of much of the Minories district and of Finsbury Square. He was also an artist and draughtsman of considerable merit. He left a number of drawings for various projects, now mostly in the Soane Museum, London, and portraits of his contemporaries, now in the British Museum. Sir John Soane was among his pupils.

Danish architecture and design. Early influences in historical times came from the more advanced societies in the South. The Romanesque style appears in Viborg Cathedral and in the church at Kalundborg, and the Renaissance (via the Low Countries) in a number of late sixteenth- and early seventeenth-century noble palaces such as those at Rosenborg and Frederiksborg. Later, Baroque and Rococo influences were felt as in Charlottenborg and the Amalienborg palaces.

However, it is twentieth-century Danish design that has given Denmark such an important place in the history of architecture. No other country of comparable size has made so significant a contribution to the modern movement. Owing to the comparative scarcity of timber in Denmark, its architecture and design owe less to a long tradition of working in wood than those of other Scandinavian countries. This scarcity led Danish designers to experiment boldly with metals and ceramics. Their work is now known and commissioned throughout the world. The houses designed by Gunnar Jensen, Finn Monies, Berge Glahn, Ole Helweg, Sørensen, Udsen, Palle Jacobsen, Jørgen Bo, and others, have received wide acclaim, while furniture and household equipment designed by Arne Jacobsen, Poul Kjaerholm, Torsten Johansson, Erik Herløw, Thormond Olesen, Hans Wegner, and Finn Juhl are major Danish exports. These designs have been marketed by unusually enterprising and imaginative furniture manufacturers such as C W F France Fritz Hansens, and manufacturers of cutlery and kitchen ware such as Dansk Designs and Georg Jensen.

Cathedral of Viborg, Mid-Jutland, founded in 1130, rebuilt 1862–76

Kronborg Castle at Elsinore, built in the sixteenth century

Painted Danish furniture, early nineteenth century

A family house in Denmark designed by Professor Arne Jacobsen

Vases designed by Per Lütken

Modern Danish interior with furniture by Borge Mogensen

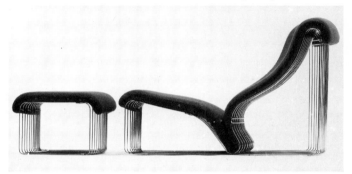

Chair and footstool designed by Verner Panton

Dannatt, Trevor (*b* 1920). British architect and industrial designer. He was educated at the Polytechnic School of Architecture. After early experience in Maxwell Fry's office and with the London County Council, he started his own practice in 1952 designing houses in Hampstead and Cambridge, and the Blackheath Congregational Church.

Dannatt was associate architect with Sir Leslie Martin for various university projects (Leicester, London). His work includes houses, showrooms, welfare homes, exhibitions, and further work at Leicester University and Bootham School Hall, York (RIBA Award). He won an international architectural competition in 1967 for a conference centre and hotel in Riyadh, Saudi Arabia.

Davenport. A small desk with a sloping top on a case of drawers. It first appeared at the end of the eighteenth century. The name probably derives from an entry in the Gillow records. 'Captain Davenport, a desk.' Most known examples are in mahogany or rosewood, and the davenport shown in the illustration is typical of those made at the beginning of the Victorian era. The sloping and hinged top encloses a well and small drawers; at the back is a drawer which pulls out to the right-hand side, fitted for writing implements.

'Artichoke' ceiling light, designed by Poul Henningsen

Hall at Bootham School, York, designed by Trevor Dannatt

Early Victorian davenport

The whole top slides forward for the writer's convenience and there are drawers and cupboards below at each side. It is an unusually useful desk for small modern rooms and, as such, is in increasing demand. The term davenport is also used in America for a sofa.

Davis, Alexander Jackson (1803–92). New York-trained American architect. In 1828 Davis became the partner of the Neo-classical architect Ithiel Town, who was nineteen years his senior. With Town, Davis built a series of Greek public buildings in the early 1830s, that included state capitols for Connecticut (1827–31), Indiana (1831–5), and North Carolina (1833), and a sub-treasury (1833) and customs house (1835) for New York.

From the mid-1830s, however, the picturesque potential of the Hudson valley, which it was then fashionable to compare with the Rhine, was just being realized; and for his richer private clients, Davis provided the micro-castle (Sunnyside, Washington, 1836, 'as full of angles as an old cocked hat') or the macro-castle (Lynd-hurst, 1838, for a former mayor

of New York City). He also built a series of Gothic academic institutions, beginning with New York University (1837). His smaller houses were in accord with the ideas of A J Downing (qv), and in 1851 the two collaborated to develop a picturesque residential estate for Llewellyn Haskell at West Orange, New Jersey.

Day, Lucienne (b 1917). British industrial designer. The wife of Robin Day (qv). She was born in Surrey, and after studying at the Royal College of Art, taught at Beckenham Art School. She began private practice in 1948 and quickly established a reputation as a textile designer, her first design (for Heal's, for whom she still works) being produced in 1950. Mrs Day has since designed china for Rosenthal Porzellan AG, wallpapers for German, Norwegian, and British firms, wall-coverings, carpets, and table linen, as well as various special furnishing fabrics for architectural schemes. She has won many international awards, including the Gran Premio at the Milan Triennale (for textiles).

Day, Robin (b 1915). British furniture and industrial designer. He was born at High Wycombe and, after working in local furniture factories, studied at the Royal College of Art. In 1949 he won the first prize (with Clive Latimer) in the New York Museum of Modern Art's international furniture design competition. He won gold medals at the Milan Triennales of 1951 and 1954, and various other awards. He has designed furniture for many important modern buildings, and has done pioneer work in injection-moulded plastic chairs which have had worldwide success.

Day-bed. A form of couch or sofa intended for sleep during the day and used in the principal rooms of houses since the Middle Ages. Edward IV prepared a room in Windsor Castle for the governor of Holland which contained 'a couch with feather beds, hanged about like a tent, knit like a net.' Few early day-beds were as elaborate as this, and usually consisted of a rectangular stuffed pallet or mattress supported on a frame of four or more legs and with a sloping headboard. This form was common throughout Elizabethan and Stuart times, and fine Stuart examples with carved frames still exist.

Seventeenth- and early eighteenth-century day-beds had long seats and sloping backs; both were usually caned and fitted with cushions or upholstered. These gave way to designs usually described as couches (qv).

Twentieth-century day-beds are less emphatically chairs for reclining upon during the day. Foam-filled upholstery and modern springing has increased their versatility. Now the day-bed is generally a dual- or treble-purpose piece of furniture, used as a sofa or an extra bed for the night.

Deal (Danish, *deel* 'plank'). A word which can be used for both a type of wood and a measurement. As a measurement it refers to a piece of square-sawn softwood generally 2 to 4 in thick, 9 to 11 in wide, and at least 8 ft long. It was used in connection with softwoods, especially fir and pine. The modern use of the word includes these woods regardless of measurement, and there can be red, yellow and white deal according to the colour of the wood.

Deal was used for German

Coffee set by Lucienne Day

Chairs by Robin Day for Hille

New York University, Washington Square, designed by A J Davis, 1837

Walnut day-bed dating from 1660–80

Irish decanter made about 1810

furniture from the sixteenth to the eighteenth century and as a carcase for veneers in all European countries during the same period, though it was not as satisfactory as the more expensive oak.

Today it is used for all types of constructional purposes – doors, roofs, and so on – as well as for shelves, packing cases, and furniture. It is also popular for laminated timbers.

From an economic point of view, deal is probably the most important of all woods. In fact, it is so popular that the world is threatened with a softwood famine.

Decanter. A stoppered glass bottle from which wines, cordials, and spirits are poured into drinking glasses. Decanters served two purposes. One (decanting) was to

remove the last of the natural sediment before wine was poured into a glass, the other was to display the drink on the table.

Decanters were developed from the wine jug or carafe at the end of the seventeenth century and are referred to in the 1680s. A few have survived: they are usually heavy, of very elegant proportions, and shaped like an onion. Other variations were cruciform and octagonal.

From 1750 the long-necked, mallet-shaped decanter came into fashion, often engraved with the name of the contents on a simulated label. A little later, slim shapes were preferred with the result that the late eighteenth-century type was tapering. The neck ring which appeared on wine bottles to secure the cork with wire now became a grip for the neck of a decanter. As many as five rings were applied, and in a few cases these are serpentine. The end of the eighteenth century saw the end of good glass-blower's shapes.

Decanters in thick glass were again produced in the nineteenth century, but now they were elaborately cut. The bodies were gadrooned or cut in diamond, lozenge, and trellis designs which greatly enhanced the sparkling look of the wine. Some are highly attractive, others unpleasantly over-adorned. Then an onion shape which had none of the elegance of its prototypes returned to fashion

Decastyle (Italian *decastilo*). A portico supported by ten columns along the front.

Deck-chair by Ernest Race

Deck-chair. A collapsible form of chair used on shipboard, at resorts, and in parks and gardens. Over the years it has acquired a conventional form – wooden side members with an adjustable slung canvas seat and back-rest.

A similar type of chair is the campaign or desert chair, in tubular metal and canvas. This was developed from Italian wartime experiments, and became fashionable in post-war interiors.

The Lady Chapel at Ely Cathedral, Cambridgeshire

The tomb of Queen Eleanor in Decorated style, in Westminster Abbey

Decorated style. Also known as the Middle Pointed or Mid-Gothic style. This is considered by many authorities the most accomplished and fully realized phase of Gothic architecture.

The Decorated style began about 1275 and lasted until 1375, though it was still occasionally employed at the end of the fourteenth century. Its main distinguishing characteristic is the form of decoration used in windows and, to a lesser degree, doorways. Windows, even in domestic architecture, became far more decorative, and ornament became an integral element in the construction. It was mainly based upon circles and quatrefoils and other geometric motifs, and was never angular but always cursive in feeling.

The same features and motifs are to be seen in doorways, in which the decorative effect is heightened by the frequently attenuated and enriched Gothic weather-mouldings or drip-stones, used above the heads of doorways and niches.

Mouldings in the Decorated

style are also complex in structure. Their effect is based upon a subtle and intricate play of light and shade, achieved by the juxtaposition of concave and convex mouldings, which are frequently separated by narrow fillets of contrasting section.

King's Cloister, Windsor

Modern decanter

A silver inkstand made by Paul de Lamerie in 1733

Gatehouse of Château d'Anet by Philibert de l'Orme, 1552–9

De Lamerie, Paul (1688–1751). The greatest English silversmith. His working life – some 40 years – coincided with the efflorescence of English Rococo silver design, and his work is its highest expression. In 1712 he was admitted a freeman of the Goldsmiths' Company, for whom he supplied several orders; in 1717 he was admitted to the Livery, and in 1742 he was elected second warden. He was held in great esteem by his contemporaries, and only his death in 1751 prevented him attaining the highest distinctions open to a man in his profession.

De Lamerie was a second-generation immigrant of the French Huguenot stock which supplied England with so many superb silversmiths, and although he never visited France his work

displays marked French characteristics. He took to the Rococo style easily, but his work in a more restrained vein was equally happy. Despite the variety of his designs they are always highly inventive and the workmanship is always of the highest standard; a superb example is the silver dolphin-mounted chandelier which he made for the Fishmongers' Company. He was a prolific worker and the wide range of his wares is illustrated by a list of his stock, auctioned at his death by a Mr Langford. The notice in the *Advertiser* includes: 'Tables, Terreens (sic) and Covers, Breadbaskets, Sauceboats, Tea-Kettles, Canisters, Coffee-pots . . .'

The Sale also included his designs and tools and his 'Valuable Collection of Prints.'

Delft. A town in Holland near Rotterdam, famous for its tin-enamelled earthenware. The Dutch East India Company was responsible for bringing porcelain from the Far East to Europe. The demand for it became so great that the Dutch began to copy it, in earthenware with a tin glaze, imitating very skilfully the Eastern styles and colouring.

The English soon began to copy the Dutch ware, which in England became known as Delft. It was made from the late sixteenth century until the end of the eighteenth. English Delft was made in London, Bristol, and Liverpool, and in the eighteenth century, Delft ware was also made in Glasgow and in Ireland.

Large and handsome chargers were produced, frequently decorated with freehand paintings of royalty as well as with formalized representations of fruit and

Blue and white modern Delft jar

flowers. Many useful objects were also made, such as wine bottles, posset pots, and candleholders. Delft was extremely decorative in a rough sort of way, and though much of the blue and white ware is monotonous, polychrome Delft possesses great charm. The additional colours were a clear yellow, a brick red, green, and purple.

De l'Orme, Philibert (c 1510–70). French architect and architectural writer, born in Lyon. De l'Orme was the son of a master mason, under whom he received his early training. He went to Rome in 1533 and studied there for a further three years. On his return to Lyon he attached himself to Cardinal Bellay, with whom he went to Paris, and for whom he began the Château St Maurles-Fosses.

In 1547 he designed the tomb of Francis I in St Denis, and the following year was given charge of the Château of Fontainebleau, an appointment he held until 1559, when Catherine de Medici replaced him by Primaticcio.

His works include extensions to the Tuileries Palace, Paris (1565, now destroyed); the Château of Anet built (1552–9)

for Diane de Poitiers; and extensions to Chenonceaux (1557) in the Loire valley. At Anet the chapel and entrance are still standing, and part is now incorporated into the Ecole de Beaux-Arts in Paris. At Chenonceaux, de l'Orme designed the bridge over the river Cher, which does much to make the château one of the loveliest in France. He also published *Nouvelles Inventions* (1561) and *Architecture* (1567).

Demi-column. An attached column, half of which is sunk into the wall.

De Morgan, William French (1839–1917). British novelist, artist-potter, and friend of William Morris. Before becoming interested in pottery, William de Morgan worked for some years in stained glass (1864–9). He began making pottery at 40 Fitzroy Square, London, and his first work was strongly influenced by Persian and Syrian pottery of the sixteenth and seventeenth centuries.

Later he moved to Chelsea, and it was there that he rediscovered the secret of reduced lustre decoration. He made many

Coloured tiles by William de Morgan

cream-coloured chargers and vases decorated boldly with red lustre in heraldic-looking designs incorporating animals and birds. Later he built a studio at Merton Abbey, where he worked from 1882–8. Then for the next ten years he ran the Sands End Pottery at Fulham with the architect Halsey Ricardo.

As well as his chargers and vases, de Morgan designed a great many ceramic tiles, which were produced in quantity at the Sands End Pottery. Many of these were in the blue and green Persian colourings that he admired so much, and were boldly drawn in 'pine-cone' or Paisley patterns; others were much like the textile designs of William Morris.

Three of de Morgan's best-known decorators at the Sands End Pottery were Joe Juster and Charles and Fred ' Passenger, whose initials can often be seen on the bases of de Morgan pottery. In Lichfield Cathedral a chapel is decorated with de Morgan tiles, and his work is in many public and private collections.

Denby pottery. In 1809 a pottery was started at this village in Derbyshire by a potter called Jager. In 1812 it came into the possession of Joseph Bourne, whose descendants have continued the business down to the present day. The early products of the factory were salt-glazed stoneware hunting jugs and Reform spirit flasks, as well as stoneware for domestic use.

Marks included BELPER AND DENBY, BOURNE POTTERIES, and BOURNE AND SON.

Today the firm specializes in well-designed fireproof kitchen ware: casseroles and dishes, tea and coffee pots, and so on. These are strong and simple in shape and colouring, and harmonize with the cottage atmosphere now so popular in the kitchen. The most popular colour-scheme is probably brown lined with pale blue, but there is also green

Modern Denby pottery

Arcaded oak chest by Thomas Dennis, Ipswich, Massachusetts, c 1675

lined with cream, and blue lined with a deeper cream.

Dennis, Thomas (*b* 1638). Dennis is considered the most important American furniture-maker of his time. He was born in England, and learned his trade there as a joiner and carver before emigrating to America. In 1663 he was working in Portsmouth, New Hampshire, and by 1688 in Ipswich, Massachusetts. His specialities were heavily carved wainscot chairs and chests with late Tudor and Jacobean ornamentation. Recent investigations suggest that many works attributed to him may, in fact, have been made by apprentices.

Dentils on a cornice

Dentil, dentel (Latin, *denticulus* 'a small tooth'). An ornamental device which when repeated was thought to resemble teeth. Dentil mouldings are seen in Ionic, Corinthian, and Composite cornices, and were much used for cornice mouldings in rooms and on chimney-pieces, doorcases etc.

Depressed arch. See **Drop arch.**

Derby porcelain. The factory at Derby in England produced ware from about 1750 to 1770. In 1770 William Duesbury, who was running it, bought the factory at Chelsea, and the two were amalgamated. The earliest Derby productions seem to have been cream jugs in the style of

the 'goat and bee' jugs of Chelsea, but other useful ware was made, as well as decorative figures (some quite large) copied from Meissen models. After the amalgamation with Chelsea the output consisted mainly of useful ware, but some figures continued to be made, still usually copies of Meissen originals.

A number of marks were used, the earliest being the word Derby incised, or a D with the date 1750 below it. Other marks used later, from 1760 to 1770, were a gold anchor with a crown above it, in blue, purple, or gold; or a crown with a mark rather like the crossed swords of Meissen below it, and with a D below that. The Chelsea-Derby marks (1770–84) were a D enclosing an anchor in red or gold, or alternatively an anchor with a D beside it.

The present Royal Crown Derby Porcelain Company was established in 1876, and still makes china with designs dating from that time and earlier. Perhaps the most popular designs today are oriental blue-and-white designs copied from eighteenth-century models, and hand-painted 'Imari' patterns reminiscent of Japanese textiles and brocades. Modern designs are also produced.

Derbyshire chair. A distinctive type of English chair, found in Derbyshire and Yorkshire during the seventeenth century. A side chair with an open back, it had a top and cross rail both decorated with a distinctive central hoop and carved decoration; alternatively it had an arcaded back consisting of two or three arches on turned balusters. The uprights were crowned with small scrolls, and turned decoration was applied along their length.

Derby group, c 1765

Design Centre. This centre for the permanent selective display of well-designed British goods was opened in the Haymarket, London, in 1956. It operates under the aegis of the Council of Industrial Design, which is an official body set up in 1944 'to promote by all practicable means the products of British industry.' The Centre, which was the first of its kind in the world, provides a constantly changing shop-window for modern design, and has done much to increase awareness of design quality in everyday things.

Desk. A piece of furniture for writing which has a flat or gently sloping top for the convenient support of books and writing materials. Medieval desks with steep sloping fronts developed from ecclesiastical lecterns and were common in university

Derbyshire chair, 17th century

Chippendale writing table, a forerunner of the modern office desk

Above, setting for George VI Memorial in Carlton Gardens and, below, houses in Welwyn Garden City by Louis de Soissons

colleges. Books were so scarce that they were often secured to the library desk by chains.

Apart from this lectern type of desk, a small, portable domestic desk was the only piece of furniture made expressly for writing from the Middle Ages to the late seventeenth century. After 1700 the functions of the desk were incorporated into several other pieces of furniture, notably the bureau, the kneehold writing table and the secrétaire. Small portable desks continued to be made and were often richly decorated and fitted inside with drawers and pigeon-holes. The sloping lids of eighteenth-century examples opened outwards to rest upon lopers and provide a flat writing surface.

From a conjunction of portable and lectern desks grew the sturdy type used by school-children. These, though usually found only from early Victorian times, have early sixteenth-century precursors such as oak desks carved with Gothic tracery and the small attractive walnut writing desks standing on slender cabriole legs, which were made for ladies at the beginning of the eighteenth century.

The term desk is now also used for the flat-topped type found in offices. Flat-topped desks are correctly called writing tables if they were made before

the twentieth century. But desks in the antique-dealer's sense of the word (ie with sloping fronts) are still being made for domestic use. Office desks are usually made of mahogany, walnut, oak, or elm (solid or veneer); and in the last few years a great deal of teak has been used. Heat- and spirit-resistant finishes are becoming more common, and the leather tops seen on antique writing tables have largely been replaced by leather-substitutes and Formica. Metal is usually present in some way in a modern desk: brass fittings, for instance, aluminium drawer handles, or a steel frame. And of course a wide variety of special fittings is available.

The demand for an 'office-in-the-home' desk is increasing. This kind of desk usually has a drop-ledge for writing and hinged doors which swing shut when work is over. The desk can then remain in the living-room as if it were a cupboard or cocktail cabinet. In general, scientific attention is being paid to the needs of the desk-user, and desk-design is progressing correspondingly.

De Soissons, Louis (1890–1962). Canadian architect, born in Montreal and educated at the Royal Academy Schools and Ecole des Beaux Arts, Paris. De

Soissons built up a large practice in domestic and industrial architecture, but he is chiefly known for his work at Welwyn Garden City, where he established a neo-Georgian manner in harmony with the existing landscape.

Despite many detractors amongst protagonists of the modern movement, the development of Welwyn has had many lessons for town planners in Britain and abroad. It has also had a profound if largely unrecognized influence on the planning of New Towns, particularly in its respect for landscape, its recognition of human scale and values, its well-planned town centre, and above all in its successful achievement of a sense of neighbourhood. De Soissons was also responsible for work for other authorities, including Plymouth, Dartmouth, Exmouth, and Teignmouth, and for Cheltenham College. One of his best-known works is the setting for the King George VI Memorial in Carlton Gardens, which can be seen by all travellers along the Mall in London.

De Stijl. Dutch art and design movement founded in 1917. Its leading practitioners included Piet Mondrian, Theo van Doesburg, J J P Oud, and Gerrit Rietveld.

De Stijl architecture and design derived from the Neo-plasticist painting of Mondrian and van Doesburg, which in turn owed much to Cubism. De Stijl architecture is characterized by right angles and cubic forms, smooth unmarked surfaces, and strong primary colours augmented by black, white, and grey.

The most celebrated De Stijl building was Rietveld's Schröder House in Utrecht (1924), on which he collaborated with interior decorator Schröder-Schrader. Oud's Café de Unie, Rotterdam (1924–5, destroyed 1940), was the other outstanding example. Many other architects drew heavily on De Stijl, and Dudok's villas at Allegonda, Katwijk, and de Vonk, Noordwijkerhout (where the interior was by Theo van Doesburg), are closely related to it. It was in

Modern desk designed by Robin Day

Schroeder House, Utrecht, designed by Gerrit Rietveld, 1924

many respects a precursor of functionalism and the International style.

Devlin, Stuart (*b* 1913). Australian gold and silver designer and sculptor. Born at Geelong in Australia, Devlin won the first of many scholarships to the Gooden Institute of Technology, when he was thirteen. He then embarked on silversmithing with a firm in Melbourne. In 1958 he left Australia to take up a scholarship at the Royal College of Art in London, where he studied light engineering and gold- and silversmithing. Between 1960 and 1965 he studied and lectured in America and Australia, where he won the competition for the new decimal coinage with designs of Australian wild animals.

In 1965 Devlin decided to set up his workshop in London, the traditional world centre of his

craft. The Worshipful Company of Goldsmiths had previously (1960) commissioned Devlin to make a large silver centrepiece to commemorate the tercentenary of the Royal Society. It now also has a number of Devlin's designs in its permanent collection in London. Devlin was made a Freeman of the Guild in 1966.

His work has included cutlery, brandy warmers, candelabra, ceremonial regalia, maces for universities, and, more recently, jewellery.

Besides the numerous awards that he has received, Devlin has exhibited with the Goldsmiths' Company in Europe and America.

De Wolfe, Elsie (Lady Mendl) (*c* 1870–1950). America's first woman decorator; she is credited with having invented the profession. In 1904, after a career in the theatre, she opened a decorating shop in New York which became an immediate success. Her first big commission was carried out a year later, when she designed the interiors of the newly founded Colony Club, the first women's club in New York. Her success in this project established her career. She later decorated one floor of Henry Frick's Fifth Avenue Mansion, now the Frick Museum. She acquired the Villa Trianon in Versailles and restored it to its former splendour. In the boom years after World War I she became an influential trendsetter. Venetian mirrors, zebra skins, white upholstery against coloured walls and vice versa, were her stock-in-trade. She married the British diplomat Sir Charles Mendl in 1926. The Elsie de Wolfe award is given to outstanding designers and decorators.

Silver candelabrum by Devlin

Dial. An external instrument face on which can be read revolutions, pressure, etc; especially the face of a clock or watch: whence the word can also mean a timepiece of any kind, such as a sundial.

The chief feature of any dial is its set of markings, which in the case of a clock or watch is the chapter ring or circle inscribed with the hours (chapters). European and American chapters were in Roman numerals.

Clock dials from the fifteenth to the seventeenth centuries were surprisingly alike. They were mostly in brass, though sometimes in iron and painted, and the chapter ring was engraved or picked out in black. The hands were simple in early clocks, but became more elaborate – often pierced and scrolled – in the seventeenth century. The remainder of the dial, usually square or round, was decorated by floral and figure engraving, though rare clocks had lavishly bejewelled dials.

The last major decorative feature of the dial was the spandrel piece. This engraved metal ornament framed the chapter ring at the four corners of square dials, and gave much decorative scope. In the earliest period (from 1690) a winged cherub and a crown supported by cherubs was common. These gave way successively to masks amongst flowers, arabesque scrollwork, Rococo foliage, dolphins, and figures symbolizing

the four seasons (1760–1800).

By 1700 it had become common to wind clocks through holes cut in the dial, and these remained usual until the early 1800s. Painted and enamel dials were common from 1700, while on brass-faced clocks the chapter ring was black on a silvered (or sometimes silver) ground. The enamel round the winding holes chipped easily; the Victorians protected them with slender metal frames.

With some notable exceptions such as the work of Breguet, nineteenth-century dials are neither beautiful nor legible, and tend to be poor imitations of eighteenth-century designs. Modern design of clock dials is, however, often of the highest quality.

The design of watch dials closely follows that of clocks. Watch dials were engraved, inlaid with gold and precious stones, and, in the eighteenth century, were often made of coloured enamels. Modern watch dials have returned to simple, pleasing, severe designs in which the numerals are sometimes replaced by marks.

Diaper, diapering, diaperwork. These terms are now usually applied to a diamond-shaped pattern on walls and other surfaces. In earlier times, however, the term 'diaperwork' was used of a pattern of squares composed of flowers that was carved or painted on to a plain

Brass dial of a sixteenth-century German table clock

131

Diaperwork in Lincoln Cathedral with detail, below

surface. This early diaperwork, which appears in the Early English and Perpendicular styles, supposedly derived from a type of cloth worked at Ypres in Belgium, whence d'Ypres, dyaper, diaper.

Diastyle. The arrangement of columns in classical architecture by which space between columns is three diameters of a single shaft. Not to be confused with distyle (qv).

Die. A term used in classical architecture to describe the part of the pedestal between the base-moulding and the cornice.

Dinanderie. A term rather loosely used to describe both medieval European brasswork and, by extension, brass from India and the Levant. The word derives from the French town of Dinant (formerly Dinand in Belgium), which was a centre for the production of brass kitchen utensils.

Brass candlestick, 13th century

Dining table. Dining tables used in medieval and Renaissance great halls were usually long enough to accommodate a large number of people. Until the fifteenth century they were trestle tables that could be dismantled after use, and even with the advent of fixed or 'joyned' tables the trestle type remained in use until the seventeenth century.

'Joyned' tables, ie those of a joined construction, are now known in antique dealers' jargon as refectory tables (qv). Many could be made longer with extra lengths of board that could be pulled out from underneath the top.

At the end of the seventeenth century, dining became a more private occasion, held in special rooms. The tables were proportionately smaller, usually of the round or oval gate-leg (qv) variety.

Most eighteenth-century examples have cabriole legs and a variety of extra sections, drop leaves, or additional rounded ends to increase the surface area.

Regency dining tables were of pillar and claw construction. Most of them were very elegant and are much sought after today.

During the Victorian era, the increasing use of Honduras mahogany, which is wider and stronger than the West Indian, so affected the size and design of

Dining-room in Inveraray Castle: Robert Morris, late 18th century

tables that a dining table became known as a mahogany. In the course of the nineteenth century, the reeded legs of most tables became increasingly bulbous and ornate.

Smaller families and lack of space have led to the production of smaller tables that are much lighter in structure. Most are still of wood, but metal stands with glass or perspex tops are gaining in popularity.

Diocletian window. A semi-circular window divided by vertical mullions into three lights. It was resurrected by Palladio and others, and was so named because of its use in the Baths of Diocletian at Rome. It became a characteristic feature of Palladianism.

Dipteral. The term used in classical architecture for a double peristyle or double row of columns set around a Greek temple or courtyard. Where the inner of these two rows is omitted the term 'pseudodipteral' is used.

Marble-topped dining table and chairs by Eero Saarinen

Small French Gothic ivory diptych of the fourteenth century

Divan in a modern bed-sitting-room

Diptych. Any folding object consisting of two leaves. It is commonly used to describe folding altar-pieces with two leaves, painted on both sides, and the pocket-sized ivory and wood tablets of the Middle Ages, many of which were superbly carved with religious subjects.

Directoire (1795–99). The government ('directory') of the French Republic, set up soon after the fall of Robespierre and lasting until the *coup d'état* by Napoleon Bonaparte. The Directoire style is conventionally dated to the last five years of the eighteenth century. Although the style is a distinct one, it is little more than a continuation of the last severe Louis XVI phase, *le style Etrusque*. The simple, Neo-classical furniture of the Directoire period was made by *ébénistes* whose businesses had survived the excesses of the Revolution, the death or exile of their principal patrons, and the cult of austere republican virtue.

Directoire furniture and *objets d'art* are extremely simple in form. The woods and metals are of inferior quality to those of previous decades, and though the results are still pleasing they do not reach the standard set in other periods.

The Directoire style gave way to Empire (qv).

Discharging arch. Also known as the relieving arch. The term is applied to an arch formed in a wall in order to relieve or discharge the weight of solid wall which would otherwise bear directly upon the wall or support below.

Dished seat. A concave wooden seat, slightly lower than the seat rail; the space is filled with a cushion.

Distemper. Water-thinned paint for house decoration. Distemper has been used for about 400 years. Strictly speaking, the term should be reserved for paints in which the binding medium is glue or a similar material. Paints of this type remain more or less soluble in water; they are more suitable for ceilings than walls, better for interior surfaces than exteriors.

Oil-bound distempers, in which the binding material is an emulsion of oil or varnish, are more correctly called water paints. These have been developed in the last 50 years. They are usually supplied in paste form and diluted; 1 cwt covers about 450 square yd. To a limited extent, they are washable and suitable for outdoor use.

Emulsion paint, developed still more recently, is different again: its binding medium is a dispersion of synthetic resin. It is completely washable; and the appropriate types can be used both indoors and out.

Distressed. Contemporary euphemism for a piece of furniture which has been made to look older than it is by artificial means. The word was once used by cabinetmakers to describe wood grain damaged in the cutting of veneer.

Distyle. A portico with two columns.

Divan (Persian, *devan* 'a customs house'). A word first used in English in 1586 but only recently used to describe a bed without head- or foot-board.

The Turkish council of state of 1586 was called the Divan, and by extension the word came to mean a council chamber. By 1702 it had become the term for a raised part of the room, often cushioned, for sitting. By 1848 it meant a smoking-room furnished with day-beds, and from this it came to be applied to the bed itself.

Because divans take up little space and can easily be disguised as day-beds, they are commonly found in bed-sitting-rooms.

Dodecastyle. A portico with twelve columns.

Dog-legged staircase. A common form of staircase in which there is no well between two parallel flights of stairs, wide-angled winders making the necessary turns at the half or quarter landing.

Dog-tooth. In architecture, a repeated ornamental motif used in the transitional period between

Mahogany Directoire furniture in a French bedroom

Directoire secrétaire à abattant

Dog-tooth moulding

An English doll's house made in 1760

the Norman and Early English styles. In its simpler form, from which the name comes, the dog-tooth device consisted of wedge-shaped or pyramidal carvings on arches, doorways, etc. The term was also applied to star-shaped or four-leafed ornamental devices carved within the simpler mouldings of arches.

Dogwood. *Cornus.* Often referred to as boxwood. The American dogwood is a pinkish wood occasionally employed for decorative work such as turnery and inlays. Dogwood was used in this way mainly during the sixteenth and seventeenth centuries. It is seldom if ever used today in America because of strict conservation laws to preserve the tree.

Dole or food cupboard. See **Cupboard.**

Regency dolphin furniture in the Royal Pavilion, Brighton

Doll's house. One of the earliest recorded dolls' houses was made for the daughter of the Duke of Bavaria in 1558. In the seventeenth century they became popular, though expensive, toys, and amazingly detailed examples were made in Germany, closely modelled on real houses. But the doll's house was most remarkable in seventeenth-century Holland; children had wonderfully accurate copies of their parents' houses, complete with replicas of the furniture. Examples are to be seen in the Rijksmuseum, at The Hague and at Utrecht.

Dolls' houses were made in Britain and America from the beginning of the eighteenth century, though few have survived with their contents intact. Between 1700 and 1750 several were designed by architects. The doll's house at Nostell Priory was designed by Robert Adam while he was building the house, and its furniture is by Chippendale. The fittings of the period are meticulously finished and every detail has been included. Dolls' houses of this calibre give us the best possible idea of the furnishing of a real eighteenth-century house.

The expense and quality of most early dolls' houses suggest that they were for the enjoyment of adults rather than children. Victorian dolls' houses, seldom so magnificent, were definitely nursery toys, and many have survived almost intact.

The doll's house is still popular in many modern nurseries. It may be gabled and 'traditional' or flat-roofed and 'contemporary' with furniture to match. A twentieth-century invention is the build-it-yourself doll's house which arrives in units which the child can assemble.

Dolphin. As a decorative motif, the dolphin has been commonly used by maritime nations since the Greco-Roman period. It was adopted by early Christian artists as a symbol of love (dolphins are capable of strong attachment to human beings) and continued to be popular in succeeding centuries, above all during the Italian Renaissance. It was used extensively in the early Georgian period and in eighteenth-century France. It was a favourite motif of Madame de Pompadour, for whom ormolu-workers made dolphin candlesticks and other objects.

The dolphin, in common with the ram, the eagle, the sphinx, and the lion became an important motif in Regency furniture and

Dolphin lamp-post

decoration. The dolphin device was most frequently incorporated into the legs of chairs and tables or the bases of cabinets and was usually carved and gilded. It was also produced in cast-iron for lamp-posts etc.

Dome. A curved ceiling or roof. The word derives from the Italian *duomo*, a cathedral, and presumably the frequency with which cathedrals in fact supported domes caused the word to become synonymous with dome in western Europe.

Radcliffe Camera: Gibbs, 1737–49

Onion dome: Nash, 1815

The dome of St Paul's Cathedral showing the internal structure

Although the outlines of domes vary enormously from bulbous (onion) to pointed, each rises from a circular base. The transition from a square or polygonal body to the circular base of the dome is effected by the use of pendentives and squinches (qqv), which fill the vacant corners, connecting the apexes of the arches into a continuous base. In the majority of cases a drum is erected on the base; this does not occur in the shallow saucer dome, which has a flat curve and rests directly on the body of the building. In order that the dome should be effective from both outside and inside, architects have had to design domes of dual construction, ie with two domes, one internal and the other external. St Peter's in Rome is one such example; St Paul's in London has a third, intermediary dome supporting the lantern.

The domes of the Pantheon in Rome (*c* AD 112) and Sta Sophia in Constantinople are undoubtedly the greatest surviving from Antiquity.

Domical vault. A dome placed directly upon a bay. It is not a dome proper but a semi-circular groined vault.

Donegal carpets. Hand-knotted carpets were first made in County Donegal in 1898, and four factories, Killybegs, Kilcar, Crolly, and Anagarry were founded. The raw materials came from England; dyeing and finishing were all done there. Carpets of this early period are seldom distinguished, and reflect the influence of William Morris. The colours are usually a watery blue-green, yellow, and beige. Although they cannot stand comparison with French and Spanish carpets of the same type, they are nevertheless decorative. The Killybegs factory survived into the 1950s when it experienced a revival, producing excellent modern hand-knotted carpets.

Door. In its simplest form, a planked, hinged screen made to protect an opening in the exterior of a building against inclement weather or unwelcome visitors. Interior doors, usually of lighter construction, were made to provide privacy.

Early doorways usually carried little decoration and even when church doorways had become highly ornamented, doors remained plain. In the Middle Ages doors were usually constructed by the wood-pegging (later iron-railing) together of two sets of planks, vertical outside, horizontal within. Some cottage doors are still made in this manner in remote rural areas of Europe.

Gradually more sophisticated and decorative use was made of door surfaces. Panelling was introduced in the sixteenth century, glazed panels in the seventeenth. With the increasing use of carpenters and joiners in the eighteenth century, the door was

Norman door and doorway at Southwell Minster

Panelled double door set into a looking-glass frame

A Donegal carpet with circular design and floral motifs

Modern door and screened porch by Ernö Goldfinger

treated in a manner similar to the elaborate panelling of the walls; in the decorative schemes of William Kent and Adam, external and internal doors were an integrated element in the decorative scheme. In Adam houses there are magnificently constructed, but essentially simple, panelled mahogany doors; their restrained decoration provides an effective contrast with the elaborately carved and painted doorcases.

In Victorian times the door became a weighty, dignified object, and the joinery was correspondingly heavy and ornate. Dark mahogany was the favoured wood.

The flush wooden door has become increasingly popular amongst modern architects and designers. In commercial buildings, factories, laboratories, schools, and exhibition halls, metal doors (often framing armour glass panels) have largely replaced the more elaborate doors of earlier times. The space-saving sliding door for closets, cupboards, and kitchen units is also widely used, especially in apartments.

Doorcase. The wooden framework which contains a hinged door. In Georgian times the doorcase was a feature of considerable importance in interior decoration, and skilled carvers as well as carpenters were employed in their construction. Pediments – triangular, broken, and segmental were placed over the doorcases of both rooms and exteriors.

Doorcase, eighteenth century

In modern times the doorcase is a much simpler feature. In many buildings it is not used at all, the doors being hung on the side walls of openings.

Door furniture. The metal mounts, locks, handles, knockers, and hinges on doors. Medieval iron-workers were highly skilled and the most primitive furniture often carried massive, elaborate hinges and locks of iron. Door hinges were long and were sometimes engraved. In the seventeenth century the double 'cock's head' hinge was popular, but in the eighteenth century it gave way to a shorter 'strap' hinge decorated in the contemporary manner. Victorian hinges were much smaller; they were usually sunk in the door frame, and eventually became entirely hidden.

Handles were made first in iron, later in steel, brass, and in the eighteenth and nineteenth centuries, gilt bronze, porcelain, or enamel. They were most commonly knob-shaped, but handles in the form of loops or acorns were made too. The modern lever-like handle is a nineteenth-century innovation, but it has never completely superseded the knob. Twentieth-century door-handles are generally made of metal, plastic, or china; designs range from the ornate reproduction style to the more austere lever type. Matching finger-plates were first made by the early Victorians; today they are still produced by manufacturers of door-knobs, though they have been more or less discarded by makers of lever handles.

Door-knockers first appeared in the late Middle Ages; the large 'closing' or 'sanctuary' rings may have been used for this purpose. Knockers were certainly well-established on front doors by the fifteenth century, and were generally vertical in shape with a pivot at the top. There were fantastic shapes too: a knocker in the form of a human face is said to have given Brasenose College, Oxford, its name. Extravagant designs abounded in Renaissance Italy. Knockers were ornate in eighteenth-century France and Germany; dolphins (qv) were especially popular.

In the present century, door-bells have tended to replace door-knockers, which retain a decorative and emergency value. Fish and animal heads still adorn many doors. Also common is a simple horizontal bar, often attached to the letter plate.

Doric Temple of Concord, Agrigento, Sicily

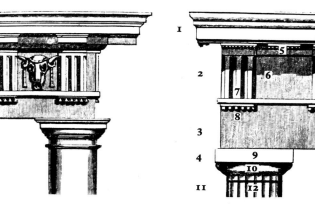

Entablatures of the Roman (left) and Greek Doric Orders: **1** *cornice* **2** *frieze* **3** *architrave* **4** *capital* **5** *mutule* **6** *metope* **7** *triglyph* **8** *guttae* **9** *abacus* **10** *echinus* **11** *shaft* **12** *arris between flutes*

Doorstops. See **Paperweight.**

Doric order. The earliest and simplest of the classical orders established by the Greeks. The Greek Doric shaft carried 20 flutings, each rising through less than a semi-circle in depth to a sharply defined edge. The column had no base and its height was between 4 and $6\frac{1}{2}$ diameters. The capital had a plain square abacus and a slightly curved echinus. Over the architrave of the entablature was a plain fillet called the tenia. The frieze was ornamented by flat projections, with three incisions in each, which are called triglyphs; and the spaces between triglyphs are called metopes. Beneath the triglyphs and the tenia of the architrave were small drops or guttae. A broad fillet called the capital of the triglyphs ran along the top of the frieze. Below the cornice were blocks called mutules, one over each metope and each triglyph. Doric ranked second of the Roman orders. Roman Doric is so different from the Greek original as to be virtually a separate order. In particular, it is higher (about 7 diameters) and the column is more slender and stands upon a base.

Antique brass door-knocker

Modern door-knob

Dormer on a chapel, c 1350

A medieval dormitory in a school

Dormer in a tiled roof

Dormer, dormer window. A window set vertically in the sloping roof of a house, having its own flat or pitched roof. Dormers do not seem to have been built before the fourteenth century. In their earliest form they were virtually the gabled continuation of a bay window, but later they were frequently placed behind parapets and given segmental or triangular pediments.

Dormitory. A sleeping apartment for several people. The word was originally used mainly for the sleeping quarters of monks, but since the nineteenth century it has more usually been applied to the equivalent rooms in boarding schools and other institutions.

Dormitory town. A term first used scoffingly or, at best, in a mildly deprecating manner, of a town on the periphery of a metropolis, ie a place to which urban office workers retired only to sleep. It has now become an entirely non-pejorative descriptive term in town planning.

Dossel (Latin *dorsarium*). Tapestries, sometimes richly embroidered, which were hung on the wall (usually the eastern wall)

Salt-glazed Doulton jug, c 1870

of a church chancel. The term was at one time used for the covering of a seat-back, especially when it was executed in carpet work.

Doulton pottery. In 1815 John Doulton (1793–1873) started his pottery in Lambeth, London, with John Watts. They made brown salt-glazed stoneware mugs, bottles, jugs, etc, with relief mouldings of hunting scenes and other rustic subjects. Later the factory turned out drainpipes, insulators, and sanitary ware.

The Doulton factory prospered, and in the 1870s much decorative 'art pottery' was produced as a result of co-operation with the Lambeth School of Art. In 1877 an earthenware factory was taken over in Burslem and much good-class domestic and useful ware produced.

In 1901 King Edward VII granted the potteries the right to use the word 'Royal' in describing their manufactures. About this time, too, the Royal Doulton Potteries rediscovered the long-lost glazing and colouring secrets of Sung and Ming dynasty Chinese potters. *Rouge flambé*, *sang de boeuf*, and crackle glazes were now obtained; some of their effects were displayed for the first time at the St Louis Exhibition in 1904.

Doulton Toby jugs continue to be popular.

Marks include the words Doulton and Lambeth in various arrangements.

Dovecote. In the Middle Ages, pigeons were a staple diet, and dovecotes, built of stone and often beehive-shaped, were an essential adjunct to monasteries, manor houses, and farms. A few of these survive but in the last 300 years dovecotes have lost their architectural importance and now often consist of simply a white-painted façade with many doors, giving on to a pigeon loft behind.

Dovetail. A joiner's device whereby two pieces of timber can be slotted together without recourse to nails or pegs. It is most frequently employed in making drawers for chests. In the eighteenth century, dovetailing became something of a fine art and the units were made so accurately that glue was unnecessary.

Dovetail joint

Dowel. A term usually applied to a peg which is set into holes or sockets in order to link two units together. A wooden dowel can be used to unite two parts of the leg of a chair; a metal dowel is usually employed to link the corner section of a marble kerb to the front section.

Downing, Andrew Jackson (1815–52). American landscape gardener and architectural writer whose books *Cottage Residences* (1842) and *Architecture of Country Houses* (1850) revolutionized the design of small houses in America. He advocated picturesque sites, and picturesque houses to complement them – houses of the sort already being built by Downing's friend, A J Davis. His ideal was board-and-

Dovecote made of stone

batten construction, because of its simplicity, the contrast it provided to the smoothness of Greek Revival houses, its cheapness, and perhaps because of its distinctively American character. Downing held that exteriors should be irregular, and surfaces painted and patterned. Planning should also be irregular, but above all practical, and Downing incorporated verandas into angles in the plan instead of projecting them under porticos. He treated questions of style very casually, although displaying a preference for Italian farm houses and various forms of Gothic; in general, Downing's bracketted cottages had a style of their own.

Dragon on an early Ming dish

Dragon. A large, winged, fire-breathing, snake-like beast, common to the mythologies of West and East. In the West, the tales of St George and St Michael, of Beowulf, Arthur, Tristram, and Lancelot all supplied stories of dragon-slaying which appeared in art for century after century. The dragon became the ensign of the later Roman Empire and is now incorporated in the armorials of the Prince of Wales.

In China, however, the dragon is even more important: it was both the symbol of the country and the badge of the Imperial family. The dragon appears in Chinese decorative arts in many guises, and has many symbolic attributes. A favourite scene is

Dorothy Draper

the dragon perpetually in pursuit of a flaming pearl, a common motif in carpets. Dragons are found embroidered on imperial and Mandarin costumes and on banners, painted on porcelain, carved in jade, and inlaid in gold on bronze. In Japanese art the dragon plays a similar role.

Draper, Dorothy (1889–1969). American interior decorator. Dorothy Draper was a nationally syndicated columnist and founder of Dorothy Draper and Company, Inc. In 1941 she directed *Good Housekeeping* magazine's Studio of Architectural Building and Furnishing. At the 1964–5 New York World's Fair she designed the Dorothy Draper Dream House. Her work ranged from decorating the homes of society leaders to restyling tenement buildings. She was the author of *Entertaining is Fun* and 365 *Decorating Ideas*. Her company is one of America's leading design firms.

Draperies. The American term for heavy fabric, usually hung in loose folds at windows. Drapes

is a common but unfashionable alternative name.

Drawing-room. The modern term deriving from the earlier 'withdrawing room' encountered by all readers of eighteenth-century plays, novels, and plans. See **Parlour.**

Draw table or **draw-leaf table.** A heavy oak table with extending leaves, popular in the late sixteenth and throughout the seventeenth century, when the best examples were made. The leaves were drawn out from beneath the table top to create a larger area, sometimes double the size.

Dressed stone is the term applied to stone after it has been cut (ie dressed) by the mason to present a smooth plane on its outer surface. The term is also used when stone is cut or shaped by a craftsman for a particular use specified by designer or architect.

Dresser. Medieval dressers are identical to cupboards – used for storage and display – and were the principal pieces of dining-hall furniture. Gothic dressers, which were of considerable social importance, were often of great height, very richly carved, and hung with embroidered covers and drapery. By the mid-seventeenth century they had become much smaller and were seldom elaborately carved. The commonest form was long and low, with three or four drawers and baluster or reel-turned legs in front and two plain legs behind. These became the dining-room sideboards of the mid-eighteenth century.

Another seventeenth-century

Early eighteenth-century oak dresser with three drawers

dresser had a superstructure of open shelves, hooks for hanging cups, and sometimes small drawers at the sides. It was popular throughout the eighteenth century, though mainly in country districts.

In Wales a more complex three-tier dresser, called a tridarn, was common. Many English country-made examples are today erroneously labelled as Welsh.

In the nineteenth century, dressers again became sumptuous and, to modern taste, over-ornate display pieces. Again they were richly carved with romanticized historical subjects. Nowadays a few modern dressers are made on the Continent, in Holland in particular. But in most houses they have been superseded by adaptable wall-units.

Dressing. A term frequently encountered in descriptions of eighteenth-century buildings. It signifies the use of a material to provide contrast in surfaces. 'Brick with stone dressings' is the phrase most frequently used, and indicates that a brick wall is embellished by the use of stone for window architraves, pilasters, cornices, string courses, quoins, balustrades, and other decorative elements in the façade. The term is also used, though more rarely, of wooden pilasters or cornices, other ways of achieving con-

trasts; namely (*a*) painting brilliant white, and (*b*) rubbing and gauging bricks, which are then in sharp contrast to the more commonplace stock brick of the walling.

Dressing-table. Also called a toilet-table. The first tables used especially for making the toilet appeared only at the end of the seventeenth century. They were no more than side-tables with a kneehole frieze and five small drawers, and were undoubtedly also used for other purposes when necessary. Such tables,

A Gothic French dresser, c 1500, with fine tracery carving

Oak drawer table and bench, 1500–50

Lacquer dressing-table with a folding top incorporating a mirror; mid-eighteenth century

made in walnut and of increasingly elegant design, commonly on cabriole legs, were made throughout the reigns of Queen Anne and George I. But by 1750 the first mahogany tables were made with fittings specifically designed as aids to dressing and making up.

Thereafter, such fittings were common to all dressing-tables and, with some variations, consisted of a central rising or hinged mirror which could be adjusted by the user and surrounded by open and lidded wells and compartments to hold bottles, pins, etc. These features appeared on flat-topped tables on tall legs, conforming in design to the fashion of the day. They also occurred – but more rarely – in the top drawer of a chest or knee-hole table, pieces of furniture which – but for the toilet fittings – would have been equally suitable for bed- or drawing-room. The knee-hole variety is especially common in America.

Drew, Jane Beverly (*b* 1911). British architect. After early training at the A A Schools in London, Jane Drew began to specialize in tropical building with Peter Koinange in Kenya. Later, after designing houses and offices in England, she joined her husband Maxwell Fry in West Africa as assistant town planning adviser to the four British West African colonies (1944–5). This led to much work abroad. In Ghana she designed schools, housing and colleges, and in Nigeria she worked with her husband on the great Ibadan University. She has also worked in Kuwait, on a 1,000-bed hospital and clinic at Ahmadi. In India she designed hospitals, housing, and a large high school, and was senior architect to the Chandigarh project (1951–4). Other commissions took her to Singapore and Ceylon; and in South Persia she was consultant on important housing and town-planning projects and a variety of buildings (hospital additions, clinics, cinemas, and nurses' homes). After working in London and teaching in the USA in 1961 she was Bemis Professor at the Massachusetts Institute of Technology. She has designed hospitals and housing in Mauritius as well as in England. For long closely associated with the Institute of Contemporary Arts, she designed interiors of galleries, club rooms, and a theatre in the Institute's quarters in Carlton House Terrace. She has designed with Maxwell Fry the Open University at Milton Keynes.

Jane Drew has lectured on tropical architecture in India, Ceylon, Turkey, Canada, Puerto Rico, West Africa, Iran, and America, and continues to teach at Harvard and Brussels Universities.

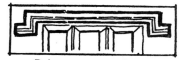

Dripstone over a window

Dripstone. An outer moulding which, in section, projects beyond the inner mouldings and wall or window surfaces of a building in order to protect them

Jane Drew

from rainwater. The shape of the dripstone section is designed to cast off the water with maximum efficiency. The dripstone frequently terminates in a down-turned finial.

Drop. Usually a garland or a cluster of ornamental motifs suspended from a point or 'nail' on a wall or in a panel or pilaster. The wheat-ear drop, for example, is often used in the narrow side sections of wall panelling, the side panels of chimney-pieces, and the pilasters of chimney-pieces.

Drop arch. A two-centred arch of greater width than its radii. It is also known as a depressed arch.

Drum. One of the circular blocks of stone which form part of the shaft of a column. The term is also applied to the ring or neck of brick or stone which supports a dome.

Drum table. The drum table is often called a circular library

Modern dressing-table with triple mirror

University College at Ibadan, designed by Jane Drew and Maxwell Fry

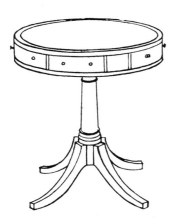

A Sheraton drum table, c *1800*

table, and was common at the very end of the eighteenth century and during the Regency period. The top is circular and has drawers all round the frieze. These are either wedge-shaped or alternatively real and dummy. Wedge-shaped drawers usually have slots and runners underneath to guide them in and out.

Drum tables almost invariably rotate on centre pedestals. Though tables with fixed tops do occur, most are rotating tables that have been simply altered. The woods used are commonly mahogany, satinwood, and rosewood. The top is often covered with tooled leather panels. See also **Rent table.**

Dry sink. A low kitchen cabinet produced in America, particularly during the nineteenth century. The top surface, usually made of marble, was intended to hold a pitcher and wash-basin. Under the sink was enclosed storage space. This

utilitarian piece was generally made of pine or maple. Today, antique dry sinks are much in demand in country houses, where they are commonly used in living- or dining-rooms to hold plants on the top and to provide storage space below.

Duchesse. A type of late eighteenth-century couch. It consisted of two tub-backed or bergère chairs fastened to a stool. Each component could be used separately. Sheraton devised a draped version, calling it a Duchess bed.

Duct (Latin, *ducere* 'to lead'). A channel which conveys water from one point to another, usually within a building. The term is now more generally applied to any built-in channel carrying electric cables, water pipes, etc.

Dudok, Willem Marinus (*b* 1884). Dutch architect, born in Amsterdam into a musical family and intended for a military career. After training at the military academy at Breda, he served for eight years in the army before becoming a municipal engineer at Leiden. In 1915 Dudok was appointed director of municipal works at Hilversum, where his most ambitious work was the famous town hall built between 1928 and 1931. He also designed many other buildings which influenced European architecture, including the theatre at Utrecht, the remarkable Bijenkorf store at Rotterdam (1928–30), the Dutch students' hostel in Paris, and steelworks at Velsen-Ijmuiden, as well as

schools, housing schemes, factories, and office buildings. His work is marked by what the American critic Lewis Mumford has aptly called 'a quality of spaciousness and freedom that derives from simple masses broken by shadow and clear spaces penetrated by light.' Mumford adds that Dudok's Hilversum town hall served as 'a living link between the great town halls and guild-halls of the past.'

Dumb-waiter. 'We had dumb-waiters so our conversation was not under any restraint by ye Servants being in ye room' is an entry by Miss Mary Hamilton in her *Diary* for 1784. The dumb-waiter is a table of two or more tiers, usually circular with a central pillar support and tripod or quadruple legs. It was used as an extra table at the corner of the dining table, carrying bottles, cheeses, and other items needed at the conclusion of the meal, and it was also used when the servants had been dismissed from the room. Sometimes there were several dumb-

W M Dudok

waiters loaded with dishes and wines for the whole meal. In the eighteenth century, meals lasted far longer than they do today, and the presence of servants must often have been an irksome restriction upon confidential conversations.

The dumb-waiter first appeared in England in the early eighteenth century, but does not figure in Chippendale's *Gentleman and Cabinet-Maker's Director,* although bills of sale from

Eastern façade of the town hall at Hilversum, Holland, by Dudok, 1928

Sheraton's Duchess bed

Inside the Royal Dutch Steelworks building by Dudok

Chippendale dumb-waiter, c 1760

his firm do exist for these pieces. Sheraton's *Cabinet Dictionary* of 1803 illustrates two elaborate dumb-waiters, one of which is no more than a copy of a Louis XVI wine table, and the other so elaborately fitted that it was probably never made. By the early 1800s the dumb-waiter was being replaced by butler's trays which in turn gave way to the trolley.

Dummy board figure. The dummy board figure was a decorative whim of the seventeenth and eighteenth centuries. A board was cut in silhouette and the front painted with a figure, animal, or object. These were used purely for decoration and served to create the illusion of 'company' in an otherwise empty room or corridor. Early figures were attached to the walls, but most of those that have survived are set in block feet which made it possible to move them from room to room.

The most popular figures were of servants, usually busy about their tasks. Dogs, cats, and children are also found in large numbers. A class peculiar to England is the dummy board soldier, whose bright tunic made a colourful addition to a dark staircase or corridor. By the 1820s the vogue for these figures had passed.

Dunlap. The Dunlap family of American cabinetmakers worked in Chester and Salisbury, New Hampshire, in the late eighteenth and early nineteenth centuries. They made Queen Anne and Chippendale furniture. Dunlap pieces can usually be recognized by their slender-ankled cabriole legs, the towering galleries on their broad cornices, and their borders of large-scale intaglio fans combined with reversed S-scrolls. Much of the Dunlaps' work was in curly maple.

Dutch and Belgian architecture. It is convenient to consider the architecture of the Low Countries as a whole since their existence as separate states is a recent event; for Belgium was only formed as a separate state from the Netherlands in 1830. Both nations were for centuries part of larger empires; Holland achieving independence only after throwing off Spanish rule in the 1570s. Few Roman buildings survive in either country; nor is the Romanesque period well represented. But there are magnificent examples of Gothic architecture throughout the Low Countries, notably the cathedrals of Bruges, Brussels, Ghent, and Louvain. Industry and civic pride led to the early establishment of a forceful and flourishing municipal architecture. Civic buildings fall into three groups: (1) town halls, which were the municipal senate houses and courts of justice; (2) trade halls or market-houses, especially cloth halls for cloth was the staple industry of the Middle Ages; and (3) guild-halls, or meeting-places for guilds or associated trades of the cities. The trade halls seem to have been the earliest group and the Cloth Hall at Ypres was the most beautiful; thanks to two major wars it is also the most

Chest on chest by Dunlap

Dummy board figure of a servant girl holding a watch

The West Frisian Museum in Hoorn

The Peace Palace at The Hague

The law-courts at Brussels

The town hall at Gouda

battered. The town halls in the cities already mentioned are of considerable size and beauty, that at Brussels being the most magnificent in Belgium and far superior to any comparable building in Holland.

Because of the continuous interchange of ideas and craftsmen between England and the Low Countries, Renaissance influences in Holland and Belgium resulted in buildings similar to those in Tudor and Jacobean England. English domestic architecture in seventeenth- and early eighteenth-century England derived more directly from the houses of the Dutch burghers than from Italian princes and merchants. The sixteenth-century religious division between the Catholic South and the Protestant Netherlands had important effects on architecture. Baroque influences were enthusiastically accepted by the Catholic Belgians but rejected by the more austere Dutch. The Jesuit church in Antwerp, the church of Nôtre-Dame du Beguinage in Brussels, St Michel in Louvain, and St Loup in Namur were seventeenth-century Belgian Baroque structures, as was the renowned group of Baroque guild houses in the Grande Place at Brussels.

In the Age of Reason, the formal approach to architecture throughout Europe determined the style of most buildings in the Low Countries, such as the Brussels Bourse (1874) and lawcourts (1866–83). Here, too, however, the links of the northern provinces with north Germany are to be seen in the railway station at Amsterdam, designed by Cuypers in 1884.

In the twentieth century the work of Dutch architects has had a considerable influence on the development of the modern movement in northern Europe. The most important figure at first was H P Berlage (1856–1934), designer of the Amsterdam Bourse (1899–1903). This trend

Apartment block by van den Broek and Bakema, 1960

was carried on and extended from civic buildings to factories by W M Dudok (qv), designer of Hilversum town hall, and by the partners J B Bakema and J H van den Broek (qqv).

Dutch barn. In Britain, originally a hay barn with open sides; it consisted of a curved roof, constructed of corrugated iron or asbestos sections, raised on cast-iron or steel stanchions. During recent years, however, Dutch barns have become larger and more enclosed, and are often made of asbestos sections.

In America, Pennsylvania Dutch barns are enclosed wood structures and are characterised by painted hex signs. They were built by the Amish farmers, mainly in Lancaster County. See **Barn.**

Dutch door. A door divided horizontally into an upper and a lower section. Each of the two parts is hinged and they can be opened independently or together. The Dutch door is also known as a stable door.

Dutch furniture. Dutch fur-

A Crendon Dutch barn

niture forms a distinctive and attractive class of its own from the end of the seventeenth to the beginning of the nineteenth century, and during this period much excellent work was produced. Until the late 1600s it differed little from furniture in France, England, and central Europe. The exceptions were cabinets and chests, which, with tortoiseshell inlay, waved ebony mouldings, and the use of ivory, display the influence of the Spanish occupation. These pieces were still made in the early part of the eighteenth century and are sometimes lined with oil paintings by well-known flower or landscape painters.

The use of marquetry flowers, birds, and figures inlaid on a rich burr-walnut ground is typical of Dutch furniture from the end of the seventeenth century. Dutch marquetry is seldom of the best quality, and never rivals the fine work produced in London and Paris, but it retains a charm wholly its own and is quite unmistakable. Symmetry is an essential ingredient but is never obtrusive. Baskets of flowers, urns, or bouquets gathered by ribbons form the central subjects, and delicate branches of leaves and flowers fill the rest of the veneered surface. Apart from marquetry, plain burr or straight-grained walnut is common, and a pale golden-yellow oak was used for cheap furniture.

The design of Dutch furniture throughout the eighteenth century is based partly on French and partly on English styles, while retaining its native character. Chairs were similar to the French provincial types but were mostly inlaid with marquetry. Early eighteenth-century tables and chests were sometimes made in eccentric shapes. Rococo influences appear in the bombé or serpentine fronts and the elaborately curved and shaped sides and bases. Until 1760 the feet were usually ball and claw, ebonized, and often of a disproportionately large size. Drawers were constructed with coarse dovetails, with nails, or with a combination of the two. Locks were large and simple, and had square tumblers.

With the Neo-classical revival, Dutch furniture began to follow Louis XVI designs closely. Satinwood was preferred to walnut, and commodes and cupboards were often embellished with panels of Japanese black-and-gold lacquer. A limited use was made of ormolu mounts, and the standard of cabinetmaking was high. After 1800 some Dutch furniture in the Empire style was made. Nineteenth-century Dutch furniture was similar to furniture in other parts of Europe, but was seldom of fine quality.

Despite the excellence of their work, few eighteenth-century Dutch furniture-makers are known by name. The best makers seem to have migrated to Paris, where the rewards of their skill were far greater. A celebrated case is 'B V R B' – Bernhard van Risen Burgh; one of the greatest *ébénistes* of Louis XV's reign.

Modern Dutch furniture is clean-lined and substantial, strongly influenced by Scandinavian work.

Dutch gold. A copper-zinc alloy that was used as a cheap imitation gold leaf. It could be beaten like gold and was very effective when new, but because the oxidization of the copper produced small spots on the surface, it had to be very heavily lacquered, giving it a far coarser appearance than gold leaf.

Duvet. Type of quilt, of continental origin with washable covers. Replaces sheets, blankets etc.

Top, Dutch bureau cabinet in floral marquetry, mid eighteenth century; centre, a side cabinet with Japanese lacquer panels in satinwood, late eighteenth century: bottom, modern swivel chair and foot-rest

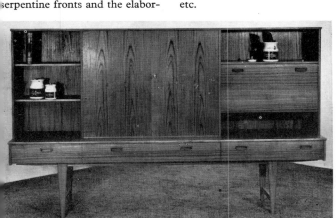

Modern Dutch teak storage unit

Eagle. The size and power of the eagle has made it a favourite decorative motif since at least Roman times, and has caused it to be used as a symbol of many nations, including ancient Greece and Rome, Germany, Spain, France, and the United States. It was in the middle of the eighteenth century, however, that the eagle became a popular device in the ornamentation of furniture and clocks.

The French employed it largely as a cresting for clocks, looking glasses, and cabinets in the late eighteenth century. The English used the motif more widely. English console tables of the 1730s and 1740s were sometimes supported on the head and wings of an eagle perched on rocks, which formed the base. Eagles also appear as clock and looking-glass crestings, as the central motif in the popular broken pediment cornice to cabinets and bookcases (1730–50), and in many other guises. In the United States the eagle was especially popular after the adoption of the Constitution in 1788, when it became a patriotic emblem much used on looking-glasses, banjo clocks, and cabinet work.

Eames, Charles (*b* 1907). American architect and industrial designer. Eames is one of the most influential furniture designers of this century, mainly because of his revolutionary designs for chairs marketed by the Herman Miller Furniture Company. Eames's first major achievement was winning an international furniture design competition sponsored by the New York Museum of Modern Art in 1939. At the time he was conducting an experimental design department at Cranbrook. He and Eero Saarinen submitted a moulded plywood chair in which a single stressed ply skin was manipulated to form seat, back, and arms, attached to a light metal underframe.

Eames's chairs were shown at the Museum of Modern Art in 1946, and two years later he was given a grant by the museum for further experiments with shell forms for chairs. He has since designed many different chair forms, most of which have acquired international fame and become something like status symbols in offices and homes. These include the fibreglass shell chair, the wire-cage chair, and the lounge chair and ottoman.

Early English style. The term describing the first stages in the development of English Gothic architecture, ie the style established between the end of the twelfth and the beginning of the fourteenth century; it succeeded the Norman style and merged into the Decorated. The most salient features of Early English are the deeply cut mouldings of pointed windows, giving a strong contrast of light and shadow, the wider use of circular windows, and the use of longer and narrower lancet windows without tracery. Flying buttresses

Charles Eames

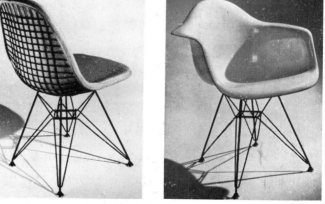

Top, desk designed by Charles Eames; centre left, chair in vinyl and wire upholstered with foam rubber; right, glass fibre and chrome wire, both 1948; below, moulded plywood lounge chair and ottoman, 1956

Early English. *The nave and aisle of Lincoln Cathedral built between 1209 and 1253*

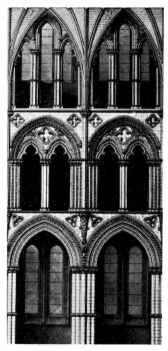

The Presbytery, Ely Cathedral

were also first introduced in this style. The term was coined by Thomas Rickman (1776–1841), a noted architect and writer, in his authoritative book *An Attempt to Discriminate the Styles of Architecture from the Conquest to the Reformation.*

Earthenware. Literally, ware made of baked earth or clay. The term earthenware can be applied to any kind of pottery that is neither stoneware nor porcelain. It is always opaque and tends to be brittle, chipping and cracking easily.

The most primitive kind of earthenware was made of clay baked at a low temperature. It was red or buff or dark brown, varying in colour according to the colour of the clay used and the degree of firing. It was also porous. To make earthenware non-porous it must be covered with a coating of some sort of glaze. The earliest type of glaze was made of lead. Maiolica, Faience, and Delft (qqv) were tin-glazed. In the eighteenth century Josiah Wedgwood perfected his Queensware – a high-quality cream-coloured earthenware from which all our present-day earthenware is directly descended.

Eastlake, Charles Lock (1833–1906). British architect and furniture designer. The coinage 'The Eastlake Style' originated in America, and described the plain 'medieval' furniture which the designer was mainly responsible for popularizing on both sides of the Atlantic in the 1870s and early 1880s.

The designs were ponderous and heavy, in what was termed Early English or Modern Gothic. Eastlake's book *Hints on Household Taste* (1868) was widely read and became something of a popular guide to aspiring interior designers.

Easton, John Murray, FRIBA (*b* 1889). British architect. After early training in Aberdeen, Easton came to London and at the age of 30 started in practice with Howard M Robertson. They were later joined in partnership between 1929 and 1940 by E Stanley Hall. Thus originated the well-known firm of Easton & Robertson, Cusdin, Preston, and Smith, which has one of the largest and most diverse practices in Europe. Among the buildings designed by the firm have been British pavilions for international exhibitions (Paris 1925, Brussels 1935, Johannesburg 1936, New York 1939), and many academic and commercial projects, including much work at Cambridge University, the Hatfield Training College (1948), and Reading University (1949). The firm also designed the Shell building on the South Bank, London.

American easy chair made in New York, 1800–10

Easy chair. The name originally given to the comfortable winged armchairs, upholstered all over, that were introduced to England in the late seventeenth century.

Similar chairs were made in America in the eighteenth century. The word is now used as a generic term for most upholstered, overstuffed chairs.

Modern earthenware made by Wedgwood

The Royal Horticultural Society's hall, designed by J M Easton, 1927

A Louis XVI bureau plat by J H Riesener, mahogany with ormolu mounts

Egg and tongue

Egg and dart

Eaves. The section of a sloping roof over-hanging the vertical face of the wall it protects. The guttering is normally attached to the eaves. In seventeenth- and some early eighteenth-century buildings the rafters of the roof are left to show on the underside of eaves. In the Regency period when eaves became both more emphatic and more decorative, these rafters were covered by eaves boards or fascias, and their decorative effect was enhanced by the introduction of supporting arms or brackets.

Ebéniste. The general term for a furniture-maker in France, but usually applied to makers of cabinet furniture rather than of chairs and other seat furniture – like the English term cabinet-maker. Ebénistes belonged to various guilds, the chief one being that of the *menuisiers-ébénistes*, an old guild which protected its members against the cheaper work of foreign craftsmen and, from 1741, did much to raise the standard of French furniture-making till the Revolution. From 1741 all members were ordered to sign their work, and a committee, the *juré des menuisiers-ébénistes*, was set up by the guild to pass each piece before it was sold. The makers signed with an iron stamp of their name or initials. The *juré* stamped its own initials J M E on approved pieces.

Ebonize. To stain and polish a close-grained wood so that it looks like ebony. It was an eighteenth century process.

Ebony. *Diospyros*. An exceptionally hard, black wood with a tight grain; from the seventeenth century it was much used in furniture-making as a veneer. It was usually imported from Ceylon and India, at first mainly to Holland, but later to England, France, and America as well. There are several species of ebony used for furniture: macassar ebony, with its irregular markings, African and Ceylon ebony, and marblewood. Ebony of a pure jet black was prized for small veneer panels and the backs of hairbrushes, for which it is still used.

Echinus. The convex or ovolo moulding beneath the abacus (qv) of the Doric capital. The term is often applied to the egg-and-anchor or egg-and-tongue motif frequently carved to ornament the curve of the echinus.

Ecuelle. A shallow dish for food, generally low and with flat side-handles. As the name suggests, it is of French origin, but it was found in other countries in the seventeenth and early eighteenth centuries.

Edge roll. The term used in Gothic architecture for a bead moulding on an external angle.

Egg-and-anchor, egg-and-dart, egg-and-tongue. Motifs employed in the carving of ovolo mouldings, first used on the Ionic order of the fourth century BC. The pattern is one of a projecting oval alternating with a pointed dart or arrowhead; the variety of interpretations of the dart accounts for the different names. There is no standard size or treatment for the pattern which is on occasion enriched so that the egg becomes a leaf.

Egyptian architecture. The architecture of ancient Egypt, in common with its other arts, was dominated by an intense preoccupation with the after-life. This fact alone is significant enough to give the history of Egyptian building an entirely different emphasis from that of other cultures, for it ensured that the most important of all buildings was not the palace or temple but the tomb or mausoleum. This fact, combined with abundance of first-rate building materials in the form of lime-stone and granite, which Egyptian masons learned to hew into blocks suitable for the erection of huge buildings, conditioned Egyptian architecture.

Preoccupation with life after death ensured that houses and other secular buildings occupied a minor place in the history of Egyptian architecture. They were built of far less durable materials, mainly bricks, dried under the

A Louis XV-Louis XVI Transitional bonheur du jour

Silver gilt écuelle, Paris hallmark, 1672

*Atid Pillar, from the Great Court
at Medinet-Habou*

Section of temple at Kalabsche

The Pyramid of Cheops at Giza

Temple at Abu Simbel

*Pillar from Rhamession,
Thebes*

fierce sun, and local timber.

Remains of prehistoric cemeteries (ie prior to 4000 BC) have been found in Upper Egypt, and brickwork of the Predynastic period (4000–3200 BC) has also been uncovered. But the history of Egyptian architecture effectively begins with the establishment of the first dynasty c 3200 BC. For the first time the areas adjacent to the river Nile came under unified military control, and the systematic development of the vast Nile Valley was seriously undertaken by means of a national system of canals and irrigation. With increased authority, the kings began to build themselves magnificent tombs. Thanks to the quality of the limestone and Egyptian skill in

quarrying it, many of the tombs from this time onwards have survived, the best known being the Pyramids, which are enlarged and refined versions of the primitive, sloping-sided *mastaba* tombs of ancient Egypt. As temples proliferated throughout the Nile Valley, they gradually acquired their characteristic form of 'battered' or tapering walls, immensely heavy and portentous columns set in pairs or in colonnades, and carved obelisks or pylons. Carved representations of rulers, animals, and battle scenes gave relief and pattern to the immense planes of the great temples. There is a famous group of buildings at Giza, near Cairo, dating from the fourth dynasty (2680–2565 BC),

the Cheops Temple and Pyramid; notably numerous temples at Karnak (from c 2470 BC).

For posterity, the Ramesside period and twentieth dynasties (1314–1085 BC) has provided the greatest interest, mainly because of the building operations carried on throughout the Nile Valley, including those at Karnak and Thebes, during the long reign of Rameses II. The temples cut from rock at Abu Simbel, with their carved 65 ft figures of the king, also date from the time of Rameses II.

The decline of Egyptian greatness dates from the upheavals which followed the death of Rameses II, although remarkable buildings were erected after that in the Sudan. The Roman and

Arab conquests led to the imposition of non-indigenous styles. With the decay of Arab culture, Egypt declined into a profound cultural and economic slough, always dependent upon foreign protection, or suffering foreign occupation.

The chief modern influences upon Egyptian architecture have been French. The tall blocks of flats in Cairo and Alexandria are more reminiscent of Marseilles than of other European cities.

Egyptian style. Interest in ancient Egypt was stirred by Napoleon's expedition in 1798. Though something of a fiasco, it had an undoubted romantic appeal, and Egyptian motifs became familiar through a book

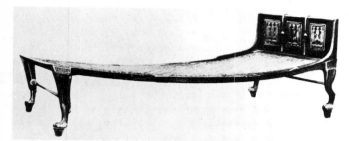

Egyptian wooden bed, XVIII Dynasty

Egyptian style Regency armchair of painted beech-wood

Breakfront mahogany bookcase attributed to Thomas Elfe of Charleston

by the archaeologist Baron de Denon, who had accompanied the expedition; his *Voyage dans la basse et la haute Egypte* (1802) contained well over a hundred illustrations.

The main influences were confined to decoration and ornament. Sphinx, crocodile, lotus, and papyrus were welcomed as novelties. In French and English furniture design though, comparatively little was made along the lines of Egyptian furniture, which remained largely unknown. However, Thomas Hope and George Smith both included Egyptian-style furniture in their major books.

Eiffel, Alexandre Gustave (1832 –1923). A notable French engin-

eer who was born at Dijon and studied at the Ecole Centrale. His iron bridges and other structures (ranging from the vast lock structure of the Panama Canal to the Bon Marché store in Paris) are now seen to be major contributions to the modern movement in architecture. Yet his most renowned work is the 984 ft tower named after him, which was erected in the Champ de Mars in Paris, in the two years preceding the Paris Exhibition of 1889. The tower was greatly disliked by Parisians, but has now come to be appreciated as a major contribution to architecture.

Elbow chair. An armchair. The term elbow was used for the arm of a chair in the seventeenth and eighteenth centuries.

Electroplate. Method of laying silver on to a base metal by electrolysis which was perfected and patented in 1840 by the Elkington family of Birmingham. They also developed the galvanoplastic method – electro-typing – by which elaborate metal objects could be rapidly and successfully reproduced.

Elers 'red porcelain' teapot, c 1700

Elers ware. A fine stoneware ranging in colour from buff through varying shades of red to dark brown. It was made at the end of the seventeenth century by the Elers brothers, David and John Philip, who came to England from Holland. They established a factory at Bradwell Wood in Staffordshire c 1694.

The Elers brothers tried to discover the Chinese secret of porcelain manufacture, and the teapots and other ware that they

made were imitations of the so-called 'red porcelain' being imported into Britain along with consignments of tea.

The Elers brothers did not mark their work.

Elevation. A drawing representing one plane, wall, side, or section of a building, showing the outline treatment of doors, windows, and other features, but lacking depth, relief, or indication of shadow.

Elfe, Thomas (active 1747–75). A leading cabinetmaker of Charleston, South Carolina. His work in the Queen Anne and Chippendale styles is usually recognized by the 'Elfe fret', a looped design resembling horizontal figures of eight. Elfe worked extensively for Charleston families, and about 1,500 pieces are documented in his account books of 1768–75.

Elizabethan furniture. Under Elizabeth I, who reigned from 1558 till 1603, England became prosperous and great. The age was a great one for building, and consequently there was an increased demand for furniture.

The principal wood used was oak, much embellished by a

primitive marquetry of flowers, and sometimes figures in pale woods, particularly pear and apple, and a hard ebony-like wood known as bog-oak.

Common forms of furniture still to be found are buffets, credence tables, dining tables, long- and joint-stools, arm- and single chairs (seldom found before Elizabeth's reign), and court cupboards. A very typical chair of the period was the farthingale chair, named after the voluminous dresses which its

Regency elbow chair in mahogany

Elizabethan oak armchair, inlaid with holly and bog-oak

Writing desk inlaid with the 'nonsuch' design, 1550–1600

width was supposed to accommodate. Perhaps the best-known surviving type of Elizabethan furniture is the bed. This was a forerunner of the four-poster, with elaborately carved marquetry headboards and massive footposts, often in the form of griffins and similar fabulous beasts.

The styles common at the beginning of the reign were those to be found throughout Europe, largely based on French and Italian models. By 1600 the influence of Renaissance classicism appeared in the vogue for turned columnar chair- and table-legs.

Elizabethan silver.

During Henry VIII's reign, Gothic was still the dominant style in England, and Gothic architectural forms were employed by metal workers. Gradually Italian Renaissance ornament was introduced. Scrolling leaves and flowers, putti, and classical details were preferred, and ornamental ideas were disseminated by pattern-plates and books im-

ported from Germany and Flanders. Holbein's visits to England were important, for he designed plate and was himself a trained silversmith. During Henry's reign – and later Elizabeth's (1558–1603) – English silver attained a very high standard. It was frequently gilded, sometimes inset with precious stones, and embossed and engraved with elaborate decoration. Some of the shapes – especially for standing cups – are both ingenious and highly inventive, and many exotic materials were incorporated into pieces; Rhenish stoneware, rock crystal, ivory, marble, ostrich eggs, oriental porcelain, and coconuts were among the most popular. Ewers and basins, flagons, tankards, and dishes were made of plate, but undoubtedly the most important household objects were the standing cup and cover, and the standing salt. It is fortunate that, despite the tendency to melt down 'old-fashioned' plate in the intervening centuries, so many of these superb *tours-de-force* have survived.

Ell, el, L. A North American term sometimes used as a measure of length, but also applied to a lean-to addition or wing of a clapboard house, so placed that the two parts together are in the shape of an L.

In the clapboard farmhouses of the New England immigrants, the ell often contained the kitchen.

Elm-wood. *Ulmus*. Hardwood varying from a dark to a pale brown. It was employed extensively for longbows in the Middle Ages, and also for domestic utensils and furniture of all kinds in the eighteenth century. It was used in conjunction with yew-wood for the seats of Windsor armchairs, and for tables, bookcases, and other cabinet furniture. When pollarded, it produces a rich burr effect as on rare and much-prized eighteenth-century bureaux, dressing-tables, and desks. Like walnut and beech, elm is particularly vulnerable to attacks by woodworm.

Embattled. Fortified structures and Gothic furniture with small crenellations along the top are often described as being embattled.

Embossing. See **Silver, decorative techniques.**

Embrasure. The term used to describe the interval (or void) between two merlons or crenelles (solids) of a battlement. In Western fortifications the embrasure was normally half the measure of the merlon. The word

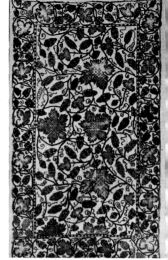

A linen pillow-cover embroidered in black silk, 1550–1600

is also used to describe the steeply sloping sides of a window opening in a turret, narrowing through the thickness of the wall to a slit through which archers could fire at attackers.

Embroidery. The craft of working patterns with a needle and thread on to a fabric base. Embroidery is a vast subject: it has been practised throughout the world over thousands of years. On the other hand the basic stitches are common to all times and places, most of the apparently formidable number being merely elaborations of a few types.

Babylon had a reputation for beautiful embroidery, but all examples have long since

*Left, Elizabethan cup and cover in silver gilt, London, 1590–1;
right the Mostyn salt, late sixteenth century*

Details of a bed curtain in cotton and linen twill, embroidered in green wools, late seventeenth century

Italian openwork cover in coloured silk gimp, silver gilt and thread, late sixteenth century

French Empire table veneered in thuya wood, c 1800

French wall hanging of wool on linen and silk, late seventeenth century

A panel embroidered in 'Berlin wools', c 1850

perished. Some Egyptian work has survived, though the Egyptians are known not to have thought very highly of the craft.

The earliest surviving medieval embroidery is a maniple from St Cuthbert's tomb at Durham, dating from the first half of the tenth century. A great deal of fine English embroidery was made during the thirteenth and fourteenth centuries, it was known as *opus anglicum* and exported throughout Europe.

Until the sixteenth century embroidery was done primarily for ecclesiastical vestments; much of it was carried out in convents and at court. Its employment for domestic linens, bed-hangings, pillow and cushion covers, and clothing (bodices, coifs, vests, cuffs) reflected the slow growth of a wider prosperity. The earliest English domestic work is Elizabethan and portrays native flora and fauna. In Italy a great variety of splendid embroidery, such as cut or applied work, was done.

In the eighteenth century, the luxury of embroidered clothing reached new heights. Rococo and chinoiserie influences were particularly strong in French work. But in the nineteenth century industrialization affected all crafts adversely and the dominance of a sober-minded middle class led to a decline in the use of sumptuous silks and gold thread. However, despite lower standards, a vast amount of embroidery was produced in the Victorian era. In recent years

there has been a revival of interest in the domestic arts, and embroidery is coming back into favour.

Empire. The French Empire period in design and decoration is usually taken to cover the years 1800 to 1830 and includes the Consulate (1799–1804) and the reigns of Napoleon I (1804–15), Louis XVIII (1815–24), and Charles X (1824–30). The style was at first a continuation of the last and simplest Louis XVI phase.

In furniture, the woods used until about 1820 were mahogany and, more commonly still, fruitwoods of a mahogany-like colour. All the designs were based on an elaboration of the rectangle. Ormolu mounts were not much used and were of inferior quality. The remarkable charm of this furniture derives from its basic simplicity, and its use of attractively figured wood. The only new pieces of furniture developed were chairs and canapés. Ornamental marquetry and ormolu was based on Greek and Roman motifs, popular since the eighteenth-century discovery of Herculaneum and Pompeii with the addition of a large number of Egyptian motifs, popularized by Napoleon's expedition to Egypt.

The late Empire style of Charles X's reign was better in execution and richer in design; satin-wood, maple, and particularly *bois clair* (light-coloured fruitwood) replaced mahogany and mahogany colours. After

A bois clair Empire chair

1830 the simplicity of the Empire style was lost in an ever-increasing desire for ornamentation, which resulted in the elaborate marquetry and carved furniture of the Victorian period.

Among the finest productions of Empire France were the tapestries and carpets from Aubusson and other factories which had survived the Revolution. Carpets were designed on a giant central patera, surrounded by borders of lotus, sunflowers, daisies, and similar floral motifs, the colouring being chiefly in attractive shades of green, yellow, and red. Empire tapestries, of which few remain, were similarly coloured and usually depicted classical subjects. Empire metalwork was also fine, particularly

brass and ormolu candlesticks, table furniture, dressing-table sets, and chandeliers. Although metalworkers were no longer strictly supervised by guilds as in the eighteenth century, they inherited the skills of their predecessors, whose work was never surpassed. The principal metalworker of the Empire period was Thomire.

Furniture-makers, too, were no longer supervised by guilds, but many fine firms existed, particularly that of Jacob Frères. The first member of the family had been the greatest seat-furniture-maker in the Louis XVI period, and the family kept up his high standards of craftsmanship and were also among the most advanced in their designs.

Enamel. A hard, vitreous compound of silica glass, minium and potash, which is stained by the chemical combination of metallic oxides while melted in a crucible. The result, when burnished, gives a brilliantly coloured and decorative surface to metal, porcelain, or other materials to which it is applied.

The ancient Egyptians and Assyrians seem to have applied it only to brick and pottery, but the effect, as at the palace of Rameses III at Tell el-Yehudia in the Nile Delta, has seldom been equalled. It was first applied to metal in ancient

A Louis XVI parquetry encoignure in kingwood and tulipwood

Greece. Three distinct techniques are known: *cloisonné*, in which the enamel is divided by strips (cloisons) soldered to the base; *champlevé*, in which the base is gouged out to receive the enamel; and a more recent innovation, *basse-taille*, in which the base is engraved in bas-relief, the translucent enamel displaying the design beneath.

Celtic and Saxon enamelling dates from the sixth century, the finest Saxon example being the Ardagh chalice in the Dublin Museum. From Ireland, enamelling was taken to Byzantium. Centuries later, it was practised in Cologne, England, Spain, and Limoges in France. Byzantine production was considerable, reaching its peak in the altarpiece in the Pala d'Oro, St Mark's, Venice, thought to have come from Constantinople in 1105. At Limoges output was also large, and has continued till modern times. All over Europe, in fact, enamelling has been practised for at least six centuries.

In China, and later Japan, enamel was extensively employed as an alternative to porcelain. The cloisonné method was almost always used, and imitation of oriental wares led to the development of English and French painted enamels in the eighteenth century. The decoration was added to a white ground enamel on a copper base, and the

finest work came from the short-lived Battersea factory, from Bilston, and from parts of Staffordshire. Enamelling is still much used today and remains unequalled for jewellery.

Encarpa or **encarpus.** A sculptured festoon or a frieze of fruit and flowers.

Encaustic (from the Greek for 'burnt in'). This term was applied to the ancient method of painting with wax as a main ingredient, for the wax required heat to melt it. Encaustic painting was used by the Greeks, Romans, and Egyptians.

The word 'encaustic' is often applied to the inlaid tiles used in medieval monasteries, and also to the nineteenth-century copies made by such firms as Minton; and was much used by architects in the past century.

Wedgwood decorated some of

Encaustic tile, c 1275

A Limoges enamel tazza and cover dating from the sixteenth century

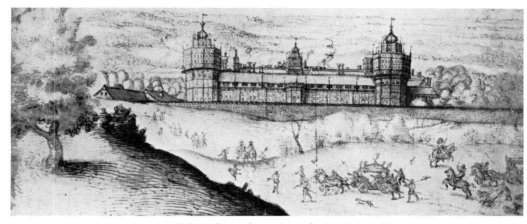

Nonsuch Palace, Surrey begun in 1538, demolished 1687

his black basalt ware with red-and-white encaustic painting, in imitation of that used on Greek and Etruscan vases.

Encoignure. The French term for a corner cupboard. Encoignures were commonly made in pairs and *en suite* with a commode. They almost invariably had marble tops and metal mounts. Unlike many corner cupboards made in other countries they were not intended to be hung on a wall. They had one door, occasionally two, and stood on three feet, sometimes there was a fourth, partly hidden foot at the centre front, beneath the apron. Whether flat-fronted or bombé, most encoignures had a detachable series of shelves above; most have been lost.

In their *Universal System*, Ince and Mayhew show 'encoinears' as corner cupboards with a series of graduated shelves above.

Endive. The modern name for a small scrolled motif that resembles the curly leaf of an endive plant.

Enfilade. A suite of intercommunicating rooms with doorways opposite one another. The main rooms were commonly arranged in this way during the Renaissance, and the practice persisted throughout the eighteenth century.

Engaged column. A column either attached to a wall or with only half its diameter free of the wall.

English architecture. None of the earliest rude dwellings now remain, but their structure was undoubtedly similar to those found today in more or less primitive communities. Far more conjecture has been expended on the great prehistoric monuments of Stonehenge and Maiden

Castle, which are the first permanent man-made structures still standing in Britain.

With the Roman occupation an immense amount of building was done throughout Britain, but too little has survived to indicate how basically southern European buildings were adapted to the more severe climate of northern Europe. The most important remains are as follows: a fairly well-preserved amphitheatre at Caerwent in Monmouthshire; public buildings, villas (centrally heated), and a theatre at St Albans; public baths at Bath; and the fragmentary remains, mostly foundations, of various pagan basilicas and temples. Christian remains are rare, although the foundations of a basilica have been excavated at Silchester.

There is even less evidence about the nature of the early Anglo-Saxon settlements; only with the development of Christian architecture does the picture change. See **Anglo-Saxon architecture.**

The first abbey at Westminster was completed and dedicated in AD 1065, a year before the Norman Conquest. Most major

English cathedrals are grouped under the general classification of Post-Conquest buildings (Chichester, Durham, Ely, Gloucester, Norwich). The Norman style (qv) is the English version of Romanesque.

The first secular buildings of any significance were Norman castles, which were established as military outposts at strategic points, each under a virtually all-powerful local lord. These castles varied considerably in construction; the shell-keep type

at Arundel and Ludlow, the rectangular-keep type at Rochester, and the round-keep, seen in its most picturesque form at Windsor, despite the raising of the Round Tower to its present commanding position in the nineteenth century. Smaller fortified houses were also built; one of the best-preserved is Little Wenham Hall in Suffolk, which is essentially a miniature castle of the thirteenth century, brick-built and remaining substantially as it was in the time of

Little Wenham Hall, Suffolk, c 1270–80

Elevation of part of Longleat, from Britton's 'Architectural Antiquities'

Lincoln Cathedral from the west

Westminster Abbey from the south-west

King Edward I.

Gothic church architecture in England passed through the succeeding stages of Early English, Decorated, and Perpendicular (qqv). Coincident with the rise of this ecclesiastical architecture was the development of collegiate architecture, especially at Oxford and Cambridge. These buildings too were monastic and ecclesiastical in style.

Military and ecclesiastical styles predominated for centuries. A number of late fifteenth-century buildings marked a changing attitude, mostly manor-houses, either in stone, as at Cothay Manor in Somerset, or half-timbered as at Ockwell in Berkshire. But only in Tudor times did domestic architecture assume an independent significance. Domestic buildings acquired new comforts and occasionally rose to magnificence, notably at Hampton Court (1520). This new development was to be seen throughout the nation, from Compton Wynyates in Warwickshire to Sutton Place in Surrey, from Hengrave Hall in Suffolk to Layer Marney in Essex. Other examples were the now diminished palace of Audley End and wholly vanished palace of Nonsuch.

Renaissance influences were also at work, cross-currents of Italianate and Gothic design often uniting in strange, dichotomous harmonies. Longleat in Wiltshire, with its pilasters and large windows, displays the first exotic impact of the Renaissance. Later came Hardwick Hall in Derbyshire, undoubtedly the most remarkable of all Britain's sixteenth-century houses, its symmetry, spaciousness, and vast areas of glass exhibiting a majestic domesticity. The trend was also followed in the lesser houses of the rising gentry, farm-houses acquiring porches and larger windows, manor-houses acquiring pilasters and curving gables. All the new influences in their noblest and most pleasing domestic form are present in Montacute House, Somerset. Smaller houses and cottages of the period also displayed remarkable advances in both construction and the provision of amenities.

The first individual architect to influence English domestic building was Inigo Jones (qv (1573–1652), who has been called the father of English architecture

Audley End, Essex, 1603–16

The Banqueting House, Whitehall, London: Inigo Jones, 1619–22

Fountain Court, Hampton Court: Sir Christopher Wren, 1689–94

Lindsey House, Lincoln's Inn Fields, London, 1640

Houghton Hall, Norfolk: Colen Campbell, 1722–32

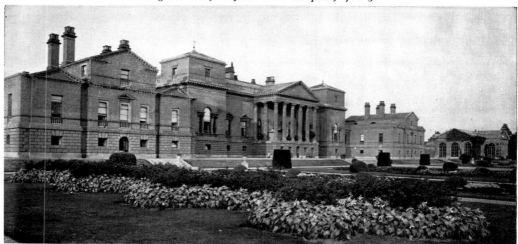

Holkham Hall, Norfolk: William Kent, begun 1734

Wilton House, Wiltshire, south façade: Isaac de Caus and Inigo Jones, begun c 1632

Jones introduced new and revolutionary theories into English architecture, particularly into urban building. His works are supreme examples of the art of adapting Italian Renaissance prototypes to the needs and climate of the North.

Jones was followed by a group who established the architectural canon out of which the Georgian tradition developed. Jones's younger collaborators, John Webb and Roger Pratt, were followed by Christopher Wren (qqv), the most renowned of all English architects, who gradually introduced what might be called a Baroque interpretation of the classic Renaissance forms of Jones and his colleagues.

Jones and Wren created great opportunities for British architects and their successors were often remarkable men. The most original was Sir John Vanbrugh (qv), soldier, author, and playwright, who succeeded Wren at the Office of Works and created a group of stupendous houses. Ecclesiastical buildings of note were designed by Nicholas Hawksmoor, Thomas Archer, James Gibbs (qqv), and others, but the eighteenth century was nonetheless primarily distinguished for secular buildings. The growing wealth of England made possible the most prolific and ostentatious era in private house building ever known. Apart from the Vanbrugh palaces, the list includes most of the so-called Stately Homes. These houses are usually grouped under the headings: (1) Baroque, 1692–c 1725; (2) Palladian, 1715–60; (3) Rococo, 1745–60.

The Baroque includes Ditchley, Oxfordshire (1720–26; architect, James Gibbs); Castle Howard, Yorkshire (1699–1712), and Blenheim Palace, Oxfordshire (1705–24), both by Vanburgh; and Easton Neston, Northamptonshire (completed 1702; architect, Hawksmoor).

The greater Palladian houses include Wanstead, Essex (1715–20), and Houghton Hall, Norfolk (1722–32), both by Campbell (qv); Holkham Hall, Norfolk (1734–64; architect, Kent (qv)); and Wrotham Park, Kent (1754; architect, Isaac Ware (qv)).

Georgian Rococo includes a greater variety of houses, ranging from the Gothick of Horace Walpole's house Strawberry Hill (1750 onwards) to the *chinoiserie* of Claydon House in Buckinghamshire (1768–71).

Meanwhile the small English house was changing but slightly in its form, although timber construction had now given way to the use of local materials, predominantly brick in the southern counties.

A new form of domestic architecture was gradually evolved which was adaptable to houses, mansions and lodges. This style, known generically as Georgian, spanned the period from about 1700 to about 1830. Thus the term covers such variations as the earlier, steeper-roofed style now known as 'Queen Anne' and 'Regency', with its more horizontal emphasis and use of slates, wider eaves, and decorative ironwork for balconies. The later years of the Georgian era (from 1760 onwards) witnessed a reaction against the formality of earlier Georgian influences. This was foreshadowed by the extravagances of Strawberry Hill and Claydon, but also appeared in works by Sir William Chambers (qv) and the adaptable James Wyatt (qv).

Although he remodelled both Osterley Park and Syon House, Robert Adam (qv) was above all

Mereworth Castle, Kent: Colen Campbell, c 1722–5

Uppark, Sussex, probably by William Talman, 1685–90

Syon House, Middlesex, interior by Robert Adam, from 1762

Osterley Park, Middlesex, remodelled by Robert Adam, from 1761

a decorative genius who exercized a lasting influence on English (and Scottish) interior design.

But by the turn of the century there were unmistakable signs of disintegration in the classical tradition, although Sir John Soane (qv) (1753–1837), one of the most remarkable and creative of architects, was in active practice. Soane's development of a logical and functional architecture was not taken up, his teachings were lost in the Gothic Revival, given its initial impetus by James Wyatt's work at Fonthill Abbey.

Before dealing with the technical and aesthetic cross-currents of nineteenth-century architecture, it is important to notice the work of John Nash (1752–1835) (qv). He is above all remembered for his unusual town- and country-planning enterprises. The first was at Blaise Hamlet in Dorset where he grouped cottage-type houses together in what is now seen as a forerunner of the garden suburb. Later in his great scheme for Regent Street and Regent's Park he created one of the most exciting urban vistas in Europe. During the Regency period (1800–30) the Greek Revival (qv) was the most important architectural manner, well shown in the collegiate buildings of William Wilkins (1778–1839, qv) at Cambridge and at University College, London.

Conflicts between rival schools of architecture were to persist throughout the reign of Queen Victoria. In its earliest stages the battle was between the adherents of Neo-classicism and advocates of a revived medieval Gothic (qv). Many architects found it possible to produce designs in both styles. Thus Sir Charles Barry (qv) (1795–1860), who preferred the classical manner, could, when necessary, design in a complex style of Gothic, as he did to win the competition for the Houses of Parliament. In carrying out this commission, Barry's colleague in charge of decoration was Augustus Pugin (qv) (1812–52), whose influence on the decorative arts in Britain was as momentous as that of Adam almost a century before.

This passion for the Gothic was fostered by the 1818 Act for building new churches, by which a million pounds was made available for the construction of over 200 Anglican churches. Although Soane, who was one of the Commissioners, and other architects such as William Inwood (1771–1843, qv), designer of St Pancras Church, favoured the Greek temple manner, the majority of the churches were in the style now known as Commissioner's Gothic. This spate of ecclesiastical architecture did much to promote the wholesale

Kedleston Hall, Derbyshire, north front: James Paine, begun 1757

The Royal Pavilion, Brighton: John Nash, from 1815

The British Museum, Bloomsbury: Smirke, 1823–47

acceptance of the Gothic revival from 1840 in other buildings, from hotels to town halls.

Architects working in the Gothic style included Gilbert Scott (qv), G F Bodley, J L Pearson, and William Butterfield (qv).

The Neo-Grecians continued to gain important commissions; the British Museum, by Sir Robert Smirke (qv); the Athenaeum and the famous Screen at Hyde Park Corner, by Decimus Burton (qv). The style recommended itself to the new banks and insurance companies as well as to the civic authorities of the provinces, with their yearning for town halls that would give substantial proof of their wealth and prosperity. These buildings were typified by Manchester Town Hall (now the Art Gallery), designed by Barry, and Birmingham Town Hall, designed by Joseph Hansom (1803–82).

Happily, the Georgian town-planning tradition was not wholly extinguished. Much advanced building was carried out in London, notably in Pimlico and Belgravia by the remarkable builder-architect Thomas Cubitt (1788–1855 qv).

Meanwhile a vast new industrial and commercial architecture was arising. The West India Docks and the London Docks, both begun at the turn of the century, possessed a melancholy magnificence which was to be echoed throughout the century in warehouses, factories, mills, and similar buildings. Their

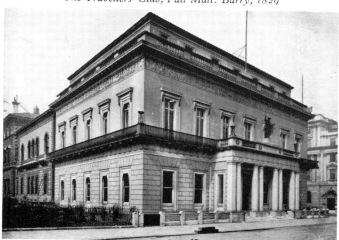

The Travellers' Club, Pall Mall: Barry, 1829

No 13 Lincoln's Inn Fields: Sir John Soane, 1812

Athenaeum Club, Pall Mall: Decimus Burton, 1829–30

College of Surgeons, Lincoln's Inn Fields: Dance the Younger, 1806–13

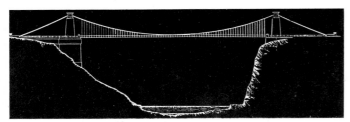

Clifton Suspension Bridge: Isambard Kingdom Brunel, 1829

Tower Bridge: Sir Horace Jones and Sir John Wolfe Barry, 1886-94

qualities are too rarely seen in other large nineteenth-century buildings.

Engineers were also making a remarkable contribution to certain aspects of architecture. The bridge-builders Thomas Telford (1757–1834), Sir Marc Isambard Brunel (1769–1849)

and his son, Isambard Kingdom Brunel (1806–59, qqv), are the outstanding figures. An important influence was exercized by the building for the 1851 Great Exhibition, designed by Sir Joseph Paxton (qv), erected in Hyde Park, and later transferred to Sydenham as the Crystal

Palace. The full significance of this magnificent building, its qualities deriving solely and successfully from its structural shell, was not grasped for many years.

Yet the Great Exhibition of 1851 had other, less happy consequences. The exhibition showed, as never before, the capabilities of machine mass-production. Henceforth any filigreed, neo-Gothic motif in timber, iron, or glass could be reproduced by the hundred thousand – and was.

This ushered in the High Victorian Gothic, a style which not only dominated churches and chapels, but also commercial and domestic architecture. Only an occasional revolutionary return to simplicity was made in the midst of this proliferating neo-Gothic mediocrity. Among these few buildings is the design by Philip Webb (1831–1915) for the Red House at Bexley Heath in Kent, built for William Morris (qqv) in 1859–60.

Ironically, church-building expanded throughout the later nineteenth century, in a world dominated by commerce and armies of underpaid workers lost to religion. Architects carried out commissions for variants on medieval Gothic with energy and dedication. But the very brashness and the success of this latter-day Gothic disseminated among the mercantile classes by the tortured and pretentious houses of C J Richardson produced an inevitable reaction.

Webb has already been mentioned. Others followed, most notably Richard Norman Shaw (1831–1912, qv). Shaw's designs in many manners, had enormous influence on domestic architecture in Britain and abroad, for he was commissioned by prosperous artists and magnates alike to build them large new houses. Although Shaw did not initiate the Queen Anne revival, his use of red brick and careful detailing in an archaic manner, and his

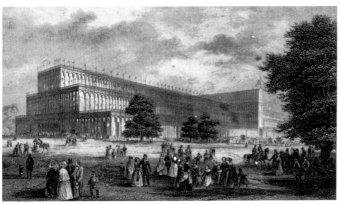

The Crystal Palace in Hyde Park: Paxton, 1851, destroyed 1936

Albert Memorial, Kensington: Sir George Gilbert Scott, 1864-72

The Law Courts: G E Street, 1874-83

country rectory, from 'The Englishman's House' by C J Richardson

Houses in Queen's Gate: Charles James Richardson, 1860

anifold commissions from the
70s, led to the almost exclusive
plication of this label to his
ork. Webb, not Norman Shaw,
is really the major innovator.
Webb's work was continued
the most important of nine-
enth-century English architects
ter Soane and Nash: C F A
oysey (1857–1941, qv), who re-
rded himself less as an inno-
tor than as one who sought for
line of continuity and sanity
om the 1820s. Thus his houses

can still be seen as rational,
practical designs, as they were at
the time when they were built,
between 1888 and World War I.
Voysey can now be recognized
as the first of Britain's modern
architects, though it can be
argued that this distinction is
shared by a Scot, Charles Rennie
Mackintosh (qv), architect of the
Glasgow School of Art.

Other architects of this period
who were mainly concerned with
domestic work were M H Baillie

Scott (1865–1945) and C R
Ashbee (1863–1942), both of
whom were in revolt against
High Victorian Gothic.

Sir Edwin Lutyens (qv) (1869–
1944) is now chiefly remembered
for his Neo-Georgian houses and
his work in the development of
the Hampstead Garden Suburb,
and his designs for the Viceroy's
House at New Delhi. Charming
and inventive as it was, his
architecture can scarcely be
called modern. However, his

House designed by Norman Shaw

A house by C F A Voysey, late nineteenth century

The Red House, Bexley Heath, Kent: Philip Webb, 1859

Headquarters building for London Transport: Charles Holden

The Market Square, Harlow New Town: Frederick Gibberd, begun 1950

Clarendon School, Oxhey, Hertfordshire: C H Aslin, 1950s

work in the Hampstead Garden Suburb continued a tradition in which English practitioners had excelled since the time of Nash. Similar 'ideal villages' and 'garden cities' had been developed in the North, at Port Sunlight from 1888, and by Sir Raymond Unwin at Earswick, near York, and at Letchworth. This work was to make its mark on the New Towns scheme initiated on so imaginative a scale after World War II.

England's contribution to the modern movement has been curiously uneven. On the one hand there have been vast and mainly successful programmes for new schools and New Towns, with a high standard of design and achievement. On the other hand, the building of new universities and university extensions and new office blocks and hotels, cannot compare with similar projects completed in America and on the Continent. Exceptions are such projects as the Elephant and Castle development in London, Castrol House, and perhaps half a dozen other schemes. Many small houses of high quality have been built, yet few blocks of flats of any great distinction apart from those designed by the official architects of the GLC. Neither do the great civic projects, such as the area around St Paul's Cathedral, offer convincing evidence that the lessons of the inter-war years have been learned – or that planners have yet begun to cope with the greatest of all the problems of modern building development: the motor car.

English bond. A method of laying bricks in alternate rows ('courses') of headers (ends) and stretchers (longer sides).

English furniture. Furniture-making has always been one of the glories of English craftsmanship. English furniture design from 1700 to 1820 was of such excellence as to be almost worthy of the title 'fine art', and boasted makers such as Chippendale and Sheraton, whose names are as familiar to us as Reynolds Gainsborough, and Turner.

Until the Restoration of Charles II in 1660, English furniture-making was similar to that in the rest of Western Europe. Oak and walnut were the favourite woods, marquetry was of coarse floral kind, cabinet-work was strong but seldom elegant. Economic growth brought about a great expansion in building during the late seventeenth century, and with it a desire for more furniture and greater attention to ornament and technical skill in production.

The first great craftsman to influence English furniture design was a Huguenot refugee from Louis XIV's court, Daniel Marot (d 1752, qv). Marot largely determined London styles in the last decade of the seventeenth

Castrol House, London: Gollins, Melvin, Ward, and Partners, 1957-63

The Vickers Millbank Tower: Ronald Ward and Partners, 1959-63

Development scheme at Elephant and Castle, London: Ernö Goldfinger

century. Oak was supplanted by the popular golden-brown imported walnut, and this was enriched with mouldings of gold-leaf on a gesso ground. In the reigns of Queen Anne and George I these materials were almost universal, and were used as the sole decoration in a style of grand simplicity.

The early eighteenth-century 'Age of Walnut' ended with the advent of mahogany, imported chiefly from Honduras and Cuba. During the reign of George II, Thomas Chippendale (1718–79) rose to prominence; his three editions of *The Gentleman and Cabinet-Maker's Director* were the most typical English expression of the Rococo style which had been in vogue in Paris since 1720. The use of slender curving foliage ornament; *chinoiserie*, Gothic, the accent on restless movement, are all attributable to Chippendale, though other fine cabinetmakers, many almost unknown today, translated his designs into what is now known as 'Chippendale furniture.'

Chippendale himself went on to make much of his finest work in the 1770s, working in the Neo-classical style. The British genius of the Neo-classical was the architect Robert Adam (1728 –92), who himself designed much severe, rectangular furniture, richly embellished with marquetry and gilt-metal mounts. Unlike William Kent, an architect of the 1730s and 1740s whose excursion into furniture-design had little effect on the national style, Adam exercized a dominant influence on all grades of furniture-making.

Before 1800, however, the designs of Hepplewhite (d 1786) guided middle-class taste; though they show little originality. With Thomas Sheraton (1751–1806), and the increasing use of satinwood, Neo-classicism was taken to its limit as a style of slender elegance and sophistication. For most of his life Sheraton was purely a designer (unlike Chippendale, who was also the owner of a large cabinet-making business), and his designs were executed by a host of London and provincial makers.

It is difficult to keep in mind the eighteenth-century way of furnishing today, when furniture is very rarely made to individual specifications. People of relatively modest means went to inspect the stock-in-trade of the local cabinetmaker, or one in London, not only for furniture but for upholstery, wallpapers, carpets, etc. They made a selection which the cabinetmaker would send and sometimes personally install. But the very rich behaved quite differently. The chosen cabinetmaker, usually assisted by an architect, was called to the house and asked to

Seventeenth century: **1** *Charles II walnut stool with upholstered seat* **2** *Early oak 'Turner's' armchair with sturdy turned posts and plank seat* **3** *Mid-century oak country chair with panelled back* **4** *Carved hall cupboard* **5** *Leather studded side chair* **6** *William and Mary table with drawers, turned legs and continuous curving stretcher* **7** *Upholstered William and Mary settee* **8** *Queen Anne walnut bureau cabinet with open fall-front* **9** *William and Mary centre table*

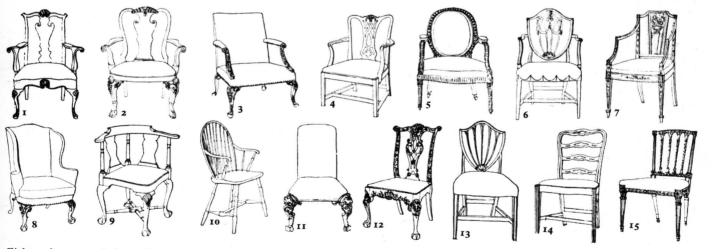

Eighteenth century chairs: **1** *Queen Anne chair with carved back splat and cabriole leg* **2** *Larger more heavily carved, early Georgian* **3** *Chippendale's version of French chairs* **4** *Chippendale's Gothick, with latticework splat* **5** *Adam style elbow chair with upholstered back and seat* **6** *Hepplewhite shield back with inlaid decoration* **7** *Sheraton, late eighteenth century* **8** *Early wing chair with claw and ball feet* **9** *Queen Anne corner chair with upholstered seat* **10** *Windsor chair with wooden seat and spindle back* **11** *George I chair on lion-shaped legs* **12** *Richly carved Chippendale rococo chair* **13** *Hepplewhite shield back side chair* **14** *Chippendale ladderback in Chinese style* **15** *Sheraton chair*

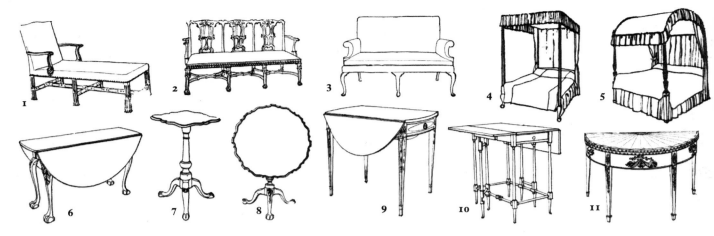

Eighteenth century: **1** *Chinese Chippendale chaise longue and* **2** *Chair-back settee with upholstered seat* **3** *Queen Anne settee on cabriole legs with roll-over arm* **4** *Early eighteenth-century four-poster bed on claw and ball feet* **5** *Field or tent bed with arched frame, late eighteenth* *century* **6** *Drop leaf dining table on cabriole legs* **7** *Tripod candlestand* **8** *Tilt-top table with a pie crust edge* **9** *Classic Pembroke drop leaf table* **10** *Spider-leg table, a lighter version of the older gate-leg* **11** *Late eighteenth century gaming table with folded top*

submit drawings for the proposed furnishings, or designs from his catalogue were discussed and altered to the patron's choice. The work was put in hand both at the cabinetmaker's shop and at the house, usually by specially hired craftsmen but sometimes by the estate carpenter.

All too little is known about individual eighteenth-century furniture-makers. Sir Ambrose Heal noted at least 4,000 makers, though even more may have existed. St Martin's Lane was the centre of the great cabinet shops, and Chippendale was established there for most of his working life. Occasional refer-ences to such shops in contemporary diaries, and notices of auctions or of damage by fire – a constant London hazard – indicate that they contained huge stocks of furniture, timber, and craftsmen's tools. According to one diary entry, a single firm employed 200 men.

Individual craftsmen were employed for each aspect of furniture-building, and drawers, carcase veneering, mounts, and gilding were all separate tasks. The whole was supervised by the cabinetmaker himself, though he seldom did any work with his own hands.

Identification of pieces is always tentative, except in the rare instances where the original accounts survive or a trade label is found inside the piece – and even these have been faked. Chairs, especially from 1780 to 1830, are often found with the maker's initials stamped on the seat rails; but even then identification is not certain. Other attributions are made on the basis of designs in the cabinetmakers' catalogue. The problem here is that many subscribers to Chippendale's *Gentleman and Cabinet-Maker's Director* were well-known cabinetmakers who no doubt copied its designs for their own clients.

If the English had adopted the French system of signing their work, attributions would be fa[r] simpler. The French *ébéniste* worked in a set style, and man[y] pieces can be identified at [a] glance. English makers were un-doubtedly more adaptable. Man[y] almost unknown makers were o[f] the first rank; on the other hand even the most famous firms pro-duced simple items for servants[] rooms.

The construction of Englis[h] furniture was unequalled any-where. Dovetails (drawer joints[) were finer than on the Continent and chair seats were held b[y] struts rather than pegs as i[n] France. The interior of cabinet work was excellent, and usuall[y] in oak. The French equivalent i[s]

Eighteenth-century chests and secretaries: **1** *Queen Anne fall-front desk on a frame* **2** *Late eighteenth-century desk with tambour panels* **3** *Mid-century pedestal library table with tooled leather top* **4** *Queen Anne dressing-table and* **5** *More elaborately carved version by Chippendale* **6** *Early tallboy on bracket feet* **7** *Bureau bookcase with broken pediment* **8** *Late eighteenth-century secretary bookcase* **9** *Early bookcase on bun feet* **10** *George II bureau cabinet with a bombé base* **11** *George III breakfront bookcase, with flat and* **12** *with swan-necked pediment*

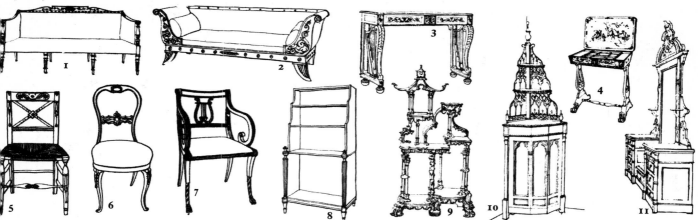

Nineteenth century: **1** *Classic Sheraton settee* **2** *Gilded Regency sofa with scrolled ends* **3** *Regency console table on harp supports* **4** *Work-table lacquered in the Chinese style* **5** *Late Victorian rush seated chair in the Sheraton style* **6** *Mid-century rosewood balloon back chair*

7 *Regency lyre-back elbow chair on sabre legs* **8** *Small Regency open book cabinet* **9** *Chinese-style Victorian whatnot with mirror-backed shelves* **10** *Victorian corner whatnot with graduated shelves over a cupboard* **11** *Late Victorian dresser with large mirror and drawers*

careless, and more often of a cheap softwood. English furniture was also more functional and better lasting than that made on the Continent. And even though factory mass production from early Victorian times resulted in more slip-shod work, the drawer of a Victorian chest moves more smoothly than any other made before or since.

The discovery of Egyptian art, and Napoleon's abortive expedition to the Nile, gave an impetus to the Regency style of 1800–20. A new wood, rosewood, was used, and Regency furniture was enriched by a return to carved ornament, which had been discarded after the rococo extravagance of Chippen-

dale's first designs.

By the end of the Regency era, strict eighteenth-century canons of sound proportions and craftsmanship were giving way to mass production on the one hand and a search for novelty on the other. The lead given by the Prince Regent in his Royal Pavilion at Brighton encouraged esoteric designs and exotic woods – calamander, amboyna, maple, and others, as well as rosewood – and gave rise to a craze for inlaying in metal, seen at its most exuberant in the tops of card tables and sofa tables. Yet the period undoubtedly produced much handsome and vigorously designed furniture which has become part of the national heritage.

During the reign of William IV the Regency tradition gradually gave way to a heavier, more sombre manner. Within 20 years of Queen Victoria's accession to the throne in 1837, the decline (hastened by the Great Exhibition of 1851) was absolute. Machine-produced furniture was in the worst possible taste, hideously overdecorated; but the new middle-class market absorbed all that the new furniture manufactories could produce.

In the 1870s William Morris' influence fostered a revival of craftsmanship as significant in furniture design as in architecture. The results are seen in the supremely simple household furniture designed by Ernest Gimson, C F Annesley Voysey, and later, Ambrose Heal. Morris' own contribution to furniture design was small: all the furniture for his firm, Morris & Co, was designed by Philip Webb.

It was only in the twentieth

century that the influence of Morris and his followers made itself felt in mass-production designs. Ambrose Heal's most notable successor was Gordon Russell who, in his factory at Broadway in the Cotswolds, made furniture as well-designed, well-finished, and truly representative of our own time as any furniture produced in other countries. Above all, he managed to apply the traditions of individual craftsmanship to modified mass-production. Fortunately, after World War II Russell was appointed the first director of the newly-established Council of Industrial Design. In this position he was able to encourage a new school of furniture-designers, including Robin Day, Ernest Race, Christopher Heal, and others.

English glass. The art of glass-making was brought to England by the Romans, but it may well have been lost after the Romans withdrew. The earliest glassmaker known by name is a Frenchman, Laurence Vitrearius, who bought land near Chiddingfold, Surrey, in 1226; he provided both clear and coloured glass for Westminster Abbey in 1240. From that time, window glass and simple utensils in a crude, rather bubbly green forest glass were made in several centres throughout the country.

During the sixteenth century the demand for expensive Venetian glass was so great that in 1549 Jean Carré, a businessman from Antwerp and Arras, brought over some Venetian glassworkers. The venture failed, but in 1570 Carré brought over more workmen to start a glass-

house at Crutched Friars. The following year Jacopo Verzelini (qv), a Venetian-trained glass-worker, arrived from Antwerp as manager. Verzelini was so successful that jealous English glassmakers were probably responsible for burning down Crutched Friars in 1575.

In 1615 Sir Robert Mansell, a retired admiral, entered the industry, and by 1623 had obtained a monopoly that included the manufacture of window glass and looking-glasses in England, Scotland, and Wales. Mansell died in 1656.

After the Restoration of 1660 there was an increased demand for luxuries and a growth of interest in scientific experiment.

An English engraved wineglass, dated 1580, probably by Verzelini

A goblet with gadrooned base to the bowl and raspberry prunts, c 1675

Glass bowl with enamel painting by William Beilby, dated 1763

Vase by James Bovell, 1876

The monopoly passed to the Duke of Buckingham, who started a factory in Greenwich to make glass resembling 'Rock Crystal', and in 1663 opened another glasshouse at Vauxhall which became famous for its mirrors. The demand for Venetian glass became so great that the embargo on importing it was lifted. Imported glass was, however, fragile and expensive, and when in 1673 George Ravenscroft (qv) set up an experimental glasshouse in the Savoy to try and produce a stronger glass with English ingredients, the Glass Sellers' Company backed him.

By the end of the century nearly 30 English glasshouses were producing Ravenscroft's new glass. This had become so heavy that it was now impossible to blow hollow stems and knops, and although some Venetian and Baroque elements still appeared on expensive ceremonial pieces,

drinking glasses were left completely undecorated. Interest was created by a variety of stem furniture incorporating balusters and different shaped knops. An occasional elongated bubble of air (a tear) is found in the base of the bowl or the stem (see **Air twist**).

There were great changes in forms and styles of drinking glasses during the eighteenth century, for a variety of social, political, technical, and economic reasons. Glasses became smaller and there was a bigger variety of bowl formations to suit the new fashion for stronger drinks like port laced with brandy, hollands (gin), and potent cordials. The influx of German influences and skilled craftsmen was responsible for the introduction of the moulded 'silesian' or pedestal stem and the techniques of engraving and cutting. Glasses were already becoming lighter and more decorative when an excise tax was imposed on raw materials (1745). As a result, the heavy lead content in each batch was reduced and glass became more watery-looking and lighter. Decoration now became elaborate and varied. Air twist stems were more complicated and sophisticated. Wheel engraving of bowls became common and, since there were many social and political drinking clubs, was often symbolic. The best-known examples are the Jacobite glasses with a rose and bud for the Old and New Pretender, but there were also Williamite, Hanoverian, and Masonic glasses. After each toast it was customary to thump the table in acclamation so, as an economy measure, stumpy glasses with heavy flat feet were devised. They were known as Firing glasses, because the thumps were said to resemble the rattle of musketry fire.

In imitation of porcelain, which was in great demand,

opaque white glass was produced in similar forms, and blue, green, and amethyst glass also became popular. Contrary to popular belief, this was made all over England and was not confined to the Bristol area. The most outstanding enamellers on clear glass were William and Mary Beilby (qv).

The cutting of glass, which had started rather tentatively on the thickest part of glasses, the heavier sweetmeat dishes, and candelabra, was still developing when the tax on glass was doubled in 1777. Many frustrated glassworkers and cutters emigrated to Ireland (see **Irish glass**).

The nineteenth century produced many revivals (Gothic, Greek, Venetian, Roman, etc) and an Arts and Crafts movement whose aim was a return to medieval craftsmanship. But there was also a love of novelty for its own sake which encouraged the production of colourful and bizarre fancy glass. In Britain there were no outstanding figures like Gallé or Tiffany, but forms of glass were none the less affected by the Art Nouveau movement. James Powell of Whitefriars produced some very delicately tinted iridescent glass, and other designs subtly combined green glass with silver mounts.

Since the 1930s, when Steve[n]s and Williams employed a you[ng] architect, Keith Murray, [to] design their commercial wa[re,] many other factories have f[ol]lowed suit. Of the freelan[ce] artists working in glass, two w[ho] have become international[ly] known must be mentione[d,] Laurence Whistler, with his d[elicate] stippling of goblets, and Jo[hn] Hutton, with his magnifice[nt] engraving of windows f[or] Coventry Cathedral and t[he] National Library at Ottawa.

Cut glass goblet, 19th century

Glasses and decanter designed by W J Wilson

An early Iron Age burial urn with wheel-turned decoration

Slipware dish made by Thomas Toft, seventeenth century

An English Delft barber's bowl, decorated in underglaze blue, made at Lambeth c 1690–1700

Stoneware jug of the type made by Dwight, Fulham, 1675–1700

English pottery and porcelain. Pottery has been made in England for over 3,000 years. The earliest Stone Age pottery was crudely formed by hand: urn-shaped vessels made to contain the ashes of the dead, and small bowls and beakers for food and drink. These are sometimes still dug up from ancient burial grounds.

When the Romans occupied Britain, they imported much red stoneware from the Continent, and they also taught the Britons to make earthenware of a much more refined type. During the Dark Ages, however, Roman skills were forgotten; little pottery survives from this period. As late as Elizabethan times, English pottery was very coarse and crude. It was strictly utilitarian and was only used by the peasants, and in the kitchens of wealthier people. The ware was sometimes decorated with a slip different in colour from the body and sometimes glazed with a lead glaze, yellow, brown, or green in colour.

Slip-decorated ware continued to be made and became gradually more technically proficient. The best examples are the elaborate chargers of Thomas Toft and his contemporaries, made in the reign of Charles II.

The first English tin-enamelled earthenware was made in the late sixteenth century. It was called Delft in England because it was an imitation of the ware made at Delft in the Netherlands. The tin glaze gave the ware a whitish appearance. When it was decorated the colours used were blue, yellow, green, and manganese brown. The manufacture of Delft continued in England until the end of the eighteenth century.

Stoneware was made from 1672, when John Dwight of Fulham started copying German wine jugs. This stoneware was either brown or grey. In the early eighteenth century, potters concentrated on producing a whiter stoneware, in an effort to discover the secret of making Chinese porcelain. The result was salt-glazed stoneware, which continued to be made throughout the eighteenth century. It was hard and strong and could be very precisely moulded. The glaze has a pleasant orange-peel texture.

The greatest developments in the history of English pottery took place in the eighteenth century and were largely due to Josiah Wedgwood, unquestionably the father of the present-day pottery industry. Among Wedg-

wood's many inventions, and perhaps his greatest achievement, was a cream-coloured earthenware he called Queensware. This was quickly copied by potters all over the country, notably at Leeds and Liverpool, and much of present-day tableware derives directly from it. Wedgwood was also responsible for introducing other kinds of pottery. His Jasperware (a refined unglazed stoneware), and his black basaltware, became world-famous and are still made to this day.

Different parts of England are known for particular kinds of pottery. Sunderland, for instance, produced a very distinctive white ware decorated with transfer printing and the addition of a pinkish (gold) lustre. Liverpool became famous for its transfer printing. The firm of Sadler and Green decorated much of Wedgwood's Queensware in this manner. Delft was made in Liverpool, Bristol, and London. Staffordshire has always produced a variety of wares and is still the heart of the British pottery industry.

Porcelain was not made in England until the middle of the eighteenth century. The first factory seems to have been in operation at Chelsea in 1744, followed a little later by other factories at Bow, Plymouth, Bristol, Lowestoft, Worcester, Derby, and Coalport. In the early nineteenth century, factories were started at Nantgarw and Swansea. These are only the most celebrated of the British porcelain factories. The documentation of early factories is almost non-existent and it is only through old sale catalogues and letters that something of their history can be pieced together.

The Derby factory seems to have been started about 1745, and continued with various changes and takeovers until in 1890 it became the Royal Crown Derby Porcelain Company.

Early Chelsea ware was copied from the work of contemporary silversmiths, and also from white Chinese porcelain. Later it followed Meissen originals. The Derby factory took over Chelsea in 1770 and the work soon showed the marked influence of the famous French factory at Sèvres. Figures with elaborate bocages were made at Chelsea and during the Chelsea-Derby period.

The Bow factory drew its inspiration from Meissen, though a certain amount of transfer printing was also done. Quantities of figures were made, many of them copies of Meissen or

Fulham stoneware tankard with silver rim by James Osburn, 1733

A Nottingham stoneware mug; 'Sarah Hole Novb ye 19th 1720'

A porcelain mug made at Liverpool c 1760, with black transfer

A Jasperware vase made by Josiah Wedgwood, c 1780

A Lowestoft porcelain mug, painted on white, made about 1790

Earthenware jug, transfer-printed and painted, Liverpool, 1804

A Longton Hall porcelain teapot with an Italian landscape, c 1755

A Leeds creamware teapot with a portrait of George III, c 1770

A late 18th-century Leeds chestnut basket, cream-coloured earthenware

A group of Sunderland lustre jugs

Chelsea figures – though for a time the factory did employ a modeller called Mr Tebo who had worked for Wedgwood. The figures made at Bow were rather coarser in modelling than those made at Chelsea, and the bocage backgrounds were cruder.

Porcelain was made at Lowestoft from 1756 until about 1803. Much blue-and-white as well as polychrome ware was produced. Charming little painted scenes were sometimes used as decoration, but most of the ware was decorated with flowers in either an oriental or French style.

The Worcester factory grew from a small factory started at Bristol in 1748. Worcester was important for the manufacture of fine-quality tableware, and it has continued in production to this day. The early work of the factory was inspired by the craft of the silversmith and by oriental porcelain, and much work was thrown as well as moulded. A great deal of the early work was decorated in underglaze blue, a colour that was much used at this factory later on as well. By 1755, natural sprays of flowers such as those used in decoration at Meissen were being painted. A couple of years later transfer printing came into wide use. Soon afterwards coloured backgrounds were used for decoration (as at Sèvres), the commonest being the famous

Worcester scale blue. Much porcelain was decorated with armorial bearings, and such pieces were frequently specially commissioned.

The porcelain made in the 1770s at Worcester is of a very high quality indeed. The body is very thin and delicate. A little later, many fluted shapes came into use; these were sparingly decorated with little flowers, either painted in colours or gilded. The nineteenth-century productions of the Worcester factory were more restrained in decoration than those of most of their contemporaries.

Spode (Copeland) and Minton were the most famous of the Staffordshire porcelain factories. Both firms still make very high-quality ware. In 1863, Minton began the 'acid gold process' in which acid is used to produce a gold pattern in bas-relief.

Spode's Royal College shape, designed by Neal French and David White in 1958, was one of the first signs of an enterprising design policy among the old-established potteries. David Queensberry's designs for Midwinter have had considerable success, and simple informal designs are now being produced by Wedgwood, Royal Worcester, Royal Crown Derby, and other firms best known for traditional shapes and decorations.

A Jackfield earthenware cow milk-jug, about 1800

A porcelain dish, hand-painted in many colours, Swansea, c 1820

Wedgwood plate with feather-edge and Liverpool Birds print

A hand-painted porcelain plate made by Minton, 19th century

Spode earthenware plate, c 1819

Spode Apollo bone china, designed by Neal French and David White

A stoneware vase: Leach, 1954

Plate designed by Paolozzi

A George III silver épergne, made in 1768

Nowadays, pottery and earthenware is just as acceptable on the table as bone china. Denby produces some excellent plain tableware, 'Peasantware'. Imaginative earthenware is being produced by Portmeirion, Rye, Briglin, and Honiton, among the smaller potteries, and innumerable potters throughout the country are producing individual designs.

Entablature (Italian *intavolutura*, an object placed on a table). The uppermost part of a classical order above the capital (qv). It normally consists of three members; the architrave, frieze, and cornice. It is often richly moulded, carved, or otherwise decorated.

Entasis. On classical columns, the subtle swelling given to the middle section, ie between the top and bottom of the shaft. This is an optical necessity. If the column tapered uniformly, it would, in fact, appear to have concave sides. The entasis was first introduced by the Greeks for the Doric order.

Epergne. A table centre-piece, usually silver, for 'relishes' and condiments. The name comes from the French word to economize – *épargner* – and relates to the use of the épergne as a table holder for salt, pickles, sauces, and the like. The épergne became popular in the first half of the eighteenth century and went out of fashion at the beginning of the nineteenth. Early épergnes tend to be compact and solid, but by 1750 light, elegant, and large épergnes were made with slender branches holding the baskets and dishes and a double-tiered pagoda top hung with bells.

Shortly after 1760, with the Neo-classical revival, the épergne became simplified once more, and its piercing reverted to more regular patterns. In wealthy houses a second pair of épergnes was used for desserts, usually with eight small suspended baskets and a large central bowl or basket standing on scrolled feet some 4 in high.

Epistyle (Greek, *epi* 'on', *stulos* 'a column'). In classical architecture, the lowest division of the entablature, otherwise known as the architrave (qv).

Equilateral arch. Another name for a pointed arch, in which the two centres describe arcs of radii equal to the span.

Ercolani, Lucian R (*b* 1888). The chairman of Ercol Furniture. He was born in Italy and taken to England at the age of three. He studied design at the Shoreditch Technical Institute. In his early twenties he was successively designer for two High Wycombe furniture manufacturers and teacher of advanced furniture-design classes at the

Lucian Ercolani

Modern Windsor chair made by Ercol in elm and beech

Govancroft's 'Lunar' range

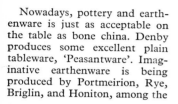

'Westbury', modern pottery by Langley

Raymond Erith

Morley Hall, Wareside, Hertfordshire, designed by Erith

Ralph Erskine

High Wycombe Technical Institute. In his early thirties he founded Furniture Industries Ltd, which now sells under the name of its associated company, Ercol. In his youth he was much impressed by the simple furniture made by early settlers in America, by the woodwork of the American Quaker and Shaker communities, and by the Windsor chair. His great achievement is to have mass produced furniture which looks craftsman-made.

Erith, Raymond Charles (*b* 1904). A British architect who has aroused both hostility and enthusiasm by his scholarly practice and development of the Georgian idiom. Yet some of his buildings are substantial contributions to any history of modern domestic architecture, indicating the lessons in town planning to

A house in Sweden designed by Ralph Erskine

be learned from the Regency genuis for serene, neighbourly, practical houses and estates. Erith has explored these themes in his designs for small houses in Essex and Suffolk. His design for the Hampstead public house, Jack Straw's Castle, with a castellated, weatherboarded façade, also caused controversy. His most considerable commission has been for the reconstruction of Nos 10, 11, and 12 Downing Street and the Old Treasury Building in Whitehall. Erith has also been responsible for the design of much collegiate building.

Erskine, Ralph (*b* 1914). A British architect trained in England and now practising in Sweden, where his reputation and achievements rank with those of the foremost Scandi-

Interior of a house at Jädraas, designed by Erskine

Houses for forestry workers at Jädraas, designed by Erskine

The Etruscan Room at Osterley, Middlesex, designed by Robert Adam

A Louis XVI mahogany commode by Beneman in le style Etrusque

navian architects. He was born in Mill Hill, educated at Saffron Walden Friend's School, and trained at the Polytechnic School of Architecture. He began practice as a surveyor and moved to Sweden in the late 1930s.

His versatility is revealed by a list of some of his works: a factory for making cardboard at Fors, north of Stockholm; a sports hotel in Lapland, a remarkable example of a building effectively related to its terrain; a highly sophisticated shopping centre in Lulea, an industrial city almost within the Arctic circle; and numerous private houses.

Escritoire. Like its early forms 'scriptor' and 'scrutoire', a general term for furniture intended for writing. See **Bureau** and **Writing table**.

Escutcheon. A term borrowed from heraldry, in which it refers to the shield which carries armorial bearings. It describes the metal plate fitted over the keyhole of a door and pivoting on a screw or rivet.

A Louis XVI étagère in satinwood with Sèvres biscuit medallions

Etagère. The French term for a set of open shelves, either in the form of a table or attached to a wall as a hanging bookshelf. The term has been appropriated by the English-speaking world and is often used of any small table with open tiers, such as the 'what-not'. In France these pieces appeared at the end of the eighteenth century and have remained popular ever since.

Etruscan style. A decorative style derived from Roman antiquities and especially Etruscan ornament. The plates of Sir William Hamilton's collection (*Antiquités Etrusques, Grecques et Romaines*), published in 1766, appears to have been the original source of this style. However, the Adam brothers claimed to be the English innovators, and they undoubtedly applied Etruscan ideas in several of their houses – the most notable and only extant example being the Etruscan Room at Osterley.

The *style Etrusque* in France was probably derived from the Adams'; it affected French decorative ideas only in the last few years of the eighteenth century. Its most pleasing expression was the exceptional severity and purity of line in Riesener's late furniture and in the furniture of his successor as maker to the crown, Beneman.

Eustyle (Greek, *eu* 'well', *stulos* 'column'). A wide spacing for columns, a full $2\frac{1}{4}$ diameters apart.

Ewer. A jug with a wide spout and handle, decorated and made *en suite* with a basin or deep dish. In medieval times a servant known as a ewerer took water to guests at table so that they could wash their hands. Later the ewer

increased in size and was used primarily for personal ablutions.

Exedra. A term from classical architecture now used to describe a large niche or recess in a wall, or angular projections to the main building such as a porch or chapel. Its earlier meanings too were varied but rather more particular: a vestibule of a house or recess in a gymnasium, or a palaestra in which discussions

were held. In this last form the exedra was provided with raised seats.

Extrados. The outer or upper edge of the curve of an arch.

Eye. Most commonly used of a small circular window, though it refers to the centre of any architectural feature, for example, the eye of an Ionic volute or the eye of a dome.

Ewer made by Pierre Harache in 1697 for the Vintners Company

Medallion of Fabergé by Pocock

Two antique faience pigeon-shaped tureens, Strasbourg and Marseilles

Faenza waisted albarello c 1480

Fabergé, Carl (1846–1920). A descendant of Swiss immigrants to Russia, he was the favourite jeweller of the Tsars as well as of every court in Europe. Fabergé is especially known for his Easter eggs in precious stones and enamel, which he made for the imperial family to exchange as presents, and also for miniature animals carved from the innumerable semi-precious stones of his adopted country, for heavy ribbed gold cigarette cases, and for enchanting jewelled flowers.

As most of his work was portable and precious, much was carried away by émigrés during the Russian Revolution. Fabergé objects now command prices far in excess of their intrinsic value.

Fabric. The basic structure of a building. Now more generally

Fabergé ribbed gold cigarette case

used for woven materials, whether of natural or synthetic fibres.

Façade. The front elevation or face of a building; this term is normally used only of fairly substantial buildings.

Facets. A furniture decoration of the late sixteenth and early seventeenth century. Facets were small, many-sided pieces of wood, commonly of lozenge shape, that were applied to flat areas of domestic furniture.

Facia, fascia (Latin, a strip or band). A term with at least three meanings. (1) A timber batten used to cover the ends of rafters which are left bare at the eaves of a roof; the rainwater guttering is fixed to the facia. (2) An element in the architrave as evolved in the Ionic and Corinthian orders; ie a flat vertical band between two horizontal mouldings. (3) The board above a shop window carrying the name of the proprietor or lessee.

Faience, fayence. The name given by the French to tin-enamelled earthenware. This kind of pottery was made all over

Europe from the sixteenth to the eighteenth centuries; the English version is called Delft, and the Italian maiolica (qqv). The word faience derives from Faenza, one of the most important centres in Italy for the manufacture of maiolica. In France, faience was made throughout the length and breadth of the country: at Aprey, Lille, Lyons, Marseilles, Moustiers, Nevers, Quimper, Rouen, Sceaux, Sèvres, Strasbourg, and many other places.

There were two main sorts of French faience, *faience blanche*, which, as the name suggests, was undecorated, and faience painted with coloured decoration. The early ware was painted with metallic oxides, which were applied to the raw glaze and fired. The colours were blue, yellow, orange, and brown. Later faience was decorated on top of the glaze and refired again at a lower temperature, so that brighter enamel colours could be used, including red and pink.

The French faience industry went into a decline at the end of the eighteenth century, as a result of competition from English Wedgwood creamware and native porcelain.

Faience is still made in many districts in France. The pro-

ductions of the potteries are mainly rather unskilful copies of traditional peasant pottery, made almost entirely for the tourist trade.

Fall-front. A flap on the front of a piece of writing furniture. It can be let down and is usually supported by lopers or quadrant stays so that it forms a level surface for writing. The flap encloses numerous drawers, cupboards, pigeon-holes, and other writing facilities.

The earliest English fall-fronts were probably made c 1660, though even earlier examples were made on the Continent. Rectangular, in walnut, and with drawers in the lower part, the fall-front cabinet was a common piece of furniture in the reigns

French Interior Decoration. *A set of mahogany fauteuils by Jacob Frères and a small table, c 1800, in a vestibule leading to the garden*

Louis XVI marquetry secrétaire à abattant (fall-front secretary)

Louis XVI mother-of-pearl fans with painted leaves

of William and Mary, Queen Anne, and George I, but it gradually gave way to a smaller fall-front, found in secrétaire cabinets from the mid-eighteenth century. The upper parts became bookcases with glazed doors, and the fall-front, some 9 in high and no longer filling the whole

of the top, opened to reveal narrow drawers and pigeon-holes, all of which could be pulled forward for the writer's convenience. Below, cupboard doors often replaced the earlier drawers.

The finest examples of the fall-front occur on French cabinets of the Louis XV and Louis XVI era – the *secrétaire à abattant*. Among the finest in existence are examples by the royal cabinetmaker, J H Riesener.

Famille jaune, noire, rose, verte. Types of Chinese porcelain (qv) made under the Ch'ing dynasty (1644–1912), mainly for the export trade. They are called by French names because the first literature about Chinese porcelain was written in French. The earliest of these categories is the *verte*, so called because of the predominance of green in the polychrome designs. In the most spectacular of the *famille verte* pieces, the enamelling is brilliant in colour, with an almost jewel-like intensity, and the designs are broad in treatment, with a delicate refinement lacking in

the more decorated wares. In *famille jaune* ware the predominant colour is yellow.

Famille rose was painted with an opaque pink enamel of European origin. This was used as early as the last decade of the seventeenth century, but was not made in large quantities until the eighteenth century. *Famille noire* ware, with its lustrous black background, was often over-decorated, and though it has a rarity value it is much less attractive than the other types.

Fan. The fan has been known since Egyptian times, when rigid frames on long handles edged with feathers were used in religious and court ceremonies. Roman ladies favoured small ivory fans. The ceremonial type in silver and silver gilt was adopted by the Church in the Middle Ages, and examples are still carried in papal processions.

Folding fans came originally from China or Japan, and Catherine de Medici is credited with having introduced the fashion to Europe. These fans comprise narrow strips of rigid material (the sticks), fixed at one end with a rivet and embellished with a folded semi-circle of vellum, paper, lace, or silk (the mount), fixed across the free ends of the sticks.

Huguenot fan-makers took the craft to London and Holland in 1685, and the next hundred years saw the zenith of fan-making and decoration. A new type of folding fan evolved in which the sticks or blades were linked not with a mount but with silk ribbons. The blades of these *brisé* fans were either intricately carved or left plain for painting. Noted artists, including Angelica Kauffman, painted mounts and blades, and their works are valued by collectors, as are the *vernis martin* (qv) fans with their lacquered sticks.

Mass-production in the nine-

teenth century ended fan-making as a craft, and the best fans of that period are those made in imitation of earlier French types.

Fanlight. A window above a door; it was frequently shaped like an open fan. Such windows received a great deal of attention from eighteenth-century architects, and provided decorative entrances to smaller houses. The term is now applied to any window, whatever its shape, above a door.

Fan spandrels. Ornamental corner fillings, found below the centre drawer of some late eighteenth-century sideboards.

Fan vaulting. A very late form of Gothic vaulting of which there are only about 25 English examples. The most famous are the Chapel of King's College, Cambridge, and Henry VII's chapel. The vault is composed of inverted solid half-cones, or cones (as in Henry VII's chapel), in between which are small flat areas on the surface of the vault. The cones have concave sides and are decorated with a fanlike pattern of tracery and ribs, all springing from the inverted apex of the cone. Decorative pendants suspended from the apex are a further elaboration of this highly-wrought form of vaulting.

A famille rose plate painted in ruby black, reign of Yung Chêng

A famille verte plate, made for Emperor K'ang Hsi

A famille jaune vase, painted 'on the biscuit' with flowering trees, yellow ground, reign of K'ang Hsi

A famille noire vase, with painted birds and plum-blossom on a black ground, reign of K'ang Hsi

A Regency fanlight

Oak farthingale chair with turkey work back and seat, c 1650

Farthingale chair. The nineteenth-century name for the upright, upholstered, armless chairs that were common throughout Europe in the seventeenth century. Both back and seat were padded. There is no evidence to support or confound the idea that these chairs were made to accommodate the huge farthingale, fashionable skirts in Elizabethan and Jacobean England – though ladies could certainly not hope to wedge themselves between the arms of any other chair.

Fascia. See **Facia.**

Fauteuil. The French term for an armchair. There can be little doubt that mid-eighteenth-century French chairs have never been surpassed for elegance and comfort.

The French chair developed in the seventeenth century on typical European lines: made in walnut or oak, turned rather than carved, heavy and of massive build.

In Louis XIV's reign the chair became lighter, was very often carved and gilded, and was decorated with heavy Baroque foliage. This gave way in the Régence period to the extravagant early Rococo forms best seen in the Musée des Arts Décoratifs in the Louvre, Paris, where the exceptionally curved frames are encrusted with rocks, flames, shells, branches of flowers, and scrollwork.

By 1750 a more sober but extremely graceful form was being made, all the lines curving and with cabriole legs.

The increasing social influence of women was largely responsible for the rapid changes in chair design. In the 1730s the wide hoops of the dresses forced the *menuisiers* to set back the arm supports of *fauteuils*. The informality of French society after the death of Louis XIV enabled women to order more comfortable chairs; the *fauteuil* of the Louis XV period, with its short legs and deep feather cushions, padded back, and curved arms, is still among the most comfortable of all chairs.

The Louis XVI *fauteuil* was less comfortable. It was built on straight, classical lines but was much lighter in structure than such a chair would have been 30 years earlier. It often closely resembled English Sheraton chairs, and resemblances between English and French work continue to be found in the Directoire and Empire periods (1795–1830); some Regency and Empire chairs are difficult to tell apart. Gilt frames were largely replaced by polished woods, and on late chairs, ormolu mounts are also found.

The tapestry covers often found on French chairs are usually nineteenth century. It was more common to cover French eighteenth-century chairs in silks, satins, damasks, and velvets, very few of which have survived. French chairs are held together by wooden pegs, which join all members of the chair, and four of which project on the underside of the chair, where the leg joins the seat-rail. (English and American chairs, by contrast, are strengthened by struts at each corner of the underframe, or with overlapping blocks.)

The practice of signing fauteuils and other chairs was common in France from the 1740s in the same way that cabinet furniture was signed. The J M E stamp (the approval mark of the *menuisiers-ébénistes'* jury) is seldom found on chairs, however. The greatest chair-makers of the Louis XV period were Tilliard and Lebas, though other makers often rivalled their work. In the Louis XVI period the craft was dominated by the incomparable Georges Jacob, maker to the Crown, whose sons worked for Napoleon and Charles X.

Nowadays, upholstered theatre seats are referred to as fauteuils.

Federal period. Term used to describe American furniture from *c* 1780 to *c* 1830, notably that of Duncan Phyfe and Samuel McIntire (qqv). See **American furniture.**

Fender. The earliest fenders date from the end of the seventeenth century. At first the fender was a guard to prevent ashes from spreading, but by 1700 the fender proper had evolved as a separate guard to stop logs and cinders from rolling on to the floor. With predominantly wooden interiors, such fireguards were essential.

Early fenders were commonly of brass, with little decoration. By the 1750s Rococo influence had been felt in all aspects of

A Charles X fauteuil in bois clair

interior furnishing, and scrollwork and boss decoration was added to fenders, which were designed *en suite* with the apron of the grate.

The fender had a straight front with rounded corners or a serpentine front, matching the shape of the grate apron. The increasingly elaborate style of the 1770s, and Adam's influence in particular, gave rise to delicately pierced and decorated fenders of a beauty which has never been surpassed. Fenders were made of brass, copper, steel, with pierced decoration and sometimes even silver. The motifs in the decoration were usually repeated on the fireplace, grate, and fire-irons. Cast-iron was used in the nineteenth century.

Fenestration (Latin, *fenestra* 'a window'). The term used to describe the way in which windows are set out in an architectural façade or elevation. It is now more generally used to describe the general effect of such an arrangement, particularly those façades in which glazing divisions and subdivisions are a considerable decorative factor in the visual appeal of a street, square, circus, or crescent. The decorative appeal of fenestration was wholly ignored by the Victorians who replaced small panes of glass and their enclosing glazing bars with sheets of plate glass.

Tapestry covered Louis XV fauteuil, signed by Falconet

A Louis XVI fauteuil with a painted frame

Two late eighteenth-century fenders; above, pierced and engraved steel; below, engraved brass

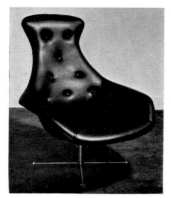

Fibreglass chair by Nigel Walters

Festoon. A chain of fruit, flowers, or drapery hung between two points. Festoons of drapery were commonly used in Georgian and even more often in Victorian interior decorations. Festoons of fruit and flowers as a decorative theme, especially in the borders of carpets and tapestries or carved on furniture, have been popular since the seventeenth century.

Fibreglass. The basic components of glass – silicone, sand, etc – can be transformed by artificial processes into a fibrous form. To make a fibreglass fabric, the materials are fused into a marble-like substance, then melted into a filament and drawn on to a drum or wheel. The filament is spun, woven, and finished in the normal way. The fabric is often printed.

In America, fibreglass fabrics have been in domestic use since 1951, and in Europe slightly later.

Spun fibreglass, sealed between two sheets of glass, has acoustic and heat-conserving properties.

Fibreglass is perhaps better known as a rigid, load-bearing material: for cars, boats, sanitary fittings, chairs, and so on. These are, in fact, made of segments of glass fibre bound with polyester resins which are poured into moulds and set. Antique garden urns, chimney-pieces, etc, are being reproduced in fibreglass.

Fiddleback. A term applied to chair splats, which resemble the musical instrument in shape. They were first designed for walnut chairs, *c* 1700, in conjunction with hooped and undulating uprights, and cabriole legs. They have been extremely popular in America since Colonial times. Fiddleback is also the name given to a decorative veneer with an undulating grain, usually mahogany or maple.

Fiddlehead. The ornamental scroll so called because of its resemblance to the terminal scroll at the head of a violin. It occurred most spectacularly in the scroll work on the bow of a ship but was also used on cabinet furniture and in wrought-iron decoration.

Field bed. The portable beds used from the Middle Ages to the mid-nineteenth century. 'Field bed' and 'tent bed' were used interchangeably in the mid-eighteenth century and thereafter the term 'tent bed' was more commonly used. The field bed was a collapsible bed that was used for travelling. Early examples probably dating from the sixteenth century had canopies; these were usually of the wagon tilt variety, consisting of a hooped framework over which hangings were arranged. During the eighteenth century, travellers frequently took tent beds with them, especially on their journeys abroad.

Fielded panel. A term normally used to describe a feature of Renaissance decoration: a panel in which most of the carved surface is raised above the face of the panel or frame. Fielded panels in the seventeenth and eighteenth centuries were simpler, frequently little more than plain panels raised above bevelled frames or moulding.

Figure. Characteristic marking on wood. See articles on specific woods.

Figurehead. The carved figure placed at the prow of a sailing ship from the earliest times until the last days of sail. Many were of considerable artistic merit, and others were expressive and vital pieces of folk art. Some of the best examples are to be found at Mystic Seaport, the museum in Connecticut, and at the Maritime Museum at Greenwich, England.

Filigree. A delicate, pierced scroll design in gold, silver, other metals, and later paper. Filigree has been a popular decorative motif from very early times, especially in jewellery and small *objets de vertu*.

An interesting type of filigree decoration is scrolled paperwork, first practised in the fifteenth century when paper was used as a substitute for precious metals. Though it is found in the sixteenth and seventeenth centuries, the finest work was done in the last half of the eighteenth, when it became an occupation for

A wooden figurehead, 1807

fashionable ladies. The scrolls of paper were arranged in any number of delicate designs (the edges gilded, silvered, or painted) and applied in particular to tea-caddies or other small boxes.

Fillet. A word with two meanings. To a carpenter a fillet is almost any narrow piece of rectangular-sectioned wood used as a raised strip or ridge. To

New England field bed dating from 1790–1800

A gold filigree bracelet c 1800

inials on the marquetry case of a late seventeenth-century bracket clock

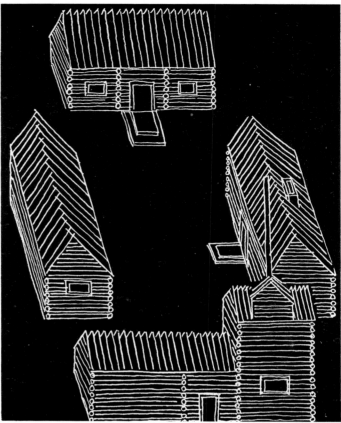

The enclosed rectangular farmyard and double-cabin type of dwelling

chitects, however, a fillet is a arrow flat strip used to separate two curved mouldings or two utes of a column. The term is so applied to a band used to rminate a series of mouldings.

inial. A decorative feature, of ood, stone, or metal, used to mphasize the terminal points a gable, pinnacle, turret, gateost, bed tester, clock, or cabinet rnice. Finials are usually aditional objects such as balls, ns, or obelisks, but can also be rvings of exotic shape. They e an important decorative ement in oriental architecture, rticularly that of China.

innish architecture. The tellectual enterprise of Finnish ventieth-century architects has nded to obscure the fact that inland has a long tradition of digenous architecture. The ry remoteness of the country s meant that outside influences ve been relatively weak. None e less, Finland did absorb and reinterpret the two great movements of modern times: the classicism of the eighteenth century and the 'modern movement' of the present century.

Stone fortresses and castles were built early in Finnish history, not as strongholds of individual lords but rather as Finnish national strongpoints and administrative outposts. These fortresses were usually sited on islands, or man-moated headlands which were cut off from the mainland. The oldest are the castles of Turku and Viipuri. Hämeenlinna, a square castle erected by the Teutonic knights, was at one time within the Swedish kingdom, and remains Finland's only medieval castle built of brick. From medieval times until the eighteenth century, these forts were of importance as Finland was fought over by Sweden and Russia. One fortified town, Hamina, was still being added to in the first half of the eighteenth century; it still exists, its streets radiating from

an administrative core. The island fortress of Suomenlinna, 'The Gibraltar of the North', was built even later, but little now remains of what must have been a spectacular military and architectural *tour de force*.

The adoption of Christianity led to the building of a notable group of medieval churches, in both wood and stone. The first sizable church was Turku Cathedral, stone-built with a brick choir. But the most memorable ecclesiastical buildings are the beautiful wooden churches built between 1600 and 1820, which were developed in what was virtually an unbroken tradition over the centuries. The magnificent 12-sided wooden church at Vimpeli, built in 1807 to the designs of Jacob Rijf, represents a fitting climax to this architectural development.

In domestic building, abundance of timber conditioned architectural development. Finland's earliest houses were inevitably log cabins; later built by an ingenious system of interlocking logs. A particular feature of these mainly agricultural buildings was the double-cabin system, in which the household was separated from livestock by a rudimentary partition which

later developed into an entrance hall of increasing sophistication. This double-cabin system was also used in larger houses, and reached its apogee in the formal two-storeyed houses of the eighteenth century, built round a courtyard enclosed by barns, stables, and other out-buildings.

Villas and larger houses were built later in Finland than in most European countries. The best-preserved manorial mansion is that of Louhisaari, which dates from 1655 and is reminiscent of Dutch buildings in its steep-

Plan of Hamina, a fortress town built in the early eighteenth century and ased upon the Renaissance type of Italian city plan. Centre is the town all. Almost all the private dwellings are single-storeyed wooden houses

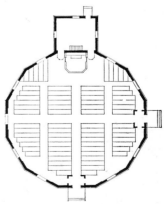

The plan of a 12-sided wooden church at Vimpeli built in 1807 to the drawings of Jacob Rijf

Original drawings for the Senate House, Helsinki, by C L Engel. This section was built in 1818–22

The main building, Louhisaari manor house, seventeenth century

Italian, and Carl Ludvig Enge a German who came to Finlar after working in St Petersbur Finnish manorial houses we far simpler than their counte parts elsewhere in Europe, ar their restrained decoration ar modest size makes them e tremely sympathetic. The mano houses of the province of Kareli with their splendid colonnade are particularly reminiscent North American colonial house

Neo-classical urban archite ture is to be seen mainly Turku, the former capital, ar Helsinki (formerly Helsingfors There are many fine buildings Turku, notably the old universi building (1802–15) and the At Academy (designed 1832–3 b Bassi). But Helsinki is still mo interesting. In just over 25 yea Johan Albert Ehrenström, politician, and Engel, his arch tect, adviser, and colleagu transformed it into one of th finest capital cities in Europ Ehrenström, as a town-planne mapped out a remarkable city the Empire style, much of happily preserved, notably th magnificent colonnaded Senat House, the university library, an the cathedral. The adjacent res dential developments, which wer constructed in timber in simu ation of stone, have now unfortu nately disappeared.

During the half-centur following the deaths of these tw makers of modern Helsinki, th

pitched dormer-dominated roof. The wars of the eighteenth century, the Russian occupation, and the compulsory migration of the aristocracy to Sweden, curtailed Finland's architectural development. Not until the later eighteenth century did merchants and industrialists begin to build mansions for themselves. The most impressive were designed by C F Schröder, a German master-builder-architect who settled in Turku. Mustio and Fagervik, two of these handsome manor-houses, are still standing. Mustio is a magnificent example of timber-building, reminiscent of timbered colonial mansions in the southern USA.

Thanks to its comparative remoteness, Finland was late in receiving eighteenth-century influences. Neo-classical forms dominated the architecture throughout the first half of the nineteenth century; the chief architects were Charles Bassi, an

Helsinki Cathedral, designed by C L Engel, started in 1830

The University Library, designed by C L Engel, built in 1836–4

An administrative building at Erottaja, Helsinki, by Hoijer, 1889

The main entrance to Helsinki railway station, designed by Eliel Saarinen, built in 1906–16. The sculpture is by Emil Wikstrom

pace of building operations slowed down. Like architects elsewhere in Europe, the Finns built in a variety of historical styles without achieving a satisfactory synthesis. Yet even the most self-indulgent excesses of Finnish ornamentation were restrained by comparison with those practised elsewhere. Not until 1872 was Finnish architectural training given a national basis with the founding of the Polytechnic Institute (now the Institute of Technology) in Helsinki.

A spate of new buildings in the last quarter of the nineteenth century, mainly under the aegis of Carl Theodor Höijer, brought Helsinki into line with metropolitan development in other countries. Large administrative blocks were built, based on a heavy revival of Italianate forms, and a modern administrative and commercial city was created.

A native preoccupation with simplicity and restraint predisposed Finnish architects towards the modern movement, and many of her architects have

The concert and congress hall, Helsinki, by Alvar Aalto, built in 1955–8

The Stock Exchange, Helsinki, designed by Lars Sonck, 1911

The tower at Helsinki Stadium by Y Lindegren and T Jäntti, 1934-52

The Tuberculosis Sanatorium at Paimio by Alvar Aalto, 1929-33

Apartments at Tapiola, outside Helsinki, by Viljo Rewell, 1955

achieved international fame. Among notable figures are Lars Sonck (1870–1956), architect of the Helsinki Mortgage Bank building (1908) and Stock Exchange (1911); and Eliel Saarinen (1873–1950), who built Helsinki railway station (1906–16). Most renowned of all is Alvar Aalto (*b* 1898), one of the major figures of the modern movement.

These and other architects less well known outside Finland, including J S Siren, Uno Ullberg, Erik Bryggman, and Erkki Huttunen, have also built a remarkable number of hospitals, sanatoria, offices, churches, departmental stores, schools, and museums. Among many outstanding buildings are the Hel-

sinki Stadium (originally built for the cancelled 1940 Olympic Games and later used for the 1952 Games), designed by Yrjö Lindegren and Toivo Jäntii, and the Finnish National Theatre in Helsinki (1954), designed by Kaija and Heikki Siren. But it is in housing developments that Finland has excelled. 'Chain' houses, studio terraces, flats, apartment blocks, and mass-housing projects in remote areas have put Finland in the forefront of modern domestic architecture. Finland, indeed, is one of the few nations in the world with an architecture which has both a recognizable national idiom and an important place in the history of the International style.

Fir. The true fir, *abies species*, grows throughout the northern hemisphere. It produces a whiteish softwood of little importance to furniture-making though used for carcases of the cheaper sorts of furniture.

Douglas fir, *pseudo tsuga taxifolia*, is an important furniture wood, but is not really a fir at all. It is also called Oregon pine or Columbian pine. It is honey-coloured with reddish growth rings, and is one of the strongest softwoods. It is quite often used for modern furniture.

Fire-back. At least as early as the sixteenth century, ironmasters were producing firebacks. In shape, rectangular,

Douglas fir chair by Heritage

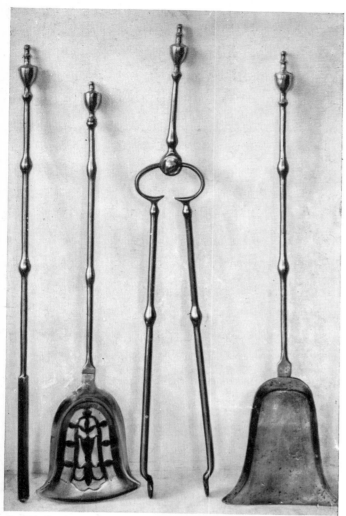

English fire-irons of Adam period. Left: a set in cast brass and steel c 1780, shovel with honeysuckle motif. Right: steel shovel, brass top

An Adam fireplace in white marble and polished steel, the basket grate with a pierced serpentine apron, c 1785

Modern circular fireplace with hood and flue suspended over an open hearth set in brick surround

square, or a variation on these forms, they were used to protect the brickwork behind the fire. They were made of white iron which had been moulded by being poured molten into boards held in sand.

The decoration of fire-backs remained constant for almost three centuries, consisting of coats of arms, animal and flower motifs, and topical and allegorical subjects. The date and the owner's name or initials were also common, normally in conjunction with armorials; many examples still exist.

Fire-irons. Although fire-irons were used during the Middle Ages, few early examples have survived. The late seventeenth century saw the first decorative sets in iron with delicate foliate and scroll motifs similar to those found on contemporary chairs and wall-carvings. A set consisted of shovel, poker, and tongs

for coal fires; a rare additional piece, known as a fire-fork and resembling a large toasting-fork, was sometimes used for wood fires.

In the eighteenth century, iron gave way to brass and steel (silver ornament was also occasionally used), and decoration was in keeping with the prevailing fashion. While fire-irons changed little in design, early sets can often be identified by the width and generous splay of the mouth of the shovel. In the eighteenth and nineteenth centuries many fire-irons were made *en suite* with fenders.

Fireplace. Until ornamental marble and metal fireplaces were introduced at the end of the seventeenth century, fireplaces were permanent architectural features. In early days they were used for cooking as well as for warmth, and in colonial times the cold of New England was

alleviated by a large wood-burning stone fireplace, around which a family's indoor life revolved.

Early marble and stone fireplaces followed contemporary interior design, and continued to do so throughout the next two centuries. Coloured marbles, inset with semi-precious stones, became fashionable in the second half of the eighteenth century, and pierced steel or gilt-metal plates were also used. Ceramic plaques were sometimes incorporated and because such fireplaces could be moved, a large number have survived from now demolished houses.

Victorian fireplaces are commonly of stone, and often superbly carved with animals and flowers of Baroque inspiration. Victorian fireplaces were, however, larger than the marble ones of the late eighteenth century and are thus far less easy to fit into modern living quarters.

Marble fireplaces are still being made, and brick and natural stone fireplaces are also popular.

Fire-screen. Central heating has made the fire-screen unnecessary, but the large open fires common until the end of the last century made small portable screens a convenience. There were two main forms of fire-screen. The earlier, the cheval or horse screen, on trestle legs and with a rising central panel held between fixed sides, was popular by the late seventeenth century. The frames were in walnut, mahogany, or giltwood, while the sliding panels were decorated in a number of ways with needlework, tapestry, painted canvas, paper or leather, Japanese and Chinese lacquers, and many kinds of textile.

A minor variant of the fire-screen consisted of wooden objects shaped like large ping-pong

Façade of Collegiate Church at Salzburg by Fischer von Erlach, c 1696

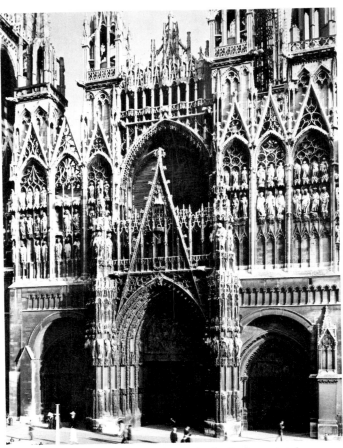

Façade of Notre-Dame, Rouen, in the flamboyant style

Prince Eugène of Savoy's Palace, Vienna, by Fischer von Erlach, c 1695

bats which fitted into slots in the back of chairs to save the head overheating.

The late seventeenth century evolved the slender pole screen which was popular during the next hundred years; it was a single stem or pole on narrow feet, supporting a sliding and adjustable banner large enough to protect only the face from the heat of the fire. The decorative banners and stems changed with prevailing fashions. Fire-screen stems were often used later to support table-tops as in many 'genuine' tripod tables sold by antique dealers since 1900.

There was a revival of interest in the decorative fire-screen in the 1920s and 1930s. They were frequently hand-painted.

Fischer von Erlach, Johann Bernhard (1656–1723). One of the greatest of central European Baroque architects. He was born in Graz and, while studying sculpture during a three-year stay in Rome, came under the influence of Borromini and began to study architecture.

During the last 30 years of his life he was responsible for the design of a considerable number of grand palatial buildings and churches, including the Imperial Palace at Schönbrunn near Vienna (c 1700), the Clam-Gallas Palace in Prague (1707), and the Schwarzenberg Palace, which was completed after his death. He was also responsible for the great collegiate church at Salzburg, commissioned by the prince-archbishop of Salzburg.

Flambeau. A flaming urn or incense-burner used as a decorative motif in furniture. It occurs at the end of the seventeenth century and was common throughout the eighteenth century. Usually in ormolu or carved and gilt wood, it was a finial to tall pieces of furniture such as the bureau cabinet, and to long-case clocks of the period 1700–40.

Flamboyant. Architectural term that describes the last phase of the French Gothic style. The exuberance of Flamboyant design and its long curving lines are quite unlike anything in English Gothic.

Flared header. The term used to describe the dark and apparently glazed end-face of a brick which has been burned black and vitrified while in the kiln.

17th-century fleur-de-lis hanging,

A Spode plate with fleur-de-lis

A fleuron in a floor mosaic

This occurs because of its close proximity to the furnace and the consequent chemical action of the salts in the brick.

Flat arch. Term used to describe an arch with only a slight rise or camber; it occurs most frequently in brick structures. Occasionally, as when used above a door or window-frame, an arch is constructed from a completely flat underside. Such arches sometimes need to be reinforced with a metal bar.

Chatham House, St James's Square, London, designed by Flitcroft, 1734

Flat chasing. See **Silver, decorative techniques.**

Flatware. The English term for spoons, forks, and other flat pieces of silver except knives.

Flèche (French, 'arrow'). A slender spire that rises from a roof ridge, especially at the junction of nave and transept. It is also known as a spirelet.

Flemish bond. A method of bricklaying whereby bricks are laid alternately in courses of headers (ends) and stretchers (longer sides).

Fleur-de-lis (or **lys**). Despite its almost exclusively Gallic connotations, the fleur-de-lis is a heraldic device used in armorial bearings in many countries. The device is sometimes thought to have derived from the white lily, but more probably comes from the white iris. The fleur-de-lis invariably consists of an erect central flower with two subsidiary petals falling or folding outwards.

Fleuron. A floral device used in architecture and decoration.

Flight. Each set or series of stairs or steps between landings and/or floors of a building, or levels outside.

Flint. A hard stone, among the purest forms of silica. Flint seams are usually found in the upper and middle layers of chalk formations, but are also found in clay.

Sea-washed flints, usually known as pebbles (up to $2\frac{1}{2}$ in in diameter) and cobbles (between $2\frac{1}{2}$ and 9 in in length) are normally included under this heading, although they differ considerably from flints.

In building, flints and pebbles can be laid in their natural state, but this necessitates the use of a considerable quantity of mortar. Flints are, therefore, often used after splitting or 'knapping', a skilled craft now in decline because flint is now less extensively used. The appearance of a wall of knapped flints is vastly different from one built of the stones in their natural state, presenting as it does a multitude of light-reflecting facets.

Flitcroft, Henry (1697–1769). British architect in the Palladian tradition. The son of a gardener to King William III at Hampton Court. Flitcroft became architectural assistant to Lord Burlington in his early twenties. He prepared drawings for several Burlington projects, including Tottenham Park, Wiltshire, and the dormitory of Westminster School. Thanks to Burlington's patronage in 1726, Flitcroft was appointed clerk of the works, and 20 years later became comptroller of the works. Among the London buildings he designed were St Giles-in-the-Field Church, St Olave's in Tooley Street, and houses, including 10 St James's Square (now Chatham House) in 1734, and houses in Bloomsbury. He partly rebuilt Woburn Abbey for the Duke of Bedford in 1747–61, and enlarged Wentworth Woodhouse for the Earl of Malton from about 1735. He also added various buildings at Stourhead in Wiltshire, including the Temple of Hercules (1755–6), the Temple of Apollo (c 1765), and Alfred's Tower.

Flock wallpaper. Flocking on to cloth was used during the Middle Ages to improve the surface appearance of inferior cloth, the technique being to apply powdered cloth to the surface by means of an adhesive. The practice was justly frowned on, as the intention was to disguise shoddy material. Flock was sometimes used as an embellishment to embossed and painted leather wall-hangings.

The introduction of flocking on to paper, as an imitation of velvet, began about the beginning of the seventeenth century. By 1926 the Painters Stainers' Company claimed flock wallpaper as their monopoly. The pieces of paper, printed with a design in adhesive, were passed through a box containing the wool flock. Powdered chalk was

Eighteenth-century flock wallpaper

181

Floor of inlaid wood in the Mirror Room of Pommersfelden in Bavaria

Above: gleaming quarry tiles in a cottage
Below: a modern floor of marble and stone in different shapes

Mosaic floor at the Roman villa, Fishbourne, Sussex

sometimes used as an alternative to wool, and occasionally powdered silk or shells, or metallic dust were used. Successive layers of the flock could be built up to look like cut velvet, and a two- or three-colour effect could be given in the same way, or by overprinting with wood blocks or stencils.

Although early flock papers were crude, by the middle of the eighteenth century, superb wall-hangings were being made, either completely flocked or with flocking enriching parts of painted or wood-block printed papers. The original blocks are still being used to reproduce old designs.

Floor. The term applied to (1) the basic plane or surface of any room or house; and (2) a storey of a house or other building.

The history of architecture can largely be traced through the history of floors – from the mud floors of the first hovels, then to the first timber and tiled floors, and later the magnificence of marble and mosaics.

In the present century, the pace of building has accelerated, and new materials, techniques, and finishes for flooring have been developed. The most common underlay is concrete, in the form of a cement/sand screed. There have also been advances in the development of resin-based sealers and hardeners, and there is a growing tendency to regard the floor as a composite whole instead of a basic structure plus sub-floor plus topping plus final covering.

Flooring. This century has seen the introduction of synthetic materials for flooring, but traditional materials are still popular. Only the most recent developments are listed here.

Wood floors may be of soft-wood, used mainly in board form as a base for other floor coverings, or hardwood, which ranges in colour from pale ivory to deep brown. The wood is made up as strip, block, parquet or mosaic flooring. New methods of making wood blocks have been developed in the last few years, and the range of imported timber increases all the time. Before World War II, good wood floors were generally used in the living area of the house, while other hard floorings were confined to halls, kitchens, and nurseries. But in the last few years, the decorative possibilities of linoleum, vinyl, cork, and other materials have been realized.

The popularity of tiles for floors is rising. Among the simplest, cheapest type are quarry tiles made from natural clays or marls in shades of red, brown, buff, blue or black. These are cold, slippery, and noisy – but very hard-wearing and pleasantly rustic in appearance. There is also great demand for Provençal *curvil ligne* tiles made of terracotta, for ceramic floor tiles, and for semi-vitrified and fully-vitrified tiles.

Meanwhile, terrazzo flooring is becoming warmer, more resilient, and altogether more suitable for domestic use: ceramic mosaic chips are being set in a matrix of epoxy resin, synthetic rubber, or vinyl, to form tiles or flooring *in situ*. Vitreous glass mosaic is being made in Italy, and honed marble is available for the well-to-do.

In its natural form, cork has the advantage of warmth, quietness, hard wear, and safety (because it is not slippery). But it is vulnerable to grease and absorbs dirt easily. Nowadays it is often combined with synthetic materials to overcome these disadvantages.

Linoleum, which is basically canvas coated with linseed oil, has the advantages of being flexible and acid-resistant.

Rubber is warmer and quieter than most synthetic floorings, but possesses certain natural disadvantages: a tendency to deteriorate when exposed to direct sunlight, and a lack of resistance to oil and grease. Synthetic rubbers have none of these failings.

Thermoplastic materials are a post-war development. The best ones are made of plastic vinyl coating (PVC) combined with asbestos or some other filler. Thermoplastic (asphalt) tiles are very cheap; but they are brittle and tend to crack if they are not laid on a flat sub-floor. The colour range is large but rather muddy. These tiles are now being superseded by the semi-flexible vinyl asbestos type. The colour choice is large, and the tiles are designed for really heavy wear.

Flexible plastic vinyl coating is responsible for a great flooring revolution. It is produced in tile or sheet form, in an enormous range of qualities, colours, and designs which encourage imaginative floor-schemes – eg hopscotch squares for the nursery floor, and 'do-it-yourself' versions of seventeenth-century flag-and-marble floors.

The newest development of all is the 'pure' vinyl tile, with little or no filler, which gives it a translucent effect.

The distinctions between these types of hard flooring are not always clear-cut. Linoleum, rubbers, and corks are often combined with a resin of vinyl polymer to form a complex structure with a durable surface, a resilient underlay and often a load-bearing intermediate membrane.

Floriated.
The term applied to any surface decorated with floral motifs. The word was most frequently used of tracery.

Floris,
Cornelis (1514–75). A Flemish architect and sculptor,

A Victorian flower arrangement made of shells, under a glass dome

sometimes known as Cornelis de Vriendt. After studying in Italy he returned to his native land and designed several public buildings, the most notable of which were the handsome town halls of Antwerp (1561–5) and the Hague (1565).

Flower arrangement.
The stylized single lotus in a vase of ancient Egypt; the Ikebana of the Japanese; the profusion of a Dutch still life; the white and green confections inspired originally by Constance Spry – flowers have always played an important role in decoration. Lilies and jasmine feature in early Italian paintings of interiors. Abraham Bosschaert (born about 1580) was one of the earliest painters of flower arrangements *per se*, followed through the years by a whole host of distinguished artists.

Fashions in flower arrangement have varied almost as much as styles in dress or interior decoration, and the art continues to command great attention at flower shows all over the world.

Flowers, artificial.
Four hundred years ago Francis Bacon said that a garden is 'the purest of human pleasures'. Perhaps, then, it is inevitable that men and women should so often have

Modern artificial flowers

to imitate God and make artificial flowers that are intended to deceive the eye – a harmless pleasure that can never produce great art, but an exercise of skill and ingenuity that is most pleasing where the deception is not entirely complete. The carved wooden flowers of Grinling Gibbons are almost lifelike, but not quite. The waxed paper cabbage roses and bi-coloured tulips originated by Constance Spry are more flamboyant than real, and the painted shell flower groups, glass-domed in the eighteenth and nineteenth centuries, delight because of their primness and sheer artificiality. Equally, the chilly white Parian ware lilies, trapped under glass on neglected graves, deceive no one.

Making flowers from feathers was a favourite nineteenth-century occupation; so were flowers fashioned out of leather and fabric. Today artificial flowers are more attractively made of beaded glass and paper. The most popular are made of plastic and, arranged in mixed bouquets, can really be quite difficult to distinguish from the real thing.

'April', by Pieter Casteels, from 'Twelve Months of Flowers', published by Robert Furber in 1730

Flower prints.
The earliest known flower prints were used to illustrate botanical books soon after the invention of printing; they were often printed in red. They were fairly crude woodcuts, bearing little resemblance to the actual flower, possibly because they were cut on small rectangular blocks of pearwood into which the flower had to be fitted.

However, a folio of flower prints published in Basle in 1542 was vastly superior in technique and accuracy. They were drawn from nature by Albrecht Meyer, and the blocks cut by V R Speckle. The woodcuts were coloured in by hand. Variations on Meyer's and Speckle's woodcuts appeared in herbals in many countries. One of the best known was John Gerard's *Herball* (1597). This book, together with John Parkinson's *Paradisus* (1629), which showed folio full-page groups of flowers, were for many years the best of their kind.

In 1730, a London nurseryman, Robert Furber, produced a very expensive catalogue, issued to subscribers only, called *Twelve Months of Flowers*. This consisted of 12 hand-coloured copper engravings of groups of flowers, with a thirteenth plate of the 450 subscribers' names (headed by the Duke of Ancaster) surrounded by a floral border. The catalogue was evidently a success since Furber published a sequel, *Twelve Months of Fruit*, two years later. These early eighteenth-century seedsman's catalogues, many copies of which may have been thrown away at once, represent the starting-point for most modern collectors of coloured flower prints.

The great age for flower books and prints was from 1730 to 1830, although a number of excellent reproductions appeared between 1830 and 1860. At first the method of reproduction was exclusively copper engraving, but between 1790 and 1830 many were engraved in aquatint, mezzotint, or stipple engraving; this is the finest period of flower-printing. From 1830 the lithograph, or print taken from a stone, superseded the earlier forms of printing. Most flower prints are hand-coloured, but a very few are printed wholly or partly in colour. The aquatint and mezzotint processes tend to produce more satisfactory pictures, while the stipple engraving used by the French in the Napoleonic period, together with a form of colour printing, was unrivalled both for artistry and for faithfulness of reproduction. Furber's prints were from paintings by a Flemish artist Pieter Casteels, who came to England in 1708. And many of the finest flower prints of the eighteenth century are either from Dutch or German books, or if published in England are the work of foreign artists. George Ehret, who illustrated Dutch, German and English works, is perhaps the most famous of these.

French flower prints are probably the best known of all. This is largely because of one artist, P J Redouté. Redouté worked over a very long period (about 1765–1835), was *persona grata* successively with Louis XVI and his court, with the Empress Josephine, and finally with the French court after the restoration. Hence he had the opportunity to create thousands of flower prints, and is known to many who have never heard of Van Huysum. His drawings are fine, yet those of Van Spaendonck, who was his teacher, or of his contemporaries Turpin or Prevost, are equally good; for the collector they have the

Connolly's Folly, Co Kildare, designed by Richard Cassels in 1740

additional merit of being almost unknown. Redouté engravings have been reprinted so often that they tend to seem hackneyed.

The most famous English flower prints come from Doctor Thornton's *The Temple of Flora* (1708). They are very large, and all either aquatints, mezzotints, or a combination of the two. They are true flower pictures with a romanticism appropriate to the age in which they appeared. Well-known RA's such as Reinagle, Cosway, and Henderson were the artists.

Victorian lithographs are still a cheap buy for collectors, but it is impossible to pretend that they are in the same class.

Flush bead. A panel decoration in which a bead moulding is sunk into the surface, so that the tip of the bead is flush with the surrounding panel.

Elevation and half-section of Doric and Ionic columns, showing flutes

Flute. A groove, usually semi-circular or segmental in section, introduced into plain surfaces for relief and decoration. The term is most frequently applied to the shafts of columns of the various orders, but is also commonly used of furniture.

Fluting. A series of flutes.

Flying finials. The three finials that adorn the pediments of long-case clocks and tallboys of the mid- and late eighteenth century.

Flying shore. An interior device in building or, more frequently, re-building, much seen after World War II. Timber supports are fixed well above ground level between the external (and frequently, after bombing, internal) walls of buildings, thus preventing them from collapsing.

Foil, foiled, foils, foliation. Variants of the term foil, which is used of the small arcs composing the cusp or projecting points in Gothic tracery, arches, and panels. Such a cusped arch is said to be foiled. A three-lobed example is called a trefoil.

Folly. An extravagant architectural structure, built without practical purpose as a gesture or joke. Follies often take the form of a classical or Gothic ruin, tower or obelisk. Together with arbours and classical temples, follies were mainly erected within a private park in a quiet glade, on a hillock, or to give, in an avenue, a focal point to a vista. Many towers were prominently positioned on hills as landmarks.

Font (Latin, *fons* 'a spring'). A receptacle or vessel normally placed near the west end of a church, but occasionally in the baptistry, it contains the consecrated water used in baptism. In early times fonts were of sufficient size to allow for the complete immersion of infants, but gradually these gave way to small, shallow basins up to 18 in deep and 2 ft wide. In Norman times fonts were mainly plain, either square or circular, and made of lead. Some examples survive, but lead was supplanted by stone, and Gothic examples were lavishly decorated. Late Gothic fonts are frequently octagonal. Early font-covers were little more than plain lids (kept sealed by a

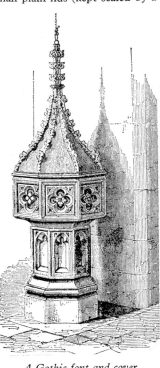

A Gothic font and cover

The font at Coventry Cathedral, designed by Sir Basil Spence, 1961; carved boulder from the Holy Land on a bronze and black marble base

The Palazzo del Laterano, Rome, designed by Domenico Fontana

Constitution of 1236), but were later highly ornamented and carried to a considerable height in the form of spires, greatly enriched by carving.

Fontaine, Pierre François Léonard (1762–1853). A French architect and architectural historian of the Napoleonic era usually discussed in connection with Charles Percier, with whom Fontaine trained in Paris. Both architects later travelled to Rome to further their studies. During the Revolution, Fontaine fled to England, but on the accession of Napoleon, Fontaine and Percier were made the emperor's chief architects. They were responsible for the restoration of Malmaison and for much work on Parisian projects such as the Louvre, the Tuileries, and the Palais Royal. They were also assiduous historians, and jointly compiled and illustrated many important architectural volumes about the antiquities of Rome.

Fontana, Carlo (1634–1714). An Italian Baroque architect and architectural historian. After training in Rome, Fontana began to work about 1660 as clerk of works, draughtsman, and assistant to Bernini, seconding him in many building projects in Rome. Fontana's name is chiefly associated with the Palazzo Montecitorio, which was originally begun by Bernini for the family of Pope Innocent X in 1650, and was continued for 40 years later by Fontana. Fontana designed the church of San Biagio in Piazza Capizucchi, many chapels in Rome, and the

Entrance of Palazzo Montecitorio, Rome, by Carlo Fontana, 1694–7

Malmaison, restored by Fontaine and Percier

Jesuit Sanctuary at Loyola in Spain. The classical inspiration of Roman architecture at the end of the seventeenth century is largely attributed to Fontana. He also compiled lavish and erudite monographs, including the *Templum Vaticanum* (1694).

Fontana, Domenico (1543–1607). An Italian architect whose career reads like a picaresque novel. While studying architecture in Rome he came to the notice of Cardinal Montalto. This provided Fontana with a powerful patron, for the Cardinal became Pope Sixtus V, who made Fontana chief architect to the Vatican. In this capacity he was responsible for impressive additions to the Vatican (the library), Lateran, and Quirinal palaces. He was also responsible for the gigantic Egyptian obelisk in St Peter's Square, of which he wrote a grandiloquent description.

Pope Sixtus V died in 1590, after which Fontana hit upon the notion of transforming the Colosseum into a factory, which outraged the Romans, even though they were relatively careless of the fate of their antiquities. After this Fontana transferred his interests to Naples, and was responsible for starting the building of the royal palace in that city.

Footstool with an embroidered cover and tassels, nineteenth century

The forecourt of Blenheim Palace, Oxfordshire, 1705–20

Cour du Cheval-Blanc at the Château de Fontainebleau, 1528–40

Footstool. In the early 1700s there was a relaxation of the rules of etiquette governing sitting at court and elsewhere. Comfortable chairs were developed and it became increasingly fashionable for men to sprawl in comfort when not in the company of ladies. By the mid-eighteenth century ladies also began to assume relaxed attitudes, and the footstool was invented as an aid. Gout, a prevalent ailment when port was drunk by the bottle, also necessitated a footstool, and several early examples are known. It was not, however, until the early nineteenth century that the footstool became really common. Early examples still exist; covered in their original needlework of flowers or animals.

The footstool has grown larger in the present century. It has become a stool for the legs as well as the feet, a luxurious extension for an easy chair, upholstered to match. Examples are Arne Jaconsen's renowned chair-with-stool and the famous Charles Eames' black hide-covered two-piece chaise-longue.

Forecourt. A walled or railed enclosure in front of a house. Here carriages used to arrive to set down their passengers. The French fortified castle, the *château fort*, was gradually transformed into a residence, or *château de plaisance,* in which a forecourt was thrown outwards from the main fabric; and this in turn influenced the development of the forecourt in Britain. Forecourts gradually became more domesticated, and were frequently graced by decorative ironwork of a high order, culminating in large and magnificent gateways.

In more recent times the forecourt has been adapted by many modern architects to form an introductory setting for a group of houses; vistas and visual surprises as well as a place for parking cars. These modern forecourts have even been built with traditional materials, cobbles, granite setts, stone slabs and gravel. But modern architects generally prefer a vista broken by trees and plots of grass to the unrelieved expanse in front of great houses in the past.

Formeret. The term occasionally used for the decorative arched ribs on a vertical wall where it meets the vault.

Formica. The trade name for a rigid laminated plastic material sold all over the world. Formica laminate was the result of research by Dr Leo Baekeland, J P Wright, and D J O'Conor, the American engineer who discovered the process in 1913 by taking sheets of paper, dipping them in resins, and pressing them under heat.

At first the new material was used only for electrical insulation, and in 1913 O'Conor and H A Faber established the Formica Insulation Co in Cin-

The forecourt of Hatfield House, Hertfordshire, 1606–11

cinnati. This was the origin of the present Formica company.

Apart from the many uses in industry that have since been discovered for Formica, nowadays in most houses, hotels, and ships, it finds a place because it provides a scratch- and heat-resistant surface; it is not affected by very dry conditions and is impervious to water. It comes in veneers, thicker panels with the characteristic surface on both sides, and board, surfaced on one side. It has either a matt or a glossy finish, and some types of Formica are suitable for use outside.

As for the patterns (the patterned paper is the top layer of the laminate, just below the transparent surface), marbles have been seen in Formica laminate since its early days in America in the 1920s, and these and mottles, plain colours, simulated tweed, linen, and wood are still the popular standbys.

There is also a range of bold designs intended for large wall areas in modern houses.

Fornasetti, Piero (*b* 1913). Italian designer, one of the few post-war designers to work in an uninhibitedly decorative style. He was born in Milan, and studied painting and sculpture at the academy there, and afterwards in South Africa. He used the most up-to-date methods of photographic application of designs to plastics, porcelain, and textile surfaces, and exported tables and china. His black and white motifs – urns, the architectural orders, classical figures, and ruins in classical landscapes have had a very wide appeal.

Forum. An open space in almost every town developed under Roman influence; eg the Forum Romanum and Forum of Trajan. These spaces were usually surrounded by public buildings, and frequently by colonnaded perambulatories. From the forum derived a major

Black and White Fornasetti mug

Italian contribution to town-planning, the piazza, now increasingly seen in new urban developments throughout the world.

Fosse (Latin, *fossa, fodere* 'to dig'). A ditch or moat dug for

The fountain at Schloss Linderhof, Bavaria, built by Ludwig II

Fountain by Orazio Oliviero at Villa d'Este, Tivoli, 16th century

purposes of fortification. The earthworks thrown up in the course of the excavation were known as a scarp or escarpment.

Fountains. The earliest fountains were purely functional; providing water for drinking or

Modern fountain by Franta Belsky

washing. Soon they became recognized meeting-places, and the very special part they played in domestic life led to their elaboration and embellishment. Decorative fountains are to be seen in Egyptian paintings and on Etruscan vases, and they were part of everyday life in classical Greece. They are just as popular today and form an integral part of a city and garden layout. The fountains of the Moorish Gardens in Granada are probably the oldest fountains that survive in their original form; those at Versailles are perhaps the most famous, and are admired by millions every year, as are the Fontana di Trevi in Roma, the fountains at the Villa d'Este and the Manniken-Piś in Brussels.

Four-centred arch. An architectural term used to describe a depressed pointed arch evolved from radii described from four centres. The two smaller radii are those on the springing line of the arch, as shown in the diagram.

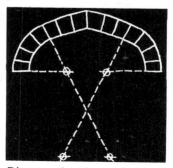
Diagram of a four-centred arch

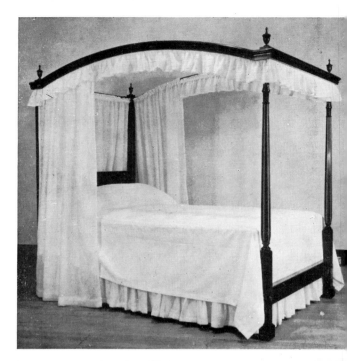

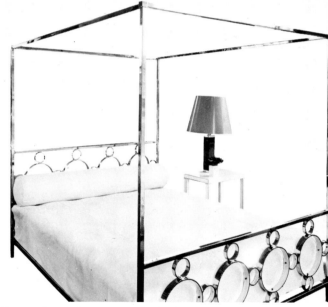

A late eighteenth century four-poster bed with flowered tapestry hangings and carved flowers on the tester, around the posts, and in the flutes

Top: modern mahogany reproduction four-poster bed. Bottom: steel four-poster bed designed by Albrizzi

Four-poster. The evolution of the bed was surprisingly slow, and four posts were seldom used until the middle of the eighteenth century. Up to then the bed had to serve as a miniature room in the corridor-space of the upper floor of a house. The two-post bed with carved or panelled headboard existed for 200 years before the smaller and more elegant four-poster was introduced because of its lightness and mobility. By 1750 bedrooms were self-contained and private.

Both Chippendale and Hepple-white designed and executed beautiful four-posters, and they still appear in the third edition of Sheraton's *Drawing Book* of 1802. The Victorians had little use for such beds, and those that survive are seldom comparable to the tall, airy four-posters profusely upholstered and with painted or gilded frames, common before 1800.

Lately there has been a revival of interest in the four-poster, both in reproductions of antique beds and in bright, mobile, modern versions made for smaller rooms. Wood and/or metal is still used, but the hangings have become purely decorative now that insulating properties are no longer needed.

Fowke, Francis (1823–65). British architect, curiously little known despite the fact that he was responsible for much of the development in South Kensington under royal patronage. His most notable achievement was the design of the Albert Hall, which was not built until after his death. Fowke took up the practice of architecture between 1867 and 1871, after a career in the Royal Engineers in which he attained the rank of captain. Apart from the Albert Hall, Fowke also designed part of the Imperial Institute blocks (later added to and merged in buildings by Colcutt and Aston Webb) and part of the Victoria and Albert Museum.

Fowler, Charles (1791–1867). One of the eminent architect-engineers of the Victorian era. His original sense of structure

The Royal Albert Hall, Kensington, designed by Francis Fowke

d planning place him, in the words of Sir John Summerson, longside engineers like Rennie nd Telford.' Fowler's chief orks are mainly markets, inuding Covent Garden (1828–) and Hungerford (1831–3) in ondon, the Higher and Lower arkets in Exeter (1835–8), and e New Market at Gravesend 818–22).

owler, John Beresford (b 06). One of London's leading terior decorators. He was eduted at Felsted, but did not tend any recognized art school.

He trained himself for his future profession by visiting art galleries and the Victoria and Albert Museum.

Fowler first worked as an office boy in St James's, then moved to Thornton Smith's, Soho Square, well-known decorators of the 1920s, to paint Chinese wallpapers. Soon he was a freelance, painting screens among other activities for Mrs Guy Bethell of Eldons, another well-known decorator.

He then worked in the decorative furniture department of Peter Jones. In 1938 he went

Top: Lower Court of Hungerford Market, by Charles Fowler, built 831–3. Bottom: Covent Garden Market, also by Fowler, built 1828–30

Two views of a drawing-room decorated by John Fowler

into partnership with Lady (Sibyl) Colefax, a social figure of the thirties and forties, and a woman of great taste and business acumen. Before she died in 1950, Mrs Claude Lancaster (formerly Nancy Tree) became a partner in Sibyl Colefax & John Fowler Ltd of Brook Street.

The firm is known for beautifully hand-painted wallpapers and old furniture. John Fowler prefers decorating in a traditional

style and much of his work is in private country houses. He prefers the original and handmade to the mass produced, likes eighteenth-century Gothick and *chinoiserie*, and has always been a champion of the Regency style.

He is adviser to the National Trust for the decoration of their historic houses and has decorated Wallington in Northumberland, Sudbury House in Derbyshire, and Clandon House in Surrey.

Pennsylvania Dutch Fractur birth certificate, Northampton County, 1794

Fractur. American folk art. Fractur are manuscripts made by the Pennsylvania Germans during the eighteenth and early nineteenth century. The name derives from a sixteenth-century German Gothic script with broken lines, and ultimately from the Latin *fractura*, meaning a break.

Fractur are probably inspired by medieval manuscripts. They are mostly certificates of birth, baptism, and marriage, house blessings, etc. They were written and decorated entirely by hand and vary from the crude to the extremely fine, the latter usually the work of schoolmasters and ministers. The decorations are naïve and full of symbolism – and of conventionalized flowers, figures, angels, and birds, all in strong bright colours.

Frame. The use of the picture frame as a structure independent of the painted panel first arose in the sixteenth century. Until then, and still occasionally during the next hundred years, painted wooden panels and conjoined frames were set into the room panelling. Early frames were carved, coloured or gilded. The two great periods of ornamental frame-making evolved around the naturalistic carvings of Grinling Gibbons and his followers in the late seventeenth century and the Rococo phase half a century later, when frames tended to vie with the pictures as works of art.

The late eighteenth and nineteenth centuries saw extensive use made of composition ornament and the gilded frames of both pictures and mirrors became progressively heavier and heavier.

During recent years artist-craftsmen have transformed the traditional frame. New materials, such as metals and moulded plastic, and the use of undecorated minimal-width frames, now relate more closely to twentieth-century art.

Framed structure. Timber frames for houses were introduced in the very early stages of most civilizations, and in Britain the cruck frame was followed by the more complex box frame, but with the introduction in the nineteenth century of cast-iron, the potentialities of framed structures were vastly increased in size and scope.

Cast-iron framing, sometimes free-standing, transformed commercial and industrial architecture. At the turn of the century, steel- and concrete-framed structures became common. Auguste Perret (1874–1954) devoted himself throughout his career to advancing the technicalities of reinforced concrete to be used, like timber, on the frame-and-panel method. He was probably the first architect in domestic architecture to show the structure in a pleasing manner.

In framed structures, the load is distributed over the frames, and the walls merely serve the purpose of weather-proofing, and may thus be made of glass or metal, with suitable insulating materials. With the optional absence of internal walls, the

Modern paintings in modern fram

'free plan' comes into its ov in modern architecture.

Franklin stove. A stove-cur fireplace invented by Benjam

A Chippendale rococo frame for an overmantel mirror with two panels

Reinforced concrete framing on apartment block, No 25b rue Fran lin, Paris, by Auguste Perret, 19

The church of St Front, Périgueux, 1120

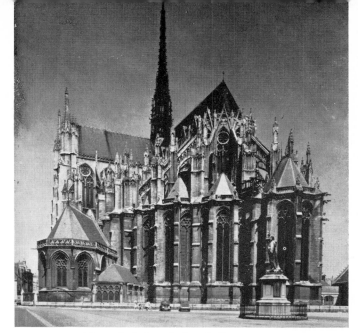

The cathedral at Amiens, built 1220–57

ranklin in the mid-eighteenth ntury. The stove was made of st iron and attached to the imney by a metal pipe. It was ood-burning, but could also urn coal, was extremely func-onal, and remains popular in merican country houses, to which it gives a period flavour. The term is also loosely applied in America to all ornamental types of small covered iron stoves.

French architecture. This can be divided surprisingly clean-ly into the two major classifi-cations of religious and secular, and more easily than Italian or British architecture into the four temporal divisions of medieval, Renaissance, Neo-classical, and modern.

In divisions both of style and period, France has been deeply influenced by Italy and England, although the influence of English architecture has been curiously underrated by all but specialist students.

The first great works of French architecture are the religious buildings of the Middle Ages. These derived from Romanesque and Byzantine structures. Later, the twelfth-century church builders of Pro-vence adopted and adapted Eastern methods in order to build pointed arches. By these means it was possible to provide vaulting more simply with a wider span, to distribute the weight of roofing more evenly, to render the vaulting virtually self-supporting, and to increase the height of the roof. The only drawback to this practice was that the roofing was usually of timber, which was far less suit-able in northern climates than in the sunshine of the South and the Near East.

The cathedral of St Nazaire at Carcassonne, built at the be-ginning of the twelfth century, is a typical and interesting example of the combination of two kinds of arches: round arches for the aisles, taken over from the Romans, and a pointed arch to span the nave.

The materials available and the state of technical knowledge conditioned the development of church architecture in France as in other countries. Byzantine in-fluences were slow to disappear. In the south-west, for instance, domes were still being built in churches at the same time as the Gothic style was being developed farther to the north.

The church of St Front in Périgueux is a typical if extreme example of the continuing vitality of Gothic (qv) which gradually evolved into a style which has become the classic provincial form of French ecclesiastical architecture; a typical example is St Sernin at Toulouse.

Alongside these smaller churches are the great Gothic cathedrals of the twelfth and thirteenth centuries, from which English and German Gothic derived. The names of these cathedrals are part of the French heritage: Chartres (mainly twelfth-century but not com-pleted until 1260); Rheims (1211 –41); and Amiens (1220–57).

St Sernin, Toulouse, 1080–96

The south front of the cathedral at Chartres, 1194–1260

The cathedral at Rheims, built 1211–90

The oldest and best known of these Gothic cathedrals, is Notre Dame, the cathedral of Paris, built between 1163 and 1214. It has, however, been argued that its architects and masons were not yet fully assured in the handling of the Gothic idiom. For most visitors to France, Notre Dame, although the finest example of the first, urgent, vital phase of French Gothic, lacks the simple grandeur of Chartres. None the less, a French adage has it that the perfect cathedral would have the towers of Chartres (despite their differences – one thirteenth century, the other sixteenth century), the front of Notre Dame, the nave of Amiens, and sculpture from Rheims.

The Château de Blois, on the Loire

Many of these great Gothic cathedrals were not, however, built as quickly as Paris and Rheims. The cathedral of Troyes, for instance, took three centuries to build and almost spanned the entire development of Gothic: it was begun at the very beginning of the thirteenth century and not completed until well into the sixteenth century, so that the sixteenth-century exterior is among the most flamboyantly decorated in the whole of France. It is impossible to avoid mentioning the soaring beauty of Bourges, for many visitors the most majestic cathedral in the country, and Orléans, remarkable in being the last Gothic cathedral built in Europe: it was begun in 1601 by Henry IV of France and finished over two centuries later.

The building of the cathedrals of Troyes and Orléans overlaps the beginnings of Renaissance ecclesiastical architecture in France, which can fairly be dated from the building of St Eustace in Paris (basically Gothic in structure but with Renaissance details), the foundation stones of which were laid in 1532. But the best known Renaissance churches are the Dôme des Invalides in Paris, built between 1680 and 1706 by Jules Hardouin-Mansart (1647–1708), and the Panthéon, begun in 1755 and not finished unt[il] after the death of its architec[t] Soufflot. The Invalides is some[what] reminiscent of St Paul'[s] but marred for some critics b[y] the fact that the dome was some[thing] of an afterthought almo[st] overpowering the classical two[-]storey pedimented base. Th[e] Panthéon is now regarded as on[e] of the greatest Renaissanc[e] churches in Europe.

Among French churche[s] which are notably influenced b[y] Palladian principles, referenc[e] should be made to the church [of] St Suplice in Paris, which has [a] pleasing, emphatically Italianat[e] façade of unusual restraint.

French secular architectur[e] followed the usual Europea[n] course, rude dwellings evolvin[g] through the kingpost-and-rafter stage to the more sophisticate[d] dwellings of stone and bric[k] Fortresses are the only secula[r] buildings of any size which hav[e] survived from the Middle Age[s].

With Renaissance influenc[e] moving steadily northward[s] across the Alps, changes bega[n] to appear in the nature of build[-]ings. These first became pro[-]nounced in the reign of Charle[s] VIII (1483–98), who invade[d] Italy and was evidently impresse[d] by her palaces and churches. Th[e] movement gained even greate[r] strength and splendour unde[r]

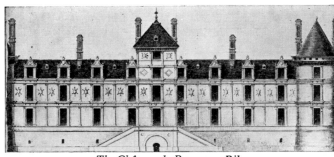

The Château de Bury near Bilos

The Dôme des Invalides, Paris: J H Mansart, 1680–1706

The Château de Chambord, built 1519–33

Francis I (1515–47).

The châteaux (qv) of the Loire show the impact of these influences in chronological order, the *château fort* giving way to the *château de plaisance*. The château of Blois, above the river Loire, is perhaps the supreme example of this branch of French archi-tecture, its diverse structural elements being assembled over almost four centuries.

With the aid of Italian archi-tects, including Serlio and Vig-nola, Francis I also raised the picturesque group of buildings at Fontainebleau, his personal palace, and the château of Chambord (1519–33). This has 400 rooms within and massive round towers without, four standing at the extremes of a vast rectangular plan with further towers concentrated at the centre of the long façade, thus investing the château with both Renais-sance and medieval qualities. Chambord is undoubtedly the most impressive of all the French châteaux.

Francis I also furthered the rebuilding of the Louvre in Paris, the principal residence of the kings of France. Here Pierre Lescot (1510–78), probably in-fluenced by Serlio, supervised the rebuilding of one of the most influential buildings in European history.

But perhaps the most widely influential of the châteaux was that of Bury, near Bilos, a much smaller building than most of the earlier châteaux, which be-came a prototype for innumer-able later seignorial dwellings, its influence persisting into the nineteenth century.

The next major royal influ-ence was Henry IV (1589–1610). The Tuileries had been begun in 1564 by Catherine de Medici from designs by Philibert de l'Orme, one of France's greatest architects. Under Henry they were continued from designs by Du Cerceau, who surpassed de l'Orme's considerable achieve-ment. The Tuileries were later linked with the Louvre by order of Henry IV.

The reign of Louis XIV (1643–1715) witnessed a return to classicism. François Mansart, or Mansard (1598–1666), and his great-nephew Jules Hardouin-Mansart were two great figures of the period. François Mansart is one of the most interesting and curious figures in French architecture: an arrogant, obstin-ate man of genius who threw away commissions rather than compromise his artistic integrity. His buildings are of pronounced ingenuity and beauty, and include several urban mansions (*hôtels*) for aristocratic patrons, the re-building of the château of Blois for the duc d'Orléans, and the

The rue des Saussaies, Paris, designed by Le Jeune

Pavillon d'Horloge at the Louvre, Paris: Lemercier, 1624–54

The church of La Madeleine, Paris: Vignon, 1806–42

The Eiffel Tower, 1889

design of new châteaux, including the still intact Château de Maisons or Maisons-Laffitte. Mansart also designed churches, including the church of Ste Marie de la Visitation in the rue St Antoine, Paris, and the chapel of Fresnes.

Mansart was a contemporary of Louis Le Vau, a more adaptable, resilient, and flamboyant architect. Le Vau did more work than Mansart, but to less effect, although he greatly developed housing on the Ile St Louis, much of it by his own schemes. He is chiefly renowned for his work at Versailles and the Louvre.

Louis XIV, backed by his adviser Jean-Baptiste Colbert, looked towards Italy for his architectural exemplars and even invited Bernini to Paris to prepare designs for a further extension of the Louvre. These plans were never adopted. Instead a plan by Charles Perrault, a medical man and architectural dilettante, was decided upon, and this provided the present east front.

Versailles was the Sun King's most impressive offering to posterity; its echoes of Italian *palazzi*, allied with a tempered Baroque, comprise a design that greatly influenced all subsequent palace architecture. Versailles, designed in part by Le Vau and Jules Hardouin-Mansart, with decorations by Le Brun, and garden landscaped by Le Nôtre, was the great achievement of Louis XIV's reign. Jules Hardouin-Mansart was chief architect for public works and was responsible for both the Place Vendôme and the Place des Victoires, thus paving the way for Napoleon's great rebuilding schemes over a century later. These were inevitably secular rather than ecclesiastical, although the Madeleine was erected during Napoleon's reign. During and after the Empire period, many magnificent buildings were built, mainly in Paris. The Palais Bourbon, the Bourse, and other great institutions were built to the glory of the Republic; but it is in the street-planning of the centre of Paris that the work of Baron Georges-Eugène Haussmann under the Second Empire made such an impressive mark on urban planning. The domestic architecture of the nineteenth century (based upon a city of *appartements* rather than separate houses) has given Paris a uniformity lacking in almost all other modern cities – avenues of tall terrace houses of considerable variety in design, far more interesting than their contemporary counterparts in other countries.

France also had its mid-nineteenth-century Gothic Revival, Viollet-le-Duc being the outstanding figure. But the new forms made possible by reinforced concrete construction were adopted in France earlier than in most other European countries. In this technological revolution, the work of Auguste Perret was outstanding, and his theories were elaborated by his pupil, the world-famous Le Corbusier. Corbusier, although Swiss by birth,

Arc de Triomphe de l'Etoile, Paris: Chalgrin and others, 1806–36

Ecole des Beaux Arts, Paris, 1820–62

The monastery of La Tourette, Eveux, near Lyons: Le Corbusier, 195

UNESCO building in Paris: Bernard Zehrfuss with Breuer and Nervi

Notre-Dame du Haut, Ronchamp: Le Corbusier, 1950–54

took up residence in Paris in 1922 and became identified with modern French architecture. His most notable work in France is undoubtedly the Unité d'Habitation in Marseilles, a great block of flats which is virtually a town in itself. These designs have provoked considerable controversy, which continues.

French casement door, window. These are usually more elongated than ordinary casements. Usually open as two vertical halves without a vertical centre-post.

French chair. This term was probably first used *c* 1660 to describe the high-backed Carolean chairs made in the current French fashion. The name appeared again a century later when Chippendale included eight designs for French chairs in his *Director* (1762). These were all upholstered with padded arm-rests, but otherwise exhibited important differences: some had elegantly rectangular backs and seats with concave wooden supports connecting arm-rest to

seat; others had pretty shaped backs which were 'open below at the back which made them very light, without having bad effect.' These had delicately wrought carving on the frame and unemphatic cabriole legs.

French corner chair. A curious form of seating which seems to have been made only by the cabinetmaking partnership of William Ince (qv) and John Mayhew. The design was reproduced in their manual and trade pattern book, *The Universal System of Household Furniture*, published in parts between 1759 and 1762 as a counterblast to Chippendale's *Director*. The French corner chair had a broad and deep upholstered seat with a semi-serpentine sweep to the front, an upholstered back, and one scrolled side. It appears to have been an uncomfortable seat, to say the least, although it doubtless displayed to advantage the voluminous dresses of the time.

French foot. A bracket foot which splays outwards, usually

in a tapering form. The French foot is to be seen in simple and decorative forms on many commodes. The simpler version was adapted by English and American cabinetmakers and was well suited to what has come to be regarded as a typical eighteenth-century English chest of drawers.

French furniture. For most people these words evoke the eighteenth and early nineteenth centuries, the greatest period for French furniture; but it must not be forgotten that from the fifteenth century much fine furniture was made in Paris and the provincial capitals. At its best, early French furniture was characterized by a refinement of carving and a technical brilliance seldom achieved elsewhere. However, it was not until the late seventeenth century that French furniture began to develop on noticeably different lines from that of the rest of Europe.

Gothic and Renaissance furni-

ture-making in France was good, but inferior to that of Italy; the style was uniform throughout Europe, and for decorative effect the skill of the wood-carver was essential. In 1608, Henry IV of France established Flemish craftsmen at the Louvre, and from this beginning was to spring the later glories of Paris as a furniture-making centre and leader of style.

From 1680 to 1780 French furniture-makers achieved a standard equalled only in England and greatly superior to that of the rest of Europe. Louis XIV (1643–1715) established the *Manufacture Royale des Meubles de la Couronne* at Gobelins in 1662, under the directorship of the brilliant artist-designer Charles Le Brun. There Italian and Flemish craftsmen initiated what was to become the tradition of French craftsmanship.

Late Louis XIV style: 1670–1710. The principal royal furniture-maker was André Charles

Seventeenth century: **1** *Burgundian chair with upholstered needlepoint seat* **2** *Louis XIV commode in kingwood veneer with metal* **3** *Kneehole desk decorated with metal inlay*

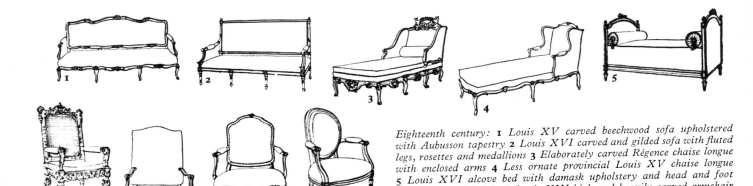

Eighteenth century: **1** *Louis XV carved beechwood sofa upholstered with Aubusson tapestry* **2** *Louis XVI carved and gilded sofa with fluted legs, rosettes and medallions* **3** *Elaborately carved Régence chaise longue with enclosed arms* **4** *Less ornate provincial Louis XV chaise longue* **5** *Louis XVI alcove bed with damask upholstery and head and foot boards of equal height* **6** *Louis XIV high and heavily carved armchair* **7** *Régence chair with gracefully curved members* **8** *Louis XV chair combining elegance and comfort, the high point of French eighteenth-century furniture* **9** *Louis XVI chair introducing more classical lines*

Boulle (qv). The dignified and classical designs of the period are to be seen at their best in the *bureaux plats*, armoires, and commodes by Boulle in the Louvre. Marquetry, common in Europe from the sixteenth century, was adapted to the use of brass and tortoiseshell inlay. Much Baroque and classical furniture was produced in solid silver for Versailles, but was melted down in 1689 and 1709 in order to assist a treasury drained by constant warfare.

Régence style: 1710–30. At Louis XIV's death in 1715, his grandson Louis XV was still a child. There was no distinctive style during the eight-year Regency, but it has given its name to the whole period between the collapse of Le Brun's classicism and the full flowering of the Rococo. The reaction against the severe and magnificent mid-Louis XIV style had started by 1700, with the earliest anti-classical designs of Jean Berain. The greatest furniture-maker of this period, Charles Cressent, early made use of the new freedom of design to relieve the solemnity of existing styles; and largely through his Rococo designs the commode came into greater prominence than before.

While Louis XIV commodes, chairs, and *bureaux plats* are to be found today (though seldom of the first quality), Régence furniture is more common, and both commodes (in kingwood, purpleheart, or rosewood) and chairs (in walnut or beechwood) can be seen in salerooms and antique dealers' shops.

The brass-tortoiseshell inlay boulle needed protection at the corners. This led to the making of metal mounts of ormolu (gilt bronze) which, by Régence times, and especially in the work of Cressent, spread from corners and feet to become part of the overall decorative scheme.

Louis XV style: 1730–70. Nicolas Pineau, a designer, returned from Russia in 1726 and at once became the leading designer in Paris. His exploitation of the still evolving Rococo style led to the full flowering of the Louis XV style – one of bold asymmetry, slender scrollwork, curves in place of straight lines – which is the one distinctive French style that was entirely native in conception.

The wealth of the upper and middle classes gave rise to an ever-increasing demand for good furniture. Makers are found in increasingly large numbers in Paris and to some extent in provincial cities (eg the Nogaret family at Lyons), though many worked outside the jurisdiction of the professional guild, the *Corporation des Menuisiers-Ebénistes.* (*Menuisier* – maker of beds, chairs, etc from plain carved wood; *ébéniste* – maker of veneered cabinet furniture.) From 1741, masters of the corporation (which throughout the century was strictly limited to 985 members) were compelled to sign their furniture, and this has been of immense help in the study, of eighteenth-century methods and makers.

Nearly 180 woods were avail-able for veneers and parquetry (geometric inlay) was very common, reaching a remarkably high standard in the furniture of makers like Migeon.

Chairs, with their entirely curved frames, were now usually gilded – a practice less frequent in earlier periods, though common in England – and decorated with floral carving of a high order. Makers like Tilliard and Lebas dominated this field. Lacquer from Japan was prized more highly than almost any other imported commodity: it was used on furniture, and some pieces were even sent to the East to be lacquered. In France, the brothers Martin used the decorative varnish japanning known as *vernis martin*, though purely 'chinoiserie' furniture, such as was made in England by Chippendale, is almost unknown in France.

Louis XVI style: 1770–90. A reaction against the extravagances of Rococo was apparent as early as 1750. The ruins of Pompeii and Herculaneum, new-

Eighteenth century: **1** *Half round or demi-lune commode; the central tier of drawers is flanked by cabinets* **2** *Slender Louis XV cabriole-legged table with marble top and metal mounts* **3** *Typical Louis XV bureau plat with three drawers in the frieze* **4** *A bonheur du jour with slightly cabriole legs but otherwise rectilinear super-structure and metal mounts* **5** *Louis XVI tapered leg tric-trac and reading table, the book rest shown in upright position* **6** *Tall carved fall-front cabinet revealing small compartments* **7** *Louis XVI commode with concealed drawers* **8** *Commode-secrétaire with a handle to operate the rising mechanism*

Nineteenth century: **1** *Satinwood table with sphinx supports* **2** *Table with oval mahogany top and metal sabre legs* **3** *X-shaped legs on a painted table with gilt edging* **4** *Mahogany table with bronze supports on a solid base* **5** *Plant stand on a three columned circular base* **6** *Cabriole-legged plant table* **7** *Table with scrolled ornament* **8** *Dressing table with bronze mounts and sabre legs* **9** *Night table with pillar supports on floor level stretchers* **10** *Marble-top table with gold and white decoration and* reeded legs **11** *Mahogany console table with bronze mounts on a solid base* **12** *Console table with marble shelf and brass inlay* **13** *Plain mahogany sideboard with marble top* **14** *Tall night table with a tambour front above a cupboard* **15** *Mahogany secretary with a drop front revealing shelves and drawers* **16** *Drop front secretary with brass mounts* **17** *Fruitwood chest of drawers* **18** *Mahogany library bookcase* **19** *Low mahogany secretary with drop front* **20** *Mahogany bookcase with broken pediment*

ly discovered, were a revelation to Europe, and slender, severe, yet attractive late classical forms profoundly influenced French designers. The new style was preferred by wealthy Parisians. For the first time, the Court was not responsible for a change in taste, and in fact continued to favour the Rococo long after the classical revival had become ubiquitous.

The transitional style between the Louis XV and Louis XVI styles was at once enchanting and awkward (reminiscent of the Régence), with straight-fronted commodes on curved legs, and chairs with curved backs and straight legs. Many of the greatest *ébénistes* were working at this time, including Dubois, Lacroix, Oeben, and the incomparable Bernhard van Risen Burgh.

By 1750 the growing preference for small, intimate rooms had led to a demand for new types of furniture. A host of small tables, *bureaux*, chairs, and side-cabinets (all with confusing and often illogical names) came into being. The fall-front secrétaire – common in Europe in the late seventeenth century – was rediscovered as the *secrétaire à abattant* and became one of the chief pieces of furniture, on a par with the commode. Marquetry (pictorial inlay) replaced parquetry, and the commonest

ground veneer was the lovely tulipwood, with its red and yellow figuring.

The Austrian Queen Marie Antoinette favoured German craftsmen, and this last great age of French furniture-making was dominated by Jean Henri Riesener.

The financial difficulties of the Crown led to a reduction in the previously over-lavish royal orders for furniture. This increased the speed with which 'Etruscan' influences – *le style étrusque* – swept Paris. Anglomania also attacked France at this time, with the result that mahogany replaced kingwood and tulipwood. Ormolu mounts were severe but of superb quality. In chairs the same simplicity was evident, and the greatest of all chair-makers, Georges Jacob, reigned supreme.

Directoire style: 1790–1800. A continuation of *style étrusque* simplicity.

Empire style: 1800–30. This style flourished in the reigns of Napoleon I (1804–15), Louis XVIII (1815–24), and Charles X (1824–30). A few great makers continued to flourish in this period, notably Georges Jacob's family, who turned from chair-making to *ébénisterie* of a very high order. Ormolu mounts by Pierre Philippe Thomire were excellent and the wood (often fruitwood in place of the more

expensive mahogany) was well chosen. The basic style – still Etruscan – was supplemented by Egyptian and other motifs as a result of Napoleon's expedition to Egypt and further discoveries of classical works of art.

By 1825 (Charles X period) the vogue for *bois clair* and other pale yellow woods was at its height. Parquetry was used to a limited extent, and the use of ormolu was often avoided. There was further simplification after 1830 with the importation of the Biedermeier fruitwood furniture style from Germany.

Notes on construction in the eighteenth century: The principal difference between the construction of French and other European furniture is in the use of round narrow pegs to hold joints. Pegs are found in chairs, where four hold each leg to the seat-rail, and in all forms of cabinet furniture. They are always used on the backs of commodes, secrétaires, and the like until early 1800s.

Dovetails (interlocking fan-shaped joints on drawers, etc) were as broad as in Holland, and not until the mid-nineteenth century did they become as narrow as those used in England from about 1720.

Drawer linings were in walnut before 1740, when they gradually gave way to oak, or sometimes pine. But in the finest Louis XVI

furniture, mahogany, cedar, and even tulipwood veneered on oak are not uncommon even for the insides of drawers. Eighteenth-century drawer linings normally had rounded tops; later work had straight-cut tops with sharp edges.

Gilt side-tables were invariably carved out of oak in France, whereas their English counterparts were in pine, and this difference is often the only way of distinguishing one from the other.

Porcelain, mounted in ormolu on tables and cabinets, is hardly ever found outside France. Many fine cabinets from 1750 were so mounted in Sèvres, and this practice continued throughout the nineteenth century.

The standard of cabinet carcase-making in France is considered inferior to that of England, with the notable exception of pieces by Riesener, whose work was always of the highest quality. Apart from drawers, the carcase was seldom of oak and usually of cheap fruitwoods and pine. The exterior of French furniture was usually lavishly constructed, the interior rather skimped and inadequate.

The locks of eighteenth-century French furniture, common on small and large drawers, worked on a different principle from those of the rest of Europe, and until 1820 the key had to be

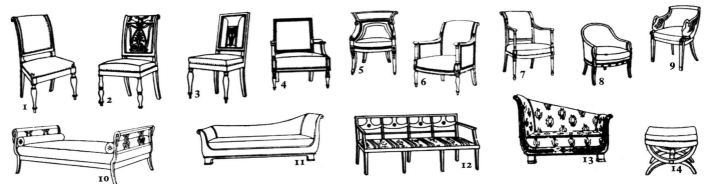

Nineteenth century: Side chairs by the Jacob brothers with turned legs **1** *with upholstered seat and back* **2** *with anthemion back and* **3** *carved back splay and padded seat* **4** *Open sided square armchair with painted frame* **5** *Mahogany desk chair with sabre legs* **6** *Armchair with closed sides, scrolled back and painted frame* **7** *Painted mahogany armchair with open sides* **8** *Upholstered 'gondola' chair with a continuous back and arms* **9** *Swans-head arm supports on a 'gondola' chair* **10** *Low mahogany bed with carved lyre motifs instead of boards, and swan-headed bed posts* **11** *Chaise longue with upholstered back and scrolled ends* **12** *Directoire chairback settee with padded seat and straight legs* **13** *Upholstered seat with carved scrolled ends and high back* **14** *Roman-inspired crossed legged curule stool with upholstered seat*

turned twice to lock or unlock. Secrétaires normally contain an oak safe box in the cupboard beneath the fall-front. These are seldom of great strength, and were probably to safeguard secrets from prying servants rather than professional thieves.

Upholstery was better understood in France than elsewhere from 1740 until at least 1800. Chairs were covered in a great variety of materials, but rarely in tapestry. Most older seat furniture now found with tapestry was re-covered in the late nineteenth century.

The webbing holding French chair-seat upholstery is broad and forms a complete interlocking pattern. Louis XV chairs – the most comfortable ever made – were the first to be sprung, though it is now rare to find them with the original springing.

Middle and late nineteenth century. In France, as elsewhere, the development of machine mass production led to the manufacture of vulgar, bulky, over-ornate furniture. At the same time, the styles of the eighteenth century were increasingly appreciated. This started the remarkable industry for reproductions, so common today in Europe and America. In France, Henri Dasson, working about 1850, was the leading copyist of his day. This tendency to copy traditional furniture was more pronounced in French cabinet-makers than in those of any other country in Europe. This nostalgia produced the generally depressing mélange to be seen in the Napoleon III style, a manner composed of oddments from the treasured pieces of earlier eras.

The Modern Movement was comparatively slow to make any impact upon the applied arts in France, although the furniture designs of Charles Plumet (1861–1928) and Tony Selmersheim owed much to the Art Nouveau designs introduced by Victor Horta in Brussels in 1893. Edmund de Goncourt caustically described these designs as the 'yachting style.'

The influence of the simple furniture of Van de Velde (a Belgian and follower of William Morris) dates from the opening by S Bing, a German art dealer, of a shop in the Rue de Provence in 1896.

When the modern movement did influence the design of French furniture, its impact was strong and lasting, in particular through the work of the French-Swiss Architect-designer Le Corbusier.

French heading. A term applied to a decorative curtain-heading in the form of pinch pleats, box pleats, or a variation of the two. Curtains have been made like this for centuries, but more in France than elsewhere, hence the name. Since the late 1950s this type of heading has been universally fashionable.

French headings are sewn by hand and, for best results, on a curtain which has a lining, and an interlining of 'bump' (wadding) to give extra body. This type of curtain can be fitted with rings and hung from antique brass or wooden rods: a more modern effect can be obtained with the type of nylon runner which can be inlaid into the ceiling plaster, so that no unsightly rail can be seen when the curtain is drawn open. A wooden rod can also be obtained which is inlaid with this invisible runner.

French interior decoration. The importance of French interior designers from 1670 to 1820 can hardly be exaggerated. Their influence is still strongly felt; they set standards and devised themes which have never been rivalled.

The fashion for painted walls was common from medieval times, but Le Brun, director of the Gobelins royal workshops from the 1670s was responsible for the first unified style of interior painted design. This court style of massive classicism, reflecting the as yet unsullied glory of Louis XIV, was blended with Baroque exuberance. Le Brun's designs for a mural panel at Versailles are as symbolic of the Sun King's reign as his designs for Gobelins tapestries of the king's victories and the triumphs of the classical gods. The Galerie des Glaces at Versailles is now all that remains of the most resplendent grandeur of the age. The silver furniture was melted down to finance the king's wars; the remaining furniture and fittings dispersed by the Revolution.

Jean La Pautre was a contemporary of Le Brun. Classical and heavy, sumptuous and elab-orate, his work ranged from portrait cabinets on giltwood stands to ewers of crystal and gold, from fireplaces to picture frames supported by griffins, vases, and Corinthian columns.

By 1700 Jean Berain, one of the greatest of all designers, had begun to introduce Rococo lightness. His designs were open, airy, and fanciful: slender vases with fruit and pheasants, trophies of love, strapwork, female masks, *Commedia del' Arte* actors, *singeries* (monkeys as men), and other elegant follies. Classical motifs remain, but their heaviness has disappeared. Berain's designs were ideal for painted panels and by about 1710 carved oak panelling had temporarily gone out of fashion.

Daniel Marot, in both Paris and London, emphasized the formalized elegance of arabesques, strapwork, and other early Rococo elements. His ceiling designs are a triumph of lightness. The painter Watteau and the designers Gillot, Oudry, and Openord contributed to this elegance. Watteau wall-panels are a miracle of opulent elegance – classical conceits framed by strapwork and chains of flowers of extreme attenuation.

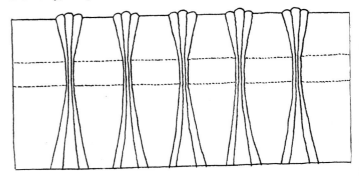

Drawing of a French heading on a curtain

A wall panel by Charles le Brun at Versailles showing Louis XIV, last half of the seventeenth century

Design for a wall in Régence style by Nicolas Pineau, early 18th century Below, design for a Louis XVI wall by Lalonde, late 18th century

It was the designer Nicolas Pineau who introduced the pure Rococo in the 1730s. His designs, mostly for furniture, show a bold use of the interplay of curves, while always preserving a symmetrical overall design.

In the 1740s Jules Aurèle Meissonnier developed the high Rococo of unfettered asymmetry. Few of his interior designs exist today except on paper. The lodges by Cuvilliés in the grounds of Nymphenburg in Bavaria are perhaps closest to the Rococo of Meissonnier's imagination.

The plump young women of the painter François Boucher epitomize the Rococo in the 1750s. By this time it was already under attack by designers and architects like Soufflot, protagonists of the Neo-classical revival. Under Louis XVI, Neo-classicism became the predominant style.

De la Rottière, Charles de Wailly, the painters Fragonard and Moreau le Jeune, and the designer Lalonde all worked in the simplified Neo-classical style which, while using many of Le Brun's motifs, created an elegance based on straight lines and geometric balance. The cabriole leg gave way to the fluted and tapering leg, and Boucher's nubile maidens to slender Roman Vestal Virgins.

With Charles de la Fosse, the prolific Lalonde dominated furniture design before the Revolution and, with Desprez and Salembier, carried classical simplicity into interior design. Painted panelling and tall ceilings were still favoured, but simpler carved oak rooms were now used to best effect. By the Napoleonic period the interior designs of the eighteenth century had been completely abandoned.

The Empire style was even more emphatically classical than its predecessor. The excavations at Pompeii and Herculaneum showed for the first time classical interiors with their original furniture still *in situ*. Greek, Roman, and later Egyptian colours, decorative motifs, and above all furniture, dominated French interiors even more than British. The bronze furniture of the ancient world was copied in timber – sometimes with curious results, eg the sabre-legged chair, which is hardly a form suited to timber construction, though seen to perfection on Greek vases.

The painter David, fascinated by the classical discoveries, did much to popularize the Empire

A Louis XIV wall-panel by Jean Berain, c 1700

style at Napoleon's court, his portrait of Madame Récamier epitomizing the epoch.

Both Napoleon and the Empress Josephine used personal decorative motifs which became part of the Empire style. The bee, denoting the ceaseless activity of the Emperor; the laurel wreath, the eagle, and, for Josephine, the graceful swan's neck were used on some of the most beautiful Empire furniture.

At Malmaison, Josephine's room, the Tent Room, was festooned with stiffly regimented drapery, the original intention being to remind her that Napoleon led a soldier's life. The draped room has been one of the elements of French decoration ever since.

Two remarkable men dominated Empire design and defined the Empire style which so long impressed the nineteenth century and is still fashionable today. Charles Percier, who won the Premier Grand Prix de Rome in 1786, and Pierre Fontaine, his partner, published *Recueil des décorations interieures* (1812), which became a standard work on Empire design. They were made directors of design to the Paris Opera and architects to Napoleon; they designed and built the famous Arc de Triomphe du Carrousel. Their best interior decorations were severely Greek, and employed the motifs of late classical design as faithfully as possible.

The last great designer of the Empire was Charles Pierre Joseph Normand, also a winner of the Premier Grand Prix de Rome. Normand's designs, somewhat reminiscent of Robert Adam, were of an almost overornate complexity; they were published in his book *Nouveau Parallèle des ordres d'architecture* (1819).

After the Empire, interior decoration was largely determined by technical advances and the rising influence of the *bourgeoisie*. Houses were no longer being built on the grand scale inspired by châteaux, and therefore the bourgeois taste for luxury was modulated into a taste for comfort. This attitude was imported from England and developed quickly in France, because of the falling price of fabrics, which made them accessible to large numbers. The mechanical manufacture of products such as wallpapers, fabrics, and carpets proved to be the downfall of the artisan; but the decorator now had a much wider range of choices.

The Restoration (1815) was characterized by the amount of furniture copied from the pre-Revolution period, and dozens of Louis XVI drawing-rooms were faithfully reproduced. Comfort, however, was still the first consideration; sprung chairs appeared and stoves replaced log fires. There was a vogue for

A salon in the 1920–30 style, arranged by M Jacques Doucet: gondola-shaped sofa made by Coard, African-inspired table and cut velvet chairs

transformed furniture – desks equipped with drawing-boards, work-tables-cum-desks. Colours in fashion followed those of opaline glass; blue, mauve, and pink were used both for fabrics and paint. Some of Balzac's novels are informative; for example, his description of a woman's apartment which is furnished with Jacob chairs, covered with striped materials, and brightened with opaline windows. The walls of Restoration rooms were hung with wallpapers of repeated multi-coloured subjects against a background of grey and white. The most popular subjects were classical scenes or fables, or military campaigns.

During Charles X's reign (1824–30) light-coloured woods came into fashion; elm, the fruitwoods, maple, and ash were the most commonly used, and were combined with darker woods, such as rosewood or amaranth. But this period was short-lived, and at the end of the reign, the

Living room with ornately draped curtains, designed by Madelaine Castaing. The painted cane sabre legged chairs are Empire style

Modern Paris apartment designed by Patrick Hart and André Laborde. Bolsters are piled high in the seating well

literary Romanticism of Scott and Hugo brought the Middle Ages back into fashion. The 'cathedral' style became the rage: chairs took on this form, wainscots had ogives up to the ceiling, and even clocks adopted the lines of Gothic-style windows.

A little later, chairs were covered in drapery, flounces of material, fringes, and braids. The upholsterer became the dominant figure.

During the Second Empire, interiors were darkened by door curtains, lace curtains, undercurtains, thick double curtains, voluminous curtain loops of wool, and bed-drapery. Doorframes were lined with artificial marble; there were black chairs of papier-mâché, decked with painted flowers, and small round tables encrusted with mother-of-pearl. Green plants in abundance were found in every room. Chairs covered in quilted materials were to be found side by side with relics of past centuries: Louis XIII, Louis XV, and Louis XVI in particular. Unfortunately the copies were overdone – garishly gilded, with disproportionate legs – and thus curved furniture became too convex; bronzes were also very much distorted. The use of gas for lighting led to the introduction of chandeliers with branches holding frosted glass globes. The colours, turkey red, gold, and dark green were particularly favoured.

As a reaction against constant borrowing from the past, l'Art Nouveau was created. Displayed at the Exhibition of 1900, it reflected the need to start afresh at all costs. Iron was used much as it was being used in the new architecture: this malleable metal enabled even the most eccentric fantasies to be realized, such as the entrances to the *Métro*, some of which still exist today, by the architect Guimard. The curvilinear floral Art Nouveau style found practitioners in decorators like Majerelle and Drufrêne, and master glassmakers like Gallé and Tiffany. But their vogue did not last long, and the taste of this odd period led on to the furniture of Ruhlman and the lacquerwork of Dunand.

In 1925 the Exhibition of Arts Décoratifs contained many designs showing the influence of Cubism and other geometric painting styles. Furniture of Cubist inspiration was right-angled, and no adornments or embossing were allowed on the walls: they were meant to be smooth. Beige became the predominant colour.

After World War II there was yet another fashion in interiors – this time for the styles of the nineteenth century. Charles X and Napoleon III pieces, thanks to their relatively modest proportions, easily found places in modern interiors. The armchairs called *crapauds* are popular because they are so comfortable. Several Parisian decorators have

introduced a fashion for English furniture; its mahogany blends well with the dark green and bright red of the nineteenth century.

The lines of Scandinavian design have also strongly influenced modern French decoration, though traditional suites are still characterized by borrowings from the eighteenth century.

French order. Many architects have sought to add their own variant of the classical orders to the architectural repertory. Philibert de l'Orme (qv), the famous sixteenth-century French architect, added a fifth, now called the French order, to those established by Vitruvius and Serlio. In the French order the shaft of the column is enriched by rings of stone, an idea derived from the use of rusticated columns in the Palazzo Thiene, Vicenza, and the more exotic columns employed in the portico of the Villa Santa Sofia, Pedemonte, by Palladio, who was de l'Orme's almost exact contemporary.

French-polishing. A process in furniture-making which has a chequered and controversial history. The process was introduced towards the end of the eighteenth century, and by the early years of the nineteenth was widespread in the furniture trade. A transparent gum was applied to the surface of timber to be polished, and by continuous physical labour, the wood could be given a highly glazed appearance, so that its grain and markings were inordinately emphasized. Yet, as critics pointed out, it was the gum that was manipulated and polished rather than the wood. In 1836 the Angelo Nicholsons, in their book *The Practical Cabinet-Maker, Upholsterer and Complete Decorator*, praised the process as 'a new and admirable mode of polishing or varnishing, by which means it is not so much necessary to polish the surface of the wood itself.' But by 1872, Charles L Eastlake's *Hints on Household Taste* condemned the practice on the grounds that 'the present system of French-polishing, or literally, varnishing, furniture is destructive of all artistic effect in its appearance, because the surface of wood thus lacquered can never change its colour or acquire that rich hue which is one of the chief charms of old cabinet-work.' A century later the controversy continues, even though French-polishing is now done mechanically in large furniture

A wafer box painted in blue on white made at Rouen in the late eighteenth century

factories. Certainly French-polishing contributed to some of the more lamentable aspects of Victorian furniture.

French porcelain. The first soft-paste French porcelain was made at Rouen towards the end of the seventeenth century. Pieces that can be attributed with certainty to Rouen were decorated in blue, with designs very like those of the faience that was being made there at the same time. The early pieces were unmarked, but unidentifiable pseudo-Chinese characters appear on some. A few pieces attributed to the Rouen factory were marked with the letters A P.

A little later in the century (c 1690) soft-paste porcelain was made at St Cloud, very much in the style of Rouen. Some of the St Cloud productions were marked with a flaming sun, usually in blue. Polychrome decorated porcelain in imitation of oriental styles was made, many of the shapes being inspired by the work of the silversmiths. Small boxes and walking-stick handles, and statuettes of oriental figures, were also made at St

A jug and cover enamelled with celadon green, with a silver mount, made at St Cloud, c 1730

A mug, painted in imitation of a Japanese Kakiyemon design, made at Chantilly c 1730

A figure of a Chinaman made at Mennecy in 1740

A teapot made at the Mennecy factory c 1760

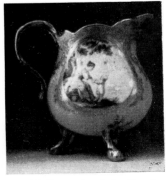

A milk jug painted by Boucher with a rose Pompadour ground, Sèvres c 1765

An octagonal plate painted in grisaille, made at Sèvres in 1786

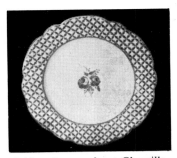

A blue plate made at Chantilly, second half of eighteenth century

A plate from a Limoges dessert service, c 1900

Cloud. Production ceased in 1773 when the factory was destroyed by fire.

In 1725 a porcelain factory was established at Chantilly. The early products were exotic in character but gradually became more Westernized in design. European flowers such as pansies were gradually introduced among the more exotic plants, and European animals and birds crept into the Chinese-inspired vegetation. Marks used at Chantilly include a hunting horn in red or blue or sometimes incised, occasionally accompanied by letters or dates. Some of the most delicate and enchanting of French porcelain was made at Chantilly.

A soft-paste porcelain factory under the patronage of the duc de Villeroy was established at Mennecy, near the Château de Villeroy, in 1735. Much exquisite work, mainly copied from oriental ware and china, was produced at St Cloud and Meissen. The factory specialized in making delicate little boxes, knife-handles, and knick-knacks for the dressing-table, decorated with beautifully painted flowers and birds. The mark used was an impressed or pencilled D V. When the lease of the factory expired in 1773, the establishment moved to Bourg la Reine and the mark was changed to B R.

The soft-paste porcelain factory at Vincennes, which was to become the most important in France, was started by two workmen from Chantilly in 1738. After various vicissitudes the factory seems to have become well established by 1750, employing as many as a hundred workmen and girls. One of the specialities at Vincennes was porcelain flowers, very delicate and true to life in colouring and form. These were sometimes mounted on wires for stalks and sometimes applied to the sides of vases and other objects.

In 1752 the king invested a lot of money in the porcelain factory. It became known as the

Royal Porcelain Factory and the king confirmed his permission to use two interlaced Ls (one reversed) as a mark. In 1756 the factory was removed to Sèvres. Porcelain was not allowed to be made elsewhere, and various restrictions were placed on other factories. However, about 1766 the restrictions were somewhat relaxed, and the manufacture of porcelain was again permitted to other factories; however the use of gilding was not, and not more than one colour was supposed to be used.

Under royal patronage Sèvres produced a vast number of grand dinner services, vases, and presentation pieces for celebrated people. The king himself encouraged visitors at his court to spend their money on porcelain. The flower-painting at Sèvres was always of a high quality and about 1749 the *bleu du roi*, a rich blue enamel for ground colour, was introduced. This was followed by other coloured grounds; among them turquoise, yellow, pea-green, and the famous *rose Pompadour*. The grounds were enriched by elaborate gilding. Panels were left white so that they could be filled in with paintings of flowers, or (more rarely) with figure or animal subjects. The workmanship was of the highest quality and no expense or trouble was spared to produce the finest possible ware.

After the Revolution, a severer Neo-classical style was followed by the 'Egyptian' revival. Designs became heavy, and there was much complicated naturalistic painting, hardly any of the plate or other piece of ware being

A bowl, probably painted by Mutel, with gros bleu ground, made at Vincennes in 1735

left white at all. In the nineteenth century many old designs were brought out and copied again. It was at Sèvres in the nineteenth century that the technique known as *pâte sur pâte* ('paste on paste') was discovered. The factory is still in production today.

There were many small factories making porcelain of both hard and soft paste in and around Paris. Hard-paste porcelain was also made at Strasbourg, Lunéville, Marseilles, and elsewhere.

In 1776 a hard-paste factory was started at Limoges, at first to make white porcelain for decoration at Sèvres. Later much good quality tableware was made and decorated at Limoges on a commercial scale. Most of the decoration was rather simple, either gilded patterns or sprays of flowers.

French provincial style. The remarkable quantity of French provincial furniture seen outside France in the nineteenth century testifies to the esteem in which it has been held for over a hundred years. The high prices now paid for it affirms this continuing appreciation especially in the United States. It is a favourite style of interior decoration in America, where traditional pieces are reproduced and built-in cupboards and other modern pieces have panels decorated with the curved moulding of the French provincial style.

Provincial furniture of the eighteenth century in France owed its design to the prevailing Paris fashions – the classical and Baroque of Louis XIV, the Rococo of Louis XV, the Neo-classical of Louis XVI. Though they followed each new trend, provincial craftsmen made furniture with a charm and individuality all its own.

The chief characteristic of this furniture is its use of woods – chiefly pale, honey-coloured walnut, indigenous to France, and to a lesser extent native beech, elm, chestnut, cherry, and apple-woods. The wood was selected

French provincial furniture: **1** Armoire with rococo carving, c 1800
2 Four-poster bed from Brittany, 1830 **3** Dresser from Lorraine with
carving on the doors and drawers **4** Breton oak bench **5** Provençal settee
with chair back **6** Breton armchair with rush seat **7** Chest from Nancy
8 Provençal Louis XV side table with cabriole legs and hoof feet

Top; a Louis XIV écuelle and cover, made in Paris in 1680. Bottom; a
Louis XV soup tureen from the Berkeley Castle dinner service

show its colour and grain to best advantage and was simply carved in the prevailing taste.

The principal styles are those of Provence, Alsace, Normandy, Brittany, and Burgundy. The accompanying illustrations show clearly the simple but individual styles.

French silver. The craft of silver-making is of great antiquity in France. The earliest known ordinance in any country relating to goldsmiths' marks was that of Philip Le Hardi in 1275, and Montpellier instituted an alphabetical system of marks in 1427. However, few examples dating from before the seventeenth century have survived, mainly because silver was so often melted down by royal decree to refill a depleted treasury.

During the reigns of Louis XIV and Louis XV, French silversmiths attained pre-eminence, both in quality and quantity of their work. They made silver for many of the courts of Europe; the largest surviving services are for that reason to be found in Russia and Portugal, the French having melted theirs own.

The Louis XIV bowl (écuelle)

illustrated, in the simple style which persisted into the early eighteenth century, is typically French. Even furniture was produced in silver for Versailles, but was melted down in 1689 and 1709 to help pay for Louis XIV's wars.

At the end of Louis XIV's reign the dignified, simple forms of the early 1700s gave way to flamboyant Rococo designs. The

Berkeley Castle dinner service in the illustration was made by Jacques Roettiers in Paris between 1735 and 1738; it represents the point of transition between the two styles.

The Rococo, fully established by 1740, was ably interpreted by such makers as the Germains, father and son, the Besniers, Lenhendrick, and many others.

The Revolution of 1789 was

responsible for the destruction of practically all this superb silver, but the First Empire from 1804 saw the re-emergence of Paris silversmiths. They used simpler forms again, with much gilding. The two outstanding makers were Biennais, goldsmith to Napoleon, and Odiot. Much of their work embodies motifs derived from Napoleon's Egyptian campaign, such as the winged

The Berkeley Castle dinner service, made by Jacques Roettiers in Paris, 1735–8

A small silver-gilt Empire chocolate pot, by Martin-Guillaume Biennais, c 1805

sphinx on the chocolate pot by Biennais.

Far more of this silver has survived, whereas fine French silver of the eighteenth century and earlier is practically non-existent outside museums.

French stool. This was a seeming innovation by the partners Ince & Mayhew and was also shown in their book *The Universal System of Household Furniture* (1762). But there is little to distinguish these so-called French stools from the more soberly named window-

seats or dressing-stools. Ince & Mayhew did, however, make some of these stools with an upholstered decorative panelled back, in which form they doubtless had a vogue as boudoir sofas, from which they are in any case indistinguishable.

Fresco. A term often applied erroneously to all forms of painting on walls or ceilings or even to paintings on very large canvases or panels which are then affixed to walls. These may properly be termed mural paintings, whereas a fresco painting is one executed on a plaster wall while the plaster is still fresh (Italian *fresco*). The plaster surface is applied to a basic wall structure, usually of brick or stone, which must be quite dry. The technique of fresco painting is of considerable antiquity, and, thanks to the skills of the ancient plasterers and artists, many frescos from earlier civilizations survive in good condition.

The correct procedure for ensuring a technically perfect fresco painting is among the most complex in the whole repertory of painting techniques. First the plaster is made from lime and water, the quantities usually depending as much on the artist's idiosyncratic beliefs as on established formulas. The complexities are multiplied by the fact

Part of a fresco by Annibale Carracci in the Palazzo Farnese, Rome

that this plaster mixture must be prepared several months (up to a year) before the painting is started. Several applications of the plaster are made to the wall, but only the primary coat of the *arriccio* (*arricciatúra*, rough casting), which is about half-an-inch in depth, is given to the entire area of the projected painting. The penultimate and final coats of the plaster, known as the *intonachi* (*intonacare*, to plaster), are applied only to the area which is to be painted at once. This is chemically imperative since the plaster must on no

account be dry when painting is begun; much of the beauty and almost all the clarity and durability of fresco painting derive from the protective film of crystal that forms as the plaster dries.

Needless to say, the water paints used in fresco work are also a matter of individual taste and conviction. They are mainly earth and mineral pigment mixed with distilled water, for experience has shown that these are best suited for combination with the plaster in the chemical reaction which takes place.

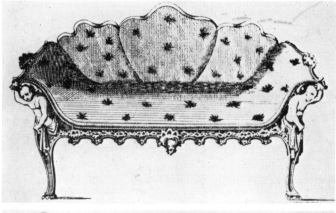

Two designs for a French stool, from the Universal System of Household Furniture by Ince and Mayhew, 1762

Detail of the fresco of The Fire in the Borgo by Raphael and his pupil 1517 in St Peter's, Rome, showing the façade of Old St Peter's on left

American primitive fresco of a tropical shore in a hall at Wintherthur

technically successful, the work of the artist and his craftsmen becomes part of the wall and will last as long as the wall stands.

Obviously fresco painting must be swiftly done, as the artist is engaged in a race against time. The great fresco painters have usually made only minimal outlines for their paintings (by indenting the plaster) before applying their pigments to the wall.

The origins of fresco painting are unknown. The ancient Egyptians practised the art and so did the Romans. The most famous frescos in the Western world are Michelangelo's in the Sistine Chapel, Rome, and Giotto's in the Scrovegni Chapel, Padua. Other Italian masters of fresco painting included Masaccio and Piero della Francesca.

Fresco painting was gradually supplanted by the less complicated method of painting in tempera.

Fret. A popular decorative frieze pattern also known as a key pattern, Greek key, or Greek fret. It is a small repeating design of interlocking horizontal and vertical lines. It was particularly favoured in the early Georgian and Neo-classical periods.

Fretwork. Also known as cutwork and lattice-work. These terms are used in furniture making to describe a strip or panel of simple or highly complex patterns, usually repeated, which is cut out and either applied to a solid surface or employed as a decorative ornamental element in its own right, eg as galleries for tables or pedestals. Fretwork was much used by most of the eighteenth-century cabinetmakers and was normally made of two or three thicknesses of veneer, usually mahogany, which were glued together and cut by special saw. The term is also used of decorative patterns of this type which are applied to the glass doors of cabinets or bookcases.

A further use of the word is to describe metalwork with a fretted appearance. This is used for the backs of garden seats or, in lattice-work, for side panels of summer-houses, fencing, and bridges.

The heyday of fretwork was during the eighteenth-century vogue for *chinoiserie* and the Gothick, when intricate patterns were incorporated into tables and cabinets, and applied to the friezes, drawers, doors, and aprons of chests and commodes.

Frieze. A term used in classical architecture to denote the middle element in the entablature, between cornice and architrave. In interior design the same term is used of a continuous panel, or strip of decoration which is set below the cornice or ceiling and above any panelling or picture-railing. It may be carved, plastered, or painted.

Robert Adam was perhaps the most important influence in making the frieze a major element in interior decoration. Outstanding examples of his designs for friezes can be seen at Osterley, and his work there and elsewhere was widely copied by metropolitan and provincial builders.

The term is also frequently employed in furniture-making (with perhaps less justification), where it describes the timber band below a cabinet top; this was often carved or painted with a repeat motif.

Fringe. A furnishing trimming used mainly for decoration, although when chairs and beds began to be upholstered it was used to conceal the joins where the material and wooden framework met.

Fringes decorated the cushions of rich Elizabethans, and were later used more freely on Jacobean chairs. The early surviving fringes are of silk and metal threads, hung straight from a netted heading of silk. In addition to the deep fringe, carried round to the lower edge of chair-seats and arms, a narrow fringe – termed *molet* in French – served to edge chair-cushions.

Tasselled fringes, popular during the Restoration period, were of floss-silk balls or of tassels, attached to a pre-woven base.

In William III's reign, when elaborate draperies in carved wood became fashionable as bed-canopies, fringes made of velvet and damask were pasted on to the wood.

Most fringes were made by gentlewomen at home, but some were imported from Italy. In time trimmings became richer and more lavish and were often very expensive; a point was reached during Queen Anne's reign when the upholstery and trimmings of beds were more important than the actual framework.

Perhaps because of this over-popularity, fringes then went out of fashion. They were revived under French influence during the last years of the eighteenth century, and continued to be used widely throughout the Victorian period, though braiding took the place of fringes on chairs.

Fretwork railings on an eighteenth-century chinoiserie bridge

A collection of Sunderland frog mugs

Frog mug. In the late eighteenth and the nineteenth century many 'frog' mugs were made. These were mugs with a frog, toad, or newt, or sometimes a group of such creatures in the bottom of the mug or appearing to climb up the side. The animals were realistically modelled and coloured, usually in brown, yellow, or green (though pink and black ones sometimes appear in Sunderland mugs). These mugs, given full to drinkers, must have raised many a bucolic laugh when the dismayed users drank down to the level of the creature in the bottom.

Frog mugs came in several shapes and different kinds of ware. Lustre and transfer-decorated frog mugs were made at Sunderland. Prattware frog mugs were made in Staffordshire. The Leeds pottery made some in their pearlware.

Similar 'joke' chamber pots were also made.

Frosted rustication. A decorative treatment of masonry in which the surface of the stone is carved in imitation of icicles. It was most popular in the eighteenth century.

Fry, Edwin Maxwell (*b* 1899). British architect and town-planner. Maxwell Fry was educated at Liverpool Institute and the Liverpool University School of Architecture. In the early 1930s he became the leader of the small group of architects and designers who founded the Mars Group (Modern Architectural Research) which substantially advanced the theory and practice of modern architecture in England.

The links established by the Mars Group with similar movements on the Continent brought Fry into touch with the leading figures working in France and Germany – Le Corbusier, Walter Gropius, and others. After Gropius had to leave Germany he became Maxwell Fry's partner for a time before he moved on to Harvard University.

Gropius and Fry built the first modern school in England (1936). Their Impington Village College was a forerunner of the schools in Hertfordshire and, more recently, those produced by the Clasp system, which have so impressed Continental planners. Fry also built a series of houses (Sun House, Hampstead, is the best known) and blocks of apartments; the Kensal Road Flats set new standards in design and accommodation. He also found time to write a best-seller, *Fine Building*, and later, with Jane Drew (qv), *Architecture for Children*.

The war took him to West Africa, where, with Jane Drew (now his wife and partner), he planned and built schools and colleges in Ghana and the first West African University at Ibadan, Nigeria. Then Fry and his wife, with Le Corbusier, designed the now-celebrated capital city of the Indian Punjab, Chandigarh (1951–4).

He returned to work on university buildings at Liverpool and a large complex of offices and social buildings at St Helens, Lancashire, for Pilkington Brothers, the glassmakers. He built the headquarters of Rolls-Royce at Derby, and a variety of housing schemes in London.

In the same period he took a leading part in a comprehensive development plan for Gibraltar. In Mauritius he designed the Government Centre in the capital Port Louis, and initiated plans for a large hospital in the north of the island.

He and Jane Drew are now engaged upon designs for the Open University at the new town of Milton Keynes.

Fulham. In 1671 John Dwight of Fulham, London, was granted a patent for the manufacture of earthenware. Dwight's hard, strong ware was much like the salt-glazed stoneware made at Cologne at about the same time. Dwight modelled some beautiful busts and figures in this hard grey ware. The pottery he owned also made many mugs, jugs, and Bellarmines (see **Cologne stoneware**). After his death in 1737, his widow continued to run the pottery until 1746, when it went bankrupt. It then changed hands several times.

Fuller, Richard Buckminster (*b* 1895). American engineer, designer-architect, professor of design at Southern Illinois University. He was educated in Milton, Massachusetts, Harvard University, and the US Naval Academy.

Like Luigi Nervi and Le Corbusier, Buckminster Fuller is one of the few revolutionaries in design who have lived to see their ideas being put into practice by others.

Fuller's revolutionary theories concern the dome, which has been a structural challenge to designers from Michaelangelo and Palladio to Vanbrugh and Wren. Fuller calls himself a Comprehensive Designer, and has some claim to the title, for he is engineer, mathematician, inventor, designer, writer, and philosopher. The form of construction that he has evolved is termed the 'geodesic dome.' This has ceased to be a mathematical theory and become hard fact. Thousands of these structures have been built, and they are being increasingly used by soldiers, contractors, businessmen, and planners of mass housing projects in the underdeveloped countries.

The geodesic dome combines the structural virtues of the tetrahedron and the sphere (the tetrahedron is a four-sided shape ie a pyramid; a sphere is the shape which encloses most space and is best suited to resist

Maxwell Fry

The Arts Building at University College, Ibadan, by Maxwell Fry

A grey stoneware mug, the upper part glazed brown, Fulham, 172

Buckminster Fuller

external pressures). By utilizing a skeletal tetrahedral form as the frame for his dome, Fuller has evolved an architectural form which seems to offer solutions to many of the world's housing, protective, and storage problems.

Fuller domes have been used in military operations and manœuvres in the Pacific and the Arctic. The US Marine Corps has air-lifted a 35 ft diameter, magnesium-framed dome, enclosing 1,200 cubic feet clear span space, with the ease of a half-ton crate. The dome has also done much to render campaign tents for the US Army and Marine Corps obsolete, and a Marine general described the new shelters as the first basic improvement in mobile military shelters in 2,500 years.

In 1953 the first large-scale permanent dome structure was erected for the Ford Rotunda. This was a geodesic structure using only 8½ tons of aluminium and spanning 93 ft, and was assembled in 30 days. It is estimated that conventional domes would have used 160 tons of steel. A dome auditorium in Hawaii seating over 2,000 people with a span of 145 ft was erected in two days.

Adventurous householders are following Fuller's own example and constructing homes within domes. Geodesic domes are also being used for garages and other urban structures; botanical gardens, banks, lecture halls, and community pools. Fuller believes that large urban areas could function healthily and efficiently under these domes.

Fumed oak. Oak furniture that was exposed to ammonia fumes, a treatment that eventually turned the oak to an unnatural yellow colour. It was used around the turn of the century, but its popularity vanished in the 1920s.

Functionalism. An architectural theory neatly and misguidingly summed up in the axiom 'form follows function.' The idea that internal structure should be expressed on the exterior, and that both should be part of comprehensive and integrated building method, was understood by architects to whom it was both a theory and a discipline. But in its name a mass of inferior work has been perpetrated by men who have taken it literally and have erected buildings that have scarcely seen a drawing-board. It is not an especially modern theory and was first articulated by the French architect and theorist Viollet-le-Duc, who called for rationalism of structure in architectural design in the mid-nineteenth century.

Furnishing fabrics. A term loosely used of both upholstery and curtain fabrics, but for the purposes of this entry confined to woven fabrics. The recent addition of man-made fibres to the list of fabrics for furnishing is perhaps the only great innovation for 500 years. The art of silk-weaving spread to Constantinople from China in about the sixth century, and thence to Genoa, Milan, and Venice. Coarser fabrics were probably woven even earlier throughout Europe, and few crafts are older.

Medieval and Renaissance inventories have many references to upholstery and the value placed on textiles. Through the traders of fifteenth- and sixteenth-century Venice, pile knotted carpets arrived from Asia Minor and spread throughout Europe. The rich householder of the fifteenth and sixteenth centuries could also buy silk and wool velvets from Utrecht and Brussels, linen velvets from Italy, silks from northern Italy and France, and tapestries from Brussels and France. With the influx of Flemish weavers, an English silk industry was operating at Canterbury and Spitalfields. Wool was interwoven with the silk, and these designs were more spacious than those of Genoa, but otherwise almost undistinguishable. Tapestries were woven at Soho and Hatton Garden by 1700, and velvets also at Spitalfields.

The eighteenth-century records of the *Garde Meuble* in France demonstrate the continuing importance of furnishing fabrics. With the exception of the Louis XV period, the whole eighteenth century conception of furniture and furnishings was based on sumptuously opulent and ingeniously designed upholstery. Fringes, ribbons, galloons, and other rich trimmings were commonplace, and the superb Lyon silks were heavily woven with gold and silver thread. For upholstery purposes, horsehair was woven at intervals into the back of silk fabrics. (The practice still continues.) The royal upholsterers, notably Delobel, Sallior, and Capin, were more famous in their day than even the greatest *ébénistes*.

The nineteenth-century development of spinning and weaving machinery revolutionized weaving techniques. Many of the cloths developed as a result are still used today for high-quality work.

Man-made fibres for furnishing, pioneered largely in America, were the innovation of the twentieth century. The first to influence furnishing fabrics was the viscose rayon. It was used with cotton and is now widely used for brocade, or brocatelles (mock brocades). Acetate was an invention which has the advantages of cheapness, and amenability to dyeing. It is used in brocades, in curtain linings, and on its own as a printed sateen.

Nylon was the first truly synthetic fibre, often added to wool and cotton in upholstery fabrics because it resists abrasion. Terylene has been widely used for curtain nets and sheers, although it can never entirely replace cotton for nets, voiles, and laces. Fibreglass has been used as a curtain fabric, its drip-dry and virtually indestructible qualities making it an important utilitarian material.

The following traditional upholstery and curtain cloths are still used and are unsurpassed for quality work. Frieze: a pure worsted cloth with a pronounced diagonal weave. Coach or covet cloths: very tightly woven wool cloths with a felted top surface. Blissé: usually a silk cloth woven with a ruched effect. Bourrette: a rough silk cloth with a tweed-like weave. Horsehair: used a great deal in the nineteenth century, still obtainable, now woven in small geometric patterns on a cotton warp. Moquette: a firm cloth with a looped top surface – the best being a high-quality cloth finely woven of pure worsted. Pure silk velvets; Utrecht velvet, always of wool, and meant to last a lifetime; and linen velvets, which for sheer understated luxury and beauty are hard to beat. Modern woven upholstery and curtain cloths rely on texture for their appeal. This can be produced by the yarn itself (eg bouclé) – so that the experimental spinning of fibres is of great importance. Then again, the mixture of fibres used plays a vital part in the appearance of the cloth; for example, wool and worsted from many parts of the world either are used in the same spun yarn, or put together in the weaving. The length of the staple and the feel, appearance, and wearing qualities of the different fibres vary greatly. Wool, linen, mohair, cotton, silk, and synthetics are all used together to produce specific effects.

Fustic or **fustick.** *Chlorophora tinctoria* or yellow wood. This is a tropical wood that, because of its attractive yellowish tones, was generally employed for inlay work. However, Sheraton (*Cabinet Dictionary*, 1803) considered it unsuitable for furniture because prolonged exposure changed its distinctive colour to a dull brown.

Roam House, Carbondale, Illinois, designed by Buckminster Fuller, 1959

House of the Seven Gables, Salem, Massachusetts

A variety of gables in the market place at Rostock, Germany

Gable. The part of an outer wall supporting a pitched or ridged roof. This area is usually triangular, although Dutch gables offer a more varied elevation. The roof-line extending beyond the gable wall is known as the verge. During the Regency era, the gables of roof-lines of low pitch were frequently invested with the mouldings appropriate to a pediment.

Gabled hip. A small gable above a hipped roof.

Gablet. A miniature gable, frequently seen over buttresses or niches.

Gabriel family. A family of French architects who built many important works for the kings of France. The first architect in the family was Jacques

Gabriel, father of **Gabriel, Jacques Jules** (1667–1742), who became *architecte du Roi* in 1687 and *premier architecte* to Louis XV in 1735. In a lifetime of considerable industry he designed churches, government buildings, town halls, bridges, and houses, and was also involved in major town-planning projects. Among his most notable designs are the Hôtel de Ville at Rennes

(1734–43), the archbishop's palace at Blois (1725), and the Place Royale (1730–60) at Bordeaux, where he also designed the Bourse. His outstanding achievement was the façade of the cathedral at La Rochelle (1740). **Gabriel, Jacques-Ange** (1698–1782), his son, became *architecte du roi* on his father's death in 1742, having already designed the Gallery of

Hôtel de Ville, Rennes, by Jacques Jules Gabriel, 1734–43

Ecole Militaire, Paris, designed by Jacques-Ange Gabriel, 1751

Gallery. *The gallery used as an armoury in the Jacobean mansion Hatfield House in Hertfordshire, home of the Cecils*

The Petit Trianon, Versailles, designed by Jacques-Ange Gabriel, 1751

The Norman Galilee chapel at the west end of Durham Cathedral

Ulysses at Fontainebleau (1737). Like his father he was deeply involved in town-planning projects, the most famous of which was his Place Louis XV (1753), now Place de la Concorde. His most important building was the Petit Trianon (1763–9), a building in a pure classical style, and a charming miniature in an age of spectacular royal display. The last of Gabriel's major buildings was the Ecole Militaire (1751), which was still being built at his death. His son, **Gabriel-Ange-Antoine** (1735–81) was *Contrôleur des Bâtiments du roi* (1761–75) and predeceased his father.

Gadroon, gadrooning. Also known as knurling and nulling. These are terms applied to a form of carving on the edges of tables, desks, and other furniture – a repetitive pattern of lobed ornament of convex or sometimes oblong curves. Gadrooning was a characteristic of Elizabethan oak furniture-making, and later of early Georgian cabinetmaking. This form of carving was well suited to Rococo decoration. It was especially common, however, as a decoration for silver, and was used extensively during the reign of William and Mary.

Gainsborough chair. The modern term for a type of chair that was described by Chippendale and his contemporaries as a French chair (qv). It has an upholstered back, seat and elbow pads, the arms are open, and the concave wooden arm supports are usually fluted.

Galilee. A small porch or chapel at the entrance to a medieval church or cathedral. The term was also apparently applied to the nave, or the western portion of the nave, which was sometimes set apart from the rest of the church by a step or other demarcating feature.

Galilei, Alessandro (1691–1737). Anglo-Italian architect, born in Florence. He was brought to England by the Hon John Molesworth and introduced to the English aristocracy. Despite this patronage he had little success in either England or Ireland, where he did some work on the Molesworths' home near Dublin. He married an Englishwoman in 1718, but returned to Florence the following year and became surveyor of the ducal buildings. He also designed the churches of San Giovanni dei Fiorentini and San Giovanni Laterano in Rome.

Gallé, Emile (1846–1904). The leader of the 'School of Nancy', one of the most important centres of the Art Nouveau movement in France. Gallé is best known as a glass-designer, although his furniture designs are also among the finest of the period.

Gallé's father was a dealer in glass and faience, and Emile studied techniques of production and decoration at Meisenthal and St Clement. He was a keen student of the chemistry of glass, and also an enthusiastic botanist. His father handed over his affairs to his son in 1874, and Emile started producing his own glass. His early work culminated in the Paris Exhibition of 1878, where he showed enamelled glass with designs based on historical sources, glass enamelled with floral motifs, and carved glass of a very personal and experimental nature. One of his innovations at the Exhibition was *claire de lune* glass with a fine sapphire tint which altered as light was directed on to it.

By 1884, Gallé had perfected many new designs, mostly with enamelled conventional motifs, which he showed at the Paris Exhibition of that year. He was now employing numerous artists and craftsmen, and was able to produce table surfaces on a commercial scale in the 1880s. He again had tremendous success at the Paris Exhibition in 1889.

Gallé had now found his own style, inspired by oriental design and his love of nature, which he combined to create a personal version of Art Nouveau in glass. His products include cased glass

A Gainsborough chair

vases carved with naturalistic décor; marquetry of glass, inlaid with plant motifs; glass enamelled with fish, birds, and the simple wild flowers of Lorraine; and vases resembling hardstones often in simple forms. Some of his pieces were mounted in bronze at his workshops; others in various metals, by the retailers who sold his products. All hi

Queen Anne circular salt trenchers with bands of broad gadrooning

Gallé by Victor Prouvé, 189

glass was signed, usually in full. Many pieces were inscribed with quotations from the French poets, the *Verreries Parlantes*. The designs were often in series, the same motifs being reproduced on different shapes; some were unique and of some only a very limited number were produced.

Gallé accepted commercial necessities and by the use of acid made quantities of cased 'nature vases.' He was a very successful businessman, and by 1900 was employing some 300 people.

In the early 1880s he started producing furniture. This was pure Art Nouveau in design, with the supports and surfaces carved in the form of plants, usually with fine floral marquetry inlay.

Gallé died in 1904, but the firm carried on under the ownership of his married daughters until 1935. Without his genius the quality declined. The commercial, insipid 'post-Gallé' designs are not to be confused with Gallé's own work, though each piece is signed *Gallé*, etched with acid, usually against a frosted ground.

Gallé established a great demand for his 'nature style' glass, and had numerous mediocre imitators. But the new status he had given to glass also influenced designers such as Tiffany, Dammouse, Marinot, and Decorchment, who became internationally recognized.

Gallery. A term of many meanings, frequently applied to almost any covered space set aside for

Top: vase with floral glass marquetry. Bottom: large vase in 'clair de lune' with enamelled flowers. Both by Gallé

The gallery at Exeter Cathedral, c 1300

Modern art gallery, designed by Richard Burton

promenading. In earlier times the gallery was open along one side. The word can also mean a building or room devoted to the display of works of art, or a combination of the two meanings

– a room in a great house set aside for strolling and lounging in in bad weather, which was embellished with works of art. The gallery was sometimes on the upper floor, extending the

The gallery at Aston Hall, Birmingham, built 1618–35

Modern house with galleries around a central well

whole length of the house: in other houses it was situated on the ground floor. The word can also be used for a projecting area such as the minstrel's gallery in palatial Tudor establishments, and has since been used in this sense in theatres or cinemas. The gallery in a church is known as a tribune.

In furniture, a gallery is a brass or wooden rail, or decorated run of metal or wood, used as a protective edging to a writing-table, sideboard, or small table.

Gambrel roof.

A distinctive form of roof seen frequently in late seventeenth- and eighteenth-century tiled and weather-boarded mills. The upper part of the roof is more obtusely angled than the lower part, giving the roof the silhouette of a mansard roof. The ends, however, are gabled, or have a gablet above a sloping end. The American gambrel, a straightforward Mansard roof, is still used.

Games-board, -table.

The use of boards and tables for games is of great antiquity, but only a few have survived even from medieval times. There is an interesting stone nine-men's Morris board at Repton School, and there are others in museums. But by the late seventeenth century both games-boards and games-tables were well enough made and valued to survive.

There are two particularly interesting types of table. The most common is the card-table, designed with a folding top to pack away neatly as a side-table, with an interior playing surface of baize or needlework. The second and more interesting type is the combined chess and backgammon table, introduced in the eighteenth century. A sliding square in the top revealed a veneered well for backgammon,

The Custom House, Dublin, designed by James Gandon and built in 1781–91

while the underside of the top was chequered for draughts or chess; the well is usually of ebony and ivory or coloured fruitwoods. An interesting late eighteenth-century north Italian table of this sort has the added refinement of built-in dice which can be 'thrown' by pulling cords at either side of the table.

Other specialized tables have also survived. Tables for *tric-trac* are common in France, although very few card-tables were made until the end of the eighteenth century, when France was swept by Anglomania, and even the card-tables were closely based on designs by Hepplewhite and Robert Adam.

Games-boards (really portable tops of games-tables) closely followed table designs and have survived to this day in miniature chess sets similar to those imported from China by the East India Company.

The number of card-tables now being made is comparatively small, and most follow the old folding top principle, or are reproductions of old designs.

Gandon, James (1743–1823).

English architect and draughts-man, the most notable of all the architects who built Georgian Dublin. Gandon was born in London of Huguenot parentage. He studied drawing and then became a pupil of Sir William Chambers. He began to practise

independently as an architect i 1764–5, and won a competitio for a design for Nottinghan County Hall and Prison in 176 In 1781 he moved to Irelan (after turning down an invitatio to practise in Russia) in order

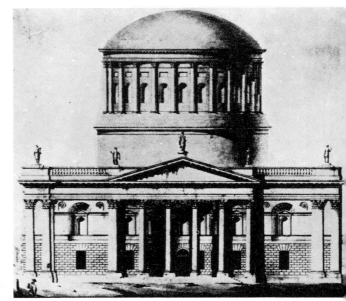

The Four Courts, Dublin: the centre block by James Gandon

A gambrel roof on the Webb House, Weathersfield, Connecticut

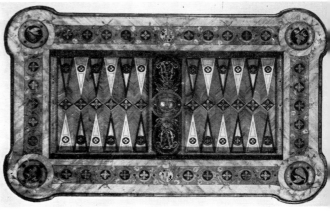

A late 18th-century Italian games table showing the backgammon we

A view of Welwyn Garden City, designed by Louis de Soissons in 1922

The formal gardens of the Villa Lante at Bagnaia, near Viterbo, Italy

superintend the construction of the projected docks, Custom House, Warehouses, and other buildings in Dublin. His Custom House, built between 1781 and 1791, is one of Dublin's outstanding buildings; others in the city by Gandon include the Four Courts, also on the banks of the Liffey, and the Parliament House (now the Bank of Ireland).

Garage (French, *garer* 'to shelter'). A word coined by the French in the early days of the motor car. Reputedly first used in 1902.

Garde du vin. A term applied by Hepplewhite to a cellaret which stood under a sideboard or side-table, 'generally made of mahogany hooped with brass and lacquered; the inner part is divided with partitions, and lined with lead for bottles; they may be of any shape' (*Guide*, 1788).

Garden city. A term first used in America with reference to a particular development of Long Island, New York, in 1869. But it was popularized by Ebenezer Howard (qv) in his book *To-morrow: a peaceful path to Real Reform* (1898); and has remained identified with the English movement of the late nineteenth and early twentieth centuries, especially the planning of Letchworth (1903) and Welwyn Garden City (1919), both in Hertfordshire. Here the object was to create a rationally planned environment combining urban amenities with pleasant surroundings and access to the countryside. In the United States, despite a large number of company-sponsored housing

schemes for employees, there has been no garden city on English lines; Radburn in New Jersey, by Clarence Stein and Henry Wright, came closest to Howard's original idea.

Garden design. Gardening has played a part in human life from very early times, and scenes of beautiful, tranquil Roman gardens appear in the wall-paintings of Pompeii. The most important gardens of the ancient world were undoubtedly those of Persia, where both parklands and small gardens were cultivated; the Hanging Gardens of

Babylon were one of the Seven Wonders of the World. The influence of Persian gardens was felt in India, where the gardens of the Taj Mahal in Agra and Nishat Bagh in Kashmir are still in existence. Gardens were brought to the West by the North African Moors who ruled Spain; the secluded pleasure gardens of Alhambra and Generalife in Granada have survived.

However, after the collapse of the Roman Empire, in Europe there was for centuries neither leisure nor space enough to cultivate gardens. Only in secluded places such as some

monasteries was the art practised to some extent. By the sixteenth century, great gardens were again being laid out, and Renaissance and Baroque gardens in Italy are without parallel for beauty and sophistication of design. The garden was seen as an extension of the house, consisting of out-of-doors rooms bounded by clipped hedges, waterways, stone-work, and plants in pots, all formally arranged. Among the greatest Renaissance gardens are the Villa d'Este at Tivoli, near Rome, filled with fountains and delightful terraces, and the Villa Medici in Rome. The garden of

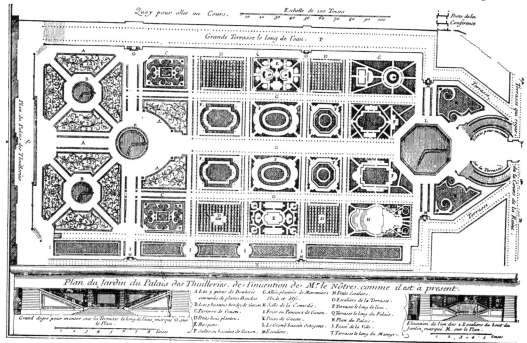

A plan of the Tuileries gardens in Paris, designed by Le Nôtre

The Fountain of Latona at Versailles designed by Le Nôtre

Park of Woburn Abbey, Bedfordshire, by Repton, late 18th century

the Villa Aldobrandini at Frascati, a precursor of the Picturesque, is among the greatest Italian Baroque gardens.

The European ascendancy of France, the brilliance of the Sun King (Louis XIV), and the inspiration of André Le Nôtre (qv) ensured that the French style in gardening in the late seventeenth century became supreme throughout Europe. Prior to this France had followed Italy, as is shown by reconstructions of the beautiful and intricate parterres of the Château Villandry in the Loire valley. Le Nôtre, perhaps the greatest of all garden designers, opened the confined French garden to the countryside. He left parterres but cut *allées* through the woods and positioned sculptures and fountains at major vantage points.

The landscape gardening of England was the next important development. This was to sweep across Europe, and even made some impact on America. It was William Kent (1685–1748; qv) who freed the English garden from French domination. He

began the process of sweeping away the gravelled parterres and clipped *allées* of Le Nôtre, thus making possible the transformation of the English gardens into a 'natural' landscape. This process derived in part from the influence of landscape painters, notably Claude and Poussin. In place of arbitrary patterns imposed upon the landscape, Kent used trees, meadows, and above all water to create an impression of harmony, seemingly without artifice.

After Kent came the two best known of English gardeners: Lancelot 'Capability' Brown (1716–83) and Humphry Repton (1732–1818). Brown's influence made Romanticism the gardening mode for over half a century. His theories encouraged the introduction of ruins, follies, temples, urns, and the rest of the garden architecture which has embellished and enlivened scores of gardens, from Chambers' Pagoda at Kew (c 1761) to those resplendent copies of the antique in the gardens at Stourhead. In lesser houses too, the shrubbery

was arranged in imitation of the rich man's park, and villas were surrounded by winding paths and bosky laurels.

The nineteenth century witnessed a great increase in the popularity of gardening. Greensward was cut up into innumerable flower-beds, but carpet bedding was all too often a kaleidoscope of unfortunately matched colours, involving the maximum of labour and yielding the minimum of beauty. Gertrude Jekyll, who evolved the herbaceous, or mixed, border, led a return to higher standards. She and William Robertson displayed a fine sense of colour and line, and their use of the flowering tree and grey-leaved shrub created the soft but definite design of the modern English garden.

America, though without the great historic gardens of Britain and the Continent, was not entirely outside the mainstream of development. Early American gardens were designed like those of the English cottages and manors that the settlers had left,

and this established a tradition that remained unchanged until Thomas Jefferson landscaped Monticello. The impetus of the landscaping movement flagged, however, until the mid-nineteenth-century work of Andrew Jackson Downing (qv). In its magnolia and cypress gardens America has something which is unique and in its way highly spectacular.

Garden furniture. Isolated examples of furniture probably made for use in gardens, or in alfresco settings, occur in Italy and elsewhere before the eighteenth century. Styles followed current designs, though in the eighteenth century particular use was made of Chinese motifs, including bamboo itself.

By 1800 iron was commonly used. Chairs, stools, and benches were made, but the latter were most popular, and many survive. By 1830 a revived Rococo was the most important element in garden furniture design, remaining in fashion for most of the century. The exuberant pierced

A modern herbaceous border with plants boldly grouped and graded

Concrete used decoratively for paving and pots in a modern garden

and scrolled designs and curvaceous outlines added a touch of romantic splendour suitable to the age of Keats and Byron, while discomfort was avoided by using piles of cushions and draped velvet.

The mass production of most nineteenth-century furniture led to the manufacture of garden furniture in cast-iron rather than the more delicate wrought-iron of the late eighteenth century. The early Victorians were so enthusiastic about making 'a great many copies from an exceedingly good pattern' (W Burge, *Art Applied to Industry*, 1846) that thousands of uncomfortable 'rustic' garden seats in cast-iron were manufactured.

Today's garden furniture manufacturers mainly use wood, aluminium, tubular steel, cane, and willow. Cast-iron furniture is usually painted white, and most tubular steel is nylon-coated. More emphasis is laid on lightness and comfort than on decoration, and plastic materials such as polyester and fibreglass are gaining in popularity. Many designs would also be suitable for indoors.

Garderobe. A French term used mainly in Provence to describe a form of the Louis XV armoire with two panelled doors.

Rustic garden furniture for out-doors and summer houses from an early nineteenth-century book

The term was adapted and anglicized to describe a small room designed and fitted for the hanging of clothes. The garde-robe was normally used also as a dressing-room, and was *en suite* with the first-floor dining and bedroom apartment. The term is also used of the privy built into the walls of medieval fortifications; it normally projected beyond the curtain walls so that it discharged into the moat ditch.

Gardner, James (*b* 1907). British designer of unusual range and versatility. Gardner started by designing jewellery for Cartier but after six years began to specialize in graphic work and advertising illustrations. In the early post-war years he began to establish his own exhibition style with the 'Britain Can Make

A mid-eighteenth-century garden seat from Fountains Abbey, Yorkshire

A wheelbarrow seat designed by Sir Edwin Lutyens

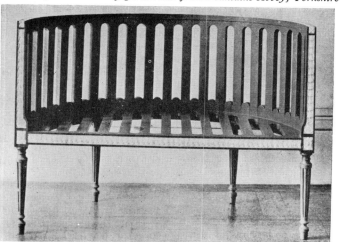

A green and white painted garden seat of Adam design

Light wire furniture on a circular paved area

James Gardner

The Evoluon Museum, Eindhoven, Holland, designed by James Gardner

Gatehouse, Battle Abbey, 1338

It' exhibition for the Council of Industrial Design.

In addition to being a co-ordinating designer for the 1951 Festival of Britain on the South Bank, Gardner was responsible for planning and carrying out the Festival Gardens project in Battersea Park. For it he designed the largest tent in the world, an open-air theatre, a showboat, cane furniture, the Tree Walk, fountains, and illuminations, etc.

He is probably best known for his British Government Pavilion at the Brussels International Exhibition in 1958.

He designed interiors and fittings for many aircraft, including the BEA fleet. He was the first designer to replace the traditional window curtain with integral blinds, he developed the seat-back table, and is responsible for the styling of internationally adopted aircraft seats.

He has undertaken the complete design of museums, including theme, research, planning, and exhibits. Examples include the Pilkington Glass Museum at St Helens, Lancashire, the New Commonwealth Institute in Kensington, London, and the 'Evoluon' at Eindhoven in Holland, generally accepted as the most advanced display treatment of technology in the world.

Gardner has also designed the housing and instrumentation layouts for the Marsden Caesium

Radio-Therapy unit; the interior of the 'Hall of Fame for American Football' in the USA for architect Edward Stone (qv); the illumination of the Cheddar Caves, and the 'pop' Britain Today section of Montreal Expo 1967. He has written and illustrated children's books in the Puffin series, and in 1960 published *Exhibition and Display*.

Gargoyle (Old French, *gargouille* 'throat'). A spout, usually of stone, incorporated into medieval buildings; its function was to discharge the rainwater from the parapet gutter well clear of those likely to be standing or walking beneath the walls. The spout was usually carved into a grotesque representation of an animal or human head, the water coming out of the mouth.

Garnier, Charles (1825–98). A French architect. After studying in Rome and Athens, Garnier, then 36 years old, won the competition for the Paris Opera House, which was not, however, completed until 14 years later.

He also designed the Casino at Monte Carlo.

Garret. Originally the topmost open chamber in a turret or watchtower. Only the roof afforded protection, the walls being open or pierced and unglazed to provide a full view of the surrounding countryside. The term gradually came to be applied to the room or attic in the roof, but is now little used owing to its literary associations with poverty and tragedy.

Garth. An archaic term, now rarely used except in dialect. It refers to the close or yard of a house, and is sometimes used of a garden or small enclosed field. The term has collegiate associations, and is used to describe an open space within a cloistered surround.

Gate, gatehouse, gateway. The gateway, with its accompanying piers and gates, is one of the many architectural features which derive from early attempts to fortify houses. The gate-

houses and gateways of medieval times were formidable structures. Those intended primarily for military purposes were normally single archways, wide enough to allow the passage of carts, but so designed that scope

A gothic gate in Ireland

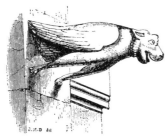

A medieval stone gargoyle

The Opera House, Paris, by Charles Garnier, 1861, completed 1875

White painted picket gate

The gateway to Cooling Castle, Kent, built c 1335

The gateway to Trinity College, Cambridge, built in 1337

for surveillance and means of defence were readily available. Thus a strong door and portcullis were constructed on each side of the gatehouse, and the ceiling was pierced, both for supervision and for defence-by-attack. Such simple archways were flanked by towers, pierced with loop-holes, and topped by crenellated parapets.

The gatehouses of large houses, collegiate buildings, and ecclesiastical establishments were also of considerable size and solidity, partly to impress, partly for defence. Here, too, the gatehouse was often a low square tower, frequently with a turret containing a staircase or with turrets at each corner of the gatehouse tower. Side entrances for pedestrians were introduced, and chapels were frequently added to the gatehouses of ecclesiastical buildings.

Increasing social stability made these vast defensive structures unnecessary. The gatehouse became an elaborated entrance, with superb oriel windows and resplendent finials or cupolas

The gatehouse at Charlecote Park in Warwickshire

The Tudor gatehouse at Sissinghurst Castle, Kent

A Renaissance gate at the Villa Lante, Bagnaia, Italy

A late seventeenth-century marquetry gate-leg desk with the legs closed

A late seventeenth-century gate at Petworth House, Sussex

A Charles I oak gate-leg table in extended position

added to the turrets and façades.

In the course of time the gate-house became detached from the house, on the outer side of an entrance courtyard. The earlier gatehouses had massive wooden-planked doors, strengthened by iron bars; these were now super-seded by stone and/or brick piers flanking iron or wooden gates of increasing distinction. Ultimately the gateway became as much an outward sign of wealth and status as a new brick façade or a painted or plasterwork ceiling.

This desire for discreet osten-tation promoted the production of iron gates, hand-wrought by master smiths. The most famous of these smiths, who worked in England, was Jean Tijou, a French craftsman employed by Wren. Tijou's gates in St Paul's Cathedral and at Hampton Court are justly renowned, and his eighteenth-century successors also produced many magnificent gates.

Gate-leg table. A table with at least one, usually two, folding leaves which are supported on pivoted legs with stretchers at top and bottom. The simplest form is a square or oval-topped table on four legs, two fixed and two on a pivot or wooden hinges. The table is of good proportions in both open and closed positions. A more complex form has additional pivoted legs to form supports which, when not in use, fold in neatly beside the fixed legs; this does, however, make the legs look rather crowded.

The gate-leg was in use at least as early as the sixteenth century, but was not common till the early seventeenth, when many tables were supported in this way. Very large dining tables were made with two gate-legs on either side.

A rare table of this period is the coach table, the narrow two foot top of which is hinged at the centre on trestle legs; it has a simple gate-leg when open, but when closed takes up very little space indeed.

The familiar gate-leg table of oak (and occasionally fruitwood) went out of fashion c 1720 returning briefly in a lighter form c 1760. It was introduced to America c 1650 and remained popular until the middle of the eighteenth century.

The Sagrada Familia Church Barcelona: Antonio Gaudi, 1920's

The vaulting over the main altar in the Sagrada Familia, Barcelona

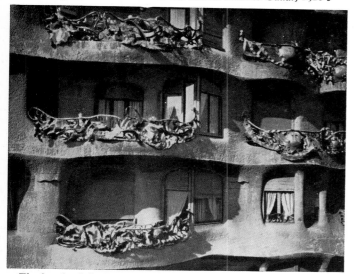

The façade of the Milá House, Barcelona: Antonio Gaudi 1905–10

Gaudí, Antoni (1852–1926). A Spanish architect, designer of some of the most fantastic buildings in modern Europe. The most notable is the Sagrada Familia church in Barcelona. Before it was finished, he was killed by being run over by a trolley bus. Gaudí took over the design and construction of this building in his early thirties; the architect Villar y Lozano had prepared the original designs. The work was spread over many years, but from the turn of the century, Gaudí began to change the designs in a radical, revolutionary, and extraordinary manner, taking the motifs of four great towers from his earlier design prepared for the Palacio Güell, near Barcelona (1885–9).

These towers are unlike anything in traditional ecclesiastical architecture – they are akin to the fantastic imaginings of an illustrator of fairy-tales. The spires are warped, gnarled, sculptural, and the most highly individualistic of all church spires. Some writers have called them the most naturalistic of all architectural exercises; others look on them as the wilful extravaganzas of a self-indulgent artist. Recent studies of the man and his works have sought to establish their logical basis, founded on mathematical calculation and practical building techniques. Yet despite his apologists and explainers, Gaudí remains an architectural phenomenon, outside all conventions, traditions, and move-

ments. Amongst Gaudí's other works are the Güell Park, begun in 1900, the Casa Milá (1905–10), and Casa Battló (1905–7).

Gauged brickwork. A term applied to brickwork which has been built with extreme attention to accuracy in laying and finish in pointing.

Gazebo. A shelter, summerhouse, or belvedere built at a vantage point to command a prospect over surrounding countryside or at a strategic point within a garden to close a terrace or path. The derivation of the word is uncertain; it was probably a dog Latin expression coined in eighteenth-century exchanges between gardening en-

thusiasts. The term has occasionally been used of a cupola or lantern built on the roof of a house to command a vista over the landscape.

Geometrical staircase. A form of staircase built within a circular or elliptically shaped well or tower in which a continuous handrail is employed without a newel-post. The stairs are built into the wall and each stair rests, in part, on the one beneath it. A secondary handrail is frequently inserted in the wall of the staircase well.

Georgian architecture. A descriptive term applied to British architecture of the reigns of George I, II, III, and IV:

One of the two gazebos at Montacute House, Somerset, begun 1588

The portico of St Paul's Church, Covent Garden: Inigo Jones, 1631

A house in Prince Street, Bristol: probably William Halfpenny, 1741

Horse Guards, Whitehall: William Kent, 1742–52

Kenwood House, Hampstead, London: Robert Adam, 1766

Redland chapel, Bristol, Thomas Paty and William Halfpenny c 1720

that is, the period from 1714 to 1830, from the Palladian movement to the decline of Regency architecture.

The origins of Georgian architecture are discernible almost a century before George I came to the throne. This is seen most clearly in the work of Inigo Jones (1573–1652) who was mainly responsible for introducing to England the revolutionary theories of Palladio (1518–80).

Jones's Banqueting Hall, Whitehall (1619–22), was one of the most influential buildings ever erected in Britain. Here most of the basic elements of the Georgian tradition appeared.

Early Georgian architecture was chiefly the aesthetic province of wealthy and aristocratic patrons, notably Lord Burlington (1695–1753). Aided by his protégé, William Kent, and with the enthusiastic co-operation of a group of architects which included Colen Campbell, Giacomo Leoni, and Henry Flitcroft, Burlington formed a Palladian circle that dominated English architecture.

Other architects outside Burlington's group helped to establish the new style, notably James Paine (about 1716–89) and Sir Robert Taylor (1714–88), who, in the words of a later commentator, 'nearly divided the practice of the profession between them till Mr Robert Adam entered the lists.'

The Palladian aesthetic was propagandized by Burlington's publications, by the majestic *Vitruvius Britannicus* folios of Colen Campbell (the first volume

of which, in 1715, anticipated Burlington's own Palladian enthusiasm), and, more widely, by the copy-books and pattern-books written by architects for their own advancement and published in large numbers in London. By this means even remote country builders were enabled to copy the authorized elevations of the Neo-Palladian enthusiasts.

Batty Langley was perhaps the most notable and assertive of these publicists, and his *City and Country Workman's Treasury of Design, or The Art of Working the Ornamental Parts of Architecture,* originally published in 1741, went through several editions.

Other architects, from Isaac Ware to Sir William Chambers, continued the tradition of publishing designs they admired, sometimes their own, frequently works by their friends.

These publications were bought and studied to an extent that would be unthinkable to a small country builder of our own time. Such was the enthusiasm for architecture in the Georgian era that scarcely a bricklayer, let alone a man of fashion, could afford to be ignorant of the subject. Thus a continuous exchange of ideas took place: merchants, squires, and parsons were prepared to discuss details of buildings and styles with their builders, bricklayers, and masons. And the publications helped to formulate a coherent discipline in architecture, based upon notions of orderliness and proportion.

An early and important result

Nostell Priory, Yorkshire, by Paine, 1735–50; left wing Adam, 1766

of this discipline was the London squares, which were built on areas leased by patrician landowners for development by speculative builders. Here, too, a prototype is to be found in the early work of Inigo Jones, in his Covent Garden piazza project pivoted on his design for St Paul's Church. Other developments followed in the last decades of the seventeenth century (notably in Bloomsbury and St James's), but the major developments were to take place under the Georges. Hanover Square was built from 1717, Grosvenor Square between 1721 and 1735, Cavendish Square from 1720. Similar developments followed until the middle of the century, when the building boom began to slacken.

The revolution started by Jones and Burlington influenced not only domestic architecture but also churches, institutional buildings, royal residences, and

even warehouses and customs houses, barracks, and theatres.

The ecclesiastical architecture of the Georgian era represents a special chapter to the history of British building. Many of the churches were built to replace those destroyed in the Great Fire half a century earlier. By an Act of 1709, 50 new churches were to be built in London – and were built, albeit spasmodically. The aged Sir Christopher Wren, who initiated this vast rebuilding programme, was succeeded by architects such as James Gibbs, Henry Flitcroft, and Nicholas Hawksmoor. Many of London's most cherished churches date from this time, including St Mary-le-Strand (1714–17), St Martin-in-the-Fields (1726), both designed by Gibbs; Christ Church, Spitalfields (1723), and St Mary Woolnoth (1716), two of six churches designed by Nicholas Hawksmoor; St John, Smith Square (1721–8), by Thomas Archer, who practised a highly individual Baroque art; and St Giles-in-the-Fields (1731–3), designed by Henry Flitcroft.

Ambitious essays in provincial town-planning were another major contribution of Georgian architecture. The Woods of Bath and dozens of other building contractors were responsible for this.

Inevitably though, the admirable orderliness of Georgian architecture presaged its decline. Discipline is first cousin to monotony, and by 1750 many buildings presented a dull uniformity in planning and elevation.

In retrospect it can be seen how dramatically Robert Adam revolutionized and revivified a declining, or at least stultifying, tradition in the second half of the century His skills and originality as a designer were combined with a daring decorative sense and an ability to adapt in a manner at once sensitive

York Terrace, Regent's Park, London, designed by John Nash and built by James Burton. Begun c *1733*

Design for the north front of the Bank of England: Sir John Soane, begun 1792

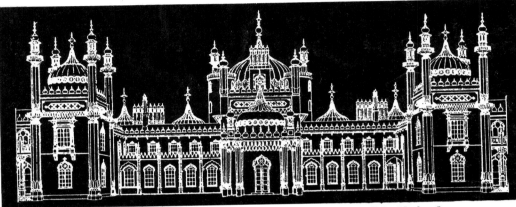

The west front of the Royal Pavilion, Brighton, redesigned by John Nash, 1825

Despite the rise of a new industrial middle class *c* 1800, the classical tradition was powerful enough to influence building for almost another half-century. This is true, for example, of buildings as diverse as theatres and docks. Haymarket Theatre (designed by John Nash in 1820) and Drury Lane (designed by Benjamin Wyatt in 1811) are the only London theatres of the period that have survived, but there are also a number of charming small theatres in the provinces.

Docks are a different matter. Despite the World War II blitz, enough of these vast and complex structures remain to remind us of the immense energy and imagination of the Georgian architect-engineer. The West India Dock is still the most impressive, designed by Ralph Walker and John Rennie and begun in 1800. Others are the London Dock (built 1802), the Surrey Docks (built 1804), and the East India Dock (built 1805).

Amongst the first of these versatile architect-engineers was Robert Mylne (1736–1811), who designed Blackfriars Bridge (demolished 1868), planned the Gloucester and Berkeley Ship Canals, and improved drainage systems in the Fen country. He also acted as surveyor to St Paul's Cathedral and designed a number of houses.

John Nash (1752–1835) made a remarkable, if uneven, contribution to the growth of London. To the Prince Regent and Nash we owe the spectacular development, between 1811 and 1835, of an earlier Regent Street (now demolished) and of Regent's Park, fortunately still preserved. To Nash must be given much of the credit for the reinterpretation of an earlier classical idiom – quite different from that of Adam, far less scholarly and fastidious, but magnificently ro-

and ingenious, old buildings to new demands. His work at Syon, Osterley, Harewood, Kenwood, and other aristocratic houses is part of that legendary period, the Augustan Age – the description applied to the architecture of the three decades after 1750.

But the Adam manner was essentially aristocratic. Although his innovations were transmitted to the more plebeian world by means of pattern-books (notably William Pain's *Practical Builder*, 1774), they were comparatively slow in filtering down from the upper reaches of society. An army of local builders continued to erect imitations of smaller Palladian villas and mansions in a manner they had thoroughly

mastered, for the gentry and middle class.

Adam's great rival, Sir William Chambers, also had a considerable practice, and his designs for Somerset House are a reminder that the older, conservative Georgian tradition carried on alongside Adam projects like the Adelphi.

Even within the Georgian discipline there were excesses and oddities, especially such as the *Chinoiserie* and Gothick – the latter extravagantly initiated by Horace Walpole's Strawberry Hill villa, gothicized between 1750 and 1790. 'Gothick' foreshadowed the later, far heavier versions of Gothic, which were to dominate so much Victorian

architecture, the later Moorish exoticism of Pepys Cockerel at Sezincote in Gloucestershire (*c* 1805), and John Nash's remodelling of the Royal Pavilion (1815–21) in a supposedly Hindu style.

The Adam brothers had many rivals and detractors apart from Sir William Chambers. Among the more important of these was James Wyatt (1746–1813), a follower of Chambers, a prolific, brilliant but unreliable and superficial designer, who was accused by the Adams, with some justification, of plagiarism.

However, in his Gothic work at Fonthill Abbey (1796–1807) and Ashridge Park (1803–13), Wyatt anticipated the heavier nineteenth-century Gothic.

Chester Terrace, Regent's Park, London: John Nash, 1825

Dulwich College Art Gallery, London: Sir John Soane, 1811–14

University College, London: William Wilkins, 1826

A decorative panel designed by Pergolesi, c 1790

oust and scenic. By using pilasters, pediments, and wide overhanging eaves, canopies, wrought- and cast-iron balconies, and stucco, Nash began a transformation of the rather sober late eighteenth-century architecture into gayer and more exotic forms. Unfortunately the Victorians took up his fancies and translated them into heavy and doleful brick travesties of his fanciful elevations.

To Nash and his copyists we owe not only the palatial terraces of Regent's Park, but considerable areas of spa and coastal owns, from Cheltenham to Brighton. The Georgian tradition thus faded in a splendid swansong of townscapes every bit as well planned as those of the early Georgians.

Sir John Soane (1753–1837), one of the most remarkable architects in English history, is now seen to be one of the seminal figures of the modern movement. His designs, in a highly personal style, showing a preoccupation with shallow domes and clerestory windows, are seen at their best in his plans for the Bank of England, started in 1792. His Dulwich College Art Gallery (1811–14) is one of the most impressive smaller buildings of the late Georgian period.

The designs by William Wilkins (1778–1839) for University College, London (1826–7), and Downing College, Cambridge (1807–21), close the Georgian era. His safe and pedantic design for the National Gallery (1834–8), outside the scope of this entry chronologically, is a fitting finale to a declining architectural tradition.

Georgian decoration. Magnificent Georgian interior decoration is still to be seen in many great country houses, eg William Kent's work at Chatsworth and on the cube rooms at Wilton; Lightfoot's Rococo carving at Claydon, and Robert Adam's designs at Kedlestone.

The craftsmen employed on such work were often Italian, some of whom, like Pergolesi, were to become famous. The inspiration for the designers, themselves mostly English, came largely from France.

However, a strong English classical influence deriving from Christopher Wren was felt in the early Georgian period. Among the first designers to profit from Wren's work was James Gibbs, who had also studied in Italy. He published many designs, not only for doors, porticos, and garden urns, but also for memorial tablets. All his work is simple, grand, and well

Alexander Place, South Kensington, by Basevi, c 1827–30

A design for the side of a room with carved panels inset with tapestry in the Louis XIV style, a carved Louis XV frieze, and a dado: William and John Halfpenny, c 1836–40

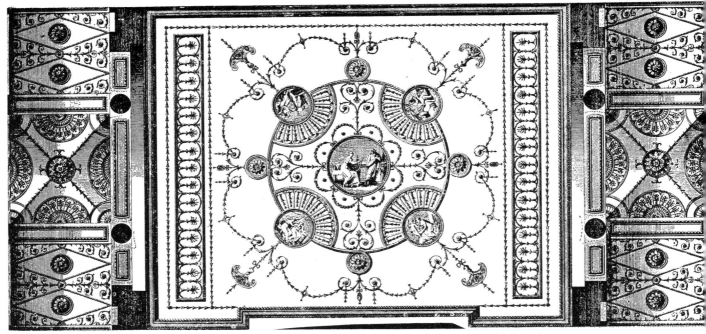

The ceiling of the library in a house in St James's Square, London: Robert and John Adam, 1770

Top: state drawing-room. Bottom: a French bed and wardrobe. Both from George Smith's collection of Designs for Household Furniture, 1808

proportioned, using adapted classical themes, slightly relieved by motifs from the nascent French Rococo of Jean Louis Berain and Nicolas Pineau.

William Kent the architect carried this classical feeling almost to the mid-Georgian period. But his influence, though great at the time, was short-lived, and the superb but heavy rooms he designed soon gave way to the light, fantastic folly of the Rococo.

The brothers Batty and Thomas Langley were perhaps the first open advocates of Pineau's Rococo. Recent research has shown that much of their work was plagiarism; it does, however, indicate the sources of the English Rococo fever of the 1750s.

After Batty Langley came many designers, both of furniture and interior decoration, who followed the prevailing fashions for Chinese, Gothic, and pure Rococo in their most extreme and impractical forms. Edwards & Darly, Matthias Lock, Thomas Johnson, Copeland, and others are known by their published designs.

Lock began to publish his designs in 1740, at first in close imitation of Johnson. At the same time the publications of Ince & Mayhew and Thomas Chippendale were available to an ever-larger public in books often sold in monthly instalments.

The work of these designers was largely concerned with furni-

ture. Other less well-know writers also publicized Rococo designs for the insides and out sides of houses. Such was Willia Halfpenny, who, with his son published in 1750–2 New Design for Chinese Temples, Triumpho Arches, Garden Seats, Paling etc. This included somewhat ur inspired Rococo wall panels an ceilings largely in the Chines taste. Halfpenny's earlier roo and panel designs, derived fror William Kent, do displa strength and grandeur, wit masks and swags of fruit, archi traves with lion masks and skin and decorated broken pediment as door-crestings.

The reaction to Rococo in terior design was led by Rober Adam. Adam's brilliant adap tation of the newly discovere Roman and Greek styles fror Pompeii was principally use

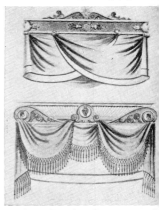

Designs for drawing room win dow cornices: Smith, 1808

'Borders for paper hangings' from Chippendale's 1762 edition of 'The Gentleman and Cabinet-maker's Director'

A side-table of carved and gilded pine with eagle headed scrolled legs and a scagliola top, 1730

between 1760 and 1790 on such houses as Kenwood, White's Club in St James's Street, London; and in many superb English country houses such as Kedlestone in Derbyshire.

Adam's decorative themes were delicate, intricate, and above all elegant – entirely suitable for an age inclined to comfortable but elegant living; sumptuous display of fine works of art, and conspicuous opulence. No aspect of interior decoration escaped Adam's pen, and the felicity of his imagination ranged over windows, fireplaces, carpets, ceilings, light-fittings, and furniture. He was thus able to create harmonious rooms that were light and colourful as well as graceful.

Towards the end of the century, Adam's influence continued to be felt in the Roman arabesque designs of Pergolesi and the paintings and decorative panels of Angelica Kauffmann. Cipriani also added a multitude of attenuated arabesque elements to available themes, but neither he nor Pergolesi bettered the work of Robert Adam.

This elaborate style was swept away by Neo-classical Etruscan severity of French styles from c 1785, and the bold, realistic, and heavier Roman and Egyptian designs of such Regency architects and designers as George Smith, John Nash, James Wyatt, and Sir John Soane.

The Regency period was one of impoverished invention. No new style was created: 'Regency' is rather a collection of earlier ideas blended with recent innovations.

'Regency Gothic' was the apotheosis of this muddle, and resulted in Horace Walpole's splendid but hardly progressive Strawberry Hill villa. Walpole, an avid and discriminating collector, was typical of this age of antiquarians, devoted to a splendid past rather than the search for 'modern' ideas, that had impelled previous generations.

Georgian furniture.

This period (1714–1830) was one of great advances in quality, extremes of good and bad taste, and unparalleled experiment in design, methods, and utility.

The early Georgian period, from 1714 to 1740, was a continuation of the grand, simple, and typically English design period. Queen Anne chairs and tables with cabriole legs, simple mouldings to edges, gilding on expensive mirror-frames and matching pier tables, large book or display cabinets, and sofas and library chairs covered in needlework done by the ladies of the household.

At first, walnut was the chief veneer wood; it was only slowly replaced by the expensive mahogany imported from Cuba and Honduras. The straight-grained Virginia walnut closely resembled mahogany, and the transition from one wood to another was not in itself revolutionary. By 1740 mahogany was the chief wood. Almost immune to woodworm and very hard wearing, it was used for both the veneer and the carcase of expensive pieces.

The influence of the French Rococo of the 1720s was not seriously felt in England until twenty years later. This was the first and most remarkable of the mid-Georgian styles (1740–90). With Chippendale's first *Director* in 1754, and the publication of Thomas Johnson's furniture designs and similar works in the early 1750s, there was a wide range of subjects and styles to choose from – pure Rococo, *chinoiserie*, and Gothic, as well as the simple early Georgian style which changed only in replacing straight chamfered legs with cabriole legs.

Chippendale's designs were a product of his inventive age rather than its archetype. A host of other craftsmen such as Vile & Cobb, and Ince & Mayhew, all produced work of the highest order.

Only one architect, William Kent, seriously influenced the design of early Georgian furniture, and then only furniture made for the very rich.

In the mid-Georgian period, Robert Adam exercised a much greater influence on fashion. By 1760 a strong reaction against the Rococo was apparent. Adam's knowledge of late Roman decoration at Pompeii enabled him to provide a great variety of delicate and elegant designs for interiors and their furnishings.

Mahogany now gave way to satinwood and other paler and more colourful woods imported from the East. Inlay became common in both woods and marbles, and the Neo-classical designs demanded of craftsmen not only decorative surfaces but also elegant proportions.

Furniture became less obtrusive. Dining chairs were lighter and smaller, and tables stood on thin tapering legs. The tables contained fitted drawers

A design for a window guard from Cottingham's 'Directory', 1824

A George I giltwood chair in the style of William Kent

Designs for console tables and a clock case by Matthias Lock, 1746

A commode of oak japanned in gold on a black ground, c 1760–70

for complicated toilet operations – male and female – and for ink, pen, and sand, etc.

Wall-mirrors became part of the architectural features of a room, and their frames part of the wall panelling.

Towards the end of the mid-Georgian period, the designs of George Hepplewhite, who was working at the same time as Robert Adam, were intended for a wider market, not (as in the case of Adam) simply for the rich. It would be fair to say that Hepplewhite's ideas are an adaptation to utilitarian needs of Adam's genius. Though famous for his heart-shaped chair-back, and for sober, elegant designs for the middle class, he was, in fact, inferior in ingenuity to most contemporary designers.

The late Georgian period (1790–1830) witnessed many changes. It began with Sheraton, an erratic but brilliant designer whose best work influenced much Regency furniture.

Satinwood continued to be used until about 1810 as a favourite decorative surface veneer. The cost of the Napoleonic Wars caused wood marquetry to be replaced by cheaper painted decoration on cabinet furniture, especially tables and bookcases.

From 1810, rosewood became the most popular veneer, relieved by simple inlay of ebony, brass, or boxwood. Gilding was used only as a relief, and almost never for a whole surface, with the exception of the well-known convex mirror capped by an eagle with outstretched wings.

Sheraton, George Smith, Thomas Hope, and many others played a part in creating English design. The Empire style in France was in part copied from England, and was in turn re-copied by the English.

Regency furniture became still less sturdy. Chairs, often beechwood grained to resemble rosewood, were smaller than ever, and consequently seldom as strong. Small book cabinets took the place of the large breakfront bookcases of the 1780s, and large numbers of small tables and cabinets were made.

The last phase of Georgian furniture is a sad one. The advent of factory methods and mass production slowly put out of business the craftsmen working for private patrons. The desire for novelty, the misuse of Rococo and Baroque, and the bad taste of the newly dominant mercantile classes disastrously lowered standards of taste throughout the nation. Ill-formed carved designs decorated both chairs and tables, and the Egyptian and Grecian motifs of the Regency degenerated into meaningless arabesques, added without regard to the requirements of the basic design.

Carving in Georgian furniture

A side-table of carved mahogany in the Gothick manner, c 1750

A George II giltwood pier-glass in the manner of Thomas Johnson

A commode attributed to Willian Moore of Dublin, c 1776–80

A side-table with a painted top and carved and gilded legs, c 1780

1 Pembroke table in satinwood, narquetry decoration, c 1780

1 mahogany cabinet on stand, prtoise-shell and carved ivory

reached its apogee in the 1750s and 1760s. The stylistic complexities of the Rococo called forth ever more ingenious techniques, and in no age has the wood-carver been a more vital figure.

Thomas Johnson's published designs were abused by some of his contemporaries as impossible to execute, but in his dedications Johnson always claimed that he himself could produce them all. The few extant examples which are known from his hand show that he was indeed a marvellous carver. However, there were many others of comparable skill.

The chains of leaves, flowers, and fruit which cascade down the sides of mirrors or the corners of commodes were at times in full relief; birds and animals appear in barely arrested movement. However skilled the best work, there was a great mass of technically less proficient carving which still conveys the charm and imagination of the period.

No part of the chair frame escaped the carver's attention, including some backs so involved and boldly decorated that they are uncomfortable, even painful, to lean against, an unusual state of affairs with eighteenth-century furniture. Delicate carved borders of egg-and-dart, bead-and-reel, etc, were applied to the edges of legs and the seat-rail, while interlaced ribbons, flowers, and shells adorned the backs.

Carving had begun in early Georgian furniture as a continuation of the simple acanthus leaf and shell adornment common in the reign of Queen Anne and earlier. After the great mid-Georgian period it practically disappeared in Sheraton's furniture, but was used to some extent in the 1790s on Adam's, and the

1810s on Thomas Hope's.

Adam and Hepplewhite carving relied on Roman motifs – the honeysuckle, patera, elongated laurel-leaf, and so on – applied in moderation to surfaces far less exotic and mobile than those of Chippendale's Rococo. Regency carving also repeated Roman and Greek motifs including caryatids. Egyptian features were added, and sphinxes, along with some earlier Georgian motifs such as egg-and-dart (in itself a motif of great antiquity). The resulting combinations were often somewhat incongruous.

Regency carving was seldom as skilled as that of the mid-

Georgian period, and is usually larger and less detailed.

Many superbly inventive and useful pieces were created in the Georgian period: the sideboard fitted for silver and wine bottles, the toilet or dressing-table, specialized games-tables, the davenport.

Chippendale and others adapted Continental, especially French, originals such as the *tricoteuse* in their design-books, usually acknowledging their origins. The publications of Sheraton in particular are full of such plagiarisms.

It must not be forgotten, however, that in the 1780s the French

A cabinet on a stand designed by Robert Adam, 1771, in marquetry of various woods and set with marble intarsia panels, dated 1709

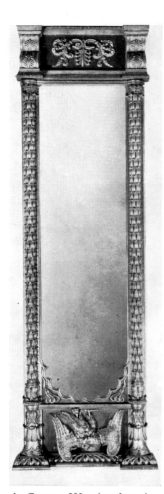

A George IV pier-glass in a painted and giltwood frame with mixed early Georgian, Regency and Gothic motifs

Top: a claw-table of carved mahogany, c 1760. Bottom: a painted armchair with a cane seat in the style of Sheraton, c 1800

A caster made by Paul de Lamerie, London hallmark for 1734–5

A tea-caddy by Shaw and Priest, London hallmark for 1759–60

took over many English designs for their own use. Dumb-waiters and tripod tables very closely based on their English originals were made to satisfy the then fashionable Parisian Anglomania. Mahogany attracted the French traveller's attention by its widespread use in England (despite its considerable expense), and it soon became popular in France.

Any review of the Georgian tradition in furniture and decoration must end with a reference to the forms patronized by George IV as regent and later king. Exotic woods, metal inlay, and bold motifs deriving from classical and Egyptian sources were the handsome features of a style that was debased and declined in the hands of the Victorians.

Georgian silver. The Georgian tradition of simple forms and restrained decoration was well exemplified in the gold- and silver-work of the eighteenth century. Much of the silver-smithing tradition derived from the Continent, for English work was greatly influenced by French and Dutch models. A major influence was the influx of Huguenot craftsmen into London which followed on the revocation of the Treaty of Nantes in 1685. These craftsmen brought with them a comparatively new manner, remarkable for its simplicity and reticence.

Inevitably, therefore, much English silver of the 1690s is indistinguishable from that produced in France. The immigrants gave a new vitality to English silversmithing and produced some of the greatest smiths in the history of English silver, including the Courtauld dynasty and Paul de Lamerie, greatest of all silversmiths of the early eighteenth century.

The silverware produced in England during the first half of the eighteenth century, particu-

larly ware for domestic use, has never been surpassed for purity of form and skill in chasing and engraving.

Fine pieces of armorial and decorative silver were also made by English and Anglo-French craftsmen, notably Simon Gribelin, who also published pattern-books which passed on his expertise to lesser craftsmen.

The rise of the mercantile class, which vied with the aristocracy in display, kept silver-smiths (as well as builders and cabinetmakers) busily employed. Even two centuries later, the quantity of silverware produced seems prodigious.

European classicism imposed a superficial uniformity on many types of design, although national characteristics and traditions gradually established indigenous stylistic traditions. This was especially true in engraving, in which English silversmiths surpassed all their European rivals. Georgian forms are simple, even austere, and decoration is limited to formal pattern-making.

Soon after the middle years of the century the cult of *chinoiserie*

The painted top of one of a pair of late eighteenth-century side-tables

A silver gilt salver by Farren, London hallmark for 1733–4

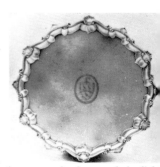

An engraved salver made by John Carter, 1770

A tankard engraved with arms and crest by Benjamin Brewood, 1759

A fluted jug made by John Parker with Edward Wakelin, 1771

began to make its mark on English silver. So, too, did Rococo influences, so that for a time silver design was cursively unpredictable.

A Neo-classical tradition was reimposed by Robert Adam and his imitators, who borrowed motifs from antiquities (mostly in marble) and applied them to silverware. This Neo-classicism dominated the applied arts of the last quarter of the eighteenth century, although its application to silver was more emphatic in England than in France.

'Bright-cut' engraving was widely used to enliven plain surfaces, and medallions (echoing the *paterae* of architects and cabinetmakers) were stamped upon a variety of silver. Indeed, almost all the decorative motifs of architecture and interior decoration are to be found in the silverware of the period.

The pendulum of taste swung yet again at the end of the period. The silver produced in the last year of George IV was clearly moving towards the more ornate and resplendent forms and complex engraving of the Victorian silversmith.

Germain. A family of French silversmiths working in the reigns of Louis XIV and XV. **Pierre Germain** (1645–84) worked ex-

tensively for the Sun King, but most of his royal pieces disappeared as a result of Louis' later economies, which involved melting down much silver. **Thomas Germain** (1673–1748), Pierre's son, was a superb silver-smith and also dabbled in architecture. After working in Italy he became established at the court of Louis XV, and he also worked for several foreign monarchs. Some of his silver appears in the background of contemporary portraits of him and his wife by Largillière. From this, and some extant works, it can be deduced that his style was extremely lavish. He left a prosperous practice to his son, **François Thomas Germain** (1726–91), who, despite commissions from the courts of France, Russia, and Portugal, went bankrupt in 1765. His work is in a florid Rococo vein. A distant relation, **Pierre Germain**, was publishing designs in this same style in 1748.

German and Bohemian glass.
After the collapse of the Roman Empire the heavily wooded areas along the great rivers continued to make a green 'forest' glass. A distinctive Teutonic form of decoration appeared, incorporating blobs of glass which had been coaxed

into 'claws.' In the early sixteenth century these developed into the well-known globular-bowled *Roemers*, probably one of the most famous forms of wine glass ever devised; it is still in use today. There was also a vogue in the sixteenth century for drinking from joke glasses in the form of pigs, bears, boots, etc.

By the middle of the sixteenth century, émigré Venetian workmen had introduced clear and brilliantly coloured glass into Germany and Bohemia. Most of this was gaily enamelled with designs ranging from peasant scenes to coats of arms and double-headed imperial eagles.

At the beginning of the seventeenth century, Casper Lehmann, court lapidary to Rudolf II at Prague, redeveloped the ancient technique of wheel engraving on glass. His pupil Schwanhardt moved to Nuremberg, which became a famous centre for such work, and here too 'Zwarzlot', the delicate use of black and sepia enamels to decorate tall covered goblets, was devised by a former painter of stained glass, Johann Schaper (1621–70).

As the quality of German and Bohemian glass steadily improved from the end of the seventeenth century, it made deeper cutting possible. The work of Bohemian and Silesian glass-cutters was unsurpassed and was exported all over Europe, even reaching Persia and the East.

From about 1727, when Bohemian glassmakers delivered twelve cut crystal chandeliers to Louis XV, this type of chandelier became a more or less mandatory adornment for palaces.

The Alexandrian and Roman technique of 'gold-sandwich' glass or 'Zwischengoldglas' (see **Verre églomisé**) became a fashionable mode of decoration for faceted beakers during the early eighteenth century. This technique involves engraving gold foil with a needle and then enclosing it between two tightly fitting layers of glass.

During the first half of the nineteenth century there were some fascinating developments in Bohemian coloured glass, such as 'Hyalith', non-transparent black glass, and 'Lythyalin', a polished, opaque, multi-coloured marble glass. Ultramarine blue glass was also popular, as was staining in red and yellow, and the use of white and coloured alabaster glass, painted in enamels and adorned with gilding. Also in great demand was 'flashed' glass in which thin layers of

A wheel-engraved Roemer, c 1700

A coloured enamelled glass, 1673

Silesian engraved goblet, c 1690

A tea set made by George Ashford and Co of Sheffield, 1800–1

Goblet by Casper Lehmann, c 1605

Zwischengoldglas tumbler, c 1730

Black vase with etchings, c 1910

Lead crystal by Pravec, 1970

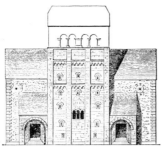

The 9th-century church of St Georg, Reichenau, Lake Constance

The Romanesque Marienkirche at Trèves, 1190–1212

contrasting colours were cut through with sloping cuts to reveal the inner coatings.

The *Jugendstil* or Art Nouveau movement at the end of the century, and Tiffany's success with iridescent glass in America, inspired a similar interest in colour fluctuations, especially on the part of Louis Lobmeyer in Vienna and the Lötz Witwe glasshouse in Bohemia.

Since the 1930s the influence of the Bauhaus and designers like Wilhelm Wagenfeld have set high standards in functional forms in Germany. In Czechoslovakia, since the reorganization of the glass industry after World War II, young artists have been encouraged to experiment with varied and exciting new techniques.

German architecture. In their earlier history the German people were content to take over and copy the buildings left to them by their Roman rulers. The emergence of the round-arched style was first seen in the reign of Charlemagne, who gave Western architecture its first

great creative impulse. It was he who insisted on the building of new churches in stone and not in wood.

The greatest monument to this policy is the chapel of Charlemagne's palace at Aix-la-Chapelle; based upon San Vitale in Ravenna, it was begun in 792, and dedicated in 805. This is one of the few Carolingian buildings still standing, and remains virtually unchanged. Under Charlemagne and later under the Otos and the Hohenstaufens (1138–1268), the Romanesque style (qv) was highly developed.

Knowledge of the earliest German churches derives mainly from the plan of the monastery of St Gall, now in Switzerland,

but once within the dominions of Charlemagne – for whom legend says, the plans were prepared. We see something of what St Gall represented in the remaining fabric of a similar, but smaller, late ninth-century church, St Georg. Built for the monks of Oberzell, and still standing on the island of Reichenau in Lake Constance, this is a rustic version of the early Christian churches and is now chiefly renowned for its remarkable tenth-century wall-paintings.

From those early examples gradually developed what is now recognized as the early German style, represented in such churches as that at Gernrode in

The cathedral at Worms, dedicated in 1110, finished by 1200

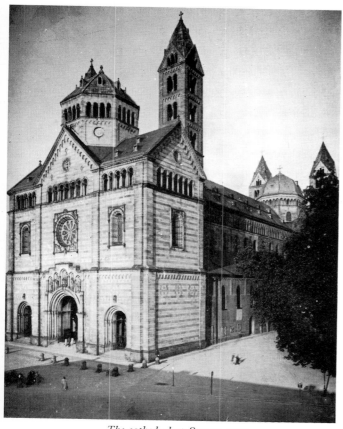

The cathedral at Speyer, 1030

The medieval convent of St Pantaleon at Cologne

the Harz Mountains and the abbey of Corvey in Westphalia. Here an unusual feature appears, indigenous to German churches: an emphatic frontispiece connecting two towers, completely hiding the church behind it. This characteristic reappears on the famous Gothic cathedral at Strasbourg. In the thirteenth century the pointed style was introduced from France.

But the Romanesque tradition died hard. The Gothic pointed arch and emphatic buttress were taken over, but they were grafted on to what remained basically Romanesque structures. The cathedral at Limburg on the Lahn, with its pair of impressive four-gabled towers almost overpowering the slender spire, is a striking example. The church at Trier also shows the persistence of the tradition in the face of fire, decay, and reconstructions (1190–1212).

The three great and typical buildings of the early Middle Ages are the Rhenish cathedrals of Mainz, Worms, and Speyer. With its two domes, four circular towers, and strongly emphasized pilaster-like buttresses, the cathedral at Worms, dedicated in 1110, is probably the best known. Much of the plan and silhouette

of its original structure survives, in spite of considerable alterations over the centuries. Here the Romanesque tradition is seen in majestic decline, with ornament unnecessarily added to forceful and harmonious proportions. Yet the total effect is magnificent, and the building represents the final flowering of the Romanesque, its verticality hinting at the pointed style of French Gothic.

A particular feature of Rhenish church architecture is the evolution of the spire, which seems to have been added to German church towers earlier than in other countries. The transition can be seen in the elevations shown in the trio reproduced; the medieval hipped roof at Minden; the four gables in the cathedral tower at Paderborn (c 1050); and the church spire at Soest (c 1200).

Despite the emergence of the pointed style, the influence of Italian church architecture remained strong, and the church at Rosheim in Alsace has a façade that would not be out of place in Venice or Verona. More frequently, the Italian and German styles are merged, as in the twelfth-century abbey church of Marmoutier, also in Alsace. Here

a bold yet subtle interplay of tower and gable, belfry and turret, has produced one of the most handsome Romanesque buildings in northern Europe.

From this period also dates the double church or chapel. In this a second storey was introduced so that two congregations – notables in the upper storey, retainers in the lower – could

listen to the same service. Such a plan is to be seen in the church at Schwartz Rheindorf and the chapel of Nuremberg Castle.

Little remains of the domestic architecture of these times, but a few buildings survived until the Second World War, which suggested that some earlier houses were of considerable distinction. In such domestic architecture

Left: an early example of the German medieval façade screen, on a church at Minden. Centre: the mid-11th century cathedral at Paderborn. Right: a church at Soest, built c 1200

The west front of Cologne Cathedral, begun in 1242, but not raised to the height originally intended until 1880

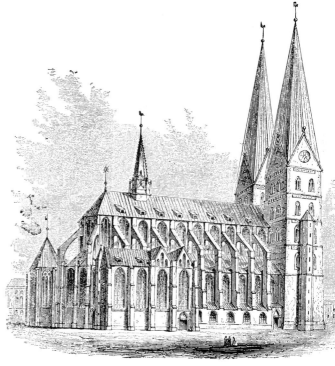

The thirteenth-century brick Marienkirche in Lübeck

The medieval Marienkirche at Mühlhausen

the motifs of ecclesiastical styles were taken over and adapted to secular use.

An interesting example of the transition between Gothic and Romanesque is the church of Geinhausen, probably started in the middle of the thirteenth century but not completed until 100 years later. Here simple spires are combined with Gothic arches in a highly individual manner, as if the German builders were determined to reduce to a minimum their debt to French prototypes.

The purely French style is first seen in the small church of St Elizabeth at Marburg, begun in 1235, and the church at Altenburg, near Cologne, begun in 1255; this is virtually a copy of the French abbey of Pontigny, and this is curiously similar in many respects to Tintern Abbey in England.

Then came the great German Gothic cathedrals, which rank amongst the noblest buildings of the Western world. The greatest is the cathedral at Cologne, but there are also superb examples at Freiburg, Strasbourg, and Vienna.

The cathedral at Cologne was begun in 1242, and its chancel was dedicated in 1322. It is without doubt the first German building which was totally committed to French Gothic. It unashamedly follows the great prototype of Amiens, although departing from its model in many important design features, and probably comprising a more disciplined final form – which to some critics has a chilly rigidity. The world-famous 515 ft two-tower west front was not raised to the height envisaged by the architects until 1880, thanks to the efforts of Sulpice Boisserée, an eminent French art collector and historian.

This French conception of the two-tower cathedral façade was not widely copied in Germany. Instead, German burghers set out to display their wealth and piety by constructing giant single towers. Those at Freiburg and Ulm, although separated by a century, are typical, if grandiose examples. The height of the spire at Freiburg, begun in 1283, is 385 ft; here a richly ornamented spire is set upon an octagonal intermediary tower which in turn rests upon a square base tower

More representative of medieval German church building is Ratisbon, one of the smaller cathedrals, but also one of the most pleasing in both design and interior proportions.

German designers worked out solutions to church-building problems which were later imitated in other countries. Thus the flat-roofed choir was first introduced in the Franciscan church at Salzburg, and was probably a model for Henry VII's chapel at Westminster, built half

The twelfth-century abbey church at Marmoutier

The Haus zum Engel, a noble's Renaissance house in Bergzabern

The façade of the Knight Hall of the Knight of the Teutonic Order in the Castle of Marienburg

a century later. The double-tower church of St Laurence at Nuremberg, begun in 1275 but not completed until two centuries later, had a similar choir.

For many visitors to Germany, the most authentically German of all these churches is not the vast cathedral of Cologne but the beautiful Marienkirche at Mühlhausen.

Secular building in medieval Germany remained unremarkable in both extent and design. Many Rhenish castles offered picturesque silhouettes, but these were basically little more than agglomerations of military and other features created over the centuries. Few of the towns and cities built civic halls to compare with those in France and the Low Countries. The most notable was the Kaufhaus at Mainz, destroyed in 1812. Houses of the wealthier citizens in the towns were of the high-gabled, elaborately ornamented styles made popular in German opera and fiction, but few survive as works of architectural distinction. There are still some in Nuremberg despite the ravages of two great wars.

The brick churches of north-eastern Germany, especially Lübeck and Danzig, deserve to be mentioned. At Lübeck the cathedral, the small Marienkirche (both built in the thirteenth century), and many smaller churches were built of brick. These, and the Marienkirche in Danzig, were in the pointed style, their interiors plastered and simulated to give the impression of a pattern of stone. Elsewhere in eastern Prussia builders made a determined attempt to emulate Western Gothic which led them into certain extravagances of style. This appears in both secular and ecclesiastical architecture, from the exotic church of St Mary in Brandenburg to the headquarters, or Knight Hall, of the Knights of the Teutonic Order in the Castle of Marienburg.

The Renaissance had curiously little direct influence upon German building, largely because the country itself was savaged by the wars of the Reformation, followed by the still greater devastation of the Thirty Years' War (1618–48). As a result,

The Charlottenburg Castle, Berlin, built in 1696

The Liebfrauenkirche at Dresden, possibly by Behr, 1726–45

Germany was left weak and divided, with hundreds of petty rulers intent upon imitating the glories of Versailles. Certainly Frederick the Great (1712–86) was a confirmed Francophil, and after the Seven Years' War devoted himself to building what were virtually French palaces; he also embellished with mixed results Berlin churches with classical porticos. A more national expression of German architecture is the Hofburg in Vienna.

In ecclesiastical architecture, the influence of Palladio and the Renaissance is most clearly seen in the mid-eighteenth-century Liebfrauenkirche at Dresden (1726–45). This is a square, domed church of considerable

distinction, marred only by the unwarranted opulence and inelegance of the interior. In Vienna the church of San Carlo Borromeo, built in 1716, also shows the strong influence of the Renaissance. A number of other handsome churches deriving from St Peter's in Rome were built, notably Salzburg Cathedral (started in 1614) and Munich Cathedral.

The greatest German contribution to eighteenth-century European architecture was German Baroque, especially the churches and palaces of southern Germany.

Baroque tendencies had been seen in Germany long before – for instance, at Salzburg Cathed-

ral – but the movement was arrested by the Thirty Years' War and did not reappear again until the later years of the seventeenth century. This happened under the influence of the Italian Baroque of Borromini and Guarini.

By the beginning of the eighteenth century, however, a number of German architects were working in an opulent theatrical style that satisfied the pretensions of their princely patrons, both religious and secular.

Fischer von Erlach was the first of these architects with his projects for the Austrian court at the Hofburg and Schönbrunn, respectively in and just outside Vienna. His designs for the Hofburg were never realized, but Schönbrunn, much altered, follows the original layout. He was also responsible for the two Salzburg churches, the Dreifaltigkeitskirche and the Collegiate Church. Just as many ambitious secular buildings were erected. These were mainly palaces for the many German princes and princelings who were anxious to copy the glories of Versailles and Schönbrunn on however modest a scale.

The most splendid of these Baroque palaces, and one worthy of any great royal house, was at Würzburg. Designed by Balthasar Neumann for the Schönborn family, it was begun in 1719 and built – in the French manner, round a *cour d'honneur* – over several decades.

The uncompleted Zwinger Palace in Dresden was designed for Augustus the Strong by Daniel Pöppelmann, who worked on it between 1711 and 1722. It was probably the most extravagantly planned of all these palaces. The mildly exotic Japanese Palace, with its concave roof, was built in the same city and for the same prince between 1715 and 1717.

The Brandenburg Gate in Berlin (1789–93), designed by K G Langhans, a theatre in Potsdam, also by Langhans (1795), and a theatre in Danzig (1789–1801) are typical if grandiose demonstrations of the *fin de siècle* romantic classicism that dominated late eighteenth-century European architecture.

The new century opened with a number of major works. The most notable architects were David Gilly (1748–1808), his short-lived son Friedrich (1771–1800), Leo von Klenze (1784–1864), Friedrich von Gärtner (1792–1847), and Karl Friedrich von Schinkel (1781–1841). Klenze was the architect of part of the royal palace in Munich, and of the War Office (1824–6) and the Glyptothek (sculpture gallery).

Schinkel was one of the most prolific and significant architects in Europe in the first half of the century. Despite his comparatively short life, his buildings and teachings exerted considerable influence long after his death, and he is justly regarded as one

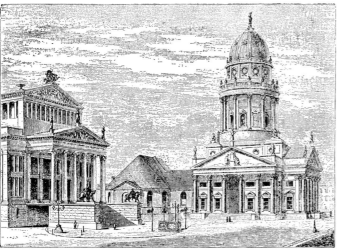

The Gens-d'armes Platz, Berlin, showing a church and theatre

The Altes Museum in Berlin: Karl Friedrich von Schinkel, 1822–30

The Schauspielhaus in East Berlin: Schinkel, 1818–21

of the makers of the modern movement. Beginning as a designer of theatre sets, Schinkel made his mark only with his project for the Berlin Schauspielhaus (1819–21). His masterpiece was the vast, colonnaded Berlin Altes Museum (1824–8).

Schinkel's original handling of the antique orders was continued by his pupils and followers, the most important of whom was F A Stüler (1800–65), designer of the Neue Museum (1843–55). Others were Ludwig Persius (1803–45), who also worked at Potsdam; and Gottfried Semper (1803–79), architect of the first Dresden Opera House (1837–41) and its successor after the destruction of the original by fire.

Schinkel's influence gradually declined with the rise of the French Second Empire manner, which affected European architecture from Austria to Scandinavia. The establishment of Berlin in 1871 as the imperial capital of a unified Germany led to a centralization of cultural influences as well as government. This gave considerable opportunities to one of Schinkel's assistants, Friedrich Hitzig (1811–81), who designed the Exchange, one of the earliest Neo-Baroque buildings of the late nineteenth century, and the Neo-classical Reichsbank (1871–76).

In Germany, as elsewhere, exponents of various historical styles competed with one another while the technological advances of the century were incorporated without question. The use of iron in buildings was less widespread in Germany than in Great Britain and the United States. Only gradually, during the last decades of the century, did German architects begin to feel their way towards a greater simplicity in design.

Meanwhile, buildings in a quite different spirit were being erected in Bavaria. On the initiative of Ludwig II of Bavaria in the 1870s and 1880s, a fantastic and extravagant Rococo revival took place. And even in Berlin, the Reichstag building by P Wallot (1841–1912), and the cathedral by Julius Raschdorf (1823–1914), added a grandiose theatrical quality to the Unter den Linden.

The technological revolution really got under way in the early twentieth century. The most important figure was Peter Behrens (1868–1940), who learned much from the Belgian architect Henry van de Velde (1863–1957). (Van de Velde moved to Berlin in 1899 and became head of the Weimar School of Arts and Crafts, later the Bauhaus, in 1902.) Although Behrens's contribution to the modern movement in Europe and the USA is widely acknowledged, it is still underrated.

Even more famous are Professor Walter Gropius (1883–1969), head of the Bauhaus and later active as an architect and teacher in the USA, and Ludwig Mies van der Rohe (1886–1969), whose later career was also in America, where his buildings have had enormous influence.

Gropius and Mies van der Rohe created the kind of buildings that is in most people's minds typical of modern architecture. Such buildings are now increasingly grouped under the label of 'the International style.' This is in many ways an apt title, for what Behrens, Gropius, and others had started was gradually taken up by followers, disciples, and imitators, so that a near-uniform style was practised by architects throughout the world.

The post-war reconstruction programmes in Berlin and other devastated German cities encouraged German architects who combined practical ability with social and aesthetic commitment.

Schloss Linderhof in Bavaria: George Dollmann, 1870–8

A house in Dessau: Walter Gropius, 1926

Building in Dusseldorf: H Hentrich and H Petschnigg, 1957–60

Memorial church among the ruins, Berlin, by Egon Eiermann, 1961

Above: an office building in Goslar: K W Kramer, 1957–8 Below: a house at Lörbach, Odenwald: Waldemar Lippert, 1957–8

The church of Mary the Queen in Saarbrücken: R Schwarz, 1956–9

These were expressed in vast housing projects, schools, hospitals, theatres, and concert halls. Only a few of these achievements can be listed here: the rebuilding of the Hanse quarter of Berlin; the outstanding school buildings in Offenbach by Adolf Bayer, Friedel Steinmeyer, and Fritz Nowotny; the Gymnasium in Dortmund by Friedrich Krämer; the Mannheim National Theatre by Gerhard Weber; the Berlin Philharmonic building by Hans Scharoun; the lightweight tent-like structures evolved by Otto Frei; the Liederhalle at Stuttgart by Adolf Abel and Rolf Gutbrod; and the Beethoven Hall at Bonn by Siegfried Wolske.

German furniture. In the late seventeenth century a distinctively German furniture succeeded the common European styles of Gothic and Baroque. The national style was of considerable diversity (partly thanks to the political fragmentation of Germany) and continued to borrow heavily from England, France, and Italy; but it none the less displayed a growing unity.

Typical of the period 1670 to 1720 are massive wardrobes, relics of medieval all-purpose cupboards. They are sometimes of great decorative merit, mostly veneered in walnut and other golden coloured fruitwoods, and relieved by rich and imaginative applied scroll and strapwork carving.

From 1720 the French Rococo influence was paramount – revolutionizing the native style as drastically in Germany as elsewhere in Europe. The electors of Bavaria at Munich were

A walnut cupboard made in Nuremberg, 1676

A marquetry commode made by David Roentgen for Versailles, c 1775

fortunate in being able to employ the Frenchman François Cuvilliés, whose work in Munich and Nymphenburg was among the best of its kind in all Europe. Native craftsmen were employed on the lavish, often gilt, furniture which was closely modelled on French styles. At the same time, the vogue for Chinese lacquer and wallpapers (used in the Amalienburg and the Pagodenburg) created a demand for *chinoiserie* japanned furniture of

all kinds.

By the mid-eighteenth century, the Rococo pervaded even provincial German work, but the earlier panelled styles were adapted to it to create a unique German style. This was somewhat ponderous in comparison with French work and in some respects resembled north Italian marquetry. There is a white lacquer commode (now at Potsdam), made *c* 1750, which could easily be mistaken for Venetian

work; and the same applies to other less elaborate pieces.

By 1770 the Germans were interpreting the Neo-classical style in much the same way as the Italians did. The severity of the straight line was relieved by marquetry panels of richly figured burr walnut and other decorative native woods. The outline (especially in commodes and bureaux) was adapted as a series of straight surfaces on different planes: projecting drawers, canted (angled) corners, and even W-shaped fronts were common.

Germany produced two of the world's greatest furniture-makers: Abraham and David Roentgen of Neuweid. Abraham (1711–93) actually worked in England from 1731 to 1738, and his son David styled himself 'Englischer Kabinettmacher', though it is unlikely that he ever came to England. Both brought to their furniture the craftsmanship of England, the elegance of French design, and the centuries-old German experience of pictorial inlay. The Germans had always excelled at marquetry, but the Roentgens' marquetry furniture was unsurpassed in the history of cabinetmaking. The very finest work of the family was done by David between 1770 and 1790.

The reputation of German craftsmen is demonstrated by the number of highly skilled men who accompanied Marie Antoinette to France and succeeded in making prosperous careers. Such famous *ébénistes* as Benneman, Weisweiler, and the incomparable Riesener were Germans.

The Napoleonic Wars impoverished Germany and damaged the furniture trade in the nineteenth century, but this very poverty itself gave rise to the simple and charming 'Biedermeier' style of the 1830s and 1840s. Its employment of lemon-

coloured woods and post-Empire lines represents a native adaptation of the Charles X style of *bois clair* furniture in France.

The Biedermeier tradition eventually went down before the nineteenth-century taste for historical revivals, and most of the furniture and interiors of late nineteenth-century Germany are virtually indistinguishable from those of the rest of Europe.

During the first decade of the twentieth century, a remarkably versatile artist-turned-architect, Peter Behrens (1868–1940), was designing houses, factories, and office buildings far in advance of their time. His work included designs for a wide range of industrial and domestic fittings, from street-lamps to tableware, and he perhaps contributed more to the introduction of high standards into machine-made design than any other man.

The most notable of Behrens' followers was Walter Gropius, whose influence has been enormously influential both in Germany and abroad. From 1919, at first in Weimar, later in Dessau (1925–8), a group of art students of *Das Staatliche Bauhaus*, started and led by Gropius as an extension of the Weimar School of Arts and Crafts, began to design experimental machine-made chairs, tables, desks, lighting fitments, and household equipment. More to the point,

A white lacquer commode with gilt carving, Munich, 1750

Biedermeier library table

A metal and canvas chair designed by Marcel Breuer, 1926

A tubular steel and cane chair by Mies van der Rohe, 1927

A stove of green lead-glazed tiles, made at Nuremberg, c 1450

A tin-glazed earthenware dish made at Hamburg, 1648

German seventeenth-century grey stoneware salt-glazed jug

A porcelain cup and saucer made at Meissen c 1730–40

Enamelled earthenware armorial jug from Durlach, late 18th century

A porcelain cup and saucer made at Vienna, 1800

they made an energetic attempt to market their designs through normal industrial organizations and their merchandising outlets.

Soon after moving to the United States, Gropius joined forces with an ex-Bauhaus student and teacher, Marcel Breuer (b 1902), an architect of Hungarian origin. Breuer, like Gropius, worked for a time in London before settling in the USA. Breuer consistently designed furniture of considerable flexibility and originality. Whilst teaching at the Bauhaus he had designed a range of tubular steel furniture which is still marketed throughout the world, and has been the prototype for almost all subsequent tubular metal furniture. His influence on twentieth-century office furniture and interior design would be difficult to exaggerate. Despite his residence in the USA, his work has made him a major force in contemporary German design.

German pottery and porcelain.
The earliest interesting examples of German pottery are earthenware tiles of the mid-fourteenth century. These tiles were specially made for the construction of great wood-burning stoves used for heating. Tiles were made in many places, Nuremberg being perhaps the most famous. The early ones were often modelled in relief, and were covered in a green lead glaze; but brown and yellow glazes were used later. Later, also, panels of tin-glazed tiles were inserted; these were painted

with Biblical and other scenes, in the blues, yellows, browns, and greens used by the manufacturers of Delft ware.

An early type of salt-glazed stoneware was developed which took the form of round-bellied jugs decorated on the neck with a bearded face in relief. These were exported in some quantity to England (containing spirits) and copied by John Dwight of Fulham and others.

At Hanau, near Frankfurt, a factory was started by two Dutchmen in 1661. It manufactured tin-glazed earthenware very much in the manner of the Dutch Delft, for which it is sometimes mistaken. Similar ware was made at Ansbach (where much porcelain was later made); at Höchst, Fulda, and Cassel, and also in Berlin and many other places.

But Germany is more famous as the first European country to manufacture true (hard-paste) porcelain. Augustus the Strong (1670–1733), the Elector of Saxony, was passionately interested in oriental porcelain. He was an avid collector and spent enormous sums on acquiring rare and beautiful pieces. Legend has it that he once swapped a regiment of dragoons with the King of Prussia for a set of 48 vases. He employed two men, von Tschirnhausen and Böttger, who collaborated in an effort to analyse the secret of Chinese porcelain. By 1710 they had succeeded, and a factory had been started at Meissen, not far from Dresden. Despite rigorous

precautions, the secret of porcelain manufacture could not be kept, and a factory was set up in Vienna a few years later. Within a very few years there were several European centres.

The earliest Meissen porcelain was decorated with enamel colours, and it was not until 1725 that the Germans discovered how to use cobalt blue under the glaze – despite the fact that there were extensive deposits of cobalt in Saxony.

In 1731 Joachim Kändler, who became the most famous of all German porcelain modellers, came to the factory. During his time there (he stayed until his death in 1774) he was responsible for the modelling of over 1,000 different figures, as well as for designing elaborate table services and vases.

Though the factory suffered somewhat from Prussian occupation during the Seven Years' War, Meissen was usually prosperous, and long remained the most important porcelain-making centre in Europe.

The styles of decoration changed with the times; influences included the oriental, Rococo, and Baroque, and the Neo-classical style of Louis XVI. The factory continued in production throughout the nineteenth century, though the wares turned out were both inferior in design and decoration; even the body of the clay changed for the worse as the original sources of supply gave out. The output of the factory was enormous, and Meissen porcelain was exported all over the world.

The second porcelain factory

A biscuit porcelain group made at Meissen, after C G Jüchtzer, c 1790

Ghiordes rug with a prayer arch at either end

Top: a porcelain group made in Vienna, late 18th century. Bottom: group 'Poetry', Frankenthal, c 1770

to be started in Europe was at Vienna. Experiments were going on there as early as 1716, but the factory did not really get going until two refugees from Meissen joined it, Christoph Hunger in 1717 and Samuel Stölzel in 1719. However, Stölzel returned to the Meissen factory the following year, taking with him one of the best of the Viennese enamellers.

The Vienna factory had a career beset with difficulties and setbacks, but nevertheless produced some fine work, particularly in the period 1750–84. The Baroque influence of the early years gave way to the lighter Rococo style. Later, under the influence of work carried out at Sèvres, Neo-classical shapes and decorations appeared. In the last years of the factory, until its closure in 1864, work of elaborate dullness was produced with an over-use of colour and gilding.

Mention must be made of the porcelain factory at Nymphenburg near Munich, because it was here that Anton Bustelli worked. After Kändler, he was the most famous of all the modellers who worked in Germany. Tableware was also made at Nymphenburg. Other porcelain centres were Fürstenburg, Frankenthal, and Kloster Veilsdorf, and many other small factories existed.

Gesso. A preparation of paste composed of extremely finely powdered chalk or whiting mixed with linseed oil and size (or glue). It was used as a base for the decorative gilding of woodwork objects such as furniture and picture frames. After setting, the composition was solid yet very easy to carve. Although gesso was known in medieval times, it was not widely used until the late seventeenth century, when gilt gesso furniture became fashionable.

Ghiordes rugs. The weaving at Ghiordes, in the west of Turkey, is among the best found in Asia Minor. Rugs, especially prayer rugs, with their high-stepped niche or arch to the field, were made from at least the seventeenth century. Ghiordes carpets are often 12 or 14 ft in length and are of a predominantly puce or wine-red colour (also described as magenta) which is very distinctive.

Giant order. An order of pilasters carried through the whole height of a façade, and thus uniting several storeys. Michelangelo made the first spectacular use of this on his Palazzo dei Conservatori and Palazzo del Senatore on the Capitol, Rome.

Gibberd, Frederick (*b* 1908). British architect, town-planning consultant, and landscape designer; a past principal of the

Giant order pilasters at White Pine, Tennessee, 1840

239

Frederick Gibberd

Architectural Association School. He was educated at King Henry VIII School, Coventry, and started in private practice in London (1930).

As an architect Gibberd has avoided specializing and has designed most kinds of buildings. His larger works include the central area buildings at London Airport; the new Ulster Hospital in Belfast; Hinkley Point nuclear power station; and the new Roman Catholic Cathedral for Liverpool, won in open competition and opened in 1967. He is probably best known for his work in town design. Since 1949 he has been continuously responsible for the design of Harlow New Town. He is also planning consultant to the towns of Bury St Edmunds, Stratford-upon-Avon, and Leamington Spa; and he has designed civic centres for St Albans, Hull, and Doncaster.

Gibberd's most recent work includes a monastery for Douai Abbey in Berkshire, a market for Newmarket, the master plan for Haverhill in Suffolk, and the Memorial University of St John's, Newfoundland. He is also working on a museum for Kingston-upon-Hull, a city hall for St Albans, and an extension of Norwich town centre.

His work as landscape designer includes Queen's Gardens, Hull, and the new giant reservoirs, Tryweryn in Wales, and Derwent in Cumberland.

Publications: *Town and Village* (1953); *The Architecture of England* (1938); *Town Design* (1953); *Modern Flats* (1958; with F R S Yorke).

Gibbons, Grinling (1648-1721). English wood-carver. Gibbons's origins remain a matter of some mystery, the existing theories ranging from Dutch parentage and birth in Amsterdam to English parentage and birth in London. What is certain is that Gibbons's talents were recognized while he was still a young man and that he was recommended by John Evelyn to Charles II, who commissioned him to execute a considerable amount of ornamental woodwork. He also worked for Sir Christopher Wren.

Gibbons was responsible for the ornamental carving in the chapel at Windsor, much work in the choir of St Paul's, and the baptismal fonts in St James's Church, Piccadilly. He was also the carver most sought-after by the great landowners who were embellishing their country houses, and his work is to be

Grinling Gibbons

Harlow Civic Centre, Essex, with the town hall in the background finished in 1963; New Town, designed by Gibberd, begun in 1949

Carving in Wood at Petworth House, Sussex, by Grinling Gibbons. Detail shown above

Choir stalls in St Paul's Cathedral, carved in wood by Grinling Gibbons

James Gibbs

almost exclusively on his work as a wood-carver, he also created the life-size bronze statue representing James II in the dress of a Roman emperor, and designed the base of the statue of Charles I at Charing Cross in London.

Gibbs, James (1682–1754). British architect. Gibbs was born near Aberdeen where he received his early education. He travelled in Holland, France, and Italy, where he began to study architecture under Carlo Fontana, surveyor to Pope Clement XI. He remained in Rome for several years, undergoing a training in classical architectural design unmatched by any of his contemporaries in England.

Gibbs returned to England in 1700 and quickly found patrons among the Tory nobility. Within five years, mainly thanks to Edward Harley, Earl of Oxford,

seen at Burleigh, Chatsworth, Petworth, and elsewhere.

Whereas carvers copied antique models, Gibbons took his subjects straight from nature. Birds, flowers, foliage, and fruit abound in his work which is characterized by an extreme fineness of carving, a deep elaboration of detail, and a wonderfully delicate and realistic touch. He was appointed master carver in wood to George I in 1714.

Although Gibbons's fame rests

Gibbs had become one of the Commissioners for Building Fifty New Churches. He was personally responsible for the design of St Mary-le-Strand (1714–17), St Martin-in-the-Fields (1722–6), and the steeple of St Clement

St Mary-le-Strand, London, designed by James Gibbs, 1714–17

Gibbs' own wooden model for St Martin-in-the-Fields, 1722–6

The interior of St Mary-le-Strand, designed by James Gibbs, 1714–17

The interior of St Martin-in-the-Fields: James Gibbs 1722–6

The Salon, or cube room, of Sudbrook Park, Surrey: Gibbs 1726–8

Danes (1719) which replaced Wren's wooden cupola. He also designed the charming little church of St Peter in Vere Street (1722–4).

Gibbs built up a considerable practice as an architect of country houses. Many of these were reproduced in his first publication, *A Book of Architecture* (1728), which was followed by other volumes in 1732 and 1747; the last, *Bibliotheca Radcliviana*, contained the designs for his masterpiece, the Radcliffe Camera at Oxford. He also designed the Senate House at Cambridge (1722–30) and the New Buildings for King's College

(1724–49), both illustrated in *A Book of Architecture*. His books were widely used as pattern-books by speculative builders of houses for the new mercantile aristocracy.

Gibbs was a remarkably assured and eclectic architect. His early work, especially parts of St Mary-le-Strand, shows evidence of his deep interest in Italian Baroque, but he was also responsive to the Palladianism of Lord Burlington and his circle. Gibbs appreciated the work of Wren and Hawksmoor, and it has been suggested that the original conception of the central dome for the Radcliffe

Library building was due to Hawksmoor rather than Gibbs.

Gibbs died a bachelor and comparatively wealthy, owning a number of houses in London which he left to friends and patrons.

Gibbs surround. A heavy ornamental window surround with a triple keystoned head and intermittent stone blocks on the jambs. It was popularized by James Gibbs (qv).

Gibson, Sir Donald Evelyn Edward (*b* 1908). British architect and town-planner. Gibson was born in Manchester and studied there at the University School of Architecture. His reputation was established after World War II by his imaginative yet practical supervision of the

rebuilding of devastated Coventry; he was chief architect of the city from 1939 to 1955. From 1955 to 1958 he was chief architect of Nottinghamshire, where he inaugurated the now world famous CLASP system of prefabricated school buildings; he later adapted and extended it for use in military construction after his appointment in 1958 as director general of works in the War Department. He was knighted in 1962, and became director general of research and development in the Ministry of Public Building and Works.

After the merger of the armed forces' works services with the Civil Ministry of Works, Gibson became the controller-general. During this period he presented to the Government the White Paper on the Agreement Board

Sir Donald Gibson

CLASP system, Nottingham 195

Sigfried Giedion

now established in Britain to test new methods of construction. This is linked with similar bodies in other European countries. Gibson became a member of its council.

Giedion, Sigfried (*b* 1893). Swiss-born art, architectural, and social historian and critic. Giedion was born in Langnau and studied engineering before

Woolworth building, New York

turning to the history of art. In 1928 he was appointed general secretary of CIAM (International Congresses for Modern Architecture), the foundation of which marks the beginning of academic studies of modern architecture. After teaching at Harvard in 1946, he was appointed professor of art history at the Zürich Federal Institute of Technology.

Giedion's first book remains his best known and most widely influential publication. *Space, Time, and Architecture* (1914) was based on a series of lectures given in the USA in 1928–39, in which Giedion sought to trace, from the Renaissance to the present day, mankind's striving towards a sense of unity between architecture and related contemporary studies. He has since published *Mechanization Takes Command* (1948), a study of mechanization since the early days of the Industrial Revolution.

Gilbert, Cass (1859–1934). American architect, born in Zanesville, Ohio. He is chiefly remembered as a designer of skyscrapers, especially the 52-storey, 792 ft Woolworth building with its late Gothic overtones, built in New York in 1913.

Gilbert had a wide and prosperous practice, and his other buildings include the Capitol at St Paul, Minnesota; the New York Custom House; public library buildings at St Louis and Detroit; and buildings for the universities of Minnesota and Texas. He was president of the American Institute of Architects in 1908–9.

Gilding. No historian has traced the origin of this craft. Herodotus says that it was practised amongst the ancient Egyptians, and his assertion has been proved by discoveries made in the tombs of the Pharaohs. Long before 1500 BC, craftsmen in the Nile valley discovered that gold was an extremely workable medium and experimented by beating the metal into wafers of such delicacy that they could be applied to plaster and, presumably, wood. The essential processes of gilding have remained unchanged through the intervening centuries, although variants achieving similar effects at less cost have since been introduced.

The application of gilding to wooden rather than stone and plaster surfaces offered far greater scope to later craftsmen. Two main processes were developed: (1) water gilding, which

Gilded decoration in the Single Cube room at Wilton House

is invariably applied to a gesso base, enables the surface to be burnished and offers a greater lustre than (2) oil gilding, which is more durable and less subject to climatic conditions. See also **Giltwood.**

These processes are outlined in *A Treatise on Japanning, Varnishing, and Guilding*, by John Stalker and George Parker, published in 1688 (reprinted in facsimile by Tiranti in 1960). There are comparatively few differences between their recipes and the processes which had already been practised for centuries, although the authors did advance the new claim that a good ground for oil gilding could be made from paint-pot scrapings. This gives a rough-and-ready background which is still used by some craftsmen.

Gilded leather was used for screens and furniture during the fifteenth century, particularly in Italy and Spain. By the eighteenth century the craft was practised more extensively, a gold lacquer varnish being applied to a silver-leaf surface.

In our own time the method most widely employed for the gilding of picture frames, pel-

mets, pilasters, book-bindings, and other objects is to apply thin and comparatively small areas of gold-leaf to the surface affixed by specially prepared adhesives. For the gilding of mirrors and clear glass and ceramic surfaces, the more usual process is to apply a powdered form of gold. For gilding of metal surfaces an electrochemical deposition process is used that is similar to the process employed in silver-plating. Some metallic surfaces are still gilded by the fire-gilding process, known in the Middle Ages, in which an amalgam of mercury and gold is applied to the surface to be gilded.

Gill, Irving John (1870–1936). American architect who, after training in the Chicago offices of Alder & Sullivan, set up his own practice in San Diego, where he began to design buildings inspired by the early Spanish missions and *haciendas*.

Gill reinterpreted the timber-built originals in masonry and stucco finishes. Because of their simplicity of form these Spanish colonial houses have a deceptively modern appearance: their large window areas and geometrical

A house in Los Angeles designed by Irving Gill, 1915–16

A Louis XIV giltwood table

A gate by Gimson, c 1897

volumes give them a remarkable similarity to the Viennese houses being built at about the same time by the Austrian architect Adolf Loos. The interiors designed by Gill anticipate the oriental styles that influenced Californian interiors of the thirties and forties. Gill also designed the First Church of Christ Scientist (1904–7) and other buildings in San Diego.

Gillow. A dynasty of British cabinetmakers, furniture-makers, and upholsterers started by Robert Gillow, a joiner who, in 1695, set up in business as a carpenter at Lancaster.

In 1757 Gillow took into partnership a son, Richard (1734–1811), who was a trained architect and surveyor. The firm was responsible for much architectural work in Lancaster, designing the Custom House in 1764. Richard was succeeded by his son, another Richard (1773–1849).

The firm never abandoned cabinet-making and was in large part responsible for its renaissance in the Edwardian era.

The London branch of Gillow was opened in 1761 in Oxford Street (then the Tyburn Road), and remained there until 1906, becoming in time the Waring & Gillow of today.

Giltwood. A term that describes any form of gilding applied to wood. The usual eighteenth-century method was to carve the wood, then to apply gesso (qv), and carve it, and finally to gild the finished object using either water or an oil technique.

The word giltwood is also incorrectly used for silver-leaf, which is applied to gesso on wood and then coloured with lacquer to simulate gold.

Gimson, Ernest (1864–1919). English craftsman and furniture designer. Gimson was born in Leicester, trained at Leicester School of Art, and became assistant to an architect in the city, Isaac Barradale.

When he was 20, Gimson was profoundly influenced by the ideas of William Morris. After a brief period in London in the 1890s, during which he attempted but failed to sell furniture commercially, he set up as a craftsman-cabinetmaker at Pinbury in Gloucestershire, and later at the nearby village of Sapperton.

His feeling for the traditional use of timber, his resolute rejection of industrial production methods, and his lifelong devotion to the teachings of Morris, have given Gimson a permanent and significant place in the history of the Arts and Crafts movement in England. He gradually enlarged the scope of his craftsmanship to include textiles, plasterwork, and metalwork, but he is now chiefly known for his simple and beautifully made furniture, particularly his ladder-back chairs.

A Victorian gipsy table

Gipsy table. A small round table on a tripod stand, late nineteenth century in origin. The top was covered with either cloth or beaded embroidery, and hung with elaborate beaded or tatted fringes.

Girandole or **gerondole.** A form of wall candelabra, of French inspiration in both name and design. The earliest elaborate English girandoles are those of the period of Thomas Johnson (*Twelve Girandoles*, 1775), Chip

An armchair by Gimson, c 1880

A George III giltwood centre table with a marble top

An American eagle mounted girandole looking glass, c 1800

ation, especially in the designs of Thomas Johnson, who delighted in *Barlow's Fable* drawings and commonly used animals (especially squirrels) and birds.

In the Neo-classical period, girandoles were made with a severity that was relieved by elegant attentuated lines, often carved with chains of husks, laurel leaves, and fan motifs. On occasions the now rectangular or oval mirrors were replaced by pictures.

By 1800 girandoles were less frequently made, and were to some extent replaced by carved wall-lights with typical wheatear, eagle, and Grecian motifs.

Girard, Alexander Hayden (*b* 1907). American architect and designer. After an unusually cosmopolitan training in architectural offices in Florence, Rome, London, Paris, and New York, Girard began to practise in Florence, staying there from 1930 to 1932. He then went back to New York, where he worked for five years before moving to Detroit in 1937. He has designed a remarkable range of industrial and commercial buildings, including offices for the Ford Motor Company and private houses in Michigan and elsewhere.

His preoccupation with industrial design has taken him into other spheres, and he has been responsible for numerous exhibitions of home furnishings, textiles, and ornamental arts for the Museum of Modern Art, Herman Miller, the Furniture Museum at Grand Rapids, etc. He lives in Santa Fé, New Mexico.

Glass, ancient and medieval. Glass as an independent substance in use for small objects such as beads seems to have originated in western Asia about 3000 BC or even earlier. Actual small vessels do not occur until about 1500 BC. The Egyptian glass-making industry appears to have been founded by Asian workers brought back after the Egyptian Pharaoh Tuthmosis III began his conquests of western Asia in 1481 BC.

The art of glassmaking soon spread to Syria and Mesopotamia, Greece, Rhodes, Cyprus, and Italy. From Syria, Phoenician traders carried it all over the ancient world.

The famous city of Alexandria, founded in 332 BC, became renowned for glasshouses in which very advanced techniques were practised. The Egyptian love of semi-precious stones and their

A dark blue and turquoise vase, Egyptian, XVIII dynasty

A Roman opaque blue jug with 'dragged' decoration

great skill in cutting them, also appears in the brilliant colours they used for small unguent bottles and mosaic plaques (see also **Miliefiori**). Bowls were ground and polished with a lapidary's wheel, which was also used to cut figures and vessels from raw blocks of glass. Egyptians achieved the amazing feat of sandwiching incised gold-leaf between two tightly fitting glass bowls (see also **Verre églomisé**). Egyptian glass was so highly prized that when Augustus conquered Alexandria, he took skilled Egyptian craftsmen back to Italy. One of the most famous of all glass pieces, the Portland Vase, was almost certainly made as a cinerary urn for a Roman emperor by an Egyptian in Italy, during the late first century BC or early first century AD.

The discovery of glass-blowing changed glass from a luxury item

pendale, and their contemporaries, working in the Rococo style. Girandoles have one or more candle branches springing from a giltwood frame enclosing a small, usually asymmetrical

mirror, which served to reflect the candle flame. The term is sometimes applied to similar pieces without mirrors.

Rococo girandoles often carry amusingly fanciful carved decor-

The bedroom of a house in Santa Fé designed by Alexander Girard

A Mesopotamian or Persian bottle, probably ninth century

A Saracen enamelled mosque lamp, early sixteenth century

to an everyday material. It probably started on the Phoenician coast somewhere around 100 BC. The new technique, by which glass was blown into moulds and later free blown, inspired more imaginative shapes, and the application of molten glass for trailed decoration.

The term 'Roman glass' covers glass made not only in Italy but throughout the Roman Empire. With the disintegration of the Empire in the fifth century, the art of fine glassmaking deteriorated in western Europe; only in the eastern Mediterranean, Syria, Persia, Mesopotamia, and Egypt ,did it continue to be practised with a high level of skill. Soon after these countries were conquered by the Moslems in the seventh century, a distinctive and decorative style, the Islamic, appeared. Typical manifestations are the long-necked flasks with globular bodies and the various forms of cutting, which include bevelling in oval facets, incised linear decoration, and a deep

relief cutting which stands right out from the rest of the surface, which has been ground down. Tin-glazed lustre earthenware may have suggested the polychrome and lustre decoration of glass. However, it was in the thirteenth and fourteenth centuries that the most renowned vitreous enamelling and gilding of Islamic glass was carried out on beakers, pilgrim flasks, and above all mosque lamp-holders. One of the most famous centres of glassmaking was Damascus, and when the Mongol conqueror Tamerlane captured the city in 1400, he sent back some of the finest craftsmen to work at his capital in Samarkand. Others fled to Venice (still a big centre of glassmaking) and other lands, bringing to a close the great period of Islamic glassmaking.

See the articles on American, English, German and Bohemian, Irish, Netherlandish, Swedish, and Venetian glass.

Glass in architecture. Although clear and coloured glass was for centuries used for windows, the technical difficulties of glassmaking limited the size of pieces made. Glass was also very expensive. Not until the beginning of the nineteenth century was it both easily available and relatively cheap.

The art of coloured or stained glass dates from antiquity, but not until early medieval times is such work found in Europe. Throughout the Middle Ages, stained glass was held in place by lead, a fact which imposed severe limitations upon the artist. Nevertheless, medieval stained glass windows are probably the greatest achievements of the artist in glass, and Chartres, the Sainte Chapelle in Paris, the lower Basilica of the church of St Francis in Assisi, and many

others, contain windows fit to stand beside any examples of 'fine' art.

It was not until well into the nineteenth century that architects could begin to think of glass as a major element in their designs. Le Corbusier summed up this and similar technical difficulties by saying that the history of building is a record of architects' ceaseless battle for light against the laws of gravity.

Wide spans of glass on any scale were first employed in Paris in shops, greenhouses, and conservatories. As early as 1829, the Galerie Orléans in Paris was built over the garden of the Palais Royal to designs by Fontaine. Thomas Hopper had built a large Gothic conservatory for the Prince Regent at Carlton House in London as early as 1811. This was surpassed by the handsome unadorned greenhouse designed by Charles Rohault de Fleury at the Jardin des Plantes in Paris, built in 1833.

The possibilities of such roofing for large department stores were soon recognized, and a series of such stores was built from the 1840s.

The Great Conservatory at Chatsworth (277 ft by 123 ft), designed for the sixth Duke of Devonshire by his gardener, Joseph Paxton, was virtually a miniature prototype for the building finally chosen for the Great Exhibition of 1851 in Hyde Park; it was later removed to Sydenham and destroyed by fire in 1936. Paxton's Crystal Palace was undoubtedly the first great building to show the full potential of glass in architecture. It owed nothing to traditional forms, but was a logical solution to the problem in hand; the provision of a vast exhibition hall with few obstructing pillars and

A stained-glass panel from Sées Cathedral, Normandy, 1250–75

wall divisions. Paxton's building was followed by the Palm House in Kew Gardens, designed by Decimus Burton and built by the Irish engineer Richard Turner in 1845.

Paxton's innovations were enthusiastically taken up and developed by other architects, particularly the architects of the new Railway Age, who readily covered their great structures with transparent roofs supported by iron and steel. The Oxford Midland Station was built by Fox and Henderson, engineers of the Crystal Palace. Although comparatively small, it indicated the possibilities of prefabricated

Detail of the roofs of the Crystal Palace, designed by Sir Joseph Paxton in 1851

Conservatories at Alton Towers, created by Lord Shrewsbury, 1814–27

The central nave of Paddington Station: I K Brunel and D Wyatt, 1854

Glazing waggons used to lay the 300,000 panes at Crystal Palace

A glass bridge at Sheffield University: Gollins Partners, 1963

glass-and-iron components. Paddington Station, designed by Brunel and Wyatt in 1854, and Lime Street Station in Liverpool, designed by Richard Turner, took the process a stage further. The Gare de L'Est in Paris, designed by R A Duquesney and built in 1847–52, was one of the most ambitious and successful of the early iron-and-glass stations.

The London Coal Exchange (1846–9), designed by the corporation architect James Bunstone Bunning, and the great Bon Marché stores in Paris (1876), designed by Boileau and Eiffel, were also influential structures.

The history of building in glass in the twentieth century is a record of architects' attempts to create complete façades in glass, frequently ignoring questions of climate, heat loss, and acoustics. Such architectural ambitions were encouraged by the use of a cast-iron (later steel) framework for buildings. A number of buildings indicated the possibilities of large-scale buildings in glass: in the USA, large office-blocks built by Louis Sullivan and the architects of the Chicago School; the Brussels Maison du Peuple, designed by Horta (1897); and the AEG Berlin building designed by Behrens (1909).

In the pre-World War I period, these experiments were continued, notably by Walter Gropius with his designs for the Fagus factory at Alfeld (1911) and a model factory at Cologne, finished in 1914. In the inter-war years glass was still more widely used in building. Two major architects, inspired by Gropius, made glass one of the main elements in the International style: Le Corbusier, with his Salvation Army Hostel in Paris (1932), and Ludwig Mies van der Rohe with his series of published projects and his later buildings, mostly in USA.

Mies's major buildings are now symbols of the International style and the Age of Glass and Steel. With his designs for the Lake Shore Drive Apartment in Chicago (1951), and the Seagram Building in New York (1956), Mies van der Rohe takes a place of special honour in this story.

Other buildings which demonstrate the imaginative use of glass in building must include Lever House (1952) and the Carbide Building (1960), both in New York, designed by Skidmore, Owings, and Merrill, and the UN Secretariat building, designed by Wallace Harrison in association with Le Corbusier and others (1947–50). Nor should Frank Lloyd Wright's work, including the remarkable building for the Research Tower of the Johnson's Wax company in Racine (1951), be overlooked in any discussion of the use of glass in modern architecture.

Glastonbury chair. A late sixteenth-century oak folding armchair with X-shaped legs,

Architect Philip Johnson's glass house in Connecticut, 1949

Oak Glastonbury chair

Stoneware jar; Han Dynasty (206 BC – AD 220). Transparent greenish glaze on top half

and arms pinned to the back uprights and to the seat rail. The back may be plain; or is decorated with carving of two round arches of guilloche pattern (qv) enclosing a sunburst and lozenge ornament.

Glaze. A glassy coating applied to pottery, stoneware, or porcelain, rendering it non-porous and impervious to liquids.

The kind of glaze used on early pottery such as slipware was made from galena (sulphide of lead). This was ground to a fine powder and dusted on to the unbaked ware. In the heat of the kiln a silicate was formed by the reaction of the silica in the body of the ware, leaving it covered in a smooth, shiny, yellowish surface. This was a dangerous process, and potter's asthma and lead-poisoning were common among the operatives, who breathed in a certain amount of the dust as they shook it over the objects they were glazing.

In England, *c* 1750, Enoch

Modern glazed pottery by Arabia

Booth of Tunstall devised a less dangerous way of dealing with the lead, by grinding it up under water with calcined flints and clay. This resulted in a creamy liquid into which the already fired biscuit ware was dipped, coating it much more evenly than was possible by the older method.

A leadless glaze was introduced, *c* 1820, but it was not until the very end of the nineteenth century that the use of lead for glazing was forbidden by law.

In the eighteenth century, salt-glazing was also common. This was used on a fine, hard, white stoneware made of clay, with the addition of a silicious sand and calcined flint. The body was fired to a higher temperature than ordinary earthenware, and when the kiln was red-hot, ordinary salt was shovelled in through the top of the furnace. The salt vaporized and covered the ware inside with a colourless soda glaze, characterized by a pock-marked or orange-peel surface.

Another kind of glaze used on earthenware was a white enamel made of binoxide of tin, into which the ware was dipped. This was a very old method of glazing, used even in Assyria and Babylon. It was adopted by the Italians in the fifteenth century for *maiolica*; and copied by the French (*faïence*) and Dutch and English (Delft).

The glaze on hard-paste porcelain was made from powdered feldspathic rock, which fuses into the body of the porcelain at a very high temperature, giving a brilliant, almost glass-like hardness of surface. The Chinese were the first to experiment with the colouring of glazes. They added many different substances, and succeeded in obtaining an amazingly large range of colourings and effects. Sometimes the glaze was put on after the first firing; if this was done, the temperature of the second firing was slightly lower, and a flux was added to the feldspathic rock to lower its melting point. This sort of glaze can be detected by the fact that it seems thicker, and has minute bubbles in suspension.

The glaze on soft porcelain was usually added after the primary firing. It was usually thickish lead glaze, sometimes running and gathering in drops or in the hollows of the object.

Glazing. The fitting of glass in window frames, lanterns, skylights, and other frameworks made to receive glass.

'The Rape of Proserpina' Gobelin by Joseph-Marie Vien, from the series of tapestries 'The Lover of the Gods', woven in 1757

Glazing bars. The thin bars of wood or metal which divide the framework of a window or door, and are moulded or cast so that they can receive and secure the panes of glass.

Globe. Ancient Greek and early Arab astronomers used versions of the astrolabe, by means of which they sought to record the movements of heavenly bodies. This was followed by the complicated open metal structure of the armillary globe, which was in turn succeeded by elementary versions of those globes most familiar today, the celestial (showing the sky) and the terrestrial (showing the earth). Special cartographical sections were engraved for application to spherical surfaces, and Mercator's projections were in use in the sixteenth century.

In the seventeenth century, study of both forms of globe was part of a gentleman's education, and the publication of Joseph Moxon's *Tutor to Astronomy and Geography* (1659) led to a growing production of globes and their stands. By the middle of the eighteenth century this was a flourishing craft in which cartographer and cabinetmaker combined to produce work of superb quality, much of which was exported.

Most of the stands used for the globe were made of mahogany. Stands of simply turned,

reeded, or fluted supports were made; so were stands with elaborate motifs, from dolphins and lions to tripods carved with acanthus.

Glyph. A vertical V-cut groove which was one of the motifs of Greek architecture. A triglyph is a panel with two glyphs and two half glyphs; the latter has bevelled edges.

Gobelin. The name of a family of French dyers, later to become the most notable tapestry house in French history. Gilles and Jehan (died 1476) Gobelin were

Castlemaine globe by Moxon, 1679

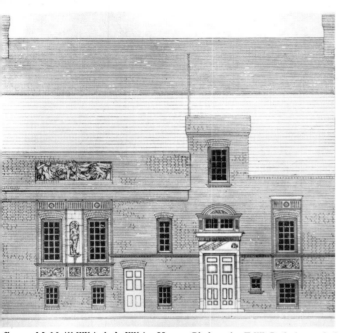

James McNeill Whistler's White House, Chelsea, by E W Godwin, c 1878

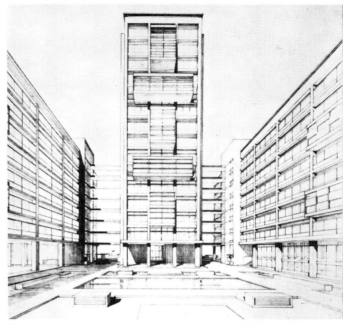

Elephant and Castle development, London, by E Goldfinger, begun 1961

the members of the family who set up their business as dyers in the middle years of the fifteenth century at the Faubourg St. Marcel in Paris, on the Bièvre. After some years, in 1529, the firm began to make the tapestries which have since acquired international renown.

Even at an early date, the

Gobelin tapestries became so widely celebrated throughout regal and ducal circles in France that in 1662 the manufactory was bought by Colbert on behalf of Louis XIV. From then on, court painters such as Le Brun were commissioned to prepare designs for the royal tapestries, which continued to be woven by

the Gobelin works. An upholstery works was later added by royal decree.

The factory was closed from 1694 to 1697, due to Louis XIV's financial troubles, and again during the Revolution, but in the early years of the nineteenth century it reopened, and in 1826 the manufacture of carpets was added to the firm's activities. Later in the century, a second establishment, of similar scope to that of Gobelin, was opened at Beauvais. Both factories continue to be operated under the patronage of the state.

Goddard foot. See Bracket foot.

Godwin. E W (1833–86). A British architect and designer, one of the foremost practitioners of High Victorian Gothic, exemplified in his unusual and handsome warehouse building at Stock Croft, Bristol (about 1862), and in his town halls at Northampton (1861–4) and Congleton, Cheshire (1864–7). He also designed a number of houses in Chelsea for avant-garde artists, including Whistler, for whom he built the White House in Tite Street.

Godwin was in the forefront of those who sought to free the Victorian interior from over-fussiness, and both in Bristol and London he showed considerable taste as a decorator, and also designed wallpapers and furniture in the Japanese taste. His much-publicized relationship with Ellen Terry drew him

into the world of the theatre, and he became a leading set designer.

Goldfinger, Ernö (b 1902). British architect, born in Budapest. Goldfinger studied at the Beaux Arts, Paris, under Auguste Perret, and set up in practice in Paris in 1924 with André Sive. After executing various design

London offices by Goldfinger, 1955

Congleton Town Hall, Cheshire, designed by E W Godwin, 1864–7

projects in France, he settled in London (1934) and designed shops for Paul and Marjorie Abbatt and houses in Essex, Sussex, and London, including a terrace of three houses in Hampstead (1937-9), one of which was designed for his own use.

After World War II Goldfinger designed the Shoreditch neighbourhood unit, newspaper offices, and numerous small houses, offices, and factories throughout Britain. One of his most notable projects has been a large complex of offices and a cinema at the Elephant and Castle, London, begun 1961. Other work has included offices and showroom for Hille at Watford, Haggerston Comprehensive School, and tourist offices for French Railways in Piccadilly (with Charlotte Perriand) and at the Champs Elysées (with Pierre Forestier). He has also been involved in projects for housing developments in Poplar and North Kensington.

Gold leaf. Decoration worked in extremely thin sheets of beaten gold. For the history and technique, see **Gilding.**

Gollins, Melvin, Ward, and Partners. British architectural practice and partnership founded in 1946 by Frank Gollins (born in Birmingham in 1910) and James Melvin (born in Edinburgh in 1912). It was later joined by Edmund Ward (born in Barrow-in-Furness in 1912). In 1963 B J Mayes, W R Headley, and A W Smith also joined.

The partnership's first major works included schools for the Hertfordshire County Architect in the Hill's frame system building, and local authority flats and housing for Lambeth. Subsequent work in the early years was largely on educational projects for other local authorities.

Terrace of three houses at Hampstead Heath, London, designed by Ernö Goldfinger, 1933

In 1953 the firm won an open competition for the redevelopment of the central area of Sheffield University. The first building completed (in 1959) was the new university library, and various buildings for the different departments have been completed since. Other work includes Castrol House, London; the Royal Alfred Seamen's Home at Belvedere, Kent; the BOAC/

The main entrance of Sheffield University Library, 1955

BEA freight terminal and Boadicea House at London Heathrow Airport; new buildings at the Royal Military Academy at Sandhurst and the Royal Military College of Science at Shrivenham; an extension to the Cambridge University Library; a terminal unit for BOAC at the John F Kennedy Airport in New York; the redevelopment of Covent Garden Market at Nine Elms; extensions to the Royal Opera House; and the development of Victoria Station. The partnership's activities also include important hospital work.

Gombroon ware. This was once a general term for Persian pottery. Gombroon was a port on the Persian Gulf, and in the seventeenth century it was a very important trading centre. Pottery was one of the items exported.

The term Gombroon ware is still applied to a particular kind of Persian ware, translucent and decorated with pierced ornament filled in with the glaze (like the rice-patterned porcelain of China). This delicate ware was made as early as the tenth century, but early examples are now very rare. The most frequently seen specimens of Gombroon ware date from the eighteenth and early nineteenth centuries.

Loughborough College of Education. All three designed by Gollins, Melvin, Ward and Partners

Royal Alfred Merchant Seamen's Home, Belvedere, Erith, Kent, 1955-9

G-plan upholstered corner seating unit, 1972

Teapot from the Royal Pavilion tea set designed by R Y Goodden, 1951

Gomme, E. Buckinghamshire furniture firm founded in 1898 by Ebenezer Gomme, a craftsman chairmaker who served his apprenticeship in various High Wycombe workshops. The firm has remained within the family ever since.

During World War I the Gommes' reputation for sound and accurate workmanship won them orders for the celebrated DH 9, an aircraft mainly made of wood. After the war the company established itself as one of the largest furniture firms in the country.

During World War II Gomme's played a leading role in the production of the de Havilland Mosquito, and the sturdiness and precision this demanded provided invaluable experience.

The G-Plan range of furniture was first introduced in 1953. It promoted a relative simplicity of style, then known as 'contemporary' which commanded popularity on a very considerable scale, a success aided by the then-revolutionary way it was advertised and marketed. Gomme's was, in fact, one of the first manufacturers to create brand furniture.

Good, Joseph Henry (1775–1857). English architect. Good was the son of a Somerset clergyman and became a student of Sir John Soane. After setting up on his own, he quickly built up a varied practice, which included the design of London churches (St Andrew's, Holborn, 1818, destroyed in 1941; St Paul's, Bunhill Row. Finsbury, 1839); the Armourers' and Braziers' Hall; schools and houses; and official work at the Royal Pavilion, Brighton (including the Queen's stables, 1832), and Kensington Palace, where he was clerk of the works. He was one of the original fellows of the Institute of British Architects.

Goodden, Robert Yorke (*b* 1909). British industrial designer, educated at Harrow and the Architectural Association.

After war service in the RNVR, he designed the sports section of the 'Britain Can Make It' Exhibition (1946). Later (with R D Russell and R Guyatt) he was responsible for the Lion and Unicorn Pavilion at the Festival of Britain (1951). The success of these exhibitions led him increasingly into industrial design,

including special commissions for gold- and silversmithing, and for a wide range of domestic silverware.

In 1948 Goodden was appointed professor at the Royal College of Art, with responsibility for silversmithing, jewellery, and glass. His work has included the blue-and-gold silk for the hangings of Westminster Abbey for the Coronation (designed in collaboration with Warner & Sons); china for Wedgwood, Grosvenor House, and SS *Oriana*; the large series of mural decorations in metal foils and

Perspex sheet for the tourist lounge of SS *Canberra*; and, in collaboration with R D Russell, the reorganization of the Western Sculpture Galleries in the British Museum, and, more recently, the Print Room Gallery and Gallery of Oriental Art.

Goodhart-Rendel, Harry Stuart (1887–1959). British architect; Slade professor of fine art at Oxford 1933–6, president of the Royal Institute of British Architects 1937–9. After leaving Cambridge, where he studied music, Goodhart-Rendel became

The Armourers' and Braziers' Hall, London, by Joseph Henry Good, 1840

Hay's Wharf, London Bridge, designed by H S Goodhart-Rendel, 1931

Nebraska State Capitol by Bertram Grosvenor Goodhue, 1922

The Corridor, High Street, Bath, designed by Goodridge, 1825

engrossed by the study and practice of architecture. His work is characterized by a fastidious attempt to bridge the gap between Georgian and modern architecture, and by his own deep sympathy for the Augustan Age. These interests are shown in his book *English Architecture since the Regency* (1953), by an earlier monograph on Hawksmoor, and by his love for Hatchlands in Surrey, the Adam house which he inherited and left to the National Trust.

Despite these tastes, which made him a successful and sympathetic post-war restorer of All Souls, Langham Place, London, and the Dulwich Picture Gallery, his practice was wide-ranging; it included a monastery, churches, warehouses, factories, and town and country houses. His most notable commercial building was Hay's Wharf, by London Bridge.

Goodhue, Bertram Grosvenor (1869–1924). American architect. Goodhue first established his reputation with designs for the San Diego Exhibition in 1915. He was responsible for the revival of the Spanish Colonial style in Californian domestic architecture. In the last decade of his life he moved towards what Professor Henry Russell-Hitchcock calls 'an eclectic sort of semi-modernism' with designs for the Nebraska State Capitol in Lincoln. Its most distinctive feature is the high tower which takes the place of the dome usually considered imperative for state capitol buildings.

Goodison, Benjamin. One of the most eminent of British cabinetmakers during the reign of George II. Little is known of his early life, but records of his activities between 1727 and 1767 (the year in which it is generally assumed that he died) are frequently met with in accounts for work done for the royal palaces.

He had workshops at Long Acre, where he was in partnership with his nephew Benjamin Farran. Details of the furniture he made for a number of aristocratic patrons are documented in bills and accounts. For example, there are letters from Goodison to Thomas Coke, first Earl of Leicester, about furniture supplied to Holkham. It is there still, and shows Goodison's debt to the style evolved by William Kent. Goodison had the same penchant for handsome, boldly designed furniture of Baroque tendency, with emphatic and ornately carved centrepieces of shells, heads, crowns, and other motifs from antiquity.

The most famous assembly of Goodison's furniture is at Longford Castle, home of Viscount Folkestone. Here, between 1737 and 1747, Goodison supplied the first and second viscounts with a remarkable variety of furniture, including pedestals, mirrors, seats, day-beds, and stools. He also supplied Frederick, Prince of Wales, with mirrors and tables for Hampton Court Palace. And he also made the prince's coffin.

The most generous of Goodison's patrons was probably the Duchess of Marlborough, who utilized his services as both cabinetmaker and agent; he bought a house in Dover Street on her behalf and made a number of alterations for her.

Goodridge, Henry Edmund (about 1800–63). British architect. The son of a builder in Bath, Goodridge built up a successful practice in Bath and south-west England, and worthily carried on the tradition of classical building in Bath established by the Woods. In later life,

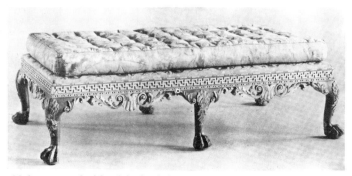

Mahogany stool with original upholstery, attributed to B Goodison, c 1740

Original design for Bristol Roman Catholic Cathedral by Goodridge, 1839

Design for a Grecian style lodge, from Goodwin's 'Domestic Architecture'

Interior design for Manchester Town Hall by Goodwin, 1833

The west front of Chartres Cathedral, 1194–1260

however, he turned increasingly to Gothic.

His work in Bath included buildings at Prior Park and the Lansdowne Tower for William Beckford (1825–6). He also designed, enlarged, and altered various ecclesiastical buildings in Somerset and Wiltshire, including the Roman Catholic cathedral in Bristol (1839–48).

Goodwin, Francis (1784–1835). British architect. Goodwin was born at King's Lynn in Norfolk, and early showed considerable energy and application in entering architectural competitions, including that for the new House of Commons in 1833. He gained awards in several of these competitions, without being invited to carry out his designs. He prepared similarly abortive designs for work in Dublin.

His ability to design in almost any manner from classical Greek to Gothic helped him to establish a profitable practice in the Midlands and the North. During the 1820s he was one of the most prolific architects in England, and carried out enough work to provide reputations for half a

dozen lesser men. He designed several Gothic churches, including St Peter's, Ashton-under-Lyne, Staffordshire; St George's, Kidderminster; Holy Trinity, Burton-on-Trent; St James's, Oldham; St Leonard's, Bilston; St Paul's, Walsall; and St George's, Hulme.

Goodwin was also responsible for a considerable amount of civic work, including the town hall and assembly rooms in the Greek classical manner at Manchester, later demolished, and the Exchange, Bradford. He also built numerous houses in the north of England and in Ireland.

Goss's armorial china. This was made by William Henry Goss (1833–1906) in Stoke-on-Trent from about 1858. An ivory-coloured porcelain body was fashioned into small cups, jugs, and vases and decorated with the arms of various towns. These must have sold in hundreds of thousands to the holiday trippers of the last century.

In addition to this armorial china, Goss produced figures in Parian ware, some of them modelled by a craftsman called

Gallimore, who came from the Irish factory at Belleek. Other products of the factory were classical figures, vases, ear-rings, brooches, and 'jewelled' porcelain sometimes considered to be superior to that produced at the Sèvres factory.

Gothic. The artistic style of the high Middle Ages, and in architecture the predominant style in western Europe from c 1150 to c 1500, superseding Romanesque (qv). Its most obvious features are the rib vault, the flying buttress, and the pointed arch. The pointed arch was derived from Middle Eastern Islamic architecture, and was occasionally used in Romanesque buildings; the important characteristic of Gothic was the fusion of the three elements mentioned above. Advances in vaulting and buttressing, in conjunction with the pointed arch – a more flexible form than the typical Romanesque round arch – made possible buildings of unprecedented height. They also made thick load-bearing walls unnecessary, so that large areas of window space could be filled with stained

glass, and the building flooded with light. Generally speaking, decoration became increasingly elaborate over the centuries, a particular feature being amazingly elaborate and fluid stone tracery.

Gothic originated in France. The Abbey of St Denis, near Paris, is usually considered the first true Gothic building (1144), followed in short order by the cathedral of Notre-Dame (from 1163). The great cathedrals of Chartres and Reims represent the culmination of the whole style. In England, some features of Gothic were anticipated at Durham Cathedral in the early twelfth century. England became the other major centre of Gothic, developing through Early English and Decorated to Perpendicular (qqv). Although largely superseded by Baroque and Palladian styles, Gothic never died out, and the English 'gothick' and Gothic revival (qv) had a European influence in the nineteenth century. Outside France and England, Gothic was mainly inspired by French examples, eg at Cologne and Strasbourg in Germany, and

Salisbury Cathedral, Wiltshire, 1220-1260

Siena Cathedral from the south-west, 1226-1380

The south transept of Westminster Abbey, 1245-66

Burgos, Toledo, and León in Spain. In the late Middle Ages, national styles did develop in these countries, and the hall church (qv) was a distinctive German contribution to Gothic. In Italy, where the classical tradition was most persistent, Gothic never became predominant, though Siena Cathedral is a great example of the style; and it was in Italy that the Renaissance gave birth to a version of Roman architecture that spread all over Europe in place of Gothic.

By the seventeenth century this great medieval architecture had become so despised that it was dismissed as 'Gothic' – that is, the barbarous architecture of the Goths, who were erroneously credited with the destruction of Roman architecture. Despite the reinstatement of the style, the name has stuck, though its pejorative connotations are forgotten.

See also the articles on the various national architectures.

Gothick, a fanciful aspect of the Gothic revival (qv), should logically be dealt with under the same heading. What started as a lighthearted and fanciful revival ('gothick') gradually became debased, and then, after a period of disfavour, burst once again into full flower (the Gothic revival) in different, far heavier forms and for very different reasons.

Gothic detail has had a continuing fascination for English artists, topographical draughtsmen, and dilettanti. Even after

true Gothic had been displaced from the architectural canon by Renaissance classicism, Gothic buildings were still being built; but they were isolated examples of deliberately anachronistic intent, and made no impact on the dominant classical-Palladian dogma.

In the middle years of the eighteenth century, however, a group of dilettante scholars, poets, architects, landscape gardeners, and other admirers of 'the picturesque' began to turn back to the Gothic style. To them it was redolent of romance, mystery, and pleasing gloom.

The self-conscious, self-indulgent melancholy induced by the consideration of sham ruins and mock-medievalism in all forms caused a revival of Gothic – with differences.

The most dedicated of the dilettanti was Horace Walpole, who, between 1750 and his death in 1797, enlarged and transformed Strawberry Hill, his villa at Twickenham, into 'a little gothick castle.' By the time he had put the finishing touch to his house by adding a gothic tower, Strawberry Hill had become one of the landmarks in the history of the English house. For, from the superficial and affected experiments of Walpole, many of the heavy-handed excesses of the High Victorian Gothic revival of a hundred years later can be traced.

The antiquarian enthusiasm of Walpole, his architect Richard Bentley, and a small group of admiring friends led to a revival of interest in Gothic among cabinetmakers and architects from Chippendale to Wyatt. All were willing to oblige with highly individual renderings of the Gothic manner, few scholarly, some tortuous, all ingenious.

Chippendale's pattern-book, *The Gentleman and Cabinet-Maker's Director*, first published in 1754, included Gothic designs for chairs and bookcases, and even organs. So too did Ince and Mayhew's *Universal System of Household Furniture*, published in 1762.

Gothick – the eighteenth-century spelling, satisfyingly appropriate for this fanciful adaptation of the medieval style – had a vigorous if fairly short-lived heyday. By the third edition of Chippendale's work, published in 1762, the allusions to Gothick were already being toned down, although the engravings were retained. The style retained its hold over cabinetmakers and decorators until the 1780s, and then, after a decline, experienced

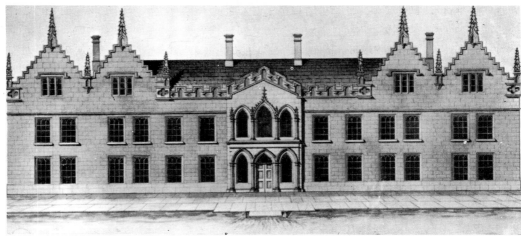

Casewick House, Lincolnshire, rebuilt in 1621 and redesigned in the Gothick style by William Legg, 1785

a fanciful but debased swan-song in the Regency. This was particularly evident in architecture, for mock-battlements and quatrefoil windows suited the Regency mood of eclectic extravagance; hence the prevalence of gothick gatehouses and lodges.

Gothick, despite its excess, was frequently charming. In mock castles (especially in Ireland), country villas, and rectories, the gothick manner – with its ogee curves, pointed Venetian windows, and multifarious forms of castellation – offered wide

decorative scope.

In the nineteenth century, under the combined influences of Sir Walter Scott's novels and Ruskin's moralizing approach to the arts, Gothic was to become heavier and far less fanciful. This second Gothic Revival is one of

Strawberry Hill, Twickenham redesigned by Horace Walpole, 1748–77

A thirteenth-century style manor house with Gothick tracery windows

A small Gothic Revival house in Somerset, c 1820–30

A pair of country-made Gothick chairs, c 1840

A Gothick carved mahogany china-cabinet on stand, 1760–70

the least appealing forms of Victorian architecture in Europe and America. Many churches were built; and a superabundance of villas with pointed doors and windows, but little else to recall the glory of pure Gothic or the fantasies of affected gothick. See also **English architecture.**

Gouge. The woodworker's basic tool, also used by wood-carvers. It consists of a steel, straight or curved, fitted into a simple wooden handle. Gouges are of various sizes and shapes. Where necessary, the gouge is struck with a mallet, but in more exacting carving it can be manipulated with extreme delicacy.

Gougework is a term applied to the mainly repetitive patterns carved by early craftsmen.

Gouthière, Pierre (1740–1806). One of the most renowned of French artist-craftsmen in metals. He worked chiefly in bronze and his incomparable metal fitments were in great demand by eighteenth-century French *ébénistes.*

Graffito, Sgraffito. Italian word meaning 'scribbling' or 'scratching.' Graffiti – casual drawings and writings on buildings – survive in great numbers from ancient times; those of Pompeii are well known, but there are also many from Egypt and Rome.

Sgraffito is a decorative technique which involves scratching through one layer (eg of stucco) so that a design appears in the different material and or colour of the layer beneath. For sgraffito in pottery, see **Slipware.**

Grainger, Richard (1798-1861). British speculative builder. Grainger was the son of a harbour porter at Newcastle-upon-Tyne, and made an enormous fortune as a result of his work in the development of Newcastle. He was remarkable – almost unique – in restricting his interests to building. He made no pretensions, yet he must have been a man of uncommon sagacity and foresight, for he commissioned designs which transformed Newcastle from a comparatively small Northern coaling port into a great industrial seaport. For most of his architectural plans and elevations Grainger commissioned John Dobson, and it is to their imagination and energy that the city owes much of its still-evident civic grandeur.

Graining. The term applied to painting on wood that simulates the natural grain of various timbers. Rosewood was most frequently imitated; followed by walnut and maplewood. Graining has a long history, dating from ancient Egypt. Its heyday was the Regency era, when much beech furniture was made to look like rosewood. The results were often charming and accurate. Graining was used on both chairs and cabinet furniture, mainly in order to make a relatively cheap wood appear expensive, but on occasions the figuring of rosewood and walnut was heightened by partial graining.

Grandmother clock. A small long-case clock (qv).

Grand Rapids furniture. Grand Rapids, Michigan, was one of the first major American centres for the production of machine-made furniture. Many furniture factories have operated there since the second half of the nineteenth century, although after World War II many firms moved to the South. The term 'Grand Rapids' suggests popularly priced, mass-produced furniture.

Grange. A term frequently applied to larger Victorian houses; a literary expression of the self-conscious medievalism of the period. The word was originally used of the remote farms attached to medieval monasteries.

Granite. One of the most valuable and durable of all stone formations used in building. Granite is a grey or pinkish grey rock of quartz, felspar, mica, and other constituents; its crystalline composition causes the surface to glint in sunlight or after rain.

Granite can be worked in blocks of considerable size, a fact which, allied with its immense durability, has made it a valued stone for piers, breakwaters, and other rugged structures. A variant, Shap Granite, is widely used as an ornamental stone.

A Victorian Gothic house, c 1860

Eldon Square, Newcastle-upon-Tyne, designed by John Dobson, and built by Richard Grainger, 1825-31

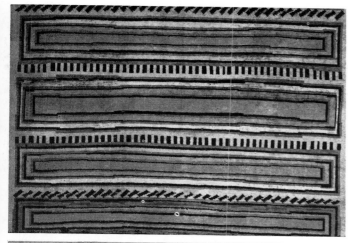

Above: detail of a carpet. Below: painted saving box, and pencil or glove box. Both by Duncan Grant for Omega Workshops, c 1914

Viola Gråsten and one of her fabric designs

taking inscriptional cutting and presenting a handsome weather-proof façade.

Grant, Duncan (*b* 1885). British artist. Grant and Vanessa Bell established a free-flowing colour-ful decorative manner which had considerable influence on textile and pottery design between the two World Wars. Grant was born in Rothiemurchus, Inverness-shire, and studied decoration at Westminster School of Art. After a very brief sojourn at the Slade, he took a studio in Fitzroy Square, Bloomsbury, and began to design textiles, china, and pottery.

Before World War I, Grant's work was commissioned by the Omega Workshops, organized by Roger Fry for the production

and sale of decorative and applied art for the home. Grant also designed decorative panels for the country house of St John Hutchinson, and decorated rooms for John Maynard Keynes, Leonard and Virginia Woolf, and others of the Bloomsbury Group, a famous literary-artistic coterie to which Grant himself be-longed.

Grass-paper, grasscloth. A wall-covering paper with loosely woven grass glued or stitched to it.

The Chinese were the first to use reeds and rice straw with which to make paper, about 2,000 years ago. In Europe, the first paper to be manufactured from a mixture of grass, lime tree bark, and other fibres (as opposed to the traditional cotton and linen) was in France; this was issued in 1784, in the form of a small book of poems.

Grass wallpapers are now made mostly in Japan. Some are also made in South Korea, where the raw materials are grown. Today, universally popular, they are still hand-made from grass, reeds, hemp, and even climbing plants such as honeysuckle. They are woven, sewn, or glued together by craftsmen working at home, and collected by exporters in the cities.

Gråsten, Viola (*b* 1910). Swedish textile and rug designer. She was born in Finland and trained at the College of Industrial Art, Helsinki. In 1949 she took Swedish nationality.

Grasten's designs for long-pile rugs, woven by Friends of the Finnish Handicraft, brought her to the notice of an admiring inter-national public at the Paris Exhibition of 1937, where she won a gold medal. During the war she designed for Elsa Gull-berg Ltd of Sweden, and after the war for the textile department of the Nordiska Co in Stockholm.

In 1956 she became director and pattern-designer for the textile firm of Mölnlycke, Göte-borg. Her freelance work includes designs for Tidstrand woollen mills and Kasthall carpet works. Her rug designs owe much to Finnish folk art, as do those for her printed textiles for furnishing fabrics and clothes.

Grate. A receptacle in which coal is burned, usually made of iron or steel and in an open basket form. Originally the grate was little more than a grid, fitted above the hearth and into the chimney recess.

Gradually the grate became a more decorative unit. By the early eighteenth century, steel and wrought-iron grates incor-porating columns, coats of arms, finials, and other motifs and devices, were widely used in the mansions of the wealthy.

Chippendale's *Director* of 1754 contains elaborate versions, and at Luton Hoo, Robert Adam designed grates in brass and steel that are masterpieces of delicate form and pattern.

In the small villas and terrace houses of the Regency period, the chimney-space was narrower. This led to the introduction of the hob-grate, which was in effect mass-produced, and usually made of cast-iron. Many of these hob-grates have a good deal of charm, with decorative bas-reliefs, reeding, and patterns on the side panels.

Gray, Milner (*b* 1889). English industrial and graphic designer. After training at Goldsmith's College, Gray served in World War I and set up as a graphic designer in 1921. He had con-siderable success, but gradually became more interested in pack-aging and exhibition design. This led to the formation of Design Research Unit, of which organ-ization he became joint senior partner with Misha Black (qv).

During World War II, Gray was head of the Ministry of Information's Exhibitions Branch. He was also a leading figure in establishing the Society of Industrial Artists and De-signers, of which he has twice been president.

Georgian steel dog grate, 1740

Mid-19th-century cast-iron grate

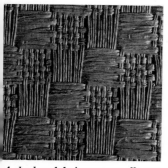

A checkered design grass wallpaper

Milner Gray

*Port and sherry decanters in blue
and ruby glass by Milner Gray*

For D R U he has specialized in exhibition and interior design, domestic and industrial equipment, plastics, ceramics, glass, and silver; and he has been responsible for the development of house-styles for many leading British companies and corporations, including British Railways, Watney Mann and. ICI Groups, Ilford Limited, and the Ministry of Technology. He designed the royal coat of arms for use at the coronation of Queen Elizabeth II.

Greek architecture. The so-called Golden Age of Greek architecture extended from about 480 to 320 BC, although a distinctively Greek architecture had begun over two centuries before 480 and lasted until the land was overrun by the Romans in 146 BC. On the other hand, Roman influence made itself felt as soon as Greece began to decline, about the time of the death of Alexander the Great (323 BC). The period from 323 until the Roman occu-pation is usually known as Graeco-Roman or Hellenistic. These five centuries established an architectural style which has left its mark on all the nations of the West, and its familiar motifs are to be seen from Leningrad to Washington DC.

Greek architecture was at all times distinguished by purity of form rather than ingenuity or technological innovation. Roman architects copied and debased Greek prototypes but they possessed technical skills far superior to those of the Greeks.

The early Greek architects based much of their structural practice upon the timber buildings. Their incurious elaboration of these timber prototypes gave to their stone and marble buildings many characteristics which are now admired, but the same fact demonstrates how timid they were in technical experiment. Thus the low pitch of the roofs on their greatest buildings, and their inability to evolve arched forms commensurate with their aesthetic ambitions, limited the range of their construction. Even the decorative elements in their architecture derived directly from techniques developed in building in timber. For example, the repeated pattern of three grooves on the Doric frieze comes from cuts made in the ends of transverse beams. The dentil motif in cornices is another legacy from timber construction. It is all the more astonishing that the simple grandeur and beauty of the more important Greek buildings is unsurpassed.

The construction of Greek temples, theatres, formal colonnades, and public buildings was carried out mainly in marble or limestone. Roofs were covered with tiles of burnt clay or with marble. The wall surfaces – even those of marble – were frequently embellished with richly coloured decorations, now vanished – but replaced by a patina of age which has greatly enriched the original materials. The finish and detailing of buildings was of an unusually high order.

The development of the Greek temple is inseparably involved with the growth of the Greek community, an increasing pressure towards more democratic rule, and the gradual evolution of the city-state. Hence buildings are free from the monolithic characteristics of Egyptian and Minoan temples, and the replacement of the inner hearth by the exterior altar allowed the Greek temple to become a community centre. This sense of the

The theatre and Temple of Apollo at Delphi, c 490 BC

The Temple of Zeus at Olympia, c 460 BC

Columns and a frieze in the Doric Order

The Erechtheum on the Acropolis, Athens, c 421–405 BC

The Ionic Temple of Niké Apteros on the Acropolis at Athens, 427 BC

community is evident in all Greek architecture, sacred and secular.

The world-famous complex of buildings on the plateau of the Acropolis in Athens epitomizes the full beauty of Greek architecture for millions of visitors. The most important buildings are the Parthenon, dedicated to Athena and built in the decade after 447 BC (though sculptures were not completed until 432); the Erechtheum, erected by aristocratic families to counteract the strength of the democratic cult of Athena – a superb synthesis with its famous caryatids of sculpture and architecture; and the small Ionic temple to Athena, built towards the end of the fifth century BC.

Delphi, to which pilgrims made their way seeking answers to their problems from the oracle,

is perhaps still more memorable, set in an appropriately majestic landscape. Here are to be seen the reconstructed remains of a circular building designed by Theodorus (its purpose is unknown), the portico built in honour of Apollo, the treasury built to celebrate the victory over the Persians at Marathon (c 490), and the Temple of Apollo, the most splendid of over 30 buildings originally built within the sacred precincts of the Apollonic section of Delphi.

Other well-known examples of Greek architecture are the earthquake-shattered Temple of Zeus at Olympia (built c 460) and the Temple of Apollo in Corinth (c 650).

Beauty of proportion and precise and beautiful decorative detail are the hallmarks of Greek architecture. The columnar forms

originating in Doris, Ionia, and Corinthos reappear time and again in Western architecture (see **Doric, Ionian, Corinthian**).

Secular Greek architecture is a less rewarding study. The domestic architecture of Athens, even in the imperialistic period under Pericles, consisted mainly of small two-storey houses, insanitarily built in narrow, cramped alleyways, many of them within sight of the Acropolis.

After the fall of the Roman Empire, Greece became a cultural backwater, although the interplay of classical Greek and Byzantine influences gave rise to some of the most pleasing of all European ecclesiastical buildings. With their red-painted flattened domes and white exteriors, the churches are simple and pic-

Corinthian capitals in the Theatre of Dionysus, Athens, 350–325 BC

An engraving of the Parthenon, Athens, 447–432 BC

The Byzantine church of Pantanassa Mystos in the Peloponnese, 1427

The church of Panaghia Kitriani, Island of Sifnos

The Byzantine church of St Theodore's in the Agora, Athens

turesque. They are to be found throughout the Greek islands.

Contemporary Greek architecture is evolving its own forms within the context of the international movement, and its architects are among the most adventurous in Europe. The best known is probably Professor Constantinos Doxiadis, who evolved the science of Ekistics, or the study of urban development and environment. Doxiadis was appointed chief town planning officer for Greater Athens in 1937, and has since held many important town-planning appointments in Greece. He has been planning adviser to various governments, including Ghana, India, and Iraq, and is responsible for the vast Eastwick development in Philadelphia, USA.

Other eminent Greek architects include Aris Konstantinidis, whose hotels on Andros and other Greek islands are among the finest buildings of their kind

A late Helladic krater, c 1375–1200 BC, found in Cyprus

in Europe, and Pericles Sakalarion, who is responsible for many projects in Athens and other cities, including the vast and imaginative Lido development outside Athens.

Greek cross. In ecclesiastical architecture this is a cross plan with four equal arms. It was used for Byzantine churches and revived during the Renaissance.

Greek key. An alternative name for the classical fret or key pattern (qv).

Greek pottery. Greek culture had its roots in the Minoan civilization of Crete, which was at its height c 1700 BC. Here art in many forms flourished. Cretan pottery was smooth unglazed earthenware, often decorated with white or red painting on a black ground. The black pigment made a protective surface covering, but not a true glaze.

Later Cretan pottery was usually painted in only one colour, red, brown, or black, on a buff body. The pigment was fired to a slight gloss, giving the impression of a glaze, though technically it was not: the ware remained porous. The decoration on this early pottery – cups, jugs, dishes – was freely drawn in the form of shells, cuttlefish, birds, animals, and even human beings.

By 1400 BC, tribes of Hellenes had moved southwards through the country we now call Greece

and had overthrown the Minoans. The pottery made in the new Mycenean culture owed much to the Minoans, but the designs became much more geometric.

Between 1000 and 700 BC, jugs, cups, wine-jars, etc, were covered in horizontal bands of strictly geometric decoration, borders of zigzag lines, checks, and the now familiar 'Greek key' pattern. Occasionally a stripe or band would contain a frieze of repetitive figures or animals drawn in a very primitive and stylized way. The colouring was brown or black, sometimes on a light ground, though more often the background was black, with buff or red painting.

The Greeks made their pottery to be used, not for decoration. The 'vase', as a purely ornamental object, is a much later conception.

By the eighth century BC Greek potters had evolved some basic forms which were well suited to the Greek way of life, and they stuck to these, with little variation, for four or five hundred years. The main objects were as follows. The *hydria*, or water-carrying pot, had a narrow neck (to avoid spilling), a bulbous body, and three handles. The *krater* was a wide-mouthed vessel for mixing. The *amphora* was used for the storage of wine. *Oinochoai* were jugs for holding oil or wine.

Greek cups were large, since the wine was drunk diluted

(about two-thirds water). They were either rather deep with a flat base (*kotylai*), or wide and shallow with pedestal bases and flat feet (*kylikes*). Horizontal handles were added to these cups because the Greeks took their meals lying on a couch, and it is easier to lift a heavy cup from a horizontal position with the thumb than with the forefinger.

Aryballoi were small ball-shaped bottles with a narrow neck and a flat disc top. They were used to hold the olive-oil

A round-mouthed jug of the geometric period, 750–700 BC

Panathenaic amphora, showing the goddess Athena, c 550 BC

Attic red figured Hydria, c 410 BC

A Corinthian aryballoi, 130–100 BC

that the Greeks used to clean themselves with (they had no soap), and were carried suspended from a string round the wrist. They are surprisingly light and delicate to handle, and though unglazed are smoother than eggshells and very pleasant to the touch.

Greek potters compensated for the softness and fragility of their material by subtly thickening the parts most likely to be chipped or broken, for example the rim round the top, and the foot. The handles were big and strong, and because they were placed exactly where they were needed, they were suited to the balance of the hand. They do not seem clumsy or an afterthought; they were, indeed, an integral, functional part of a functional piece of household equipment.

In the seventh century BC, with the expansion of the Greek Empire and trade links with Egypt, Syria, and Asia, Greek pottery underwent certain modifications. Polychrome painting was introduced and the technique of using black-painted figures with incised internal details began to be practised (the 'black-figure style'). Corinth was a centre for this form of decoration, and the factories there exported pottery all over the Mediterranean.

During the first half of the sixth century BC, Athenian potters captured the export market, and until about 400 BC made ware decorated with red figures on a black background (the 'red-figure' style). The Attic clay burned to a bright orangey red, which the Corinthian clay (deficient in iron) did not. The later Corinthian potters covered their pots with a slip containing red ochre in an attempt to hide the deficiency. Even so, by about 550 BC the output of the Corinthian potteries had declined to a mere trickle, just enough to satisfy local demands.

After the geometric decorations of the ninth to eighth century BC, seventh- to sixth-century BC Corinthian decorations showed Eastern influences, lotus-buds and other Egyptian and Assyrian motifs appearing in the designs. The Corinthian painters used animal and human forms on their black-figure vases.

This technique was also used for the vases filled with oil that were given as prizes in the Panathenaic Games (late sixth century to late fourth century BC). These vases were decorated on one side with a figure of Athena carrying a shield, and on the other with figures of athletes taking part in various sports.

Most of the Athenian pottery was decorated by the red-figure technique. The subjects were many and varied: gods and goddesses disporting themselves, horses, winged griffins (qv), satyrs and maenads, and other mythological creatures. Hunting and warlike subjects were painted as well as more peaceful occupations such as music-making and dancing. Erotic subjects were also popular.

The painting was often very

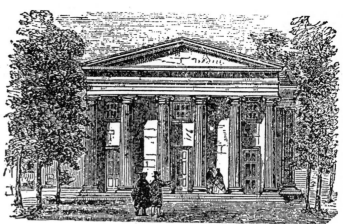

Downing College, Cambridge, after designs by Wilkins, 1806–11

The main gate of Chester Castle, by Thomas Harrison, 1793–1820

detailed and precise, so that it is possible to see exactly what kind of clothes the figures wore and how they did their hair. Many of the Attic vases are signed, so that even the names of the painters have come down to us.

Athens was defeated by Sparta in 404 BC. It must have been a time of great upheaval, and the arts suffered. Some of the Greek potters fled to Italy, but their later work is of little interest.

Greek revival. An architectural movement which developed within the larger framework of the classical revival of the late eighteenth and early nineteenth centuries. A variety of influences contributed to the Greek revival, most of them arising from the desire of aristocrats and architects to make the Grand Tour in order to study the buildings of antiquity. Many books were published as a result of such travels. *The Antiquities of Athens* (1762), by James ('Athenian') Stuart and Nicholas Revett, was of particular importance in publicizing specifically Greek styles, as opposed to the Roman and Renaissance which represented 'classicism' for most people.

The Greek revival made only slow headway until after 1790, but the publication of two additional volumes of *The Antiquities of Athens* in 1789 and 1795, and the arrival of the Elgin Marbles in England in 1801, intensified interest in Greek architecture. Another factor was the travels of such architects as Samuel Pepys Cockerell, Robert Smirke, and William Wilkins. As a result many new large buildings in both western Europe and America began to show Greek revival influences. A few examples are Chester Castle, designed by Thomas Harrison and built between 1793 and 1820; Downing College (1806–11), designed by Wilkins; the demolished Greek Doric Nelson Column in Dublin (1808–9), also by Wilkins; and Covent Garden Theatre (1808–9), designed by Robert Smirke. In America one of the most notable examples is Andalusia,' (in Bucks county, Pennsylvania) designed by Thomas V Walter.

These influences also affected domestic architecture. Contributory factors were the growing use of slate for roofing, which allowed for a lower pitch of roof, as in Greek temple construction, and the use of stucco for exterior walls, which enabled Greek decorative motifs to be inexpensively incised or added to friezes and pilasters.

Green Belt. A method of controlling urban development: a limit is placed upon building and a ring of rural or semi-rural land deliberately maintained around the built-up area. The notion is scarcely as modern as is often believed, for such plans were used in the late sixteenth century for the curtailment of metropolitan growth.

The modern interpretation of the phrase derives from the theories of Ebenezer Howard (qv) in the early years of this century. This was in connection with Howard's championship of garden city developments, put into practice at Letchworth and Welwyn in Hertfordshire.

In Britain the Green Belt idea received further authoritative backing in the Greater London Plan, compiled by Sir Patrick Abercrombie and J H Forshaw in 1944. But during recent years, the Green Belt theory and practice has been subjected to severe criticism, most forcefully in Dr Peter Hall's book, *London 2000*, and in sections of the South East Development Plan.

See **Garden city.**

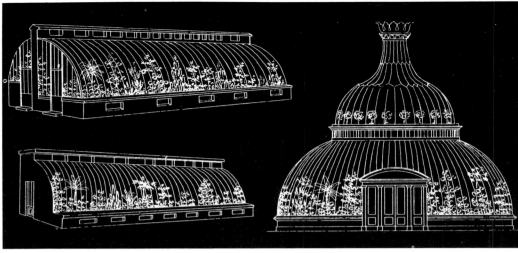

Three designs for greenhouses from M Boitard's 'L'art de Composer et Décorer les Jardins', c 1800

Greenhouse. There have been small, partly glazed houses in Britain since the sixteenth century. They were originally for the overwintering of orange trees, the much-prized foreign 'greens' – for evergreens – which were probably first grown in the reign of Elizabeth I. These greens gave them their name.

During the seventeenth century, thanks to French influence, orange-houses became elegant, architect-designed objects, with the new and elegant name of orangeries. Orangeries were built by many distinguished architects until early in the nineteenth century. Then the great variety of tender foreign plants being imported, and new techniques of glazing, made the old formal orange-house (which inevitably had a high proportion of wood and masonry to glass) obsolete.

The most remarkable developments in greenhouse construction as we know it were sparked off by the vast, glass-walled, glass-roofed Serres des Jardins du Musée d'Histoire Naturelle, built by Rouhault Fils in Brussels. The idea was taken up by the sixth Duke of Devonshire, and his gardener Joseph Paxton, at Chatsworth in Derbyshire. Paxton's *Magazine of Botany* (1834) showed glasshouse constructions of wood, glass, and iron. Yet these were the merest outlines of what were to come: with Decimus Burton as architectural consultant, Paxton built the vast curvilinear Great Conservatory (1836–41), 277 ft long, 123 ft wide, and 67 ft high. The building was heated by eight boilers, fed by fuel carried on a small tramway, and supplied hot water for seven miles of four-inch iron piping.

Decimus Burton, in collaboration with the Dublin iron-founder Richard Turner, was also engaged in erecting vast greenhouse structures based on Paxton's work at Chatsworth. Burton's greatest achievement was the Palm House at Kew.

Greenhouses have ceased to be the perquisite of the rich, and many firms now supply low-priced, prefabricated greenhouses.

Greenway, Francis Howard (1777–1837). British architect. Greenway was the son of a Gloucestershire mason, and his life-story is strange and chequered. Greenway was a pupil of John Nash in Carmarthen before setting up in business in Bristol with two older brothers. In the manner of the time, they engaged in speculative building. Greenway designed the hotel and assembly rooms at Clifton, but then he and both of his brothers became involved in bankruptcy

The Greenhouse at Chatsworth, from Paxton's 'Magazine of Botany'

The Palm House, Kew Gardens, designed by Decimus Burton, 1845

St James's Church, Sydney, designed by Greenway as a courthouse

St Luke's Liverpool, New South Wales, by Greenway, 1818–25

proceedings.

Greenway was accused of forgery, pleaded guilty, and in 1812 was sentenced to be hanged. The sentence was commuted to transportation for life, and Greenway arrived in Australia as a convict in 1814. There he came under the patronage of Governor Macquarie, who was then engaged in ambitious building plans for the development of the colony. Macquarie had already requested the dispatch of a competent architect from England, and when Greenway arrived sensibly armed with letters of introduction, he was able to start work almost immediately on the governor's plans for the city of Sydney.

Greenway at first worked without fees of any kind, but he quickly made himself indispensable, and was soon fairly prosperous. He was appointed government architect in 1816, and during the following year prepared a plan for the future development of Sydney. He was responsible for what are now among the most historic, handsome, and carefully preserved buildings in the city, including the Hyde Park Barracks, begun in 1817 and finished in 1819 (for which he received an absolute pardon); St James's Church; St Matthew's (at Windsor, New South Wales); St Luke's (at Liverpool, New South Wales); the Court House, Sydney, the Macquarie Tower, and the stables for Government House, also in Sydney.

Greenway's buildings are characterized by a bold and majestic simplicity, and are among the most forthright expressions of the Georgian canon to be found in the Commonwealth. Thanks to the work of the National Trust of Australia, their merits have been recognized and steps taken to preserve them. Greenway's last years were clouded by setbacks. He was dismissed in 1819, and again went bankrupt in 1824. He died in obscurity in Australia.

Griffin, griffon, gryphon. One of the most ancient of all grotesque devices, deriving from the mythological bestiary. The griffin has the head, wings, and forelegs of an eagle, and the rear quarters of a lion (or sometimes a serpent). The head was frequently used on its own in architectural and heraldic decoration, and in this form is distinguished from the more mundane eagle by emphatically pointed ears and a pronounced tuft beneath the beak.

The griffin appeared in aristocratic quarterings for centuries; but was most widely employed as a decorative motif during the late Italian Renaissance. It was resuscitated by Adam and his contemporaries, and was also widely used as a decorative device in the Empire and Regency styles, when griffin supports were particularly popular for console tables, side-tables, and sideboards.

Grille. A latticed screen, used as a decorative protection for windows, cabinets, fanlights, and other openings. Wrought-iron grilles for window-openings were used in the seventeenth century, but few have survived. In the eighteenth century, grilles were widely used as decorative additions to glazed fanlights, usually in wrought-iron, cast-iron, or for special purposes, lead.

In cabinetmaking brass grilles were employed for the fronts of bookcases and glass cabinets; they were usually of a simple criss-cross design and were especially popular during the late eighteenth century and the Regency period. Occasionally

A gilt chair with griffin arm supports, c 1805

A grisaille painting in fresco by Giovanni Battista Tiepolo, 1755–60

more complex interwoven designs were used.

Grisaille. A form of decorative painting in tones of grey, widely used for decorative panels in late eighteenth-century interiors. Many famous Italian decorative painters accepted the challenge to make these experiments in monotone, including painters with such widely different techniques as Tiepolo and Guardi. Grisailles were carried out in oils, gouaches, and tempera.

Groag, Jacqueline (*b* 1903). Designer of textiles, wallpapers, carpets, and plastics. Born in Prague, she later lived in Vienna, and studied at the Academy of Applied Art. She married the Austrian architect Jacques Groag, and moved with him to Paris and then to London.

She has consistently and ingeniously exploited the decorative possibilities of simple geometric motifs, frequently in highly complex designs. Influences on her include the Bauhaus, the work of Paul Klee, and the Wiener Werkstätte.

At the Paris Exhibition of 1937 she gained a gold medal, and she has exhibited in Milan, Zurich, and New York, as well as in London.

Groin, groined vault. A term used to denote the arris (sharp edge) formed by the intersection of two curved sections in a vault. Ribs following this line are known as groin ribs.

The groined or cross vault is formed by the intersection of two tunnel vaults.

Gropius, Walter (1883–1969). German-American architect. Gropius has been one of the most

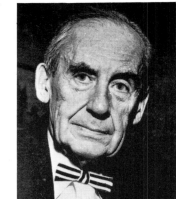

Walter Gropius

influential twentieth-century architects, though he has perhaps exerted this influence more through his teaching than his buildings.

He was born in Berlin, the son of an architect and the great-nephew of the eminent Berlin architect Martin Gropius (1824–80), who was also head of the School of Arts and Crafts in Berlin. Walter Gropius was

Jacqueline Groag and her design for laminated plastic, 1963

The glass-walled staircase by Gropius and Meyer, Cologne, 1914

trained in Munich and later in Berlin, where he became one of several eminent architects to pass through the drawing-offices of Peter Behrens.

During his three years in Behrens' office, Gropius prepared plans for standardizing, mass-producing, and financing small houses, a subject which remained a lifelong interest. He set up on his own in 1910, and in 1911 came into prominence with an unusually advanced steel and glass design (worked out in collaboration with Adolf Meyer) for the Fagus factory at Alfeld an der Leine.

The lightness and structural novelty of this building (which has been described by Professor Pevsner as 'the fulfilment of the spirit of today') were repeated in the designs prepared by the two architects in 1914 for a model factory for the Deutscher Werkbund Exhibition at Cologne. With its spiral staircases enclosed within two glazed end-towers, and with its general effect of weightlessness and symmetry, this building made a great impression, and would probably have been even more influential had war not engulfed Europe. In the meantime, Gropius had also established a reputation as an industrial designer, having designed various domestic fitments and advised on locomotive and automobile body design.

During the war years Gropius was invited by the Grand Duke of Saxe-Weimar to prepare plans for reorganizing the Weimar Art Schools. As a result the Bauhaus (qv) was founded in 1919 with Gropius as director. He held this position until 1928. During the years of his directorship Gropius revolutionized the teaching of industrial design in Germany. Many of the practical teaching

The Assembly Hall, Village College, Impington, Cambridgeshire, by Walter Gropius and Maxwell Fry, 1936

methods now employed throughout the world were Bauhaus innovations, especially the procedures which encouraged students to design prototypes which were suitable for mass-production and might engage the interest of manufacturers.

Gropius had continued his architectural practice (notably with his designs for the school buildings at Dessau in 1925–6), for he believed that the instructors themselves must be involved in current technological problems. But in 1928 he resigned his directorship of the school to give all his time to his practice. He was one of the chief co-ordinators for a large housing development at Karlsruhe (1927–8), and also for one at Siemensstadt near Berlin, a complex which influenced many European housing developments during the inter-war years.

The advent of Nazism caused Gropius to leave Germany, and he settled for a time in England. There he worked with Maxwell Fry, and their partnership was responsible for the remarkable Impington Village College buildings in Cambridgeshire. In 1937

Gropius moved on to the USA, taking up the professorship of architecture at Harvard.

He continued his architectural work in partnership with Marcel Breuer, a former pupil and master at the Bauhaus. The partnership, which lasted until 1941, was responsible for a number of private houses, exhibition buildings, and a housing development near Pittsburgh.

Gropius had long proclaimed his belief that architecture was essentially a team effort, and his successful partnerships with Meyer, Fry, and Breuer had shown his capacity to work with other architects. In 1945 he took a new step forward by entering into partnership with seven younger architects, the group being called The Architects' Collaborative.

TAC, as it was soon known, has a considerable number of architectural achievements to its credit, including the Harvard University Graduate Center (1949–50) and the McCormick Building (1953). It also built a number of private residences, for to the end of his life Gropius consistently demonstrated his

interest in smaller units of domestic architecture as well as in larger housing developments.

Gros point. A form of coarse stitch much employed by French needle-workers for the coverings of chairs and settees.

Grotesque. A decorative mask or figure of a mythological beast or a human. Regency and Empire decorators were greatly addicted to the use of a wide range of grotesques from ancient legendary sources on walls and furniture.

Grotto. A favoured ornament for parks and gardens in the eighteenth and early nineteenth century. Grottoes usually consisted of caves below ground or of summer-houses above ground; those above ground were always made to look as subterranean as possible, being built of glass, roots, or slag, and decorated with shells, rock-crystal, etc.

Grottoes were built as part of the reaction against the formal garden. For the generation of Pope and Kent the perfect garden was no longer an en-

House in Old Church Street, Chelsea, designed by Walter Gropius, 1936

An artificial grotto summer-house built of clinker and shells

closure with gravel walks and geometrical flowerbeds, but a landscape, a park, in which everything appeared as natural as possible. Part of the fantasy was that temples, ruins, and grottoes 'just happened' to be in exactly the right places.

Grottoes were popular with the improvers of parks partly because of their associations. Centaurs and satyrs might have lived there in ancient times; later, they might have given refuge to a hermit. They were thus well suited to the tastes of imaginative readers of Virgil and Horace – and the gothick horror novels.

Grottoes at Stourhead and at Goldeney, Bristol, have figures of Neptune and nymphs. Those at Pontypool and Burley are fitted up as habitations for hermits. Indeed, some grottoes were lived in by paid hermits, employed to grow their beards and sell their dried-pea beads for the wonderment of visitors.

An enduring appeal of grottoes was their materials. They provided a genteel occupation for unemployed aristocrats, who could (and did) spend weeks sticking shells and pebbles into damp plaster, making colourful patterns. Pope had one of the earliest grottoes, at Twickenham, and friends of his at Cheddar shot down stalactites for him with their blunderbusses.

Grottoes continued to be popular long after other eighteenth-century fads had faded. A good many still exist, but most have been slowly picked to pieces.

Grouped columns. Three or four columns or sections of columns joined around a central axis.

Grouped columns on a corbel-head

Grumbold, Robert (1639–1720). The best known of a family of Northamptonshire masons. Grumbold was one of the most important figures in the architectural development of the university buildings at Cambridge between 1670 and his death.

His first contribution was made, in partnership with another mason, with work on Clare Hall, starting in 1669; in 1716 he was rebuilding the fountain at Trinity College. Between those dates he had come under the influence of Wren and Hawksmoor, and had rapidly progressed from craftsman to acknowledged architect. As early as 1682 he designed (and later built) the hall and buttery additions to Clare Hall.

His later designs include a projected design for a new chapel for St John's College, and a stone bridge for the same college, finished in 1712. He also probably designed the chapel of St Catherine's Hall as well as other buildings for Clare Hall, Peterhouse, and the Civil Law School.

Guarini, Guarino (1624–83). Italian architect, mathematician, philosopher, and priest. Guarini was born in Modena, and in his mid-teens travelled to Rome as a novitiate in the Theatine Order. He returned to his native city in 1647 and, after ordination, took up a lectureship in philosophy. In common with other gifted divines of his time, he showed an early interest in architecture, and designed a church and palace in Messina, neither of which is now standing. In 1662 he travelled to Paris, where his versatility was displayed by designs for Sainte Anne la Royale (1662; destroyed in 1823) and theological teachings and writings, notably the *Placita Philosophica* (Paris, 1665).

Most of Guarini's major works are in Turin, where he was installed as architectural adviser to Carlo Emanuele II of Savoy. His ecclesiastical works include S Sidone (1667–90) and S Lorenzo (1668–87), his secular buildings the Collegio dei Nobili (1678) and Palazzo Carignano (1679).

Guarini's theory and practice, documented in his treatise *Architettara Civile*, greatly influenced the late Baroque architects of southern Germany and Austria. Guarini uses forms – such as the pendentive and pilaster – for visual effects in which their actual function is totally disregarded or deliberately flouted.

The Fountain, Trinity College, Cambridge, by Robert Grumbold, 1716

The cupola of S Lorenzo, Turin, by Guarino Guarini, 1668–87; for interior see 'B' frontispiece

Capella della SS Sidone, Turin by Guarini, 1667–90

An example of a guilloche moulding of raised and incised ornament

Wedgwood Coronation Mug designed by Richard Guyatt

A good example of Guarini's style is the chapel of the Cathedral of SS Sidone. The chapel, which reputedly shelters the relic of the Holy Shroud, was begun by Amedeo di Castellamante in 1655. Guarini took over in 1667, and significantly changed his predecessor's plan, particularly in his creation of spatial effects. These are seen at their most dramatic in the ribbing of the dome, in which an emphatic diminution of scale makes it seem much higher than it actually is. Guarini specialized in these effects in the domes of other churches he designed, notably S Lorenzo, and he was also a master of simulated effects of space and depth in his treatment of interior walls and ceilings.

Gubbio. An Italian town in the duchy of Urbino, where Giorgio Andreoli made his famous majolica from *c* 1500 to 1541. He made earthenware plates and dishes, and other large and important pieces, which were richly ornamented with lustrous coloured metallic glazes, notably a splendid ruby. These lustred pieces from Gubbio were superior to any

other ware of a similar type being produced elsewhere.

The subjects varied from heraldic designs, trophies, and similar motifs to carefully painted pictures of the Judgement of Paris and other classical scenes. Reproductions of this ware were made in the last century by Carocci Fabbri & Co, and also by the Marchese Ginori's factory at Doccia, near Florence.

Guéridon. In France this term was first applied to lamp-stands during the reign of Louis XIV. In the eighteenth century the term took on the additional meaning of a small circular tea-table, the *table en guéridon*.

In Britain the term guéridon is more commonly applied to a specialised form of lamp-stand: the circular tray held by an ebonised negro with gilt decoration, introduced in the sixteenth century. Often called Moors or Blackamoors (qv), these were popular until the late nineteenth century.

Guilloche. A decorative motif deriving from continuous scroll patterns. It was used as an ornamental device for friezes in classical architecture, and basically consists of two (occasionally more) bands twisted one within the other. The spaces thus created were normally filled with a simple rose pattern or, later, with a raised semi-sphere.

The motif was used in furniture-making from the middle of the sixteenth century, and was particularly popular in the Regency era. In Victorian furniture, simplified guilloche mould-

ings in wood and metal were frequently used.

Guinea pit or **guinea hole.** One of the recesses carved in eighteenth-century card-tables to hold coins during play. The corner depressions are usually for candlesticks.

Guttae (Latin, 'drops'). The row of small drops below the triglyphs on a Doric entablature.

Gutter. A slightly sloping channel, formerly constructed of lead but nowadays mostly of zinc, which is used to collect and dispose of rainwater. Until the middle of the eighteenth century, gutters were normally made of lead, and were incorporated within the cornices. In the Regency period the gutter was formed within the overhanging eaves. In houses or terraces of houses, the gutter between two pitched roofs (known as the valley gutter) conveys rainwater to the drainpipe.

Guyatt, Richard (*b* 1914). British graphic designer. Guyatt was born in Spain, but was educated at Charterhouse. After leaving school he worked in an advertising agency, and as a freelance designer in London and Paris.

After serving in the war he became an exhibition designer, and helped to start Cockade Ltd with Sir Stephen Tallents. He was co-designer, with Robert Goodden and Dick Russell, of the Lion and Unicorn Pavilion at the Festival of Britain in 1951.

In 1948 Guyatt was appointed

professor of graphic design at the Royal College of Art. He has also been consultant to Wedgwood, and is a member of the Post Office Stamp Advisory Committee and the Bank of England Design Committee, and continues with his freelance practice as a designer.

Gwynn, John (*d* 1786). British architect. Gwynn was born in Shrewsbury and was one of the many eighteenth-century carpenters and masons who became architects and writers. His reputation was made as the author of *Essay on Harmony as it relates chiefly to Situation and Building* (1734), which was followed by works on design, surveying, and other aspects of building. The last was *London and Westminster Improved* (1766), a book of remarkable foresight to which Gwynn's friend, Dr Johnson, contributed a dedication to the king.

As an architect, Gwynn is chiefly remembered for bridges. After an unsuccessful submission in the 1759 competition for Blackfriars Bridge, Gwynn designed the English Bridge at Shrewsbury (1769–74, demolished 1925); the bridge at Worcester (1771–80); and Magdalen Bridge (1772–82) at Oxford, where he was surveyor. In that capacity he designed the new Markets (1773–4) and the Workhouse. He died at Worcester.

Three Graces, Gubbio plate, 1525

Magdalen Bridge, Oxford, designed by John Gwynn, 1772–82

John Gwynn by Zoffany

Ha-ha. A peculiarly English contribution to the history and development of garden design. The ha-ha is a form of sunken trench or ditch with a wall or fence in its depths. This allowed cattle and sheep to come right up to the garden but not inside it. They thus formed part of the vista, which was not spoiled by visible fences.

There are many versions of the story of how this kind of ditch came to be known as a ha-ha. The first known picture of one is an engraving in John James's *Theory and Practice of Gardening* (1712). 'At present,' he writes, 'we frequently make through views called Ah, Ah, which are openings in the walls, without grilles, to the very level of the walks, with a large and deep ditch at the foot of them . . . which surprises the eye upon coming near it and makes one cry Ah! Ah! from whence it takes its name.'

William Kent was undoubtedly responsible for popularizing the ha-ha. 'He leaped the fence, and saw that all nature was a garden,' said Horace Walpole. The full exploitation of the ha-ha was left to Lancelot (Capability) Brown, who swept away the formal garden and used ha-has to give views of aristocratic estates beyond the confines of the lawn.

Glass bowl by Hald, 1948

Hakewill, Henry (1771–1830). English architect, chiefly known for his ecclesiastical designs and for his work at Rugby School, where he was responsible for several school buildings and the chapel. He also designed a number of buildings in the Middle Temple in his capacity as architect to the Benchers.

Hakewill was the son of a painter and decorator, and studied at the Royal Academy Schools. He was a leading exponent of the Gothic manner, as in his designs for Rendlesham House, Suffolk, and Rugby. He also designed St Peter's, Eaton Square, London (1824). His original plans were used again by his son James to rebuild the church after it was gutted by fire in 1836.

Hald, Edward (*b* 1883). Swedish glass-designer; his masterly appreciation of the intrinsic qualities of glass, and the designs appropriate to it, has influenced glass design throughout the world.

Hald trained as a painter at Johan Rohde's School in Copenhagen, at the Artists' League School in Stockholm, and also with Matisse. Influenced by the current demand for improved industrial products, he began work with Orrefors glassworks in 1917. He produced many remarkable pieces of art glass in the Graal technique, developed at Orrefors between 1915–20. (The Graal technique took Emile Gallé's layering technique a stage further, melting etched, cut, or engraved patterns into the glass.) Hald's prolific and original work for Orrefors helped to establish a world-wide reputation for Swedish glass. He was managing director of the factory from 1933 to 1944. He has also done ceramic designs for Karls-

Rugby School, Warwickshire, designed by Henry Hakewill, 1809

St Peter's, Eaton Square, London, by Hakewill, first built 1824–7

Ha-Ha. *Capability Brown laid out the curving ha-ha, dividing lawn from park, at Petworth House, Sussex, 1753–63*

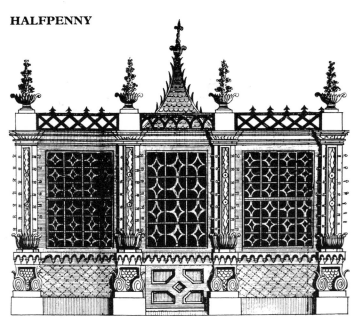

'A Green House in the Chinese Taste', designed by Halfpenny, 1750

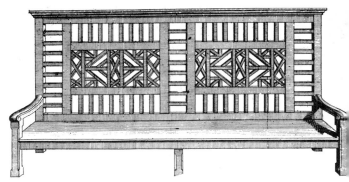

A 'Garden Seat in the Chinese Taste', 1750

Window design by Halfpenny

krona and Rörstrand, and his work is represented in museums in Sweden, Norway, Denmark, New York, Paris, and London.

In 1925 he won the Grand Prix in Paris, and since then he has won many awards.

Halfpenny, William (d 1755). English architect and author of

architectural pattern-books. Halfpenny's origins and early career are obscure, but his first published drawings suggest that he moved to Bristol from Richmond in Surrey (where he apparently worked as both gardener and carpenter).

Halfpenny prepared designs for Bristol Exchange and Infirm-

ary, but neither was accepted. The Coopers' Hall is certainly to Halfpenny's designs, and so may be the Assembly Rooms.

His wider reputation rests on his pattern-books. He was a prolific writer and publisher, from his earliest *Magnum in Parvo, or the Marrow of Architecture* (1722) to *The Country Gentleman's Pocket Companion and Builder's Assistant*, written with his son John and published in 1753.

Halfpenny is chiefly known for designs in the Chinese taste, many of which have a fanciful charm, and for less successful attempts to publicize a highly personal version of 'gothick.'

Holy Trinity Church, Leeds, by William Halfpenny, 1722–7

The Coopers' Hall, King Street, Bristol, by Halfpenny, 1743–4

The half-timbered White Horse Inn in Kallstadt, Germany

Timber patterns on the gatehouse at Stokesay Castle, Shropshire

Half-timbering. A form of framework used in the construction of dwellings in which the wall timbers were widely spaced. Such half-timbered buildings had more or less rectangular framework, with few if any diagonal braces. The intervening spaces were filled with wattle-and-daub, rubble, brick, stone, or any handy material suitable for infilling. The resulting construction, half timber and half infilling, gave rise to the term.

Hall. A term whose meaning has gradually changed. The early hall was the main and often the only room within the keep of early fortified manor-houses. Such halls had open roofs and were the core of the house, with sleeping chamber(s) at one end, and kitchen and buttery at the other. As England became wealthier, the hall developed into an apartment of increasing comfort and splendour. The central hall remained the focal point of larger houses until the sixteenth century.

The spread of Renaissance ideas changed the plans of houses. The hall gradually became an ante-chamber or entrance-room (complete with

The Marble Hall at Weston Park, Staffordshire, 1898

The hall of a small house

A walnut hall chair, George I

staircase to the upper chambers) leading to the principal ground floor apartments of the house.

Hall chair. An uncomfortable all-wood chair introduced at the beginning of the eighteenth century. These chairs were placed in halls and corridors, where they were used by servants and strangers. They were generally carved or painted in a formal style; many owners had their coats of arms painted on the backs.

Hall church. An airy church in which the nave and aisles are of equal or approximately equal height.

Hall cupboard. An oak cupboard in two stages, the upper being less tall and slightly recessed, so that there was a narrow shelf in front. At the top was a projecting cornice resting upon bulbous supports at the sides; these became progressively lighter, and finally became pendant knobs. The hall cupboard was originally called a cupboard or a press (a name still used). The finest examples were made in the first half of the seventeenth century. Walnut and japanned cabinets then became more popular, and hall cupboards were found only in poorer households, and in the provinces, where they continued to be made until the early eighteenth century.

Hallett, William (1707–81). One of the most successful Georgian cabinetmakers, with workshops in Newport Street, and later in St Martin's Lane, next to the workshops of William Vile, the court cabinetmaker. There is reason to believe that Hallett had some business connection with Vile.

Hallett was responsible for some of the furniture at Holkham, and had a wealthy clientèle. Even the hard-to-please Horace Walpole was moved to high

Hallmarks on a silver tankard by John Elston, Exeter, 1706. L to r. Elston's mark, Britannia silver marks, Exeter's castle, date letter

commendation of Hallett's work.

Halling, Else (b 1899). Norwegian weaver and textile designer whose work probably helped to improve standards in Norwegian weaving more than that of any other designer of her generation.

Halling trained at the state SCIA and Frank Stoltenberg's weaving school, and afterwards taught and ran weaving schools at Trondheim and in Oslo. In 1951 she became the director of the Norsk Billedvev tapestry studio, and wove a number of large tapestries after cartoons by artists. Her study of old Norwegian fabrics, and her concern with yarn and colour, have revived this old skill and brought it into the modern craft tradition.

Hallmarks. The hallmarking system was established in order to protect the goldsmiths' trade, and to ensure that the buyers of precious objects were not cheated. It is one of the oldest forms of consumer protection and is an invaluable guide to the collector of old silver, enabling him to date a piece of silver with complete accuracy.

Pure silver in its natural state is too soft to be worked without the use of an alloy to give it additional strength. One of the most important reasons for the development of the hallmarking system was to ensure that the goldsmith was using the correct amount of alloy. In England this amount was regulated as early as 1238, when the standard was established as being that of the coinage (the Sterling standard, qv). Every troy pound was to contain 11 ounces 2 pennyweights of pure silver and 18 pennyweights of alloy. The standard was raised from 1697 to 1720, and lowered between 1542 and 1560, and from 1920 onwards.

The English hallmarking system dates from 1300. The wardens of the London goldsmiths were ordered to mark all plate with a leopard's head before it left the goldsmith's hands. This mark is still used for **London** plate, the only period

when its use lapsed being from 1697 to 1720, when the standard was raised.

In 1363 there was a further regulation of the trade. All gold smiths were required to use mark known to those surveying their work. These were original based on the medieval shop sign used by particular goldsmith Such marks continued to b employed until the late seven teenth century, and were use in conjunction with letters unt the eighteenth century. Initial were also in evidence at an earl date (certainly before the la fifteenth century), and in 169 the maker's mark changed b order to the first two letters of th maker's name. This caused con siderable confusion in an alread confused period after 1720, whe the manufacture of silver in bot the 'old' and 'new' standard wa allowed, and from 1730 onl initials were used. The record of the Goldsmiths' Compan since 1697 are virtually complet except for those of the larg plate workers between 1758 an 1773, and the small plate worker registered between 1738 an 1758.

In 1478 the use of a dat letter as a separate mark ap peared, possibly as the result an Act of 1477 making th Goldsmiths' Company respon sible as a body for penaltie inflicted on wardens who marke silver of an illegal standar Since Saint Dunstan was th patron saint of English gold smiths, the date letter wa changed each year on the saint day, May 19, but since th Restoration of 1660 it has bee changed on May 29. The Londo cycle lasts for a period of 2 years and omits J, I, V or U W, X, Y, and Z.

Yet another hallmark wa added to the existing three 1544, a lion passant gardan This was probably introduce to emphasize the continuing hig standard of plate in an era debased currency. Original crowned until 1550, the lic passant gardant faced left fro 1550 to 1821; since 1821 it ha been a lion passant, with th head facing to the front.

A carved Jacobean hall cupboard with strapwork decoration

Hallmarks for 1964–5. L to r, the maker's initials, English sterling mark, London's leopard's head, and the date letter

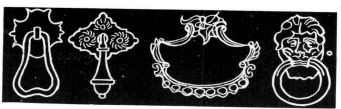

Drop handles: L to r, medieval, iron; baroque, brass; rococo, ormolu; Classical Revival, brass

In 1697 the standard of purity was raised in order to discourage the manufacture of plate. Every troy pound was to contain 11 ounces 2 pennyweights. The leopard's head and the lion were exchanged for a seated figure of Britannia to the left and a lion's head erased (with a jagged neck ending in three points) and in profile, facing left. The old standard and marks were revived in 1720, but the Britannia figure and the lion's head erased sometimes appear on silver made after that date. The Britannia figure can easily be confused with the Hibernia figure, used on Dublin plate since 1731.

In December 1784 all plate was further marked with the sovereign's head in profile, signifying that all plate brought for assay was dutiable. This mark was used until 1890, when the duty was abolished.

English provincial plate was also subject to assay, but generally speaking the finest pieces were always made in London. In Dublin the assay was established as early as 1605; the crowned harp was used as one of its hallmarks. (See **Irish silver.**)

Early American plate is not immediately datable. This is largely because colonial, state, and federal governments did not regulate the goldsmiths in any way, although both Boston and New York had societies or guilds of goldsmiths that enforced a very strict apprenticeship. In the absence of any definite system of hallmarking the only guides to the dating of early American silver are the presentation dates on commemorative pieces and the use of a goldsmith's mark. The English standard of silver was used, and the goldsmiths' marks were similar to those of their English contemporaries.

Seventeenth-century American goldsmiths marked their work with their initials, and in the eighteenth century full surnames were occasionally used. In nineteenth-century Philadelphia and New York there was some use of pseudo-English hallmarks, and after 1860 the silver in America was usually marked Sterling. The first American assay office on the English pattern was established in Baltimore in 1814.

Continental hallmarking is extremely complicated because of the irregularities caused by political and social upheavals. However, the goldsmiths' trade in Paris was regulated from 1260, and these regulations and subsequent controls were codified by Louis XIV in 1679 and remained almost unaltered until the Revolution of 1789. They were broadly similar to those of other European countries, and the original standard of 1260 was equal to that of the English Sterling standard. Later a higher standard than that of sterling was introduced, and a very rigid and strictly regulated guild system was in operation until 1791. The Parisian guild was limited to 500 members in the eighteenth century, and French silver of the period carries four marks: a maker's mark, to show that the maker in question is an admitted master of the guild of goldsmiths; the mark of the guild warden, certifying the standard of silver and the good quality of the workmanship; and a charge and a discharge mark, both tax marks that were obligatory from 1677 to 1774.

Hall settee. A piece similar to the hall chair (qv) in design, but able to accommodate two or more people. This characteristic eighteenth-century piece was usually of mahogany and not upholstered. In pattern-books, designs for hall settees are also recommended for gardens and summer-houses.

Hammer beam. A cross-member in a timbered roof which helps to distribute the load of the roof throughout the wall. The hammer beam is horizontal and supports an arched brace which rises to the collar immediately below the ridge of the roof. The hammer beam is, in turn, supported by another brace.

Handle. In its basic form a knob or bun, which later developed into highly decorative door and drawer pulls in wood, metal, glass, and other materials. The design of handles has always received attention from decorators and architects, so that the provenance of many pieces of furniture can be more readily determined by the craftsmanship of the handles than by examination of the piece itself.

Since the seventeenth century, decorative handles have been most commonly made of brass in England and of ormolu in France, but in earlier times, iron was more generally used.

Hanging shelves. Literary references indicate that hanging shelves existed in the Middle Ages, though they were not in widespread use until the very late seventeenth century. They were illustrated in many contemporary trade catalogues, and fine examples exist with delicate fretwork ends and compartments, shallow drawers, pagoda tops, and other variations.

Hardboard. Any board made from compressed wood pulp. Owing to its lightness, durability, and ease of working, hardboard is increasingly used for internal walls, doors, partitions, screens, and ceilings which have no great stresses imposed upon them.

Hardwick family. Like many similarly successful family con-

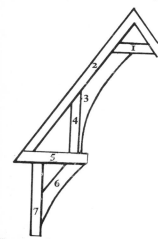

Hammer beam construction: 1 collar beam 2 principal rafter 3 arched brace 4 strut 5 hammer beam 6 brace 7 wall post

Euston arch, London, by Philip Hardwick the Elder, 1835

Grosvenor Hotel, Victoria Station, by Philip Hardwick the Elder, 1835

Redwood Library, Newport, Rhode Island, by Harrison, 1748–51

cerns in the eighteenth century, this remarkably successful dynasty of British architects was begun by a mason-turned-architect. The founder, **Thomas Hardwick** (dates unknown), ran a stonemason's business at New Brentford in Middlesex, and later set up as an architect. He was responsible for rebuilding the nave of St Laurence's Church, Brentford, Middlesex (1764), and he also rebuilt Hanwell Church, Middlesex (1781).

His younger son, **Thomas Hardwick** (1752–1829), studied at the Royal Academy Schools, and then became a pupil of Sir William Chambers, for whose work he had a lifelong admiration; he wrote a laudatory monograph of Chambers (1825). Hardwick travelled in Italy and then established his own practice. He became architect to St Bartholomew's Hospital and clerk of the works at Hampton Court.

He designed St Marylebone New Church (1813–17), St John's Chapel, and St John's Wood Church (1814), and restored and repaired several other churches. He also had a very extensive and successful practice as a surveyor.

His son, **Philip Hardwick** (1792–1870), was the most famous member of the Hardwick family. His fame as an architect rests on one monumental work, the gateway to Euston Station (demolished in 1964). He had a highly successful career, and was in charge of numerous important building projects, including wharves and warehouses at St Katherine's Dock (1827–8); the Goldsmith's Hall (1829–35); the Victoria Station (Grosvenor) Hotel (1835); and Curzon Street

Station, Birmingham (1838). He worked with his son, **Philip Charles Hardwick** (1822–92), on the hall and library of Lincoln's Inn (1843–4), a forerunner of much neo-Tudor building in Victorian England. Philip Charles Hardwick was also the architect of the Great Western Hotel at Paddington (1851) – a mock-Louis XIV pile.

Hardwood. A general term for the timber taken from any broadleaved tree. Historically important hardwoods are oak, elm, and chestnut. The most widely used hardwoods in modern furniture-making are West African woods such as mahogany, sapele, and obeche, and the ubiquitous teak from Burma. Beech, birch, oak, and elm are also commonly used.

Harewood. A figured sycamore or maple, sometimes known as silver-grey sycamore, which was frequently dyed by eighteenth-century cabinetmakers for use in inlay and marquetry work. It provided a contrasting veneer to rosewood and mahogany.

Harlequin table. A pembroke or writing-table with a small, oblong, boxlike superstructure fitted with drawers and pigeon holes. This entire receptacle was concealed within the body of the table or raised as a superstructure by means of weights. It was introduced in the late eighteenth century.

Harmonic proportions. In architectural theory these are scales of measurement applied to a sequence of rooms. The scale is directly related to the proportions of musical harmony, which were regarded as perfect, and therefore a fit guide to the spatial harmony of rooms. The system was invented in antiquity and revived during the Renaissance, first by Alberti and most notably by Palladio.

Harrison, Peter (1722–1775). The earliest named American architect. He was born in Yorkshire, England, and established himself in Newport, Rhode Island, as a sea captain, entrepreneur, and surveyor; he further established his position by a lucrative marriage.

Harrison's buildings show a knowledge of English architectural developments previously

unusual in the Thirteen Colonies. They show how important printed treatises were in disseminating this information. Most of Harrison's work derived from Gibbs's *Book of Architecture*, and it reaches heights of lavishness (the Touro Synagogue, Newport, Rhode Island, 1759–63), elegance (St Michael's Church, Charleston, 1751), and ingenuity (King's Chapel, Boston) which would have been remarkable even for Gibbs. Harrison's earliest work, the Redwood Library at Newport (1748), is derived from Palladio's Venetian churches, but carries an unbroken entablature round all four sides, above both the Doric portico and the wings. This remarkably early temple-like arrangement shows that Harrison also knew Colen Campbell's *Vitruvius Britannicus*; it foreshadows Jefferson's Virginia State Capitol of 1789.

Harrison, Thomas (1744–1829). British architect who was born in Richmond, Yorkshire, the son of a carpenter. His early talent for mathematics and draughtsmanship brought him to the notice of Sir Laurence

Skerton Bridge, Lancaster, designed by Thomas Harrison, 1783–8

Dundas, who made it possible for him to travel in Italy.

In 1783, on the strength of his Roman studies and drawings, he was commissioned to design the five-arched Skerton Bridge at Lancaster to span the river Lune. He also rebuilt Lancaster Castle as a county gaol in the Gothic manner.

Harrison also worked at Chester, where he designed another county gaol, this time as part of the rebuilding of Chester Castle (1793–1820), which also included the county courts and treasury. The gaol is a massive stone structure in a heavy and forbidding version of the Doric style; it was the first prison built on Jeremy Bentham's panopticon principle, the cells encircling the warders' central well. Harrison also designed the Grosvenor Bridge in Chester, which had a single 200 ft span, then the greatest in Europe.

He designed a number of private houses in the north of England, notably the Gothic Hardwick Grange in Shropshire for Lord Hill, and Broomhall in Fife for the Earl of Elgin.

His lesser claims to fame are that he prompted his patron, the Earl of Elgin, to acquire the treasures from the Acropolis now in the British Museum, and that he prepared designs for the Russian ambassador for a lighthouse on the Black Sea coast.

Haunch. The part of the extrados (qv) between the springing of the arch and the apex or crown.

Haussman, Baron Georges-Eugène (1809–91). French town-planner. Haussman, the son of a textile manufacturer at Colmar, entered the civil service in 1831 and spent the next 22 years in the provinces. In 1853

Etoile, Paris, with radiating roads as laid out by Haussmann

he was appointed Prefect of the Seine, a position he held until 1870. 'Paris as we know it,' writes John Russell in his book on the city, 'is very largely the creation of Haussman. We cannot turn on a tap or take an omnibus, or buy a cut of beef without falling in with his plans. Nor is there anywhere in Paris, from the Bois to Vincennes, and from the Buttes-Chaumont to the Parc Montsouris, that does not bear the imprint of his heavy Alsatian thumb.' Haussman's energy, determination, and ruthlessness

swept away the city of Balzac and set the pattern for nineteenth-century Paris. With the assistance of Alphand he demolished thousands of smaller houses and gardens, replacing them with avenues and *places*. He replanned and rebuilt public buildings from *mairies* to railway stations, and developed new boulevards. He introduced new concepts of urban landscape gardening, including the Bois de Boulogne, and instituted new water and sewerage systems, cemeteries and canals. These vast projects inevitably aroused a tremendous amount of controversy and criticism, and under strong pressure Haussman finally resigned and was transferred to a relatively obscure post. His dictatorial decrees and demoniacal energies made Paris into a modern city, but his departure from power was unlamented.

Hawksley, Anthony (*b* 1921). British silversmith, born in Coventry. Hawksley trained at Maidstone College of Art and the Royal College of Art. After leaving the Royal College in 1951, he began to work on his own, but also taught for two years at Birmingham College of Art. He is now visiting lecturer at the Oxford School of Art.

He has exhibited in London, Edinburgh, Zurich, Stuttgart, Philadelphia, and Vienna. Special commissions include silver for Queens, St Hugh's, Magdalene, and Keble Colleges, Oxford, and numerous private collections. Hawksley's hanging cross in steel, copper, and glass at St Francis, Cowley, is a notable contribution to architectural metalwork. He also designs and makes jewellery.

Hawksmoor or **Hawkesmore,** Nicholas (1661–1736).

Anthony Hawksley and one of his designs for a pepperpot

Nicolas Hawksmoor

The Mausoleum at Castle Howard, Yorkshire, by Hawksmoor, 1727–8

St Mary, Woolnoth, London, by Hawksmoor, 1716–27

All Souls College, Oxford, designed by Hawksmoor, 1715–40

English architect. Hawksmoor, as the name is usually spelled, was one of the most original and powerful of English architects, a master of the Baroque style, which he interpreted in a highly personal native idiom.

Hawksmoor was born into a farming family in Nottinghamshire, probably at Ragnall. Nothing is known of his early education, but after working as a clerk in Doncaster, his architectural ambitions brought him to the notice of Sir Christopher Wren, to whom he became clerk and assistant, measuring and drawing, and supervising contracts and tenders.

As far as is known, his first official position was as deputy surveyor (to Wren) at Chelsea Hospital (1682). He also helped Wren on the palace at Winchester designed for Charles II; the palace remained unfinished.

Hawksmoor soon became indispensable to Wren, helping his master in the design and construction of the post-Fire London churches, as well as designing some himself. He also gave unstinted help with the planning of St Paul's Cathedral, for which he was making designs from 1691 until 1712. Wren procured for Hawksmoor the post of clerk of the works at Kensington Palace (1689) and Greenwich Hospital (1698). Hawksmoor retained the Greenwich appointment until his death.

Hawksmoor's abilities inevitably brought him to the notice of Vanbrugh, who had been comptroller of the works since 1702, for Hawksmoor had exactly the kind of technical knowledge that Vanbrugh – an amateur of genius – needed to carry out his vast projects. Hawksmoor worked closely with Vanbrugh at Greenwich Hospital, Castle Howard, and Blenheim. At Blenheim he was first employed as assistant surveyor, but after Vanbrugh quarrelled bitterly with Sarah, Duchess of Marlborough, he became architect in charge.

Vanbrugh undoubtedly owed much to Hawksmoor, and in part acknowledged his debt by making Hawksmoor his deputy as comptroller of the works (1721). It is arguable that both Wren and Vanbrugh owed much more than has generally been realized to Hawksmoor's creative genius – a supposition which gains support as more is discovered about Hawksmoor, a reticent but passionately committed architect.

Hawksmoor's own quality can be seen in the six churches which he designed as part of the post-Fire building programme. These six churches were St Alfege, Greenwich (1712–14); St Anne, Limehouse (1712–24); St George-in-the-East, Wapping (1715–23); St Mary, Woolnoth (1716–27); St George's, Bloomsbury (1720–30); and – probably Hawksmoor's most remarkable achievement – Christ Church, Spitalfields (1723–9). Most of the churches have been altered, or suffered damage in World War II; but sufficient documentary evidence remains to demonstrate Hawksmoor's unique contribution to English ecclesiastical architecture.

His secular architecture was equally personal and wide-ranging. He made a lifelong attempt to fuse two major styles: the Roman civic-monumental manner and English Gothic. His published plans for transforming the centres of Oxford and Cambridge make it clear that Hawksmoor wanted to give the university towns something of the heroic set-piece quality of ancient Rome, as well as the movement and surprise occasioned by unexpected vistas. His Roman inclinations and

St Anne's, Limehouse, London, by Hawksmoor, 1712–24

Gothicism, allied with his extensive technical knowledge, made him a formidable force in his prime.

During the last 20 years of Hawksmoor's life, he was somewhat overshadowed by Lord Burlington's more formal Palladianism. This caused him considerable bitterness – a bitterness expressed in his communications with his patron Lord Carlisle.

Hawksmoor's buildings form a group unparalleled in England, ranging from his early and

Ambrose Heal

decorous treatment of Easton Neston in Northamptonshire (1702) to the grandeur of the Mausoleum at Castle Howard (1729–36); from the originality of the Clarendon Building at Oxford (1712–15) to his part in Blenheim, culminating in his own designs for the Triumphal Gateway (built in 1722–3).

Header. The end face of a brick, normally laid as part of a header-and-stretcher course. An exception is the heading bond (qv).

Heading bond. A term applied to a method or pattern of brick-laying, whereby only the end faces of the bricks were seen. Such a system gives greater flexibility in course-laying, and facilitates the construction of curved or serpentine walls.

Heal, Sir Ambrose (1872–1959). British furniture-designer and cabinetmaker, and one of the leaders of the modern movement in Britain. Heal was educated at Marlborough, and when he was 21 entered the family business, now a famous London store. Five years later, the first catalogue of *Heal's Plain Oak Furniture* was produced under his direction, beginning the revival of simple domestic furniture in Britain.

At the Paris Exhibition of 1900 Heal showed bedroom furniture which he had designed in conjunction with Cecil Brewer. The furniture was widely acclaimed, particularly a wardrobe in fumed and waxed oak, with inlays of pewter and ebony, and awarded a prize. To contemporary eyes these pieces may seem dated and even affected, but compared with rival products of the same period, they had a lightness and simplicity which had not been seen in English cabinetmaking for well over a century.

Heal applied the same fresh visions to beds and bedding, the basic products of his firm, and his experiments strengthened his determination to have done with ponderous and dull pieces. His lifetime spanned the history of the modern movement, from its beginnings under the influence of William Morris, Philip Webb, and Charles Voysey to the postwar founding of the Council of Industrial Design. He was knighted in 1933.

Heal's other interests were literary and historical. In 1925 he published an account of London tradesmen's cards of the eighteenth century, and in 1931 an account of English writing masters and their copy-books.

Wardrobe designed by Ambrose Heal, from the Paris Exhibition, 1900

He also wrote studies of English goldsmiths and the signboards of old London shops. His most important books were based on his collection of trade-cards of early cabinetmakers, and *The London Furniture Makers* (1953) is a valuable record of over 2,500 cabinetmakers, upholsterers, carvers, and gilders from 1660 to 1840.

Sir Ambrose died in 1959. His son Anthony, born in 1907, had succeeded him as chairman of the firm some seven years before, after serving an apprenticeship with Gordon Russell and studying in Germany. His younger brother Christopher, born in 1911, studied economics and architecture at Cambridge, and textile and furniture design at the Central School, before joining the firm in 1934. He has designed many printed fabrics and numerous sets of furniture, including a series of modular sectional bedroom units.

Helix (plural helices). An architectural term for any spiral-like ornament. Because the word is also used to describe the external rim of the ear, it has been applied to the ear-like curve of caulicoli (qv).

Bedroom with modular sectional furniture by Christopher Heal, 1965

Helm roof of Stompting Church

Jug by R Hennell, 1852

Modern coffee pot by R and G Hennell

Hellenic and Hellenistic architecture. Terms that are easily confused, describing the two periods into which Greek architecture is conventionally divided. Hellenic spans the period from *c* 700 BC to the death of Alexander the Great in 323 BC. Hellenistic describes all later Greek architecture, and the buildings of the Mediterranean basin influenced by classical Greek prototypes. Hellenistic forms dominated the architecture of the eastern Mediterranean until the Romans evolved their own style (based on reinterpretation of Greek forms) in the first and second centuries AD.

Helm roof. A form of gabled spire peculiar to Romanesque architecture. The four gables formed a base for an attenuated pyramidal pinnacle or spire.

Hemicycle. Any structure built on a semi-circular plan.

Hennell family. During the past 240 years, there have been no fewer than 21 members of the Hennell family working as silversmiths; this is a remarkable record even in a trade traditionally practised over several generations.

Lion's claw salt-cellar. From a set made by David Hennell, 1737

David Hennell, first silversmith in the family, was born in Newport Pagnell in 1712. Unlike many contemporary silversmiths, he was of native English descent. In 1728 he was apprenticed to Edward Wood, a smith specializing in making salts. When his seven years were up, David Hennell entered his own mark, DH, at Goldsmiths' Hall, and soon set up a business nearby, in Foster Lane. In 1736 his half-brother William became David's apprentice, but never appears to have registered his own mark. David seems to have specialized in making salts; one of the earliest known examples is an octagonal trencher salt dated 1736. Soon the Rococo was influencing even small wares such as salts, and in 1740 David made a fine set of four salts, with shell feet. His most characteristic product, however, was a circular salt with everted gadrooned rim, on claw or hoof feet. One fine early set of 1737 has splendid chased lion knuckles and lion paw feet. The Wood and the Hennell workshops, which were near neighbours, dominated mid-eighteenth century salt design and probably made most of the salts sold in the trade.

David Hennell had 15 children, and his fifth son, Robert, who was one of the few to survive into adulthood, became a fine silversmith. He completed his apprenticeship to his father in 1763, and at once father and son entered a joint mark, in a cross-like punch. David and Robert worked together until about 1773, when David apparently retired and Robert entered his mark alone, describing himself as a 'Salt Maker of 16 Foster Lane.'

Robert also made some small jugs, teapots, and a particularly fine épergne in the Adam taste (1786). The finely engraved tea-table silver made by Robert Hennell may have been decorated by his nephew, also named Robert, whom he took as an apprentice in 1778. This second Robert was simultaneously apprenticed to an engraver, John Houle. Robert possibly worked mainly as an engraver, for he did not enter his mark as a plate-worker until 1809, using RH in a cut-cornered oblong. He moved to the Strand, and his son and grandson, both of them called Robert, and another grandson, worked in that area until 1877. A descendant of this line of the family, Thomas (1903–45), was a well-known artist.

Meanwhile, Robert Hennell of Foster Lane (his mark is RH in an oval punch) took his own sons into the business. The eldest, David, was born in 1767, and by 1795 Robert decided to include his name in the mark, registering RH over DH, which was easily distinguishable from the cross mark used by Robert and his father. The business flourished, and besides pierced salts and mustard pots, turned out elegant tea-table wares; the Hennells made some of the first tea-services in the elegant Adam and early Regency styles. In 1802 the youngest son, Samuel, had his mark added to those of his father and brother, but the middle son, Robert, does not appear to have completed his indentures.

David seems to have left the manufacturing side of the business *c* 1804 (or perhaps earlier, in 1802, when Robert and Samuel entered a joint mark). Robert died in 1811 at the age of 70, and then Samuel registered his own mark, SH, in distinctive, scooped oblong. He worked on, mostly alone, though in 1814 he did register a mark with John Terry, a nephew by marriage. Samuel died in 1837, by which time yet another Robert was conducting a flourishing business for the family in Bloomsbury, though he did not register a mark as a silversmith. R & G Hennell still have premises there, and since the 1830s they have been making beautiful jewellery as well as silverware.

Hepplewhite, George (*d* 1786). English cabinetmaker and furniture-designer. Hepplewhite's origins are obscure, and little is known of his early working life. He nonetheless became one of a group of cabinetmakers who made English furniture design famous in the late eighteenth century.

Although his name has been given to a wide range of furniture, no authenticated pieces of 'Hepplewhite' furniture have been identified as the work of the London firm which he founded in Redcross Street, St Giles's,

Sofa published in Cabinet-Makers' and Upholsterers' Guide, 1788

Sheraton design for chairs in the Herculaneum style

A Hepplewhite chair

A knifecase by Hepplewhite

Cripplegate. Hepplewhite owes his fame to his *Cabinet-Makers' and Upholsterers' Guide*, published two years after his death by his widow, Alice Hepplewhite, trading under the title of A Hepplewhite & Company. The furniture shown in the *Guide* was intended to be made in mahogany and satinwood, and was somewhat lighter in construction than those of Chippendale. The Hepplewhite style is thus based upon the book rather than any pieces known to be by the author.

Heptastyle (Greek, *hepta* 'seven', *stulos* 'column'). A term used to describe a Greek portico with seven columns supporting the pediment.

Herculaneum. A somewhat ornate chair, deriving in design and ornament from remains of Roman furniture discovered at Herculaneum and Pompeii. Sheraton coined the name. The chairs were decorated with an abundance of classical motifs copied from Roman sculpture, paintsings, and carvings.

Heritage, Robert (*b* 1927). British furniture designer. Heritage was born in Birmingham and educated there at King Edward's Grammar School. He entered the industrial design department of Birmingham College of Art in 1942, specializing in light metalwork. He then studied at the Royal College of Art in the furniture school, under Professor R D Russell. He was staff designer to a furniture manufacturer before starting his own practice in 1935, which he combined with teaching at two London art schools. He was made a Royal Designer for Industry in 1963.

Herm or **term.** A statue or ornamental treatment of a supporting pier; it represents the head and torso of a man, usually Hermes, upon a tapering four-sided base. This device was very popular in ancient Greece, and Athens was full of such statues, which were used for boundary markers. In the eighteenth century, they were used to mark the boundaries of gardens.

Herringbone. A pattern much used by bricklayers for walls and paths. It was first employed during the seventeenth century, for the infilling for walls and timber-framed houses. As the earlier wattle and daub or lath and plaster decayed, bricks, which had become cheaper, were used for infilling panels. The herringbone or chevron pattern was used both vertically and horizontally.

The pattern was also employed during the eighteenth century in the veneer or walnut furniture.

Hexastyle (Greek, *hexa* 'six'; *stulos* 'column'). A classical Greek temple portico with six columns.

Hickory. A tree indigenous to North America; a member of the genus *Carya*. Its vernacular name is a contraction of pohickery, a word widely used in the South. The tree is graceful, and the timber was highly suitable for furniture made by travelling joiners and cabinetmakers, especially cupboards, stools, chests, candlestands, and chairs.

Robert Heritage and his Oregon chair 1962

Herm in a country garden

Above: modern living-room designed by David Hicks. Below: the Q4 Room on the liner Queen Elizabeth II

A walnut veneered highboy with birch and maple ends; 1700–20

David Hicks

Hicks, David (*b* 1929). British decorator and designer, educated at Charterhouse and the Central School of Arts and Crafts. He worked for a short time in advertising, in the studios of J Walter Thompson, and then started on his own as a decorator. In 1956 he helped to start the firm of Hicks and Parr in Lowndes Street, and when the partnership ended in 1960, founded his present company, David Hicks Ltd.

He has designed many restaurants, motels, and the Q4 Room on the *Queen Elizabeth II*, as well as private houses in England and America. He was responsible for two suites of rooms at Windsor Castle, for Princess Anne and Prince Charles, and a private suite at Buckingham Palace for Prince Charles. His other activities include designs for carpets, fabrics, and tiles. He has written several books on decorating.

Highboy. A term of American origin and usage, applied to a piece of furniture made throughout the eighteenth century. This derived from the Queen Anne and William and Mary tallboy, and consisted of a chest of drawers mounted on a stand fitted with drawers. The highboy remained in favour in the United States long after the tallboy had fallen into disuse in England. They were made in great numbers and in various timbers, and they were frequently painted and then lacquered.

Hildebrandt, Johann Lukas von (1668–1745). Austrian architect. Hildebrandt was born in Genoa; his father was an officer in the Imperial army, then stationed in the city, and his mother an Italian.

Hildebrandt's early training was as a military engineer, but he also studied architecture under Carlo Fontana in Rome. He settled in Vienna in 1696, and in 1699 was appointed chief architect to the court. His first notable building was the Palais Schwarzenberg (1700–15); Hildebrandt prepared the plans, although the building was completed by his great rival at court, Fischer von Erlach. Hildebrandt's range was wide, and although his originality was less evident than that of his rival, his close (and costly) attention to Baroque decorative detail was renowned. The chief buildings designed by Hildebrandt include the Schloss Belvedere (1721–2)

The Lower Belvedere, Vienna, designed by Hildebrandt, 1714

Victorian style bedroom designed by John Hill

The Upper Belvedere, Vienna, by Lukas von Hildebrandt, 1721–2

for Prince Eugene and the Daun-Kinsky Palace (1713–16), both in Vienna; and the Schloss Mirabell in Salzburg. He also designed churches, most notably the Laurenzkirche at Gabel in northern Bohemia (1699), and his last great work, Slift Kloolerbruck in Moravia (begun 1740).

Hill, John (*b* 1905). British interior designer and decorator. Hill, the son of a West of England cloth manufacturer, was educated at Marlborough and Cambridge. He then became a trainee with Green & Abbott, of which he is now managing director.

Hill has been consistently preoccupied with the twin problems of colour and pattern, and was one of the first members of his profession to perceive the decorative values of revived and simplified Victoriana. He has initiated the design of fabrics and wallpapers to match his decorative inventions. He began by working mainly for private patrons, but publication of examples of his work brought him to the notice of hoteliers and the railways. In this sphere he began by redecorating the Royal and Pavilion Hotels at Scarborough, and since the end of the war has been almost exclusively concerned with work on hotels throughout Britain.

Hill, Oliver (1887–1968). British architect. Advised by Sir Edwin Lutyens, Oliver Hill started his career in the workshops of a well-known firm of builders, where he acquired at first hand the feeling for material that characterized his subsequent work. He also attended the evening school of the Architectural Association.

One of Hill's first commissions was the reconstruction of a large country house in Berkshire and the layout of the gardens of Moor Close. Between the world wars he was occupied in designing private houses, and often their gardens and furniture as

John Hill

well. His works fall into two categories, those recalling the Palladian environment, and those – his personal preference – in the contemporary idiom.

Hill's interest in experiments

Oliver Hill

Joldwynds in Surrey, designed by Oliver Hill, 1935

Stone table and chairs designed by Oliver Hill, 1933

Lord Nelson's funeral car, designed by John William Hiort

with new materials and processes led to the Exhibition of Industrial Design at Dorland Hall in 1933, and subsequently to his appointment as architect of the British pavilion at the Paris International Exhibition in 1937, where he was also in charge of display. He was also responsible for the Cotswold Tradition Exhibition of 1951.

Apart from houses, Hill designed the Midland Hotel at Morecambe and all its equipment, the Whitwood Mere School in the East Riding, the award-winning Newbury Park Station, and the exterior of the Weymouth Pavilion Theatre.

Hinge. A fitment, formerly of wood but now usually of metal, used as a means of hanging and/or opening lids and doors. The earliest hinges were wooden pin hinges, found in twelfth-century chests. Later, metal hinges of the butterfly type were frequently used for food and clothes' chests. As metalworkers became more adept, hinges became more decorative and ingenious. The strap hinges of the sixteenth and seventeenth centuries, frequently employing fleur-de-lis and other motifs, gave much scope to craftsmen, although the moving parts of the simple hinge mechanism remained basically un-

changed. Thus, the widely-used wrought-iron hinges of the eighteenth century were little more than elaborations of the butterfly hinge of two centuries earlier, with various refinements, such as chamfering the edges of the mounts, introduced to display the craftsman's skills. The earlier wrought-iron hinges were gradually supplanted by more resplendent versions in brass and, in exceptional cases, silver.

Modern machine-made hinges have the same basic construction, although lightweight metals are employed.

Hiort, John William (1772–1861). Hiort, son of a Swedish father and English mother, was born in London and became the most important early nineteenth-century designer of official ceremonies, spectacles, and festivals. His range extended from arranging funerals of great public figures (including Pitt and Nelson) to designing such ephemeral structures as a triumphal arch in the Gothic manner for the coronation banquet of George IV.

Hiort came to this position of eminence by a curious route, beginning with a brief apprenticeship to an engineer and miniaturist, and progressing via a clerkship in the Office of Works to the post of chief examining clerk (1815–32). As such, he was responsible for the planning of an unusual variety of official spectacles, grave and gay, ecclesiastical and secular, regal and

plebeian. The position also offered him considerable scope for the exercise of skill and tact as an architectural entrepreneur in widely different spheres. He supervised the restoration of Westminster Hall (in co-operation with J B Papworth and Thomas Gayfere, master mason to Westminster Abbey), and also the construction of lodges, cottages, conservatories, stables, an aviary, and other domestic structures for Prince Leopold and Princess Charlotte at their Claremont estate in Surrey. In these projects he was again aided by Papworth.

Hiort practised with some success as an architect in his own right, and designed houses for Lord Bexley in Kent and Westminster, and for other notabilities in London. He was also a businessman of considerable ingenuity and acumen. After inventing and patenting his project

The funeral procession of Lord Nelson from Greenwich to Whitehall, organised by Hiort

The hipped roof of Hugh May's Eltham Lodge, 1663–4

Half-hipped roof on a brick and flint barn

r building circular flues (used Buckingham Palace), he unded the London, Surrey, d Kent Safety Brick Company 825). After his retirement from e Office of Works in 1832, he moved to Bath, but returned London to publicize his later ventions in connection with the nstruction of chimneys. He

ish inscribed 'ave Maria gra ena', Manises, sixteenth century

rug-jar, painted in lustre and ue. Manises, fifteenth century

wrote a treatise on this subject in which he recommended circular or oval flues as easier to clean than square flues and better adapted to allowing smoke to escape. He died in Kensington aged 89.

Hipped roof. The term applied to a roof with a sloping end instead of the traditional gable. Where the end is gabled and hipped, the term half-hipped is used.

Hip tile. A roofing tile shaped and fired for the particular purpose of covering the hip on a tiled hipped roof.

Hispano-Moresque pottery. The Moors introduced into Spain the ceramic arts of glazing with tin oxide, and of lustred decoration. Exactly when this happened is unknown, but the first reference to the appearance of lustred pottery is by the geographer Edrisi, who wrote of a 'golden ware' made at Calatayud, in Aragon, in 1154. Ibn Sa'id (1214–86) refers to the golden pottery made at Murcia, Almeria, and Malaga. However, none of it has survived.

Malaga was in the kingdom of Granada, the last stronghold of the Moors in Spain. Here in the fourteenth and fifteenth centuries, much beautiful lustred ware was produced. The body of the ware was rather coarse, and fired to a warm, buffish pink. It was glazed with oxide of tin, giving a creamish opaque surface, and the main colours used for decoration were blue and a pale straw-gold (obtained from silver). The early designs were based on Kufic script, plant forms, and arabesques. The Alhambra, the great palace of the Moors at Granada (begun 1273), was decorated with lustred wall-tiles. Two large and handsome vases were discovered there; they were cream and blue with gold lustre and were decorated with strapwork and arabesques surrounding gazelles. They probably date from the early fifteenth

century.

When Ferdinand and Isabella conquered Malaga in 1487, the industry declined, though pottery was made at Malaga until the beginning of the sixteenth century.

It is known that 'golden ware' was made at Manises near Valencia from 1383. This became famous throughout Europe and North Africa. Large chargers were made, as well as drug-pots, vases, and plates. The decoration – gold lustre, sometimes used alone and sometimes combined with blue and manganese – consisted of rather more naturalistic plant-forms than those used at Malaga. The designs also incorporated heraldic beasts, lions, and eagles, and later deer and antelopes. Armorial bearings were often the central motif. Sometimes ruby, violet, and opalescent lustre were used with astonishingly rich results. Blue and manganese gradually ceased to be used from c 1500, and later productions are much more nondescript.

In the fourteenth century, pottery was made at Paterna, near Valencia. This was decorated with green and purple Moorish and Near Eastern designs. A deeper, coppery-gold lustre was used in the seventeenth and eighteenth centuries, when a great deal of rather coarse ware for everyday use was made. The technique of using lustre decoration persisted, and is used to this day. William de Morgan (qv) was strongly influenced by Hispano-Moresque pottery.

Hitchcock, Henry Russell (*b* 1903). American architectural historian. Hitchcock was born in Boston, Massachusetts, and educated at Harvard, graduating in 1924. He was appointed assistant professor of art at Vassar College in 1927, and between 1928 and 1948 was in turn assistant, associate, and full professor at the Wesleyan University, Middletown, Connecticut. He was lecturer in architecture at the Massachusetts Institute of Tech-

nology (1946–8), and appointed director of Smith College Museum of Art (1949–55). He has also been lecturer in architecture at New York and Yale University.

Hitchcock's researches and publications have done much to unravel the complicated aesthetic and economic influences which shaped the history of architecture in the nineteenth and twentieth centuries, especially in Britain. He has also been one of the most lucid of guides to the development of modern architecture. His publications include works on the architecture of Frank Lloyd Wright, J J P Oud, and H H Richardson, *The International Movement in Architecture*, a two-volume history of *Early Victorian Architecture in Britain* (1945), and *Architecture of the 19th and 20th Centuries* (1958).

Hitchcock, Lambert (1795–1852). A Connecticut cabinet-maker who established a factory at Hitchcocksville in 1825, and gave his name to a chair widely copied in New England, New York, and Ohio. With its broad pillow-back band, the Hitchcock chair owed much to Sheraton

Hitchcock chair, c 1836

The White House, Washington, designed by James Hoban, 1792

Hogarth chair in a self portrait, painted in 1764

originals, including its turned and splayed legs, and caned seats. The chairs were painted to simulate rosewood, and were frequently stencilled with floral motifs.

Hoban, James (c 1760-1831). Irish-American architect. After an early training in Dublin, Hoban emigrated to America in 1789, and after working as an itinerant architect in Charleston and the Deep South, moved to Washington in 1792. There he soon began to make a considerable reputation, and there he remained for the rest of his life, working on the designs of several public buildings of importance. His most important commission was the design of the White House, which he was also responsible for rebuilding after its destruction by the British forces in 1814. He also acted as adviser and supervisor during the building of the Capitol in Washington, from original designs by Dr William Thornton, the doctor-engineer.

Hoffmann, Josef (1870–1956). Austrian architect and craftsman. Although Hoffmann trained as

an architect in Vienna under Otto Wagner (qv) and designed a number of notable buildings, his interests lay predominantly in the applied arts and crafts and decoration. In 1903 these interests led him to establish the Wiener Werkstätte, which resembled the English arts and crafts movement in outlook and aims.

Hoffmann's first building of consequence was the Purkersdorf Sanatorium (1903), but the building which gave him something of a European reputation was a luxurious mansion on the outskirts of Brussels. In this, the Palais Stoclet, many features derive from Wagner prototypes, but the marble-walled interiors are wholly Hoffmann's.

The publicity attending the Palais Stoclet brought Hoffmann commissions for other mansions, including buildings in Vienna and Hietzing, and he also built low-cost flats in Vienna.

Hogarth chair. A name that became current in the second half of the nineteenth century. It describes the type of bent back (qv), single, or arm chairs that Hogarth included in many interiors, and in his own self-portrait.

Hogarth frame. A decorated black-and-gilt frame used for eighteenth-century engravings.

Holabird and Roche. William Holabird (1854–1923) and Martin Roche (1855–1927), American architectural partnership. Both men were Chicago-educated and trained in the office of the engineer William Le Baron Jenney, who discovered 'skyscraper construction.' Holabird and Roche's Tacoma Building, Chicago (1887–9), was the first to give clear aesthetic expression to Jenney's technique. All the walls were carried on a metal frame, the floors acting as

Charles Holden

shelves; this was expressed by minimal amount of exterio cladding, and by oriels runnin the full height of the building

Holden, Charles Henry (1875 1960). British , architect an town-planner. Holden was bor in Bolton and trained in Man chester before moving to Londor He entered the drawing-office c H P Adam, with whom he wa later to enter partnership. Whe he was 30 he won the top awar in an open competition fc Bristol Central Library. Tw years later the firm of Adams

The Palais Stoclet, Brussels, by Joseph Hoffman, 1905–11

Building in Chicago, Illinois, designed by Holabird and Roche

Senate House, London University by Holden, opened 1936

Arnos Grove station, designed by Charles Holden, 1932

Sudbury Town station booking hall, designed by Holden, 1931

An aerial view of Holford's plan for the St Paul's redevelopment

Lord Holford

Holden, & Pearson was formed, and the partnership established a practice of considerable range, geographical and technical. This included the British Medical Association building in London, and many Underground stations and buildings, among them the St James's Park headquarters of London Transport. During World War I Holden was appointed architectural adviser to the Imperial War Graves Commission. His most important – and controversial – building was the Senate House and related buildings for London University in Bloomsbury. He was responsible, with W G (now Lord) Holford for the town-planning report on the development of the City of London, published in 1947.

Holford, Lord (b 1907). Architect and planner. William Graham Holford was born in Johannesburg, South Africa, and educated at the Diocesan College, Cape Town, and the University of Liverpool School of Archi-

tecture. After further studies at the British School at Rome (1930 –3) he was appointed lecturer in architecture at Liverpool University, and two years later became the architect responsible for development work in distressed areas of north-east England. In 1936 he was appointed Lever professor of civic design at Liverpool. During the war he

was attached to the Ministry of Supply as chief technical officer to the Ministry of Town and Country Planning.

In 1946 Holford, along with C H Holden (qv), became planning consultant to the City of London Corporation; he was also attached to the University of Liverpool in a similar capacity. In 1948 he was appointed professor of town-planning in the University of London.

Holford has acted as planning consultant on projects for the London County Council, the cities of Pretoria, Canberra, and Cambridge (with H M Wright), and the universities of Exeter and Kent. As a result of fierce controversies over his published plans for the redevelopment of areas around St Paul's Cathedral and for Piccadilly Circus, Holford became widely known as one of the formative influences of twentieth-century British urban planning. He was knighted in 1953 and made a Life Peer in 1965.

Holland. The traditional fine woven linen used for roller-blinds. It is manilla in colour,

usually with a bottom border of macramé lace and a hand-woven linen cord and weight.

Holland, with a highly-glazed finish, is still used for roller-blinds, but is now made in several pale colours and stripes.

Holland, Henry (1745–1806). British architect. Holland, one of the greatest architects of the

The west front of the Queen's Building, University of Exeter, by Holford

285

Henry Holland

eighteenth century, was the son of Henry Holland, a prosperous master-builder of Fulham, London. Having shown promise as an embryonic architect, Holland became assistant to the ageing Lancelot (Capability) Brown in 1771. Brown was an old friend of Holland *père*, whose commercial success prompted the family to build a substantial house in Mayfair, London, where Brown and the young Holland set up in business. He married Brown's daughter Bridget in 1773.

In 1771, with capital borrowed from his father, Holland took a lease in Chelsea of nearly 90 acres (subsequently enlarged), and there began as a speculative property developer. Here he built himself a handsome and substantial villa, Sloane Place, and began the planning and building of houses in the Hans Town development. Meanwhile, thanks to his connections with Brown, he had come into contact with several aristocratic patrons of the Devonshire House set, and in 1776 was commissioned to draw up plans for the design of Brooks's Club in St James's Street. This building led to wider recognition of Holland's skill as an architect, and also greatly enlarged his social contacts. He formed a lasting friendship with Charles James Fox, and, more significantly, was brought to the notice of the Prince of Wales (later George IV). Brooks's, now restored, is the least impaired of Holland's work in London.

Soon after the Prince of Wales came of age in 1783, he set about the rebuilding of his dilapidated Carlton House Terrace property and chose Holland as his architect.

Holland's work at Carlton

Brook's Club, St James's Street, designed by Holland

House is known only through engravings, sketch-books, and the furniture removed from Carlton House before its demolition. These pieces, designed by Holland, show his consummate ability as a decorative artist.

Holland went on to design other buildings for the prince, who was soon occupied with schemes for enlarging a property at Brighton to provide a suitable domestic setting for his mistress, Mrs Fitzherbert. Holland's first building for the Pavilion at Brighton had a plan and structure typical of the architect's sane approach to his task – th[e] difficult task of designing buil[d]ings at once modestly palati[al] and opulently comfortable. A[ll] Holland's designs were huma[n] in scale; the needs of everyda[y] living were not subordinated t[o] displays of wealth and splendou[r.] His sober yet distinguishe[d] designs for the Pavilion we[re] unfortunately to be swept awa[y] only a few years later.

Althorp in Northamptonshi[re] was the first of Holland's majo[r] commissions arising from h[is] connections with the leadin[g] Whigs. At Althorp, Holland r[e-]

The Ionic portico at Broadlands, Hampshire, added by Holland, 1780

The anteroom at Althorp, Northamptonshire, by Holland, c 1788

Wenvoe Castle, Glamorganshire, by Henry Holland, 1780

The refaced south wall of Woburn Abbey, designed by Holland, c 1787

ased an earlier structure and ave the façade a discreet and istinguished sobriety; within, he house was given a magnificent riple library and a group of andsome reception rooms. Iolland's skills as a decorator vere also given full scope, and he Blue Boudoir remains one of he most exquisite of all English nteriors.

Holland also did a considerble amount of work at Bedford Iouse in Bloomsbury and Woburn Abbey in Bedfordshire. At Woburn he was responsible for dding stable blocks, a conervatory, a dairy, cottages, a iding school, and numerous ther buildings to the structure esigned by Henry Flitcroft in he middle years of the century. Iolland's continuing delight in he decorative side of his work s exemplified by the Chinese Dairy – a delightful essay in hinoiserie. In 1788 he designed new Ionic portico, vestibule, nd inner hall, for Lord Palmerton at Broadlands in Hamphire. The two apartments proided what was in effect a gallery or Palmerston's collection of ntique statuary.

For many students, however, outhill in Bedfordshire, rebuilt in 1794 for the brewer Samuel Whitbread, remains Holland's most pleasing and personal achievement. The long, low lines of this house, with its projecting, pedimented central block, Ionic-columned loggias, and two-storey terminal pavilion, make it an influential building in the history of English domestic architecture; its emphasis on the two-storey elevation shaped many smaller villa developments during the Regency years.

Two other Holland projects must be mentioned. His designs for the Drury Lane Theatre, prepared for Richard Brinsley Sheridan between 1791 and 1794, resulted in a magnificent building, reputedly 'one of the most beautiful playhouses in the world.' And the most curious of his speculative schemes was his conversion of Albany, a house he had designed for the Duke of York. The duke, having overspent his allowances, was forced to give up the building. Holland, with the aid of the builder Andrew Copland, then converted it into the existing residential chambers.

As a designer of interiors, Holland was influenced by French prototypes, although he did not travel abroad until his reputation was firmly established, after the building of Brooks's. Despite these influences, he evolved what could be termed an English version of Neo-classicism. He also adopted and refined a Greco-Roman decorative style which had much in common with Robert Adam's manner.

Hollow wall. An alternative to the more usual building term, 'cavity wall', used to describe the method employed to put up modern brick walls. The description can apply to walls of any section, but the normal hollow wall is the 11 in, which is formed by laying two skins of $4\frac{1}{2}$ in bricks with 2 in of air space between. The space ensures greater sound-proofing and reduces the likelihood of damp penetration. The two skins of the wall are pegged at specific points by metal ties, to give the structure greater strength and stability.

Hollow-ware. Silver which is raised on a stake or spun. The term covers a wide range of objects from the hollow coffee-pot to a tray classed as hollow-ware because of the method of manufacture used.

Holly. *Ilex aquifolium.* This is one of the whitest woods. It was used for such skilled work as inlay in the sixteenth and seventeenth centuries, and marquetry during the late seventeenth and early eighteenth centuries. Dyed black, holly was sometimes used for the ornamentation of cabinets.

Honeysuckle. The common name of the *Lonicera* genus, and one of the most ubiquitous of all decorative motifs, deriving from the Greek anthemion. It was first revived during the Renaissance, and even more vigorously during the Empire and Regency periods. It is seen in friezes, and frequently in cast-iron versions for the balconies of houses.

Hood. A term applied to any canopy projecting over a door or window, but most commonly to a semi-spherical or curved canopy.

On long-case clocks, the hood is the upper movable part of the case, enclosing the dial and mechanism. A rising hood was one that slid upwards; when the increased height of the cases made this impractical, a hood that pulled forward was used for a time. Later the fitting of a hinged door became standard practice.

Hood mould. A protective moulding, curved in section and mainly found in Gothic architecture; it was placed above a door or window to throw off rainwater. The hood mould originally followed the pointed curve of an arch and was continued horizontally beyond the door or window opening, frequently in the form of a string course (qv). In later periods of building, the hood mould was often adapted to classical and more mundane curves, and door and window shapes.

The Albany, Piccadilly, converted by Holland into residential chambers

Hood mould over a doorway

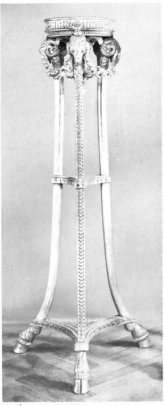

Hoof foot on a torchère, c 1770

Hoof foot. A foot that is most commonly found in conjunction with the cabriole leg on English furniture of the early eighteenth century. It made its first appearance around 1680.

The device is as old as the early Egyptian dynasties in both solid and cloven form. The cloven foot of English decorative work was most common in Chippendale Rococo.

Hooke, Robert (1635–1703). English scientist and architect.

Hall screen in the Merchant Taylor's Hall, London, by Hooke, 1673

Deepdene, Surrey, Hope's country house; the interior is furnished in Greek and Egyptian styles

Although his scientific work was more important, Hooke has a secure place in the history of English architecture. His career as an architect did not begin until he was 30. Before that, after being educated at Westminster School and Christ Church, Oxford, he had made his reputation as a scientific theorist. In 1662 he was appointed curator of experiments to the Royal Society, and professor of geometry at Gresham College. Later (1677–82) he was secretary of the Royal Society.

After the Fire of London (1666), Hooke produced plans for rebuilding the city, and was appointed one of its three post-Fire surveyors. In this capacity he worked with Wren, with whom he had long been friendly as a fellow-member of the Royal Society. Wren and Hooke undoubtedly worked together on the design of the Monument on Fish Hill and the rebuilding of the Navy Office. Hooke's chief architectural work was in connection with the rebuilding of the City churches, in which he played a considerable part as a surveyor. He was also made surveyor to the Dean and Chapter of Westminster.

In addition to ecclesiastical work in the City, at Westminster, and at Canterbury, Hooke carried out a number of private commissions. He designed such houses as Shenfield Place in Essex, Montagu House in Bloomsbury for Ralph Montagu (later Duke of Montagu), and Colyton in Devonshire for Sir Walter Young. Hooke was also concerned with additions and alterations to the Bethlehem Hospital in Moorfields and Magdalene College, Cambridge.

Hoop-back. A chair-back in which the top rail forms a continuous curve with the uprights. The form was used horizontally in Windsor chairs dating from the late eighteenth century and later, giving a continuous back and arm rail; but in these chairs it was more usually known as a bow-back (qv).

The American hoop-back is a Windsor chair with a horizontal arm rail bow and another upright bow fitted across the back of the arm rail. Both are fitted with spindles, those positione at the back being continuou between the two bows.

Hope, Thomas (c 1770–1831 British patron and propagandis Thanks to his father's wealth Hope was able to indulge h interest in the arts. As a youn man he travelled widely i Europe and the Near East, a quiring a considerable knowledg of architecture and a passion f Egyptian antiquities.

The French occupation of th Low Countries in 1795 force the Hopes to leave their busines and home in Amsterdam an Haarlem and to re-establis themselves in England. Thom Hope took a house built b Adam off Portland Place, an set himself up as a patron of th arts, adding to the house picture gallery designed by hir self. This gallery was built the Greek revival manne Hope's main interest outsi Egyptian design and decoratio

In 1806 Hope bought a hou in Surrey, known originally The Deep Dene (later as Dee dene). He began to enlarge th country house in much the san manner as he had his Lond house, once again employir either Peter or William Atkins (or both) as supervisor and co tractor. An extensive and detail description of Deepdene and i contents is given in *Neale's Vie of the Seats of Noblemen a Gentlemen* (second series). T interior decoration of the hou seems to have been divided b

Mahogany table inlaid with ebony and silver, by Hope

Penrhyn Castle, Caernarvonshire, designed by Hopper, 1827–47

Library at Penrhyn Castle with Norman arches and ornamented ceiling

tween Grecian and Egyptian motifs; the contents of the Sculpture Gallery, however, were remarkable for their catholicity, ranging from a figure of Augustus to a bust of the Duke of Wellington.

Although Hope's gallery in London was well known, he is now chiefly remembered for his singular attempt to introduce into Regency England a form of 'pale yellow furniture relieved by masses of black and gold', based on antique Egyptian models. In the attempt he played a notable part in popularizing motifs ranging from rams' and eagles' heads to a veritable legion of Nerfertiti-topped pilasters.

Hope published several books on his chosen studies, the most influential being *Household Furniture and Interior Decoration from Designs by Thomas Hope* (1807). But despite his wealth and his claims to act as an arbiter of architectural designs, Hope's portentous judgements on all aesthetic matters made him a ready target for contemporary wits. His influence upon English and French furniture design

Armchair by Hope, 1807

was nonetheless of some importance, and the mock-antiquities of Hope and others played a part in the disintegration of the Neo-classical traditions. Many of the less felicitous aspects of decoration, and the more daunting Victorian furniture designs, can be traced to Hope's dogmatizing, if not to his taste. Unlike many Victorian craftsmen, he never fell into bathos, because of his wide knowledge of antique models and fine feeling for the arts.

Hopper, Thomas (1776–1856). British architect. Hopper, the son of a surveyor in Rochester, Kent, was a talented and somewhat contumacious architect. He owed much of his early success to the Prince Regent's interest in a *cottage orné* in Fulham designed by him. As a result he was commissioned to undertake additions to the Regent's own establishment at Carlton House, including a conservatory in the Gothic manner. He published proposals and counter-proposals after awards had been made to others for the General Post Office (Sir Robert Smirke) and the Houses of Parliament (Sir Charles Barry). Despite these *contretemps*, Hopper was a highly successful architect with a reputation extending to Russia; the Emperor Alexander I offered him employment, but Hopper remained at home, occupied with a large practice which included the official surveyorship of Essex. His most notable buildings were probably Penrhyn and Margam Castles in Wales, and the Essex County Gaol at Chelmsford.

The main staircase at Penrhyn Castle

Horn armchairs with padded seats

Detail of an inlaid floor designed by Horta

Hopper light. Also called a hopper window or hopper casement. A window which follows the conventional casement construction, but is hinged to allow the upper part of the window to open for ventilation.

Horn furniture. Furniture of extravagant form, characterized by the use of horns and antlers for arms. The horn chair was an oddity that probably derived from the 'rural chairs' projected by Robert Manwaring in his *Cabinet and Chair-Maker's Real Friend and Companion*; these incorporated carved members representing tree-trunks and rockeries. In Britain horn chairs persisted into the early Victorian era, and similar furniture enjoyed some popularity in early nineteenth-century French decorative schemes.

Horse-brasses or **amulets.** These are used as decorations for harnesses to bring good luck and ward off evil spirits and sickness.

Horse exercising machine. See **Chamber horse.**

Horseshoe arch. An arch used in Islamic architecture and known variously as horseshoe, Islamic, and Moorish. It may be round or pointed.

Horta, Victor (1861–1947). Belgian architect. Horta was born in Ghent, and studied at Ghent Academy and the Brussels Académie des Beaux-Arts. He then worked in the office of Alphonse Balat, a successful architect working in the Neoclassical style. Horta's own predilections were formed by the teachings of Viollet-le-Duc (qv),

and his first buildings – a group of three small houses in the Rue des Douze Chambres in Ghent (1886) – exemplified his master's theories of rationality in design.

These simple designs show no signs of the influences that were to transform Horta's work during the next few years. Brussels was a centre for discussion of *avant-garde* ideas, in particular the nascent Art Nouveau style; and Horta soon became deeply involved. Soon he became the chief practitioner of Art Nouveau in Belgium.

Horta was in charge of the interior decoration and furnishings of the buildings he designed, and had considerable opportunities to display his inventive genius. His designs for the Maison Tassel in the Rue P E Janson, Brussels (1893), have frequently been called the first true examples of the Art Nouveau. Here the typical rhythms of this cursive style were given the fullest scope, and their cumulative effect is that of revolutionary declaration of be-

lief in new forms, techniques, and materials. This is also evident in Horta's use of ironwork, both structurally and decoratively – from the wrought-iron hand-rails of staircases and balconies to the unashamed iron framework for a glazed interior winter garden.

Horta practised the new style in other buildings, notably in designs for the Hotel Solvay in the Avenue Louise, Brussels (1895–1900), where he was in charge of every detail of decoration and furnishing. The result is the fullest statement of Horta's authority as an interpreter of Art Nouveau.

These commissions made Horta's reputation, and he was responsible for many houses in and around Brussels, all carried out in the manner he had made his own. Yet he was far more than a decorative master: he was one of the most searching and serious of all the architects seeking new and more rational structural forms. In his designs for the Maison du Peuple in

Horseshoe and cusped arches in the mosque at Cordova

The Maison du Peuple, Brussels, designed by Horta, 1896–9

Ebenezer Howard

ɔrussels (1896–9), and in two ɔepartment stores 'A l'Innova-on', Brussels (1901), and 'Grand ʒazar' in Frankfurt (1903), the ɔecorative mannerisms of Art Nouveau accompany a striving ɔr the lightness of structure that ʋas later to characterize the work ɔf Gropius and Mies van der ʒohe.

Horta was appointed a pro-ɛssor of the Académie des ʒeaux-Arts in Brussels in 1912, ɔut in 1916 he went to the USA. ^here he was greatly influenced ʋy the work of US architects; ɔr on his return to Brussels ʌter World War I, his work was naracterized by a rectilinear ɛmplicity, even austerity, in ɔmplete contrast to his previous ɔecorative work. His later work, ɔtably the concrete Palais des ʒeaux-Arts in Brussels, 1922 to ɔ28, places him amongst the in-ʌuential progenitors of the ɔodern movement and the Inter-ɔtional style. He was appointed ɛad of the Académie des Beaux-ɔrts in 1927, a position he held ɔr four years.

Howard, Ebenezer (1850–1928). Town-planner, publicist, and founder of the garden city movement. Howard was born in London, and after working as a junior clerk, emigrated to the USA at the age of 20. Four years later he returned as a trained shorthand reporter, which was thereafter his chosen career if not his major interest. In 1898 he published *To-Morrow: a Peaceful Path to Real Reform* (currently available under the title *Garden Cities of Tomorrow*), which made a significant impact on the garden city idea, and ultimately on the post-war development of the New Towns. In his book Howard advocated the building of towns with a population of between 30,000 and 60,000, surrounded by agricultural belts, and commercially and industrially as nearly self-supporting as possible. The book led to the founding of the Garden City Association (now the Town and Country Planning Association), and to the formation of kindred societies and associations elsewhere, culminating in the International Garden City Federation (later renamed the International Federation for Housing and Town Planning); Howard was the first president. Howard's writings and energetic idealism led to the foundation of the two well-known garden towns: Letchworth in 1903, and Welwyn in 1920. He was knighted in 1927 and died at Welwyn Garden City the following year.

Howell, Killick, Partridge, and Amis. British architectural partnership. It was formed by four young architects who met in 1950 as a result of their work in the housing division of the

Spiral staircase in Wolfson Block, St Anne's College, Oxford, designed by Howell, Killick, Partridge and Amis

London County Council architect's department, during which time they designed the Roe-hampton housing scheme. W G Howell and J A Killick started the practice, and were joined by J A Partridge in 1959, and S F Amis in 1960. The partnership's works include a number of housing projects and university extension developments, including the faculty of commerce and social science at Birmingham University; St Antony's College and St Anne's College at Oxford; and the University Centre, Sidney Sussex College, and Darwin College at Cambridge.

Huguenot silver. The term Huguenot silver should properly be restricted to silver made by immigrant Protestant craftsmen who fled from France at the end of the seventeenth century. In fact, it is applied to all English silver between about 1685 and 1730 that shows French influence.

For several years before Louis XIV ended French tolerance of Protestantism by the Revocation of the Edict of Nantes (1685), there had been a trickle of Huguenot refugees from France. After 1685 the trickle became a torrent. Most of the Huguenots

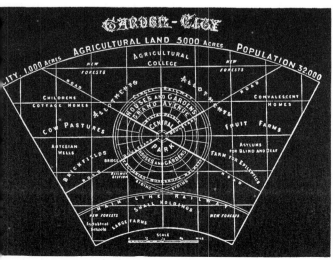

Diagrammatic representation of the ideal Garden City by Howard, 1898

The Wolfson Block at St Anne's College, Oxford, 1964

Sugar caster: de Lamerie, 1719

Jug by W Fawdery, 1722

One of a pair of candlesticks made by Pierre Harache, 1685

were craftsmen – lacemakers, silk weavers, gold- and silversmiths – who sought religious freedom and peace in England and Flanders, Ireland and America.

Many silversmiths found their way to London. They came from all over France: Pierre Harache from Rouen, Louis Mettayer from Poitou, Pierre Platel from Lorraine, David Willaume from Metz. Later their craft traditions were carried on by their sons, and by craftsmen of Huguenot descent who were brought up in England from childhood, such as the renowned Paul de Lamerie.

The fact that many of the first wave of Huguenot refugees came from the provinces of France probably accounts for the establishment of the formal, more restrained, Régence styles in England, rather than the fashionable, almost Rococo, flamboyance that was already sweeping Paris. Not that the Huguenots found themselves particularly welcome in London. During the 1680s, and indeed until as late as 1711, London silversmiths frequently attempted to drive out the foreigners, or at least to prevent them from becoming free of the Goldsmiths' Company, and so able to set up in business on their own account. This hostility did not deter London silversmiths from making use of Huguenot designs and Huguenot skills.

English silver badly needed a new stimulus. London craftsmen were overwhelmed with orders, but their repertoire of Dutch-influenced chased designs, their own rather naïve *chinoiseries*, their interpretation of the Baroque, and their often inadequate standards of workmanship, did not wholly satisfy their rich, display-conscious patrons. Possibly, even without the influx of refugees, silversmiths would soon have turned to France for inspiration. The new ideas and, much more important, the skill of the Huguenots at applied decoration, chasing, and engraving, were most timely. They introduced many improvements in the forms of silverwares, and – most important of all – devoted meticulous attention to detail in ornament. They gave the two-handled cup and cover a new importance, introduced the tall helmet-shaped ewer, and made wide use of the baluster form for candlesticks, casters, cups, and jugs. They were probably mainly responsible for the increased employment of hexagonal and octagonal forms for pots, jugs, and salvers.

The decorative skills of the Huguenots are undeniable. They

Design for Metropolitan Museum of Art, New York, by R M Hunt

introduced the motifs of the French Régence style, with its formal yet delicate applied strapwork, flowerheads, husks, diapers, and shells. Their attention to detail has already been noted, and their engraving – used for both border decoration and coats of arms within Baroque cartouches – revived a skill that had been almost lost in England. They also perfected the cut-cardwork that had first been introduced some 40 years before, making elaborate silhouettes by piercing and overlaying layer upon layer to achieve intricate and satisfying applied detail. Their standard of casting was also exceptionally high. Cast and chased details were used for ornament as well as for bold flying scroll handles, finials, and even objects such as candlesticks.

Among English silversmiths there was a growing tendency towards simplicity, with ornament restricted to fluting and gadrooning. The Huguenots helped to formalize this style, flattening flutes and subduing bold foliate chasing into formal acanthus borders, turning caryatid handles into elegant bold scrolls or harp-shapes, turning bulging curves into slightly tapered ones, and making form and ornament subservient to proportion and regularity.

The impact of Huguenot design and craftsmanship coincided with the enforcement of the higher, Britannia Standard for silver. But the demand for silver objects remained high. Tea, coffee, and chocolate fostered the demand; casters for sugar and spice were needed; mugs and tankards, punch bowls and wine cisterns, salvers and waiters, dishes, plates, and ewers, and a dozen other domestic wares as well as more formal cups and covers, consumed silver fast. And the Huguenot influence was all for much heavier plate – of heavy gauge, made weightier with applied ornament and mouldings, and often cast. The higher cost of the Britannia Standard silver in no way

deterred the silversmith from using heavy metal and much ornament, for many patrons were prepared to pay the higher price.

By the end of Queen Anne's reign, native and Huguenot styles had blended to create an elegant style in which the most sought-after of all old English silver was made. Some wares, it is true, remained very much the province of individual English or Huguenot silversmiths. Few of the Huguenots, for instance, even those of the second generation born in England, made tankards; while silversmiths of Huguenot extraction seem to have made most of the helmet-shaped jugs and ewers. Up to about 1710 the nationality of the silversmith is often evident even without inspecting his mark. (Tea and coffee wares are an exception.) Later, the marriage of styles makes questions of origin very difficult to answer. For the silver detective, assessing how much is English and how much Huguenot is an absorbing pursuit.

Hunt, Richard Morris (1827-95). American architect, trained in Paris at the Ecole des Beaux Arts (1845–54), after which he worked under Lefuel for a year on the most important commission of the day, the New Louvre.

He returned to the USA in 1855, though he visited Europe again in the 1860s.

Hunt was undoubtedly the best-trained, most competent architect of the decade following the Civil War; but his works are overshadowed by those of architects far less accomplished but far more original. The details of his New York Tribune Building (1875) shows that he was by no means a copyist, and his Stuyvesant flats in New York City (1869–70) have all the suavity of contemporary French design and none of the bombast it acquired in England or America. Hunt could mass picturesque elements upon a solid base with unsurpassed ingenuity, as in his Vanderbilt Mansion in New

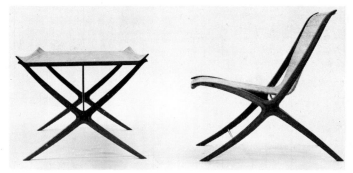

Chair and table by P Hvidt and O Molgaard-Nielsen, 1960

St George's Church, Sheffield, designed by William Hurst, 1821–5

York City (1879–80). He failed in that he tried to solve architectural problems in exclusively aesthetic terms; the Tribune building is the earliest proper skyscraper, yet its articulation is handled beautifully but entirely inappropriately.

Hunting-chair. A form of armchair which seems to have derived its specialist name from a reference in Sheraton's *Cabinet Dictionary* (1803). In this it is described as 'stuffed all over, except the legs, which are of mahogany.' The chair was in effect an adjustable day-bed, for it was fitted with a sliding frame which could be pulled out to form a foot-rest 'for one that is fatigued as hunters usually are.' The term was short-lived, and seems to have passed away with its coiner. No illustrations of it appear to have survived.

Hunting table or **hunter's sideboard.** A tall sideboard table at which huntsmen could stand up to take refreshments. It was made in the southern states of America from the mid-eighteenth to the early nineteenth centuries.

Two versions exist, one a table with only a deep frieze, the other with either drawers or cupboards;

this type is perhaps better known as a hunt sideboard.

Hurst, William (1787–1844). British architect. Hurst was born in Doncaster, where he became assistant to an architectural firm of which he was later to become junior partner. Woodhead & Hurst were responsible for much building in Yorkshire and Derbyshire. Among their major achievements were the churches of St George, Sheffield (1821–5), Christchurch, Doncaster (1827–9), and St Thomas, Chesterfield (1830–1). Their secular practice was concentrated mainly in and around Sheffield, and included a musical hall, the grammar school (1825; later demolished), and additions to the town hall (later the court house). The ecclesiastical side of the practice continued to flourish after the death of Woodhead, with many more churches in the two counties.

Husk. A small three-lobed ornament taken from the dry ripe husks of oats or other seeds. Chains of husks were popular in plasterwork decoration and inlay, especially on chairs and cabinet furniture.

Hutch (from the French *huche*). Basically, a chest. But the term

is a fairly expansive and flexible one which seems to have been applied to many medieval chests or small cupboards. It covered receptacles that could store clothes or food, and was presumably the prototype for the later hanging larder cupboard. The hutch in its earliest form was hung or placed on a stand, and had pierced or decoratively carved doors. In American usage the word is applied to dressers with a superstructure of open shelves.

Hvidt, Peter (*b* 1916). Danish architect and furniture designer whose work has done much to establish the international reputation of modern Danish furniture.

Hvidt trained as a cabinetmaker and designer at the School of Applied Art for cabinetmakers in Copenhagen, staying on between 1942 and 1945 as an instructor. In 1944 he set up his own office with the designer Orla Mølgaard-Nielsen (*b* 1907). Together they have designed furniture for France and Son, Fritz Hansen, and Soborg. They have exhibited in America, England, France, Germany, and Italy, where they won awards at the Milan Triennale.

Hypar and **hyperbolic paraboloid.** Hypars, or umbrella-shaped structures, have had considerable influence upon the growth of what are now generally termed 'shell-designs' in architecture. Basically, the hypar is an

umbrella-like shape which can be used either in a conventional manner as a roof structure or in plural, segmental, or even up-ended forms depending on the size and functions of the building. Elaborations of the basic hypar, or shell-roof, into more complex hyperbolic paraboloids have resulted in some of the most spectacular modern buildings; among the most famous are the churches, laboratories, warehouses, hotels, and other buildings designed by Felix Candela. The best-known shell-structure in England is the Commonwealth Institute at Holland Park, London, designed by the firm of Matthew, Johnson-Marshall, and Partners.

Hypocaust heating. A system evolved by the Romans for the heating of houses and baths which combined many of the advantages of both modern convected hot air and radiated heat. A *hypocausis* or furnace was built underground and the hot air from it carried, by means of *cuniculi* or flues, to the rooms to be heated. The flues also acted as radiators.

Hypostyle. A term usually applied to a hall of which the flat roof is built upon grouped columns. The structure seems to have originated in ancient Egypt and reached its fullest architectural expression in the hypostyle hall at Karnak in the early Eighteenth Dynasty (1570–1450 BC).

Hyperbolic parabola on Mausoleum at Karachi by R Squire and Hartnell

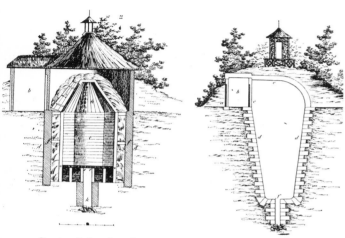

Sectional drawing of a typical nineteenth-century ice-house

Ice or **crackle glass.** So called because of its resemblance to broken or cracked ice. This effect, developed in seventeenth-century Venice, was achieved by two methods. Either the vessel was suddenly cooled by plunging

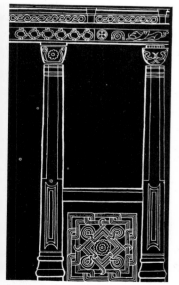

Iconostasis at St Luke of Siros

it into cold water, reheated, and then blown, a process which produced minute cracks and gave a frosted appearance; or while the glass was still molten it was rolled on to broken fragments of glass which were then partly remelted.

Ice-house. A structure in which an elementary form of refrigeration was carried out; it was frequently attached or adjacent to large houses. Normally it consisted of a cellar with hollow walls, floors, roof, and double doors, or a separate structure in the form of an inverted hollow cone. Ice-houses were increasingly used during the seventeenth and eighteenth centuries. In his *Encyclopedia of Villa, Farm, and Cottage Architecture* (1836), Loudon gives elaborate instructions for the building of ice-houses suitable for private houses, farm-houses, and inns.

Iconostasis. The screen in Byzantine churches which separates nave from sanctuary. The iconostasis was at first a columnar

screen with a parapet supporting sculpture or other decorations; later its divisive function became more emphatic, three doors piercing the screen. After the fifteenth century the iconostasis was essentially a wall which was decorated with icons.

Ictinus. Greek architect. Ictinus lived during the second half of the fifth century BC, and, in collaboration with Callicrates, designed the Parthenon at Athens. It was begun in 447 BC by order of Pericles, and finished in 438 BC; Phidias, the master sculptor, apparently supervised the work throughout. Ictinus wrote a book, no longer extant but quoted by Vitruvius, on the building of the Parthenon. Other buildings, for the designs of which Ictinus was probably solely responsible, were the Temple of Apollo at Bassae, near Phigalia in Arcadia, and the Telesterion or hall of initiation

Doric column from the Parthenon

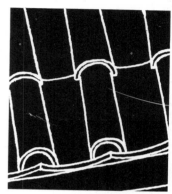

Imbrex tiling on a roof

at Eleusis. Remains of both buildings still exist.

Imbrex. A convex-shaped roofing tile which was used in ancient architecture to cover the gaps or joints between flat or concave tiles. The term derives from Latin *imber*, a shower, indicating the facility with which the tile threw off rainfall. The imbrex section has been incorporated into many forms of modern sheet-roofing in asbestos and metal, and the same principle is used in the curved pantile.

Imbrication. An arrangement of decorative motifs resembling overlapping formalized fish-scales. It was widely used in ancient Roman architecture, and was revived during the Renaissance, and again in Empire and Regency decoration.

Impost. The upper course of a wall, or topmost part of a pier or pilaster, on which the base of an arch rests, and from which the arch springs.

Ince, William, and **Mayhew,** John. English cabinetmakers. The names of these two eighteenth-century craftsmen are in-

Ivory. *A hanging cabinet decorated with carved ivory figures and medallions; it was made for Sir Robert Walpole in 1743*

An Ince and Mayhew design for a corner cupboard, an 'Ecoineur'

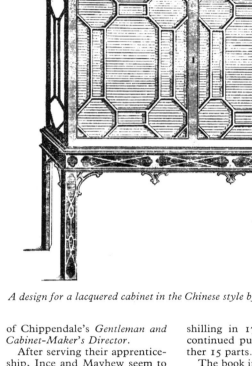

A design for a lacquered cabinet in the Chinese style by Ince and Mayhew

market in mind. The engravings were the work of Mathias Darly, who had engraved most of the designs in the *Director*.

Although Ince and Mayhew were accused of plagiarizing Chippendale's designs, and did occasionally borrow heavily from him, they were evidently skilful and inventive craftsmen in their own right. Their self-confident designs, based ostensibly upon what they termed 'the raffle leaf', and doubtless owing something to Hogarth's *Analysis of Beauty*, published in 1753, were undoubtedly of the same genre as Chippendale's but added a youthful gaiety and brash ebullience which is not without charm. They were certainly amongst the most successful cabinetmakers and upholsterers of their time. Their curious bastardized Anglo-French nomenclature for the pieces they designed also has its charms: *ecoineurs* (corner cabinets); *voiders* (trays); *illuminares* (candlestands); *un grand sofa* (sic). *The Universal System* included a section on tripods and metalwork, a subject not covered in the *Director*.

Many of Ince and Mayhew's designs, especially those catering for the taste for Rococo motifs and *chinoiserie*, have considerable verve and audacity. They are also authoritative and at ease when dealing with fret designs, whether applied to the doors of bookcases or used for tray frames or galleries or chair backs.

variably linked, because they were joint authors of a well-known pattern-book. *The Universal System of Household Furniture*, which was issued in parts between 1759 and 1763, is perhaps more accurately described as a trade catalogue; it was undoubtedly intended to compete with the third edition of Chippendale's *Gentleman and Cabinet-Maker's Director*.

After serving their apprenticeship, Ince and Mayhew seem to have set up their own workshop in Carnaby Market while they were still young men. The first part of *The Universal System*, dedicated to the Duke of Marlborough, was published at one shilling in 1759, and the work continued publication for a further 15 parts.

The book in its final form provided subscribers with only half of the 200 plates supplied by the *Director* and with considerably less technical guidance, but the preface carried a French translation, plainly with the foreign

Inchbald, Michael (*b* 1920). British interior designer. Inchbald was trained as an architect. He has won several awards for his designs, and his furniture has been selected for exhibition in New York and at the Milan Triennale and at the London

A chair by Ince and Mayhew

A drawing-room designed by Michael Inchbald

Michael Inchbald

Design Centre.

Inchbald has been responsible for many decorative schemes for hotels, offices, and commercial projects, including rooms at the Savoy Hotel, Claridges, and the New Berkeley Hotel. He has also designed a range of staterooms for the liners *Franconia* and *Carmania*, as well as three public rooms in the *Windsor Castle* and the Queen's Room on the *Queen Elizabeth II*.

Indian architecture. This simple term scarcely does justice to a subject that is both complex and various – historically, geographically, and racially.

The early history of architecture in the vast Indian subcontinent is dominated by its great religions: Buddhism, Hinduism, and Islam. Ruins of ancient Buddhist shrines, built over 5,000 years ago, have been discovered, but the most extensive remains of Buddhist shrines or *topes* are those at Sanchi in Bhopal. Many of these, dating

Detail of a pillar at Avantipore

from *c* 300 BC, were made known to the West by the archaeological publications of General Sir Alexander Cunningham in the mid-nineteenth century. Other Buddhist temples, known as *chaitya* caves, were usually hewn out of solid rock and supported by enormous shafts. Those at Nasik, Bedsa, and Ajanta, in the area between Bombay and Poona, have been well documented. These holy caverns or halls are comparable to early Christian churches, although much smaller than the early abbeys and cathedrals. A wide nave usually leads to an apse containing the *chaitya* or shrine. Other early buildings were the *viharas* or Buddhist monasteries of southern India, pyramidal in elevation and of no outstanding architectural interest.

Farther north, in Kashmir, the remains of a somewhat different form of religious building exist. These are the Jain temples. Although the religious beliefs of Jains and Buddhists were not dissimilar, the Jain temples were above ground and seem to have been more architecturally impressive. The temples were built within courtyards, the walls of which were far more sophisticated in decorative treatment than the southern Buddhist temples. The decorative motifs employed in the embellishment of the temples were complex and richly detailed. The courtyards frequently enclosed shallow water-gardens.

Hindu architecture has generally been classified into three styles: the Dravidian temples in the area of the Madras Presidency (Tamil Nadu); the Chalukyan, represented by remains in the Kalvan area; and the northern or Indo-Aryan style. Although these styles are interrelated, each has its own clearly defined characteristics. The Dravidian temples were built by the Tamil-speaking peoples and added extreme richness or ornament to the traditional stepped pyramidal forms. The Chalukyan style produced the great temple at Halebid with its myriad sculptures, the whole constructed out of the local volcanic potstone. The northern style, as practised by the Sanskrit-speaking peoples, spread over a far greater area: from the provinces of Dharwar in the west to Orissa in the east. It has left few monuments of any great size and is influenced by Moslem styles, as in the elevation of the Temple of Vishveshwar.

Most of northern India was conquered by the Moslems to-

One of the group of thirty temples at Khajuraho, 10th century

The east front of the Central Pavilion at Halebid

The Taj Mahal, near Agra, 1630–53

The elevation of Jamma Masjid, Ahmedabad, 1424

wards the end of the twelfth century. This led to the destruction of many ancient Hindu temples and the building of new mosques to the glory of Allah. The fusion of local styles with the Moslem manner, originating from Persia, produced somewhat hybrid buildings in what is generally known as the Indian Saracenic style. Over the centuries, however, the style gradually evolved into the splendid Mogul or Mughal style seen in

tombs, mosques, forts, and palaces, many of which are still standing. Notable examples of Mogul architecture are the great mosques at Delhi (1198) and Jaunpur (1438), and mosques at Ahmedabad. Other buildings include the fort at Agra (1566) and the Taj Mahal, also at Agra, built in the middle years of the seventeenth century.

The Taj Mahal was almost the last of the great Mogul buildings, for India became increasingly subject to native wars and the incursions of European merchant adventurers and troops. After the British domination had begun (c 1745) the architecture of India was once again that of its conquerors. At first, the Greek revival version of the later Georgian manner was employed; this style, with its shadowy porticoes and wide canopies, happened to be well adjusted to the climate. It was followed by the less felicitous influences of the Gothic revival under Sir George Gilbert Scott. Finally, the palatial Neo-Georgian manner of the joint architects of the

New Delhi complex, Sir Edwin Lutyens and Sir Herbert Baker, provided a fitting background for the last few days of British rule.

Western influences have not, however, diminished with the departure of the British. The Franco-Swiss architect Le Corbusier was responsible for the planning of Chandigarh, the new capital of the Punjab, where he sought to impose Western ideas on an Eastern climate. Many well-known Indian and European architects and engineers helped in the design and evolution of the new capital. Maxwell Fry, Jane Drew, Pierre Jeanneret, P N Thapar, and P L Verma have worked under the direction of Le Corbusier, who was here able to put into practice his theories of the town as a living organism.

The Capitol is the commanding feature of the town and is set at the head of a slope in a 250-acre enclave. It comprises the secretariat, high court, governor's residence, and assembly chambers. Le Corbusier firmly rejected the traditional ideal of locating government buildings in the centre of the town, assigning them to the northernmost corner, where government can function undisturbed.

The Capitol is approached by the main 300 ft wide avenue lined with trees on either side. Important banks, government offices, and hotels are located on this road. The four-storey high court is famous for its parasol-like roof, a new method of securing protection from the sun in the tropics. The roof stands clear of the walls, projecting 26 ft all along. The entire building has multi-patterned sun-breakers which protect it from the sun and wind. They are so designed that the rays of the summer sun are kept out all the time, while the oblique rays of the winter sun can have free play in heating room interiors.

The city centre has been planned both as a commercial and civic centre, the idea being very Indian – that of a central *Chowk,* with the most important buildings, such as the town hall, the central library, the post and telegraph offices, banks, etc grouped around it. The *Chowk* is open only to pedestrian traffic.

Tomb detail, I'timad-ud-Daulah

The Secretariat building at Chandigarh by Le Corbusier

Indian carpets. Carpet-making was introduced to India by the Mogul princes in the sixteenth century. It was entirely based on Persian work, with Persian designs and weavers from Herat. The industry flourished until the early years of the seventeenth century, but the designs deteriorated once it was cut off from its Persian sources. However, the technique was often impeccable, and luxurious rugs were made with well over two thousand knots to the square inch. Agra and Warangal produced some of the better work of the nineteenth century. The quality today is generally poor.

Industrialized building. 'Industrialized', 'factory', or 'system' building are terms applied to new methods of production in building. The object has been to modernize the industry by adopting some of the car industry's techniques in prefabrication and conveyor-belt assembly. By reducing the amount of work that has to be done on the site, by borrowing some of the techniques of mass-production, by the kind of rationalization which is commonplace in other industries, and by turning the site itself into a kind of factory or factory extension, industrialized building has achieved good enough results to be widely utilized. Basically all industrialized building systems can be divided into two categories. (1) Those which are known as *in situ* systems use fast-hardening concrete cavity walls and other structural methods to speed up work on the site. (2) Prefabricated systems enable factory-made components, large or small, to be delivered to the site at the appropriate moment for incorporating into the growing building.

In either case the builder has to invest at least three times as much in plant and equipment as he does for houses built by conventional methods. In addition, if he prefabricates in an off-site factory, he has to pay for carrying the finished parts to the site, a much more expensive business than dumping lorry-loads of sand and gravel there. So, even on sites where several hundred houes are to be built at a time, the cost of a factory-built house is apt to prove uneconomical. Only a mass market brings down the price per unit. Part of the trouble is that systems vary considerably in method, material, and manpower demands, and thus differ

greatly in what they can offer.

There are even more advanced methods. Plastics manufacturers now provide shells of glass-reinforced polyester that are suitable for basic structures anywhere in the world. Shells are light enough for two trucks to be able to transport housing units for 112 people which can be assembled by a two-man delivery team in one working day.

Inglenook. A term derived from the Scottish *ingle*, meaning a fire upon a hearth. Inglenook refers to a wide nook or chimney corner beside the ingle in which high wooden settles were placed. The arrangement creates an intimate and cosy scene; after two hundred years of disuse it was resurrected by the Edwardians as a central motif of their cottage style.

Inlay. Inlaying is basically the ornamentation of one material by the insertion of a contrasting material. The term is generally applied to the cabinetmaker's technique for decorating the surfaces of furniture with decorative motifs set into the wood. The design is established by the contrast of timbers (or veneers) of different grain or by the contrast of different textures or materials. Thus inlays, though usually in wood, have been made with metal, ranging from pewter to brass, and more exotic materials such as ivory and tortoiseshell. The basic technique

was known to the ancient Egyptians. Inlay was used on oak in the sixteenth and seventeenth centuries, but its supreme expression is in Regency and Empire work.

In its simplest form the technique was quite straightforward: decorative material was set into the solid surface, which was cut to the shape appropriate to receive the motif(s). As the

A chest inlaid with ivory in the Lombardic Carthusian style

Guéridon with inlaid Sèvres panels

...isting up prefabricated wall

Dutch cabinet inlaid with floral marquetry

Norman interlacing arches

cabinetmaker's craft became more sophisticated, the technique was elaborated: veneers of various coloured woods were assembled into complex decorative patterns, employing geometrical, floral, and arabesque motifs which were deployed against a ground of darker colour. Thus satinwood, harewood, holly, acacia, sycamore, and fruit woods were contrasted with mahogany, walnut, and later rosewood, in this technique of 'markatree' – later revised to marquetry – a process which dates from the increased popularity of walnut furniture in the latter half of the seventeenth century. In the early eighteenth century the French *ébenistes*, led by André Charles Boulle, became preoccupied with inlay and marquetry, and developed techniques for inlaying brass into wood, known as boulle or buhl (qv).

During the periods when inlay was widely practised, table-tops, bureaux, and clock-cases were usually the objects chosen to demonstrate the craftsman's skill. During the Regency era, a metallic inlay of a form more simple than Boulle's became popular, especially for the decoration of sofa-table and dining-table tops and the supports of writing-tables.

See also the articles on marquetry and parquetry.

Intaglio. A process by which a design is cut, engraved, or stamped into a surface, so that an impression can be made on a softer surface, giving a design in relief. In varying forms the process is used in many crafts, from jewellery design to printing: in certain divisions of jewellery design, for example signet rings, the resulting intaglio is an end in itself. The process was first used by the ancient Assyrians and Egyptians for making seals. Hard stones, such as onyx, were engraved in depth and then used for stamping initials, monograms, or devices upon wax. This has remained one of the most important purposes of the intaglio process. In printing, intaglio is a process in which the printing-ink is retained in the recesses of plates made by the craft or process engraver until the plate is applied to paper; an impression is made on the paper by the pressure of the proofing or printing machine.

Intarsia or **tarsia.** A type of mosaic made up of different coloured woods and popular in Italy during the fifteenth and sixteenth centuries. It was used to decorate small rooms such as studies in palaces and choirs of churches.

Intercolumniation. The space between columns, as in a colonnade. In ancient times the distance was supposedly calculated from the lower diameter of the columns, depending upon the order employed; but in practice it was apt to vary.

Interlacing arch. Interlacing arches are a means of surface decoration mainly found in Norman work. Each series of pilasters carries a pair of arches, springing right and left to the next pilaster but one, and so crossing the arches carried by the intermediate pilasters. In England, interlacing arches are found in the aisles at Durham Cathedral and on the west front of Southwell Minster.

International style. A term first used in 1932, when the American architect Philip Johnson, in association with Henry Russell Hitchcock, the architectural historian, arranged an exhibition of international architecture at New York's Museum of Modern Art. In the catalogue produced for the exhibition which showed the work of Mies van der Rohe, Frank Lloyd Wright, Le Corbusier, Gropius and others, the term International style was first used. It rapidly caught on, and although many critics protested at the implications of such an all-embrac

A house in Brno, Czechoslovakia: Mies van der Rohe, 1930

A seaside house on Long Island, New York: Marcel Breuer

The five main ratios of intercolumniation, established by Vitruvius

1½ diameters PYCNOSTYLE
2¼ diameters EUSTYLE
3 diameters DIASTYLE
2 diameters SYSTYLE
3½ diameters ARAEOSTYLE

The five main ratios of intercolumniation, established by Vitruvius

Frank Lloyd Wright's headquarters at Taliesin, Arizona

Unité d'Habitation, Marseilles: Le Corbusier, 1947–52

ing description, the term was apposite and succinct enough to become an accepted term.

The International style originated in the tentative works of such disparate architects as C F A Voysey, Louis H Sullivan, and Adolf Loos, and has flourished down to our own time. Architecturally, the term defines the efforts of architects in many countries to evolve simpler and more logical forms of construction and expression. To Henry Russell Hitchcock its essential feature is the conception of architecture as volume rather than mass, with regularity rather than axial symmetry as the controlling element in the design. But to most laymen the style is typified by its apparent emphasis on rectilinear silhouettes, most clearly seen in the buildings designed by Mies van de Rohe.

The earliest examples of the style are probably the domestic projects of Adolf Loos and the commercial buildings of Sullivan.

Gradually, the logic of the style, its suitability to current building technology, and improved methods of communication caused its international adoption. Despite nationalistic departures in the 1930s, it has become the characteristic modern style, reaching its fullest international influence in the 1950s as a result of Mies's work in America.

Interpenetration(s). A motif
originally evolved by fifteenth-century European carvers. Interpenetrations are mouldings which intersect or appear to intersect or pierce each other.

Interrupted arch or **pediment.** An alternative term, more widely used in the USA than in Britain, for the broken arch or pediment. The apex or topmost curve of such features is omitted, allowing the introduction of a bust or some other decorative motif.

Intrados. The inner curve of an arch, balanced by the outer curve or extrados (qv). It is also known as a soffit.

Inwood, William (c 1771–1843), and Henry William (1794–1843). This unusual father-son partnership was responsible for many Greek revival churches and chapels in London.

Henry William was trained in his father's office, but later travelled widely in Greece, studying ancient buildings. On his return he studied at the Royal Academy schools before joining his father's practice. Thanks to the knowledge he had gained on his travels, the younger Inwood was able to make their joint enterprises uncommonly scholarly versions of the Greek manner.

The Inwoods designed a number of churches in north London, notably St Pancras New Church, one of the most distinguished and influential of all Greek revival buildings in England. They also designed All Saints Chapel, Camden Town, and St Peter's Chapel in Regent Square, Bloomsbury.

Both Inwoods were also authors. The son published *The Erechtheum at Athens* (1827) and a work on the architecture of Greece, Egypt, and other coun-

tries. The elder Inwood published the well-known *Tables for the Purchasing of Estates*, which continued to appear in new editions long after his death. The Inwoods died in the same month in 1843: the son drowned en route for Spain, and the father died in his house in Marylebone.

Ionic order. The early development of the Ionic order occurred among the Greeks on the west coast of Asia Minor (Ionia); not until c 500 BC was the order used in Greek temple architecture on the mainland. Two of the finest examples are on the Acropolis of Athens: the

St Peter's Chapel, Regent Square, London: W and H W Inwood, 1824

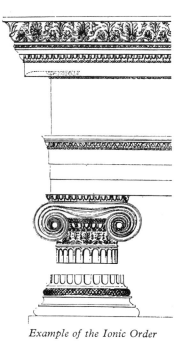

Example of the Ionic Order

arrises as in the Doric order. The column is slender, and rests upon an Attic base composed of two torus mouldings with a scotia and fillet between; at the very bottom is a square plinth. Directly above the semi-circular heads of the flutings is a bead moulding, over which there is an echinus decorated with egg and dart motifs. The two volutes at the front and back are cushioned on the echinus; they are joined at the sides by a concave pillow which is usually enlivened with small decorations such as bead mouldings.

Though Vitruvius formulated rules for the order, its origin remains a matter of speculation. None of the existing theories can be termed definitive, mainly because of the paucity of early examples which would show the stages by which the order gradually developed. The basic spiral motif has long been employed as a decorative device even by most primitive peoples. See **Orders.**

temples of the Erechtheum (421–405 BC) and Niké Apteros (427 BC).

The shaft of the Ionic column has 24 flutings (early examples have been found with as many as 40), and all are separated by flat areas or fillets, but not

Bunratty Castle, Co Clare; fifteenth-century fortress

Irish architecture. As in most other European countries, the earliest Irish buildings of any consequence were for defensive or ecclesiastical purposes. St Patrick's mission (usually but controversially dated 432–61 AD) introduced Christianity into Ireland, and led to the efflorescence of Irish monasticism during the sixth and seventh centuries. Hundreds of monasteries were built, but they were a good deal more primitive than their European counterparts, being little more than adaptations of earlier fortified enclosures of church, library, refectory, workshops, and huts. During the seventh and eighth centuries, conically-roofed fortified round towers were added to serve as belfries, watchtowers, and rallying-points for defence. Although primitive, these settlements housed scholars and craftsmen whose achievements, ranging from book-illustration to metalwork, made them famous throughout Europe. The masterpiece of this monastic culture was undoubtedly the *Book of Kells*, now in Trinity College, Dublin. Churches remained simple one-chamber structures, although the richness of their woven hangings and paintings doubtless made the interiors highly colourful.

After the Anglo-Norman conquest of Ireland in 1169–70, Romanesque influences were for a time in evidence in ecclesiastical architecture, although the two post-conquest Dublin cathedrals of Christ Church, begun in 1172, and St Patrick's,

Part of the sixth century monastic buildings, Glendalough, Wicklow

St Kevin's 'kitchen', monastic building at Glendalough, Co Wicklow

The exterior of Russborough House in Co Wicklow, designed by Richard Cassels, built 1741

gun two decades later, are milar in style to contemporary thedrals in England. Under nglish influence other Gothic urches were also built, including Kilkenny Cathedral nid-thirteenth century) and beys in Muckros, Holycross, d other centres. Understand-ly enough, in the troubled nturies that followed, there was tle secular building. Queen izabeth I founded Trinity ollege, Dublin, in 1592, but w academic buildings of note se to consolidate the foundan. Kilmainham Hospital in Dublin (1680) is one of the few notable buildings before 1700.

During the eighteenth century, however, a vast programme of public and private building was initiated by the Anglo-Irish ruling class. Some of the finest classical post-Palladian architecture in Europe was produced. Great houses were built (Powerscourt, Castletown, Russborough); houses and castles were enlarged and gothicized (Birr, Glin, Lismore, and scores of others); and Dublin itself was spectacularly enriched. Trinity College (1752–60); the Custom House (1781–91); the Four Courts (1785); Parliament House (1785); later the Bank of Ireland, and the General Post Office (1814) were built alongside squares and terraces which carried on the Georgian urban tradition already established in London. The Anglo-Irish nobility also built many fine town houses to complement their country mansions. Although most of the smaller terrace houses imitated London's domestic elevations, later Anglo-Irish architects developed a one-storey Regency house of considerable visual charm which is virtually indigenous to Ireland.

This burst of building activity, which transformed Dublin in less than a century into a fully European capital, was directed by a group of architects of unusual imagination and versatility. Most of them were uprooted from England by exigent patrons. The most important was James Gandon, although the native-born Francis Johnston and the German-born Richard Cassels (later Castle) designed many fine buildings. Other English architects made their contri-

The General Post Office, Dublin; the main front by Francis Johnston

The Four Courts, Dublin, by James Gandon, 1786–96

Mussenden Temple in Co Derry, built in 1783 as a library

Castleward House, Co Down, designed by Bernard Ward in 1765

A typical Regency single-storey terrace house in Dublin, c 1830–60

Dublin Bus Station, designed by Michael Scott

The new Abbey Theatre, Dublin, by Michael Scott and Partners, 1966

bution to the Irish scene, most notably perhaps Sir William Chambers, whose Casino (1757–71), at Marino near Clontarf remains one of the most pleasing of Ireland's Georgian buildings. John Nash was responsible for many of Ireland's more exotic private houses.

The pace of building slowed down in the nineteenth century, in part because of Ireland's poverty and political instability. A number of ecclesiastical buildings were built, including the Anglican Cathedral in Cork (1863–70), and various public buildings were erected in Dublin, including the National Gallery (1854–64) and the National Library (1884).

Twentieth-century Irish architecture reflects the stylistic conflicts which have dominated all European architecture. The Bel-

fast City Hall (1896–1902) and the Parliament Buildings Stormont, near Belfast (1928–32), are examples of Neo-Georgian institutional architecture. More recently, thanks to the influence of native-born architects, including Raymond McGrath, Michael Scott (Dublin bus station), Desmond Fitzgerald (Dublin airport), and others, Dublin and other Irish cities now possess outstanding examples of modern architecture.

Irish Chippendale. The modern term for a style of mid-eighteenth-century Irish furniture resembling Chippendale. The carving was rather imprecise and there are certain characteristic features such as over-deep aprons on tables and a preponderance of lion masks and elongated paw feet.

Merrion Square in Dublin, built in the eighteenth century

A Cork water jug, c *1780*

Irish glass.

Lead glass was probably first made in Ireland c 1690, and developed along similar lines to glass in England. After 1780 many skilled craftsmen and cutters, frustrated by the heavy excise taxes in England, emigrated to Ireland, initiating what is known as the Anglo-Irish period. It was not until 1825, when an excise tax was finally imposed on Ireland, that her glass industry began to decline.

An early immigrant was a Bristol manufacturer, Benjamin Edwards, who set up a glasshouse in Belfast in 1776. The best known Irish glasshouse is Waterford, founded by two businessmen brothers, George and William Penrose, in 1783. It was first controlled by John Hill, a skilled glassmaker from Stourbridge who is said to have recruited some 50 English craftsmen who brought with them all the necessary formulas and designs. From its inception Waterford prided itself on the high quality and clarity of its glass and the variety of its ware, which included all manner of tableware, smelling-salts bottles, candlesticks, lustres, and chandeliers.

It is often difficult to be sure which glasshouse was responsible for the heavily cut glass which was produced in great quantities during the late eighteenth and the early nineteenth century: glassworkers were notoriously itinerant, taking secret formulas with them and copying successful designs. Fortunately some of the Irish glasshouses impressed some of the bases of their decanters, sugar basins, and jugs with identifiable trademarks.

Irish silver.

There were fine Irish silversmiths in the Middle Ages, but it was not until 1605 that the Dublin silversmiths were reorganized and an assay established. In the seventeenth century, political upheavals led to a massive destruction of Irish plate, and only in the very late seventeenth century was silver made and preserved in any quantity.

Dublin was the main centre, and the crowned harp of Dublin appears on the finest pieces, the majority of which were made in the eighteenth century. Silver was also made in Cork.

Irish silver was strongly influenced by English styles, but Irish patrons were less wealthy than their English counterparts, and styles therefore tended to be simpler and sometimes several years behind contemporary London fashion.

The immigrant Huguenot

Two-handled Irish cup made by Christopher Hartwick, 1701

Waiter with fine cast and chased border decorated with shells and small heads. Made in Dublin in 1751

A cut glass 'canoe' bowl, late eighteenth century

A delicately pierced dish ring typical of late eighteenth-century Irish silver

A kitchen pepper, probably Cork

Part of the section of the Mosque of Ibn Touloun at Cairo

Lattice-work balcony at Cairo

Column capital in the Alhambra

silversmiths were never as important in Dublin as they were in London, but the flourishing book trade in eighteenth-century Dublin did supply some fine engravers for Irish plate.

Two-handled cups without covers were very popular in the early eighteenth century. Tripod cream jugs and sugar bowls, decorated with lion masks, were fashionable *c* 1760. Irish silversmiths liked decoration of this type with fanciful embossing, but their execution of Rococo decoration tended to be rather poor by comparison with contemporary London work. Dish rings, made to protect the table from hot tableware, were a common feature of Irish silver from the mid-eighteenth century. These spool-shaped objects were beautifully pierced and gave rise to some very fine decoration. Neo-classical designs were late in coming to Ireland, and were still being produced at the begin-

ning of the nineteenth century, when London smiths were creating much more massive forms.

After the Act of Union (1800), Ireland became subject to British law. Political and social conditions were unfavourable, and Irish silver rapidly declined.

Islamic architecture. The beginnings of Islamic architecture are obscure. In a comparatively short space of time, in the early seventh century, Mahomet managed to unite his first followers, the Bedouin Arabs, and a host of other nomadic tribes. These tribes had for centuries roamed the desert, dwelling mainly in tents. They had had no urban capital or cultural centre. Yet from the seventh century onwards they conquered most of what is now known as the Middle East, North Africa, and part of Spain; and they established a distinctive architectural style throughout their dominions. This was undoubtedly partly indigenous, but owed more to Arabic skill in adapting, borrowing, and incorporating the materials and motifs

of the lands they overran. Thus in Spain, conquered in AD 711, the Islamic manner overlaid the Roman style; columns and capitals of the earlier styles were even directly incorporated in new buildings. Seven centuries later, the Arabs' successors, the Ottoman Turks, captured Constantinople (1453) and penetrated deep into Europe. Here, too, they took over an existing style – the Byzantine – and made it their own.

There were inevitably diverse elements in a style found over such a vast territory. One unifying characteristic – albeit a negative one – was that representations of men and animals were rare; at times they were frowned on for religious reasons. Islamic architecture and decoration is permeated at all levels by vigorous geometric motifs, profusely applied, mostly as flat ceramic surfaces, and frequently brilliant in colouring.

Although the Muslims invariably built their mosques by incorporating pre-Islamic structures, religious buildings did not have the same significance in the development of the Islamic style

Pillar decoration at the main mosque at Nayin, Persia, tenth century

Deylamite work at former Jorgir mosque, Isfahan, tenth century

as temples and churches have had in the development of other architectural styles. Even the structural elements of mosques follow no set layout. Each, however, contains a hall of prayer (*Mihrab*) which was usually housed under a dome and indicated the direction of Mecca; a place for ablutions; a large area for the reading of the Koran; a form of pulpit (*Mimbar*); and a minaret or slender tower from which the muezzin called the hour of prayer. The earliest minarets were the converted church towers of vanquished races.

As with all building styles conditioned by harsh sunlight, Islamic architecture is inward-looking rather than a matter of façades. High blank walls enclosed richly decorated interiors, with the most lavish decoration reserved for the interior open courts and their surrounding colonnades. Balconied windows, enclosed by lattice-work screens, were among the few devices which gave relief to Islamic façades. The lattice-work, frequently of considerable decorative charm and complexity, was a far more effective protection against sunlight than glazed windows.

A style with such diverse origins inevitably included a variety of forms. Even the arch, one of the dominant motifs in all Islamic building, is encountered in three widely differing forms: (1) the pointed arch (in Egypt and Sicily), similar to the Western pointed arch, which undoubtedly derived from Islamic prototypes; (2) the so-called keel arch, similar in section to that of an upturned boat hull (found mainly in India); and (3) the horseshoe arch, a segment of a circle rather greater than a semi-circle, which is to be seen mostly in Spain. Each form was the basis for a plethora of decorative and colourful embellishments and arabesques.

Islamic architecture is usually divided into five geographical – and stylistic – areas:

I: North African and Spanish, which was to include what is now widely known as the Moorish style.

II: Egyptian-Sicilian, which included the most splendid of the Muslim mosques, notably those of Ibn Tulun (AD 876–7) and the later Melik-el-Itasson (1356).

III: Persian-Arabian, embracing what are now Iran and Iraq; Baghdad became the cultural centre of this area, and the building of other cities encouraged the growth of arts and

Moorish wall decorations in the Alhambra, Granada, 1309–54

Honeycomb decoration at Bistam, Persia, early fourteenth century

Above: main prayer eyvan of Cheqmaq mosque, Yazd, Persia, 1436.
Below: the Bank Melli in Tabriz, Persia, designed by Foroughi

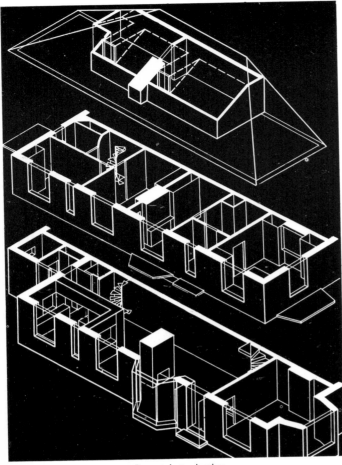

Isometric projection

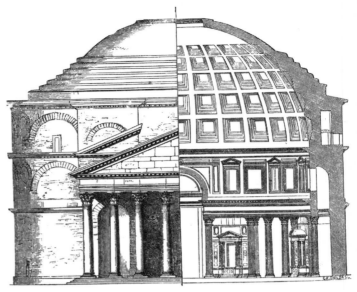

Half elevation, half section of the Pantheon, Rome

sciences. Many palaces and mosques in Baghdad were of a palatial nature in sharp contrast to earlier austerities; their domed silhouettes, keel arches, brilliant colours, and elegant minarets made them objects of great beauty.

IV: Indian architecture (qv), which flourished after the founding of Delhi by the Muslims. It owed much to Persian prototypes, although native Hindu craftsmen inevitably gave the Islamic manner their own interpretation. This medley of manners culminated in the mosques and palaces of the Mogul emperors.

V: Turkish, owing much to Byzantine influences.

Isometric projection. A graphic method employed by architects and draughtsmen to give a rough three-dimensional picture of a projected building. Verticals govern the finished drawing, for they remain vertical and are based on the true scale. Other lines are drawn from the base lines of the plan and are usually set at an angle of about 30° to the horizontal. The final

drawing, despite the inevitable distortion of curves and diagonals, is a useful indication of the building's volumes.

Italian architecture. Whereas Greek architecture was based on essentially geometrical elements (column, pediment, gable, etc), Roman architects exploited more cursive forms such as the arch, dome, and vault. Their approach to structural needs and materials was more pragmatic, leading them to utilize brickwork and concrete in an unprecedented manner. Where the Egyptians and Greeks had been concerned with temples, tombs, and palaces, the Romans built to cope with the manifold needs of a great and growing empire. Aqueducts, temples, bridges, baths, and amphitheatres were solidly and ruggedly built; and often they represented great feats of engineering (the single span of the Pont S Martin between Aosta and Ivrea is 117 ft wide). When decoration or better finishes were required, their surfaces were stuccoed or faced with the readily accessible marbles of Italy. Two centuries

before the Christian era, Roman builders constructed the remarkable spans of the concrete dome of the Italian Baths at Pompeii; and the vaulting of the Temple of Diana at Nimes was one of the great structural and architectural achievements of the ancient world. Vaulting was increasingly used during the following century, and is probably seen in its most impressive form in the Tabularium or record office in Rome, built in 78 BC.

The Romans took over the Greek orders, which they developed and debased but also made more manageable – to the despair of purists over the ensuing centuries. They applied the orders to secular buildings, disregarding the 'rules' of Greek architecture. The most characteristic Roman innovation was the Composite order, in which they sought to fuse Corinthian and Ionic elements, with mixed success. Composite arcades in which several elements were used to give unity and authority to

these Roman versions of the Greek *stoa*, or roofed colonnades, were also introduced.

The most interesting of all Roman buildings is probably the Pantheon, built *c* AD 120, in the reign of Hadrian. The Pantheon has been termed 'the apogee of Roman building', it possesses a unique grandeur and simplicity, and is the oldest roofed building in the world still standing. The dome, skilfully ornamented with deeply sunk coffers of diminishing size, has an inner span of 141 ft; this is the same as the height of the building, and adds a satisfying mathematical regularity to its simple yet subtle harmonies.

Other great Roman buildings include the magnificently vaulted Baths of Caracalla (AD 215); the Colosseum (AD 69–79), the most complex and splendid of all Roman amphitheatres; and the triumphal arch of Titus. The remains and reconstruction (in model form) of Hadrian's Villa at Tivoli (*c* AD 120–5) show something of the palatial gran-

Temple of Fortune, Rome, c 40 BC

Theodoric's Tomb, Ravenna, AD 53⁰

Medieval towers of San Gimignano

The cathedral and campanile at Lucca, begun 1060, façade 1204

deur of imperial Rome; so does Diocletian's palace at Split (Spalato) in Yugoslavia, built in AD 300, when the Roman Empire was already in decline.

The impact of Christianity on Roman building appeared mainly in early churches which were adaptations of the pagan Roman basilicas. The more spectacular forms of roof vaulting were generally replaced by less osten- tatious forms of pitched roofing. On the other hand, Christian builders made frequent and in- discriminate use of the columns of ancient temples for colon- nades in their new edifices.

The round-arched Roman- esque style, evolved between the eighth and twelfth centuries, was more interesting in northern Italy than in the south. The study of these regional aspects of the

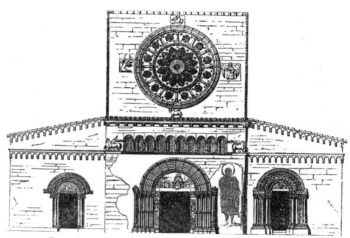

Romanesque façade of S Maria Maggiore, Toscanella

Central part of the façade of the Doge's Palace, Venice

The Cathedral, Florence; section of dome and part of nave

309

The façade of Siena Cathedral; lower half 1284–1300, upper 1377–80

The Foundling Hospital, Florence: Brunelleschi, 1421–4

The Strozzi Palace, Florence: Il Cronaca, 1489–1539

Villa Malcontenta built on the Brenta Canal, near Venice: Palladio

Romanesque has provided scholars with a subject containing very diverse features. Local building idiosyncrasies ranged from the heavier rib vaulting of the north to the admixture of Norman and Saracenic influences in Sicily; from the Byzantine elements in S Marco, Venice, to the later Romanesque of the Campanile at Pisa. One especially interesting form utilized in the development of Romanesque was the circular church based on pagan *tumuli*, although considerably increased in size.

The advent of Gothic in Italy *c* 1240 did not stimulate a comparable regional variety; in fact, the style as a whole was never fully accepted in Italy.

The Renaissance radically changed Italian architectural theories, and the influence of such men as Brunelleschi, Alberti, Sansovino, Bramante, Palladio, and Vignola was felt far beyond Italy. Andrea Palladio (1518–80) was undoubtedly the most important in European terms; in England, for example, his influence was strongly felt during both the seventeenth and the eighteenth centuries, and spread from England to North America. His studies of ancient Rome, his books, and his own designs changed the façades of the Western world.

Renaissance architecture, based upon classical forms and rules, gradually deteriorated into a monotonous use of basic components. The resulting reaction from innovators such as Michelangelo, Bernini, and Borromini, resulted in the exuberant forms of seventeenth-century Baroque.

Baroque was still based upon Greco-Roman styles; and variants upon classical architecture persisted in Italy through the eighteenth century. By the last decades of the century they had become overworked and overloaded with useless ornamentation and display. The decline continued during the nineteenth century, for Italian architects were uninfluenced by the Greek and Gothic revivals so important elsewhere in Europe.

Under Mussolini a new, emphatic, and aggressive ostentation

S Maria della Pace, Rome: Pietro da Cortona, 1656–7

Palazzo Madama Turin: Juvarra, 1718–21

Museum of Modern Art, Rome, late nineteenth century

Palace for Exhibitions, Turin: Nervi, 1948–50

Façade of railway station, Rome: L Calini, M Castellazzi, V Fadigati, E Montuori and A Pintonello, 1949–51

Olivetti Building, Milan: G A Bernascioni, A Fiocchi, M Nizzoli, 1954

appeared in the vast number of institutions built by the state. More enduring and rewarding were the new housing developments and reclamation schemes undertaken by Fascist architects and planners.

The post-war years have seen a resurgence of architectural individualism in Italy. Many commercial buildings are of international significance, notably the Pirelli building (designed by Gio Ponti, qv, and others), which demonstrated that towering office buildings need not be mere elongated blocks of concrete. The structural innovations of the great engineer-architect Pier Luigi Nervi have also shown that the most utilitarian buildings can be aesthetically satisfying. Many fine blocks of apartments have also been built.

Roman couch with bone and glass inlay

Detail of a painted walnut marriage coffer, early fourteenth century

Italian furniture and decoration.

The earliest forms of Italian furniture are those now generally known as Etruscan. They derived principally from Hellenistic design, and consist of stools, couches, chairs, footstools, tables, and various simple forms of chests. The Romans took over and adapted Greek prototypes, then declining from their earlier beauty and austerity. The more ornate Hellenistic forms suited Roman tastes, and formed the basis of all their early furniture; it is frequently difficult to distinguish between Greek and Roman furniture of these overlapping periods.

Roman furniture designs were

Roman marble table

Renaissance walnut mirror frame

uniform throughout the empire, so that couches, chairs, and tables were similar in design from Britain to North Africa. Soft furnishings were used for the coverings of beds and couches, and ranged from leather and linens to sheepskins and, later, silk. To judge from references by ancient writers, the woven fabrics were frequently highly colourful, but upholstery was virtually non-existent. Curtains were in use, but mainly as door coverings. The richness of colour of the fabrics must have been enhanced by the colours of the mosaic floors. Marius the Epicurean, writing of these floors, mentions the rich interior effects produced by the Romans' lavish expenditure on their floorings, adding that such surfaces were at their best when old. Yet Suetonius, writing during the second century AD, comments – not altogether admiringly – on the basic furnishing and contempt for luxury of at least one of the Emperor Augustus's houses.

In medieval times the heart of the larger houses was the hall, with its adjacent master-bedroom. Furnishings were still rudimentary, although there were often sumptuous hangings and patterned rugs which came from the Near East.

The paintings of Carpaccio (1486–1525) show many details of furniture and furnishings and help to clarify the gradual development of Italian interiors. Beds with elaborate carvings on posts and bases, doors with carved and decorated cases, chests frequently carrying lavish decorations – all are shown in these pictures, along with rugs and rich hangings. Italy was a great centre of international trade, and Italian homes gradually became far more cosmopolitan than those elsewhere in Europe. Decorative motifs ranged from adaptations of French and German Gothic in

the northern alpine districts to a distinctly Moorish style in the south.

A gradual simplification of form, combined with disciplined yet elaborate use of pattern, occurred under Renaissance influence in fifteenth- and sixteenth-century furniture. Most pieces were of oiled walnut. Furniture began to show signs of the architect-designer's hand: the settee, adapted from the chest, acquired a new importance; the sideboard was developed as yet another version of the chest. Chairs remained comparatively untouched by this increasing sophistication, although the X-framed, slatted Savonarola chair became widely popular. The underframes of tables were made more ingenious and decorative, although their origin in the trestle-table was still evident. Regional idiosyncrasies were marked, from the gilt furniture favoured in Tuscany to the inlaid furniture of Venice.

Later Renaissance furniture continued with these established models, but added a variety of carved motifs, also borrowed from architecture. The key-pattern, acanthus leaf, guilloche combined with pilasters, and pediments were introduced into a wide range of furniture. The transition from the classical forms of the Renaissance to the more exuberant Baroque was reflected in furniture design, with a consequent emphasis on display and luxury. Vast wall cabinets became the centrepieces of salon and bedroom. Flamboyant carvings with scrolls and swags, richly gilded, dominated the bases and pediments of these panelled pieces. Similarly elaborate decoration appeared in other furniture, from bedheads to mirror-frames.

Later, although the forms evolved by English and French craftsmen influenced Italian furniture, their austerity had little

Baroque cabinet, c 1700

appeal. Italian craftsmen reinterpreted the styles introduced by Adam and others (derived from Pompeii and Spalato) in a more exuberant fashion. Similarly, they reinterpreted influences introduced from France as a result of the Napoleonic Wars. This is reflected in descriptions such as Italian Empire and Italian Directory styles which

The Magistretti chair

Modern Italian furniture with unit seating by Mario Bellino and arc lamp by Castiglione

A small ivory and tortoiseshell cabinet housed in a cabinet on a stand, mid-eighteenth century

persisted in one form or another throughout the nineteenth century.

During the present century, Italian architects and designers have been among the leaders of the Modern Movement. Today

Italian furniture is internationally known for its inventiveness and ingenuity. Established classics, such as the Chiavari and Magistretti chairs, continue to sell throughout the world alongside extreme innovations.

Ivory. Elephant tusks, and sometimes the tusks of other animals, have been used for practical and decorative purposes from the earliest times. Archaeological discoveries have shown that ivory was used to make small objects in prehistoric times. The Egyptians were responsible for much beautiful sculpture and carving in ivory, and small ivory caskets were also made. Artists in other civilizations, from the Far East to Byzantium, used ivory for many centuries. Eskimos have long used the tusks of the walrus for small and decorative carvings, as did seamen with their scrimshaw work in the days of sail. The comparatively modest size of tusks limited the decorative use of ivory in furniture, and it was usually employed in the form of inlays, cartouches, cameos, plaques, and mounts. Italian, Spanish, and Portuguese cabinetmakers used ivory much more as an inlay material, producing very richly ornamented

effects. French cabinetmakers used ivory extensively for decorative details in the eighteenth century, and a famous English piece, a hanging cabinet made for Horace Walpole in 1743, is decorated with a group of ivory cameos and an ivory motif for the tympanum.

Ivory is still widely used in the Near East, particularly in Iran, for the decoration of small objects such as caskets and jewel-boxes.

Ivory, Thomas (c 1720–86). Irish architect. He trained as a carpenter in Cork, but in 1759 he was appointed master of architectural drawing in the Schools of the Royal Dublin Society, a position he retained until his death. As an architect, he is chiefly known by his designs for the King's Hospital or Bluecoat School in Blackhall Place (1773), and for the municipal buildings on Cork Hill, Dublin, formerly Newcomen's Bank (1781).

One of a pair of Indo-Portuguese armchairs in ivory, eighteenth century

The Bluecoat School, Dublin, by Thomas Ivory, 1773–83

A 'cow' milk jug, typical of the Jackfield pottery

The Examination Schools, Oxford, designed by Jackson

Jackfield. A pottery was founded about 1750 at Jackfield, Shropshire, England, by Maurice Thursfield. A red-bodied ware covered with a smooth and shiny black glaze was manufactured. In some cases the ware was decorated with oil gilding and with unfired painting of which only traces remain today. 'Cow' milk jugs were a typical product of this factory. The ware was unmarked, and though similar ware was made at other potteries, 'Jackfield' has become a generic term for pottery of this type.

Jackson, Sir Thomas Graham (1835–1924). British architect and architectural historian. Jackson was born in London and educated at Brighton College and Corpus and Wadham Colleges, Oxford, where he had a brilliant academic career. He entered Sir George Gilbert Scott's office in 1858, and four years later set up his own practice in London. He soon began to specialize in restoration and additions to scholastic and ecclesiastical buildings. His own scholarly interest inclined him to a form of Neo-Jacobean architecture, which was highly appreciated by his clients. His practice was one of the most extensive and successful of his time. In Oxford he was responsible for the Examination Schools and the High School for Girls, as well as extensive collegiate and ecclesiastical restoration. He was similarly occupied at Cambridge, where he also designed the Sedgwick Museum, the Law Library and other buildings.

The deliberately nostalgic architectural style favoured by Jackson made him almost an inevitable choice by governing bodies for building and enlarging school buildings, and he worked at Eton, Harrow, Winchester, Rugby, and Brighton.

Jacob, Georges (1739–1814). French cabinetmaker. Jacob was the founder of one of the most successful and long-lasting of all French furniture-making families, although his name has come to be particularly associated with the development of the Louis XVI chair.

Jacob was born at Cheny in Burgundy, of peasant stock, and is thought to have served his apprenticeship under Louis Delanois, one of the most influential French cabinetmakers in the reign of Louis XV.

Jacob's skilled craftsmanship was allied to a highly experimental technique, and he was the first of the French *menuisiers* to transform the heavier chair-shapes of the Louis XV style into the lighter Louis XVI forms. This was made possible by technical innovations in the carving, planing, and shaping of timber so that lightness could be achieved without loss of strength. Jacob was perhaps the first French craftsman to use mahogany for chair-making, and he is also credited with the introduction of the sabre-leg – which might more properly be called the reintroduction of the Etruscan leg.

Jacob armchair with carved birch frame in white and gold, and Beauvais tapestry upholstery

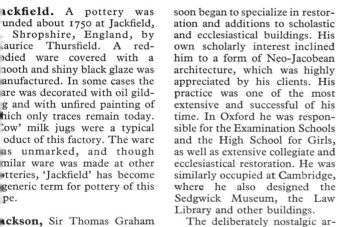

Jacobsen. *Bentwood and steel chair designed by Arne Jacobsen in 1952*

JACOBEAN ARCHITECTURE

Directoire chair by Jacob

The east front of Aston Hall, Warwickshire, possibly designed by John Thorpe, 1618–35

Jacob was unusually sensitive to currents of fashion. He played a notable part in the transition from the Louis XV to the Louis XVI style, and later he helped to introduce the Empire style. He seems to have been equally sensitive to political changes, for although he made furniture for various members of the royal family from 1775, he succeeded in surviving the Revolution.

In 1796 he made over his very considerable Parisian manufactory to his two sons, Georges and François-Honoré, who vigorously carried on the firm's business. François-Honoré established a reputation as a leading cabinetmaker under the name of Jacob Desmalter, a name which he also gave to the firm on the death of his brother in 1803. Desmalter became Napoleon's favourite cabinetmaker, and under imperial patronage the firm inevitably expanded, so much so that at its zenith it was employing over 300 workmen in several workshops. In the post-Restoration period it was further reorganized under the first Jacob's grandson, Georges-Alphonse, and continued to be successful.

Jacobean architecture. English architecture during the reign of James I (1603–25). It is transitional and somewhat heterogeneous in manner, bridging the Tudor tradition and the gradually emerging Renaissance style.

At the beginning of the reign, Elizabethan exuberance and 'gothic fancie' dominated architecture. The New Stuart court was increasingly responsive to Continental influences, felt through books on architecture

and through travel abroad.

As in the Elizabethan period, growing wealth encouraged building by the middle as well as the upper class. A considerable number of small manor-houses and yeomen's houses were built, many of the yeomen's houses being the early seventeenth-century cottages that have survived down to the present day. The building of cottages proper continued to decline.

Simplification of style, and a greater preoccupation with symmetry, were features of the planning of interiors and elevations.

This tendency was reinforced by the rise in status of the architect, who began increasingly to supervise the whole structure from the plan to completion. The quest for symmetry was responsible for the main features of the larger Jacobean house: a greater emphasis on a centrally-placed porch leading into a hall on the central axis of the house. This new plan led to a diminution in importance of the Elizabethan great hall, which now began to assume the place it has since retained, ie as a hall and not the main room or chamber of a house.

The major decorative themes of the period changed, comparatively swiftly, from Gothic to Renaissance. Columns and pilasters based upon the classical orders were introduced into buildings – sometimes with very unhappy effects, twisted and foreshortened columns being placed on squat ungainly plinths. Decorative detail for panelling, friezes, and mouldings was taken, with rather more success, from Italian and Flemish sources.

Apart from the decline in

importance of the great hall, the basic structure of the larger Jacobean house was slow to change. External changes were considerable: windows were enlarged, mullioned, square-headed, and in most cases unadorned by tracery patterns. As architects became more assured, windows were boldly continued in bays two and three storeys in height. This confidence was also expressed in dramatic gables, frequently ornamented, and soaring grouped chimneys. Much of our knowledge of Jacobean architecture derives from sets of drawings assembled by two architects: the John Thorpe (1563–1654) Collection, now in Sir John Soane's Museum, and the Huntingdon Smithson (c 1580–1628) Collection in the RIBA Library.

The most magnificent of the

great Jacobean houses is Hatfield House in Hertfordshire, built between 1607 and 1611 for Robert, Earl of Salisbury. This great E-plan house has different main façades: an austere brick-work northern entrance-front with mullioned windows, a projecting porch, and bay-windowed towers, and a vastly more elaborate south front with an ornate central entrance-porch, an arcaded ground floor incorporating an eclectic use of the orders, and a pierced stone parapet running the length of the façade.

Other notable houses of the period are Bramshill in Hampshire (1605–12), designed for Lord Zouche, incorporating an older building; Chastleton in Oxfordshire (1603–4); and, later in the reign, Aston Hall in Warwickshire (1618–35).

Bramshill, Hampshire, 1605–12

An engraving of Chastleton, Oxfordshire, 1603–4

Fountains Hall, Ripon, Yorkshire, 1611

These houses, although they represented a departure from the architectural variety and occasional vulgarity of much late-Elizabethan building, were essentially transitional in manner. They form a modest group, deriving but set apart from their Tudor prototypes, with no hint of the Italian-classical manner that was to revolutionize English architecture in the hands of Inigo Jones (qv). Yet the Queen's House at Greenwich, the first Classical house in England, was started in 1616, during the Jacobean period, though it was not completed – for Henrietta Maria, the Queen Consort – until a generation later. Although a contemporary of other early Stuart architects, Inigo Jones was no less than half a century ahead of them.

Jacobean furniture and decoration. The Tudor forms of tables, cupboards, chairs, and benches remained basically unchanged during the Jacobean period (1603–25), and oak was still the most widely used wood. But the decoration of these pieces became much simpler, and was increasingly influenced by Renaissance motifs. The doors and panels of Tudor-inspired parlour cupboards, for example, began to be carved in the Italianate manner with arabesques, scrolls, medallions, and plainer geometrical devices. Upholstery was gradually introduced, and ease and comfort became more important design considerations than an imposing formality. The farthingale chair (qv), a square, armless, padded object, was introduced at the beginning of the century. It was usually covered in velvet, or a woven woollen fabric known as 'Turkey work' because it simulated the pattern and texture of Turkey carpets. Such chairs were frequently studded with brass-headed nails.

American Jacobean furniture is very similar. It was the first furniture to be made in the colonies, and the style persisted until the last quarter of the century when Restoration influences were belatedly felt. Many of the pieces were similar to English Jacobean furniture, including trestle tables, chests, joint stools, and press cupboards;

A Jacobean court cupboard with grotesque supports

The staircase, Aston Hall, Warwickshire, early seventeenth century

An ornate ceiling at Aston Hall, Warwickshire

*Above: the Jacobean Marble Hall, Hatfield House, Hertfordshire.
Below: a 'Four Seasons' tapestry, from Hatfield, seventeenth century*

others such as the Brewster and Carver chairs, were new. Turning, carving, and applied decoration were common on both sides of the Atlantic, although in America the selection of motifs was restricted and they were executed in lower relief and with more energy. New England Jacobean furniture is sometimes referred to as Pilgrim, after the Plymouth colony.

See **American furniture.**

Jacobsen, Arne (1902–71). Danish architect and industrial designer. Jacobsen was born in Copenhagen and trained at the architectural school of the Academy of Arts, graduating in 1928. His first notable achievement as an architect was a group of small houses in the Bellevue area of Copenhagen. This project was followed by the thoughtfully designed two- and three-storey Bellavista housing estate. Here a gently-stepped plan gave each flat a pleasant prospect and a fair share of sunlight. A project for a summer theatre and restaurant, designed as an integral part of the Bellevue scheme, was undertaken but later completely altered.

Jacobsen's early work was strongly influenced by Le Corbusier, and later by Gunnar Asplund. Asplund's theories can be traced in Jacobsen's designs for several buildings of the late 1930s, notably the town halls of Aarhus (1937), designed in conjunction with Erik Møller, and Søllerød (1940–2), designed with Flemming Larsen.

After World War II, Jacobsen stepped into the front rank of internationally-known architects, designing several buildings which gained wide recognition. His preoccupation with almost classical ideas of proportion and

Arne Jacobsen

Town Hall, Aarhus: Jacobsen 1937

The south front of a house at Sorgenfri designed by Jacobsen

St Catherine's College, Cambridge, by Jacobsen, 1959

Cutlery designed by Jacobsen

and Ruthwen Jürgensen (1956), and in larger projects for communal housing, as at Soholm (1950–5).

In addition to his work as an architect, Jacobsen established a quite considerable reputation as a furniture designer, and his 'egg' and 'swan' chairs are now marketed throughout the world.

In Britain he is known for his 1959 designs for St Catherine's College, Cambridge, where he was not only responsible for the buildings but also for collegiate furniture, fabrics, tableware etc.

Jambs. The vertical side posts of a door, archway, window, or fireplace opening, carrying the lintel.

James, John (c 1672–1746). English architect, the son of a parson. James probably received a better formal education than most architects of his time. Nevertheless, he was nearing 30 before he was able to escape from his work as assistant to the master-carpenter to the Crown. He was appointed storekeeper and assistant clerk of the works at Greenwich, then (1718) joint clerk of the works with Hawksmoor. When Hawksmoor died in 1736, James succeeded him as sole clerk.

James's other appointments were as master-carpenter to St Paul's Cathedral in 1711, and in 1714 as assistant surveyor to the Cathedral authorities; in 1723 he succeeded Wren as surveyor.

James's designs are careful,

scale, allied with his experimental interest in new building techniques and profound attention to the quality of detail and finish, enhanced his national reputation. This was confirmed by his designs for the Jespersen offices in Copenhagen (1955),

the Redøvre Town Hall (1955), and the SAS building in Copenhagen (1959).

Unlike many other successful twentieth-century architects, Jacobsen maintained his interest in the design of private houses, eg those for C A Møller (1951)

unostentatious, but somewhat colourless. Although not one of the original surveyors for the Fifty New Churches, he did design St George's, Hanover Square (1713–24), which remains his most notable achievement. When Gibbs was dismissed from his surveyorship, James was offered the post, and completed the tower of St Alphege at Greenwich. In January 1715 James was made surveyor to Westminster Abbey and was responsible for completing the west towers of the Abbey.

James's private work was limited. Two houses shown in *Vitruvius Britannicus* were designed by him: a house at Twickenham (1710) and a large house, Wricklemarsh, at Black-

The 'Egg' chair designed by Arne Jacobsen, 1957

St George's church, Hanover Square, London, by John James, 1713–24

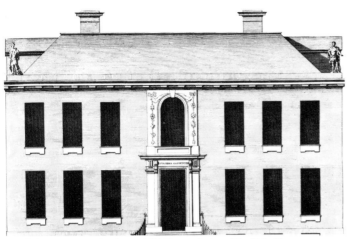

A house at Twickenham, Middlesex, designed by John James, 1710

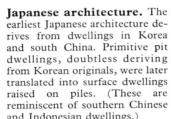

The Sanctuary of the Ise Shrine, Naiky, Archaic Period style

heath, designed for Sir Gregory Page in 1721 and demolished in 1789. He also translated several works on architecture, and Le Blond's *Theory and Practice of Gardening* (1712), outlining the theories of garden design elaborated by Le Nôtre (qv). Through James's translation, this work was of considerable significance in the development and design of some important English gardens.

Japanese architecture. The earliest Japanese architecture derives from dwellings in Korea and south China. Primitive pit dwellings, doubtless deriving from Korean originals, were later translated into surface dwellings raised on piles. (These are reminiscent of southern Chinese and Indonesian dwellings.)

Remains of a great many pit dwellings have been discovered and variously dated from the fourth or fifth centuries AD to the eighth. They are roughly of flattened circular shape and up to almost 20 ft in diameter. They are set up to 3 ft into the ground, and include a rough superstructure of poles and rudimentary thatching.

The surface dwellings were tent-like structures of bamboo and thatch, occasionally raised well above ground and reached by ladders. A vivid impression of these houses can be gained from pottery models of the fifth century in the National Museum at Tokyo. Later and more sophisticated versions of these houses were gabled, saddle-roofed with wide projecting soffits, frequently carried on carved brackets and with emphatic barge-boards.

The shrines of the Shinto religion were the earliest buildings of importance in Japan, but as most of these shrines, including the best known at Ise, were rebuilt at 20-year intervals, their early appearance is not preserved.

Buddhism was introduced into Japan from Korea in the mid-sixth century. The new religion led to the building of new monastic buildings and temples, including the seventh-century Horyuji monastery, with its pagoda and other buildings. The pagoda of Horyuji – five storeys with sweeping roofs and decorative finials – became a prototype for innumerable pagodas throughout Japan.

During succeeding centuries, Buddhist temples continued to be built in the basic forms of the Horyuji complex, but with many superficial variations. The most important Buddhist temples include those in the ancient capital of Heijo (eighth century), and temples on Mount Koya and Mount Hiyei, and at Kyoto.

Japanese domestic architecture was of the simplest construction; buildings were generally one-storeyed and made of wood, with tile-covered roofs. Timber was widely used because of its qualities of resilience and resistance against earthquakes. The dimensions of Japanese houses are based upon a modular unit derived from the standard mat or *tatami*. This is approximately 6 by 3 ft, and rooms are described as 6-mat, 8-mat, and so on according to size. The interior arrangement of the rooms allows considerable flexibility. Interior walls, frequently made of paper, are movable, allowing the speedy expansion or contraction of given areas. Domestic flexibility is further enhanced by the fact that matted rooms have no immutable purpose. The Western bedstead has no counterpart in the Japanese household; consequently the use of mattresses makes reception rooms adaptable to bedrooms at night. Ceiling heights are standardized and there are no corridors, the veranda being utilized as a passageway. Essen

Ceremonial Hall of the Kyoto Imperial Palace, eighth century

Pagoda of Buddhist temple

Buddhist temple in the Todaiji compound, Nara; mid-eighth century

Hoodo Hall of the Byodoin Temple, 1053

ial features of the Japanese house are the tokonoma, or picture recess, and the tea room, which is sometimes a separate building in the garden.

Japan possesses fine castles and palaces; but in even the most palatial complexes, human scale is recognized and accepted. The Palace of the Emperor at Kyoto, for example, is an assembly of modern pavilions with temple-like roofs. Several of the Japanese castles are of considerable size, but their decorative rather than their material qualities are dominant, with elaborate sweeping rooflines and an abundance of gilded ornament.

Modern architecture in Japan can, with some reason, be dated from the mid-nineteenth century, when the Emperor Meiji abandoned isolationism and opened the country to Western influences. European architects were invited to build in Japan, and a medley of architectural styles was introduced which has become known as Euro-Japanese. Wood was superseded in larger building projects by structural methods based on the use of reinforced concrete and steel. The manner in which the Imperial Hotel in Tokyo (built in 1916 to designs by Frank Lloyd Wright) resisted the 1923–4 earthquakes quickened the pace of Western-inspired building. After World War I, a number of younger architects formed a group and showed their own work at the Tokyo Peace Exposition in 1922. The members of the group were responsible for a number of influential modern buildings in Tokyo, including the Central Telephone Office (1926), the Asahi News Press Building (1927), and the Shirokiya Department Store (1929).

Today most Japanese buildings, apart from smaller houses, are built of reinforced concrete, and the International style has supplanted the traditional Japanese manner. This at first resulted

National indoor gymnasium in Tokyo by Kenzo Tange, 1964

Exterior view of Hamanatsu Gymnasium in Chizuoka

A gymnasium in Takamatsu, designed by Kenzo Tange, 1964

JAPANESE GARDEN DESIGN

Katswa Palace garden with stone lantern

Modern bamboo terrace and garden in Tokyo, by Horiguchi

in a number of far-from-distinguished buildings, but during recent years native architects, including Kenzo Tange, Junzo Sakakura, and Kunio Maekaua, have produced buildings of a recognizably Japanese character, based on an oriental interpretation of the simplicities of the Bauhaus style.

Japanese garden design.
The Japanese garden derived from Chinese influences, although Japanese landowners soon began to formulate their own versions of this borrowed art. An increasingly aristocratic culture gradually established the tenets which, in one form or another, have governed Japanese garden design ever since. By the twelfth century these were clearly defined, although the influence of the Chinese Zen sect and native artists later led to designs that were more mannered – based upon artists', rather than the

gardeners', conceptions of the ideal garden.

The Japanese garden has become one of the most consciously contrived of all works of art. It is based upon simple, almost symbolical interpretations (or rather translations) of natural forms, the emphasis being upon contrasts of hill and water, sand and stone. These basic structural elements are enlivened by planting. Irrespective of its size, the garden is considered as the perfect means of linking man and nature, design and decoration, art and artifice.

Because space is so valuable in the overcrowded Japanese archipelago, gardens are planned on modest lines. The celebrated garden at Ryoanji, Kyoto, is little larger than a tennis-court. The aim of the Japanese garden-planner is not to create a pleasure-ground of colour and perspective, but to evoke a mysterious landscape of different

textures: of rock, and raked sand to represent water. It is intended to evoke a mood of thoughtful contemplation, or provide a setting for quiet conversation. Colour, apart from the seaweed colours of rock and sand and bamboo leaf, is considered too jarring. Flowers are thus virtually excluded, although they have their part to play within the house. Instead, thought and time are devoted to the exact placing of stones, to raking the ripples of the sand, and to siting the single tree.

Above all other nations, the Japanese have sought to integrate house and garden, mainly by planning their garden as extensions of their house. Simple architectural and structural devices are adopted to blur the line of demarcation between indoors and out. One of these is the veranda, linking both house and garden. Bamboo blinds and wooden or stone steps and stepping-stones are further devices. Stepping-stones lead from the front gate to the entrance of the house, and from the rear of the house into the garden. The sense of integration is emphasized by the fact that Japanese houses are normally of one storey, with wide overhanging soffits. The house is normally sited in the middle of the garden, well back from the thoroughfare, and set behind a timber or bamboo protective fence. The gardener's effort is to screen his house from his neighbours rather than to display it: he tries to preserve the privacy of his family with the aid of trees and shrubs. The minuscule front garden and large back garden of Western terrace houses is virtually unknown.

Many variations on the basic elements were eventually evolved. For some gardeners the ideal

was to create, with the utmost detail, a garden evocative of an idyllic countryside. Evergreens predominated in the planting, since they were thought to evoke a greater sense of serenity than deciduous trees and flowers. For others, the solution was symbolic: a level surface on which the imposed design consisted of formal patterns – though far less formal than, say the French gardens of Le Nôtre which were largely dependent upon the interplay of sand and stone.

These various forms of garden design were studied with care, grouped, and classified. Three main classifications were established: (1) *Shin*, representing gardens in the naturalistic manner; (2) *Gyō*, a simplified version of the natural scene; and (3) *Sō* the wholly symbolical garden. Various subdivisions made the analysis still more subtle and precise.

The full realization of the *Shin* garden is wholly independent of its size and physical limitations. In the larger garden, natural features, from knolls to pools, are created artificially. To these seemingly natural features are added other artifices of the designer: stepping-stones, bridges, stone lanterns, etc. In smaller gardens these characteristics are reproduced in miniature, and in the very small ones they are symbolized by the introduction of rock, sand, miniature trees, and so on. With the growth of the tea-ceremony, the tea-house, no matter how small, has become an essential feature of the garden, completing the Japanese garden as we know it today.

Japanese interior design
Thanks to the late industrialization of Japan, she has largely avoided the transitional stage – the

Raked sand and rocks in the ancient Japanese garden at Ryoanji

A pavilion in Nishinonganji Temple compound, Kyoto, c 1600

The interior of a modern Japanese house

which mass production means bad design – undergone by Western nations. After each of the World Wars, Japanese engineer-designers have taken a leading place among those who have utilized the machine to produce well-designed objects for everyday use. During recent years, Japanese cameras, radios, and automobiles have consistently been among the best designed in the world. Modern Japanese furniture, derived from traditional prototypes, is well adapted to contemporary requirements, and has been readily accepted by the West. This is also true of their ceramics. Japan's exports reach most parts of the world, but her main overseas market is the USA.

Japanning. A process introduced into cabinetmaking in Stuart times in an attempt to emulate the hard-finish lacquering practised in the Far East. It was seen in imported cabinets and trays, and was so called because most of these pieces originated in Japan. The original process was based upon the use of the sap of the *Rhus vernicifera*, many coats of which were applied to the wooden surface in order to give a varnish of unusually resplendent finish. The closing of Japan to Western traders in the seventeenth century led to European attempts at lacquering, which was practised not only by cabinetmakers but also by dilettantes, frequently with disastrous results.

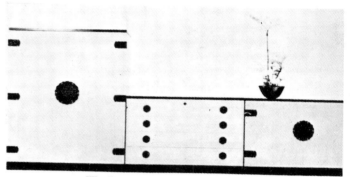

Wooden cabinet by Yomamoto-Kogyo

Japanese lacquer sho-dana (shelf cabinet), nineteenth century

Japanned lacquer cabinet, English 1800–10

A design for Japanning from 'A Treatise of Japanning and Varnishing' by John Stalker and George Parker, 1688

Reproduction of the Portland vase in Jasper made by Josiah Wedgwood

A Treatise of Japanning and Varnishing (1688), by John Stalker and George Parker, was the first important primer on the craft. Despite its overblown prose, the book was an authoritative and practical guide, seeking to correct many of the faults of cheap-jack japanners and varnishers who had gone into business to exploit the craze for lacquer. The conventional background for 'oriental' paintings was black, but increasing virtuosity led to the introduction of other coloured grounds. Whimsical and fantastic scenes, Europeanized versions of supposedly Japanese works, were painted, but English and Dutch artists were stilted and heavy-handed in their renderings – the French less so – and European work is easy to detect.

Buried in the verbosity of Stalker and Parker are precise instructions for preparing gums

Wedgwood Jasper dish, 1790

and varnishes, and applying successive coats of 'whiting and parchment size' to the object to be varnished before the painting was put on in a paste. These instructions also included the application of raised surfaces to represent mountains and other landscape features. The japanning process was applied to furniture, trays, cabinets, and looking-glass frames, and in the mid-seventeenth century was widely used for long-case clocks. The japanning craze died down from about 1770 but was revived again in Victorian times in Europe and America, when mass-produced japanned articles flooded the market.

Jardinière. An ornamental holder for displaying flowers or indoor plants. A jardinière is usually made of wire or wrought-iron but can also be of natural or coloured earthenware or carved wood. The term is early nineteenth century.

Jasperware. First introduced by Josiah Wedgwood in 1775, after many years of painstaking experiments. Many people think

of 'Wedgwood' and 'Jasper' as being synonymous. It was a hard, fine, white, unglazed stoneware, which was made into very many different objects, from elaborate vases to tiny ear-rings and plaques. The background was blue, sage green, lilac, pink, black, or (very rarely) yellow, and on it were placed friezes of classical figures and ornamentation in white relief.

Though Wedgwood tried to keep his formula a secret, Jasperware was soon copied by other potters. It is still made at the Wedgwood factory today.

Jeanneret, Charles –Edouard. See **Le Corbusier.**

Jefferson, Thomas (1743–1826). President of the USA, philosopher, and architect. Jeffer-

Example of a typical jardinière

Monticello, Charlottesville, Virginia, designed by Jefferson

son's career as an architect was based on the assumption that 'nature' provided the ultimate criterion of architectural quality. As he derived this belief from England, he designed his own house, Monticello, in Virginia, as an Anglo-Palladian villa (1769). But a trip to Europe convinced him that English architecture was vastly inferior to French; so his next work, the Virginia State Capitol at Richmond (begun 1789), was based on what he had seen of the Maison Carrée at Nîmes, a Roman temple in southern France. The Virginia State Capitol established the classical temple as the ideal form for state capitols until the 1840s, but Jefferson's own contribution was too scholarly to be exciting, and too intellectual to be really practical. As president he was responsible for the appointment of Latrobe as surveyor of public buildings in 1803 – a fortunate choice, since Latrobe's strength lay in just those areas in which Jefferson was deficient. Between 1817 and 1826 Jefferson designed the University of Virginia at Charlottesville on an extended U-plan, with a Pantheon-like library enclosing the vista. The other two sides were lined by colonnades linking temple-like pavilions. These were divided into two storeys, the bottom half for classrooms and the top for professors' living quarters, complete with a veranda which bisected the portico horizontally. This portico arrangement provided the model for countless Greek revival mansions throughout the South.

Jensen, Gerreit (active 1680–1715). The first cabinetmaker in England to achieve individual distinction. Jensen was most celebrated during the reigns of William and Mary and Queen Anne, but after his death he was largely forgotten until the present century.

Jensen had settled in London by 1680, presumably having emigrated from the Netherlands; nothing is known of his earlier life. By 1693 he had a business in St Martin's Lane. His furniture is strongly influenced by the French *ébénistes*, with whom he is known to have had direct contact. His inlaid work in ivory and metal, the medium in which he specialized, is in designs of ornate curving foliage and small geometric motifs. The work is extremely attractive, though unsophisticated when compared with contemporary French furniture.

Aerial view of Virginia University, designed by Jefferson

Jib door. A concealed door which is papered or painted in the same way as the wall, and set flush with it.

Johnson, Philip (b 1906). American architect. Johnson was born in Cleveland, Ohio, the son of an eminent lawyer. He read Greek and philosophy at Harvard, where he became interested in writings by Henry Russell Hitchcock and Le Corbusier, and descriptions of the work of Mies van der Rohe and other modern architects. These extramural interests gradually displaced his classical studies, and he decided to take up architecture as a career. In 1930 he and Hitchcock travelled throughout Europe in the course of preparing a joint book, *The International Style*, which was published two years later. On this trip Johnson met Mies van der Rohe, and from that time became Mies's most fervent disciple.

On his return from Europe, Johnson was appointed the first director of the new department of architecture and design at the Museum of Modern Art in New York. His first major exhibition was devoted to the modern architecture of Europe, and the

Philip Johnson

Example of a jib door which is almost imperceptible when closed

Philip Johnson's own house at New Canaan, Connecticut, 1949

Robert Leonhardt House, Lloyd's Neck, Long Island, New York, designed by Johnson, 1956

catalogue for that exhibition (based on the studies he had made for his book) played an important part in the development of the International style in the United States. Another catalogue, *Machine Art*, prepared for an exhibition of industrial design, was also influential.

In 1939, at the age of 33, Johnson decided to return to Harvard and study architecture with the object of practising rather than explaining. Here he came more directly under the influence of the ideas of Gropius and Mies van der Rohe. But it was to Mies's theories of design that he continued to give allegiance, as he demonstrated in the house he built as a thesis project in Cambridge, Massachusetts, and in the book he published on Mies in 1947, after he had left Harvard and returned to the Museum of Modern Art.

In 1949, as a result of a challenge arising from an argument with Mies concerning the structural possibilities of glazed buildings, Johnson designed and built his now-famous Johnson house at New Canaan, Connecticut. In this he sought to emulate Mies's design for the equally famous Edith Farnsworth house in Illinois, designed in 1946 but not completed until a year after the Johnson house. The two houses had marked similarities, but Johnson's had a classical symmetry evocative of an eighteenth century pavilion in its relationship with the surrounding parkland. Mies's building is asymmetrical and more dynamic in plan and elevation. Both houses, unusual experiments in comparatively small glazed buildings, have prompted thousands of

Pavilion at New Canaan, Connecticut, designed by Johnson, 1962

Interior of Robert Wiley house, designed by Philip Johnson, 1953

weekend holiday-house imitations throughout the world.

Johnson again drew on the Miesian aesthetic for the structural themes of his first commissions after he set up in practice in 1953. These comprised a group of houses. The first was the Wiley House in New Canaan, followed in 1956 by the Leonhardt House, with a cantilevered glass living-area projecting from the main structure of the house above a sloping hillside site. In the same year, Johnson designed the Boissonnrias House in New Canaan (1956), an exceptionally handsome and imaginative geometrical structure for indoor-outdoor living.

Although he had worked on the interiors and restaurant of Mies's Seagram Building in New York, Johnson's first major building was the Kneses Tifereth Israel Synagogue in Port Chester, New York (1954–5). This austerely dramatic structure exemplifies Johnson's contention that he is a traditionalist, owing allegiance to no single style. Indeed, in the Kneses Tifereth building he seems to be borrowing themes from Soane rather than Mies.

Since this building Johnson's practice has grown considerably, and among the more recent buildings for which he has been responsible are the Sheldon Memorial Art Gallery for the University of Nebraska (1963); the Museum for pre-Columbian Art, Dumbarton Oaks (1963); the New York State Theater (1964); and the General Motors building in New York, completed in 1970.

Johnson's buildings are characterized by urbanity, elegance, superb detailing, and finish, and a deeply thought-out feeling for the final three-dimensional mass. He has also displayed a continuing preoccupation with the relationship of his buildings –

Roofless church, New Harmony, Indiana, 1960

particularly his houses – to the surrounding landscape. He has confirmed his right to be known as a modern traditionalist, for he is undoubtedly the most eclectic of the great architects now in practice.

Johnston, Francis (1760–1829). Irish architect. Johnston was born in Armagh, and early in life gained the invaluable patronage of Richard Robinson, Archbishop of Armagh, who in 1778 sent him to work with the Dublin architects Thomas Cooley and Samuel Spoule. Johnston later returned to Armagh to work for his patron. He was reputedly responsible for the reconstruction of the cathedral and various other buildings attached to the archbishop's palace. In 1794, after the death of the archbishop, Johnston removed to Dublin, where he was appointed architect and inspector of civil buildings in the Office of Public Works. He enjoyed a considerable success in Dublin and built up a large practice. There his buildings included St George's Church (1794–1802); the Chapel Royal in Dublin Castle (1807–16); and, most widely known, the General Post Office (1815–17). He was also responsible for the design of a number of the castellated castles (notably Charleville Castle in Co Wicklow) which were built in such profusion in Ireland after the end of the Napoleonic Wars.

Joined chest. First introduced in the late fifteenth century, this chest did not become the dominant type until the sixteenth century. It was of a framed and panelled construction using mortise and tenon joints. Joined chests were without doubt an improvement upon the boarded chest, being stronger in construction and a good deal more elegant in design.

Joinery. The term applied to the lighter forms of woodwork in a building, ie doors, window-frames, staircases, cupboards, and other fitments, as distinct from the heavier structural timber members of the building.

Joint. Point where two pieces of timber are fitted together. There are several methods of strengthening joints, ie dovetail, mitre, and mortise and tenon.

Joint or **joined stool.** A sixteenth- and seventeenth-century stool of pegged construction that superseded the board or slab-ended stool. The design re-

Entrance hall of the New York Theater, Lincoln Centre, 1964

St George's church, designed by Francis Johnston, 1802–13

The General Post Office, Dublin, designed by Francis Johnston, 1815–17

Inigo Jones from a drawing by Van Dyck

The Queen's House at Greenwich, designed by Inigo Jones, 1616

sembled contemporary tables with turned or carved legs and an underframe and stretchers that were frequently unadorned. Often made in sets, those used at the dining-table could be pushed beneath it when not in use.

Joist. In flooring, a horizontally-laid member, normally of timber but now increasingly of steel or concrete. Joists are laid parallel to form the basic framework for flooring. The underside of the joists forms the framework for the ceiling of a lower floor, whether left uncovered or made the basis for a lath and plaster covering. In smaller buildings, joists are usually laid wall-to-wall, but in large steel and/or concrete structures the pattern is frequently more complex, with joists based on a grid system running from girder to girder.

Jones, Inigo (1573–1652). English architect. Although he was the great originator and innovator of classical architecture in England, remarkably little is known about Jones's early life. He was baptized in St Bartholo-mew-the-Less, Smithfield, on 19 July 1575, the son of a cloth-worker. He was reputedly apprenticed to a joiner, but the next period of his life is completely undocumented; it is now generally supposed that for part of it he was working as a 'picture maker' or decorative artist. His foreign travels undoubtedly began while he was still a young man, but who underwrote the expenses of this unknown artist remains a mystery. He probably worked for some time as a painter or copyist in Florence, but most of his time in Italy seems to have been spent in Venice. From there he is supposed to have been summoned to Copenhagen in 1603 by King Christian IV of Denmark, presumably on the basis of the reputation he made in Italy. An alternative possibility is that Jones went to Denmark in the entourage of the Earl of Rutland, appointed ambassador to Denmark in 1603. Of his work in Denmark, if any, nothing is known, although legend has credited him with the design of the Copenhagen Börs, or Exchange. This has been done on the basis of certain similarities to the London Exchange, for which Jones prepared a design, although it was still primarily that of a decorative artist rather than an architect.

During his residence in Italy, Jones certainly studied the writings and buildings of Palladio, for his annotated copy of Palladio's *I quattro libri dell' architettura* is still in existence. The lessons he had learned in the Veneto began to be applied after Ann, King Christian's sister, came to the English throne in 1603, as the wife of James I. For the queen, Jones designed and supervised the production of a number of masques, collaborating with Ben Jonson, Shakespeare's friend and rival. Decorative and stage commissions kept him close to the court, and in 1610 he was appointed surveyor to Henry, Prince of Wales, who died two years later. In 1611 Jones made his second visit to Italy, accompanying the Earl of Arundel, who was escorting the king's daughter, Princess Elizabeth, and her husband on a sightseeing tour *en route* to their splendid castle in Heidelberg. They visited the cities of the Veneto, Naples, Florence, and Rome. The Earl and Jones extended their visit, and Jones did not return to England until 1615. By that time he had wholly assimilated the Renaissance architectural aesthetic, and was evidently fully equipped to take over the duties involved in his appointment to the surveyorship of the king's works, which had become vacant.

Like Vanbrugh after him, Jones seems to have attained mastery at one bound. In 1616 he began the Queen's House at Greenwich; in 1619 he was commissioned to add a new banqueting hall to the Whitehall complex; and during the decade following 1615, he designed the rest of the small group of buildings that has given him a place among great European architects.

Inigo Jones was perhaps the most widely influential of all British architects, for his ideas were taken up by Colen Campbell in *Vitruvius Britannicus* and thus led on to Palladianism and the great Georgian tradition. Unfortunately, of over 40 works

The Banqueting Hall, Whitehall, designed by Inigo Jones, 1619

St Paul's Church, Covent Garden, designed by Inigo Jones, 1631

Double Cube room, Wilton House, designed by Inigo Jones, c 1649

The Superga, near Turin, designed by Filippo Juvarra, 1715–27

the chamber of the Trusteeship Council. Though best known for his furniture designs – the chairs having a distinctive sculptural treatment of the wooden frame – he has also designed glassware, carpets, light fittings, and refrigerators. He was awarded six gold medals at Milan Triennales during the 1950s, and has exhibited in Germany, England, France, and America.

Juvarra, Filippo (1678–1736). Italian architect. Juvarra was born at Messina, in Sicily, and was apprenticed to the family craft of silversmithing. He became interested in the study of architecture, taught himself to be a good draughtsman, and went to Rome to train under Carlo Fontana. His first employment was as a stage designer under the patronage of Cardinal Ottoboni at the theatre in the Cancelleria, Rome. Later, in Naples, he became the first designer to develop Ferdinando Bibiena's perspective effects.

In 1714 Juvarra was appointed architect to King Victor Amadeus II of Savoy. There followed two prolific decades, interrupted by a journey to Portugal, Paris, and London in 1719–20. Juvarra was probably the most accomplished and sophisticated architect of his generation. His buildings show a complete understanding of Renaissance and post-Renais-

sance architecture. His imaginative skills were matched by technical proficiency in a remarkable succession of churches, palaces, and villas in and around Turin.

The Chapel of Veneria Reale (1716–21) is an outstanding example of Juvarra's skill in combining sound planning principles with an unusual sense of 'theatre' which gives the building its remarkable spatial qualities. The Chiesa del Carmine (1732–5) broke with the Italian tradition of solid nave walls, for which Juvarra substituted tall piers and arched openings. The Superga (1715–27), a church and monastery sited on a 2,000 ft eminence outside Turin, has a dome reminiscent of St Peter's, Rome; its façades rival those of northern Baroque monasteries such as Melk.

Juvarra's town palaces included the well-known Palazzo Madama (1718–21), although the most engaging of his secular buildings is undoubtedly the hunting lodge at Stupinigi, built on a cruciform plan with two arms extended to form a great seven-sided forecourt. The central domed hall again demonstrates Juvarra's skill in utilizing the work of many craftsmen in the service of his theatrical gifts.

Juvarra died at Madrid in 1736, while working on plans for a palace for Philip V.

built to his designs, only seven now survive. These include the Queen's Chapel at St James's; St Paul's Church, Covent Garden; and parts of Wilton House in Wiltshire, including the Double Cube Room.

Juhl, Finn (b 1912). Danish architect and furniture designer.

Juhl studied architecture at the Academy of Art, Copenhagen. He set up his own office in 1945, and in the same year became principal of the Frederiksberg School of Interior Design and Decoration, a post he held until 1955. In 1951 he represented Denmark at the United Nations in New York, where he designed

'Bangkok' silk-covered chair and stool designed by Finn Juhl

The Stupinigi, a hunting lodge outside Turin, by Juvarra, begun 1719

Louis Kahn

Kahn, Louis (*b* 1901). American architect. Kahn was born in the Baltic island of Osel in Estonia, now part of the USSR. He left for the USA in his youth, and was trained as an architect at the University of Pennsylvania, Philadelphia. He first worked with the Philadelphia City Planning Commission, and later with George Howe and William Lescaze. He remained comparatively unknown until he was in his late forties, when he began a series of buildings which have brought him an international reputation. The most widely publicized has been the Richards Medical Research Building for the University of Pennsylvania (1958–60), in which the functional square towers (carrying all ducts) give the buildings a stark silhouette which has caused them to be classified as examples of the 'New Brutalism.' This is a misnomer, for these buildings are amongst the most dramatic architectural forms of our time. Kahn's other buildings include the Yale University Art Gallery, New Haven (with D Orr, 1951–3), Laboratory Towers, Philadelphia (1967), Salk Institute, San Diego, and the Palace of Congress at the Venice Biennale (1969).

Kas. A large two-door cupboard introduced to North America by Dutch settlers in the second half of the seventeenth century. It continued to be made up until the early nineteenth century. The typical kas had a cornice, bun feet, and grisaille (qv) painted

Medallions painted by Angelica Kauffman on a ceiling at Syon House

decoration of fruit, flowers, and other ornamentation.

Kauffman, Angelica (1741–1807). Swiss decorative artist, Angelica Kauffman was brought to England in 1766 by Lady Wentworth. She soon became one of a group of Continental artists, including Zucchi, Cipriani, and Bonomi, who established a considerable reputation for their painted interiors, popularized by the work of Robert Adam. Angelica quickly became known as a somewhat prudish *femme fatale* in artistic circles, and as a decorative painter. She was adept at decorating walls and ceilings with agreeable groupings of Neo-classical motifs and scenes that were delicate and graceful, if of no great artistic consequence. Her most important commissions were carried out for Adam, notably at Chandos House and Stratford House, and she executed four paintings on

Yale University Art Gallery, designed by Louis Kahn 1951–3

An Adam commode decorated by Angelica Kauffman

Keep. *The keep at medieval Scottish Blackness Castle in West Lothian*

Church of the Ascension, near Moscow, by Kazakov, 1793

The Senate, now Moscow University, designed by Kazakov, 1785

the ceiling of the vestibule at Burlington House.

With Mary Moser, Angelica Kauffman was one of the two women foundation members of the Royal Academy. In 1767 her social ambitions caused her to make a disastrous marriage to a bogus count (Frederick de Horn), whom she left after discovering his true antecedents as a butler. 14 years later, after Horn's death, she married Antonio Zucchi – again unhappily, although they were both phenomenally successful artists. The work done by Zucchi and Angelica also included much handsome painted furniture, and they exercised a considerable influence on the leading cabinetmakers, including Chippendale and

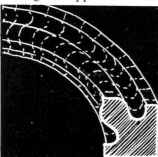

Section of a keel moulding

Hepplewhite; examples of Angelica's work on furniture are the painted medallions on a pair of sycamore commodes at Osterley. Angelica eventually moved to Rome, where she continued to reside after Zucchi's death in 1795. Her name was for a time romantically linked with that of Goethe.

Kazakov, Matvei Feodorovich (1733–1812). Russian architect. Kazakov was amongst the most eminent eighteenth-century Neoclassical architects in Russia. His practice was almost exclusively confined to Moscow. Like most of his contemporaries, he at first worked in the Baroque style practised by his mentor, Vasili Bazhenov, with whom his name is linked in the design of the Pashkov Palace, Moscow (1785–6). This manner was gradually superseded by a more individual style, well suited to the imperial and institutional buildings he designed for the Empress Catherine. For her he built the Senate (1771–85), the Petrovski Palace (1775–82), Palladian in plan but Gothic and medieval in detail, and a number of other buildings; many were destroyed in the great fire of 1812. Kazakov's most notable building is the

Church of the Ascension (1790–3). He was widely influential as an architectural teacher.

Keel arch. An alternative but little-used term for the ogee arch (qv), coined because of its likeness to an upturned keel.

Keel-moulding. A moulding with some resemblance to a boat keel; in section it is more like pointed arch.

Keene, Henry (1726–76). British architect. Keene was born in Middlesex, and was reputedly

The Guildhall, High Wycombe, Bucks, designed by Keene, 1757

e son of a carpenter. His talent ·r architecture was encouraged; ·d at the age of 20 he was pointed surveyor to the dean ·d chapter of Westminster. This ·sition provided him with valu- ·le source material for his study · Gothic architecture, which he ·as later to translate into a ·mestic 'gothick.'

Lord Halifax, who was ap- ·inted Lord Lieutenant of ·eland in 1761, made Keene ·chitect of His Majesty's works · Ireland, but his only recorded ·ork – the west front of Trinity ·ollege, Dublin – was carried out ·tween 1752 and 1759, years ·fore his appointment.

Keene's chief claim to fame is ·s skilful work (from 1750) in ·othicizing Arbury Hall, War- ·ickshire, the home of Sir Roger ·ewdigate, MP, scholar, and ·lettante. Thanks to the con- ·ued patronage of Newdigate, ·eene was able to design several ·ildings in Oxford, notably ·dditions and alterations to ·hrist Church, Magdalen, ·alliol, Worcester, and Univer- ·ty colleges. He was also respon- ·ble for the design of the ·uild hall at High Wycombe,

built in 1757.

Like many other eighteenth-century architects, Keene was a speculator in building projects. He was involved in developments in Oxford and London, chiefly in Golden Square, Soho (where he lived), and in Harley Street. Yet he seems to have died in mid-career, in debt to Newdigate and others.

Keep. The innermost tower of a medieval castle; alternatively known as donjon.

Kent, William (c1685–1748). British architect. Kent was one of several eminent eighteenth-century architects who started life in very humble circum-stances. Kent (or Cant) was born in Bridlington in Yorkshire, and was reputedly apprenticed to a coach-builder. He must have been extremely precocious, for he was taken up by three York-shire gentlemen and sent to further his studies in London, and then in Italy. In Rome, Kent became acquainted with Thomas Coke (later Earl of Leicester) and Lord Burlington; his ability to be agreeable and

useful to aristocrats was to stand him in good stead throughout his life.

Kent spent his time profitably, partly in the painting school of Benedetto Luti and partly in carrying out commissions for Burrell Massingberd and Sir John Chester who, with Sir William Wentworth, had under-written the Italian venture. Kent's commissions were many, ranging from copies of well-known paintings to busts of mythological heroes, from Nea-politan soap to fans for his patrons' wives.

He applied himself assidu-ously to his painting and won the Pope's medal; he was also the first English artist to be admitted to the Duke of Tus-cany's academy. His first major commission (1717) was to paint the ceiling of the church of S Guiliano dei Fiamminghi in Rome.

Kent returned to England in 1719, this time under the patron-age of Lord Burlington. He was soon engaged on decorative paintings at Burlington House. Thanks to Burlington's efforts he was even able to replace the

William Kent

far more talented Thornhill at Kensington Palace.

His development from history painter to architect was slow and hesitant. Even in 1724, when he and Lord Burlington published *The Designs of Inigo Jones with some Additional Designs*, his own contributions were decorative

Gothick Saloon at Arbury Hall, Warwickshire, by Keene, begun 1750

Entrance hall, Holkham Hall, Norfolk, by Kent, begun 1734

The south elevation of Holkham Hall, Norfolk, designed by William Kent, begun 1734

rather than architectural; and although he was appointed master-carpenter in 1726, his appointment a year later as inspector of paintings in the royal palaces probably demanded more of his time. One of his tasks was to restore the Rubens ceiling in the Banqueting Hall, Whitehall.

As a member of the Board of Works, however, Kent was inevitably drawn into the practice of architecture. His designs for royal buildings show his dedication to the precepts of Palladio, as interpreted by Inigo Jones; his decorative schemes, particu-

larly in the interiors of the buildings he designed, are less indebted to Palladio.

Among Kent's buildings were the Horse Guards, the Royal Mews, and the Treasury Buildings. The Horse Guards was a late design and was completed after Kent's death by his collaborator, John Vardy. It remains as one of the most pleasing of London's monuments, a compact and charming Palladian group, set off by the wide parade ground.

But it was Holkham, designed over many years for Thomas Coke, Earl of Leicester, that established Kent's lasting fame,

despite the denigration of contemporary and later critics. This great house in Norfolk was designed and built on an epic scale. The hall, with its giant Ionic colonnade of Derbyshire alabaster, monumental stairway, and statuary niches, is a noble composition by any standards.

Kent also 'improved' Rousham, a Jacobean house that belonged to his friend General Dormer. He gave the house some handsome interiors while respecting the Jacobean Gothic style of the house.

Among the least-known but most impressive of Kent's dom-

estic designs is 44 Berkeley Square, a small town house built for Lady Isabella Finch in 174 (now the premises of the Clermont Club). The great saloon on the first floor and the staircase have a magnificence unexpected in a comparatively small house

Kent also has a claim to fam as the artist who released English gardening from the excessive formality of the French garden His skills as a painter and architect enabled him to visualize landscape garden free of par terres but possessed of natural charms. In the words of Walpole 'he leaped the fence and saw that all Nature was a Garden', thu creating the English landscape garden, which has been called the nation's greatest contribution to the visual arts.

Key pattern. Ornamental pat tern based upon the ancient Greek fret. It is a continuous line with a repeating right angled motif. For about a century after 1720 the key pattern wa painted, carved or inlaid on furniture.

Keystone. The wedge-shaped stone at the summit of an arch

Brown state bedroom, Holkham Hall

The saloon of 44 Berkeley Square, designed by Kent, 1743

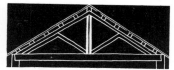

Diagram of a king-post

as the term implies, it locks the whole together. It is sometimes decoratively carved.

Kidderminster. Kidderminster may well be the earliest centre of carpet manufacture in England. Inventories show that it was producing rugs in the early seventeenth century, though no examples have yet come to light. Rather cheap, smooth-faced carpets were made at Kidderminster until 1753, when Brussels carpets (moquettes) were introduced.

King-post. The upright post, based on the tie beam in a roof structure; it acts as the main support of the ridge.

Kingwood. *Dalbergia cearensis.* Sometimes referred to as violet wood because of its distinctive colour. Kingwood was popular among craftsmen from the seventeenth century, and was employed extensively, particularly for decorative work.

Klenze, Leo von (1784–1864). German architect. Klenze was one of the leading German Neo-classical architects of the early

nineteenth century. Although he was born in Hildesheim, he came under French Empire influences when he was sent for his architectural training to the Ecole Polytechnique in Paris. In 1805 he visited Italy and England. In 1808 he was made court architect by the King of Westphalia (Napoleon's brother, Jerôme). In 1814 he was summoned by Maximilian I to Munich, where his considerable reputation was established. He was first commissioned to build the Leuchtenberg Palace (1819) and the Odeon, built a decade later; but his first major building was the Munich Glyptothek (1816–30) in the Königsplatz. This sculpture gallery, in which traces of his French training appeared, contained series of highly decorative vaulted interiors and housed a remarkable collection of antiquities. Klenze's hilltop Walhalla near Regensburg, built between 1831 and 1842, was an unashamed Neo-classical variation on the Greek temple. Next, Klenze was summoned to Russia, where he designed the Hermitage Museum in St Petersburg, built between 1839 and 1849. Among the many buildings for which Klenze was responsible after his return to Munich are the Ruhmeshalle (1843–53), the Propylaeon (1846–63), and the Königsbau section of the Royal Palace (1826–33). Klenze gradually moved away from his earlier Greek revival manner into a Neo-Renaissance

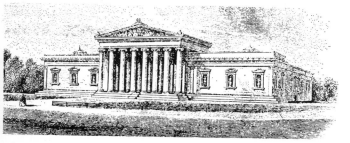

Munich Glyptothek designed by Leo von Klenze, 1816–30

The Ruhmeshalle near Munich, by Leo von Klenze, 1843–53

The Grundvig Church in Copenhagen, designed by P V J Klint

style, basing his designs on Italian *quattrocento* buildings.

Klint, Kaare (1888–1954). Danish architect and industrial designer. Klint was the son and pupil of P V J Klint, and, like his father, was at first a painter. Later he trained as an architect and designer under Carl Petersen, becoming lecturer in furniture design at Copenhagen Academy of Art in 1924. His furniture and other designs are in several Danish museums. He is most widely known for his ingenious paper lampshades, which have been widely imitated.

Klint, Peter Vilhelm Jensen (1853–1930). Danish architect. Klint was born at Skelkør, was trained as an engineer, and afterwards worked as an artist. He turned to architecture in his forties. He is known chiefly for his Grundvig Church in Copenhagen, a vast enlargement of the Gothic country church, built in yellow brick and with an organ-shaped façade. This church was started in 1920 and completed after Klint's death by his son Kaare.

Klismos. A light, elegant chair used by the ancient Greeks and probably dating from the sixth century BC. Information about the chair has been gathered

Ceiling lamp by Kaare Klint

mainly from the many illustrations of it on pottery. It had four concave, tapered, and splayed legs, and curved back uprights with a narrow concave back-rest between. It is extremely elegant, and the occupant is often shown lounging comfortably. The design was resurrected with the Greek revival (qv).

Greek Klismos chair

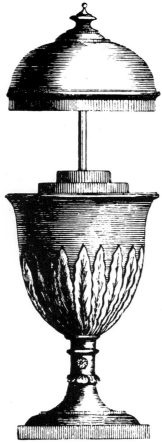

Knife case with raised lid

Kneehole. From the late seventeenth century to the present day, tables and similar pieces of furniture have been made with central recesses so that it is possible to sit close up to the surface.

Knife-cases. These were mainly made during the eighteenth century, especially the second half. They were made in pairs and in two different shapes: a knife box normally placed at either end of the sideboard, or a vase stationed on the sideboard or on the flanking pedestals. The vase type was made in the late eighteenth century.

Downton Castle, Herefordshire, designed by R P Knight, 1774

The box had a serpentine front and a sloping lid that lifted to reveal the partitions inside. Early boxes were made of shagreen or wood with decorative metal mounts; later versions such as the vases were usually inlaid, veneered, or even painted.

Knight, Richard Payne (1750–1824). English collector, connoisseur, landowner, and landscape designer. Knight was the wealthy owner of the 10,000-acre estate of Downton Castle in Herefordshire. He was also one of the leading figures in popularizing theories of the Picturesque, both in architecture and landscape design. His own castle, begun in 1774, was in the picturesque, mock-castle manner which influenced John Nash so strongly.

In 1794 Knight put forward some of his ideas in a long didactic poem, *The Landscape,* addressed to a friend and fellow Hereford landowner, Sir Uvedale Price (qv). This poem was loaded with injunctions to ambitious gardeners. A decade later Knight published *An Analytical Enquiry into the Principle of Taste,* which was basically an attack on the revolution in landscape design begun by Capability Brown and continued by Humphrey Repton. Repton considered that his own work had been deliberately overlooked in Knight's *Analytical Enquiry,* and countered with his own *Enquiry into the Changes of Taste in Landscape Gardening* in the following year.

Knight then removed to his house in Whitehall, and in 1814 was appointed Keeper of the British Museum. He is believed to have committed suicide.

Knitting-chair. Originally a term applied fairly loosely to armless Victorian tub chairs, often used for knitting. The term was first employed for a chair made specifi-

State Opera House, Unter den Linden, Berlin, by Knobelsdorff, 1741–

cally for knitting as recently as 1948, when a chair designed by Charles Addison was shown in a competition sponsored by the Scottish committee of the Council of Industrial Design. The chair has a walnut base formed by a built-in drawer for working materials.

Knob. Normally a single-stemmed handle of metal, wood, glass, or plastic; it has been used for drawers and doors of chests and cabinets. Inevitably, the design of knobs followed the stylistic characteristics of the furniture to which they were affixed. Thus elaborately-finished Louis XVI commodes carried sophisticated knobs in metal gilt, while Victorian chests of drawers carried turned knobs of solid wooden construction. In recent years the development of kitchen radio and television equipment has led to the manufacture of a wide range of plastic knobs; too many have been exotic in form and of dubious design.

Knobelsdorff, George Wenceslas (1699–1753). German architect. Knobelsdorff was appointed court architect to Frederick the Great, and his name is chiefly associated with the building of the king's Palace of Sanssouci (1745–53), one of the most delightful and elegant of all eighteenth-century regal conceits, owing much to French Rococo influences. However, Frederick's was the guiding hand in creating the lighthearted Sanssouci. Knobelsdorff's own manner, a somewhat unrelenting version of Palladianism, was better expressed in the Berlin Opera House, built in 1741–3

Pavilion at Sanssouci Palace

Knock-down furniture. form of prefabricated sectionalized furniture, known in furniture manufacturing circles a KD furniture. It was express designed for easy transport, wit a consequent emphasis upo convenience in packing, crating and shipping. Thanks to th underlying necessity for func tionalism at all stages, man forms of KD furniture have thoughtfulness and purpose i

Decorative metal door knob

Knock-down two- and three-seater sofas

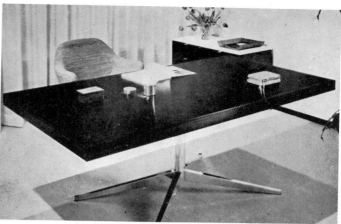

Executive desk designed by Florence Knoll

design lacking in more ambitious furniture made in the same factories.

Knocker. Door furniture, usually of brass or iron, hinged to strike against a metal plate. Knockers have often been highly

Goat's head door-knocker

decorative, carrying fauna motifs; but in recent years they have tended to be plainer in design.

Knole sofa. Term applied to a form of day bed evolved in the early seventeenth century. The name comes from Knole in Kent, the home of the Sackvilles, which houses a remarkable collection of Tudor and Stuart furniture. The Knole sofa is distinctive by reason of its high upholstered back and sides, the sides being set apart from the back and hinged by means of ratchets and corded ties. It has enjoyed a vogue at various times in this century among fashionable decorators and their clients.

Knoll, Florence (*b* 1917). American furniture designer. She was educated at Cranbrook Academy and trained at the Illinois Institute of Technology and the Architectural Association in London. She then joined Harrison and Abramovitz in New York, where she met and married Hans Knoll. They formed the firm known as Knoll International (Form International in Britain). Apart from Florence Knoll's designs, the firm commissioned furniture designs from architects and designers such as

Mies van der Rohe, Eero Saarinen, and Isamu Noguchi. The firm became internationally known, chiefly because of its success in complementing the work of architects in the design of interiors. The most remarkable of these joint ventures was the out-of-town headquarters of the Connecticut General Insurance Company designed by Skidmore, Owings, and Merrill. After Hans Knoll was killed in a car accident in 1955, Florence Knoll controlled the design operations of the Knoll company, but in 1960 she sold the business to Art Metal, continuing to act as design consultant to the group.

Knop. One of a series of knobs used alternately with cusps or rings in ornamental turning. It dates from the second half of the seventeenth century. The motif is also known as knop and cusp, and knop and ring.

Knott, Ralph (1878–1929). British architect. Knott's major claim to fame was his design for the London County Hall, prepared in 1908 while he was working as an architectural assistant in the drawing-office of Sir Aston Webb. This vast building was still in course of construction

when Knott died in 1929, although the first section of the building had been opened in 1922. It was completed in 1933.

Knuckle. The carved terminal scroll on the arms of Windsor and similar elbow chairs.

Knuckle joint. A term used in joinery and cabinetmaking to designate an interlocking joint which roughly resembles a finger joint. It is used in such elements as the separate hinged leaves of a dropleaf table.

Knurl. A term used by eighteenth-century chair-makers to describe a form of whorl foot. Tradition demands that the knurl should be carved on the *inner* side of the leg – illogically, since it remains unseen from the front.

Kremlin. A fortified tower, or series of towers, built within a Russian city; it was invariably entered by way of a triumphal gateway through which all state processions passed. The towers were usually adorned with deeply machicolated walls, and enclosed five-domed churches and belfries. The most famous Kremlin is that of Moscow.

The Kremlin, Moscow

Label moulding and stop

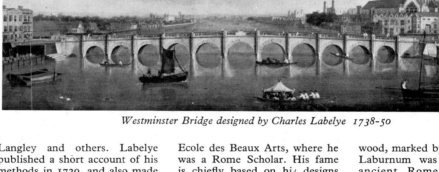

Westminster Bridge designed by Charles Labelye 1738–50

Label moulding. A medieval stone moulding made to repel rainwater. It was set on a façade, usually Gothic, and projected above and around the heads of windows and doorways. The moulding followed the line of the window-head and was sometimes continued as a string course (qv). The label is also known as a dripstone or hoodmould.

Label stop. A carved ornamented boss acting as a finial at either end of a label.

Labelye, Charles (1705–81). British architect-engineer of French origin. Labelye seems to have arrived in England at the age of 20, but nothing is known of his early training or practical experience until 1738, when he was appointed engineer in charge of the building of a new Westminster Bridge. His appointment was not well received by his English contemporaries. Labelye's use of caissons was new to English engineering. The project was attended by various setbacks, and was not opened until 1750, when it received much criticism from Batty

Langley and others. Labelye published a short account of his methods in 1739, and also made technical recommendations for improving London Bridge, the port of Sunderland, the harbour at Sandwich, and the Fens. Although naturalized in 1746, he returned to France in 1751 and apparently died there some 30 years later.

Labrouste, Henri (1801–75). French architect. Labrouste was born in Paris and trained at the

Ecole des Beaux Arts, where he was a Rome Scholar. His fame is chiefly based on his designs for the Bibliothèque Sainte-Geneviève in the Place du Panthéon (1843–50), and for the Bibliothèque Nationale in Paris (1858–68). His advanced use of steel frames encased in masonry give him a significant place in the history of modern French architecture.

Laburnum. *Laburnum anagyroides.* A yellow to pale brown

wood, marked by brown streaks. Laburnum was referred to in ancient Rome as 'Corsican ebony.' A notable use of the wood was for inlay work in the form of oyster pieces (qv) in the late seventeenth century. At the beginning of the twentieth century, craftsmen began to favour laburnum for drawer and door handles.

Lace (Latin, *laqueum* 'a noose'). Lace is made by looping, braiding, or twisting threads. As a

Exterior and interior of the Bibliothèque St Geneviève, Paris, by Henri Labrouste, 1843–50

Loos. *Mahogany and brass staircase of a house in the Michaelerplatz, Vienna, designed by Adolf Loos, 1910–11*

Brussels lace, 18th century

A Louis XIV black lacquer commode

handcraft it falls into two categories, needlepoint and pillow-lace. Needlepoint, a development of cutwork, is worked with a needle and a single thread, and ordinary embroidery stitches (especially the blanket stitch) are used to create designs. Pillow lace is made with a cushion and numerous threads wound on bobbins.

Lace-making, as it is known now, originated in fifteenth-century Italy in Venice. This was needlepoint work. Italy is also held by some to have been the birthplace of pillow or bobbin lace, a claim disputed by others on behalf of Flanders.

The great demand for fine laces – especially for wear at court – encouraged inventiveness and exquisite craftsmanship. Italian work was the most sought-after, and such high prices were paid for it that governments felt impelled to sponsor native industries, as Colbert did in France (1665).

In mid-sixteenth-century England sumptuary laws were passed prohibiting foreign gold and silver cutworks to be worn by people below a certain rank. Later, all imports of foreign cutworks were banned. Passements (*passementerie*) was the name given to the luxurious gold and silver braids worked by the Parisian makers, who until the mid-seventeenth century made no distinction between such braid and lace.

Belgian bobbin lace of the eighteenth century is amongst the finest ever made, the most important being Brussels, Mechlin, Brabant, Antwerp, and Valenciennes. Belgian refugees settled at Honiton in Somerset, England, which then became the main centre of English lace. Honiton lace continued to be fashionable until the end of the nineteenth century.

American lace was only made at Ipswich, Massachusetts. It was based upon English designs and techniques.

Broadly speaking, old lace can be classified by pattern formations: geometric in the sixteenth century, scrolled in the seventeenth, and with more complicated scrolls on a background during the eighteenth century, when the finest work was produced.

Machine-made lace was first manufactured in the late eighteenth century, but was not patented until the mid-nineteenth. Nottingham in England is one of the major centres for machine lace.

The delicate and spidery effect of lace has influenced decoration in a number of ways. Its name has been given to the net-like patterns in Venetian glass (lace glass or *vetro di trina*), while 'lacework' is a porcelain technique that was introduced in the Meissen factory in 1770. It was made of real lace that had been dropped into porcelain 'slip' and then fired so that the lace fabric burnt away, leaving the pattern in porcelain.

Lacquer. In modern times, a coloured or opaque or clear varnish, usually applied to metal or wood surfaces. Chinese lacquer was a very different substance. It was made from the sap of the tree *Rhus Vernicifera*, indigenous to China and known in Japan since the sixth century AD. This turns yellow-brown and then black on exposure to air. Occasionally the resin is worked in the solid, or applied to metal alloys or porcelain. But 'lacquer-work' usually refers to its application to an extremely thin layer of wood, usually a pine with a soft, even grain. Many thin coats of resin are applied, each in turn being dried and polished. The whole process is highly skilled and laborious, and the resulting surface is extremely hard and takes a brilliant polish. The resin may be coloured brown, buff, black, green, etc; the beautiful red Chinese lacquer is produced by the inclusion of red sulphuret of mercury. The lacquered surface was either carved or painted and gilded. It could be further enriched with built-up surfaces, or inlaid with shells or mother-of-pearl.

Chinese lacquerwork, particularly lacquered cabinets, was highly prized by the beginning of the seventeenth century. Special stands were made for them, richly carved and gilded, which are now sometimes of more value than the cabinets themselves. Chinese Coromandel screens have always interested Western collectors. Here the deeply lacquered surface was cut out in intaglio and further enriched with applied colour and gold.

Lacunaria (Latin, *lacuna* 'a hole', 'a gap'). The term applied to the recessed panels in a coffered ceiling.

Ladderback chair. A chair with horizontal back slats. It has been made since the Middle Ages, and was particularly common in the eighteenth century in both England and America, where in many instances the slats were pierced.

Lady chapel. A chapel dedicated to Our Lady, the Virgin Mary; normally used for private prayer or meditation but oc-

Venetian lace

The Lady Chapel at Long Melford, Suffolk

Lacunaria in the Pantheon

City of London Custom House by David Laing, 1813-17

"Plan and elevation for an ornamental cottage or lodge, made for a nobleman" from Laing's 'Hints for Dwellings', 1801

casionally for devotion by small gatherings. The Lady chapel in larger churches and cathedrals is usually built east of the chancel and high altar, forming a projection from the main structure. In smaller churches it may be little more than an extension of the altar.

Laing, David (1774–1856). British architect. Laing, the son of a cork cutter, was articled to Sir John Soane when he was 16. In his mid-thirties he was appointed architect and surveyor to the Board of Customs, and designed the Custom House (still standing) in Lower Thames Street (1813–17). Owing to a

subsidence occasioned by faulty piling (part of the structure had to be rebuilt in 1825), Laing was dismissed from office and forced to stop practising as an architect. The last 30 years of his life were passed in obscurity.

Before his enforced retirement, Laing had been responsible for the design of St Dunstan-in-the-East and various private houses in London, Essex, Devon, and Berkshire. He published pattern-books, including *Hints for Dwelling* (1801), which consist of original designs for cottages, farm-houses, and villas.

Lalique, René (1860–1945). French artist and industrialist.

Lalique was born at Ay in Champagne. At 20 he was apprenticed to a jewellery firm in Paris. From the age of 30 he worked as a freelance designer and exhibited at the Salon des Artistes Francais as an independent jeweller.

Lalique turned his attention to rock crystal and designed his own laboratory and salon in Paris. Its door of sculptured glass was his first architectural glass design, but it was the design of a perfume bottle for Coty that made both him and the perfume famous. In 1920 he acquired a glassworks at Wingen-sur-Moder in Alsace-Lorraine. Here he produced glass designs which caught the mood of the 1920s and were taken up by the rich and the fashionable. His work made a considerable impact at the 1925 Paris Exhibition.

After his death in 1945 his work was continued by his son Marc, who had trained with his father.

Lambrequin. Ornament derived from a formal treatment of pendant draperies with tasselled or escalloped edges. In heraldry the word describes the plumes on helmets, but its use in interior decoration probably originated in France. Lambrequins are most conspicuously used in the designs of Jean Berain and Daniel Marot.

Laminated materials are manufactured from natural or man-made substances. They are made up of a succession of layers, or *laminae*, of the same or alternating materials. In sheet form these materials have been widely used for door and wall panelling, table-tops, etc.

Lamps. The oldest lamps are simple open vessels, filled with oil and burning from a wick. This basic design was used until the development of the Argand lamp between 1780 and 1783. The attendant inconveniences of smoke, wick trimming, and re-fuelling caused the lamp to be relegated to bedrooms for the greater part of the seventeenth and eighteenth centuries; lanterns and chandeliers supplanted them in formal rooms.

New lamp designs were introduced in the late eighteenth century. Lamps were made with pedestals or hanging on chains, the latter possibly suggested by Roman lamps found in Pompeii and Herculaneum. These types antedate the greatly improved lamps of the next century, the Moderator lamp (1836) and the Duplex Burner (1865). The use

Lalique crystal vase

of paraffin was the other major change before the replacement of lamps by gas and electricity.

Modern lamps, almost exclusively wired for electricity, come in three basic forms; hanging, standing, and table.

Oil lamp with marbled glass

Modern table lamp

Lancet windows

Designers have turned their attention to this long neglected aspect of furnishing, and standards of design are currently high with Italy leading the field. The wealth of materials now available has done much to stimulate production.

Lancet arch. A pointed arch described from two centres with radii longer than the span of the arch. Sometimes known as an acute arch.

Lancet window. A tall, narrow, pointed arch window used in thirteenth-century church building. Lancet windows are frequently arranged in groups of three, as at Beverley Minster, Yorkshire.

Landing by John Nash, 1805

The artificial lake and park of Blenheim Palace, Oxfordshire, created by 'Capability' Brown

The lancet shape was used for chair backs in the mid-eighteenth century, when it became part of the gothick decorative repertoire, usually taking the form of three attached arches. Again, with the revival of interest in Gothic forms in 1800–50, it was used for the cases of table and mantel clocks.

Landing. The level platform or staging between two flights of stairs or steps.

Landscape gardening. The landscape garden has been called England's chief contribution to the arts, and has been copied all over the world.

Landscape gardening began in the eighteenth century as a revolt against the formality and artifice of garden plans in the previous century, formal plans such as those laid out by Le Nôtre at Versailles and Vaux le Vicomte, and copied to a lesser extent in England. Such set, geometric plans were popular in Tudor times and later in the box-outlined Dutch gardens introduced by William III.

The landscape gardeners set out to give gardens a completely 'natural' appearance, albeit one subtly manipulated in the interests of beauty. Parterres of

box and yew, statues, canals, and fountains were deemed unfashionable, and in the enthusiasm for the new movement many of the finest gardens of England – such as Henry Wise's great parterre at Blenheim – were ruthlessly swept away. Groves, vistas, perspectives were the order of the day, as were serpentine streams and lakes, so constructed to make them seem larger than they were.

Among the high priests of the new cult was William Kent (qv). Kent was followed by the celebrated Lancelot 'Capability' Brown (qv). Contemporary with Brown was William Shenstone, who at his estate, The Leasowes, created a park and garden on a comparatively small scale which was much admired. Later came Sir William Chambers, who developed Brown's theories, and, for novelty, introduced *chinoiserie* to the English scene, peppering his parks with pagodas – as at Kew – and spanning streams with fretwork bridges. The last of the pontiffs of the landscape gardening was Humphry Repton (qv), who was less didactic than Brown. Repton wisely reinstated the dividing line between house and park: the terrace. And unlike Brown, he did not frown on planting near the house.

By Victorian times the era of private park-planting was over, and the age of carpet-bedding, the rock-garden, and the herbaceous border, had begun. This was largely the work of two fine gardeners, Gertrude Jekyll and William Robinson.

Nowadays a revival of interest in landscape gardening on a large scale has been displayed by large organizations, and some thought at least is being given to planting around factories, housing developments, and on the borders of motorways.

Landscape panel. The cabinetmaker's term for a wooden panel with the grain running horizontally.

Langley, Batty (1696–1751). British architectural writer. Langley was born in Twickenham, the son of a local gardener, and he himself also became a gardener. Later he became a writer on architecture, garden design, and estate management; and he even opened a school for architectural drawing.

His ambitions inevitably took him into the practice of architecture, but he was far from successful. His pattern-books were, however, widely popular, and did much to disseminate the

Design for a gothick window by Batty Langley

early Georgian style among provincial builders. Many of his books provided a firm grounding in the architectural orders and were undeniably useful. Some of Langley's most extreme views, such as his championing of highly individual and esoteric forms of Gothic (some of which are to be seen in the Soane Museum), aroused the scorn of Horace Walpole; they have been largely, and to some extent unjustifiably, dismissed.

Langley's publications include *The Builders' Chest Book* (1727); *New Principles of Gardening* (1728); *Ancient Masonry, both in the Theory and in the Practice* (c 1735); *Ancient Architecture Restored and Improved by a Great Variety of Grand and Useful Designs* (1741); and *The Builder's Jewel* (1746).

Lannuier, Charles Honoré (1779–1819). A French emigré cabinetmaker who arrived in America in 1803 and set up a

Pavilion by Langley

Mahogany card table by Honoré Lannuier, c 1805

furniture shop in New York. He worked in the Louis XVI and Empire styles and is said to have influenced the designs of Duncan Phyfe (qv). Many of Lannuier's pieces had elaborate ormolu mounts, fine carving, gilding,

and wire inlay. He made a number of pieces for the Van Rensselaer family which are on display at the Albany Institute of History and Art, New York. Other works, including a sofa-table and a small ornamental

Lantern on Castle Howard, Yorkshire, by Vanburgh

Glass lantern, c 1800

stand or guéridon, are displayed in the Red Room at the White House, Washington.

Lantern. The basic form of a light enclosed by a transparent covering has been used since classical antiquity for hanging, wall, and portable lanterns.

Most early examples are of horn (hence probably the name 'lanthorn'), a material which continued to be used for utilitarian lanterns until the early nineteenth century.

The elegant glass hanging lanterns that were first made in the early eighteenth century are now much sought after. Even then they were a luxury item, with delicate copper, brass, or giltwood frames that were often octagonal or hexagonal in form.

In the Regency era, lamps replaced the lanterns used in draughty places such as staircases and passages.

In architecture a lantern is a glazed or pierced superstructure, made of timber or occasionally stone, erected on the roof of a building. It admits light to an attic storey or stair-well, or is used to improve the ventilation of the interior. A lantern is sometimes incorporated in the dome of a large house or ecclesiastical building (Castle Howard, St Paul's Cathedral), or in the top of a tower (Ely Cathedral).

Lantern clock. A small and typically English wall clock of the seventeenth and early eighteenth centuries. It has only one arm, a circular face that overlaps the upright sides of the frame, cresting, and a small domed top. The top is encased in diagonal curved bands, at the crossing of which there is a finial. Most examples antedate the invention of the

The façade of Assembly's College, Belfast, by Lanyon, 1853

The Royal College of Physicians, London, by Denys Lasdun, 1962

pendulum in the late seventeenth century, though in some, the weight-driven mechanism was subsequently replaced by a pendulum. These clocks are sometimes called birdcage clocks or, mistakenly, Cromwellian clocks.

Lanyon, Sir Charles (1813–89). British architect and civil engineer. Lanyon was born in Eastbourne, but was trained as an engineer in the Dublin Board of Works under Jacob Owen, whose daughter he married. While still in his early twenties he was appointed county surveyor of Kildare. Later he became county surveyor of Antrim, building railways and roads, notably the coast road from Larne to Portrush. His best buildings are in Belfast, and include Queens College (1846–8), the Ulster Institution (1854), and many official buildings, banks, churches, and houses. He was made president of the Royal Institute of Architects in Ireland, was knighted, became mayor of Belfast in 1862, and was elected to Parliament in 1866.

Larch. *Larix decidua.* A strong and durable European wood, varying in colour from russet to pale brown. Towards the end of the eighteenth century, larch was used for the carcase work of case furniture (qv), and for rustic furniture.

Larsen, Jack Lenor (*b* 1927). American textile designer. The recipient of many international awards, Larsen is generally considered one of the most imaginative of contemporary textile designers. Examples of his work are in many museums, including the Victoria and Albert in London and the Museum of Modern Art, New York. He was a student of architecture and interior design at Washington University, and did postgraduate research in historic textiles at Washington and Cranbrook. The firm of Jack Lenor Larsen Inc was formed in 1952 to 'explore the design possibilities of hand and power weaving.' Larsen's woven fabrics, while influenced by the rough weaves of peasant countries, are unique in their use of surface

texture. His printed fabrics are distinctive and always experimental.

Lasdun, Denys (*b* 1914). British architect. Lasdun was educated at Rugby School and trained at the Architectural Association Schools. After war service (1939–45) he worked with Wells Coates, and was a partner in the Tecton group before setting up in private practice. Among his first works were the now-famous school for Paddington (1951), and housing schemes for Bethnal Green (1955) and Paddington (1955). His work has also included designs for the Peter Robinson store in the Strand, London (1958), and luxury flats in St James's Place (1958). It is remarkable for the skill and subtlety with which he fuses an uncompromising twentieth-century austerity with an elegance in design and detailing that is unmatched in modern British architecture. These qualities are shown in the most famous of his buildings, the Royal College of Physicians, designed in 1960. Lasdun has also been

Denys Lasdun

responsible for a considerable body of academic architecture, including buildings for Fitzwilliam College and Christ's College, Cambridge, and for London University and the universities of Leicester and Liverpool. Currently his most significant works are the National Theatre being built on the South Bank of the Thames (the designs

Jack Lenor Larsen and his design for batik printed cotton velvet

Luxury flats, St James's Place, designed by Denys Lasdun, 1958

Bank of Pennsylvania, Philadelphia, by Latrobe, 1798

Latticed garden pavilion

Lattice window

were exhibited at the Sao Paulo Biennale in 1969 and received a special award), the University of East Anglia and the new headquarters for the Royal Institution of Chartered Surveyors.

Lasdun has lectured widely to schools of architecture, both in Britain and abroad.

Latin cross. The most common ecclesiastical cross plan in western Europe and America; it consists of one long (nave) arm and three short arms of equal or nearly equal length.

Latrobe, Benjamin Henry (1764–1820). Anglo-American architect. Latrobe was born in Leeds; his father was the leader of the Moravian mission in England. His career as an architect was divided between England

and America. He was at school at a Moravian College in Saxony, and returned to England to work in the Stamp Office. On his father's death in 1786 he left this sinecure and began to study architecture in Samuel Cockerell's office, supplementing this training by engineering experience under John Smeaton, the civil engineer and rebuilder of the Eddystone Lighthouse. He then practised successfully as an architect, designing many police offices (he was surveyor to the London police), and several villas in Surrey and Sussex.

After the tragic death of his wife in 1796, Latrobe seems to have suffered some form of mental upheaval, and emigrated to America. He was immediately successful, being taken up by Thomas Jefferson, and was res-

ponsible for the Bank of Pennsylvania in Philadelphia, begun in 1798, which has been called 'the first monument of the Greek revival in America.' Latrobe now made a highly successful career as one of the foremost official architects; in 1803 Jefferson appointed him surveyor of public buildings to the federal government, a position he retained until 1817. He made additions to the Capitol at Washington and was responsible for the renovation of the interior after its destruction by the British in 1814. Among his architectural works in America were the Cathedral (1804–18) and the Exchange (1815–17) in Baltimore. He also continued with his engineering projects, which included the introduction of water supplies to Pennsylvania and New Orleans.

Lattice. A term applied to any criss-cross or diamond-shaped pattern used in decoration. It has been employed in a wide variety of structures, ranging from the criss-crossed metal bars of medieval window openings to the timbered lattice-work of garden treillage. Windows with leaded diamond-shaped panes are frequently called lattice windows.

Laurana, Luciano (d 1479). Italian architect. Laurana was born in Dalmatia, but little else is known of his early life. His reputation as an architect has fluctuated, mainly because – despite Laurana's considerable reputation at the time of his death at Pesaro – his most important work, on the Palazzo Ducale, Urbino, was attributed to another architect by Vasari in his *Lives of the Artists* (1550); indeed, Laurana was unaccountably omitted from Vasari's book. This lack of documentation has also

been responsible for uncertainty in attributing to Laurana the Rocco Constanza, the citadel at Pesaro, where he was certainly active in the late 1470s.

The Palazzo Ducale, which dominates the hill-top town of

The cortile of the Palazzo Ducale, Urbino, by Luciano Laurana

Bernard Leach

Stoneware bowl by Bernard Leach, 1947

Le Corbusier

Urbino, is the work of many architects. Each made his contribution to this architectural masterpiece, the court of the great humanist and patron Duke Federigo da Montefeltro.

Laurana's task was to combine the Palazzetto della Jole and the medieval keep of Castellare. He was also responsible for the internal courtyard, one of the most elegant cortiles in existence, based on a slender variant of the Corinthian order. Many of the gracefully designed chimneypieces and door cases of the Palazzo are also attributed to Laurana.

Laurel. The laurel leaf, traditional symbol of triumph, was first used as an architectural decoration in the ancient world. It was readopted as a motif during the early Georgian period, and was found particularly in moulded detail and in friezes of cabinet work.

Lazy Susan. A revolving tray set upon a squat stand that is usually placed in the centre of a table used for informal eating. Lazy Susans provide a central cache of containers for salt, sugar,

and other condiments, preserves, and relishes that would otherwise have to be passed around. It was a late eighteenth-century American development of the dumb waiter (qv), still often used.

Leach, Bernard (*b* 1887). British potter, probably the most famous studio potter of this century. Leach studied at the Slade and also in Japan for many years. He made slipware and stoneware showing a marked oriental influence. Leach began his artistic career as a draughtsman and etcher, turning to pottery in 1911. Of his life and work in Japan, a Japanese writer has said, 'Few foreigners have been so loved and understood by Japanese.' After his return from Japan in 1920 he was greatly influenced by the work of William Staite Murray (qv), who had begun his own experiments in 1915 and had also been inspired by Sung pottery.

Leach started his pottery at St Ives in Cornwall in 1920, and here he trained many talented craftsmen, including his sons and grandson. Leach's personal mark consists of his initials, BL, in various arrangements, pencilled,

incised or impressed. The Leach pottery at St Ives has developed into a small factory for the manufacture of moderately priced domestic stoneware. The pieces are well designed and well finished. The pottery uses an impressed seal mark, a square with the corners cut off, enclosing a horizontal bar with an S-like character across it and two dots in the upper left-hand and lower right-hand corners.

Leaf scroll foot. A scroll foot decorated with formalized leaves.

Lean-to roof. A single sloping roof with its rafters resting against a higher wall.

Leather. Leather has been used for upholstery since ancient times. Chairs, chests, and screens clad in leather and studded with nail-head decoration have been made in most cultures: some still survive from Ancient Egypt.

The hides used are generally those of cattle, sheep, pigs, and goats. Goatskin is used for Moroccan leather, the elastic soft leather found on desk tops and library tables. This particular use of leather was introduced during

the Renaissance.

Its durability, colour fastness, and variety makes leather suitable as a strong chair covering, or as a thin, light covering, tooled and gilded, for small boxes and jewel cases. Leather furniture is being manufactured in increasing quantities; the most notable examples are chesterfields and Charles Eames's black hide versions of the club chair.

Le Corbusier Charles-Edouard Jeanneret (1887–1965). Swiss architect, born at La Chaux-de-Fonds. One of the great creative architectural figures of the twentieth century, although he inspired his disciples more by what he preached and designed than by what he built.

After early training in several parts of Europe – from Vienna and Munich to Athens and Paris – Le Corbusier started an independent practice in Paris in 1922. His early buildings (during what he has called his 'years of misery, and of abject, blind folly by the profession and officials') were small houses, including two in Stuttgart, denounced later by Hitler but now historical monuments. He also designed for

Leather Chesterfields in an interior by Adolf Loos

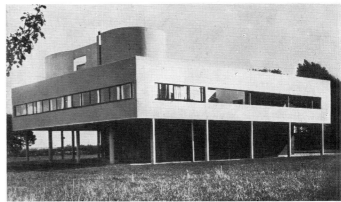

The Villa Savoie, Poissy, by Le Corbusier, 1927-31

Notre Dame du Haut, Ronchamp, by Le Corbusier, 1950-4

A drawing for Chandigarh, by Le Corbusier

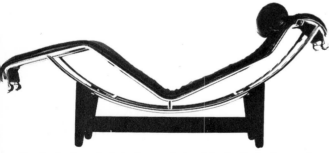

Steel tube framed chaise longue designed by Le Corbusier, 1928

The House of the Surveyor of the River Loue by Ledoux

arious exhibitions, including the 6,000 sq ft tinted Pavilion des 'emps Nouveaux in the 1937 nternational Housing Exhibition eld in Paris. He also produced evolutionary development plans r Algiers, Moscow, Rio de aneiro, and other cities, based n his theories of great blocks of ats and *la ville radieuse*.

Le Corbusier has also painted nd written prolifically. His books include *Quand les Cathédrales étaient Blanches*, a study of New York and the United States, *Vers une Architecture* (1922), and *Urbanisme* (1924). *My Work*, published in 1960 (Architectural Press), is his somewhat acrimonious autobiography.

In the last decades of his life, Le Corbusier's architectural designs received widespread recognition. His chapel at Ronchamp, the Unité d'Habitation at Marseilles (1945-50), his work on the UNO building in New York, and Chandigarh, new capital of the Punjab, confirmed his stature as one of the three modern masters, on a par with Frank Lloyd Wright and Mies van der Rohe.

Ledoux, Claude Nicholas (1736 –1806). French architect whose work has a starkness and purity which caused him to be hailed as a forerunner of the modern aesthetic. He earned his living as an engraver before studying architecture under J F Blondel. Many of his projects remained unrealized because of his over-ambitious designs, the most famous of which was his ideal city at Chaux, which he conceived on being commissioned to the salt works at Arc et Senans in Franche-Comté. Many of Ledoux's projected buildings were designed with the basic forms of cube, cylinder, pyramid, and sphere in mind. Some of his best designs were the Château de Benouille (begun 1767), the Pavillon de Louviennes (1771), the palace and gateway for Mme Thélusson (1788), the theatre at Besançon (1775-84), and the Paris Toll houses (1784-9).

Leeds ware. The ware produced at a pottery established *c* 1760 by two brothers called Green. At this early date salt-glazed stoneware was manufactured. The famous creamware came later.

Leeds creamware was very often decorated with pierced decoration imitated from the work of the contemporary silversmiths. The body is very light and the glaze has a particularly pleasing silkiness to the touch. Much of the ware was decorated with free-drawn sprays of flowers in black and red, though other colours were sometimes used. Some of the work was transfer-printed. Apart from cream-coloured earthenware, the factory made mottled and marbled ware, pearl ware, and lustred ware.

By 1820 the work of the pottery was declining and it finally closed down in 1878.

Leeds creamware transfer printed tureen and ladle

Leeds creamware cocklepot

Château de Richelieu, Poitou, designed by Jacques Lemercier, 1631

The ware was by no means always marked, but LEEDS POTTERY, impressed and in various forms, appears on many pieces.

Lemercier, Jacques (*c* 1580–1654). French architect. Lemer-cier was born in Pontoise, the son of a master-mason. He studied in Rome for several years before returning in 1617 to Paris, where he began to make a con-siderable reputation. He is generally regarded as one of the founders of French classicism, although he was undoubtedly less gifted than Mansart and Le Vau.

Lemercier's first important building was the Pavillon de l'Horloge at the Louvre (1624), but his major achievements were carried out under the patronage of Cardinal Richelieu. He de-signed the Sorbonne in 1626 for Richelieu, and designed and began to build the new town of Richelieu in Poitou in 1631. He also designed the Palais Cardinal, later known as the Palais Royal (begun in 1633). He was involved in the building of three of the greatest of Parisian churches: the Oratoire, St Roch, and Man-sart's church of Val de Grâce, which Lemercier completed (1645). He designed a number of important houses, notably the Hôtel de Liancourt, the plan of which was copied by later archi-tects. Within a comparatively restricted area, Lemercier man-aged to combine an impression of grandeur with the maximum living-space. In his work he sought to combine Roman influ-ences with the new French classical style: elements that were never completely reconciled.

L'Enfant, Pierre-Charles (1754–1825). French emigré engineer, responsible for planning the urban layout of Washington D(C) until his dismissal from publi(c) service in 1792. His plan was th(e) conventional Baroque one o(f) radiating streets, road-points and immensely long vistas focus-ing on monuments. However, i(t) was specifically French in havin(g) houses surrounded by garden(s) rather than being terraced an(d) giving directly onto the street.

Lennon, Dennis (*b* 1918). British architect and industria(l) designer. Lennon was educate(d) at Merchant Taylors' School an(d) trained as an architect at Uni-versity College, London. Afte(r) serving in World War II, h(e) worked for Maxwell Fry. H(e) became director of the Rayo(n) Industry Design Centre in 1948 and two years later started hi(s) own architectural and desig(n) practice in London.

Lennon's commissions hav(e) included the design of numerou(s) showrooms and over 30 restaur-ants. He has also been responsibl(e) for hotel interiors, including th(e) Ridgeway in Lusaka, the Cum(

Church of Val de Grâce, Paris, completed by Lemercier, 1645

Aerial view of Richelieu, Indre-et-Loire, by Lemercier, 1631

Sekers showroom, London, designed by Dennis Lennon, 1965

Dennis Lennon

berland in London, and the Albany in Birmingham, Nottingham, and Glasgow. He was consultant architect to the Royal Opera House in London. His more recent commissions have included a scheme for the development of a 35-acre site in London to house 3,500 people, with flats, houses, shops, and public houses arranged in interrelated groups; and with James Gardner (qv) the co-ordination of all aspects of design in the Cunard liner *Queen Elizabeth II*.

Le Nôtre, André (1631–1700). French landscape gardener. Le Nôtre was the son of one of the head gardeners at the Tuileries, and trained as a draughtsman under Simon Vouet, painter-in-chief to Louis XIII. He also studied architecture, possibly under Jacques Lemercier or François Mansart (qqv). He was thus amongst the best-equipped

of all landscape gardeners. While still in his twenties, Le Nôtre prepared and had accepted an alternative plan to Mansart's scheme for the orangery at Versailles. By an unusual combination of talent, tact, and wit he seems to have made his way without making enemies. He was soon enjoying royal favour, was provided with lodgings in the royal park, and received further commissions – notably at the Tuileries, for the upkeep of which he was to be responsible until the end of his life.

Despite his work for Louis XIII and Louis XIV, Le Nôtre was allowed an unusual degree of freedom in being permitted to work for various aristocratic patrons. Among his earliest commissions were those for the gardens at Wideville, the episcopal garden at Meaux, Vincennes, Bourges, Castries, and the Luxembourg Gardens (for

Gaston, duc d'Orléans). But his first great achievement was the gardens at Vaux-le-Vicomte, the palace built by Nicolas Fouquet, the king's superintendent of finance. Le Nôtre's work at Vaux brought him into closer contact with Louis XIV, and he was commissioned to design the gardens at Versailles, the Trianon, Fontainebleau, St Cloud, and Chantilly. His classical designs were mainly based on a central axis, with an emphasis, near the house, on formal artificial water-courses and fountains, and terraces and parterres

planted in complex patterns which have been compared to floral embroidery; these faded away into simpler parterres in the nearer distance, and thence into a backdrop of woodland. In brief, Le Nôtre's formal designs were in complete contrast to the 'English garden' of the following century.

Le Nôtre's work at Versailles occupied him during the rest of his life; at one stage over 1,500 workmen were under his direction. Yet there is reason to believe that he regarded Chantilly as his masterpiece. These gardens were created for Prince Louis II, known as the Grand Condé. At Chantilly a great stairway descends from the terrace to a huge water parterre. Although much of Le Nôtre's work has been destroyed, the great water parterre remains.

Le Nôtre's fame brought requests for his advice on gardens abroad, and in 1662 he travelled to London and partly redesigned the royal parks at Whitehall and Greenwich for Charles II, he also added a semi-circular formal garden to Hampton Court, and is supposed to have given advice about the garden at Chatsworth. Later in life Le Nôtre travelled to Italy, and legend has it that he advised Pope Innocent XI

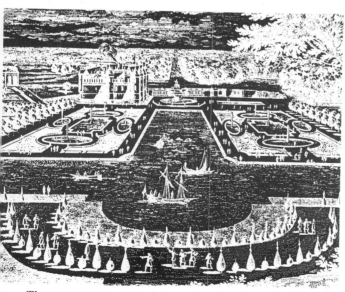

The water parterre at Chantilly, designed by André Le Nôtre

The gardens of St Cloud designed by Le Nôtre

Clandon Park, Surrey, designed by Leoni, 1731-5

on the task of redesigning the Vatican gardens in the French manner.

Le Nôtre's theories had little lasting influence on English or Italian landscape design, but he is the chief figure of the great period of classical French garden design. His enormous influence upon French landscape gardening, in both great estates and small, has persisted into our own time.

Lenox. An American pottery company. Walter Scott Lenox, the founder of the firm, became a partner in the Ceramic Art Company of Trenton, New Jersey, in 1889. He eventually took over complete control, and in 1906 established Lenox Incorporated, which became the foremost American manufacturers of fine tableware. Lenox was the first American manufacturer to produce china that could compete with good European tableware. His products helped to destroy the notion that good china could only be had from abroad; in 1917 Woodrow Wilson confirmed that this was not so by ordering a 1,700-piece Lenox dinner service for the White House. See **American Pottery**.

Leoni, Giacomo (c 1686–1746). Italian architect. Leoni was born in Venice, and after studying in his native city worked as architect to the Elector Palatine. He went to England, originally to see through the press a two-volume English edition of his book on Palladio, translated by Nicolas Dubois and published in London in 1715–16. He practised as an architect there, but was never given any kind of official appointment. This was imperative for solvency, and despite help from one or two patrons (especially from Lord Fitzwalter), Leoni seems to have lived a hand-to-mouth existence and died in impoverished circumstances. Nevertheless he built several important houses, including Argyll House in King's Road, Chelsea (1723); Clandon Park, Surrey, for Lord Onslow (1731–5); and a house in Arlington Street, Mayfair, for Lord Shannon (1738). He also designed two garden gateways which can be seen at Stowe, in Buckinghamshire.

Lescaze, William (1896–1969). American architect. Lescaze was born in Geneva and studied there under Karl Moser. After World War I he worked on the rehabilitation of devastated areas of France before emigrating to the USA, where he began to practise as an architect in Cleveland. In 1923 he set up his own firm in New York, and from the early thirties began to work with George Howe (1886–1954). Their association resulted in the design for the 33-storey Philadelphia Savings Fund Society (1932), one of the most distinguished and important buildings in the development of the skyscraper, well in advance of most buildings then under construction. Lescaze's other works include a theatre, studios, and offices for Columbia Broadcasting Studios in Hollywood (1938) and the Longfellow Building, Washington (1941). He designed Spinney Hill Homes, a complex of over 100 dwelling units at Manhasset, Long Island (1950); the Borg-Warner building in Chicago (1955); and the Church Peace Centre building, New York City (1962).

Lesene or **pilaster strip.** A pilaster without base or capital. It may have had a functional origin as a bonding course in the thin rubble walls of Anglo-Saxon architecture, but it is seen most frequently on the exteriors of late Anglo-Saxon and early Romanesque churches throughout the country.

Lethaby, William Richard (1837–1931). British architect, designer, and exponent of the Arts and Crafts movement. The chief influences on him were Norman Shaw (to whom he was both pupil and assistant), Philip Webb, and William Morris. Lethaby was active as a designer, working at furniture, fireplaces, pottery, etc. He implemented the Arts and Crafts teachings, applying Morris's principles at the London Central School of Arts and Crafts, which he founded in 1894. He was also a founder of the Art Workers' Guild and the Design in Industry Association.

In his architecture, Lethaby probably showed greatest originality in the church at Brockhampton, Hertfordshire (1900–2), and the Eagle Insurance building in Birmingham (1899). His many published works include books on Hagia Sophia, Westminster Abbey, on medieval arts and crafts; and in 1935, *Philip Webb and His Work* was published.

Philadelphia Savings Fund Society, designed by Lescaze 1932

Columbia Broadcasting Studios in Hollywood, USA, by Lescaze, 1938

Collège des Quatre Nations designed by Le Vau, 1662

Lesenes on an Anglo Saxon church tower

Le Vau, Louis (*c* 1612–70). French architect. Le Vau, the son of a master-mason, was born in Paris. Little is known of his early life and training, although he is reputed to have studied in Genoa and Rome before settling in Paris, where he designed his first known building, the Hôtel de Baufru, in his mid-twenties.

He appears to have been deeply involved in the development of important private houses on the Ile St Louis. These houses for wealthy patrons included the renowned Hôtel Lambert for Jean Baptiste Lambert, and others for well-known financiers and lawyers. Le Vau was taken up by the king's minister,

Fouquet. It was for Fouquet that Le Vau designed the most famous of all his buildings: Vaux-le-Vicomte, the most resplendent of all French châteaux, with gardens designed by Le Nôtre (qv). The château was started in 1657, and was built at an extraordinary speed.

Le Vau had succeeded Lemercier as *architecte du roi* in 1654, and survived the fall of Fouquet in 1661. He was nominated to take over the completion of the Louvre, but owing to various controversies (involving, among other things, alternative designs by Bernini), Le Vau's part was never more than that of a collaborator. He was, however, responsible for the central section of the Palace of Versailles.

Other buildings designed by Le Vau included the Collège de Quatre Nations (Palais de l'Institut) with its domed church (1661–5), and the churches of St Sulpice (1655–70) and St Louis-en-Ile (1664).

Le Vau was a major influence in the development of French classicism, second in importance only to Mansart (qv).

Leverton, Thomas (1743–1824). British architect. Leverton was born in Woodford, Essex, the son of a builder for whom he worked until able to study architecture. This transition was effected by drawings exhibited at the Royal Academy when Leverton was already in his late twenties. He was soon enjoying a highly successful practice which was to make him one of the wealthiest architects of his time. He was closely involved in the design and building of several houses in the Bedford

Eagle Insurance Building: Lethaby

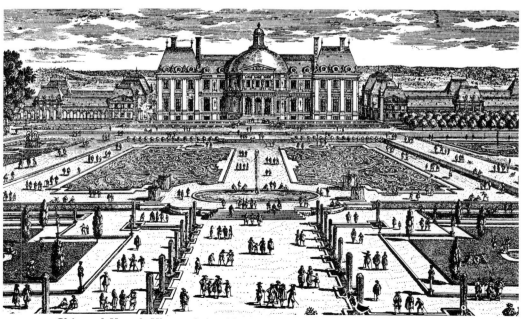

Château de Vaux-le-Vicomte designed by Le Vau, 1657–61; garden designed by Le Nôtre

The centre section of Versailles, designed by Louis Le Vau

Houses in Bedford Square designed by Thomas Leverton

Square development in London, in one of which, No 13, he lived from 1796 until his death. He designed a number of country houses, including Woodford Hall, Essex (1771), Riddleworth Hall, Norfolk (1792), and others in Hertfordshire, Kent, Hampshire, and Yorkshire. He held the post of architect to the Land Revenue authorities and was a JP for Surrey, Kent, Middlesex, and Westminster.

Libergier, Hugues (d 1263) French master mason depicted on a tomb in Rheims Cathedral holding a model of St Nicaise, Rheims Parish Church, which he designed and built c 1230; he also holds compasses, a staff, and an L-square. The stone is inscribed with the word 'Maistre'.

Library screen. During the Regency period a bookcase was evolved which incorporated a vertically-sliding silk fire screen in the carcase. George Smith sought to popularize this form of bookcase in later editions of his *Cabinet-Maker's and Upholsterer's Guide,* without a great deal of success.

Library steps. Cabinetmakers made various objects to help the eighteenth-century reader reach the higher shelves in libraries. These included library steps, as well as chairs, tables, and stools, all incorporating sets of steps. The library steps and chair was ostensibly a somewhat spare chair-form, but was hinged so that the seat could be overturned, the whole contraption becoming a set of three or four steps. Library steps were also accommodated in what appeared to be no more than a mahogany or velvet-covered pole; this could be opened out to display a built-in ladder structure of even greater flexibility than the chair-steps.

Library table. A larger than normal mid-eighteenth-century table, designed to accommodate two scholars on either side of a particularly spacious table top. The top was usually leathered, and was supported on two commodious pedestals; in some

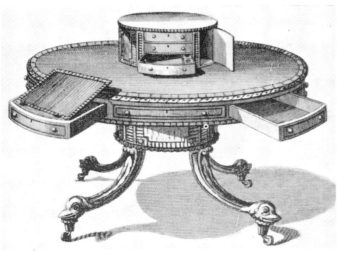

Design for a library table by Thomas Sheraton, 1803

The library table for Harewood House by Chippendale

Modern library steps

Linenfold panelling on an oak chest, 16th century

Lich gate of a country church yard

stances these carried doors, ut they might also be left open o house large folios, outsize lases, etc. The size of the brary table also allowed for a rge kneehole space. Some incorporated a prop-up flap in the ble top to facilitate the study f large books or manuscripts. Most cabinetmakers' guides of e late eighteenth century, including Sheraton's and Hepplehite's, showed a number of dividual versions of the library ble.

Lich (Lych)-gate. This term (derived from the Old English *lich*, meaning a corpse) is applied to the pitch-roofed gateway at the entrance to a church path or churchyard. Here the pallbearers could rest the coffin while awaiting the arrival of the officiating priest.

Liebes, Dorothy (1899–1972). American textile designer. Dorothy Liebes was born at Santa Rosa, California, and educated at the University of

California before going on to Columbia University, where she taught art from 1925 to 1928. She then took up interior decorating in San Francisco, and finally began designing textiles. She set up studios in San Francisco and New York, designing for such firms as Goodall-Sanford, Quaker Lace Co, Jantzen Knitting, Mills, Bates, Collins, and Aikman, DuPont, and Forstman Woollens. She was director of the Decorative Arts Exhibit at the 1939 San Francisco Exposition, and a director of the 1964–5 New York World's Fair. She won numerous design awards, including one at the Paris Exposition (1937) and the Elsie de Wolfe Award (1963).

Lierne rib. A short secondary rib inserted between the main ribs and tiercerons in later Gothic vaulting. It is of decorative rather than structural significance, issuing from neither a main springer nor a boss.

Lierne vaults are vaults in which there are a great number of lierne ribs joining the main ribs and tiercerons.

Lignum vitae. *Guaiacum officinale.* An extremely hard wood native to the West Indies and Central and South America. It is a smooth wood with a fine, regular, and tight grain that varies in colour from a deep brown to olive-green; occasionally it is almost black.

In the early sixteenth century lignum vitae was reputed to be a cure for venereal diseases. Only towards the end of the century was its suitability for turned work fully realized. Wassail bowls, goblet loving cups, and pestles and mortars were particularly common. In the late seventeenth century the wood was used for oystering (qv) and parquetry (qv), and in the eighteenth century for small detailed veneers.

Lime. *Tilia vulgaris.* A wood

favoured by carpenters because of the ease with which it could be worked. The lime was first used extensively during the Carolean period. It was a favourite material for the naturalistic carvings of Grinling Gibbons and his school.

Limed oak. Oak furniture which has been coated in lime and then brushed clean, leaving a whitened grain. It gained considerable popularity in the early twentieth century, and is still used as a means of lightening the colour of oak.

Linen cupboard. Until the mid-seventeenth century, household linens were normally stored in a deep chest, but after that date it began to be supplanted by a large shelf-fitted cupboard. See **Press.**

Linenfold panelling. Walls and chests carved to simulate the appearance of folded linen. This was an indigenous English form of decoration, extremely popular in Tudor times.

Linen press. A device for pressing the household linen. The fabrics were placed between two heavy wooden boards fixed tightly together by means of a spiral screw. Many of those found in England are of Dutch origin, notably seventeenth-century pieces on their own stands. No examples exist from before the sixteenth century.

Lintel. A stone, timber, metal, or concrete member, laid horizontally above a door or window opening to support part of the superstructure.

Lion motif; lion's mask; lion's paw foot. One of the most ancient of decorative devices in the ornamentation of furniture. It was used by the Egyptians and Persians, and was later widely adopted and adapted

Dorothy Liebes and two of her textile designs

Lion monopodia on a Regency side table

by the Romans. The lion's paw (in conjunction with the lion's mask motif) was frequently employed by Georgian furniture-makers for the decoration of chairs, the mask being used on the knees of cabriole legs and the paw at the base of the leg. The lion's paw motif was used most extensively and handsomely during the Regency period, frequently as a brass termination for the legs of chairs, stools, and dining- and writing-tables. In the Victorian era the motif became heavy and debased as a result of mass-production wood-carving methods.

Lip moulding. A small convex moulding frequently found around the edges of drawers. The curve is slightly flattened.

Liverpool porcelain. Porcelain was made in Liverpool by Richard Chaffers as early as 1756. Josiah Wedgwood is said to have complimented Chaffers on the quality of his work. The body of the ware was generally greyish in colour and rather like Worcester but inferior to it. The

Liverpool jug, c 1775

decoration was usually of oriental inspiration, both blue and white and polychrome. The ware was unmarked.

Liverpool pottery. Apart from the Delft ware made in Liverpool during the eighteenth century, much salt-glazed stoneware was made. Later on a considerable amount of blue and black transfer-printed ware was manufactured.

From the 1790s, the Herculaneum factory made creamware, lustre, basalt, and other kinds of ware similar to those being made in Staffordshire. It was sometimes marked HERCULANEUM POTTERY in a variety of forms. Liverpool is most famous for the transfer printing of Sadler and Green.

Livery cupboard. A freestanding cupboard for storing food, or an allowance or rations for overnight use – *livré* being a term denoting an allowance of beer, bread, candles, etc, delivered to members of the household. The term 'livery cupboard' came into use in the mid-sixteenth century, when 'aumbry' (qv) went out of current usage. The precise character of such cupboards is not known, but they had at least two tiers and shelf space as well as an enclosed cupboard.

Lock. The earliest forms were the heavy iron locks on medieval chests. With increasing interest in design and decoration, locks inevitably received attention from metal-craftsmen as well as locksmiths, and the locks of the Renaissance period were frequently ornate objects. By the second half of the seventeenth century, locks were highly elaborate, and complex patterns and forms were further developed in

Ashley Lodge at Somerely, near Ringwood, Hampshire

the Georgian era. Sheraton lists an impressive range of locks essential for the cabinetmaker's full repertory, including such items as box locks for tea-chests, mortise locks for outer doors, till locks for drawers, and spring locks for inner doors.

Lodge. Originally a small dwelling built by landowners for temporary accommodation during hunting forays. Later the term was applied to any small house or cottage appended to a greater house; it was usually built at the entrance to the estate or park.

Loewy, Raymond (b 1893). American industrial designer. Loewy was born in Paris and studied at various French institutions, specializing in electrical engineering. During World War I he served in the Corps of Engineers, being awarded the Croix de Guerre and Légion d'Honneur.

After the war Loewy emigrated to the United States. He was appointed art director to the Westinghouse Electric Company in 1929, and in the same year established an industrial design office. In 1932 the success of his designs for the Coldspot refrigerator brought him a national reputation; his designs for the Studebaker car made him inter-

Castellated lodge at Saffron Waldon, Essex

Raymond Loewy

Studebaker 'Avanti' designed by Raymond Loewy, 1963

...ationally known, its body design ...eing far in advance of that of ...ny other mass-production car. ...oday the firm Loewy Snaith ...nc is one of the largest of its ...ind in the world, with ten ...ivisions covering the ramifications of industrial design, and ...ffices in New York, London, ...nd Brussels. Loewy became a ...aturalized US citizen in 1938. ...e has received many inter-...ational honours and awards for ...is work as an industrial designer. ...oewy Snaith has augmented its ...asic design services with market ...esearch, housing, engineering, ...nd architectural work.

...oggia. A term applied to ...lmost any covered area adjacent ...o, or part of, a house which acts ...s a shaded open-air shelter. A ...oggia can be small, and with a ...anopy of the simplest frame ...onstruction; or it can be a ...ighly decorative colonnaded ...rcade of considerable size.

Long and short work. A method of laying stone quoins that was sometimes used in Anglo-Saxon architecture. Tall vertical stones were laid alternately with horizontal ones, and all were bonded into the wall.

Long-case clock. A clock regulated by weights and pendulum needed to be housed in a tall case; such clocks were therefore known as long-case clocks. The invention of the pendulum as a regulator of the rotation of the wheels of the clock was made in Holland by Christiaan Huygens van Zulichen in 1657. As a result, long-case clocks were soon being made in several parts of Europe. The cases offered considerable scope to the cabinet-maker, and they became highly decorative pieces of furniture, veneered and japanned. After 1878 the long-case clock gradually became known as the grand-father clock.

The Long Gallery at Hatfield House, Hertfordshire

Long gallery. An apartment for walking in during inclement weather, usually long and narrow; it frequently housed a collection of paintings. In the sixteenth and seventeenth centuries the long gallery was on an upper floor.

Longton Hall dish

Longton Hall. Reputed to be the first place in Staffordshire to make porcelain. The factory was started in 1750 by a William Jenkinson, who was joined a year later by William Littler. The business seems to have come to an end in 1760. Recent investigations have determined the site of the pottery, but its history is still not known in detail.

Two types of porcelain appear to have been made. The first was rather heavy, crude, white, but curiously translucent. It was used for vases and tableware, the dishes being often of basket-work or leaf form, with rustic handles; and there were decorative pieces in the form of fruit and vegetables after the manner of Chelsea. The other kind of porcelain was somewhat finer and more like the porcelain made at Meissen. Plates and dishes were made of this ware, painted

Ornamental wooden garden loggia

Long-case clock by Tompion, late 17th century

House at Nothartgasse, Vienna, designed by Adolf Loos, 1930

with birds and flowers, in imitation of Chelsea but inferior to it in execution. Some figures were also made. The colouring used was bright, but perhaps a little crude. Often the pieces were unmarked, but crossed L's painted in blue in various forms were sometimes used, perhaps standing for Littler Longton.

Looking-glass. See **Mirror.**

Loos, Adolf (1870–1933). Loos was born in Brno, now in Czechoslovakia, but then part of the Austrian Empire. He was the son of a stonemason and sculptor. He was educated at the Royal and

Loos by Kokoschka, 1910

Imperial Grammar School at Melk, and for three years at the department of building science in the State Technical College at Liberec in Bohemia. After military service he continued his architectural studies at the Dresden College of Technology for a further three years. He then went to the United States, where he had an uncle living in Philadelphia, before returning to Vienna at the age of 26 to take up a career as an assistant in the offices of Carl Mayreder. He soon started on a collateral career as controversialist, in 1898 publishing his first major attack on what he considered to be the sham architecture of the time. In the course of the dispute he broke with many of the leading Viennese architects, a characteristic event in his unhappy, stormy career.

On the strength of his pre-war villa designs, Loos was appointed chief architect in the Vienna department of housing in 1920. This appointment lasted less than two years, Loos resigning in disillusion. He then went to France, working intermittently in Austria, Czechoslovakia, and Germany. He became fairly well known in France, where he lectured at the Sorbonne.

On his sixtieth birthday Loos was granted a pension by the president of Czechoslovakia, Thomas Masaryk, a gesture

which symbolized the gradual recognition of Loos's significance as a theorist and practitioner. His most important buildings were private houses, notably the Steiner House in Vienna (1910). Here the austere geometry and repudiation of ornament foreshadow the modern movement. Loos's last major commission, carried out between sojourns in sanatoria, was a workers' housing estate in northern Bohemia in the early 1930s.

Loose cover. A separate cover that fits over upholstered furniture. It is usually made of a closely woven material such as linen, and has a frill around the hem.

Stretch-covers are a recent innovation; these give the appearance of upholstered furniture while remaining easy to remove for cleaning.

The loose cover is also called a slip cover.

Lopers. The sliding arms that pull out and support the fall or lid of a desk or bureau.

Lotus ornament. This decoration is as old as ancient Egypt, and has enjoyed its greatest popularity whenever there has been a revival of interest in that culture, eg in the French Empire period. The lotus ornament exists in a variety of stylized forms, the most common being the three-leaved lotus, the bud, and the palmette; the palmette evolved into the egg and dart and anthemion motifs (qv).

Loudon, John Claudius (1783–1843). Scottish landscape designer and writer. Loudon, the son of a farmer, was born in Cambuslang in Lanarkshire, and apprenticed at an early age to a nurseryman in Edinburgh. He travelled to London and at the age of 20 published an essay on laying-out public squares. In 1809 he set up his own agricultural school at Great Tew in Oxfordshire to advance his theories, which were based on a belief in the superiority of Scottish to English husbandry. The school was highly successful, but the restless Loudon sold it at a profit three years later and began to travel in Europe to further his knowledge. On returning to London he found that his investments had failed, and he thereupon began his career as one of the most remarkable and prolific of all encyclopaedists. He published an *Encyclopaedia of Agriculture* in 1825 and an *Encyclopaedia of Plants* in 1829.

J C Loudon

Three years later he began publication, in monthly parts, of the successful *Encyclopaedia of Cottage Farm and Villa Architecture*, published as a 1,138-page book in 1836.

When he was 47 Loudon married Jane Webb, a budding novelist then aged 23. From then on they collaborated in all Loudon's works, and Jane Loudon continued them after her husband's death.

Loudon's publications included a *Magazine of Natural History* and *The Architectural Magazine*, but the most important of all his publications was the *Arboretum et Fruticetum Brittanicum* in eight volumes, remarkable and unique work whose failure crippled him financially for the rest of his life.

Loudon was a major influence on the early stage of modern gardening, as a theorist and practitioner of landscape gardening, and as a writer with a scientific approach to all horticultural and agricultural problems.

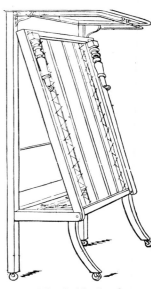

Folding bed by Loudon

generally applied to slatted wooden window shutters used as protection against the sun. The decorative value of the louvre has led to a revival in the use of these slatted wooden structures as cupboard doors and indoor screens, as well as for windows.

Love seat. A wide chair in which two people can sit side by side. Introduced during the Carolean period, it was then called a courting chair or a tête-à-tête seat. It was later sometimes S-shaped.

See also **Conversation chair.**

Lowboy. A piece of furniture popular in America throughout the eighteenth century. It was a low chest with one long drawer and usually three smaller drawers below; it was supported by cabriole legs. See **Tallboy.**

Lowestoft. The Lowestoft factory was founded in 1757 for the manufacture of soft-paste porcelain. One of the first partners was Robert Browne, who is said to have worked at Bow in order to learn the secrets of the trade. The bodies of both Bow and Lowestoft porcelain are chemically the same, so the story may be true.

Compared to the products of other mid-eighteenth-century porcelain factories, Lowestoft ware consisted of works on a rather small scale, and it was not thought very much of in its day. However, it has a definite character and a certain simple charm, and is now much sought-after. Some of the pieces are marked 'A trifle from Lowestoft' and were obviously made to sell as souvenirs to visitors to the town. Other pieces were made for presentation, and are inscribed with names and dates.

As well as the usual tea- and coffee-services and tableware, Lowestoft produced inkstands, tea-caddies, and dolls' tea sets. A great deal of blue-and-white ware was made, in the fashion of the time, after the Chinese style of decoration; and polychrome ware was also made, often in charming little sprigged and floral patterns, and sometimes even in elaborate oriental designs. The colours included a brownish indian red and strong clear pink, green, turquoise, and occasionally, on the grander pieces, gold. The factory ceased production c 1802.

Lowestoft ware was not marked with any particular distinguishing mark, but blue numerals occur inside footrings, and marks were frequently 'borrowed' from Worcester or Meissen, whose designs the Lowestoft factory freely plagiarized.

Lozenge. A diamond-shaped ornamental figure with four equal sides.

Lubetkin, Berthold (b 1901). Architect. Lubetkin was born and trained in Russia, but afterwards moved to Warsaw and Vienna before settling down for some years in Paris. There he worked under Auguste Perret (qv), the pioneer in reinforced concrete structural techniques, while continuing his architec-

Lowestoft bowl

tural studies at the Ecole des Beaux Arts. After briefly establishing a practice in Paris, Lubetkin set up in London, forming the influential Tecton Group in 1931. The half-dozen architects in the group were unusually successful, and among their earliest pre-war commissions were the Penguin Pool at the London Zoo (1933–4), the Highpoint flats in Highgate (1934–7), and the Finsbury Health Centre. Their post-war projects included the multiple blocks designed for the borough of Finsbury in the early fifties, which take a high place in Britain's post-war housing schemes.

Lucarne. A French term for a skylight or dormer window.

Ludovice, João Frederico (Johann Friedrich Ludwig, 1670–1752). German-born architect, the son of a goldsmith. After working as a goldsmith in Rome and Lisbon, Ludovice was commissioned by the King of Portugal to build a convent of modest size at Mafra. The whims of the king and his successors led to the continuous enlargement of

Louvered wardrobe doors

Louvre, louver, lover, loover (French, *l'ouvert* 'an opening'). Originally applied to an opening in a cottage roof which allowed smoke from the hearth in the middle of the room to escape. The term is now

Queen Anne lowboy with panelled cabriole legs

Penguin Pool at the London Zoo by Berthold Lubetkin, 1933-4

The library at Coimbra University designed by Ludovice, 1717-23

Two views of a lunette

Copper lustre ware made at Sunderland, early 19th century

the convent between 1717 and 1770; it finally became a grandiose complex of royal and ecclesiastical buildings, one of the largest in Europe, and an outstanding example of central European and Roman Baroque touched by Portuguese influences. Between 1717 and 1723 Ludovice also designed the library of Coimbra University.

Lunette. A semi-circular opening set in a dome or in a vaulted or coved ceiling. The term is also frequently used for a semi-circular or circular window or decorative panel set in a wall or in the tympanum of a pediment.

Lustre ware. Lustre decoration was used by potters in Spain (see **Hispano-Moresque**) and Italy (see **Gubbio**). The decoration of pottery by platinum (silver), copper, and gold (pink) lustre was practised by potters all over England, in Staffordshire, Sunderland, Liverpool, Swansea, etc. The use of silver lustre for decorations was first introduced into the United States in the early nineteenth century by Abraham Miller in Philadelphia.

Some English lustre ware was completely covered in the silver coating and was known as 'poor man's silver.' Other pieces were painted with a 'resist' decoration which showed through as white against the silver background. Sometimes the ware was covered with a canary-coloured enamel, and then the lustre decoration was applied on top of that.

All three lustre colours were used in conjunction with other forms of decoration, sometimes with plain bands of colour, sometimes with embossed or relief decoration. On some pieces the lustre was used sparingly, for bands of edgings only.

Gold produced a pink or purple lustre, and much was made at Sunderland. Copper produced an approximation to the natural colour of the metal; it was made in great quantities throughout the nineteenth century for a relatively popular market, and is sometimes very crude in form.

Lutyens, Sir Edwin Landseer (1869–1944). British architect. Lutyens was the son of an army officer turned artist, and overrespectful pupil of Sir Edwin Landseer. Lutyens had only a slight formal education, and after studying at the South Kensington (now the Royal) College of Art, was apprenticed to Sir Ernest George of George and Peto. When still in his teens he was commissioned to build a small country house near Farnham. While he was engaged on this work he was taken up by Gertrude Jekyll, the eminent landscape gardener, who commissioned him to design a country cottage, known as Munstead Wood, set in her woodland garden. The success of his early commissions, and the reputation he gained as a result of his connections with Gertrude Jekyll, led Lutyens to set up an

Sir Edwin Lutyens

Crooksbury designed by Sir Edwin Lutyens, 1890

Castle Drogo by Lutyens

Viceroy's House, New Delhi, designed by Sir Edwin Lutyens, completed 1930

independent practice at the age of 20.

He now accepted similar but more extensive country-house commissions. His houses, small and large, showed pronounced individuality, allied with a fashionable architectural nostalgia and an understanding of traditional building materials and methods. Lutyens became the most eminent English country-house architect of the day, and as his commissions grew more impressive he gradually developed a highly personal style in the 'Wrenaissance' manner. The designs of his houses have been criticized for their excessively imitative Georgian characteristics, although few have denied his inventiveness and thoroughness. His manner was perfectly suited to the ambitions of Edwardian rentiers and enlightened tycoons, and the list of his country houses matches that of the most eminent of his Georgian predecessors. Among his earlier grander houses are Nashdom at Taplow in Bucks (1905) and Heathcote in Yorkshire (1906). Typical of his later work in country houses are Gledstone Hall at Skipton in Yorkshire (1923) and the extensive development of Castle

Drogo in Devonshire (1910–30), a granite castellated structure of unusual imaginative strength. Lutyens never lost his feeling for cottage-type houses, and designed several smaller houses in the Hampstead Garden Suburb. He designed the art gallery in Johannesburg and several monumental office blocks, institutions, and official buildings, ranging from Britannic House in Finsbury Circus, London (1926), to Campion Hall at Oxford (1934). One of his most charming office buildings is the Midland Bank adjacent to St James's Church in Piccadilly, London. The building for which he is chiefly remembered is the vast Viceroy's House at New Delhi, a fitting architectural finale to the long British reign in India.

Lyons, Eric (*b* 1912). British architect. Lyons was born in London and trained at the Polytechnic School of Architecture. He began his career as architectural assistant in various private practices, which included that of Walter Gropius and Maxwell Fry. He set up in independent practice in 1945, forming his present partnership with Ivor Cunningham and Gilbert Powell in 1963. The firm acts as con-

sultant architects to Span Developments Ltd, and in that capacity has had a notable influence on standards of housing and environmental design throughout Britain. Lyons's schemes at Ham Common, Blackheath, Twickenham, Cambridge, and Weybridge have been remarkably successful architecturally, socially, and environmentally. He is currently engaged as architect to the Kensington and Chelsea Borough Council for the World's End Redevelopment Scheme, a comprehensive high-density scheme for 2,500 people. He has also designed housing and schools for a number of public bodies, including Harlow New Town, Southampton, and the Greater London Council.

Lyons is one of the few modern architects who have managed to design housing estates with the intangible qualities that characterize Georgian market towns and villages. His rare feeling for neighbourhood design, with its acknowledgement of a need for domestic privacy even in high-density developments, is linked with a highly sophisticated feeling for architectural and structural elements; this ranges from an appreciation of texture and pat-

tern to a visually satisfying deployment of trees and landscaping. Lyons has won many awards, both in Britain and abroad.

Lyre form. The curving outline of the classical lyre has frequently been included in furniture designs, especially by Adam, Sheraton, Hepplewhite, and Duncan Phyfe. Its most common use has been for the pierced back splat of a chair; an Adam design of 1775 had thin metal rods for the strings. Its sinuous curve occurs again in the contour of the scrolled sides of sofas in England and America. French designers have been particularly fond of the shape, and in the late eighteenth century, spring clocks were made in lyre-shaped cases.

Lyre table support

Eric Lyons

Span development at the Priory, Blackheath, by Eric Lyons, 1957

Lyre back chair

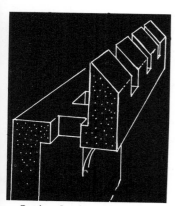

Section showing machiolation

Machicolation. A term used in medieval castle-building for the openings in the floor of a projecting parapet. Through these, missiles and molten lead could be dropped on to assailants. Machicolations were brought to the West by the Crusaders, who copied them from the Saracens.

Mackintosh, Charles Rennie (1868–1928). Scottish architect. Mackintosh was born in Glasgow

Charles Rennie Mackintosh

and studied at the Glasgow School of Art. He then became an assistant in the Glasgow architectural practice of Honeyman and Keppie. In 1891 he travelled to Italy on a scholarship grant. On his return to Scotland he executed a good deal of graphic work and metalwork in an Art Nouveau manner, gaining a modest Scottish reputation.

In 1896, while still an assistant with Honeyman and Keppie, he won a competition to design the Glasgow School of Art. This commission earned him an international reputation, thanks to the uncompromising rationality of his plan and its expression in the façades, allied with a highly original interpretation of the Scottish vernacular tradition in his treatment of the centrepiece. With this single building, Mackintosh took his place among the pioneers of the gradually evolving modern movement; he has been called 'the one real fore-runner of Le Corbusier.' Mackintosh increased his reputation with designs for the furniture and fittings of the School of Art. His chair shapes in particular, with their angular simplicities, were a breakaway from the languid cursiveness of much industrial design influenced by Art Nouveau. These designs had a considerable influence, particularly in Germany and Austria. Further commissions followed, including the series of Cranston tearooms throughout Glasgow, begun in 1897 but now mostly destroyed. Mackintosh also designed two houses, Windyhill, Kilmacolm (1899–1901), and Hill House, Helensburgh (1902–3), and a school in Scotland Street, Glasgow (1906). Between 1907 and 1909 he added a library wing to the School of Art building, an uncompromisingly stark and impressive structure. Un-

Hill House, Helensburgh, designed by Mackintosh, 1902-3

Glasgow School of Art by Charles Rennie Mackintosh, 1897-9

Maiolica. *A portrait plate from Castel Durante behind one of soldiers from Montelupo, and a Cattagiolo platter*

Bedroom chair with linen back and seat, by Mackintosh, 1900

fortunately Mackintosh had a difficult and erratic temperament which alienated friends and clients. In 1913 he left Honeyman and Keppie (in which he had been made a partner in 1904) and retired to Suffolk to paint landscapes. He later moved to London, to France, and back to London, taking no active part in the architectural developments he had done so much to shape.

Mackmurdo, Arthur Heygate (1851–1942). British designer and writer. Mackmurdo was the son of wealthy parents, and during his early studies became fascinated by the works of John Ruskin. He decided to study at Oxford so that he could attend Ruskin's lectures there, and he later travelled to Italy with his mentor. In 1880 he designed his own house at Enfield, and he was also responsible for designing other houses. In 1882 he formed the Century Guild, one of several similar associations of architects, designers, and craftsmen which were formed between 1880 and 1890. The Guild

A lampshade in macramé

An engraving of the façade of St Peter's by Maderno

sponsored a magazine, *The Hobby Horse,* in which Mackmurdo demonstrated his gift for graphic decoration, anticipating several later Art Nouveau mannerisms. As a furniture designer he was also well in advance of his time, anticipating several ideas which were later developed by Voysey (qv).

Macramé. Derived from the Arabic word for fringe, macramé is the art of decorative knotting. It is of very ancient origin and has been practised consistently, especially for making fringes. During the nineteenth century there was a macramé revival, but interest waned, and with the exception of a few places such as Sardinia and Liguria, this kind of work was little known until the late 1960s, when it became immensely popular on both sides of the Atlantic. The knotting can produce a large number of varied geometric patterns, and current interest has stimulated design so that hammocks and lampshades have now been added to the more usual repertory of fringes and bags.

Maderno, Carlo (1556–1629). Italian architect. Maderno was born at Capolago on Lake Lugano. He travelled to Rome to further his architectural studies, and took out Roman

citizenship in 1588. At first he acted as assistant to his uncle, Domenico Fontana (1543–1607), but by the opening years of the seventeenth century he had established a separate reputation as the first architect of importance in the evolution of Roman Baroque.

In 1603 Maderno's façade for S Susanna, Rome, was completed. This is a clearly Baroque structure, developed from the contradictory tendencies of Mannerism, in which the size of the bays, the orders, and the sculptural decoration all become more pronounced towards the centre. In the same year Maderno was made architect of St Peter's. His main task was to design a nave based on a Latin cross plan, supplementary and complementary to Michelangelo's centralized plan – an unfortunate commission since this addition inevitably obscured the view of the dome. The most famous of Maderno's other works are St Andrea della Valle (1608–28), with a dome second only to St Peter's in size, and the forecourt of the Palazzo Barbarini, the latter, in fact, basically to the designs of Bernini, with contributions from Borromini.

Magistretti, Vico (*b* 1920). Italian designer and architect. Magistretti trained in Milan

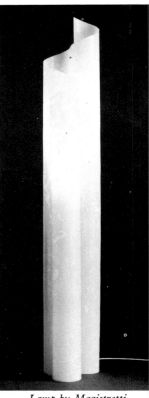

Lamp by Magistretti

before opening an office in the city in 1945. Though chiefly known for his furniture design (especially chairs, mainly in beechwood or moulded fibreglass), his work is very wide in scope, including such items as televisions and lighting fixtures. Magistretti has exhibited in New York and London, and at every Milan Triennale since 1948; he won the Grand Prix in 1948 and 1954, and a gold medal in 1957.

Mahogany. *Swietenia.* This rich coppery-red wood became popular with furniture-makers in America in about 1730, and in England about a decade later. It is easily worked, neither shrinks nor warps, and, though pinkish on cutting, soon deepens to

Magistretti stacking chairs

Bridge over River Arve, near Vessey, Geneva, by Maillart, 1936

The vestibule of the Laurentian Library by Michelangelo, 1524-6

ch red which polishes up exemely well.

Of the principal sources of mahogany, Cuba, Honduras, San Domingo, Jamaica, and Africa (Khaya), Jamaica was the first to supply England. 'Jamaican wood' in fact included mahogany from Cuba and Honduras, shipped to Europe via Jamaica, as well as the indigenous wood. Jamaican mahogany was first mentioned by John Ogilby in *America* (1671), and from this time there is evidence of the wood's use for tables and panelling. San Domingo mahogany was also exported. A lightly figured but much harder wood than the others, it was not greatly used despite the fact that it could be carved in a particularly crisp and vigorous fashion.

By 1750 the Cuban variety was the most used. The wood was easier to work than San Domingo mahogany, and the grain was more attractively figured with curls and the fiddleback pattern, the very best pieces being used for veneering. From 1750 this finely marked and easily worked wood was employed by English furniture-makers until displaced by Honduras mahogany.

This variety, which is also referred to as Baywood, from the Bay of Honduras, was, according to Sheraton (*Cabinet Dictionary*, 1803), 'the principal kind of mahogany in use amongst Cabinet makers'. Because of its combination of width, strength, and lightness, it appreciably influenced the design of furniture, making possible light chair members but also broader table tops – so much so that the term 'mahogany' came into use to describe a dining-table. Honduras mahogany was frequently used for carcase work; Cuban mahogany, which has a better surface, was then employed for the veneer.

Mahogany remained popular, although in the Regency period it was replaced for the more decorative work by satinwood and rosewood.

African mahogany, *khaya ivorensis,* is from the west coast of the continent. It too is a pale red wood that darkens with exposure. Occasionally it has a particularly good figure, and such pieces were employed for decorative veneers and other work such as turnery, mouldings, and general cabinet work.

Maillart, Robert (1872–1940). Swiss engineer, born in Berne. After studying at Zurich Technical College he worked as assistant in a number of engineering firms before setting up as an engineering consultant in 1902. He worked in Russia from 1912 until the Revolution, as a result of which he lost everything he possessed. He set up once again in Switzerland, this time in Geneva.

As early as 1901 Maillart introduced a revolutionary new conception of reinforced concrete design with his bridge at Zuoz in the Engadine. This was followed in 1905 by the Tavenasa Bridge across the Rhine. Both bridges showed how arch and road could be successfully unified in designs of the utmost logical simplicity. Many of the spans Maillart evolved were of considerable width; that at Salgina

Gorge, near Schiers, was almost 300 ft. Maillart built over 40 bridges and designed many more, several of the most spectacular never being carried out. He was also responsible for some multistorey buildings. In 1920, for a Zurich warehouse, he evolved a concrete mushroom technique foreshadowing Nervi's (qv); supporting columns were integrated with beamless floor slabs to produce a utilitarian building of considerable elegance and economy in construction.

Maiolica. The famous tinglazed earthenware made in Italy from c 1400. This ware was embellished with painted decoration – including quite simple blue geometric patterns on the white enamel background, elaborate naturalistic scenes from the Bible, mythology etc in many colours, and imitations of Isnik pottery. Traditional colours were yellows and browns of varied intensity, blues, greens, and black, and sometimes a ruby or golden lustre was used.

Tuscany and Umbria were the chief centres for maiolica, though it was also made in Venice, Padua, Gubbio, Pesaro, Faenza, and Urbino. In the eighteenth century maiolica was also made in Genoa and Castelli, and in Palermo and Caltagirone in Sicily.

Italian maiolica had a marked influence on the tin-glazed earthenware made in France (see **Faience**) and to a lesser extent on Delft pottery (qv).

Mannerism. Mannerism in architecture is principally an Italian movement of the years 1520 to 1600. It was found in other countries, but except in France and Spain it amounted to little more than a tendency towards the fanciful. The name was only given to the movement in the 1920s, when it was realized that the period between

the High Renaissance and Baroque had separate and meaningful stylistic features. Mannerism is usually seen as embodying deliberate contradictions to the rigid canons of Renaissance architecture. Michelangelo's Laurentian Library in Florence (1524-6) epitomizes the Mannerist technique: its columns are encased in niches in the walls and perched upon insubstantial consoles; they are apparently decorative only, but in fact support the roof. Guilio Romano was the other major exponent of Mannerism, and Vasari, Ammanati, and Vignola also worked in the style.

Mansard roof. A form of roof construction which makes it possible for attic rooms to be larger than in simpler forms of pitched roof construction. The Mansard roof has two sloping planes, the lower steeper than the upper; it is erroneously called after the French architect François Mansart.

Mansart, François (1598–1666). French architect. Mansart, son of a master-carpenter,

Minton tazza in imitation maiolica, c 1862

Val-de-Grâce, Paris, by F Mansart and Lemercier, 1645-67

Château de Maisons Lafitte designed by Mansart, 1642–6

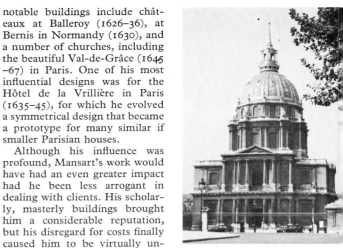

Les Invalides by J H Mansart

notable buildings include châteaux at Balleroy (1626–36), at Bernis in Normandy (1630), and a number of churches, including the beautiful Val-de-Grâce (1645–67) in Paris. One of his most influential designs was for the Hôtel de la Vrillière in Paris (1635–45), for which he evolved a symmetrical design that became a prototype for many similar if smaller Parisian houses.

Although his influence was profound, Mansart's work would have had an even greater impact had he been less arrogant in dealing with clients. His scholarly, masterly buildings brought him a considerable reputation, but his disregard for costs finally caused him to be virtually unemployed for the last decade of his life.

Mansart, Jules Hardouin (1646–1708). French architect, born Jules Hardouin. He was the great-nephew and, it is generally assumed, the pupil of François Mansart, whose surname he adopted in 1666. He was the favourite architect of Louis XIV, for whom he designed the château at Clagny (1674). The success of this commission led to his appointment as *architecte du roi* in the following year. In 1678 he was given complete control of all the royal works at Versailles; later still, he was ennobled. Apart from Versailles, Mansart's best-known designs are the Place Vendôme (from 1698) and the Chapel of the Invalides (1680–91). Despite his close connection with the crown, he also designed several châteaux for private clients, including one at Dampierre (1680).

Mansart's unbroken success aroused a good deal of envy, and he was accused of maintaining an architectural factory; yet certainly his assistants were of high standard. He was undoubtedly an architectural designer and organizer of remarkable skill.

Maple. *Acer saccharum.* Sugar maple, native of eastern Canada and New England, is the variety chiefly used for cabinetmaking, joinery, and flooring. The wood is very hard, strong, and easily workable – properties that were recognized by the early American settlers, who used it for furniture-making. It is still being used. Maple is a pale cream to yellowish brown or biscuit colour and has decorative figuring. The most distinctive form, very popular for veneering, is the bird's-eye pattern of circular dots, brownish around the outer rim but pale inside. Other varieties of maple are found in temperate climates in Europe and Asia. The English maple is another name for the English sycamore, a wood that has been employed for marquetry and veneering.

Marble-top table. Marble was used for table-tops in the

was one of the most influential of all French architects. He may have received his early training in Rennes under Gautier, but he was also clearly influenced by Salomon de Brosse (1571–1626).

Mansart was largely responsible for the introduction of Renaissance elements into French architecture. His masterpiece is undoubtedly the Château de Maisons Lafitte (1642–6), where he was given a free hand by René de Longevil. Although appointed *architecte du roi* in 1636, Mansart designed comparatively little for the town or the nobility; his commissions came mainly from the wealthy new *haute bourgeoisie*. His other

Place Vendôme, Paris, designed by J H Mansart, begun 1698

Régence giltwood marble-top table

Satellite town of Vallingby, near Stockholm, by Markelius

early Italian Renaissance, but the fashion did not take hold outside the Mediterranean countries until the early eighteenth century. Slabs of white marble were exported and then coloured in imitation of the more expensive varieties. By mid-century, native marbles were used by furniture-makers in other countries, although rare and more costly pieces were (and are) still imported from Italy.

Marbling or **marblizing.** The term applied to the *trompe-l'oeil* simulation of marble on other surfaces, usually timber or plaster. Although widely used by modern decorators, the practice has an extremely long history and was popular in ancient Rome.

Markelius, Sven Gottfried (*b* 1889). Swedish architect. After training at the Technical College and the Academy of Fine Arts in Stockholm, Markelius became assistant to Ragnar Østberg (qv). His first important commission was for the Swedish pavilion at the New York World's Fair (1939). He later gained an international reputation with his design for the concert hall at Halsingborg, and various housing developments in and around Stockholm. However, his most important project was the development of Vällingby, near Stockholm, where Markelius has been head of the town-planning department.

Marlboro' leg. The cabinet-makers' term for a square tapered leg. Late eighteenth century.

Marot, Daniel (*c* 1662–1752). French designer, engraver, and architect. Marot was born in Paris, the son of the Huguenot architect and engraver Jean Marot (1619–79). He emigrated to Holland in 1685, the year of the Revocation of the Edict of Nantes, becoming architect to William of Orange. When William became King of England, Marot followed him, stay-

A design for a state bed by Daniel Marot

ing from 1694 to 1698. He worked on the interiors of Hampton Court Palace, William's favourite residence. His designs were based on detailed knowledge of French classical design and Baroque ornament, of which he made lavish use.

On his return to the Hague, Marot designed the Schuylenberg House (1715), the Royal Library (1734–8), the Stadthuis (1733–9), and other large town houses. He published a volume of engravings in 1702, and his *Oeuvres* ten years later. This work was very popular in England, and though most of the collection belonged to his early career, it contributed to the rapid spread of Continental ideas. Marot is generally believed to have begun the fashion for elaborately draped beds with richly carved ornament and ostrich plumes at the corners.

Marquee. A corruption of marquise (qv), describing tents and other temporary awnings.

Marquetry. A method of inlaying contrasting materials

which are often both exotic and ornamental: veneers such as satinwood, rosewood, and zebrawood, but also brass, pewter, and other metals, and materials such as bone, ivory, and mother-of-pearl. Eighteenth-century cabinetmakers, particularly the French *ébénistes*, made extensive use of decorative patterns

Pictorial marquetry on a transitional Louis XV–XVI commode

Marquetry on Louis XV table

Marquise at Miami Beach, Florida

Libraries at Oxford by Martin and St John Wilson, 1961-5

and motifs for inlay work. These were mostly floral, and were particularly popular in designs for commodes.

Marquise. A French term, applied to a canopy which shelters the entrance to a public building. The device has been widely adopted in America, particularly for New York hotels. The marquise is a prominent feature of the urban scene in North America.

Martha Washington chair. A high-backed, upholstered armchair with slender open wooden armrails, and gently tapered legs; it is named after George Washington's wife.

The sewing table, also called after Martha Washington, is an oval work table with a fitted central portion of two or three drawers. The hinged leaves at either end cover deep pouches to hold sewing materials.

Martin, Sir (John) Leslie (*b* 1908). British architect. Martin was born in Manchester and

Sir Leslie Martin

Harvey Court, Cambridge, by Martin and St John Wilson, 1960-2

trained at the Manchester University School of Architecture, from which he graduated in 1930; he afterwards taught there. In 1934 he was appointed head of the School of Architecture at Hull, where he remained for five years. At this time he was in private practice, was a member of MARS (The Modern Architec-

tural Research Society), and edited *Circle* with Ben Nicholson and Naum Gabo.

Martin then left teaching for public service. He worked for the LMS Railway before moving in 1948 to the London County Council, first as deputy architect and later (1953), in succession to Sir Robert Matthew (qv), as

architect to the LCC. During this period the architects' office of the LCC was responsible for many fine school and housing projects. Martin was jointly responsible with Matthew for the Royal Festival Hall (1951).

Since 1958 Martin has been professor of architecture in Cambridge. He was also Slade professor in Oxford (1965–6). His work in association with Colin St John Wilson has included designs for new academic buildings for the University of Leicester (1958–61), for Harvey Court, Cambridge (1960–2), and for the Manor Road Libraries, Oxford (1961–5).

His more recent work includes an arts building for Hull University (1963–7), a new science development (1967–70) and a plan for the redevelopment of Wellington Square (1968), the latter for Oxford University.

Mascaroon. See **Mask.**

Mask. The exaggerated face of a human or fantastic creature used in carved decoration: for

Martha Washington chair

Lion mask on a marble-top table

Bruno Matheson

Sir Robert Matthew

xample, the satyr mask, which as particularly popular *c* 1740. architecture the mask is alled a mascaroon; it is purely ecorative and should not be nfused with the gargoyle (qv).

Mathsson, Bruno (*b* 1907). wedish furniture designer and chitect, the son of a furniture-aker, Karl Mathsson, under hom Bruno trained. He was in e vanguard of design in the 40s and 1950s; designing mfortable non-upholstered airs with laminated plywood ames and a close webbing for e seat and back. Always con-ious of the functional nature d natural properties of his aterial, Mathsson never uses loured woods. Each item of rniture receives individual eatment.

Mathsson has built several ivate houses as well as his own hibition building in Varnamo. is furniture is known inter-tionally through his individual ows and his contributions to rger exhibitions in America, urope, and Scandinavia. He as awarded the Gregor Paulson ophy in 1955.

Matthew, Sir Robert Hogg (*b* 906). Scottish architect.

Matthew studied architecture at the Edinburgh College of Art. In 1945 he became chief archi-tect and planning officer for the Department of Health in Scot-land, following this with a term as architect to the London County Council (1946–53). During this period of post-war reconstruction many housing schemes and schools were built. Matthew and Sir Leslie Martin (qv) were jointly responsible for the Royal Festival Hall.

In 1953 Matthew was ap-pointed professor of architecture at Edinburgh University. He remained in charge of the de-partment until 1968, when he became chairman of the School of the Built Environment in the University.

In 1953 Matthew also set up in private practice. The partner-ship of Robert Matthew, John-son-Marshall, and Partners, with offices in Edinburgh, London, Welwyn Garden City, and over-seas, is one of the largest and most diversified in Great Britain. Projects undertaken by the prac-tice include New Zealand House, the Commonwealth Institute, the universities of York, Bath, Ulster, and Stirling, Turnhouse Airport, and the Royal Commonwealth Swimming Pool in Edinburgh.

Two views of New Zealand House, London, by Matthew, 1963

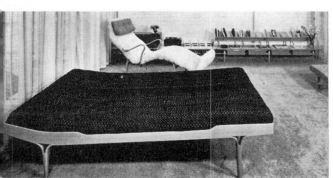

A double bed and chaise longue designed by Mathsson

Work abroad has included pro-jects in Australia, Canada, Hong Kong, Nigeria, Pakistan etc.

Matthew was president of the Royal Institute of British Archi-tects from 1962 to 1964, and was awarded the RIBA gold medal for architecture in 1970.

He has also for many years been active in the field of international architectural co-operation; he was chairman of the Union Internationale des Architectes (1961–5) and of the Common-wealth Association of Architects (1965–9).

The Mausoleum at Castle Howard by Hawksmoor, 1729-36

Pingree House, Salem, Massachusetts, by Samuel McIntire, 1804

Mausoleum. A term deriving from Mausolus, for whom a magnificent tomb in the heroic manner was erected at Halicarnassus in Greece. There is a splendid mausoleum in Britain, designed by Nicholas Hawksmoor, at Castle Howard in Yorkshire.

May, Hugh (1622–84). British architect. Little is known of May's early life apart from the fact that he was born near Chichester, and that his parents were in easy circumstances. He seems to have been a longtime associate and close companion of the Duke of Buckingham, and was a member of Charles II's court in exile. After the Restoration he was appointed paymaster of the works, supervising the financial aspects of refurbishing the royal palaces. Later on he became comptroller of the works at Windsor. After the Fire of London (1666) he was one of the king's nominees on the commission appointed to report on rebuilding the City.

May seems to have moved easily in court circles, and designed houses for several courtiers. Although overshadowed by Wren's, his houses were individual in design and remarkable for the decorative qualities of their interiors (May patronized Verrio and Grinling Gibbons). Few of May's houses survive, and much of his valuable work at Windsor is embodied in the castle fabric. His most notable houses were Eltham Lodge in Kent (1663–4) and Cassiobury Park in Hertfordshire.

Maze. A labyrinth of alleys and intercommunicating paths winding between parallel hedges. The way to the centre is bewilderingly difficult, bounded by tall, dense, and impenetrable hedges. The maze is a relic of the Renaissance formal garden, though of the many that have been constructed William III's at Hampton Court Palace, Middlesex, is the best known. There is also a maze at Hatfield House, Hertfordshire, and a newly planted one at Chatsworth in Derbyshire.

The complicated geometric designs inlaid in the floors of medieval French cathedrals are also called mazes or labyrinths.

Mazer. A bowl of polished spotted maple-wood, generally mounted with silver banding around the rim, and a silver medallion in the centre. The name apparently derives from a corruption of the word 'maple.' Fourteenth-century examples are known, and the mazer was in popular use until the mid-sixteenth century. Large numbers survive, for they were extremely useful household objects.

McIntire, Samuel (1757–1811). American wood-carver, sculptor, and architect of Salem, Massachusetts. McIntire was the son of a joiner in this shipbuilding town, and tradition has it that he began his career by carving the figureheads for ships.

McIntire's fame rests chiefly on his carving, which was always delicate and usually in the Neoclassic style. He carved interior woodwork as well as furniture made by other craftsmen. Common motifs such as wheatsheafs, fluting, and rosettes accompany McIntire's own more characteristic bunches of grapes, cornucopias, and baskets of fruit. He kept himself informed of European developments; though some of his motifs are in the Adam style, his work was mainly influenced by Hepplewhite.

McIntire built the Salem Court House (1782), and he is best known as an architect for his work on the Pingree and Pierce-Nichols houses in Salem. Most of McIntire's buildings and carving were done in the Salem area. At his death the business was carried on by his son, Samuel Field McIntire.

Carving by Samuel McIntire on a chest-on-chest

Eltham Lodge, Kent, designed by Hugh May, 1663-5

University Club, New York, by McKim, Mead, and White, 1899

The Pierpont Morgan Library, New York, by McKim, Mead and White

McKim, Mead and White. American architectural partnership, by far the most distinguished in American architecture of the 1890s, and largely responsible for the 'Academic Revival.' Charles F McKim (1847–1909) and Stanford White (1853–1906), the most influential members of the firm, had different backgrounds and aspirations. McKim had been trained at the Ecole des Beaux Arts in Paris, and returned to America on the outbreak of the Franco-Prussian War. He became H H Richardson's assistant before setting up on his own in 1892. White also worked for Richardson (1872–8), then spent a year in France before replacing Bigelow in the firm of McKim, Mead, and Bigelow. Unlike McKim, however, White was more interested in contemporary British architecture – especially Norman Shaw's – than in French work. The interior of the firm's H Victor Newcomb House, Elberon, New Jersey (1880–1), is decorated in a kind of Shavian-Japanese style that influenced American domestic interiors for the next half-century.

However, McKim went beyond Beaux Arts styling, and White beyond the shingle style. The common style which they urged was formalistic, and sometimes symmetrical, often drawing directly upon Renaissance or Palladian sources. As its most astylar, this formalism is best represented by the W G Low House, Bristol, Rhode Island (1887), still in the shingle style although nearly symmetrical. But the plan of the H A C Taylor House at Newport, Rhode Island (1885–6), is specifically Anglo-Palladian, and the house is detailed in a specifically Georgian manner. The firm also favoured the Colonial style for domestic building; eg the cricket club at Germantown.

For town houses and public buildings, McKim, Mead, and White turned to the more monumental style of the Italian Renaissance. The Villard Houses (1884), designed by their assistant Joseph B Wells (1853–90), were severe and rectilinear versions of the Cancelleria Palace in Rome. The Boston Public Library (1887), despite McKim's insistence that it derived from Alberti's Tempio Malatestiano in Rimini, has much in common with a French library of the 1840s, Labrouste's Bibliothèque Ste Genevieve in Paris. Both exhibit crisp, linear effects, beautifully moulded detail, and light-coloured stone. Above all, the Boston Library is in marked contrast to Picturesque or Richardsonian public buildings by virtue of its complete regularity. More than the products of the Beaux Arts architects, this 'American Renaissance' paved the way for Neo-classicism.

The W G Low house, Bristol, Rhode Island, designed by McKim, Mead and White, 1887

Plaster medallion in a fireplace panel

Design for a salon by Juste-Aurèle Meissonnier

Poster of furniture-makers Joseph Meeks and Sons

Meander. Another name for the Greek key pattern (qv).

Medallion. Strictly speaking, a medallion is a carved tablet that is a prominent feature of a decorative scheme. The term is more generally used to describe any round or oval figure, carved or flat, that is included in a larger scheme.

Meeks, Joseph & Sons (1797–1868). A New York firm of furniture-makers who operated for 71 years at 43 and 45 Broad Street. In 1833 Meeks issued a colour lithograph illustrating 44 items of furniture available on order. This was the first time complete furniture designs, rather than just details, were published in America. The furniture illustrated was typical French furniture of the 1820s, with large, plain surfaces, scroll supports, and projecting columns supports, and projecting columns.

Meissonnier, Juste-Aurèle (1695–1750). Painter, sculptor, architect, and designer. Meisson-

nier was born in Turin but spen[t] his working life in France, wher[e] he became champion of th[e] Rococo style. At court he de[-] signed the many decorations fo[r] masques, and, in 1726, was ap[-] pointed by Louis XV to b[e] *dessinateur du cabinet et orfèvre d[u] roi*, succeeding Berain *fils*.

Apart from his engraved de[-] signs, little can be attributed t[o] Meissonnier with confidence Much of his work was for noble[-] men outside France, giving hi[m] a wide influence. His super[b] designs embody the spirit of th[e] Rococo, charmingly light an[d] asymmetrical. He was made master-silversmith in 1724, an[d] thereafter used JOM with [a] crowned fleur-de-lis as his mar[k]. Other silversmiths and porcela[in] factories took elements from h[is] designs.

Mellor, David (*b* 1930). Britis[h] industrial designer. Mellor wa[s] born in Sheffield and educate[d] at the Sheffield College of Ar[t,] the Royal College of Art i[n] London, and the British Scho[ol] in Rome. In 1954 he opened [a] design office and workshop i[n]

David Mellor

Cutlery by Mellor

Schocken Department Stores, Chemnitz, by Mendelsohn, 1928

Eric Mendelsohn

Einstein Tower by Mendelsohn

Sheffield. His range as an industrial designer has been considerable and varied, and has included stainless steel cutlery for use in government canteens and hospitals, telephones, street lighting, and furniture. He has also carried out numerous special commissions, including candelabra for Goldsmiths' Hall and for Shell, and a bronze fountain for the botanical gardens at Cambridge.

Melon bulb. The modern term for the ornamental bulb found on table legs and bedposts of the late sixteenth and early seventeenth century.

Mendelsham chair. A late eighteenth- and early nineteenth-century type of Windsor chair, made by Daniel Day of Mendelsham, Suffolk. The seat and turned legs were of the conventional Windsor type; its peculiarity lay in the insertion of turned balls below the straight top and cross rails.

Mendelsohn, Eric (1887–1953). German architect. Mendelsohn was born in Allenstein in East Prussia, and was educated in Munich and Berlin. Early in his career, which included stage designing, he showed an unusual preoccupation with the sculptural possibilities of modern architecture. His sketchbooks were filled with highly imaginative drawings showing something of the influence of the theatre; at the time there was no expressionist theory of architecture which he could utilize. He set up in private practice in 1912, but his career was cut short by World War I, in which he served in the German Army.

In the early post-war years Mendelsohn's drawings of visionary but technically feasible projects attracted considerable attention, and as a result he was commissioned in 1919 to design the Einstein Observatory at Potsdam. The completed building aroused widespread interest and discussion, and took the architect at one step into the forefront of his profession. Important commissions followed, and Mendelsohn was responsible for a considerable number of projects, including many departmental stores. The most important were the two Schocken Stores at Stuttgart (1927) and Chemnitz (1928). Their skilful fusion of Mendelsohn's expressionism and the International style received world-wide recognition and had a considerable international influence upon department store design in the 1930s.

When Hitler took power, Mendelsohn left Germany and set up a practice in London in partnership with Serge Chermayeff. The two designed the De la Warr Pavilion at Bexhill-on-Sea (1934–6). Between 1935 and 1939 Mendelsohn did extensive work in Palestine, notably large hospital and university projects in Haifa and Jerusalem. In 1941 he settled in the United States, practising in San Francisco, where he built the Maimonides Hospital (1946), synagogues and community centres.

Merlon. On an embattled parapet the merlon is the upright part between the two embrasures or crenelles.

Metope. The square panels between the triglyphs (qv) of an entablature of the Doric order. The panels are usually plain, but sometimes carry paterae or masks.

Mews. A word originally applied to the coops where the royal hawks were mewed at Charing Cross, London. Royal stables replaced the mews on this site, and mews then became the term generally applied to the stables and accommodation to the rear of town houses.

Mezzanine or **entresol.** A low intermediate storey between two higher ones. It provides a practical way of accommodating

De la Warr Pavilion, Bexhill-on-Sea, by Mendelsohn, 1933-4

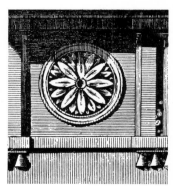

Engraving of metope

Windows for the mezzanine floor at Easton Neston by Hawksmoor

The Laurentian Library, Florence, by Michelangelo, 1524-6

more rooms within the fabric of a building when there is no need for every room to be of equal height.

Michaelangelo Buonarotti

(1475-1564). Italian architect, sculptor, painter, mystic, and poet, one of the supreme geniuses – perhaps the supreme genius – of Renaissance art.

Michelangelo was born in Florence, and at the age of 13 became apprenticed to Domenico Ghirlandaio, at that time the leading artist in the city. However, he was soon transferred to join Lorenzo the Magnificent's school of sculpture in the Medici gardens.

Michelangelo was not involved with architecture until commissioned to design the monument to Julius II in 1513 – by which time he had already established himself as a painter (Sistine chapel, 1508-12) and sculptor (*David*, 1504). His first major architectural commission (1516), for the Medici family, was to design a façade for Brunelleschi's S Lorenzo. This was rapidly followed by commissions for the New Sacristy, to house four members of the family, and the Biblioteca Laurenziana in the monastery attached to the church.

The façade of S Lorenzo, which was to have held 24 pieces of sculpture, was finally abandoned. Although a model does exist, it is without the sculptures and is unlikely to represent Michelangelo's final intentions.

The New Sacristy, or Medici Chapel, is incomplete, lacking the figures intended to accompany those of Dawn, Dusk, Night, and Day, which recline upon the sarcophagi. Nevertheless, in the New Sacristy, as in the projected Julius monument (never satisfactorily completed) and the abandoned façade, it is clear that the architecture and sculpture were to work together towards a total effect.

The new effects sought by Michelangelo were achieved in the vestibule of the library of S Lorenzo (1534–c 1560). Here a shallow, sculpturesque staircase flows down into the comparatively small but tall room. The treatment of the walls is strangely ambiguous. Wall tabernacles are curious and contradictory in form, and the coupled columns are let into the wall and apparently supported by small consoles. Yet despite appearances, they do actually support the structure.

In 1534 Michelangelo travelled to Rome, where he stayed for the last 30 years of his life. During this time he was engaged on a large number of architectural schemes, all of which were to be completed by another hand. In redesigning the Capitol, on one of the seven hills of ancient Rome, he planned the *piazza* as a triangle, with the Palazzo dei Signori at the longest side. At the centre of the inlaid pavement was to be the remounted antique bronze of Marcus Aurelius, which had survived the Middle Ages because it was believed to represent the Christian Emperor Constantine. Sadly, the design was altered by Giacomo della Porta, and Michelangelo's closely organized and emphatic treatment was sacrificed by the transformation of the *piazza* into a quadrangle. However, Michelangelo's complex treatment of the façades remains, and the giant order was used as planned. This was in fact its first appearance; it is a unifying element in the façade, and became an extremely popular device during the Baroque period.

In 1546 Michelangelo completed Sangallo's Palazzo Farnese by designing the doorway and cornice on the exterior, and the upper storey in the courtyard. In the same year he became involved with St Peter's – an involvement lasting until his death. This is the architectural work for which he is best remembered and which he himself considered the most important. He reorganized the ground plan into a combination of the central plan and the Latin cross. The building of the beautiful drum was completed before he died. The dome, which was the work of Giacomo della Porta and Domenico Fontana, is more pointed than in Michelangelo's final drawings.

His other works include fortifications at Florence (1527-30, the Porta Pia, Rome (1562), and the Sorza Chapel at Sta Maria Maggiore, Rome (c 1560).

Mies van der Rohe, Ludwig

(1886-1969). German-American architect. He was born Ludwig

The New Sacristy, Florence, by Michelangelo, 1520-34

Ludwig Mies van der Rohe

Interior of a house in Brno, Czechoslovakia, by Mies van der Rohe, 1930

Farnsworth House, Illinois, by Mies van der Rohe, 1946-50

Mies but later added his mother's name to his own. Mies, the son of a master-mason, was born in Aachen (Aix-la-Chapelle) and received no formal architectural training. But encouraged by his father, he developed a talent for drawing the architectural details required for the stone-cutting workshop. He later moved to Berlin, and worked first for Bruno Paul the furniture designer, and later in the office of Peter Behrens (qv), the most influential architect then working in Germany.

In 1911 Mies set up in independent practice and designed several houses which owed much of their inspiration to Behrens. After World War I, Mies began in earnest the spectacular career which was to make him one of the most influential architects in the world. The first demonstration of his individual manner was the German Pavilion at the Barcelona Exhibition of 1929. This embodied many of the principles on which his later work was based, and was virtually a prototype for many designs for houses which were later to become world-famous. A wide-

spreading slab roof was supported on seemingly delicate chrome-plated steel columns, travertine sections, and glass. The dramatic simplicity of the Pavilion, set among pools and a half-court enclosure, made it a landmark in modern architecture. Mies's famous Barcelona chair, introduced for use in the Pavilion, was an equally significant advance in industrial design. The Barcelona project brought Mies several commissions, including the Tugendhat House at Brno, Czechoslovakia (1930), which plainly derives from the Pavilion.

In 1930 Mies succeeded Gropius as head of the Bauhaus, but Nazi influence on the activities of the school, and its consequent removal to Dessau, culminated in a decision to close it. Finally in 1937 Mies left Germany for the United States.

In the following year he was appointed professor of architecture at the Armour (now Illinois) Institute of Technology in Chicago. His influence and practice developed rapidly. His domestic designs, notably the glass-and-metal Farnsworth

House (1946–50), and various skyscraper apartment buildings such as the Promontory Apartments (1947) and Lake Shore Drive (1951) in Chicago, were widely copied by American and European architects; so were the environmental principles manifested in his gradual development of the campus complex for the Institute. Mies's Seagram Building in New York (1956–9) is now reckoned as one of the masterpieces of modern architecture.

His buildings, with their austere, classically-proportioned elevations, emphasis upon a revealed metal framework, and use of glass, have been copied all over the world, for they were the logical outcome of all the theories put forward by adherents of the modern movement in architecture.

Milk glass. Opaque white glass made in imitation of porcelain was manufactured in Europe from the sixteenth century. The earliest was Venetian *lattimo*; German, Bohemian, and French milk glass followed during the next century. American hand-blown milk glass was not made

Seagram Building, New York, by Mies van der Rohe, 1956-9

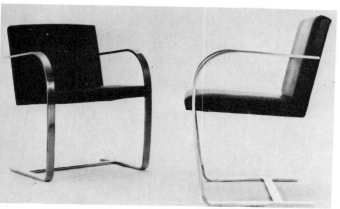

Stainless steel Brno chair by Mies van der Rohe, 1930

Barcelona chairs and stool by Mies van der Rohe, 1929

Millefiori paperweight

until the early nineteenth century. In the last decades of the century the glass was pressed on a large-scale commercial basis. 'Black milk glass' is, in fact, a deep amethyst colour.

Millefiori (Italian, 'a thousand flowers'). An ancient glass technique which probably originated in the Near East about the fifteenth century BC, and is still in use today. Rods of coloured glass are placed in a mould to form a pattern. This is then heated and drawn out into thin canes, the pattern being retained in miniature form. Sections of these canes are cut, and they can be placed together and reheated to fuse them into new designs. Glass mosaic plaques were made in this manner, and *millefiori* is an ancient form of decoration on beakers and bowls. Since the nineteenth century it has mainly been used for paperweights (qv). Today, most *millefiori* work is done in Venice.

Miller, Sanderson (1717–80). British architect. Miller, the son of a wealthy Oxfordshire merchant, was born near Edgehill in Warwickshire. After studying at Oxford he set up as a country gentleman and began to indulge his interest in architecture, landscape design, and

Hagley Hall, Worcestershire, by Sanderson Miller, 1754-60

writing. His skill as an amateur architect, with a penchant for gothick in its more picturesque forms, gave him a considerable reputation among his friends and acquaintances, for whom he always seemed willing to prepare gothick 'improvements' to country houses and landscape ruins.

Mills, Robert (1781–1855). The first American-born professionally trained architect; a pupil of Latrobe. Like Latrobe, Mills was an engineer who worked on lighthouses and waterworks, as well as an architect. From 1836 until 1851 he was government architect and engineer. This enabled him to establish classical rationalism as the style most suited both to monumental work, like the obelisk with which he furnished L'Enfant's Washington plan (1848), and to functional work such as his polygonal Lunatic Asylum at Columbia, South Carolina (1821–5). For Mills the same considerations determined the design of the small, elementally plain customs houses with which he equipped seaboard towns, and the massive

and austere government offices such as the Treasury (1836–42), which he built in Washington.

Minaret. The tower attached to a mosque. The minaret has either a gallery or a projecting balcony from which the muezzin (priest) calls the faithful to prayer by means of the traditional chant. Minarets are constructed in many forms, from the tall slender towers of Turkish form to the square Moroccan minaret with a high, built-in gallery.

Miniature furniture. Tiny models of cabinets and chests of drawers, usually not more than 12 in high, were used as samples by eighteenth-century cabinet-makers. They are of excellent craftsmanship and have long been cherished by collectors.

Mirror. In ancient times, particularly among the Romans, reflections were obtained from sheets of polished metal, usually bronze or silver, which were occasionally fashioned into a convex shape.

The method of making mirrors by using glass backed by thin

Washington Monument by Mills

sheets of metal was practised in medieval times; a guild of glass-makers was established in Nuremberg in the fourteenth century. However, it was Venetian craftsmen who developed mirror-making on a commercial scale, forming their own corporation in 1564.

The craft developed in France and England through the recruitment of Italian craftsmen, despite the severe penalties and restrictions imposed by the Venetian authorities.

The decorative possibilities of

Gothick Castle, Hagley Park, by Sanderson Miller, 1747-50

The minarets of the Blue Mosque in Istanbul

Design for a mirror by Thomas Chippendale

Water filled moat at the Château du Plessis-Bourré

mirrors were speedily recognized, and the collaboration of frame-maker and mirror-maker has made mirrors among the most splendid of all elements in interior decoration.

The modern process of silvering mirrors was discovered in the mid-nineteenth century in Germany.

Misericord. From the Latin *misericordia* 'pity.' A functional bracket hinged to the underside of the choirstall; it could be rested upon for support while standing during a service. Misericords are chiefly remarkable for their carvings of animals, and allegorical and mythological figures.

Mitre. The join made where two wooden sections meet at right angles. The term is most frequently used in frame-making.

Moat. A deep defensive ditch surrounding a castle or town. The moat was designed to impede the enemy by increasing the height of the walls – sometimes by as much as 40 ft.

Mocha ware is said to have originated at William Adams's Cobridge factory at the end of the eighteenth century. Certainly this factory and Leeds Pottery used this type of decoration on cream-coloured earthenware.

Nineteenth-century Mocha ware was a cheap, thick, white earthenware. The earlist known dated peice is in Christchurch Mansion, Ipswich, and is dated 1799. Jugs and tankards are the

most common pieces, but other items such as coffee pots, porringers, and butter dishes were also made.

The basis of the design was a broad band of coloured slip, usually blue, grey, or coffee-coloured, on which were the 'trees' or fronds of the moss agate or Mocha stone decoration.

Fable of the fox and geese on a misericord

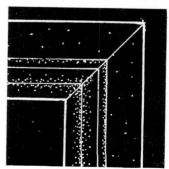

Diagram of a mitred corner

Mocha ware jug and mug

Ruins of the monastic buildings of Fontains Abbey, Yorkshire

To make the decoration the potter used a 'secret' mixture which he called 'tea'; it was said to consist of tobacco juice, turpentine, manganese, and urine. While the band of colour was still damp, the potter would drop a small quantity of this mixture on to the slip, which then spread out into the tree-like markings. Sometimes black rings were added above and below the coloured area.

This ware was made by Edge and Malkin in Burslem (1871–90) and by T G Green of Church Gresley in Derbyshire, whose firm, founded in 1864, is still in production. It is rare to find marked pieces.

Modillion. The ornamental bracket (normally console-shaped) which is used, in series, as a support for a cornice of the Corinthian or Composite order. The term is also applied to the brackets supporting the wide soffits of Regency buildings.

Module (Latin *modulus*, from *modus* 'a measure'). The attempt to establish a universally applicable unit of measurement in architecture dates from antiquity. The module was a unit of proportion upon which all subsequent measurement of a building were based. As early as the first century BC, Vitruvius, in his manual *De Architectura,* specified the modular measurement for the orders as half the diameter at the base of a column. Architects have been seeking the perfect modular measurement ever since. In more recent times considerable efforts have been made to established an internationally acceptable module in building and industrial design ('modular co-ordination'). Four inches or

ten centimetres has become a favoured module in many countries, but it has never been established as an international standard. Among the reasons for this lack of success are the individual whims of manufacturers, reluctance to change their production methods, and the understandable desire of designers to work to a smaller unit and retain their freedom.

Modulor. A scale of proportions based upon the human body and the Golden Section rule. It was devised by Le Corbusier and advocated in his book *Le Modulor* (1957).

Monastery. The early history of monasticism is still semi-legendary. It probably originated among early Christian hermits in Egypt, who had the solitude of the desert but occasionally met for communal worship. The development of buildings suitable for monastic life probably dates from the fourth century AD

when chapels and refectories were built, first by St Pachomius and later by St Benedict. In 529 AD Benedict founded Monte Cassino, the prototype for the hundreds of Benedictine monasteries built throughout Europe over succeeding centuries.

Monastic buildings inevitably varied with the forms of communal life devised by the abbots of the orders. The Cistercians established communal refectories and dormitories, whereas the Carthusians lived in separate cells, continuing the tradition established by the early hermits.

The medieval monastery might be the focus of a great agricultural estate, a centre of learning, or even an institution of political or administrative importance. Hence the development of monastic settlements from rudimentary shelters and chapels into buildings of considerable architectural interest and complexity. A monastery might consist of a church, a chapter house (for meetings of

the governing body), cloisters (covered walks or arcades), dormitories, a guest-house, workshops, a hospital, and the abbot's house, as well as a bakehouse, a brewhouse, mills, and other ancillary buildings. Some of these monastic complexes reached the size of extremely large villages.

Money pattern. A mid-eighteenth-century decoration. The money pattern consisted of a series of overlapping disks, and was so called because the disks resembled coins.

Monolith (Greek, *monos* 'one'; *lithos* 'stone'). A single stone or block of stone, set up in an unworked state or fashioned into monumental form as a pillar, column, or obelisk.

Monopodium. In furniture-making, the curious device of an animal's conjoined head and leg; the animal is usually a lion (qv). The monopodium was used as a support or decoration and was

The Monte Cassino monastery in Abbazia, Italy

Monopteral temple in the garden of Le Petit Trianon

Inverary Castle, Argyllshire, gothicized by Roger Morris, 1736

especially popular during the early nineteenth century. The motif is of Roman origin, revived by Thomas Hope (qv) in particular, in his *Household Furniture and Interior Decoration* (1807).

Monopteral. Adjective describing a temple, usually circular, which consists of a single circle of columns supporting a roof.

Monteith. A bowl, generally low and with a notched rim. It is thought to have been named after a man named Monteith who wore a notched cloak. Still-life paintings show that the Monteith was used as a cooler; glasses were up-ended in it with their bowls plunged in ice and

their stems resting within the notches. It was probably also used as a punch-bowl. In England the Monteith was at its most popular in the late seventeenth century; several fine examples with elaborate ornament have survived.

Monument (Latin, *monere* 'to remind'). A term applied to almost any form of building erected to commemorate some notability or historic event. There are many kinds of monuments, from columns to mausoleums.

Moorfield carpets. Thomas Moore's factory at Clerkenwell, London, produced the finest hand-knotted carpets made in

eighteenth-century England. On several occasions Moore worked for Robert Adam (qv); several of his carpets are still in their original positions, for example at Syon House and Osterley Park in London.

Moorish arch. See **Horseshoe arch.**

Moquette. A carpet and upholstery material made in imitation of velvet. It was woven by the same technique but with inferior wool. It was especially popular from the sixteenth to the eighteenth century and was produced in the Netherlands, Germany, France, and England. In England it was called 'Brussels

carpet' when used as a floor covering, and the factory at Kidderminster (qv) was the most productive English centre during the nineteenth century.

Morris, Roger (1695–1749). British architect. Morris was born at Wetherby in Yorkshire. In his twenties he was taken up by the Duke of Argyll, then master-general of Ordnance, and given a position in the Board of Ordnance. He was also patronized by the 'architect earl', Lord Pembroke. Morris's major works were carried out for these two noblemen. The most important were Marble Hill, Twickenham (1728), and the Palladian Bridge at Wilton (1736). He also de-

A William III Monteith bowl by Thomas Jenkins, 1700

Moorfields carpet in the hall of Osterley Park, Middlesex

Palladian Bridge at Wilton, designed by Roger Morris, 1736

Interior of the Red House, Bexley Heath, Kent, designed by Morris

signed the Council House at Chichester, Sussex (1731–3). His successful and impressive work in the Palladian manner of Colen Campbell was followed by a gothick phase. Morris was responsible for gothicizing Inveraray Castle for his first patron, the Duke of Argyll, and was engaged on the project at his death. It was completed by his relation, Robert Morris, who is better known as a writer on architectural subjects than as a practising architect.

Morris, William (1834–96). British craftsman, writer and, propagandist. Morris was born in London and educated at Marlborough College and Oxford. He intended to enter the Church, but in 1856, after

William Morris

graduating, entered the architectural drawing-office of G E Street (qv). During his time at Oxford he had become friendly with Burne-Jones, the two men sharing an enthusiasm for a romanticized medievalism. This became the keynote of Burne-Jones's paintings and Morris's prose and poetry. Morris left Street's office long before serving out his articles, married (1859), and devoted himself to supervising the building of a house at Bexley Heath in Kent. This was the famous Red House commissioned from Philip Webb (qv). Today it seems an unexceptional red brick domestic building, but at the time it represented an emphatic break with the prevailing – and overworked – architectural manners of the time. Perhaps more important, it stimulated Morris to design furniture and fabrics more to his taste than the commercially available items.

In 1862, fired by this newfound interest, Morris founded the firm of Morris, Marshall, Faulkner, and Co, with Webb and Burne-Jones as two of the partners. The firm had a strange commercial career. Thanks to Morris's romantic attitude towards craftsmanship, the prices of his products were considerably higher than those of comparable (if uglier) machine-made products. Morris, a convinced socialist, was thus caught in a dilemma: he fervently desired his furniture, textiles, and wallpaper designs to be bought by the masses, but found his market exclusively among his own *rentier* class. The problem was aggravated by the somewhat carefree nature of his commercial methods.

The influence of Morris and Co was considerable, but of a nature unforeseen by the founder. His textile and wallpaper designs remain the choice of the middle class and are little known among the workers to whose enlightenment he had devoted so much of his time and teaching. The same is true of the books he printed at the Kelmscott Press, which are the exclusive interest of wealthy collectors and book dealers.

Morris's work as a designer was conditioned by his highly romantic interpretation of the Middle Ages, but his reaction against the ugliness brought into life by the industrial revolution, then in full spate, was courageous and beneficent. His emphasis was on the virtues of simplicity and integrity in design and craftsmanship. He lectured widely from 1877, and his teachings made a considerable appeal to younger architects and designers. As often occurs with wellintentioned revolutionaries, Morris's teachings changed life, but not in the way he expected. He dreamed of a return to Merrie England and the downfall of the machine; his lectures stimulated others to investigate the aesthetic possibilities of in-

dustrial design. Morris's teachings were noted and acted upon by Peter Behrens (qv), C [ ] Voysey (qv), and other architects much more than by the world' craftsmen and workers.

Morris chair. An easy chai[r] invented by Morris, Marshal[l] Faulkner, and Co in the secon[d] half of the nineteenth century. It had a wooden frame, arm pad[s] and an adjustable back. The term is now most commonly used t[o] describe large wooden easy chair[s] with loose cushions.

Wallpaper by Morris

One of a set of six Mortlake tapestries, 1623-36

Mosaics in San Vitale, Ravenna, 6th century

Mortice (Verb: to mortise). A method of joining two separate members, usually of timber. The tenon, a projection on one member, is inserted into a cavity or hole in the other so that an exact fit is achieved.

Mortise lock. A lock which works on the basis of a tenon-and-mortice device.

Mortlake tapestry. In 1619, Sir Francis Crane, under the patronage of James I, established tapestry works at Mortlake in Surrey. The object was to emulate the magnificent tapestries woven by contemporary craftsmen in France and the Low Countries. To this end, craftsmen from these countries were brought to Mortlake by Crane and later by Charles I, who took a great interest in the progress of the Mortlake works. Despite this patronage, Mortlake tapestries never formed the basis of the native school: almost all the notable examples exhibit an unmistakably foreign character.

Morton, Alastair (1910–63). English textile designer. Morton was the son of Sir James Morton of Morton Fabrics, Carlisle. He was educated at St George's School at Harpenden, Edinburgh University, and Balliol College, Oxford; but he left before taking a degree to enter the family business. In the 1930s he showed outstanding skill as a textile designer in his own right, and also commissioned and applied abstract designs by other artists. He soon began to devote most of his time to Edinburgh Weavers, a branch of the firm started by his father, pioneering designs in fabrics that would appeal to avant-garde designers, decorators, and architects. Among the artist-designers whose work he commissioned were Ben Nicholson, Barbara Hepworth, Marino Marini, and Hans Tisdall. Morton's achievements were recognized by his election as a fellow of the Society of Industrial Artists in 1947, and as a Royal Designer for Industry in 1960.

Mosaic. An ancient decorative device, much practised by the Romans. In a mosaic, a pattern or picture is made by assembling fragments (tesserae) of multi-coloured marble, stone, glass, or pottery. The mosaic is usually incorporated in a wall or floor. The most famous is probably the mosaic of Pliny's doves in Hadrian's villa at Tivoli, near Rome; S Vitale at Ravenna has magnificent mosaics of Justinian, Theodora, and their court. The sizes of the fragments used in mosaic work have varied from time to time: from the average half-inch squares of Roman tesserae to the much smaller units of later Italian work.

Mosque. A temple used for Muslim worship. The highly

Alastair Morton and one of his fabric designs

Mosque in Istanbul

The interior of the Sultan Ahmet (Blue) Mosque, 17th century

Victorian tilt-top table with mother-of-pearl inlay

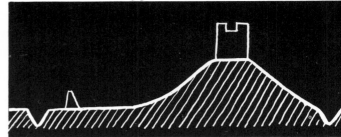

Section through a motte-and-bailey stronghold

Moulded brick chimneys

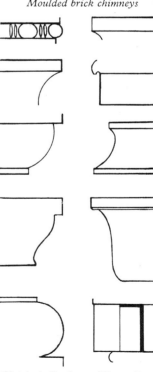

Classical Greek mouldings. Reading from top to bottom: fillet, corona, scotia, cyma recta, dentils; right: astragal, cavetto, ovolo, cyma reversa and torus

decorative and complex mosques of the seventh century onwards derived from the primitive square enclosure set up by the prophet Mohammed at Medina in AD 622. As with the buildings of other religious faiths, additions and embellishments were gradually made to the original form. The most significant addition to the mosque was the minaret (qv), from which the call to prayer was made. The final form of the mosque retained the *sahn* or open courtyard surrounded by a covered arcaded aisle (*livan*) wider on the side nearest Mecca, which also housed the sanctuary.

Mother-of-pearl. The lustrous and translucent lining of certain shells, particularly the pearl oyster, has been widely used for decorative inlay. Early Chinese black lacquer furniture was inlaid with mother-of-pearl, and there has been a collection at the Shoso-in, Japan, since the eighth century. In the west it became popular after its widespread use for decorating pistol stocks in mid-sixteenth-century Germany.

Motif. A device, symbol, or ornament which is the dominant feature in a design; the theme of a repeat-pattern used to embellish furniture, textiles, etc. Periods and styles can be characterized by their preference for particular motifs.

Motte-and-bailey. A hybrid French term applied to a man-made mound or knoll (motte), fortified in a fairly rudimentary manner by stockades or palisades, and protected by a primitive tower within a bailey. In England these motte-and-bailey strongholds were the rude predecessors of Norman castles.

Mouchette. A motif of curvilinear tracery that is similar to a curved dagger.

Moulded brickwork. For certain kinds of decorative brickwork, clay was set in shaped moulds before firing. Moulded brickwork was employed extensively in the more ambitious Elizabethan building projects. A wide variety of structural details were so treated from chimney stacks to chimney-pieces. On exterior work, moulded brick mullions and cornices were frequently plastered to simulate stonework. Moulded bricks were superseded by the softer bricks of the late seventeenth century, which could readily be cut by hand to any required shape. In the Victorian era there was a resurgence in the use of debased forms of moulded brickwork.

Moulding. A continuous decorative band created by making a projection or incision above or below a flat surface. Mouldings can be of the simplest forms, achieved by adding a simple fillet or rounded astragal section to a plane surface; more complex

Mullion in gothic window

storing blankets and linen. Most rest upon a solid base or plain bracket feet, although there are early eighteenth-century versions on stubby cabriole legs, frequently with side handles.

Mullion. The heavy vertical post in a window structure which divides the window into two or more sections or 'lights'. Mullioned windows are typical features of medieval and early Renaissance architecture.

Muntin. The vertical member in a wooden framed construction, panelled chest or door, found between the verticals at either end, which are called stiles or side posts. The muntin may thus be the central vertical or one of a series.

Mushroom swelling. Oval swelling on the legs of late seventeenth-century chairs, tables, and stools. The shape was somewhat like a mushroom, and the upper part was carved often with gadrooning (qv).

Mutule. A projecting inclined block under the corona of a Doric cornice. It corresponds to the modillion of other orders, and is probably derived from the ends of wooden beams.

Mylne, Robert (1734–1811). British architect. Mylne was one of the earliest British architects who successfully combined the functions of designer and engineer. His works ranged from domestic and ecclesiastical buildings to bridges, canals, drainage, and harbour works. He was born at Powderhall near Edinburgh, where his father was a master-mason; he acted as his father's assistant. At the age of 20 he was sent to join a younger brother in Paris. After some months he went on to Rome, where he spent four years in architectural studies, being elected to the Academy (a rare distinction for a Protestant), and also becoming a member of the academies of Florence and Bologna.

On his return to London in 1759, Mylne set about preparing designs for a bridge to be built at Blackfriars. His submissions were selected out of 70 entries, much to the annoyance of his English contemporaries, and his appointment as architect in charge of the projected structure was received with considerable hostility. The bridge he built remained in use until replaced by the present Blackfriars Bridge in 1868. Following the success of this

or 'enriched' forms are made by a multiplicity of projections and or incisions. At each period in architectural history, mouldings have been executed in a distinctive style, so that buildings can be dated fairly accurately by their mouldings alone. These range from the egg-and-tongue and bead-and-reel motifs of the ancient Greeks and Romans to the Tudor flower seen in mouldings on fifteenth-century English buildings.

Mulberry. *Morus nigra, morus alba.* The mulberry is mentioned by Evelyn in his *Sylva* (1679) as a wood used mainly as a veneer. But it was also employed for small objects as well as for bureaux and cabinet work. The actor David Garrick was presented with a commemorative box in 1769, said to have been made from Shakespeare's own mulberry tree.

Mule chest. A chest of joined construction with two or three drawers in the base. The first known examples date from the late sixteenth century. They are commodious, and were used for

'The Wick', Richmond, Surrey, designed by Mylne, 1775

project, Mylne was frequently employed to advise upon a remarkably wide range of architectural and engineering works. These included designs for the Gloucester and Berkeley Ship Canal; drainage and harbour improvements at King's Lynn, Yarmouth, and Wells in Norfolk; and a bridge at Newcastle-on-Tyne. He was appointed engineer to the New River Company; surveyor to St Paul's Cathedral, and surveyor to Canterbury

Cathedral. In 1775 he was appointed clerk of the works at Greenwich Hospital, but was dismissed by the governors seven years later after disagreement with the Hospital surveyor. He was elected a fellow of the Royal Society in 1767, and was a founder-member of the Architects' Club in 1791.

Mylne lived at Amwell in Hertfordshire, where he built himself a house which is still standing.

Robert Mylne by G Dance

London house by Mylne, 1797

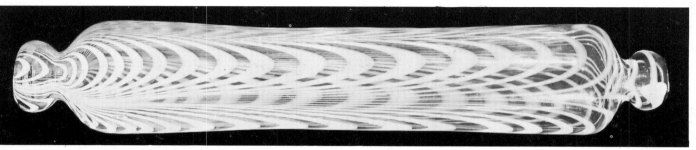

Nailsea rolling pin in clear glass with looped striations, early 18th century

ailhead. One of a series of ur-sided studs, typical archictural decoration of the late orman and Early English riods. Each resembles the ad of an old-fashioned wrought il.

In leather furniture the nailad is of aesthetic as well as tilitarian significance. In leather ork, such as chests and chairs, rass-headed nails were used to tach the leather to the carcase. his has been employed since e Gothic period, and has beome part of the work of a offerer.

Nailsea bottle, c 1800

Nailsea. A generic term for unsophisticated late eighteenth-century and nineteenth-century English glass jugs, flasks, beakers etc with mottled or trailed enamelled decoration, and the very colourful and decorative 'friggers' – glass hats, bells, pipes, rolling pins, ships etc.

These were originally made for the glassworkers' amusement, but were increasingly produced in the nineteenth century for sale at fairs and markets. The name Nailsea derives from a bottle and window glasshouse opened in the town in 1788; but Nailsea glass was produced by many other glasshouses.

Nantgarw and Swansea. A porcelain factory was started at Nantgarw in 1813 by William Billingsley (from Derby) and Samuel Walker. Billingsley made a porcelain body that was beautifully white and translucent, but it was very expensive to produce because so many of the pieces lost their shape during the firing. When Billingsley got into financial difficulties, a Swansea potter called Dillwyn arranged for the manufacture to be transferred to his factory (the Cambrian Pottery). By 1817 Billingsley had left Swansea and returned to Nantgarw, but in 1820 he went to Coalport, where

he remained until his death in 1828.

Three main types of porcelain were made: one, greenish in colour, that resembled a duck's egg; one with a finely pitted surface and a yellowish tinge; and a third with a colourless translucency. The output of the factory mainly consisted of high-quality tableware, inspired by Sèvres products; they were simple in shape and decorated with floral patterns. The Nantgarw factory marked its ware NANTGARW in capital letters, with CW for 'China Works' beneath; Swansea ware carried a trident and the word 'Swansea', usually impressed but sometimes written. Much of the plain white ware from these factories was sent to London to be decorated. There is said to be more faked Swansea and Nantgarw porcelain in circulation than any other kind of English china.

Naos. The inner chamber of a temple in ancient Greece. It was the sanctuary in which the god resided.

Narthex. In early Christian and Byzantine churches the narthex was a separate vestibule or ante-chamber across the western end of the nave and divided from it by a wall or

Nantgarw porcelain plates, early 19th century

screen of columns or railings. It was used by women and non-communicants. The term has also been applied to the enclosed antechamber (otherwise called a Galilee) at the western end of some medieval churches.

ash. *The dome of the Music Room at Brighton Pavilion with water-lily chandeliers and wall paintings of Chinese landscapes, designed by John Nash*

John Nash

Cumberland Terrace, Regent's Park, designed by John Nash, 1827

Interior of Sandridge Park in Devonshire by Nash, 1805

Nash, John (1752–1835). British architect. Nash's early life is obscure, and he did nothing to cast light upon it after he had become successful. He was probably the son of a Lambeth millwright who died when Nash was about eight. The nature of his education is unknown, but at an early age he entered the office of Sir Robert Taylor (qv) in a fairly lowly position, eventually becoming one of Taylor's assistants. In his mid-twenties, after receiving a legacy of £1,000 from an uncle, Nash set up as a builder, an event that foreshadowed his later interest in large speculative developments. His independence was short-lived: he was made bankrupt in 1783, and then repaired to Carmarthen in South Wales, possibly to join his mother. Here, in an area where his previous misfortunes were doubtless unknown, he again set up as a builder. He and his partner, Saxon, were given the job of re-roofing Carmarthen Church. Then Nash received his first important architectural commission from a local dignitary, John Vaughan, to design a bath. This modest task seems to have set Nash on his way to greater things, and in 1788 he was responsible for the design of Carmarthen Gaol, his first public building. The success of this venture made him an architect of local reputation, at least, although he was also involved in discussions attending the building of a bridge at Sunderland.

In 1796 Nash returned to London and set up in partnership with the noted landscape designer Humphry Repton; his part was to design the many architectural items called for in the landscaping of large estates. Not surprisingly, Nash began to establish a reputation as a country-house architect. From 1796 he was continuously occupied in this profession in various parts of England. In 1798 he

married a woman who ha reputedly been one of the Prin of Wales's many mistresse Nash had designed a conserv tory for the prince, and henc forth enjoyed substantial fortu and royal patronage. In 1806 was appointed architect to t Department of Woods an Forests.

Over the following years designed such country houses Ffynone, Pembrokeshire; Casin Dulwich; Southgate Grov Middlesex; Sundridge Par Kent; and Luscombe Cast Dawlish, Devon; and he ma additions to Corsham Cour Wiltshire.

By 1802 the Nash-Rept partnership had been dissolve but Nash continued to desig for country houses with unabat variety and vitality. West Gri stead Park, Sussex; Killy Moo Co Tyrone; Longmer Ha Shropshire; Cronkhill, Shro shire; Sandridge, Devon; an Lisson, Co Tyrone, were amor

Killy Moon Castle in County Tyrone, Ireland, by Nash, 1808

Lough Cutra Castle, County Galway, Ireland, by Nash, before 1817

complete hamlet of Blaise in Gloucestershire.

Meantime, in his capacity as architect to the Department of Woods and Forests, Nash had been preparing plans for the improved layout of the crown lands of Marylebone Park, a long-term project which was later to be developed into his great Regent Street and Regent's Park scheme. These place him among the great town planners of his own or any other age.

In 1813 Nash's prestige was enhanced by his appointment as surveyor-general at the express command of the Prince Regent. In this capacity Nash became involved in the remodelling of the Royal Pavilion at Brighton; and in the reconstruction of Buckingham House (later Palace). His work on Buckingham House, where he superseded Sir John Soane, led Nash into trouble, and after 1830, when George IV died, Nash was ejected from his positions. He died at his house at Cowes in 1835, the great reputation which he had established in a lifetime of professional energy, imagination, and skill, tarnished by his royal master's extravagance and his own willingness to serve that extravagance.

All Souls' Church by Nash

he more important. He also built a large number of cottages in the Picturesque manner, a form of domestic architecture in which he excelled; most notable were his designs for the

Metal frame sofa with loose cushions by George Nelson

Nash and his work are now seen in a far more sympathetic light. Although his work undoubtedly lacked distinction in the finer points of architectural detail he had a remarkable talent for town-planning; no city in the world possesses a more brilliantly imaginative conception of picturesque urban development than Regent's Park. Nash's country houses were also possessed of unusual charm, originality, and practicality.

Nave. That area west of the crossing axis of a church. It is reserved for the laity.

Table by George Nelson

Necking. Architectural term for the narrow moulding between the bottom of the capital and the shaft of the column. Also used for similarly-employed small mouldings on furniture.

Needle spire. A slender spire that rises from well within the parapet of a square tower. The base of the spire rests either directly on the tower top, or upon a small, centrally positioned structure.

Needlework. The generic term for both plain and decorative needlework, including embroidery, *gros point, petit point*, and *appliqué*.

Nelson, George (*b* 1908). American architect and furniture designer. He studied architecture at Yale. In 1946 he became head of the design office of Herman Miller and Co. In 1956 this company introduced Nelson's famous polyester shell armchair, which has a bowed, chromium-plated tubular leg section supporting a polyester shell seat. In 1957 Nelson designed an experimental house, and two years later, with Charles Eames, the pavilions of a US exhibit in Moscow. In 1967, also for the USSR, he designed the US Industrial Design Exhibit.

Part of a needlework hanging, 17th century

Building in Regent Street, London, by John Nash, 1812

The neo-classical façade of the British Museum by Sir Robert Smirke, 1823-47

Neo-classicism. Movement in art and architecture (c 1760–c 1830), in many respects a visual equivalent to the ideas of the Age of Reason. Seen merely as a shift in taste, it represented a reaction against Rococo anti-classicism, although the forms were often interpreted in a Rococo spirit; the Scottish architect Robert Adam, for example, used the well-known classical forms, but in unclassically delicate linear patterns.

Central to Neo-classical theory is the conviction that the arts should improve the mind, rather than satisfy the senses. The most pragmatic of Neo-classical buildings are therefore museums (Schinkel's Altes Museum, Berlin, 1824–8; Smirke's British Museum, London, 1825–47), conceived as temples of instruction; and a great many of the major works are civic, whether colleges, stock exchanges, or American state capitols. The urban planning of Washington, Leningrad, and Edinburgh is as much a monument to Neo-classical theory as to Neo-classical form. Buildings, like paintings, were supposed to serve a moral purpose, or at least to point a moral by commemorating a virtuous or useful life. Etienne-Louis Boullée's scheme for a cenotaph to Newton did this on a heroic scale, and the funerary monuments of Antonio Canova served the same purpose. The cult of commemoration resulted in Westminster Abbey in London, and the newly completed church of Ste Geneviève in Paris, being transformed into Neo-classical pantheons. The appeal to the mind resulted in a rational examination of the forms to be employed. The Abbé Largier pointed out that if classical architecture was a rational language, its grammar must be used neither incorrectly nor verbosely. His ideas influenced many architects to avoid superfluous elements. In J G Soufflot's church of Ste Geneviève, Paris (1757), column and entablature were used with the same regard to their structural role as the post and lintel of a primitive hut; and Sir John Soane omitted capitals and entablatures from the interiors of his Bank of England, London (1798), indicating the columns by means of lines in the plaster.

Largier's ultimate example of rational architecture was the hut, and contemporary thinkers turned to primitive society and culture (Gaelic Scotland, Teutonic Germany, Archaic Greece), finding in them a nobility and simplicity apparently lacking in their own society. The vogue for things Egyptian was also in part inspired by the cult of the primitive. The order which was most consistently revived was Greek Doric (the earliest), and it was usually given a deliberately primitive look by making the columns too short and the entablature too heavy.

Neo-classical forms were not always derived from classical architecture. Architects attempted to create ideal forms just as Neo-classical sculptors created ideal bodies. The idea might be fear, as at George Dance the Younger's Newgate Prison in London (1768), in which windowless walls, cyclopean masonry, and reliefs of fetters carved over the prisoners' entrance were calculated to daunt and deter potential inmates. It might equally well be civic virtue, as at Jefferson's State Capitol in Richmond, Virginia (1789), or wisdom, as at the same architect's University of Virginia (1817–26). Direct symbolism was also employed as in Ledoux's design for a river surveyor's house, with a cascade passing right through it. Sublimity was also a desirable quality, especially in ecclesiastical buildings; the cavernous interior of Benjamin Latrobe's Baltimore Cathedral (1805) is one of many examples.

Inevitably the ideal was believed to be located in nature – not the 'common nature' perceived by all, but a 'noble' nature – basically geometrical which it was the architect's task to reveal. Thus F Gilly's design for a theatre in Berlin (1798) was composed of a series of geometrical shapes, clearly distinguished from one another. In the stables at Chelsea Hospital, London (1814), Sir John Soane used unadorned semi-circular motifs to articulate the wall, and Boullée's cenotaph to Newton was a complete sphere. Even

An Egyptian room from 'Household Furniture' by Thomas Hope, 1807

The interior of Baltimore Cathedral by Benjamin Latrobe, 1805

Settee with Grecian motifs designed by Thomas Hope, 1807

Pier Luigi Nervi

n the ideal was classical, ying was for preference ded; architects like C R kerell in England, and iam Strickland in the USA, loyed classical models cor-ly, but also very ingeniously, create modern buildings. er designers manipulated ical forms with still more dom; furniture designers in-ably used architecture and mics as sources of designs, Josiah Wedgwood even took arble funerary urn as the ce for a soup tureen.

vi, Pier Luigi (*b* 1891). an architect-engineer. Nervi born in Sondrio, Lombardy,

gwood Jasper urn with Flax-n design, late 18th century

and graduated in engineering from the University of Bologna. He was almost 40 before his work began to be recognized outside engineering circles. Then, in the early 1930s, the significance of the exposed structure of his designs for the communal stadium at Florence was under-stood and publicized by archi-tectural theorists. They also advanced the claims of the engin-eer to be considered as an influ-ential architect, comparable with the leading practitioners of the then-emerging International style. Nervi was unique as an architect-engineer in his time, but much of his practice followed the lines established by the great bridge-builder Maillart (qv). Like Maillart's, his engineering designs were supreme examples of form following function, a theory then very much in the ascendant amongst theorists and avant-garde architects.

Nervi himself played little part in the controversies of the period; for his commissions for viaducts, bridges and other engineering works kept him continually busy. One of his most significant suc-cesses, both technical and aes-thetic, was a prototype aircraft hangar which he designed at Orvieto in 1935; further develop-ments of the idea followed after World War II with studies of loadbearing joints as elements in roof structures; and it was these that made him internationally famous as an engineer-architect who could create beautiful works via an unashamed presentation of skeletal structural forms.

These early studies in the interdependence of joists and roofs led Nervi towards even more imaginative and revolu-tionary technical experiments. He was able to give warehouses, factories, stations, and other

industrial buildings greater roof spans than had hitherto been considered feasible without heavy strengthening supports. These experiments culminated in Nervi's most spectacular work:

The Giova Ni Berta Stadium in Florence by Nervi, 1929-31

The roof of the Palazzo Dello Sport in Rome by Nervi, 1957

the Exhibition Building at Turin, built in 1948–9. After he had published a project for a sports stadium in Vienna (1953), it was inevitable that Nervi should be commissioned (1957) to design the Ite Palazzetto dello Sport for the 1960 Olympic Games in

Roof structure of the Pirelli Building in Milan by Nervi, 1958

UNESCO headquarters, Paris; Nervi, with Breuer and Zehrfuss, 19

Bottle with calligraphic scrolls

Rome. Nervi had also collaborated with other architects, notably with Gio Ponti and others on the Pirelli Building in Milan (1958) and on the new railway station at Naples (begun 1954). His other buildings include the Unesco Building (1956) and an exhibition hall (1958), both in Paris; other sports stadiums in Florence and Rome; and a second exhibition hall in Turin (1961).

Nest of drawers. A set of diminutive drawers in a superstructure on a writing-desk or dressing-table. Also the contemporary term for a very small chest of drawers of the seventeenth or eighteenth century.

Nest of tables. A set of three or four small tables; graduated in size so that they can fit one beneath the other, thus saving space.

Netherlandish glass. Before the sixteenth century, glass made in the Low Countries was virtually indistinguishable from glass made in Germany and Bohemia. The 'façon de Venise' glass which was then produced was also derivative – almost identical to the ware being made all over western Europe.

During the seventeenth century a more distinctive Netherlandish style began to develop. The ware included tall flute glasses, goblets with 'beech-nut' moulding, and tall stemmed glasses with a series of hollow knops and even greater elaboration of the highly ornate Venetian stem. However, the giant Teutonic *Roemer* remained a favourite form, and continued to be made in green glass.

The main feature of seventeenth- and eighteenth-century Netherlandish glass is its superb decoration. This falls into th distinct categories. From second quarter of the seventee century, an original and tremely fluent calligraphic s of diamond-point engraving developed by a group of amat artists. From the late seventee century to about the middle the eighteenth, wheel engrav in the German manner was fashion, as German craftsn and techniques infiltrated the Low Countries. Because its softness and light refrac qualities, English leadglass increasingly in demand; much undecorated ware imported, particularly from N castle. The third category decorating was dot stippl which started in the 1720s continued well into the n teenth century. This was an at which the Dutch artists v never surpassed.

Neumann, Johann Balth (1687–1753). German late oque architect. Neumann

Goblets with stipple and diamond point engravings, late 17th century

The Residenz at Würzburg designed by Neumann, c 1711

The interior of the Würzburg Residenz by Neumann; frescoes by Tiepolo

rn in Bohemia, and trained in
ometry, surveying, and engin-
ring at Würzburg. In 1717 he
ited Milan and Vienna.

His early appointments as
perintendent of buildings in
e bishoprics of Würzburg,
mberg, and Speyer, and in the
ctorate of Trier, were obtained
gely through the patronage of
e von Schonborn family, and
particular Prince Bishop
iedrich Carl von Schonborn.
Neumann's first work was the
ürzburg Residenz (c 1711), on
ich other architects, including
ldebrandt, collaborated. Its
gnificence is enhanced by the
ococo plasterwork of Antonio
ssi and frescos by Tiepolo.
eumann's buildings, spatially
mplex and intellectual in de-
gn, convey an immediate im-
ession of visual elegance and
ontaneity. His ingenuity in
aircase design culminated at
uchsal (1731), a masterpiece
stroyed during World War II.
e Pilgrimage Church of
erzehnheiligen (1743) is per-

haps his masterpiece with an
intense sense of movement reinforced by lavish decorations.

Neutra, Richard (1892–1970).
Austrian-born American architect. Neutra was a disciple of
Adolf Loos, and after 1911 of
Frank Lloyd Wright. From 1922
–3 he worked with Erich Mendelsohn, and in 1923 went to the
USA to work with Holabird and
Roche in Chicago, then with
Wright at Taliesin. The Lovell
House, Newport Beach, California (1927–9), derives its
regular outline and total absence
of ornament from Loos, but its
picturesque siting on the edge
of a hill, and its dramatic cantilevers, are more in the spirit of
Wright. However, its historical
importance lay in its alternate
horizontal layers of plain concrete
and glass, maintained by the
thinnest supports, which make it
one of the first International
style buildings in the USA. The
Sidney Kahn House, San Francisco, built at the height of

Two views of Vierzehnheiligen Church, Bavaria, by Neumann, 1743

The Lovell House, Los Angeles, California, by Neutra, 1929

Holiday house designed by Richard Neutra

International style influence (1940), reveals similar qualities while eliminating the Wrightian picturesqueness. After the war Neutra's Kaufmann Desert House, Palm Springs, California (1946–7), exemplified the movement away from the International style. Here the use of local materials, and the slightly less rigid planning, suggest analogies with Maybeck or the Green brothers, placing the building within the tradition emanating from west coast Spanish ranchhouses.

Newel. The post or central core into which the handrail and strings (qv) of a wooden staircase are fitted.

New Hall hand-painted porcelain teapot, and cup and saucer, late 18th century

New Hall porcelain. A hardpaste porcelain made at Shelton near Hanley, at a factory called the New Hall. A patent for the manufacture of this porcelain had been bought by a syndicate of six potters from Richard Champion of Bristol in 1781; and the porcelain is not easily distinguishable from that of the Bristol factory.

Delicate springs and festoons predominated in decoration; the most used colours being pink, red, and black. By about 1810 the hard-paste body had been given up in favour of bone china, and production ceased altogether about 1825.

The marks used on the hardpaste porcelain consisted of a swash capital N followed by the pattern number. A circular mark enclosing the words 'New Hall' was used on the later types of bone china, but the pieces are by no means always marked.

Niche. A recess, usually fairly shallow and round-headed, made in an interior or exterior wall, pier, or column. They are usually intended to hold an urn or statuary.

Nicholson, Peter (1765–1844). British architect and architectural writer. Nicholson was born at Prestonkirk in East Lothian, the son of a stonemason. Preferring woodwork, Nicholson was apprenticed to a cabinetmaker at Linton in Haddingtonshire. After serving his apprenticeship he worked for a time in Edinburgh, but in 1788 moved to London, where he taught while preparing his first book, *The Carpenter's New Guide*, published when he was only 27. He was already showing himself to be remarkably versatile and original; evolving new solutions to complicated structural problems, and engraving his own plates to

Niche for a statue in a garden

Two niches in a modern house

illustrate his theories. *The Carpenter's and Joiner's Assistant* (1793) was followed by *Principles of Architecture*, published between 1795 and 1798.

By this time Nicholson had acquired a considerable reputation, and two years after the completion of *Principles of Architecture* he returned to Scotland and set up in practice as an architect. He enjoyed a modest success in Glasgow and Partick, designing town houses and making additions to collegiate buildings. On his appointment as surveyor of Cumberland (1808) he left Glasgow for Carlisle, where he supervised the building of Thomas Telford's Courts of

Peter Nicholson

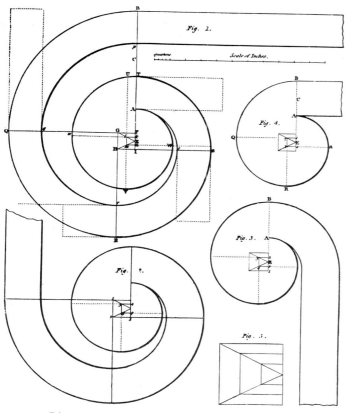

Diagrams by Peter Nicholson for the end of handrails

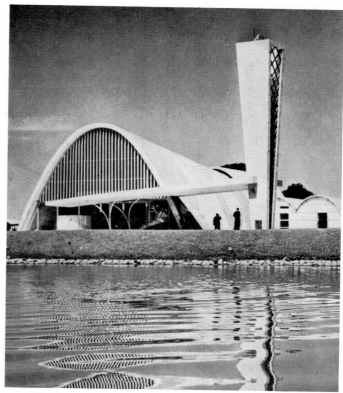

The Church of St Francis, Pampulha, by Niemeyer, 1942-3

Justice. He returned to London in 1810 and began an ambitious *Architectural Dictionary* in two volumes and a still more ambitious project for a 12-volume work dealing with architecture and engineering. His publishers were declared bankrupt after five numbers had appeared, and the work had to be abandoned at great financial loss to Nicholson.

Despite his considerable talents, and a degree of local and national recognition, Nicholson never gained the commissions he deserved. He was a prolific writer, publishing over 20 books ranging from practical guides to masonry and joinery to treatises on algebra and isometrical drawing. In 1914 he was awarded the

gold medal of the Society of Arts for his recommendations concerning handrailing, and he received a silver medal for his invention of the 'centrolinead', which has been defined as an instrument for drawing lines required to converge to an inaccessible point.

Nicking. A simple method of notching or cutting a surface. It is used as a form of decorative work on some seventeenth-century oak furniture.

Niemeyer, Oscar (*b* 1907). Brazilian architect; born Oscar Niemeyer Soares Filbo in Rio de Janeiro. He was educated at the National School of Fine Arts in the city; entered the archi-

tectural offices of Lucio Costa (qv), and his first major task was to supervise the building of the Ministry of Education and Health headquarters, one of the landmarks of modern architecture in South America; Le Corbusier was partly responsible for the design.

For a time Niemeyer was greatly influenced by Le Corbusier and by Costa, with whom he jointly designed the Brazilian Pavilion for the New York World's Fair 1939. But he soon evolved his own version of the International style, exhibited in his first major project at Pampulha, which began in 1942. The Yacht Club in this complex now ranks amongst the classics of modern architecture. In parti-

cular, Niemeyer displayed an appreciation of the dramatic possibilities of the Brazilian landscape and climate. He was less bound than most of his contemporaries by the cult of extreme angularity, being happy to employ sculptural forms such as parabolic vaulting, vast canopies, and double curves. To exploit his new and often exuberant forms to the full, Niemeyer invited the co-operation of structural design-engineers, notably Joacquim Cardoso.

Niemeyer has been one of the most prolific designers of the twentieth century, with unusually few projects that have remained as blueprints, a proof of his practicality as well as his imagination and energy. In 1956 he was

Oscar Niemeyer

Plaza of the Three Powers, Brazilia, designed by Niemeyer

The circular Cathedral of Brasilia by Oscar Niemeyer

Chapel of the Alvorado Palace, Brasilia, by Oscar Niemeyer

appointed architectural adviser to Nova Cap, the organization set up to carry out the building of Brasilia, the new capital of Brazil planned by President Juscelino Kubitschek. In 1957 Niemeyer was appointed chief architect. Among his most notable buildings in Brasilia are the president's palace, the law courts, the museum, Congress Building, and other public buildings, all planned within Costa's general scheme. In the design of these buildings and in the general architectural development of the new capital, Niemeyer worked in close co-operation with President Kubitschek, as he had in the Pampulha development project.

Niemeyer's other buildings have included his own house at Gavea and the Sul America Hospital (both 1953).

Night clock. Seventeenth- and eighteenth-century lighting was generally dim and localized, and telling the time at night presented difficulties. Several innovations were introduced to deal with the problem. Dutch Striking, the hour being repeated on the half-hour, but on a smaller bell; the more elaborate Grande Sonnerie, with a different chiming for each quarter-hour; and the illuminated or night clock. This probably originated in Italy, and bore pierced numerals on the dial, so that a light behind them could shine through.

Night table. A polite term for a night stool or close stool. This was an eighteenth-century bed-side table with tray top, made in two sections. The upper part was usually in the form of a cupboard; the lower looked like a drawer and, in fact, incorporated a pan and seat. Bow-fronted examples came to be known as 'night commodes', a term later euphemistically abbreviated to 'conmode.' In the nineteenth century a night table and bidet was adapted from three-tier bed steps.

Nomadic furniture. A term coined by Siegfried Giedion in his book *Mechanization Takes Command* (1948) as a generic term for all forms of portable furniture, from the collapsible military furniture used by commanders in the field to the mass-produced knock-down furniture of our own day.

The Italian 'campaign chair', one of the most popular items of furniture in modern interiors, was originally produced for Italian officers during the war in northern Africa. Another example of nomadic furniture, the film director's collapsible chair, has also proved popular, and has established itself as a useful piece of garden furniture.

Nonsuch chest. A form of chest which carries inlaid decoration on its sides or lid resembling Henry VIII's spectacular Palace of Nonsuch in Surrey. The inlay work was of German origin or the work of imported Flemish and north European craftsmen.

Norman architecture. Romanesque architecture was introduced to Britain by the Normans and was the prevailing style until the advent of Gothic *c* 1200. Its outstanding characteristic is the employment of round-headed arches. Early Norman in England is extremely similar to the architecture of Normandy, but the two diverged as other Continental influences were felt in England (the great west towers of Germany, the massive round piers of Burgundy); and the elongation of the nave was a purely English contribution. Taken as a whole, however, Norman architecture in England is a more coherent style than French Romanesque, which consisted of a number of regional schools.

The nave of a Norman cathedral has a gallery over the nave arcade, and a clerestory with a small passage on the wall at the foot of the windows. Crossing and west towers are frequently found. Rather crude sculptural decoration proliferated *c* 1100, and chevron or zig-zag mouldings were found on string courses, jambs, archivolts, arches, and any other available spaces. Billet, cable, nailhead, and diaper work – all standard Romanesque mouldings – were employed. So were more specifically English motifs, such as the

Nomadic military chest

Italian campaign chair

Oak Nonsuch chest inlaid with various woods, 16th century

Norman arch with chevron moulding and cushion capitals

Nottingham punch bowl in brown salt-glazed stoneware, 1750

interlacing arches (qv), used to enliven walls, at Castle Acre Priory, Norfolk, where they cross the whole façade, and the mid-twelfth-century beakhead device (qv) of a head with a beak biting a roll moulding. Some of the best-known Norman buildings are Gloucester Cathedral 1089–1100), Tewkesbury Cathedral (1123), and Durham Cathedral (1093), which possesses the first proper rib vaults in northern Europe and thus looks for-ward to Gothic architecture.

Nosing. The edge of a tread (qv) that projects beyond the riser (qv), or any other horizontal moulding projecting beyond the vertical face below.

Nottingham stoneware. Salt-glazed stoneware was made at Nottingham from *c* 1660 to the end of the eighteenth century. The earliest known dated piece is inscribed 1700, and the last 1799. The shapes of Nottingham stoneware were strong and simple, and it was well made. It was coated with a ferruginous wash of clay which burnt to a distinctive smooth brown iridescence; this gave an almost metallic appearance to the glaze. The ware was generally decorated with incised patterns, and many pieces are inscribed and dated. Though it was made by the Morleys of Mughouse Lane, it was never marked with their name.

Intricate double pieces were sometimes produced at Nottingham, with the outer layer decoratively pierced to reveal the layer below. An interesting type of jug was made in the shape of a bear. The body was covered with rough shavings or granules of clay to indicate the shagginess of the beast's fur. The head was detachable and could be used as a cup. Punch bowls, sometimes very large, were also made in the hard brown Nottingham stoneware, as were mugs, cups, teapots, and two-handled lovingcups.

Nursery furniture. The range and versatility of nursery furniture has greatly increased during the post-war years; in particular, designers have paid increasing attention to the needs of children during their transition from infancy to childhood. The design of playpens now permits considerable freedom of movement while ensuring the child's safety. The smaller chairs and tables so frequently used in nursery furniture have, however, occasioned criticisms from some child psychologists, who contend that scaled-down imitations of adult furniture could retard the child's natural growth into adolescence and maturity. The bunk bed, the most practical and popular piece of nursery furniture, seems to have aroused no such adverse reaction.

Nursing chair. The nineteenth-century (possibly older) term for a chair with an especially low seat.

Nymphaeum. A classical sanctuary consecrated to nymphs. They originally resembled grottoes, but later became architectural monuments, mostly rotundas ornamented with statues and fountains. They were used as assembly rooms and had a special significance for weddings.

The Norman nave walls of Gloucester Cathedral

Nursery table and chairs designed by Alvar Aalto

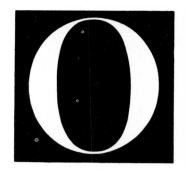

A Provençal oak commode, mid-18th century

Oak. *Quercus.* More than 300 varieties of oak have been recorded. Most medieval furniture was made of this hard wood, and the tradition of its use continued into the early Renaissance period. The English oak originally flourished in extensive forests; however, by Elizabethan times these had been so depleted by over-felling that the Crown ordered the introduction of extensive replanting.

The close of the seventeenth century witnessed the introduction of more decorative woods, after which oak was confined to rustic furniture and carcase work. Today it is used for much contract work and office furniture. See **Fumed oak.**

Oast, oast-house (Latin, *aestus* 'heat', 'fire'). A brick-built, cone-shaped kiln, originally constructed for the purpose of drying hops; a few examples are rectangular in plan and have steep pitched tiled roofs. In England during the past two centuries, oasts have become part of the Kent and Sussex scene, but many have now been converted to private houses and weekend cottages.

A Kentish oast-house

Obelisk. A tapering shaft employed for decorative or monumental purposes; it is usually made of stone and four-sided, is raised to a considerable height, and is normally finished with a cut-off pyramidal top. Obelisk forms were widely used in ancient Egypt; 'Cleopatra's Needle' in London, on the River Thames, is a famous example. Napoleon's expedition led to a revival of interest in things Egyptian in the early nineteenth century, and the obelisk was again seen in a variety of forms, from gigantic monuments to tapering obelisk-type pilasters for bookcases and cabinets. The obelisk has also gained fresh popularity in recent years as a decorative motif in interiors; obelisks have been built in marble, simulated marble, wood, and in clear and coloured Perspex.

Octastyle. The term which describes a portico with eight columns.

Oculus. A circular window.

Oeben, Jean-François (1720–63). German-born *ébéniste*. In the 1740s Oeben went to Paris, where he entered the workshop of Charles-Joseph Boulle, the surviving son of André Charles Boulle. He was patronized by Mme de Pompadour, and was appointed *ébéniste du roi* in 1754 and a *maître* of the guild in 1761. Most of the furniture bearing his *estampille* is by Riesener: Oeben himself died in 1763, soon after he had been granted the *estampille*, and Riesener continued his work, technically under Mme Oeben.

Oeben furniture is of a gay, curving Rococo design, decorated with naturalistic baskets of flowers, and later geometric designs, in elaborate marquetry and with delicate ormolu mounts. Many pieces were fitted with

Modern perspex obelisks

ingenious mechanical devices, a practice at which the Germans excelled. Typical of these is the remarkable 'table à la Bourgogne' which can be opened to reveal a multitude of devices that transforms a simple chest of drawers into a highly sophisticated, complex piece of furniture.

Oeil de boeuf. A small round window. It received its name

Small secrétaire by Oeben

Obelisk. *A silver inkstand made in the form of the Quirinal Monument in Rome, by Vicenzo Coacci, 1792*

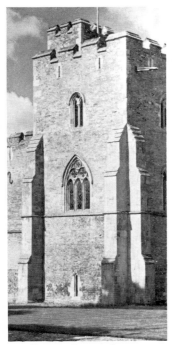

Off-set surfaces on buttresses

Aerial view of Central Park, New York, designed by Olmstead

from a small octagonal vestibule at the Palace of Versailles which was lit by one such window.

Off-set. A horizontal or sloping ledge on a wall or pier; it exists because the masonry above it is less thick than the masonry below. The edge is often moulded to prevent rainwater damaging the wall beneath.

Ogee, ogee arch. In its basic form the ogee, or ogive, is an S-shaped curve used in the profiles of mouldings. The S shape is normally flattened but sometimes has a bolder profile. The mouldings with the convex curve below are known as cyma recta (qv), those with concave below

and convex above as cyma reversa. The ogee shape is used in a double form to make the pointed or ogee arch. The ogee was introduced around 1300, becoming a major motif in Decorated Gothic. The lead roofs of the cupolas and turret-towers of many fifteenth- and sixteenth-century secular buildings were frequently ogee-shaped.

Ogival arch. Another name for a pointed Gothic arch.

Olbrich, Joseph Maria (1867–1908). Austrian architect, an outstanding pupil of Otto Wagner. Olbrich was one of the first architects to impose a linear structure upon the Art Nouveau style, as in his Sezession Gallery, Vienna (1898). He was a founder-member of the Sezession, a movement which did much to publicize modern ideas in art.

Olbrich's Vienna Gallery, and a tower, the Hochzeitsturm, at Darmstadt, are dignified in their arrangement of masses. However, taken in conjunction with this, Olbrich's houses at Mathildenhöhe, Darmstadt exhibit the persistence of the curving forms of Art Nouveau, and the lack of functional clarity that is apparent in the work of Hoffmann.

Olive, *Olea europa.* The wood of the olive tree has always been used in the Mediterranean

area, where it grows in abundance. Yellowish, with an undulating speckled figure, this decorative wood was fashionable during the late seventeenth century and was used extensively up to the beginning of the nineteenth century. It was used for turnery, ornamental veneers in the form of parquetry, boxes, and picture frames.

Olmstead, Frederick Law (1822–1903). American landscape architect. Olmstead laid out Central Park, New York (begun 1859; largely complete by 1876), in the early nineteenth-century Picturesque tradition; the plan of the commissioners of 1801 envisaged a gridiron scheme, but Olmstead, like Nash at Regent's Park in London, laid out an irregular network of water and wood, crossed by winding paths and bridges. In 1911, following the lead of Ebenezer Howard and Letchworth, he planned the garden city of Forest Hills, Long Island. His career thus spanned the entire nineteenth-century Picturesque tradition; however, between the Central Park and Forest Hills projects he was also responsible for the formal layout of the 1893 World's Exposition at Chicago, on a symmetrical scheme with regularly planned walks and lakes.

Onion foot. The American term for a large form of bun foot used on chests and cabinet stands of the seventeenth century.

Opaque twist stems. In ancient times, threads of opaque white glass were used in making vessels in the Middle East. The technique was revived by the Venetians in their *latticino* and *vitro-de-trina* in the sixteenth century, and the twist stem became increasingly popular in

Ogee arch over a doorway

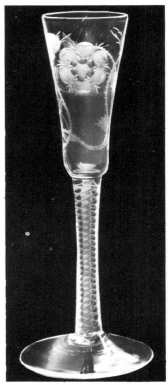

Glass with opaque twist stem

The orangery at Kensington Palace by Christopher Wren, 1689-1702

The Gothick orangery at Daylesford House, Worcestershire

the design of drinking-glasses in the eighteenth century. Well over 100 variations have been noted.

Opaque twist stems were made by placing rods of white or coloured glass upright in a mould into which clear glass was poured. This adhered to the partly re-heated rods. One end of this mass was held by pincers; the other was drawn out and twisted until the desired width or pattern was achieved, when it was cut into suitable stem lengths.

Open twist. A decorative spiral turning that was popular on post-Restoration oak furniture. A two-stranded spiral is known as double open-twist.

Opisthodomos. The architectural term for a vestibule at the back of a Greek temple, corresponding to the *pronaos* at the front. It can also refer to an enclosed space used as the treasury.

Opus Alexandrinum. A mosaic paving in which tesserae in a limited selection of colours are arranged into geometric patterns. Most of the work is Italian, dating from the Middle Ages and the Renaissance.

Opus Incertum. In Roman masonry this was a facing of irregular stones upon a concrete wall.

Opus Reticulatum (Latin, *rete* 'a net'). In Roman masonry this was a facing on a concrete wall, made with small square stones arranged in a diamond-pattern like a mesh net.

Orangery. A seventeenth-century architectural-cum-horticultural innovation, designed for the cultivation of orange trees. Sir Christopher Wren designed one of the earliest at Kensington Palace (1689–1702) for William of Orange and Queen Mary. The architectural and decorative possibilities of the orangery were quickly recognized, and these one-storey buildings, with east-to-west façades consisting almost entirely of tall windows to let in the maximum amount of sun-

light, soon became standard features of eighteenth-century domestic complexes. As the orangery soon became a social as well as a horticultural retreat, it became the object of much decorative ingenuity.

Oratory. A term first applied to a small room or chapel set aside for private devotions, usually in a private house. The term was later applied to larger public places of worship.

Order(s). A comprehensive term applied to the construction, proportion, and decoration of the columnar systems established by the architects of ancient Greece and Rome. It encompasses the base (or pedestal), shaft, capital, and entablature (or lintel) of the major orders: Doric, Ionic, Corinthian, Composite, and Tuscan. The Doric is generally considered the earliest, dating from the late sixth century BC. The Ionic probably evolved in Asia Minor at the same time, but was not found in Greece until the middle of the following century.

The Corinthian order was also in evidence during the fifth century, but was later adapted and changed in detail by Roman architects, who established the prototype for the Corinthian as used in Renaissance buildings. The Tuscan is the simplest of the orders, and was probably of Etruscan provenance. The Composite order, which never rivalled the others in popularity, was a Roman innovation combining features derived from the Ionic and Corinthian orders. Our knowledge of the Orders derives from researches described by Vitruvius in his treatises. The canon thus established was later reinforced and given absolute authority for all practical purposes by the publication of *L'Architettura* (1537–51) by Serlio, who provided detailed information concerning the correct proportion and decoration of each of the traditional orders. His dicta became the acknowledged sources of all subsequent 'classical' building.

See also articles on the various orders and their components.

The orders of architecture from Peter Nicholson's 'Dictionary of Architecture', 1862. Left to right: Greek Doric and Ionic, Corinthian and Composite

Oriel window of the gatehouse at Hengrave Hall, Suffolk, 1525-38

A Louis XV bureau plat with fine rococo ormolu mounts

Oriel (**window**). A term whose derivation is unknown. It is now applied exclusively to a form of bay window projecting from the upper storey of a building and supported on brackets or decorative corbels. In medieval times the term ('oriel') was applied to a wide variety of architectural elements.

Ormolu (French, *or moulu* 'ground gold'). The gold-coloured furniture mounts and decorative stands that were used in France from the late seventeenth century and elsewhere from the mid-eighteenth. The material was, in fact, either gilded brass or copper; nowadays it is an alloy of copper, zinc, and tin. As the name suggests, ormolu originated in France as gold or gold leaf; subsequently the term *bronze doré* became more common there, whereas in England and America 'ormolu' was retained. The mounts, corner-pieces, elaborate handles, etc were cast and later chiselled so that a very highly wrought finish could be obtained.

Orrery. An instrument showing the motions of sun, moon, and planets. It was invented by George Graham in 1710, and a copy was made for Charles Boyle, Earl of Orrery, after whom it was named. See also **Astrolabe.**

Orthographic projection (Greek, *orthos* 'straight'; *graphos* 'writing'). A method of graphic projection used by architectural draughtsmen in working drawings. Buildings, rooms, and objects are shown by points being projected at right angles to the planes of projection, based on plan and elevation.

Østberg, Ragnar (1866–1945). Swedish architect. Østberg was born in Stockholm, where he studied at the academy and technical school; later he studied in the United States. He also travelled widely in Europe and America. He returned to Sweden in 1900 and set up in practice. Few architects have achieved

Oriel window, Hengrave Hall

such fame for a single building as Østberg did with his designs for Stockholm Town Hall, built between 1910 and 1923. This building skilfully bridged the gulf between late nineteenth-century institutional heaviness and the angular austerities of the International Movement. In his design Østberg borrowed liberally from the motifs of Sweden's historical architecture and her applied arts and crafts, combining them with a romanticized view of contemporary architecture. The building, sited magnificently by the Stockholm waterside, exerted considerable influence upon architects in the 1920s, but the Bauhaus theories later made its nostalgic romanticism seem old-fashioned. In 1921

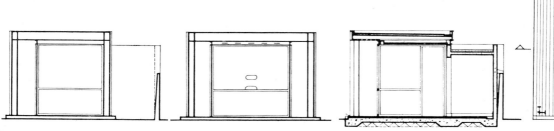

Orthographic projection of gatehouse to factory; elevations, cross section, plan

Stockholm Town Hall designed by Ragner Østberg

The Bio Health Resort in Arnhem, Holland, by J J P Oud, 1952-60

stberg was appointed professor f architecture in the Stockholm cademy. In addition to Stockolm Town Hall he also designed he Maritime Museum (1938) n Stockholm, the theatre at mea, and collegiate buildings t Uppsala University.

ttoman. A low upholstered eat that first became popular in he late eighteenth century. The onvenience of such a simple rm of seating was self-evident, nd the nineteenth century saw large number of corner and rcular versions. These deeply uttoned, practical, but heavyoking pieces occur in many lustrations of Victorian inriors. In America a great ariety of ottomans existed. In heir simplest form they are also nown as a Turkey sofa.

ud, Jacobus Johannes Pieter 890–1963). Dutch architect. ud studied in Amsterdam and Munich. After travelling and udying in Italy, he returned to Iolland and set up in practice t Leiden, his first commission eing a cinema in Purmerend,

his birthplace. During World War I he became one of the most influential members of the De Stijl group, which derived its aesthetic mainly from Cubism. Oud sought to apply those theories to architectural design. In 1918 he was appointed city architect of Rotterdam, and as such was responsible for the design of several housing estates, notably at Hoek (1925–7) and Kiefhoek (1925–30). These projects notably diminished his interest in Cubism, and he became one of the practitioners of a less angular form of design, sometimes known as Beton-Rococo. He also designed the Apostolic Church at Rotterdam (1929) and the Shell Building at The Hague (1938–42).

Overdoor. Sometimes called a *sopraporte*. It refers to a bas-relief or decorative painting placed above a door and within the framework of the door case. It is occasionally also used to describe the pediment over a doorway.

Overhang (oversailing, overjutting). Terms applied to a method of construction used in timber-framed houses. The upper storey is virtually cantilevered over a lower storey by lengthening the ceiling joists of a

lower floor in order to sustain an outer, upper wall. The method offered the dual advantages of providing one or more upper storeys of greater area and, by weighting the overhanging joists with the wall, significantly strengthening the whole structure.

Overmantle mirror. A mirror designed especially to be positioned above the fireplace, and to harmonize with the overall design. The height of the overmantle mirrors varied enormously; some were huge, filling the space between mantleshelf and cornice; others were smaller and oblong in shape. The smaller type was common from 1720, and often had two vertical divisions with a wide central and two flanking glasses. All overmantle mirrors were carved, and some had a framed picture above or candle branches at either side.

Oversailing course. A method of bricklaying or stonework in which a course of bricks or masonry is laid to project beyond the course below.

Overspill. A modern townplanning term for the section of an urban population which is superfluous or harmful to the

planning ideal, and should therefore be transferred elsewhere.

Overstuffed furniture. Seat furniture that has been upholstered so that none of the wooden seat rails is left uncovered.

Ovolo (Latin, *ovum* 'an egg'). A convex moulding a quarter round in section; used in all periods of architecture and cabinetmaking. Occasionally it is enriched with egg and dart or similar motifs. Also called a quarter round or echinus (qv).

Oxford chair. A nineteenthcentury easy chair with an upholstered back seat and open arms. It is of generous proportions, with a long seat and high back.

Oystering. A striking veneer of Dutch origin. The small branches of walnut, laburnum, and other woods are cut across to attain a distinctive circular figure. The small individual pieces are known as oyster pieces or oysterwood.

Segmental overdoor

Detail of olivewood oystering on a Carolean cabinet on stand

Overhanging top storey

Pagoda at Kew designed by Chambers, 18th century

William Pahlmann

A drawing room designed by William Pahlmann

Pagoda. A Buddhist temple or tower found in India and China. Most pagodas rise in a series of storeys, each of diminishing area and height, so that the final form is that of a gently tapering obelisk. The overhanging roofs with upturned corners make the pagoda particularly exotic to Western eyes. But not all are symmetrically built: in the octagonal pagoda in the Summer Palace of Peking, the overhanging roofs are set in pairs beneath a canopied topmost roof. The eighteenth-century cult of *chinoiserie* led to the introduction of pagoda-like forms into European architecture; Sir William Chambers's pagoda at Kew is a memorable example.

Pahlmann, William. American interior and industrial designer, born in San Antonio, Texas. Pahlmann studied in New York and Paris before joining the New York department store Lord & Taylor, for whom he was head of the interior design department from 1936–42. Since 1946 he has been president of William Pahlmann Associates, which has designed restaurants, hotels,

clubs, and homes throughout the world. Pahlmann has been associated with many now accepted furnishing innovations, and has designed a great number of furniture fabrics and wall and floor coverings. He is a member of the advisory committee of the Cooper-Hewitt Museum of Design. He received the Elsie de Wolfe Award in 1964. He has

written several books on design and decoration, including the *Pahlmann Book of Interior Design,* and also writes a syndicated newspaper column.

Paine, James (c 1716–89). British architect. Little is known of Paine's early life, although he is thought to have been born in southern England, and to have

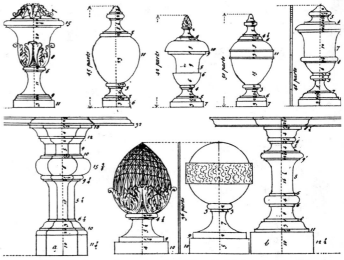

A typical page from one of William Pain's pattern-books

Padauk or **padouk.** *Pterocarpus dalbergioides.* A type of rosewood varying in colour from crimson to golden brown. The wood was employed by furniture-makers from the early eighteenth century. It is also referred to as andaman redwood, after the islands in the Indian Ocean. Padauk has mainly been used for decorative work, and was employed extensively by the French *ébénistes.*

Pad foot. See **Club foot.**

Papier-mâché. *An assortment of small objects including trays, snuff boxes, letter racks, a coaster, and a small writing box*

James Paine

An engraving of Sandbeck, Yorkshire, from James Paine's pattern book

studied and begun his architectural training in London. When still only 19, he was commissioned to prepare designs for Nostell Priory in Yorkshire. He quickly established a considerable reputation as a country house architect, especially in the Midlands and North of England, and before he was 30 had also designed the Mansion House at Doncaster (1745–8). The success of these buildings, which were ideally suited to the current Palladian taste, brought him many commissions, so that he was reputed to have 'nearly divided the practice of the profession' with Sir Robert Taylor. He held several profitable official and royal appointments, including the clerkships of the works at Greenwich (1745), Newmarket (1750), and Richmond New Park Lodge (1758). Paine was a lifelong Palladian. His designs invariably possess authoritative and distinguished elevations, and interiors that are highly practical as well as decorative. Some of his designs are extremely original in conception, as is demonstrated by Robert Adam's apparently ready accept-

ance of what was in essentials Paine's plan for Kedleston, which Adam took over from the older man. Many of the mansions built by Paine have been demolished, but existing buildings include Heath House, Wakefield, Yorkshire (1744–5); Belford, Northumberland (1754–6); the stables at Chatsworth (1758–62); and Brocket Hall, Hertfordshire (1760–70).

Paine was also a bridge-builder of note, and was responsible for earlier versions of the bridges over the Thames at Richmond (1774–7), Chertsey (1780–5), Walton (1783), and Kew (1783–9).

Pain family. A family of builders, surveyors, and architects. The most notable member was William Pain (c 1730–c 1790), the author of a series of instructional manuals. His sons, James, George, and Henry, became pupils of John Nash and later removed to Ireland, where they established a considerable family practice.

Paintbrush or **brush foot.** The American term for a furni-

Brocket Hall, Hertfordshire, by James Paine, 1760-78

ture foot carved as an upright grooved scroll turning inwards at the floor. It is of Spanish or Portuguese Baroque origin and is found on furniture of the late seventeenth and early eighteenth century. It is also known as a Spanish foot.

Painted furniture. Paint has been applied to furniture for both protection and decoration. It is a

simple way of disguising chea wood or making a cumberson object seem lighter.

Traces of paint have bee found on ancient Egyptian furn ture. During the Middle Ages was used quite extensively folk or country furniture in mar parts of Europe, a practice whi continued down to modern time It also extended to the Ne World, and some pieces a

Nostell Priory, Wakefield, Yorkshire, designed by James Paine

An 18th-century Venetian painted commode

Pennsylvania Dutch painted chest of yellow pine and poplar, 1780

highly prized, especially eighteenth- and nineteenth-century chests of Pennsylvania Dutch origin, with designs based on German folk motifs.

In England, furniture painting was most common in the late seventeenth and the eighteenth century. Japanned articles were made in imitation of oriental lacquerwork, as was also done in America. Many amateurs practised the technique, and it was popular until the nineteenth century.

Robert Adam (qv) introduced painted details on some of his furniture. This was an immediate success, and was followed by the painting of an entire piece in a pale shade, with the details of borders, garlands, arabesques,

and plaques applied afterwards.

Nowadays whitewood furniture provides opportunities for the amateur decorator to brighten up his surroundings.

Paktong. Chinese nickel silver. An alloy of copper, zinc, and nickel that was imported into the west in the second half of the eighteenth century. The Chinese had used the metal for furniture hinges and mounts, but in the west it was chiefly used for small household objects, candlesticks, and chimney furniture.

Palissy, Bernard (1510–89). French potter. Palissy began life as an apprentice glass painter, and then became a land surveyor. Around 1540, when he was living

at Saintes, he was shown a piece of maiolica or Chinese ware that fired his enthusiasm, and he made persistent attempts to emulate it. His years of failure and penury, and his eventual success through an introduction to the French court, are described in his autobiography. He enjoyed royal protection and set up a pottery in the Louvre; but his Protestant beliefs frequently brought him into danger, and he spent the last four years of his life in the Bastille. Ironically, it was for rustic pottery that he was honoured, not for fine ware such as he had striven to imitate.

Palissy's typical works were large plates and oval dishes, covered with coloured glazes of blue, green, violet, or yellow.

Small, realistically modelled forms of reptiles, insects, and shells were applied to the dishes (Palissy lectured on natural history) giving them their characteristic high-relief appearance; the undersides were of a mottled tortoiseshell. Many forgeries of Palissy ware were made during the nineteenth century.

Palladianism. The term applied to all forms of architecture deriving from the principles established by Palladio (qv) in his book *I Quattro Libri dell' Architettura*. The style is epitomized by the use of a central pediment temple-style portico with flanking wings. In Britain the term has particular relevance to the architecture of the later

An English painted corner cupboard, c 1770

Circular plate moulded in relief by Bernard Palissy, 1550-1600

The Goldsmith's Hall, London, by Philip Hardwick the Elder, 1829-35

Marble Hill at Twickenham designed by Roger Morris, 1728

Renaissance, beginning with the buildings designed by Inigo Jones (qv) in the two decades before 1650, and the eighteenth-century revival associated above all with Lord Burlington (qv). The style lasted into the Regency era, and has continued to make an especial appeal to British architects. It was adapted (in a somewhat heavy and over-weighted form) for use in much Victorian and twentieth-century institutional architecture

In America the Palladian influence was also strong, and the drawing-room at Gunstan Hall, Virginia, is one of the finest examples of Palladianism to be found in the New World. Thomas Jefferson (qv) was a practitioner of the style. There was an eighteenth-century revival of Palladianism in Italy, and the style also had some impact in Germany and Russia.

Palladian windows on the Basilica in Vicenza

Palladian window. A tripartite window, the openings of which are framed by columns or pilasters, as at Palladio's Basilica in Vicenza. The centre light is the tallest and is arched, whereas the narrower windows on either side have a straight cornice. The Palladian window is also known as a Venetian window or as a Serliana (qv).

Palladio, Andrea (1508–80). Italian architect. He was unquestionably the most influential of all European architects. Derivations of his basic designs are to be seen clearly in Whig mansions in England, hunting lodges in Germany, colonnaded mansions in the United States, and Tsarist palaces in Russia.

Palladio (born dalla Gondola) grew up in humble circumstances in Padua. While still a boy he started work as a stonemason, and he was enrolled in the craft guild of Vicenza when he was 16. His career really began c 1536, when he was patronized by an eminent poet and philosopher, Giangiorgio Trissino. Trissino encouraged the young Palladio in the study of mathematics and literature and later sent him to Rome, where in 1545 he began the studies of ancient architecture which were to form so substantial a basis for his own designs.

On his return to Vicenza, Palladio quickly established his reputation with a two-storeyed colonnaded screen for the remodelling of the somewhat over-heavy Basilica. He then began the series of buildings, secular and ecclesiastical, which were to bring him lasting fame and to provide models for international Palladianism. These buildings included a group of villas based on a plan of great simplicity. Each consisted of a central block, flanking wings which were added as simple extensions, or more subtle and visibly dramatic curving quadrants. These wings housed farm staff and implements. Within their essential unity, the villas, with their temple-form colonnaded porticos, show a remarkable diversity; they range from the majestic Rotonda (begun 1530), with its four hexastyle porticos, to the simple austerity of Foscari (Malcontenta), built in 1560.

Palladio was also responsible for the designs of some of Italy's

Drawing of the courtyard of Palazzo Thiene, Vicenza, by Palladio

Villa La Rotunda, Vicenza, by Palladio, 1560-75

S Giorgio Maggiore, Venice, by Palladio, begun 1530

Diagram of the Villa Foscari (La Malcontenta) by Palladio

noblest churches, including S Giorgio Maggiore (1560–75) and Il Redentore (1576), built in Venice. The famous Teatro Olimpico in Vicenza was started by him in 1580 and finished by Scamozzi. In 1570 he published his *I Quattro Libri dell' Architettura*, which was translated into many languages and has influenced successive generations of architects.

Palmette. A classical motif similar to a fan or stylized palm leaf. It occurs frequently in friezes. When employed alternately with the lotus flower, it forms the classical anthemion pattern (qv).

Panel. Basically a board used as a wall decoration, chair-back, or chest-top. They were often ornately carved or inlaid, and have been much used in repetitive form as panelling.

Panelling. A form of wall-covering or lining first used in England in the thirteenth century (in Windsor Castle), although known long before in France and Italy. Panelling was also used for doors and screens. The earliest panelling in England was of Norwegian pine, which was gradually supplanted by English oak. This early panelling

was extremely heavy and ornately carved. Form and decoration gradually became lighter and simpler, a tendency that reached its climax in the sixteenth century. One direct result of this was the widespread use of the simply-carved linenfold pattern.

Linenfold was replaced by floral and geometrical patterns in the next century. In the eighteenth century, pine was once again widely used for panelling, which was invariably painted, and larger panels were used. The framing of panels became much simpler,

with the popular bolection employed as a framing moulding.

The fashion for simple wood-panelled walls was also marked in American houses of colonial times. It remains a popular wall-covering in contemporary homes, when the attempt is made to

Early French Renaissance panelling in S Vincent's Church, Rouen

Panelling painted by Boucher, from the Château de Crecy

emulate the seventeenth- or eighteenth-century atmosphere, but more often for the undisguised modern library or study. The wide boards that characterized early panelling are no longer available.

Pantheon (Greek, *pan* 'all'; *theos* 'god'). The name given to any temple dedicated to the classical gods as a group, but now more generally applied to the world-famous temple in Rome, built *c* AD 125, and still standing.

Pantile. A curved form of roofing tile widely used in Mediterranean countries, and also found in parts of England and Scotland. During recent years a highly glazed pantile in brighter colours, mainly deep greens, has become popular for use in summerhouses and garden pavilions in both the United States and Europe.

Paperweights. A description of what sounds like a millefiori (qv) paperweight was written by a Venetian librarian of St Mark's *c* 1495. The first recorded exhibition of paperweights, however, took place in Vienna as late as 1845; they were

made by Pierre Bigaglia, a Venetian. By 1846 paperweights were being produced in France by the Cristalleries de Baccarat (qv), soon to be followed by St Louis and Clichy; all excelled in design and workmanship, and achieved brilliantly intense colours.

Paperweights made at these and other French factories enclosed flowers, animals, and fruits, as well as portrait busts and medallions of famous people, made from a porcellainous substance.

Stourbridge in England produced millefiori paperweights during the second half of the nineteenth century, but they tend to be larger than the French and were never executed in such brilliant colours.

Many English bottle-glass manufacturers at Stourbridge and elsewhere produced ovoid bottle-green paperweights. These usually enclosed silvery flowers growing from a pot, or sparkling cascading fountains, the chemical action of chalk producing the silvery bubbles. Larger weights, weighing up to six pounds, were used as doorstops and are often known as 'dumps' or 'dumpies'. They sometimes contain only air bubbles, formed by pricking the glass with a sharp tool before adding another gathering of glass.

In America from *c* 1850 to 1880, paperweights were made by the Boston and Sandwich Co and the New England Co, the most original enclosing almost life-sized glass fruits.

Papier-mâché. A paper-based substance which could be readily moulded into shapes and then baked. It was made by mixing quantities of paper pulp, and later paper sheets, with a fixative, chalk, and occasionally sand. The

Pantiles on a roof

baked surface was brittle and hard, and could take a high degree of polishing. The process originated in the ancient Near East. It was introduced into England from France during the seventeenth century, mainly for use in picture framing, but did not begin to acquire widespread popularity until the late eighteenth century when a Birmingham craftsman, Henry Clay, developed a version of the substance which he termed Claysware. Horace Walpole's furnish-

Paperweight

Two views of the Pantheon, Rome, AD 125

Papier-mâché Canterbury, c 1860

John Buonarotti Papworth

ings at Strawberry Hill included a writing-desk in Claysware. Birmingham became the centre of papier-mâché manufacture. The firm of Jenners and Bettridge in Birmingham specialized in papier-mâché ware, and in 1825 obtained a patent for their 'improvements' in the use of mother-of-pearl in the production process. During the early Victorian era a wide variety of objects, from firescreens and tea-trays to sewing-chairs and sofas, were made in papier-mâché. Smaller objects were frequently inlaid with mother-of-pearl.

Papworth, John Buonarotti (1775–1847). British architect. John Papworth was born in Marylebone, the son of a well-known stucco worker. He set up in private practice in his mid-twenties, his independence being made possible by successful early commissions to design houses in the Woodford and Chigwell areas of Essex.

Papworth was a prolific and versatile designer of villas, rectories, cottages, farm buildings, and lodges. He was also a developer of estates, which gave full scope to his flair for landscape gardening. He was responsible for designing the Brockley Estate in south London and the Montpellier Estate in Cheltenham. In London he also designed warehouses, factories, shopfronts, and galleries, and carried out numerous extensions and alterations to clients' houses.

Early in his career Papworth acquired a reputation as a designer of furniture and other objects connected with his work as an architect. Some of these were esoteric objects, such as a glass throne for the Shah of Persia and a sherbet service for the Pasha of Egypt. Papworth's versatility persuaded him that he had a certain affinity with Michelangelo, and he added Buonarotti to his given names.

In 1834 he was one of 12 founder-members of the Institute of British Architects. He was appointed first director of the Government School of Design, founded in 1835. He was also a writer on a wide range of subjects, his chief works being *Designs for Rural Residencies* (1818) and *Hints on Ornamental Gardening* (1832). His brother George (1781–1855) and sons John Woody (1820–70) and Wyatt Angelicus (1822–94) were all architects.

The Montpellier Pump Rooms, Cheltenham, by J B Papworth, 1825-6

Laleham Park, Middlesex, by J B Papworth, 1827-30

The gateway at Fonthill Abbey, Wiltshire, by Papworth, 1829-42

18th century parapet

Paradise. The garden or cemetery of a monastery; also the open courtyard, or atrium, surrounded by porticos.

Parapet. In its simplest form the parapet is a low-built wall at the extremities of a roof, normally an extension of the structural walls. The parapet was long used as a protective device, built high and, in fortified houses and castles, often backed by a rampart walk. Such parapets were given crenellations or battlements. Later they were decorative or fanciful items, as in 'gothic' houses.

Parcel gilt. Partly gilded. A term that has been in continuous use since the Middle Ages to describe gilded decoration upon furniture and silverware.

German parcel gilt beaker, Berlin, c 1700

Parchment or **parchemin panel.** An early sixteenth-century decorative panel that was used on chests, presses and wall panelling. Its distinctive device, known as a rib pattern, is two curved and moulded ribs that back on to each other; the spaces between carry small carved ornaments such as bunches of grapes and vine leaves.

Parclose. A screen or railing which partitions off a chapel or tomb from the main body of the church.

Pargetting, parging. Originally the simple plastering of the open sections within the timber framing of a house. The term was also applied to similar treatment of ceilings. From the sixteenth century, particularly in East Anglia, when the plastering of complete walls became general, the plaster was worked in highly decorative patterns usually involving simple floral motifs. Examples of such parging or pargetting survive on the exteriors of a number of houses in the Stour Valley area of Suffolk, notably in the village of Clare, and are occasionally found in Essex and Hertfordshire.

Parian ware. Known first as 'statuary porcelain', this fine white porcelain bisque was invented c 1845. Various companies (Copeland and Carrett, Minton, T and R Boote) claimed to have invented it, and by 1850 numerous firms, including Wedgwood, were making the same sort of body.

The fine marble-like body lent itself to detailed modelling, and great quantities of busts and statuettes were made. No Victorian drawing-room would have been thought completely furnished without its quota of sentimental maidens or gambolling *putti*. Parian ware achieved enormous popularity. The writer of a catalogue entry for the 1851 Great Exhibition in London fulsomely eulogizes 'that exquisite material in which England remains unrivalled and which is second only to marble.' American Parian ware was first produced at the Bennington Pottery in Vermont.

Parlour (Italian *parlatorio*; Norman French *parloir*). Originally a private apartment in a monastic house to which inmates and/or visitors could withdraw for conversation or conference. It was also known as the 'Speke House.' In *Piers Ploughman's Vision* the fourteenth-century

Pargetting on a house at Clare, Suffolk

poet William Langland wrote:
Now hath eche riche a rule
To eten by hymselve
In a pryvee parlour
and in *The Ancient Rites of Durham* the parlour is referred to as 'the place where merchants used to utter their wares, standing betwixt the chapter-house and the church door.' The term persists in the phrase Mayor's Parlour.

From the fourteenth to the end of the last century the term was used for a well-furnished family living-room in smaller private houses. It was often a dining-room as well, especially during the eighteenth century. In Sheraton's *The Cabinet Dictionary* (1803) it is listed under 'Dining-room' (although he does refer to parlour chairs), and in Loudon's *Encyclopaedia* (1833) the decoration of the parlour is defined as 'in a medium style, between that of a drawing-room and that of a dining-room.' Today the term is used in America especially in relation to the formal living- or reception room in historic houses, eg the Readbourne and Port Royal Parlors at Winterthur, and the East Parlor at Van Corlland House.

Parlour chair. The eighteenth-century term for a type of light chair similar to a dining-room chair, with an open back. Such chairs are illustrated in Ince and Mayhew's *Universal System of Household Furniture* (1759–63). The Victorians were very liberal with their use of the word, though it has now passed out of fashion.

Parlour cupboard. This word is now used to describe a group of heavy carved cupboards made during the sixteenth and seventeenth centuries. They ap-

Parian salt cellar by J Bell, Minton, c 1847

An oak parlour cupboard with griffin supports, early 17th century

The parterre at Blenheim Palace, Oxfordshire

pear to have originally been known simply as cupboards or presses. They were usually two-tiered; and the term includes pieces with an open lower and enclosed upper tier, but is mainly applied to those that were completely enclosed. The upper tier had two or three cupboards and an overhanging cornice that was usually supported by ornamental bulbs, though these were later replaced by carved pendants. In many cases the cupboards were arranged to give a splay front. They were usually made of oak.

Parquetry. A decorative geometric pattern of woods, first associated with flooring (an association commemorated in the word 'parquet'). Its late seven-

teenth- and early eighteenth-century use on furniture – mainly walnut furniture – was extremely decorative; oyster pieces (qv) are often found. The geometric mosaic was enhanced by contrast with the grain of different coloured veneers, either inlaid or made into a single sheet.

Parson's table. A low, square-shaped occasional table, somewhat akin in shape to early Chinese tables; it is named after Parson's School of Design in New York. Versions of this modern table were conceived independently by Joseph Platt in New York and Jean Michel Franck in Paris. It is usually made of plastic in white, black, red, and other bright colours.

Parterre. In gardens, the parterre is a level area on which flowerbeds are formally arranged in an ornamental and sometimes very intricate pattern. The beds themselves are often outlined in box, and extra colour can be supplied by coloured gravels. There are many examples of the parterre on the Continent, for example at Versailles and Vaux-le-Vicomte in France, and at Schloss Bruhl in Germany. One of the few spectacular examples in England is at Blenheim Palace.

Partners' desk. A Victorian innovation, an elaborated form of the large library tables of the eighteenth century. A double-fronted desk of larger-than-

normal dimensions enabled two people to work facing each other. Each front carries the normal complement of drawers and/or cupboards.

Partridge wood. *Andira inermis.* A Brazilian wood that was employed for parquetry and inlay work in the seventeenth and eighteenth centuries. It is hard and reddish brown in colour, with mottled streaks resembling birds' feathers. It was most popular with French *ébénistes.*

Passion, emblems of. The emblems of Christ's Passion, such as cross, nails and crown of thorns, were frequently used in medieval carving on screen panels, bench-ends and fonts.

Parquetry work on the staircase at Claydon House, Buckinghamshire

An early Louis XV kingwood parquetry commode

A modern patchwork bedspread in velvet and other fabrics

The patio of a modern house enclosed on two sides

Patchwork. The piecing together of different materials has a history at least as old as ancient Egypt. It flourished in Europe in medieval times. Though it was generally thought of as a domestic and thrifty form of needlework, the English and Dutch made a velvet patchwork that was a suitable fabric for dresses and wall and bed hangings. Fine decorative patterns in infinite variations were produced in America. Introduced by the first settlers, no doubt for utilitarian reasons, patchwork became especially popular in the eighteenth and nineteenth centuries.

Patera, paterae. Small circular disc-like ornament used in classical architecture, and later used in Western architecture and furniture. Regency cabinetmakers were particularly enamoured of paterae for decorating the friezes of cabinets, the backs of chairs, and the cornices of bookcases.

Paternosters. Small round mouldings resembling the beads of a rosary or chaplet. Also called bead or pearl mouldings.

Patina. The green film on old bronzes, produced by oxidization. The term is applied by extension to the deep colour and surface sheen of veneer and timber caused by age and many polishings.

Patio. The inner courtyard in a Spanish or Spanish-American-type house. It is open to the sky and similar to the atrium (qv). The word is now used more generally for partly enclosed paved areas.

Pavilion. (1) A decorative building, with no particular utilitarian purpose; it is usually erected as a focal-point in a park or large garden. (2) The detached wing or wings of a large house, connected to it by colonnades or walls. (3) A modern structure adjacent to a sports field in which players can change and from which spectators can watch.

Paw foot. An animal paw has been used as a terminal on table and seat legs since antiquity; it is found on ancient Egyptian furniture. The most common is the lion or bear paw, which attained its greatest popularity in the early nineteenth-century (English) Regency, and French and American Empire.

An 18th century pavilion

The Grotto Pavilion at Pushkino, near Leningrad, by Rastrelli, 1744-63

Pavilions flanking Carton, County Kildare, Ireland, designed by Richard Cassels, 1739

axton, Joseph (1803–65). ritish gardener, engineer, archict, and town-planner. Paxton as one of the most remarkable d versatile men of his time, for e started with no advantages d at the time of his death was e of the most eminent men in ngland. He was born in Bedrdshire, the son of a small rmer, and was employed at an rly age in the establishment of e 6th Duke of Devonshire as rdener, first at Chiswick and ter at Chatsworth. At the age 23 he was appointed head rdener at Chatsworth. He soon came land-agent and business viser to the duke, and their iendship resulted in travels toether on a Grand Tour empassing Switzerland, Spain, aly, and Greece.

Among Paxton's preoccupations at Chatsworth was the design of greenhouses, which were built to ever-larger dimensions as his practical knowledge and confidence increased. Early in his career he began experiments on a 'ridge and furrow' system of building large glazed structures, which eradicated the necessity for a raftered supporting roof. Paxton's largest structure of this kind, the Great Conservatory, built between 1836 and 1840, was 277 ft long, 123 ft wide, and 67 ft high, and was built on a laminated timber frame supported by hollow cast-iron columns. Another large glass building was the Lily House, built in 1849. The expertise acquired by Paxton was given still greater scope by the building

of the Great Exhibition of 1851, for which he was knighted. This vast prefabricated structure (based on a 24-foot module) was the largest building ever erected, being 1,800 ft long and 770,000 square ft in area. It was also a masterly demonstration of the use of factory-made, site-assembled units. The building was afterwards taken down and reassembled as the Crystal Palace at Sydenham; it was destroyed by fire in 1936.

Paxton's career was now in full swing. He was elected Liberal MP for Coventry in 1854, designed large mansions in England, Ireland, and France; and at the same time continued to supervise the landscaping of the Chatsworth grounds and various public parks, including that at

Birkenhead (1843–7). He was also interested in the development of railways; hydraulic engineering (including the construction of the world's highest fountain jet); and town-planning projects.

Peardrop handle. Small hinged handle resembling an elongated pear; usually made of brass. These handles occur on drawers and doors from the late seventeenth century.

Pearl ware. 'Pearl white', as Josiah Wedgwood called this body, which he introduced in 1779, was much whiter than the cream-coloured earthenware he had perfected in the 1760s. It was also heavier than creamware and had a bluish grey tinge. It was copied almost immediately by other potters, though it never achieved the popularity of Queensware.

The Leeds Pottery made some good pearl ware, including magnificent horses, some 16 in high, which were especially made for advertising display by harness-makers and chemists specializing in veterinary supplies.

Tableware, including frog mugs and jugs, was also made in pearl ware, though it was quickly superseded by the blue transfer-printed tableware introduced by Josiah Spode in the 1780s.

Pearwood. *Pyrus communis.* The traditional wood for rustic furniture. When used for inlay

The Crystal Palace designed by Paxton for the Great Exhibition of 1851

The 'conservative' wall at Chatsworth, Derbyshire, designed by Paxton, 1836–40

Pearl ware jug, Leeds

411

An early Louis XV péché-mortel

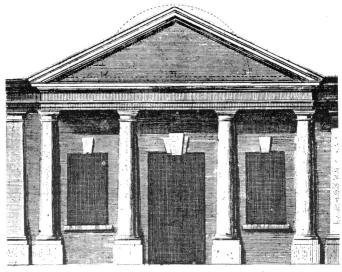

A pediment surmounting a Tuscan portico

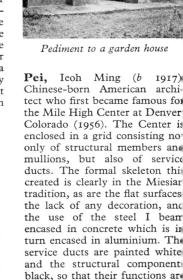

Pediment to a garden house

work in the seventeenth century it was usually stained black to make a cheap imitation of ebony. During the seventeenth and eighteenth centuries pearwood was also used for picture frames and bracket clocks. Pear and lime were the woods favoured for the carvings of Grinling Gibbons and his school.

Péché-mortel. A two-part couch described by Chippendale in his *Director* as 'made to take asunder in the Middle; one Part makes a large Easy-Chair; and the other a stool': an eighteenth-century forerunner of modern easy-chair cane footstool design.

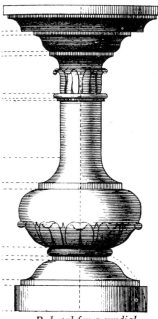

Pedestal for a sundial

Pedestal. A term first used in classical architecture, in which the pedestal is the base or substructure supporting a column of one of the architectural orders.

It was later adapted by cabinet-makers and is used in two senses. The first applies to sets of cupboards or drawers within a pedestal, used in pairs to support a table or desk. The second refers to the solitary central support of a table-top or chair, fixed or revolving.

The term is also applied to the decorative tapering bases used as supports for sculpture, as well as to the stands flanking the sideboard table of Adam design. In this the pedestals were surmounted by vase-shaped knife cases.

Pediment. A triangular-shaped gable-end applied to Greek and Roman temples, usually sup-

ported on a colonnade. This feature was widely adopted and freely adapted by Renaissance architects for interior and exterior work in domestic architecture; this tendency was reinforced by the villas of Palladio, in which the pediment was a major decorative element. The triangular pediment was elaborated into a series of ornamented variants, the triangle frequently carrying a decorative design within the tympanum or space enclosed by the sides of the triangular mouldings. Another widely used variant was the broken pediment, in which the triangle lacked an apex. Other variants carried scrolls and various decorative devices. The degree of projection of the pediment from the shell of the building was also changed. For example, the pediment over a doorcase projected only slightly from the wall, given apparent support by pilasters rather than columns.

Pei, Ieoh Ming (*b* 1917) Chinese-born American architect who first became famous for the Mile High Center at Denver Colorado (1956). The Center is enclosed in a grid consisting not only of structural members and mullions, but also of service ducts. The formal skeleton this created is clearly in the Miesian tradition, as are the flat surfaces the lack of any decoration, and the use of the steel I beam encased in concrete which is in turn encased in aluminium. The service ducts are painted white and the structural components black, so that their functions are clearly advertised on the outside.

Another of Pei's distinguished achievements was his design for the redevelopment of Philadelphia's Washington Square area (Society Hill), which was adopted in 1960. His famous streamlined towers became a fact of the

A mahogany pedestal desk by Thomas Chippendale

Redevelopment of Washington Square, Philadelphia, by Pei, 1960

Two medieval pendants from churches

A Scottish pele tower

A pendentive

broad development of this historic area, brilliantly relating the nineteenth to the twentieth-century city.

Pele tower (sometimes known as peel tower). A term indigenous to the border county of northern England and Scotland. It describes a tower built as a form of domestic fortification; most are small, consisting of little more than a keep. Pele towers were no longer built after the sixteenth century.

Pelmet. An addition at the head of a window, usually decoratively draped, designed to frame the window and complement the side curtains. In the seventeenth and eighteenth centuries, pelmets were comparatively simple decorations; the fabrics were attached to a three-sided stiffened case, usually of wood, known as a lambrequin. During the nineteenth century, however, the pelmet developed into an important feature in interior schemes, the draperies being festooned, pleated, and gathered into voluminous overhanging drapes.

Pembroke table. A term of unknown derivation, occasionally but improbably foisted on the 'architect Earl', the 9th Earl of Pembroke. The Pembroke table is a particular form of small light table with hinged side flaps.

Pendant. Ornamental plaster bosses, normally elongated, suspended from late Gothic vaulting, and, carved, in Tudor hammer-beam roof trusses.

Pendentive. The curved triangular section or concave-shaped spandrel which is made by the angle of two walls forming

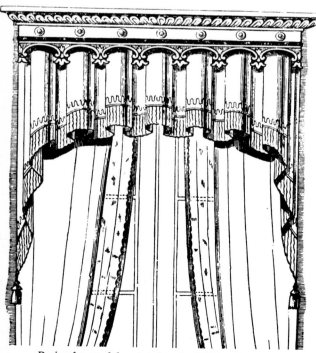

Design for an elaborate pelmet by J C Loudon, 1860

A design for a Pembroke table by Hepplewhite

A rose-covered pergola in a garden in Madrid

Perpendicular vaulting in King's College Chapel, Cambridge

part of the base of a domed roof. The pendentive is an essential strengthening element in the support of a dome. It was used most frequently in Renaissance church architecture, although it had a place in Byzantine and Romanesque churches; and it was also employed in secular architecture, following Palladio's adaptation of the temple form for domestic buildings.

Pennsylvania Dutch. See **American furniture.**

Pentastyle. Term descriptive of a temple with five columns across its front or portico.

Penthouse. Formerly a term applied to an attic structure formed by a lean-to roof added to the roof of any large building. The word is now used almost exclusively to describe self-contained, separately roofed living quarters on the top of a large apartment, building, or hotel.

Percier, Charles (1764–1838). French architect. See **Fontaine**.

Perfume burners. Elaborate and decorative vessels in which substances were placed to smoulder and give off a pleasing smell. Most were vase-shaped with ormolu mounts, and were made in the eighteenth century. They were also called essence pots or cassolets.

Pergola. A covered or part-covered garden structure, made by a double line of spaced posts supporting joists and forming a frame for climbing plants.

Peripteral. The architectural term to describe a building surrounded by a single row of pillars.

Peristyle. The term used to describe a group of columns set about a building or courtyard.

Pernambuco wood. *Caesalpinia Brasilensis*. A type of Brazil wood similar to Cuban mahogany. It is a glossy, orange-hued wood that was employed for inlay work, particularly during the seventeenth century.

Perpendicular. The last phase of English Gothic, from *c* 1360 to *c* 1550. The style is dominated by vertical and horizontal lines (hence its name), and one of the most characteristic motifs is the panel with a cusped arch-head used as a blind wall decoration, or in rows as window tracery. The windows were extremely large, and transoms were usually introduced as supports.

The naves of churches and cathedrals were usually without triforiums; they had only large clerestory windows above the nave arcades. Fan vaulting in various degrees of elaboration was a feature of Perpendicular.

The extensive Perpendicular work is in parish churches and chapels, since the major ecclesiastical buildings had already been begun in earlier Gothic style. Additions were, however, made to many cathedrals, eg a chancel at Gloucester and naves at Canterbury and Winchester. But the most famous Perpendicular buildings are chapels: King's College Chapel, Cambridge; St George's Chapel, Windsor; and Henry VIII's Chapel at Westminster Abbey.

Perrault, Claude (1613–88). French amateur architect who is known for his work on the great Colonnade du Louvre (ie east façade), begun in 1667. He was a doctor with a wide scientific training before taking up architecture. He was partly responsible for the east façade, in which the architect Le Vau and the painter Le Brun also had a hand. It is a very finely balanced façade: the central section and the two end sections are integrated by the skilful use of coupled columns which extend across the entire width. Perrault also designed the Observatory

The east façade of the Louvre, Paris, designed by Perrault, 1667

An apartment block in Paris designed by Auguste Perret, 1903

The perron leading to the piano nobile at Kedleston, Derbyshire

1667) and the Château de Sceaux (1674). In 1673 he published *Les Dix Livres d'Architecture de Vitruve* (enlarged 1684).

Perret, Auguste (1874–1954). French architect. Although most of Perret's work was done in

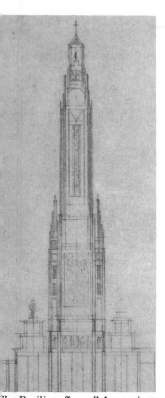

The Basilique Jean d'Arc project, Paris, by Perret, 1826

France, he was born in Brussels. He trained at the Paris Ecole des Beaux Arts, but did not stay long enough to take his final examinations. He then entered the family building business, and had started designing buildings in concrete before he was 20. About this time he began to be preoccupied with methods of reinforced concrete construction. His structural experiments were far in advance of those being carried out elsewhere, and his technical originality was widely acknowledged. Perret also showed, for example, in a design for an apartment house in Rue Franklin, Paris, that concrete could give fresh vitality and an austere simplicity to façades that were normally little more than repetitions of traditional models. His designs undoubtedly gave a highly personal distinction to the use of the new material.

Perret added a number of distinguished buildings to the French heritage, notably the Church of Notre-Dame at Le Raincy (built in 1922–3), one of the classics of modern ecclesiastical architecture and a majestically austere reinterpretation of the Gothic theme. Perret also brought the same intellectual clarity to bear upon the many villas and studios he built. In these his exactitude and distinction in planning and detailing, and his preoccupation with proportion, give his designs a certain affinity with the later steel-and-glass structures of Mies van der

Rohe. His incomparable technical skill in handling large-scale concrete structures brought Perret commissions for industrial projects throughout his life, ranging from warehouses (Casablanca, 1915) to aircraft hangars (Marseilles, 1950).

Perron. The term applied to an exterior flight of steps rising to the *piano nobile* (qv) of a house. It thus constitutes the main entrance to a house, though not necessarily the most frequently used.

Persian carpets. Carpets and rugs from Persia are the finest from the Orient. They are unequalled in technique, design,

and colour. They were manufactured in antiquity, but none have survived. There are, however, many from the sixteenth and seventeenth centuries, a great period in which Persia was ruled by Tasmak (1524–77) and Shah Abbas (1588–1629). The most important of these famous carpets and designs are the prayer rug with *mihrab* (the pattern of the Moorish arch sometimes pointed at the top); the medallion pattern with a large central design and canted corners; the vase carpet with central motif; carpets with scenes of hunting; and the garden carpet or flower carpet. The garden carpet with its massed trees and plants and a background network of stems, is

Persian carpet from Kashan with floral motifs

415

Baroque Persians supporting an entablature and balcony

A pewter teapot made by William Will (1764-96) of Philadelphia

Ornamental carving on the end panels of pews, c 1500

perhaps the most beautiful of all; the world-famous Ardabil carpet which took one man a lifetime to make, is of this type. The Persians were the only Muslim people whose carpets included men and animals (in hunting carpets), which are realistically represented; other makers limited their designs to flowers. Other centres of manufacture were Isfahan, Tabriz, Kerman, Kershan, Feraghan, Sehna, Saruk, and Herat. Herat carpets are the very best, and are particularly associated with the small recurring leaf pattern (popularly supposed to be a fish) and rosettes.

Persians. Sculptured figures of men used instead of columns as supports for a cornice.

Pew. An ecclesiastical term which has undergone several changes in definition over the centuries. Originally the pew was the raised platform, dais, or desk from which the priest addressed the congregation. Later the word was applied to enclosed seats on a low platform which were reserved for the socially important members of the congregation. Such pews were in effect small sealed-off rooms with their own panelled doors. Finally the term was applied to all forms of seating within a church which had end-panels, boards, or wainscoting, usually panelled and carved or decorated. The rows of seating thus enclosed or semi-enclosed

were arranged so that a broad passage was left down the middle of the nave, with narrower passages down each aisle and cross passage.

Pewter. Pewter is an alloy; the term is applied equally to the tin and lead of the Romans and the more various combinations of copper, zinc, antimony, bismuth, and even silver. Copper tended to strengthen the alloy; and so was used for hollow ware such as tankards and bowls, which were frequently cast in moulds. Standard proportions were drawn up by the medieval guilds but varied from country to country. If decorated at all, tankards and vessels were usually engraved whereas flatware was simply punched with dye stamps.

Phyfe or **Phyffe**, Duncan (1768-1854). American cabinet maker, considered by some the greatest of all American cabinet

Voltaire chair made by Duncan Phyfe

A mahogany couch by Duncan Phyfe, 1810

akers. He was certainly the
ost fashionable in the New
ork of his day. He employed
ore than a hundred craftsmen
his shop, and was a furniture
anufacturer rather than simply
craftsman. He was the son of
n immigrant Scotsman who
rrived in America in 1783–4.
he son was established in New
ork by 1792, and later had
remises in the fashionable Par-
tion (later Fulton) Street, which
njoyed a reputation similar to
hat of St Martin's Lane in
ondon. Phyfe's shop became
he most popular in the street.

His work was of high quality,
and he was able to provide the
well-to-do with furniture in the
European fashion: he was strongly influenced by Sheraton's
pattern-books, the furniture of
Thomas Hope, and the French
Empire furniture. Phyfe's long
career (he did not retire until
1847) spanned the whole classical
period. He produced furniture
during every phase, constructed
of the finest San Domingo
mahogany. Phyfe tables were
supported upon a vase-shaped
pedestal and sabre legs with
brass feet.

Phyfe was the leading maker
in New York in the late 1790s,
but by the 1830s the quality of
his furniture had declined considerably and he had given way
to the over-ornateness so characteristic of nineteenth-century
work. He retired and sold his
stock in 1847. He died in 1854,
leaving a considerable fortune.

Piano nobile. Literally, in
Italian, the noble floor – an essentially accurate description of the
first floor in the grander Italian
houses of the Renaissance. This
was the principal floor, one
storey above the kitchens and
service rooms on the ground
floor. It consisted of a series of
reception and ante rooms normally set out en suite. In architecture the *piano nobile* is an
essential feature of large houses
in town and country.

Piazza (Italian *piazza*; French
place; Spanish *plaza*). An Italian
term applied to any open square
or area enclosed by buildings.
This essentially Continental urban device has received increasing study during the century by
planners of New Towns, and as
a result the pedestrian precinct
has become an essential feature
of urban developments. 'Precinct'
defines the same kind of enclosure, but architects seem to
avoid it, probably because of its
ecclesiastical associations.

Picture clock. This was in
fashion at the end of the eighteenth century. It was quite
literally a picture with a clock
mechanism: a dial was incorporated somewhere in the scene,
frequently on a clock tower.
Mechanised movements oc-
curred, eg figures engaging in
some simple activity and water
apparently flowing.

Picturesque. The term originally used in landscape design to
describe a romantic man-made
garden which gives an impression
of untrammelled Nature while
incorporating a judicious assem-

Piano nobile at the Upper Belvedere, Vienna, by Hildebrandt

The Covent Garden Piazza, London, designed by Inigo Jones, 1630

The picturesque dairy at Blaise Hamlet by Nash, 1803

A pier glass and table from Chippendale's 'Director'

bly of appropriately 'rural' buildings. The term derives from publications issued in 1794 by two neighbouring Herefordshire squires. In *An Essay on the Picturesque*, Sir Uvedale Price (1747–1829) may be said to have coined the term, or at least claimed it for himself as far as posterity is concerned. In the same year Richard Payne Knight (1750–1824) issued *The Landscape – A didactic Poem*, addressed to Price. This is a sustained versified catalogue of the elements of landscape design favoured by Price and Knight. They are epitomized in the lines:

O! *waft me hence, to some*
  neglected vale;
Where, shelter'd, I may court
  the western gale.

These publications aroused the resentment of Humphry Repton, who regarded them as a slight upon his own and Capability Brown's achievements in revolutionizing English parklands and landscape gardens. Yet all four men were basically pursuing the same ideal: the taming of nature in order to make nature seem more natural. Ironically, Brown and Repton did more to inculcate ideas of the Picturesque than the two squires, who are now known only to specialist students.

Pie crust table. A small tripod table with a circular top that has a carved scalloped edge. Pie crust tables are usually made of mahogany, and date from the second half of the eighteenth century.

Pier. A word of several meanings in architecture and building. (1) A solid massive construction in stone, brick, or concrete, designed to bear a load or counter the thrust of an arch or wall. (2) The solid areas of walls between piercings by doors and windows (hence pier-glass, qv). (3) Pillars in Romanesque and Gothic architecture. (4) A land-based extension into the sea, usually built on massive lines and occasionally supported on pillars or piles.

Piercing. See **Silver, decorative techniques.**

Pier glass. A vertical looking-glass with a carved giltwood frame, designed to fit the space or pier between two windows. It was usually placed above a specially designed console or pier table.

Pier table. A form of side table designed to stand against a pier. Some were console tables, but in the late eighteenth century many were made in pairs, of light construction with semi-circular tops and slender legs.

Pietra-dura. An expensive form of mosaic made up of hard and semi-precious stones such as agate, amethyst, jasper, and lapis lazuli. It is also called Florentine mosaic work, and appears on table-tops and in inlay work on cabinets.

Pilaster. A shallow section of a pillar, based on one of the orders, built against the face of a wall; it can also be a segmental section of a column. Generally the pilaster does not project from the wall by more than one-third of its width. It was originally a structural element, acting as a form of buttress to a wall, but it later became a decorative device and was much used in Renaissance and later architecture.

Pilaster strip. See **Lesene.**

Pilgrim period. A term used in America to describe the Jacobean phase of New England furniture design.

Pillar. A vertical, free-standing structural member which bears a load. Unlike the column, which is invariably cylindrical, the pillar can be of any section – square, polygonal, or columnar – and of any material (though a timber pillar is usually called a post).

Pillar carpet. See **Chinese carpets.**

Pilotis (French, 'stilts'). Pillars beneath a building that raise it above ground level. The term was introduced to describe the architecture of Le Corbusier in particular. In this, high buildings are raised upon reinforced concrete pillars, freeing the ground-floor area for use as **car-parks**, playgrounds, etc. The *pilotis*

Pilasters on an exterior and in room scheme

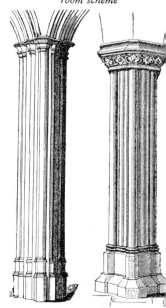

Two perpendicular pillars

Pilotis by Le Corbusier

An engraving by Piranesi of the Piazza of St Peter's Rome

system was used most dramatically in Le Corbusier's Unité d'Habitation at Marseilles, in which 38 great *pilotis* were used, each carrying a load of 2,000 tons.

Pinchbeck. A common gold substitute used for jewellery and

Ornamental pineapple

clock-making. It was invented by the clockmaker Christopher Pinchbeck in 1732, and was an alloy of copper in zinc.

Pine. *Pinus.* A variety of types of this wood is to be found in America and Europe. Pine is a softwood, easily worked, and it has always been a practical and popular choice for country furniture, as well as for building and floors.

Pineapple. A popular motif for decoration in architecture and furniture. It is commonly found in stone masonry (on gateways and garden ornaments) and finials on clocks. Silver pineapple cups (*Ananas Pokal*) were made in Germany in the late sixteenth· century. They were tall, the main body consisting of one to four pineapples and were frequently supported upon a figure and surmounted by a finial.

Pinnacle (Italian *pinacolo*). A small turret, or tapered ornamental feature, consisting of shaft and finial. It terminates or crowns a spire, or buttress, or the angle of a parapet. It was much used in Gothic architecture. Although seemingly ornamental, the pinnacle, in fact, countered the outward thrust of roof trusses.

Piranesi, Giovanni Battista (1720–78). Italian artist, born in Venice. Piranesi trained as an

engineer and architect, settling in Rome in his mid-twenties. There he became interested in the antiquities of the city and began a series of drawings and engravings of the ruins, and imaginative reconstructions of the ancient city as it might have been, which was to exert a profound influence on architects of the Neo-classical and Romantic movements. He was a staunch Roman, and in his engravings in *Della magnificenza ed architettura de' Romani* (1761), extolled the virtues of Roman architecture, arguing that it was greater than Greek architecture. He further developed this theme four years later in his book *Parere sull'architettura,* delving more deeply into the past for what he believed could be a more imaginative contemporary style. Yet his designs for the church of S Maria del Priorato at Rome (1764–6) are disappointing, in that Piranesi failed to realize the ideas implicit in his engravings.

Piscina (Latin, 'a reservoir of water'). Originally applied to the tanks or fountains of Roman baths. The word now more usually refers to the shallow stone basin in a niche near the altar; the priest uses it to wash altar vessels. It is called a pillar piscina when free-standing.

Planewood. *Platanus acerifolia.* A durable white wood. The English variety is sometimes referred to as English sycamore.

According to Sheraton, planewood was often employed in preference to beech for 'painted chairs, or the flyjoint rails of car and pembroke tables' (*Cabinet Dictionary,* 1803).

Planted moulding. A moulding that is worked independently

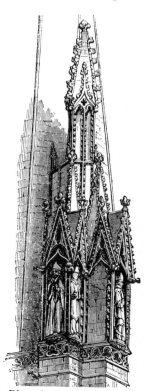

Pinnacle in Oxford, c 1280

Plaques on the Courtauld Institute at Portman Square by Adam

and then applied to the surface. Another name is stuck moulding.

Plaque. A tablet of round, oval, or rectangular shape that is used decoratively on internal and external surfaces; it may be attached or inlaid, and made of metal, porcelain, or any decorative material. Eighteenth-century Sèvres or low-relief Wedgwood ceramic plaques adorn the doors of very many cabinets and commodes.

Plasterwork. Decorative stucco work used in the interior of buildings. Plasterers have existed

Louis XVI secrétaire à abattant with Sèvres panel

since ancient times, but plasterwork acquired artistic significance only from Renaissance times. Baroque and Rococo plasterwork are supreme examples of the art. Fruit and flowers, *putti* and portrait medallions, are executed with amazing realism and delicacy. On occasion the work is in such high relief that the bird or flower is scarcely attached to the wall. The plasterers or *stuccodores* modelled the stucco while it was still wet, a procedure requiring great skill. They were frequently organized into guilds, and it is possible to identify regional schools as well as the work of individual masters. Although the art is mainly associated with southern Europe, other countries have produced skilful plasterers and schools, such as the Dublin school of the eighteenth century.

Plastic furniture. The production of plastic furniture has increased steadily since the 1940s. In plastic furniture almost unlimited variations of colour and shape are possible, and virtually any curve can be moulded into the furniture.

Plastics were first used in chair-making in 1949, when Charles Eames developed the first glass-fibre reinforced plastic chair. Back, seat, and arms were all moulded in one piece. From that time plastics were widely used as a component material, but not until the 1960s was the injection and press moulding of plastics fully exploited. Moulded polyurethane and injection moulded polypropylene are of most consequence to mass pro-

Plasterwork dining room ceiling at Osterley by Robert Adam

The hall of St Vincent's Hospital at St Stephen's Green, Dublin

The builder and his wife depicted in plasterwork Co Antrim, c 1700

Italian sculpture chair made of polyurethane

The 'Fiorenza' plastic chair designed by Motomi Kawakani

duction. Robin Day's polyprop chair (1963) is one of the most successful examples, made of polypropylene: it is strong, flexible, and cheap to manufacture, and is mass produced in 23 different countries. This chair has a metal frame, in contrast to the rigid moulding of Eero Aarnio's pastilli chair, which has no legs and sits squat upon the ground – a complete departure from traditional concepts of the chair. Inflatable seat furniture such as the Italian blow-up chair of PVC film was being made by 1967, and is now in increasing supply as manufacturers produce different versions.

Tables are also made of hard plastic, eg the Parson's table. The most recent innovation in bedding is the water bed, constructed of a pliable plastic to contain water, and dispensing with the traditional frame, mainspring, and mattress.

Plat band. An architectural term for a flat-faced moulding of greater width than projection.

Plumes on a state bed

Plinth. The lowest projecting member of a wall, column, or pedestal.

Ploughed. Term that describes a grooved surface. The name comes from the tool – the adjustable plane or plough – that is used to form the groove.

Plum. *Prunus domestica.* This is a hard and heavy wood with a brownish hue, rather similar to West Indian mahogany. It was used during the sixteenth and seventeenth centuries for rustic furniture, and occasionally for decorative work.

Plumes. Ostrich feathers were used as luxurious finials on the testers of state beds (qqv), and are also found in groups of three or five, carved in chair backs of the late eighteenth century. See **Prince of Wales feathers.**

Plum mottle. A repeating figure found on mahogany veneers; it is a small, dark, plumlike shape.

Plymouth porcelain. In 1768 William Cookworthy founded a factory at Coxside, Plymouth, for the manufacture of hard-paste porcelain; he used the kaolin he had discovered some years earlier in Cornwall. The factory was transferred to Bristol in 1770, where it remained in production for eleven years. Cookworthy retired soon after the transfer, and the factory was taken over by Richard Champion.

Early Plymouth figures are often discoloured with smoke, and many have sagged out of shape during the firing, or developed firing cracks. The paste was hard, intractable, and not at all easy to model in fine detail. The glaze was cold and

glittering. The Cookworthy figures are mostly adaptations of those made at Longton Hall (qv). They stand on Rococo scroll bases. The later figures made by Champion are technically more competent, and are mounted on a rocky mound or a square base.

Ornamental pieces were also made, and so was tableware, some of it decorated in the Oriental manner with a blue underglaze. It included armorial porcelain, made to special order.

Plywood. An industrially produced wood consisting of several thicknesses of timber glued face to face, with the grains of each pair placed at right angles. It achieves maximum strength from the accumulation of grains. Manufacturers produce plywood in such a variety of forms that it can serve many purposes. Two typical methods of construction are (a) a series of veneers glued together; and (b) a lumber core, which is a hard timber core to which a thin covering of veneers has been attached.

Plywood was first patented in America in 1865, and has been extensively used ever since. After World War II, production was greatly increased for a variety of

manufacturing techniques. Today it is an extremely useful and an occasionally pleasing material.

Pocock, William Fuller (1779–1849). British architect and decorator. Pocock was the son of a builder operating on a fairly large scale in north London, and was apprenticed to him. Later he was allowed to become

William Fuller Pocock

Plymouth porcelain figures of the four continents, 1770

Designs for the decorative treatment of a window recess by Pocock

The Water Tower at Posen, Berlin, designed by Hans Poelzig, 1910

A pointed arch

Gio Ponti

an architect and was accepted as a student at the Royal Academy Schools. Pocock's practice was unusually varied, ranging from villas to monuments, from schools to alms-houses. He was also responsible for designs for a number of buildings overseas. Unlike most architects of his time, he was concerned with the interior decoration of his buildings, and many of his Neo-classical schemes are of considerable distinction. He published a number of books on design and decoration, including *Architectural Designs for Rustic Cottages, Rural Dwellings, and Villas* (1807), *Modern Furnishings for Rooms* (1811), and *Observations on Bond of Brickwork* (1839).

Podium. A continuous projecting base or pedestal; also the raised platform surrounding the arena in an amphitheatre.

Poelzig, Hans (1869–1936). German architect and teacher whose work influenced much contemporary German architecture. He was a professor and later director of the School of Arts and Crafts in Breslau (1900–16), and professor of architecture at the Charlottenburg technical college in Berlin.

Poelzig's Water Tower at Posen (1910), built over an exhibition hall, was one of the first Expressionist buildings. After World War I he continued to design highly imaginative Expressionistic buildings like the Grosses Schauspielhaus, Berlin (1920), with its interior of dripping stalactites. His later industrial works, eg the office building for I G Farben at Frankfurt (1929), are monumental but orthodoxly modern. The office building at Breslau (1911) is remarkable for its prophetic design of horizontal bands of windows, a feature that was to become common in the 1920s.

Pointed arch. The term applied to any form of traditional Gothic arch in which the two vertical sides of the intrados curve inwards to a point. These arcs are described from centres on the springing line. The pointed arch was introduced to Europe from the Middle East at the end of the eleventh century.

Poker work. A simple method of decorating wood: the design was carved out with a hot poker, after which the charred areas were cleaned out and smoothed. The nineteenth-century Arts and Crafts Movement revived interest in this and similar techniques.

Pole screen. See under **Fire screen.**

Pompeian style. This term has been used loosely, especially in the nineteenth century, to describe furniture in the Neo-classical style. However, there have been rooms decorated in a more genuinely Pompeian style, prompted by the excavations that took place at Pompeii in the mid-eighteenth century. One such example is the ballroom at Castletown House in Eire, with small detailed decoration and a series of minute figures similar to those still to be seen at Pompeii.

Ponti, Gio (*b* 1891). Italian architect. Ponti was born in Milan, and has spent most of his life there. At first he wanted to become an artist (he has continued to draw and paint), but then turned to architecture, studying in his native city. From the first, he was preoccupied with

A seaside house designed by Gio Ponti, 1940

The Pirelli Building in Milan designed by Gio Ponti and others, 1955-9

new technological developments rather than traditional styles, although in his earlier designs he sought to link the new technology with the symmetry of Neo-classical designs. Ponti played little part in the architectural controversies of the inter-war period, and did not even join the famous *gruppo 7*, the architectural co-operative founded in 1926, which had a pronounced Milanese bias. Instead, pursuing his individual course, in 1928 he founded *Domus*. This became (and has remained) one of the world's leading magazines concerned with architecture and industrial and interior design.

For 40 years Ponti's achievements have had a profound influence upon modern Italian architecture, although, like Le Corbusier, he was more honoured abroad than at home. His early Italian commissions included the Institute of Mathematics for the University of Rome (1934) and an office building for the Montecatini Company in Milan (1936). He also designed projects in South America, Sweden, and France. In 1958 he designed the now world-famous Pirelli building in Milan, with Luigi Nervi (qv) as consulting structural engineer. This building, with its elongated hexagonal plan and superbly shaped and tapering façades, made an impact upon the city's town-planning schemes out of all proportion to its size and scope.

More recent buildings designed by Ponti, in conjunction with his partners, include a second building for the Montecatini Company, a hospital, churches, and commercial buildings in Milan, a number of public buildings for Islamabad, the new capital of Pakistan, and offices in Baghdad, where he was appointed consultant to the development board. He has lectured

The Institute of Mathematics, Rome University, by Ponti

widely in Italy and abroad.

Ponti has continued throughout his career to maintain a close and practical interest in industrial design, ranging from cutlery to bathroom fittings, and has continued to edit *Domus* with authority and energy.

Pontypool japanning. A process introduced at Pontypool, Monmouthshire, in the late nineteenth century. It involved the decoration of tin articles with bright colours and a heavy protective varnish; the designs were usually floral or landscapes.

Poole pottery. Pottery has been made on a commercial scale at Poole in Dorset, England, at least since the middle of the last century. The firm of Carter and Co was started by Jesse Carter in 1873, chiefly for the production of ceramic tiles and decorative lustre pottery inspired by Art Nouveau. Owen Carter made decorative pottery in Edwardian times, and after World War I architectural faience was made to designs by Harold Stabler.

Carter, Stabler, and Adams started the Poole Pottery, in 1921. Truda Carter was responsible for much of the pastel-coloured decorative ware that

was made during the 1920–30 period; it was ornamented by brushstroke designs of flowers on an eggshell glazed ware.

Pope, John Russell (1874–1937). American architect whose work represents two aspects of the so-called Academic Revival at the turn of the century. One is the 'American Renaissance', which he represents in the sense that he modelled his work on European High Renaissance buildings of extreme formality and symmetry. This, rather than stylistic or chronological affinities, is what his models have in common: the Hill House, Washington DC (1909), is

A Poole vase, 1930s

423

Broad Street Railway Station, Richmond, Virginia, by J R Pope, 1817

The Zwinger in Dresden designed by Pöppelmann

modelled on Inigo Jones's Queen's House at Greenwich in England; the Brazilian Embassy, Washington (1913), is modelled on Peruzzi's Palazzo Massimi in Rome.

Other buildings by Pope are essays in archaeological reconstruction. The most famous example, the Temple of Scottish Rite at Washington (1916), reconstructs the Mausoleum at Halicarnassus in a plausibly 'classical' spirit of calmness and formalism. Both of Pope's styles reflect the desire for order prevalent among his generation, which could not find satisfaction in merely following the examples of the *Ecole des Beaux Arts* in Paris.

Poplar. *Populus.* The two most important varieties of this light, soft wood are the black and white poplars. Although not particularly strong, these woods were employed in the sixteenth and seventeenth centuries for inlay work, and occasionally for marquetry.

Pöppelmann, Matthäus Daniel (1662–1736). German late Baroque architect. Pöppelmann was born in Westphalia and became court architect to Augustus the Strong, elector of Saxony, in 1705. Three years later he became a privy councillor and went abroad, visiting Rome and Vienna, where he found inspiration for the proposed Dresden Palace in the work of Carlo Fontana and Hildebrandt. On his return, designs were drawn up, but only the Zwinger, a rectangular building for fêtes and tournaments, was actually erected.

The Zwinger was a pleasure ground for the court, laid out with lawns and fountains and enclosed by fantastic gateways and single-storeyed galleries. Pöppelmann's style is clear and inventive, untouched by the florid, heavy handling that mars much Baroque work. He collaborated with Balthasar Permoser, a Bavarian sculptor who created mythological figures of remarkable vigour for the Zwinger; between them, Pöppelmann and Permoser made it a masterpiece of design and decoration. The Zwinger now survives only in reconstruction, the original having been destroyed in World War II.

Poppyhead. A carved ornamental finial for bench or pew ends, representing animals, figures, foliage, etc. 'Poupée head' is a common but incorrect version of the term.

Porcelain. A fine, extremely hard, translucent ceramic ware. The first hard-paste or true porcelain was manufactured in China in the late thirteenth century (see **Chinese porcelain**). It was made of china clay (kaolin) and feldspathic rock, and was fired at a high temperature. Europeans admired Chinese porcelain, and made many attempts to discover the secret of its manufacture; success was achieved only in the early eighteenth century at Meissen. Softpaste porcelain was made by adding powdered glass to the clay, and was fired at a lower temperature; in England boneash was also added. Present-day bone china (qv) is made by combining hard-paste porcelain with bone-ash.

Porch. A small roofed structure that decorates and protects an outside door. It is usually supported on posts or columns.

Medieval and Victorian porches

A Charles II porringer and cover, dated 1671

Porringer. Alternatively called a caudle-cup or posset-pot. This lidded, two-handled piece seems to have superseded the taller standing-cup in the seventeenth century, and survived well into the eighteenth.

Portal (Latin, *porta* 'a door or gate'). An entrance of monumental character such as are found on Gothic cathedrals and Renaissance palaces.

Portcullis. A massive protective grid, usually constructed of oak with terminals of spiked iron. It was suspended above the entrance to a castle, normally at the gatehouse doors; there was frequently a second portcullis at the inner entrance to the gatehouse. By means of vertical grooves or slides the portcullis could be swiftly lowered at the threat of enemy attack. Examples of the portcullis can be seen in England at Bodiam Castle and at the Tower of London.

Portcullis at Hever Castle

Victorian porte-cochère at the St Pancras Station Hotel, London

Porte-cochère. A covered entrance to a house which is large and wide enough to admit a carriage, allowing guests to alight before the entrance door. The device is used on a grander scale in some commercial buildings, enabling vehicles to make collections and deliveries under cover.

Porter's chair. A distinctive type of chair, found in the halls of most large country and town houses during the eighteenth century. It is leather-upholstered, with enclosed sides extending upwards into a hood so that the manservant could sit near the door while being protected from draughts.

Portfolio stand. A stand in which prints could be stored. During the eighteenth and nineteenth centuries, when print-collecting was common, these wooden stands stood in drawing-rooms so that the prints were easily accessible. Portfolios of prints could even be hired for social occasions.

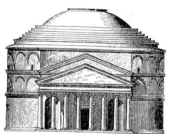

Portico on the Pantheon

Portico. The most widely used of all the decorative devices introduced into domestic architecture by Palladio, who adopted it as a result of his study of temple architecture. The portico is usually intended to impress at first sight: an imposing porch is made still more imposing by such features as a pediment supported on columns, and a wide flight of steps leading up to the portico. During the eighteenth century, a handsome portico became a mandatory element in all new mansions, and porticoes were added to the existing façades of many older houses. Throughout the nineteenth century the portico was an essential feature of almost all public buildings of consequence, from theatres and museums to town halls. They figured prominently on churches despite their pagan associations.

Portmeirion pottery. A pottery founded by Susan Williams-Ellis and her husband Euan Cooper-Willis in 1962.

A 19th century porter's chair

They took over two old-established Staffordshire pottery factories, Grays and Kirkhams. Kirkhams had been makers of scientific and chemists' pottery for many years (bleeding bowls and leech jars being in their catalogues until a comparatively recent date). Inspired by the simple and pleasing shapes of this ware, and helped by the technical skill of the pottery workers at Kirkhams, Susan Williams-Ellis designed a whole range of kitchenware, ovenware, tankards, boxes, and coffee sets. The simplicity of the shapes and the striking brilliance of the colours represented a new conception of traditional pottery.

Postern. A term that can now be applied to almost any door or gate at the rear of a house. In

Postern gate at Caernarvon

Early pottery from Acoma Indian Pueblo, New Mexico

The interior of Coleshill, Berkshire, by Sir Roger Pratt

medieval times the postern was the concealed passageway leading from the barbican, which commanded the approach to a castle, and to the main fortifications.

Pottery. A general term that originally described all objects modelled out of clay and fired in a kiln. Modern usage excludes the hardest wares, porcelain and china, so that the term now describes the various types of earthenware and stoneware (qqv).

Pouch table. See **Work table.**

Pouffe. A low, backless, and upholstered seat, introduced during the Victorian era. It is usually round, and resembles a very large footstool.

Pounced ornament. Ornament that is pricked, stamped, or punched on to a surface.

Powell and Moya. A firm of British architects established in 1946 by Philip Powell (1921–71), who was trained at the Architectural Association and worked as an assistant to Sir Frederick Gibberd. In 1946 Powell set up in practice with Hidalgo Moya (b 1920) at Los Gatos, California. Moya has also trained at the AA and had been an assistant to Gibberd. Other architects have since joined the firm.

Powell and Moya gained their first major success in 1948 when, in open competition, they won the commission for the Churchill Gardens flats in Westminster, better known as the Pimlico Development. These flats, built between 1948 and 1962, were the first post-war British housing development to gain international acclaim. After this the firm received a number of other commissions, all of which have been carried out with bold planning,

careful detailing, and sympathetic understanding of human needs. The commissions have been of unusual variety, ranging from flats and individual houses to swimming-baths and hospitals. The Chichester Festival Theatre in Sussex is by Powell and Moya, and the firm has also been outstandingly successful in their designs for collegiate buildings. They designed extensions at Brasenose, 'Christ Church', and Corpus Christi, Oxford, and at St. John's College, Cambridge. They also designed a picture gallery for Christ Church, and the new Wolfson College.

Pratt, Sir Roger (1620–85). British architect. Pratt was the son of a Norfolk squire who was also a lawyer. He intended to follow the law himself, and after leaving Magdalen College, Oxford, entered the Middle Temple in 1637. In 1640 his father died,

leaving him in extremely comfortable circumstances, whereupon he set out on a six-year Grand Tour, mainly architectural in purpose, which took him through the Low Countries, France, and Italy. To judge from his notebooks, he must have studied the buildings of Palladio, Scamozzi, and others.

Pratt was one of the pioneers of Renaissance architecture in British l, notably in his designs for Clarendon House (1664–67) in Piccadilly, built for Edward Hyde, Lord Clarendon. This was one of the most influential of all seventeenth-century houses. Although the building only stood for less than 20 years, it had a profound effect upon subsequent building throughout the country. After the Great Fire, Pratt was one of the three commissioners appointed by the king to supervise the building of the City; for his labours he received a knignt-

The Churchill Gardens development, Pimlico, London, by Powell and Moya

Coleshill, Berkshire, designed by Sir Roger Pratt, 1650, now destroyed

hood. In 1668 he married an heiress and virtually retired as an architect, though he busied himself with the rebuilding of a house he had inherited at Ryston in Norfolk.

Pratt completed Coleshill in Berkshire (1650–62), owned by Sir George Pratt, his cousin. What part he played in the original design with Inigo Jones (and Jones's pupil, John Webb) is still not known.

Pratt ware. A pale cream or white earthenware, decorated with underglaze colours. It was named after Felix Pratt, who made the ware in Staffordshire from about 1780 to 1830, but the names of at least a dozen other potters are to be found on similar objects. Pratt ware was made in Staffordshire, Yorkshire (Ferrybridge and Leeds), Newcastle upon Tyne, and Sunderland.

Pratt ware jug, c 1790

The colouring was a typical maiolica range: yellows, oranges, browns, greens, blue, black – in fact, the oxide colours capable of withstanding the high temperature needed to fuse the glazes.

There are Pratt jugs with relief decoration painted with these oxide colours. The subjects vary from rustic scenes to commemorative items, showing historical figures such as the admirals Nelson, Jervis, and Duncan, the Duke of Wellington, the Duke of York, and General Hill. As well as jugs, mugs, teapots, flasks, and cornucopias, many underglaze coloured figures were also made, some of them copies of figures made earlier by the Ralph Woods and Enoch Wood; there were also many small anonymous figures of children, gardeners, shepherds, and the like.

Prefabrication. A comparatively modern term that describes a building practice of some antiquity. Prefabrication entails making standardized parts of a structure before building starts, so that these components need only be assembled on the site.

This procedure was often followed by eighteenth-century speculative builders, who prefabricated such elements as doorcases, window frames, doors, and other joinery. One of the most spectacular demonstrations of the value of prefabrication was the design of the Crystal Palace by Joseph Paxton (qv); 900,000 sq ft of glass, 205 miles of sash bar, and other equally substantial

quantities of components were brought to Hyde Park at required times in prefabricated form. Prefabrication is now an essential factor in building economics. Its development was speeded up by the military necessities of World War II, when huts, hangars, and even the Normandy invasion harbours were prefabricated.

In America there are probably more prefabricated houses assembled than anywhere in the world, with plans ranging from simple adaptations of small early homes to modern designs.

Presbytery. Part of the east end of a church, beyond the

choir, an area reserved for the clergy. It is where the high altar is placed.

Press. A large piece of furniture for holding linen or clothes. The word was virtually interchangeable with cupboard (qv) and aumbry (qv) in the late sixteenth century. From the seventeenth century the press functioned very much as a wardrobe, clothes often being stored on movable shelves. Some presses that look like ordinary hanging wardrobes are found to contain drawers or shelves behind the tall doors. The eighteenth-century 'clothes press' had cupboard doors above, concealing shelves, and drawers in the lower part. This form was enlarged in the nineteenth century (commonly with the addition of a hanging cupboard) and called a wardrobe.

Press bed. A bed that was disguised as a press or wardrobe when not in use. The doors were usually hinged at the top, so that when they were lifted up and supported by posts they formed the tester; the bedstead unfolded from inside the body of the cupboard. Press beds are first mentioned in seventeenth-century inventories, and were still being used by servants in the early nineteenth century.

Press cupboard. A term now used mainly in America to describe a late sixteenth-century cupboard. The type is known in England as a hall cupboard (qv), though it has long been misnamed 'court cupboard.' It is in two parts, the lower of which is taller and fitted with a pair of doors. The superstructure is recessed and divided into three

Medieval oak press with iron hinges

Prince of Wales feathers

panelled cupboards; the side cupboards are sometimes positioned obliquely to the centre. The whole is crowned by a projecting cornice with carved or turned corner supports.

Prestressed concrete. A method of building construction which ensures the safety of a structure with pre-cast concrete components. Before being used, such components are subjected to artificial stresses well beyond those likely to be encountered.

Prie dieu. A small desk at which one could pray. It carried a low ledge, so placed that it was possible to kneel and still use the top for reading.

The prie dieu chair was a small, low, upholstered chair without arms, and with a narrow back that broadened out towards the top. It was made in the early nineteenth century, and though also known as a kneeling chair, was in fact used in drawing-rooms as well as for prayer.

Prince of Wales feathers. The three ostrich feathers first adopted as a crest by the Black Prince were used decoratively on chair backs in the late eight-eenth and early nineteenth centuries.

Prince wood. A seventeenth- and eighteenth-century term for the wood now called kingwood (qv); today it is applied only to a type of Central American laurel, *Cordia gerascanthus.*

Principal rafters. In a roof truss these are the main rafters between the wall plate and the ridge, dividing the length of the roof into bays.

Print room. A room in which the walls were covered with prints. The print room was a mid-eighteenth-century phenomenon introduced at a time when there was a vogue for print collecting. Each wall was decorated with prints and numerous borders, ribbons, and festoons that could be cut out of specially compiled books and then pasted on to the walls. Few of the decorations are still intact.

Pronaos. In a Greek or Roman temple this is the open vestibule at the front, corresponding to the opisthodomos (qv) at the back. The term may also refer to an enclosed space used as the treasury.

Prostyle. A portico with free-standing columns in front of a building. The alternative relationship is a portico *in antis.*

Pseudodipteral. See **Dipteral.**

Pugin, Augustus Welby Northmore (1812–52). British architect and artist. He was the son of a Frenchman, Augustus Charles Pugin (1762–1832), an architectural draughtsman who

Augustus Charles Pugin

Augustus Welby Pugin

had been attached to John Nash's (qv) office in Carmarthen and later in London, where he set up his own school of architectural drawing. It was there that the son studied before travelling, extensively with his father, helping him in the preparation of architectural drawings. Pugin sought to establish his own reputation as a theatrical and furniture designer (including

some designs for Windsor Castle), and while still in his twenties manufactured furniture to his own Gothic designs, but the enterprise failed. Following his father's death he joined the Catholic Church and set up as a church architect, designer of church furniture, author, and artist. He was a restless man, moving from London to Salisbury, and thence to Ramsgate,

The east side of Park Square, Regent's Park, by A C Pugin

Prostyle portico on Carlton House, London, by Henry Holland, 1783-5

Design for St George's, Southwark, by A W Pugin, 1838, not executed

Drawing for the Houses of Parliament by A W Pugin

where he settled. His unrelenting industry eventually led to a severe mental breakdown and he was confined to a private asylum where he died.

Pugin's most notable achievement was his Gothic contribution to Sir Charles Barry's designs for the Houses of Parliament. The collaboration was so close, and Pugin's work so authoritative, scholarly, and individual, that he was effectively co-designer of the completed building. He was without question responsible for all the Gothic decoration and detailing. Despite the great exertions required for this project, Pugin also managed to design St Chad's Cathedral, Birmingham (1839–44), and a number of other ecclesiastical buildings. He was also author of several books, notably *Contrasts* (1836), an onslaught on contemporary architecture and an advocacy of Gothic as the great Christian style. Pugin's other books include

Examples of Gothic Architecture (1831–38), *Gothic Furniture* (1835), *The True Principles of Pointed or Christian Architecture* (1841).

His practice passed to his son Edward Welby Pugin (1834–75), who acquired a considerable reputation as an ecclesiastical architect. He designed several Catholic churches and secular buildings, including convents and schools.

Pulpit. A raised stage or desk in the church nave, from which sermons are delivered; made of wood or stone. Pulpits have also been installed in refectories of monasteries, in cloisters, and even in public thoroughfares. They are frequently enriched with carving and sometimes with decorative painting.

Pulvinated frieze (Latin, *pulvinatus* 'cushion-shaped'). A convex frieze, rounded in sec-

tion, that is found in classical architecture and occasionally on case furniture of the late seventeenth and early eighteenth centuries.

Pumpkin pine. *Pinus strobus.* North American wood found from Newfoundland to Virginia. It is a pale yellow-brown colour, with thin darker lines running down the grain. Pumpkin pine has been much used for furniture and building since Colonial times. White or cork pine are alternative names.

Purfled. This describes carved ornament resembling lace, embroidery, and drapery. By extension it is applied to any lace-like effect produced by a profusion of tracery and small pinnacles.

Puritan furniture. Early Colonial furniture made in America around the middle of the seventeenth century. Styles were simple, with some carving and turning.

Purlin. A horizontal beam used in the construction of a roof. It runs parallel to the ridge beam and provides support for the common rafters or sheet roofing; it is supported by the principal rafters. There are frequently two purlins on each slope of the roof.

Purpleheart. *Peltogyne.* A Central American and British Guianan wood that has a purple colour after it is cut. Although not easy to work, this wood was used at the end of the eighteenth century for inlaying, veneer, banding, and other decorative purposes. It has been confused with rosewood.

Pycnostyle. A Greek term whose literal meaning was a sequence of columns in close succession. It is now used of a regular column spacing of one and a half diameters.

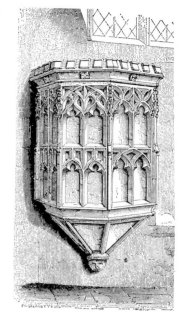

Engraving of a pulpit

Pyramid (Latin *pyramis*, pl *pyramides*). The great pyramids of Egypt were the tombs of the pharoahs of the IV to the XII Dynasties (before 3000 BC). They developed from the more modest *mastaba*, a rectangular tomb with sloping sides and a flat top, and the stepped pyramid, as at Sakkara and Meidum. The pyramid was built on a square base with the four sides sloping towards an apex, a marvel of engineering and building technique. Inside, elaborate precautions were taken to prevent intruders from finding the burial chamber and treasure room; even so, plunderers always succeeded in negotiating the endless passages and numerous false corridors.

The pyramid with its uncompromising form found little favour in subsequent centuries, although some follies (qv) were erected in the eighteenth century.

Pyramid of Caestius, Rome, 12BC

The Great Pyramids of Menkaura, Khafra and Khufu at Gizah

Quadrangle. The Great Court at Trinity College, Cambridge

Quadrangle. A square court or yard in a monastery, and later in collegiate buildings; frequently enclosed by cloisters and cells or chambers. The quadrangle is usually entered by way of a gatehouse or lodge.

Quadrant or **quadrant stay.** The curved metal device used to

Quadrapartite vault, Rouen

support the fall front of a desk; usually a quarter-circle.

Quadrature. The Italian term for illusionist decorations; the Baroque era (qv) was the heyday of quadrature. Wall paintings at Pompeii are the earliest known examples; false windows with imaginary views can still be seen there. See **Trompe-l'oeil.**

Quadriga. A chariot drawn by four horses harnessed abreast, represented in sculpture on buildings and in relief on coins. Well-known examples are the quadrigas on the triumphal arch of Hyde Park Corner, London, and the Brandenburg Gate in Berlin.

Quadripartite vault. A bay of a vault, divided into four cells by a pair of intersecting diagonal ribs.

Quarenghi, Giacomo (1744–1817). Italian architect. Quar-

The quadriga at Hyde Park Corner, London, by Adrian Jones, 1912

Quadrangle. *The view over the 15th century quadrangle at Magdalene College, Oxford, towards the New Building*

The Central Naval Museum (former Exchange) by Quarenghi, 1805-10

The English Palace at Peterhof designed by Quarenghi, 1781-9

enghi was born near Bergamo, where he studied at the academy. He became a successful artist; but became interested in architecture after studying the writings and buildings of Palladio and Bramante. His architectural career dates from his rebuilding of the Church of St Scolastica, at Subiaco near Rome, in 1771.

In 1780, Catherine the Great invited Quarenghi to St Petersburg, and he was the most influential architect in Russia until her death. His first important work, and perhaps his most typical, was the English Palace at Peterhof (1781–9), in origin an unashamedly Palladian design, but adapted in masterly fashion to Russian conditions. Quarenghi's other buildings included the Hermitage Theatre (1782–5); the Alexander Palace at Tsarskoe Selo (1792–6), intended for Catherine's grandson the future Alexander I; the Stock Exchange (1784–1801); and the Marinski Hospital (1803). Quarenghi was also responsible for a great number of more mundane buildings, including barracks, stables, and riding-schools. After Catherine's death in 1796 his influence gradually declined; despite Quarenghi's international reputation, Alexander I preferred the French architect Thomas de Thomon.

Quarrel or **quarry.** A diamond-shaped pane of glass, or a

Quartetto tables

square pane placed diagonally; the term can also be applied to a quadrangular piercing in the tracery of a window. The name probably derives from the fact that such small openings could be glazed by a single piece of glass or quarry. The term is also applied to diamond-shaped paving tiles.

Quartering. Four adjacent veneers of similar grain, symmetrically arranged.

Quartetto table. Sheraton coined this word in his *Cabinet Dictionary* (1803) to describe a nest of tables (qv).

Quatrefoil design

Quatrefoil (French, *quatre-feuille* 'four leaf'). A formalized four-leafed motif, especially the pierced pattern on the tracery of a Gothic window, divided by cusps or featherings into four leaves or lobes. Friezes of quatrefoils were frequently employed in the Perpendicular and Decorated styles.

Queen Anne style. Strictly speaking, domestic architecture built in the reign of Queen Anne (1702–14). This is typified by picturesque town or small country houses of red brick, with hipped roofs, heavy white cornices, wide window frames, and relief-work ornament. The period witnessed the introduction and establishment of Georgian architecture in England.

But the term is also used to include domestic architecture of the previous period (William and Mary), and even the English Baroque. It also includes a range of interpretations of the Palladian canon, particularly the domestic architecture of America in the first half of the eighteenth century.

A revived nineteenth-century Queen Anne style was propagated by Norman Shaw (qv) and others. It featured gay, red-brick, curly-gabled houses with white painted balconies and terra cotta panels of sunflower and lilies.

In England, furniture in the Queen Anne style was made during the first two decades of the eighteenth century. It was the heyday of walnut and decorative veneers and designs of elegant and graceful curves inspired by Netherlands Baroque

A Queen Anne house in Castle Street, Bridgwater, Somerset

A Queen Anne house in Great Marlow, Buckinghamshire

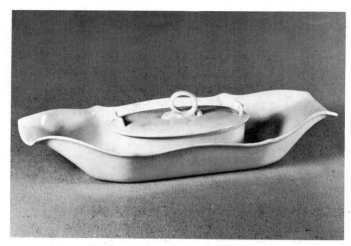

Wedgwood Queensware asparagus dish

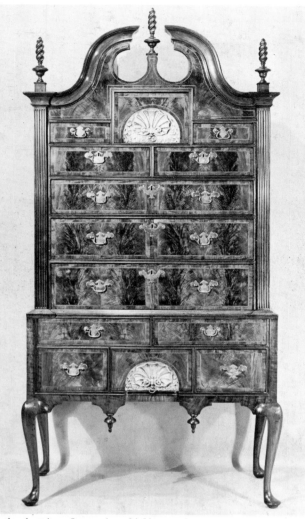

An American Queen Anne highboy made by the Woodward family

Linen quilted with silk, 1600s

seded salt-glazed stoneware, which had been widely used for tableware earlier in the eighteenth century.

In 1765 Wedgwood made a tea-service of his new creamware for Queen Charlotte, who was so delighted with it that she appointed him 'Potter to the Queen' and gave him permission to call his new invention 'Queensware', a name that has been used ever since.

A similar creamware body was soon made by many other potteries, notably at Leeds, where many fine examples were made with pierced decoration.

Some Wedgwood Queensware was made into beautifully simple classical shapes and left completely undecorated; other pieces were shipped to Liverpool to be decorated by the new transfer-printing process of Sadler and Green; and yet others were decorated with simple hand-painted borders based on geometric and floral forms.

Quilt. Originally the term applied to a light form of mattress. From the mid-seventeenth century it seems to have been used exclusively to describe a bed covering filled with soft feathers or wool, and encased between two sheets, frequently of heavy linen or calico. Quilts gradually became items of considerable decorative interest; of especial interest are patchwork quilts made from geometrically shaped pieces of colourful cloth.

Quirk. A small, sharp-edged channel, recess, or groove in a moulding or between mouldings. In Greek and Roman architecture, ovolos and ogees are usually quirked at the top; in Gothic architecture the quirk frequently occurs between mouldings.

Quoin (French, *coin* 'corner'). The external angles or corners of a building. The term is most frequently used when dressed stone or distinctive brickwork is employed on corners as a decorative feature. In timber houses, quoins are sometimes made to simulate stonework.

Diagram showing quoins

at the previous monarch, William of Orange, had taken to England. It was the era of the cabriole leg, the bun and the claw-and-ball feet, vase-shaped back splats and curving swan-

necked pediments. The same characteristics are found in American Queen Anne which begins in 1720 and continues until about 1750. During this time few new pieces of furniture appeared, but adaptations of European prototypes were responsible for the specific character of American Queen Anne. One such example to emerge was the highboy upon cabriole legs with a scrolled pediment and carved shell motifs in the centres of the upper part and the base.

Queen post. One of a pair of vertical posts in a roof truss, suitable for spans of 30–45 ft. A king post truss is suitable only for distances of 20–30 ft. Queen posts connect the main tie beam to the principal rafters.

Queensware. Josiah Wedgwood gave this name to a fine cream-coloured earthenware that he had perfected by 1763. This earthenware body soon super-

American Queen Anne chair

Ernest Race

Rabbet or **rebate.** A channel cut or sunk in a piece of wood so that the raised edge of another piece will fit into it.

Race, Ernest (1915–64). British designer. He was born in Newcastle upon Tyne and educated at St Paul's School and the Bartlett School of Architecture. After World War II he met J W Noel Jordan, a light-engineering manufacturer, with whom he formed Race Furniture Ltd.

At this time there was an acute shortage of wood, but an abundance of aluminium alloy and steel which were used in aircraft and armament manufacture. It needed the ingenuity of both designer and manufacturer to produce furniture in these new materials, and Race was a notable pioneer. His dining chair of cast aluminium, with its upholstered seat and shaped plywood back, was the first British cast-aluminium chair to go into production. His 'Antelope' chair, made of steel rod with shaped painted plywood seat, was made for the 1951

Rafters in a converted mill house

Festival of Britain and used throughout the South Bank Exhibition.

Raeburn armchair. An attractive armchair made throughout the eighteenth century. It has a plain upholstered rectangular back, short, narrow, padded arms, and wood arm supports that form a scroll or simple concave curve linking the front of the seat and the arm.

Rafters. The structural timbers, based on the wall plates at the eaves of a building, which

rise to the ridge, forming a skeletal frame-work for the support of the roof.

Rail. (1) Any bar of metal or timber which rests on a series of supporting posts, balusters, or other upright components of a fence or balustrade. (2) The horizontal member or moulding in a panelled frame for a wall or door. The term is also used as an abbreviation for the chair rail or dado rail, a moulding applied to the walls of rooms at chair-back height to protect wallpaper or paint from damage.

Rainwater heads

Rainwater head. A capacious metal receptacle placed at the top of a rainwater or 'drain' pipe; it received water from the roof gutters. Rainwater heads are now made of cast iron, but in earlier times they were often lead, and were elaborately ornamented and usually dated.

Rampart. A defensive outwork of fortified buildings. In earlier times the rampart was little more than a bank of earth, but in more sophisticated castles the term was applied to an outer wall with a crenellated parapet. On the

Romanesque. *The 11th century nave of the Basilique de la Madeleine at Vezalay, Burgundy*

Section of a rampart taken from Fournier's 'Traité des Fortifications', 1647

Rams' heads on a torchère

inner side of this wall was a raised path known as the rampart walk, which was connected by steps to the inner areas of the castle.

Ram's head. A classical motif reintroduced by the Adam brothers. It became very popular on furniture and interior decorations of the late eighteenth century.

Ranch house. A long one-storey house, usually with a low-pitched roof, and sometimes with a cellar and a low attic. This type of small family house was particularly popular in the western states of America, from which it spread to other regions.

Rastrelli, Count Bartolommeo Francesco (c 1700–70). Italian architect. Although he was born in Italy, all Rastrelli's work was carried out in Russia, to which he was taken at an early age by his father, a sculptor. He was sent to Paris to study architecture, and later to Saxony, Austria, and Italy. Rastrelli received his first major commission after the accession of Elizabeth Petrovna to the throne. In 1741 he was appointed official architect to the tsarina, and as such made a major contribution to the transformation of eighteenth-century St Petersburg into a city of great beauty.

Rastrelli's Summer Palace in St Petersburg (1741–4), although built of wood, was by far the most impressive building in the city. He was next commissioned to finish the Anichkov Palace, begun by Zemtsov (1744). His major work was the reconstruction and vast enlargement of Peterhof (1747–52). Rastrelli was circumscribed by the fact that much of the original building had to be preserved, but certain features – the terminal pavilions, the Merchants' Hall, and the staircase – show his genius as an exponent of the Rococo and as a decorator. The church at Peterhof was one of several that Rastrelli designed for Elizabeth. In these he combined Rococo with an imaginative use of Russian forms; the resulting

synthesis gave Rastrelli's work unique and gay decorative ricness. Even the matter-of-fasobriety imposed upon his dsigns for the cathedral in Kiby the nineteenth-century archtect V P Stasov, scarcely detracfrom Rastrelli's resplendedecorative interiors. His laworks were amongst his greatesthe Great Palace at Tsarkoe Se(1749–56), now known as Puskino, and the Winter PalaceSt Petersburg (1754–62). In boRastrelli had to deal with existibuildings of considerable lengwhich had to be still furthextended. He was probabhappier with the smaller paviliohe was called on to design, whisuggests that he was at heart

The Vorontsov Palace in Leningrad by Rastrelli, 1747–57

The Smolny Monastery in Leningrad by Rastrelli

The Winter Palace at Leningrad, designed by Rastrelli, 1754-62

miniaturist, forced by the exigencies of royal patronage to work in a palatial, even gargantuan, scale.

Rastrelli's influence declined on the death of Elizabeth in 1762, and the accession of Catherine II, who favoured a sober classicism.

Ravenscroft, George (1618–91). British glassmaker, the discoverer of British lead glass. In 1673 he set up an experimental glass house at the Savoy in London, and in 1674 obtained a patent from Charles II to make 'Chrystalline Glass resembling Rock Crystal.' The production of glass from British materials would obviate the need for costly and fragile Venetian imports, and therefore Ravenscroft was backed by the Glass Sellers' Company, who built him another glasshouse at Henley-on-Thames to ensure greater secrecy for his experiments. At first he used calcined flints (hence the term 'flint glass') and potash, but glass made from them suffered from 'crizzling', a progressive decomposition which produces an unsightly opaque look. To overcome this, Ravenscroft added oxide of lead. In 1677 he was authorized by the Glass Sellers to mark his glass with the famous raven's head seal, a complimentary pun on his name. In 1679, for reasons unknown, he retired.

Reading chair. A specialized form of chair, first made in the early eighteenth century. Many were used in libraries, and they are sometimes called library chairs.

The reading chair was made of walnut or mahogany, and had a pear-shaped seat upholstered in leather. The reader faced the back of the chair, on which there was a broad, curved top rail with an adjustable book rest.

Sometimes there were candlesticks and trays hinged below the arms.

Another type of reading chair, introduced in the nineteenth century, was an armchair with an adjustable book rest upon one arm. See **Cockfighting chair.**

Récamier. A chaise longue of the Directoire and Empire periods. It was a graceful piece of furniture with one end higher than the other, and was called after Mme Récamier, whose salon was one of the most brilliant of her time. There is a famous painting of her by J L David.

Redwood. *Sequoia.* A ruddy wood from the west coast of America, where it is found predominantly in the Coast Range of California and in south Oregon. Redwood is the *Sequoia sempervirens* rather than the *Sequoia gigantea* or big tree, which is the largest of all trees. Neither wood is suitable for furniture construction, but the burls in redwood give a particularly beautiful figure that is used

for veneers and small turned articles such as bowls.

Reeding, reed, reeded moulding. A form of moulding in which beads are grouped in parallel lines extremely close together. Reeding is most frequently used in mouldings attached to door frames.

Refectory table. The modern name for the very long table, typical of the late sixteenth and the seventeenth century. There are usually six or eight legs,

joined by plain rectangular stretchers fixed very close to the ground.

Regency style. The term 'Regency style' in British architecture, furniture design, and interior decoration extends over rather more than the decade of the Regency proper (1811–20). The style evolved in reaction to the somewhat heavy symmetry of the Greek revival, and its decorative liveliness and inventiveness soon made the new style popular.

Architecturally the Regency

A late Elizabethan oak refectory table

Glass bowl by Ravenscroft with raven's head on the base, c 1675

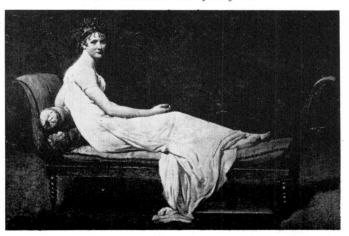

Madame Récamier reclining on her couch, painted by David

Cronkhill in Shropshire by John Nash, 1802

Part of a Regency crescent in Brighton

style is one of the most cavalierly eclectic in English history, embracing such apparent polarities as the classical and the gothick, each reinterpreted in highly individual and frequently eccentric ways, along with such exoticisms as chinoiserie and pseudo-Hindu extravaganzas like the Royal Pavilion and Sezincote. In so far as it is possible to define it, Regency was a continuation of the late eighteenth-century Greek revival. However, there were so many cross-currents of influence, from Romanticism to the Napoleonic Wars, that the gothick of Sir Walter Scott and the researches of Napoleon's experts into Egyptian antiquities were just as likely to influence a patron as recollections of Greek and Roman prototypes.

The result was a lively and entertaining miscellany of buildings in which the use of stucco was probably the closest approximation to aesthetic uniformity. The Regency style is probably seen at its most uniform in the town and country villas of the rising middle class, in the linked or semi-detached pairs of villas which grace the suburbs of larger cities, and in the stuccoed architecture which remains so engaging a feature of Regent's Park and such towns as Brighton and Cheltenham. Here are the motifs which have come to represent the Regency style: bowed fronts, canopies, ornamental ironwork, and a lavish use of the orders, particularly the Ionic and Corinthian.

Among the best-known Regency architects are John Nash (1752–1835), architect of the Regent's Park terraces; Sir John Soane (1753–1837), architect of the Bank of England; John Buonarotti Papworth (1775–1847), who carried out much work at Cheltenham; George Basevi (1794–1845), who was responsible for much of South Kensington's domestic architecture; and Decimus Burton (1800–81), who did most of his work in and around Hyde Park and Regent's Park while still a young man.

In the design of furniture the

A Regency black lacquer cabinet

Elbow chair with paw feet

Pedestal work table

Regency was equally eclectic. The austere symmetry of the eighteenth century was discarded in favour of a greater exuberance in the use of inlay and ornament. Such publications as Thomas Hope's *Household Furniture an*

Regency designs for ornamental metal work by Cottingham

A relieving arch over a doorway

Interior Decoration (1807) advocated academic interpretations of Greek, Roman, and Egyptian styles. The 'Egyptian' taste was reinforced by *Designs for Household Furniture and Interior Decoration* (1808), published by George Smith, a cabinetmaker and upholsterer, who also included Chinese and gothick designs, and derivations from the French designs of Percier and Fontaine. Smith popularized all the representative Regency motifs, and also made possible those debased versions of interesting and individual designs which the Victorian joiners made in such vast quantities. It is these that are now so often passed off by the unscrupulous as Regency designs.

Regula. On a Doric entablature, this is the short band to which the guttae (qv) are attached. It is placed just below the tenia (qv).

Reilly, Sir Charles Herbert (1874–1948). British architect and architectural teacher and writer. Reilly was born in London and educated at Merchant Taylors' School and Cambridge University. After an early training with John Belcher, he was taken into partnership. He was professor of architecture at Liverpool University (1904–33), and was a strong advocate of university training for architects. Reilly was a prolific writer on architecture; his publications include *The Theory and Practice of Architecture* (1932) and *An Outline Plan for Birkenhead* (1947), which suggested grouping small houses round urban ('Reilly') greens. He also wrote an autobiography, *Scaffolding in the Sky.*

Reilly, Sir Paul (b 1912). British design expert. Reilly was born in Liverpool, the son of Sir Charles Reilly (qv). He was educated at Winchester College, Oxford University, and the London School of Economics. After commercial experience with Venesta, the plywood importers, he made a career as a specialist editor in journalism. He joined the Council of Industrial Design in 1949 as chief information officer, became deputy director in 1957, and succeeded Sir Gordon Russell as director. He is a member of the Design panels sponsored by British Railways and the Post Office, and of the Greater London Council's Historic Buildings Board.

Relief (Italian, *rilevare* 'to raise'). Sculpture and sculptural decoration that projects from a flat surface. When the surface is

Sir Paul Reilly

worked to only a small degree it is known as low or bas-relief (qv); by contrast, high relief work stands right out from the background, being at least half in the round.

Relieving arch. An arch built into a fabric over a rectangular opening; it thus relieves the lintel of much of the weight of the wall above, and offsets the load or thrust onto the side walls. It is also known as a discharging arch.

Reliquary. A small box or shrine for sacred relics.

Renaissance. The period from *c* 1420 to *c* 1530 in western Europe; its roots were in fourteenth-century Italy, and Italian craftsmen, artists, and styles gave the lead to Europe throughout the period. Its most striking feature was the intensification of interest in classical antiquity, though in painting and sculpture, artists went far beyond classical models. A new sense of individuality and a more secular outlook appeared, both allowed artistic expression

Plasterwork in high relief, Dublin, by Robert West, 1755

Sir Charles Reilly

The interior of S Lorenzo in Florence by Brunelleschi, 1425

repeated indefinitely on the same scale, following the example of Alberti's Palazzo Rucellai, Florence (1446). Bramante drew one possible conclusion from this in the choir of S Maria del Popolo, in which the flat surfaces of wall, barrel-vault, and apse are articulated solely by means of lines, without any antique decoration whatsoever. More significant, however, was the exploitation of the circle in Bramante's 'Tempietto' in the cloisters of S Pietro in Montorio (1503), which is built to a circular plan, without dominant axes or dominant parts. Bramante's design for rebuilding the basilica of St. Peter's, Rome (c 1503), while centrally planned, assumed the dominance of the central space over the surrounding ones, thereby displaying a characteristic that was already fundamentally Baroque. The development of this church by a number of architects after Bramante's death marked the transition from the Renaissance to the Baroque (qv).

by many munificent patrons – popes and princes in Italy, and increasingly powerful monarchs in France, England, and Spain.

The ultimate sources of design were classical models, and particularly the Roman remains so abundant in Italy. These gradually became known beyond the Alps, whereas an independent interest in geometry and design remained an almost exclusively Italian prerogative.

In architecture the first great step forward was taken in Florence by Filippo Brunelleschi (1377–1446). Brunelleschi reinterpreted the traditional Florentine Gothic basilica, not only with details derived from buildings he had seen in the Roman forum, but also applying a system of geometrical proportion to determine the relationship of the parts. The result, in a church like S Lorenzo, Florence (1425), was superficially similar to the early Christian basilicas of imperial Rome, but also possessed an unparalleled clarity of articulation.

Leon Battista Alberti (1404–72) evolved a comprehensive theory of classical architecture, drawing largely on the rediscovered Roman theorist Vitruvius (qv). In a building like Alberti's S Andrea, Mantua (1472), the structural elements of classical architecture (vertical pilaster and horizontal entablature) are used exclusively to divide the façade into a geometrical scheme based on the proportion of 1:2.

By the time of Bramante (1444–1514) this system of articulating the façade by means of the classical orders had developed into a method by which each unit of an elevation or plan could be

Rennie, John (1761–1821). Scottish engineer, architect, and bridge-builder. Rennie was the son of an East Lothian farmer, and as a youth worked for a millwright. His thrift enabled him to undertake a three-year course of mathematical studies at Edinburgh University. After leaving, he set up as an independent millwright and engineer in Edinburgh, and while still in his early twenties built his first bridge, over the Water of Leith in Midlothian.

In 1784 Rennie moved to Birmingham to join Boulton and

The Villa Farnesina in Rome by Peruzzi, 1509–11

S Maria Novello, Florence, recased by Alberti, 1456–70

Southwark Bridge, London, designed by Rennie, 1815-18

St Patrick's Cathedral, New York, by James Renwick, 1859-79

Watt, acting as adviser on the mechanical engineering problems involved in building the machinery in the new Albion Flour Mills at Southwark, London. His work on this project established his professional reputation, and his mechanical and civil engineering knowledge were henceforth in considerable demand. But his main activity was bridge-building, in which he displayed a remarkable skill, energy, and diversity. He designed Kelso Bridge over the Tweed (1799), Musselburgh Bridge over the Esk, and other bridges in Lincolnshire, Staffordshire, and Scotland. But his most ambitious bridges were built in

John Rennie

London; notably Southwark Bridge (1815–17), and London Bridge, designed by Rennie and completed by his son after Rennie's death.

Rent table. A pedestal table with a circular or polygonal top, made during the second half of the eighteenth century. It has drawers painted or inlaid with letters or numbers, suggesting accounts and records. A few rent tables have removable circular panels in the centre of the top, enclosing secret drawers or a well, supposedly for money collected from tenants.

Renwick, James (1818–95). American architect. Renwick worked in many styles. His most unusual building, the Smithsonian Institute in Washington DC (1848–9), was a 'Norman' castle, so designed at the insistance of Renwick's client, Robert Dale Owen. Grace Episcopal Church, New York City (1843–6), was in fourteenth-century English Gothic style to suit Anglican tastes, while for New York City's Catholic community, Renwick built St Patrick's Cathedral (1859–79) in a type of Gothic closer to contemporary Continental models. For public buildings he worked in the fashionable Second Empire style, beginning with the Charity Hos-

pital on Blackwell's Bland, New York (1858). The extreme plasticity of his complex design for the main hall of Vassar College, Poughkeepsie, New York (1860), was an indication of the direction this style was to take in the USA despite the fact that Renwick was instructed to use the Tuileries as a model: not a very plastically modelled building, and one which in any case he can only have known from engravings. This reworking of French models (whose details he never really mastered) ranks as his most important contribution to American architecture.

Repoussé chasing. See **Silver, decorative techniques.**

Repton, Humphry (1752–1818). British landscape gardener. Repton was born at Bury St Edmunds, Suffolk, the son of an excise collector. He became a general merchant in Norwich in his early twenties, but his business quickly failed. After activities ranging from a private secretaryship to a Lord-Lieutenant of Ireland to an abortive attempt to establish a mail-coach service, Repton decided to turn his lifelong interest in gardening

Sheringham Hall, Norfolk, by Humphry Repton, 1859-79

441

One of Repton's schemes, showing before and after, taken from 'Sketches and Hints on Landscape Gardening', 1794

to advantage and, when nearly 40, he set up as 'a landscape gardener.'

Repton was aided in this enterprise by his practical knowledge of horticulture and his skill as a watercolourist. His ingenious perspectives comparing the present and potential states of would-be patrons' gardens were a powerful inducement to employ him. He bound these, with his reports, in his now-famous 'Red Books.' Thanks to his skilful manipulation of Picturesque (qv) elements, Repton soon became a fashionable and successful figure. He also had a judicious taste in domestic architecture, although he directed his commissions towards John Nash, to whom he articled his sons. Yet his own designs such as the remodelling of Welbeck Abbey and the designing of Sheringham Hall, Norfolk, showed considerable skill and ingenuity. His various publications were collected by J C Loudon (qv), and published in 1840.

Reredos. Facing or screen which covers the wall behind the altar. It is usually ornamental, and is made of wood or stone.

Respond. A term applied to the pilaster or grouped pilasters that support the impost (qv) or upper part of the wall, beam, or pier on which the arch rests. A respond is normally the end feature of an arcade or colonnade.

Restoration. The period that opened with the accession of Charles II in 1660, and closed with the Revolution of 1688. The Restoration was a time of rapid development in English furniture styles. There was a great influx of foreign ideas: French and Flemish styles were popular with the returning court, and Queen Catherine of Braganza was largely responsible for the introduction of more exotic Portuguese and Chinese influences. Accurate knowledge of French decoration was acquired from the immigrant Huguenot

craftsmen who left France after the revocation of the Edict of Nantes in 1685. Decoration became gay and frivolous, and scrolls and spiral turning abounded.

Restoration chair. A term most commonly used in America to describe Carolean chairs with high backs, one or two caned panels, and a carved framework with the heaviest concentration of ornament on the front stretcher and top rail. Sometimes there is a crown in the middle of the cresting.

Retable. A carved or painted altarpiece that stands at the back of the altar; also the ledge between the altar and the east wall.

Return. Any part of a structure that falls away from the main direction, usually at a right angle. The word is used, for example, of the part of the hood mould that turns from a downward to a horizontal plane.

Reveal. The vertical side of a door or window opening; the term is applied to both the outer wall into which the opening is inset and the vertical sides of the inner wall.

Revell, Viljo (1910–64). Finnish architect. Revell was born in Vaasa in Finland. He studied in America, in several European countries, and under Alvar Aalto (qv), becoming one of Aalto's most distinguished pupils. In 1937 he set up his own office, in which many of Finland's leading contemporary architects have been trained.

One of Revell's best known buildings is the Teollisuuskeskus (with Keijo Petäjä, completed 1952), built on the waterfront in Helsinki. This is a multi-purpose

Side chair, c 1660

The reveal of a window

The respond on a Regency villa

The Kudeneule Factory, Hanko, Finland, by Viljo Revell, 1958

The Valiala cemetery chapel group, Tampere, Finland, by Revell, 1956

building with shops on the ground level, offices on intermediate storeys, and the Palace Hotel at the top. Revell's Meilahti primary school, Helsinki (with Osmo Sipari, 1953), presented a new treatment of the subject, with its long, waving, two-storey. classroom wing constructed of reinforced concrete with brick infilling. Other notable works by Revell include housing at Tapiola, the satellite town south of Helsinki, begun in 1952; the Kudeneule textile works, Hanko (1956); Toronto City Hall (1958, with others); and the Vatiala Cemetery, with reinforced concrete chapel (1962).

Revere, Paul (1735–1818). The most famous American goldsmith. Paul Revere's father was a Frenchman who set up in Boston in 1723. The Revere marks are similar, although Paul Revere generally used *Revere*, whereas

his father used *P Revere*. He is famous not only as a goldsmith, but as a hero of the American War of Independence. He was leader of the Boston Tea Party, and his ride from Boston to Lexington, Massachusetts, is legendary. He was a skilled engraver of trade cards and book plates, and published political cartoons deriding British author-

ity. He was also a pioneer of copper plating for ships.

Revolving bookcase. A stand for books resembling, and contemporary with, a dumb waiter (qv). It had circular tiers, diminishing in size from top to bottom, that revolved around a central column. Square revolving bookcases continued to be made in the

nineteenth century.

Revolving chair. Chairs with revolving seats exist from the late Middle Ages. Only in the nineteenth century did they begin to be confined to offices.

Ribbon back chair. Or Ribband back, as Chippendale spells it in his *Director*. These chairs

Paul Revere

A silver tea set by Paul Revere, dated 1793

Ribs on the vaulting of a church by J I Pearson, 1870-80

The Stoughton house, Massachusetts, by H H Richardson, 1882-3

had wonderfully light Rococo decoration with fragile and very delicate splats like puckered ribbon. Few were made and fewer still survive.

Ribbon ornament. Crinkled ribbon was a favourite device of Rococo craftsmen, who used it in inlaid work as a bow with trailing ends tying together two marquetry twigs, as a binding for a bunch of stalks, or meandering around a stick in the rose and stick motif, a peculiarly French device. Ribbons were worked in ormolu, wound loosely around mounts or tied in bows with the loose ends streaming out, the tips always cut into a V-shape.

Carved ribbons with rosettes can be found on table edges.

Rib pattern. Curved rib device of the early sixteenth century See **Parchment panel.**

Rib, rib vault. A light projecting ridge on the groin of a vault, or on a flat ceiling. It may be structural in purpose or merely moulded for decoration.

In a rib vault, the groins are replaced by diagonal arched ribs which provide a framework on which the masonry of the infilling can be supported.

Richardson, Henry Hobson (1838–86). American architect, born in Louisiana and educated at the Ecole des Beaux Arts in Paris. H H Richardson established himself in Boston in the years following the Civil War. His particular talents for originality of detailing and attention to the nature and quality of materials, made him an important figure in a period when architects were conscious of the need for a new style. By the time of his early death, Richardson was recognized as the creator of a distinctive personal manner which at least broke away from standard European models. His career forms an instructive contrast to that of his contemporary Richard M Hunt, who was undoubtedly a talented designer but failed to provide any solution to the crisis of mid-nineteenth-century architecture.

Moving away from High Victorian Gothic *c* 1870, Richardson interested himself in early and thirteenth-century Gothic (for Trinity Church, Boston, 1872–7, the model is Spanish); and ultimately in Romanesque. The discovery of Syrian Christian architecture in 1865 provided him

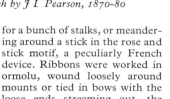
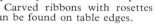

Mahogany ribband back settee based on a Chippendale design of 1762

The Marshall Field Building, Chicago, by H H Richardson, 1857-87

with models in which mass played a more important role than space. The mountainous and awe-inspiring qualities of these buildings are echoed in Richardson's small-town public libraries (eg the Crane Library at Quincy, Massachusetts, 1880–3), and in Sever Hall, Harvard College, Cambridge, Massachusetts (1878–80). Even Richardson's private houses (Glessner House, Chicago, 1885–7) are rather overwhelming. His planning varied from the formalism of the Marshall Field Wholesale Store, Chicago (1885–7), or the subdued shingle style Stoughton House, Cambridge, Massachusetts (1882–3), to the asymmetry of the Allegheny County Gaol, Pittsburgh (1884–8). Here picturesque planning is used as a means of heightening the drama created by massively rusticated walls, a characteristic which links the building to eighteenth-century prisons like Dance's Newgate in London, or Ledoux's design for Aix-en-Provence.

Richardson created a style that was widely imitated, though in the 1890s it was completely superseded by the Beaux Arts reaction. It was in some ways far too personal, and often unsuited to its task. The Marshall Field Store, although influential, was, if anything, backward-looking both technically and aesthetically.

Rickman, Thomas (1776–1841). British architect and architectural historian. Rickman was the son of a grocer and chemist at Maidenhead, Berkshire, and had a rather irregular career in medicine and commerce down to 1813. But at the same time he was teaching himself to draw, specializing in architectural subjects after prolonged examination of a very large number of ecclesiastical buildings. In 1812 he wrote an architectural history of Chester Cathedral, and began to lecture to the Liverpool Academy. In 1817 he published *An Attempt to Discriminate the Styles of Architecture in England from the Conquest to the Reformation*, in which he coined the terms Early English, Decorated, and Perpendicular, which have become standard nomenclature for English Gothic styles.

In 1818 Rickman began to practise as an architect in Liverpool, under the patronage of the iron-founder Thomas Cragg. He later opened another office in Birmingham. He built many churches in the Gothic style, and was also responsible for a number of secular buildings, notably the New Court of St John's College, Cambridge (1827–31).

Ridge. The point in a roof at which the two sloping sides meet; usually there is a continuous structural element at this point, the ridge-piece, which supports the upper ends of the rafters.

Ridge rib. In vaulting, a secondary rib that follows the longitudinal ridge of the vault, or crosses it transversely.

Riesener, Jean-Henri (1734–1806). *Ebéniste*, born at Gladbeck, near Essen, Germany. Riesener went to Paris, where he worked under Oeben, whose widow he later married. He thus gained entry into the exclusive Parisian corporation of *menuisiers-ébénistes*, into which Oeben himself had intruded through royal patronage. He became a *maître* in 1767, and *ébéniste ordinaire du roi* in 1774.

Although he had worked for Louis XVI, Riesener was not immediately ruined by the Revolution, at one stage being employed by the Directory to remove royal emblems from furniture. He was able to buy back a great deal of his own work at sales of royal furniture, but had difficulty re-selling it. He was eventually compelled to earn a living as an assessor at the law courts.

Riesener's furniture is notable for its quality; it is extremely elegant and less exaggerated than the Rococo work of Oeben, under whose *estampille* some of Riesener's work appears. Sometimes he collaborated with Merkelain, who worked out ingenious mechanical devices that enabled a single piece of furniture to serve several purposes.

Red-blue chair by Rietveld

Gerrit Rietveld

Rietveld, Gerrit (1888–1964). Dutch architect and furniture designer. Reitveld was the son of a joiner, to whom he was apprenticed (1899–1906). He went on to study jewellery design before setting up his own cabinet-making business (1911–19). During this period he took instruction in architecture under P J C Klaarhamer, and by 1919 was able to set up his own office as an architect, closing the cabinetmaking business.

In the same year, Rietveld came into contact with the De Stijl movement. The magazine *De Stijl* carried an illustration of his red-blue chair (designed in 1919), and the linear, abstract style of the chair appears again in Rietveld's best known building, the Schroeder House, Utrecht (1924). In both of these works his use of strong primary colours is also an indication of his adherence to De Stijl.

Rietveld designed a number of buildings in the Netherlands, Austria, Italy, France, and Germany, but after the demise of the *De Stijl* magazine (1931) his

St George's Church, Birmingham, by Thomas Richardson

A lacquered serpentine commode by Risen Burgh, stamped BURB

A Louis XVI commode by J H Riesener, c 1785

Turned and bentwood rocking chairs

work received little attention until the revival of interest in movement in the 1950s. Of his later buildings, the most important are the De Ploeg textile works, Bergeiyk (1956), housing developments in Hoograven, with others (1954–6), the Zonnehof Museums, Amersfoort (1959), and various private houses.

Risen Burgh, Bernhard Van (c 1700–c 1765). *Ebéniste.* An elusive man whose identity was only rediscovered in 1957. He had for many years been known to scholars and students as 'BVRB', the initials on his stamp. A *maître* of the guild before 1730, he seems to have dealt largely with *marchands-merciers* through whom private clients bought their furniture.

His work is of outstanding craftsmanship, and has a grace and elegance that places it among the finest Rococo furniture. Van Risen Burgh was one of the first *ébénistes* to encrust furniture with porcelain plaques. He worked in a style that can be described as Louis XV.

Riser. The vertical front of a step, in between two horizontal treads.

Robsjohn-Gibbings, Terence Harold (b 1905). American interior designer, born in London; he emigrated to America in 1929. Between 1943 and 1956 Robsjohn-Gibbings was sole designer for the Widdicomb Furniture Company. He is president of Robsjohn-Gibbings Ltd (New York), which specializes in designing interiors, as well as furniture, fabrics, and accessories. His publications include *Goodbye Mr Chippendale, Mona Lisa's Moustache, Homes of the Brave,* and *Furniture of Classical Greece.*

Rocaille (French, 'rockwork'). A term first used to describe the artificial grottoes of Versailles; it is now applied to the typical Rococo ornament that resembles rocks and shell-work.

Rocking chair. A chair fitted with curved bends or rockers which are attached to the legs, permitting the occupant of the chair to rock or be rocked. The device probably derived from the use of similar bends for cradles; it has been attributed to Benjamin Franklin, but is probably older.

Early rocking chairs merely had bends added to traditional

shapes. The first rocking chair specifically designed for an appropriately relaxed body posture was probably evolved in Boston, Massachusetts, in the early nineteenth century. Various types were later developed ranging from bentwood rockers with upholstered seats and backs to a metal-framed upholstered rocker, shown at the Great Exhibition in 1851, and known as Dr Calvert's Digestive Chair. The most consistently successful of all rocking chairs has undoubtedly been the bentwood chairs (qv), first designed over a century ago by the American industrial designer Michael Thonet (1796–1871).

Rockingham. The Rockingham pottery at Swinton in Yorkshire (situated on the estate of the Marquis of Rockingham) was started c 1745 by a man called Twigg. Little is known of the early work. The pottery passed through several hands, and in 1778 was taken over by Thomas Bingley and Co, who enlarged it. Earthenware and stoneware of quite good quality were made, including blue and white transfer-printed tableware, and brown tea- and coffee-services and jugs. These had a shiny brown glaze which became known as a 'Rockingham' glaze. Another product was the Cadogan teapot, a copy of an oriental original in the shape of a peach, which was filled from the base on the inkwell principle. From about 1790 to 1800 one of the Greens from the Leeds pottery (qv) was a member of the firm, and Rockingham ware became similar in character to that of Leeds. In 1806 the works were acquired by William Brameld, who was succeeded by his three sons. About 1823 Thomas Brameld began to make fine quality porcelain, and the mark of a griffin passant, the Rockingham family crest, was adopted. A large quantity of good-quality porcelain tableware was made at Rockingham in the period 1820–42, some of it in the

Rococo taste; much, however, was florid and over-ornate, with flowers in relief and gilding. Coloured grounds such as applegreen, grey, or apricot were used. Figures, animals, and other ornaments were also made.

Rococo. In origin, the anticlassical, anti-Baroque reaction against the style of Louis XIV in early eighteenth-century France.

The antipathy towards classical formalism manifested itself in a desire for convenience and intimacy; for example, in J H Mansart's Château du Val, near Paris (1674), the rooms are small, and the whole building merely a one-storey pavilion. The classical orders were used sparingly on the outside, and on the inside

Terence Robsjohn-Gibbings

Walnut credenza based on an ancient sarcophagus by Gibbings

A Rockingham saucer, c 1830–7

Rococo church by Die Wies, Bavaria, by Zimmerman, 1735-54

The marquetry side panel of a commode by David Roentgen, c 1775

only in formal rooms. In other rooms they were replaced by wooden panels with delicate mouldings. The logic of classicism was abandoned, and no division was made between walls and ceilings; in Robert de Cotte's Hôtel de la Vrillière (1713) the pilasters are panelled in such a way that all structural sense is lost, while stucco figure groups overlay the cornice. Shaped rooms, then rounded corners,

A Louis XV Rococo giltwood chair with tapestry cover

came into fashion, breaking down the division between wall and wall. Furniture, porcelain, and decorative prints echoed the motifs of the walls and ceilings to produce an effect of totality that was not possible with the classical style.

Antipathy towards the heroic and visionary preoccupations of the Baroque resulted in a corresponding interest in the human and sensual. The small scale and delightful visual charm of the exterior of François Cuvilliés Amalienburg Pavilion (1734) is matched by the sensual display of earthly delight inside. Instead of the illusion of transcendental light from above, as in a Baroque building, Rococo light is ubiquitous, flooding in from full-length french windows, and reflected in mirrors the full height of the walls, and from the surfaces of porcelain. The very popularity of porcelain owed much to its elegant informality, in contrast to the silver furniture with which Louis XIV had equipped the Galerie des Glaces.

Rejection of the heroic also led to iconographical changes. The gods of Olympus lost their popularity to the shepherds and shepherdesses of Arcadia, whose

absorption in hunting and love-making was singularly appropriate to French society of the *Régence* period. The attributes of Venus (shell, waves, reeds, mirrors) became the dominant motifs in design; for example, in the work of Juste Aurèle Meissonier (1693–1750), who became goldsmith to the king in 1724. In general, motifs were derived from nature, and, following nature's laws, were most frequently asymmetrically arranged.

The impact of the Rococo outside France was powerful but limited. The naturalism and exoticism of its motifs appeared in England, but largely confined to Vauxhall Pleasure Gardens and to Chippendale's furniture. Lord Burlington experimented with shaped rooms (although his motives were archaeological), and the most significant development in early eighteenth-century English architecture was the villa, an intimate secondary residence comparable to the Château du Val or the Amalienburg Pavilion. But the wider aesthetic implications were ignored, and there was no attempt to create a truly Rococo architecture.

The tradition of superlative stucco craftsmanship in south

Germany was revitalized by the new motifs from Paris. These were lavishly applied to fundamentally Baroque churches in Bavaria and central Europe. Here, too, the wider implications were none the less ignored.

Roentgen, David (1743–1807). German *ébéniste*, perhaps the most widely known *ébéniste* at the end of the eighteenth century, for his was the first and most successful business within Europe. He was the son of Abraham Roentgen, a cabinet-maker who had established a business at Neuwied, near Coblenz. David took it over in the late 1760s and later went to Paris, where he opened a furniture depôt in 1779.

He was patronized by Louis XVI, who appointed him *ébéniste-méchanicien du roi et de la reine*, and by Catherine II of Russia and many other European rulers. He visited Russia on several occasions, and some of his furniture is now in the Hermitage Museum, Leningrad.

Roentgen followed the general trend in taste, moving from the naturalistic flowers and ribbons of the 1770s to more severe architectural shapes. His work

A marquetry table with panels by David Roentgen, c 1785

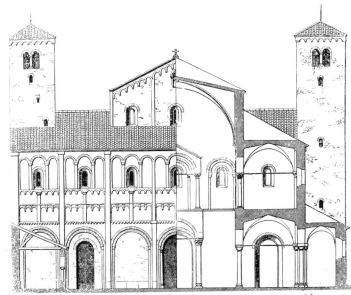

The elevation and section of the façade of the Cathedral at Novara

was also distinguished by the incorporation of mechanical devices, a feature peculiar to furniture by German craftsmen. He was completely ruined by the Revolution, and his depôt was confiscated. He fled to Berlin, where he became court furnisher to Friedrich Wilhelm II.

American easy chair with roll-over-arm, c 1700

Roll moulding. Simple convex moulding, semi-circular or more than semi-circular in section; it was used in Norman architecture, when it was known as a bowtell, and in early Gothic. A roll moulding with a slight edge on its curve is a scroll or edge moulding; one with a fillet is a roll and fillet moulding.

Roll-over-arm. The name given to upholstered arms of chairs that roll outwards to give a scrolled profile. They have been used in various forms since the seventeenth century. The earlier versions are the most elegant.

Roll-top desk. A type of Victorian desk with a curved top which could be closed over the working-top by means of a tambour device (qv). The roll-top desk was widely used in offices, and was also the most popular form of desk for the paterfamilias in the home. An earlier desk that is very similar is the French *bureau à cylindre*, on which the top is made of a solid piece of wood.

Roman architecture. See **Italian architecture.**

Romanesque. The style of ecclesiastical architecture in western Europe between *c* 1000 and *c* 1200. Romanesque was in part a response to specific social and liturgical needs; in particular the need for churches with a number of separate chapels, which in turn arose out of the cult of relics and the popularity of pilgrimages, and also from the custom that every priest should say mass every day. In Romanesque churches, these chapels were not merely walled-off areas within a single space (as in a Carolingian church), or rooms added on to the main structure (as in an Anglo-Saxon church). Instead, architects evolved a system whereby all the spaces opened into one another but

maintained separate identities through differences in scale. Chapels were normally placed at the east end of the church, and it was here that their multiplication produced the most ingenious articulations of spaces. Two types in particular stand out, epitomized by St Martin-de-Tours (997) and Cluny (rebuilt 981). At St Martin-de-Tours the chapels radiate outwards from the sanctuary, opening out into an ambulatory, which opens out into the choir, which in turn opens out into the transept. At Cluny the chapels open in echelons into the transept and into the eastward extension of the aisles.

Nor was this clarification limited to the plan. The points where the spaces interpenetrated were not holes cut in a wall, but were articulated by means of

A mid-19th century copy of a roll-top desk by Riesener

An aisle in the Romanesque church of S Philibert at Tournus

The Romanesque oratory of Saint Croix, near Arles, 11th century

The west end of S Etienne, Abbeye aux Hommes, Caen, 1066-86

vertical supports and round arches, capitals punctuating their junction. Sculpture appeared at the points of tension (the capitals), and Corinthian capitals were chosen as the model since they gave more opportunity for invention. Two types of elevation evolved; the Saxon (central German) type, originating at St Michael, Hildesheim (begun *c* 1000), and the Anglo-Norman type, originating at Jumièges (*c* 1040). At St Michael the interior space is divided into its component parts (nave, transept, etc), and then sub-divided by means of piers into a small number of large square spaces which are themselves sub-divided by columns. In the Anglo-Norman type the sub-division of the component parts is regular; although the supports could vary in detail they have in common a vertical shaft which runs from floor to ceiling. This system sub-divides the spaces into much smaller parts and makes it easier to extend them; therefore naves tend to be long.

Ceilings were soon subjected to equally logical treatment. A uniform flat (wooden) or barrel-vaulted (stone) ceiling did not provide a fitting complement to the division of spaces into clearly distinguished individual bays. At Durham (vaulting begun 1104) rib vaults were not used for structural reasons, but in order to divide each bay from its neighbours by means of transverse arches, and to assert its separateness by a crisscross of diagonals.

The adoption of a system of clearly distinguished, logically complete bays as units of design paves the way for Gothic architecture (qv).

Romayne work. Renaissance ornamental carved panels sometimes used for furniture. The panels enclose small profile heads in medallions, and scrollwork and foliage.

Rood screen, rood loft. The screen which separated the choir from the nave of a church. Above it was the rood loft; very few of these galleries survived the English Reformation because they carried the Rood, as well as other images, and were consequently destroyed as idolatrous. With the disappearance of loft and Rood, the surviving screen became synonymous with the chancel screen.

Roof (Old English *hrof*). The outside upper covering of a building, usually categorized by its basic construction or by the nature of its outer protective layer. The construction or form of a roof can be curved, pitched, or flat, and thus ranges from the dome to the horizontal roof, from the vault to the suspended roof; the various framed roofs – lean-to, pitched, hammer-beam, king-post, mansard, etc – all fall within this last category. Protective coverings include sheet metal, slate, tile, and thatch.

In the past, climatic conditions largely governed the pitch (slope) of a roof. Flat roofs – now ubiquitous – were largely confined to buildings in hot and dry climates; sloping roofs to temperate and humid regions. The Swiss chalet (qv) has a very broad, gently sloping roof that retains the snow; houses in rainy areas have the steepest pitches.

The principal longitudinal components in a basic timber-framed roof are the ridge beam, laid along the apex of the roof, the purlins, which lie along the slope of the roof, and the sole or wall plate, which lies along the top of the wall. Between the sole plate and the ridge are a series of coupled rafters; the principal rafter is placed strategically in the construction, and common rafters fill the rest of the length. Sprockets are occasionally used to give extra lift to the eaves. This is the basic construction of a small roof not more than 10 ft in span.

The other simple members in this form of construction are the tie beam spanning the sole plates, and the collar beam, a tie beam farther up the slope of the roof. More complicated constructions – king and queen posts, hammer-beam, and mansard roofs – are the subject of separate articles. See also individual roof members and constructions under separate entries.

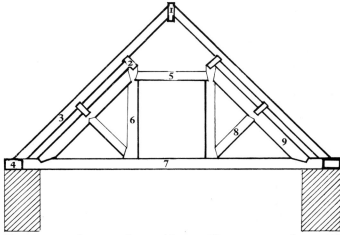

Queen post roof construction: **1** *ridge* **2** *purlin* **3** *common rafter* **4** *wall plate* **5** *collar beam* **6** *queen post* **7** *tie beam* **8** *strut* **9** *principal rafter*

The rose window at the west end of the Cathedral at Rheims

A Rudd dressing table, c 1773

Rosette. A formalized rose, carved, painted, or moulded onto a circular disc or patera. It was used singly or in series.

Rose window. A circular window in which the intricate tracery resembles a stylized rose. The most famous rose window is probably at Chartres Cathedral.

A rout chair

The form varies, so that occasionally the radiating mullions suggest a wheel.

Rosewood. *Dalbergia.* A general term applied to a variety of woods indigenous to India and South America. The name derives from the peculiar scent the wood exudes on being cut. Rosewood was popular in Europe and America for all types of furniture. The dark brown, streaked South American variety was used most by American and English furniture-makers. It was particularly popular in Georgian England for decorative work such as inlaying, banding, panelling, and veneering. It was valued in the Victorian era as a type of mahogany, and is still employed as a veneer.

Rotunda. A circular, usually domed, building or hall. The central hall of the Capitol, Washington, is an example.

Roundabout chair. A chair of ungainly design, with a circular seat and six legs. It was made in the East Indies c 1700 and

was imported to Holland; there it acquired its other name, Burgomaster chair.

In America, the term roundabout chair is used of both the English writing chair and the nineteenth-century companion chair, which had three double seats joined together on a central pivot.

Roundel. A small circular window, or any ornament that is circular. The term is also applied to an ornament used within a circular space or recess.

Roundheaded arch. See **Semi-circular arch.**

Rout chair. Chairs made to be hired out for parties and large gatherings; the term derives from the eighteenth-century revival of the word 'rout' to describe select gatherings and lively entertainments. The rout chair was small, painted, and rush-bottomed.

Rudd dressing-table. Copiously-drawered dressing-table which is shown in Hepplewhite's *Guide* (1788) and Shearer's *The Prices of Cabinet Work* (1793). The origin of the name is uncertain: it seems to have derived from either a courtesan who stood trial with two forgers in 1775, or a rather obscure eighteenth-century cabinetmaker.

Rudolph, Paul Marvin (b 1918). American architect. Rudolph studied at Harvard University under Walter Gropius. In 1958 he was appointed chairman of

the department of architecture at Yale University, and he has designed several university buildings. All Rudolph's works, from his earlier small houses at Sarasota, Florida, to his later campus buildings, have aroused controversy. It has been said that he seems likely to inherit the mantle of Frank Lloyd Wright, and there is no doubt that almost every project he undertakes divides critics into partisans and detractors.

Among his major projects have been schools at Sarasota; students' quarters at Yale; a multi-storey garage at New Haven; and the Endo Laboratories at Garden City, New York.

Rudolph – like Philip Johnson (qv) – believes in designing a building with a view to its particular purpose, without im-

Paul Rudolph

The sunken seating area in the Milam House, Florida, by Rudolph

Milam House, Florida, by Paul Rudolph

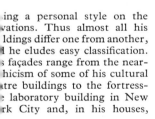

ing a personal style on the vations. Thus almost all his ldings differ one from another, he eludes easy classification. façades range from the near-hicism of some of his cultural tre buildings to the fortress-laboratory building in New rk City and, in his houses,

from the Neo-classicism of his Sarasota house to the stark angularities of the Milam house.

Rug. From ancient times this term was applied to almost any covering – for walls, tables, benches, beds etc – made from a heavy or thick material. But for

the past hundred years 'rug' has been used almost exclusively of floor-coverings. The earliest rugs were made of felt, and it has been estimated that these elementary coverings were used 25,000 years ago. Their ornamental possibilities began to be exploited at an early date, and

examples from the fourth or fifth century BC have been discovered in the Middle and Far East. Middle Eastern examples have long figured in European and North American decorative schemes, Persian rugs holding pride of place in Europe. With the development of weaving

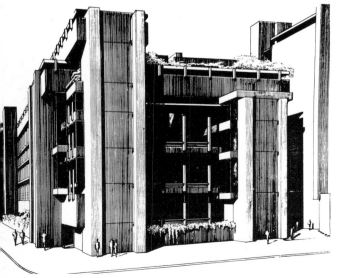

School of Art and Architecture, Yale University, by Rudolph, 1963

A Caucasian rug from Kazak

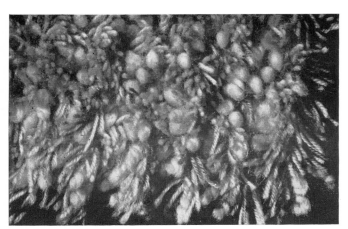

Detail of a Rya rug

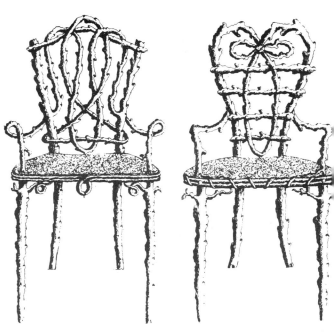

Rustic seats from William Wright's 'Grotesque Architecture'

machinery, many of the ancient motifs of rug-making were adapted for mass production, uniformity of design replacing the wayward charm inseparable from hand craft.

In more recent times, rug-making has again been widely practised as a craft. The brilliance of colour of modern hand-woven rugs is enhanced by the depths of pile now obtainable by the use of fine wools.

Rundell, Bridge & Rundell. An important silver-making firm of the Regency period. In 1785 Philip Rundell took over the firm of Theed and Pickett in Ludgate Hill, and shortly afterwards took John Bridge as a partner. From 1789 the firm enjoyed royal patronage, and the Prince Regent was to become its chief client. Paul Storr, Benjamin Smith, Digby Scott, and James Smith were among the silversmiths employed, frequently working to the designs of distinguished artists such as Flaxman and Stothard. The main emphasis was on Neo-classical silver. The firm was at

its zenith in the second decade of the nineteenth century; Philip Rundell retired in 1823, Bridge died in 1834, and in 1842 the business was closed.

Runner. A term used variously to describe the curved members of a rocking chair, the wooden guide strips at the sides of a drawer, and the supports of the fall front of a desk. The last were called lopers by cabinetmakers. The term is also applied to a strip of material used to decorate the top of a narrow table or piano.

Running dog. See **Vitruvian scroll.**

Running sideboard or **dinnerwagon.** A stand with two or three open shelves, sometimes with a gallery but more often plain. The feet often had castors attached so that the sideboard could be moved about; in America it was also called a moving sideboard. The running sideboard was popular on both sides of the Atlantic during the nineteenth century.

Rural or **rustic chairs** and **furniture.** A form of furniture designed in a deliberately rustic manner to satisfy the sophisticated eighteenth-century British taste for 'the simple life of the country' – a taste also shown in landscape gardening. Designs for such fanciful pieces were provided by Robert Manwaring in *The Cabinet and Chair Maker's Real Friend and Companion* (1765) and William Wright in *Grotesque Architecture, or Rural Amusements* (1767).

Rush seating. The weaving of rushes, one of the oldest country crafts, was used to make chair seats in medieval times, and has been practised ever since. Chip-

pendale supplied a set to Sir Roland Winn in 1766, and Sheraton's *Cabinet Dictionary* (1803) gives directions for painting them white.

Today, Italian and Spanish chairmakers make good rush seats for chairs and small settees. Common rushes of unusual robustness are used.

American variants are flag seats (flag is another word for rush) and splint seats (made from splintered wood, frequently hickory).

Russell, Sir Gordon (b 1892). British designer. Russell was brought up in the Cotswold village of Broadway, Worcestershire, where his father, S B

Russell, had bought the Lygo Arms, a Tudor inn still run h the Russell family today. He w educated at Campden Gramm School and served in the Wo cestershire Regiment durin World War I. On demobilizatio he joined his father's furnitu business, but soon began design modern pieces. In 19 he founded Gordon Russell L in association with his father an brothers (R D and D G Russell), producing simple, we designed, well-made furniture natural woods. The Arts an Crafts movement (qv) ideals infl enced much of his early work, b he began to design furniture f mass production without sac ficing his high standards. In 19

Centrepiece signed Rundell, Bridge and Rundell by Paul Storr

Rush seating on a modern beechwood settee

Sir Gordon Russell

Richard Drew Russell

the firm produced the first of a successful ten-year programme of Murphy radio cabinets (designed by R D Russell).

In 1942 Russell joined the wartime Utility Furniture Advisory Committee, which imposed new, simple, and good standards upon nationally produced furniture. The following year he was made chairman of the Board of Trade Design Panel. In 1944 he became a member of the newly-founded Council of Industrial Design, set up to promote higher standards in British industry, and later took over the directorship (1947–59). Under his leadership the CoID moved to the Haymarket, London, where the Design Centre (qv) opened to the public in 1956.

During this period Russell also helped to plan the 1951 Festival of Britain. He was knighted in 1955. From 1956 to 1966 he was a member of the British Railways Design Panel. His autobiography, *Designer's Trade,* was published in 1968.

Russell, Richard Drew (*b* 1903). British designer, educated at Dean Close School, Cheltenham, and trained at the Architectural Association School. He joined the family firm of Gordon Russell Ltd in 1929, eventually becoming director of design. In 1934, to widen his experience, he moved to Murphy Radio as chief industrial designer. In 1936 he set up in private practice, con-

tinuing to act as consultant designer to both companies.

After service in World War II, he resumed private practice. In 1948 he was appointed professor in the School of Wood, Metals, and Plastics in the Royal College of Art, continuing in the School of Furniture Design until 1964, when he became professor emeritus.

Russell collaborated with Robert Goodden (qv) in designing, building, the interior and display of the Lion and Unicorn Pavilion in the 1951 South Bank Exhibition. They continued to collaborate, redesigning the Greek galleries of the British Museum (completed in 1969), the Department of Prints and Drawings, and Gallery of Oriental Art. Russell was appointed Royal Designer for Industry in 1944, and a fellow of the Society of Industrial Artists and Designers in 1947.

Rusticated column. A column with alternating plain and rusticated blocks throughout the length of the shaft. The rustication in this case is provided by square blocks or enlarged circular sections, pitted and scored by masons to give the required impression of massive support.

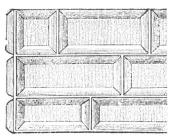

Rustication

Rustication. An elaboration on the term 'rustic work', employed by early eighteenth-century architectural writers. Rustication comprises large blocks of stone used in exterior walling, which are carved with deeply grooved edges or broad joints; it is usually employed on the lower storey of a building. The effect of massiveness was emphasized by making the rusticated blocks project beyond the general façade, sometimes by as much as a foot. The play of light upon the deep channels between the blocks enhanced the apparent thickness of the stonework, giving the building an appearance of solidity while enriching the texture of the wall. Rustication was widely employed in the Florentine palaces, notably the Strozzi and Riccardi.

Rusticated Columns

Rustication on the Spada Palace in Rome

The Greek Sculpture Gallery, British Museum, by R D Russell 1969

The Dallas International Airport for Washington designed by Eero Saarinen, 1958-63

Saarinen, Eero (1910–61). American architect. Saarinen went to the USA with his father, Eliel Saarinen (qv), when he was 12. He returned to Europe to study sculpture in Paris, but then studied architecture at Yale University. He joined his father's practice in Michigan, becoming principal partner in 1950.

Saarinen made his reputation very rapidly after World War II. His designs for the various organizations within General Motors Technical Center in Michigan (1948–56) won international recognition, as did his work at the Massachusetts Institute of Technology (1953–5). Unlike those of his contemporary Mies van der Rohe, Saarinen's buildings have no readily recognizable design-theme, confirming his own stated belief that 'in any kind of design, one has to go fearlessly ahead to the most rational, most intense consequence.' He was undoubtedly influenced by the work of other architects, from Mies van der Rohe and Felix Candela to Philip Johnson and Louis Kahn. His most notable later buildings are the Yale Hockey Rink (1953–9), Kennedy Terminal (1956–62), the T J Watson Research Center, Yorktown (1957–61), and

the Dallas Airport, Washington (1958–63). Saarinen was also responsible for the design of the US embassies in London (1955–61), and Oslo (1959).

Saarinen also designed furniture for Knoll Associates from 1946. He had earlier exhibited at the Organic Furniture Competition at the Museum of

Eero Saarinen

North Christian Church, Columbus, Indiana, by Eero Saarinen, c 1960

Stave church. *The highly decorative medieval Gol Stave church now preserved in Oslo, c 1200*

Saarinen tulip chair, 1956

Saddle cheek wings

A Salem secretary by Edmund Johnson, Salem, c 1800

Modern Art, New York (1940), winning two prizes jointly with Charles Eames. His 'tulip pedestal' and 'womb' chairs are modern classics.

Saarinen, Eliel (1873–1950). Finnish architect. Saarinen was born at Rantasalmi and trained in Helsinki, afterwards setting up in practice with Herman Gesellius and Armas Lindgren. He designed the Finnish Pavilion at the Paris Exhibition (1900), and four years later won the competition for Helsinki railway station, finished in 1914. He also won a further competition for the design of the Finnish Parliament buildings, which were never built. After a visit to the USA he settled there, enjoying success as practitioner and teacher. Saarinen's principal designs were for the Cranbrook Academy of Art (of which he was later director) and various schools, churches, and museums in the Middle West.

Helsinki Station by Saarinen

Sabicu, Sacquebi. *Lysiloma sabica.* Although this hard and durable Central American wood is difficult to work, it has been used for cabinetmaking and joinery since 1750. It is similar in colour to rosewood and in character to mahogany, and has been used in particular for veneer work in the form of bandings.

Sacristy. In ecclesiastical architecture, a room in which sacred vessels are kept, generally on the north side of the chancel. It is sometimes also used as a robing room and meeting-place for church business. In the larger well-preserved sacristies, ovens for baking communion bread are occasionally found.

Saddle-back coping. Coping that slopes down an equal distance from either side of a ridge.

Saddle-back roof. The term commonly used of a pitched roof on a tower; but it is properly defined as a normal pitched roof placed in an unusual position.

Saddle bar. An iron bar fixed horizontally across a mullioned window. Small pieces of wire were often twisted around the bar so that it would stiffen the leaded glass against the wind and support the slender stone mullions.

Saddle cheek. A term used by Hepplewhite to describe a winged easy chair in which the wings or cheeks are shaped like a saddle; the intention may have been to exclude draughts.

Saddle seat. This type of wooden seat is usually found on Windsor chairs. It has a shallow depression either side of the central ridge, and therefore re-

sembles a saddle. Saddle stools are three-legged with similar seats.

Salem rocker. A rocking chair made in New England in the early nineteenth century. It had a heavily scrolled seat, arms, and top rail, with narrow spindles in the back. The back was lower than that of the Boston rocker (qv).

Salem secretary. A characteristic piece of Federal furniture, invented by a group of cabinetmakers in Salem in the late eighteenth century. It is a bookcase-cum-secretary with a recessed shelved superstructure enclosed by two or four glazed doors, and a lower cupboarded portion that frequently contains a fall-front writing flap.

Salt-glazed stoneware. In the early eighteenth century a number of Staffordshire potters experimented with a ware they hoped would be comparable to Chinese porcelain. Taking a lead from John Dwight of Fulham, Staffordshire potters concen-

trated on making lighter and lighter coloured stoneware. Finally an almost white stoneware was achieved by John Astbury, who had the idea of adding calcined flints to the body of the sand and clay mixture. The resulting ware was then glazed with salt, which gave it a very agreeable, smooth, slightly 'orange-peely' texture. It was very strong and hard-wearing and was not easily chipped; but unlike Chinese porcelain was never translucent. It became very popular, superseding the earlier, rather clumsy Delftware, and

Salt-glazed plate

Salt-glazed stoneware teapot, 1755-60

Art glass for Iittalan Lasitendas by Timo Sarpaneva, 1966

was soon made in great quantities. It continued in production until Wedgwood's cream-coloured earthenware captured the market; by about 1770 production had almost ceased.

Tableware of all kinds was made in salt-glazed stoneware, particularly teapots, for which the relatively new habit of tea drinking had created a demand too great to be met by the import trade from China. Decorative figures were also made, as well as useful objects such as jelly moulds and salt cellars.

The first salt-glazed stoneware was buffish in colour, and was known as Crouch ware. It was ornamented with white pipeclay decorations sprigged on to the surface. The ware was made progressively paler in colour until it was a creamy white.

Teapots were cast in the most fantastic shapes – shells, camels, and even houses – as well as more conventional forms. Plates were often moulded with intricate basketwork designs in Rococo style. The first coloured salt-glazed stoneware was known as

'scratch blue'; the surface of the ware was decorated with incised patterns into which clay stained with cobalt was introduced. Much of the later salt-glazed stoneware was enamelled with jewel-like colours.

Saltires. The X-stretchers which connect the legs of chairs and tables diagonally.

Sampe, Astrid (b 1909). Swedish textile designer. Sampe trained at the Stockholm School of Arts and Crafts and the Royal College of Art, London. In 1936 she joined the Nordiska Company in Stockholm as head of its newly-formed textile department. Her designs and experiments, carried out at the Nordiska textile studio, have won Sampe an international reputation. She has carried out work for overseas textile firms, including Donald Brothers of Dundee and Knoll International Textiles of New York, and has also designed carpets and other floor coverings.

Sampler. A term applied to any piece of canvas on which embroidery was worked as a pattern, particularly for a beginner in needlework. Traditionally it contained an alphabet, embellished with various forms of flora and fauna. The chronicler Rapháel Holinshed remarked upon the skill in embroidery of the ladies at Queen Elizabeth's court, and the widespread practice of the craft in Elizabethan times was responsible for much beautiful work. Samplers were frequently used as wall decorations, and also as cushion covers.

Sanctuary (Latin, *sanctuarium* 'a holy place'). A church or part of a church considered sacred.

Sanctuary is especially associated with safety from attack and freedom of arrest, which was any man's right under medieval ecclesiastical law.

Sarcophagus. This was one of the many antique forms adapted to curious ends in the late eighteenth century. It became a wine cooler in the hands of cabinetmakers, and an outdoor jardinière in the hands of stonemasons. In *The Cabinet Dictionary* (1803) Sheraton refers to the wine cooler as 'an imitation of the figure of these ancient stone coffins.' Such coolers were normally placed beneath the dining-room sideboard. As an element in the Picturesque (qv), stone coffins were placed in landscaped gardens to induce a suitable mood of melancholy.

Sarpaneva, Timo (b 1926). Finnish glass, textile, and graphic artist and sculptor. Sarpaneva was born in Helsinki, and studied there at the Arts and Crafts School (1946–9), returning later (1953–7) as a teacher.

In 1950 he began his long association with the Iittala firm as a glass artist, the profession in which he is best known. His work always had a sculptural quality, but in 1964 he moved from an ostensible vessel form to pure sculpture. He is still working for Iittala, as well as for

Björneborg's cotton and machine shops (since 1955). For Björneborg he has designed textiles, and a range of cast-iron cooking pots which has become very popular. He has arranged a number of exhibitions in Helsinki and South America, and was responsible for the Finnish section of the World Fair at Montreal in 1967. He has won numerous awards.

Sash-window (French, *chassis* 'frame'). A wooden-framed window which contains a pair of double-hung sliding windows, raised and lowered by means of weighted cords. Sash-windows were introduced in the late seventeenth century, and the term seemed to have gained currency soon afterwards.

Satinwood. The two most important varieties of this wood are *Chloroxylon swietenia*, East Indian satinwood, and *Xanthoxylon flavium*, West Indian satinwood. These were used, mainly in the eighteenth century, for veneering fine furniture. The use of this warm yellowish wood, sometimes particularly finely figured and extremely glossy when polished, marks the transition from the solid furniture of the Chippendale period to decorative furniture with more elaborate fittings. Satinwood was also used for panelling.

A linen sampler, dated 1666

A George III satinwood table top with marquetry work

Chair by William Savery, c 1705

Satyr mask. Motif used on the knees of chairs and tables by fashionable mid-eighteenth-century cabinetmakers.

Savery, William (1721-87). American cabinetmaker, a member of the Philadelphia School. Savery worked mainly in the Queen Anne and Chippendale styles. His highboys and lowboys have been considered to be among the finest produced in the Colonial America. The knees of his chairs often carry an intaglio leaf carving.

Savonarola chair. An X-shaped folding chair made in Renaissance Italy. It consists of interlocking wooden strips with a slatted seat just above the intersection, and a low back.

Savonnerie. The most famous of all European carpet factories,

and one that established a standard of excellence to which all subsequent manufacturers have aspired. The founder, Pierre Dupont, was a successful carpet manufacturer in the workshops at the Louvre. In 1627 he acquired premises at La Savonnerie, an old soap factory on the Quai Chaillot. Work commenced there under his partner, but the works at the Louvre were not finally closed down until 1672.

Savonnerie pile carpets were said to be 'made' in the Turkish manner, using the Ghiordes knot, but the designs were strictly French. The carpets could be owned only by the French royal family, favoured foreign diplomats, and crowned heads, who were given them as presents. This rule was not relaxed until 1768, and even then prices remained so high that few could afford to buy. The factory continued to operate – with difficulty – during the Revolution, but was finally closed down in 1825.

Scagliola. An imitation marble made up of plaster of Paris, isinglass, chips of marble, and colouring. Though known to antiquity, its period of greatest popularity was the seventeenth and eighteenth centuries. The variety of its colour combinations and markings led to its use for architectural decorations and commode and table tops. See **Pietra dura.**

Scaling. A decorative surface finish resembling fish scales. It was used on mouldings in architecture, and on chair frames and console tables in cabinetmaking.

Scallop. An edge carved into a series of convex curves, resem-

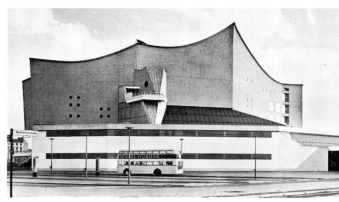

The Berlin Philharmonic Hall designed by Hans Scharoun, 1963

bling a row of scallop shells or the magnified outer curve of a shell. Late eighteenth-century tripod tables often had edges scalloped like the traditional pastry crust on a pie; hence they were called pie crust tables (qv).

Scalloped capital. A variation on the cushion capital (qv) in which each side is shaped into a series of truncated cones or scallops.

Scamozzi Ionic. A variant of the traditional Ionic order that was invented by Vicenzo Scamozzi (1552-1616). The capital has four identical faces instead of the usual two, causing the corners to be angled out at the juncture of the volutes. The abacus above has concave sides.

Scharoun, Hans (1893-1972). German architect. He lived in Bremerhaven until 1912, when he paid his first visit to Berlin to study at the technical college. It was in Berlin that he was to build many of his major works. His style developed consistently without undergoing radical changes, despite his long practice. It is strongly expressionistic, rejecting the severe geometry of the International style. Scharoun's schemes are full of wide oblique or acute angles, rounded corners, semi-circular sweeps, and irregular groupings and skylines. In Nazi Germany his work was restricted mainly to designing projects that were quite unrealizable at the time. Then, after the war, his experimental style and response to social needs again brought him to the fore. This is most clearly demonstrated in the Philharmonic Hall, West Berlin (1963). The seating in this highly-structured hall is broken up into small oblique-angled units on different levels.

His other works include the 'Romeo and Juliet' point blocks

in Stuttgart (with Wilhelm Frank, 1954-9), the Charlottenburg-Nord housing estate, Berlin (1955-61), and Geschwister-Scholl School, Westphalia (1962).

Schinkel, Karl Friedrich (1781-1841). German architect, born in Prussia. Schinkel studied architecture under Friedrich Gilly (1772-1800) at his academy in Paris. However, before he embarked upon an architectural career he established a reputation as a painter and stage designer.

Nearly all of Schinkel's architectural works are in Prussia. In the capital, Berlin, he designed a memorable collection of public buildings in a Greek revival style. The Neue Wache in the Unter den Linden (1816-18) is a severe and powerful building with a plain Doric portion and only a very restrained use of ornament. Schinkel's other works in Berlin included a cathedral, a theatre, and the Altes Museum, all designed and built before 1830.

Despite his knowledge and mastery of the Neo-classical idiom, Schinkel's feeling for theatrical effect appears in the Gothic designs that he produced concurrently with the Greek

A detail of a Savonnerie carpet with a blue and cream ground

K F Schinkel

The Neue Wache in Berlin designed by Schinkel. 1816-18

The design for the War and Foreign Offices, London, by George G Scott

works. The War Memorial on the Kreuzberg in Berlin (1819–21) is a Gothic structure made of cast-iron, demonstrating his contemporary awareness.

His later works, many of which were carried out for the future Friedrich Wilhelm II, provide further evidence of his eclecticism. They include such diverse ideas as church projects in a north Italian Romanesque style, a romantic garden design, a castellated schloss, a court gardener's house, and an advanced design for a shop with a façade of glass and vertical piers.

Scimitar or **sabre leg.** Term applied to the curved leg of a Regency chair, shaped like the curved blade of a cavalry sword. 'Waterloo leg' is an occasionally used alternative name, for obvious patriotic reasons; and 'swept leg' is also sometimes used. The scimitar leg was rectangular in section, sometimes reeded, or gently rounded in front; examples are known with paw feet. Unfortunately, the shape, although graceful, did not make for sturdiness, and most scimitar chairs have since needed

Scimitar or sabre leg

metal reinforcements at the junction of leg and seat.

Sconce. A wall light made largely to utilitarian designs until the end of the seventeenth century, when its decorative value began to be appreciated.

The candles in a sconce were supported in two different ways: on branches from a vertical back plate or wall bracket, or in sockets on a tray attached to the wall by a backplate. The first design, with enriched back plate and candle branches, was the one from which the splendid mid-eighteenth-century sconces developed; they are more usually known as girandoles (qv).

Sconces were made of metals, such as brass, copper, and silver, or in earthenware. Then, in the late seventeenth century, walnut was introduced, occasionally with a needlework panel, and afterwards one of carved giltwood.

Scotia. The architectural term for a concave moulding, particularly one at the base of a column.

Scott, Sir George Gilbert (1811–78). British architect, the son of a clergyman; he trained under Edmeston and Henry Roberts. Scott was one of the major exponents of the Gothic revival, and though never a designer of great originality or imagination, he was awarded major commissions and achieved considerable fame, largely through careful self-advertisement.

The Martyrs' Memorial in Oxford (1841) was one of his first works, based upon a fourteenth-century Eleanor Cross. It was designed in partnership with W B Moffatt (1812–87), with whom Scott had already designed workhouses, and Wanstead School in Essex. The collaboration culminated in St Giles, Camberwell, London (1842–4), which

marked Scott's coming-of-age as a Gothic revivalist. In the year of its completion Scott won the competition for the church of St Nicholas, Hamburg (1845–63), which was to bring him international recognition. The greatest part of the church was destroyed in World War II, but the spire (475 ft) and tower still dominate the church's surroundings. In Canada Scott designed the cathedral at St John's, Newfoundland, though it was not built until 40 years later by his son, also George Gilbert.

Scott was appointed architect to Ely Cathedral (1847) and to Westminster Abbey (1899), where his restorations of chapter house, monuments, and northern portal were careful and accurate but lacking in inspiration. In 1858 he was appointed to build the War and Foreign Offices in London; on Lord Palmerston's

instructions his first Gothic designs were rejected and Italian Renaissance designs demanded. But with the exception of St Pancras Station (1865, now demolished) and the Albert Memorial (1864–72) in Hyde Park, London, his secular works rarely attract much notice. The Albert Memorial was commissioned by Queen Victoria in memory of her consort, who died in 1861; it is a typical example of Victorian High Gothic.

Scott was the author of several books, including *Remarks on Secular and Domestic Architecture* (1858), *Gleanings from Westminster Abbey* (1862), and *Medieval Architecture* (1879).

Scott, Sir Giles Gilbert (1880–1960). British architect, grandson of Sir George Gilbert Scott (qv). He received early recognition for his winning Gothic design for

The west front of Liverpool Cathedral, by Giles Gilbert Scott, 190.

Screen with papered panels

Liverpool Cathedral (1904). A similar boldness of design appeared in such later buildings as the chapel at Charterhouse School (1922–7) and St Joseph, Norfolk (1910–36). Most of Scott's work was ecclesiastical, or else educational (including the new buildings of Clare College, Cambridge, and Lady Margaret Hall, Oxford). Much was banal, though two major London monuments are representative of his more inspired moments: Battersea Power Station (1932–4) beside the Thames, towering over the river and providing a model for many other power stations, and Waterloo Bridge (1939–45), with a series of shallow arches in the classical bridge-building tradition.

Scott was made a member of the Royal Academy in 1922, and was president of the Royal Institute of British Architects (1933–5). He received several honorary degrees, including one from Trinity College, Toronto, where he built a chapel.

Variants on scrolls

Scratch carving. An elementary method of decorating country furniture, ie with patterns scratched or chiselled out of the surface. Rare after 1700.

Screen. These have long been used to provide privacy and protection from both heat and draughts.

In the Middle Ages, screens usually consisted of a wooden frame on which various materials could be fixed. In the seventeenth century, large folding screens became more elaborate, being covered with velvets and rich fabrics, needlework, painted and gilded leather, and japanned decoration. Many oriental lacquer screens were imported in the eighteenth century, when they were considered an essential item in every large household. Folding screens intended as protection against draughts, or used to conceal unsightly entrances, became very large (over 6 ft in height) and often had six or more folds. See **Fire screen.**

Screens passage. In medieval buildings this passage ran along one short end of the hall, providing access to the domestic regions (buttery, kitchen, and pantry). The entrances were shielded from the hall by a screen; with the spread of Renaissance influences, this became elaborately decorated.

Scroll. A recurring motif in classical architecture, imitating in stone the appearance of rolled parchment scrolls. There are many variants of the motif, including the double scroll.

Scrolled leg. Scrolled legs are found in a very pronounced form on cabinets and side tables made c 1680–1700. After this date the device continued to be used in a more refined and elongated version, or as the basic design for some of the heavily ornamented Baroque furniture of which William Kent (qv) was the chief exponent.

Scroll foot. A foot formed as an outward scroll. At the end of the seventeenth century the scroll was heavy and pronounced (as was most ornament of the time). During the eighteenth century, when the scroll foot was often used in conjunction with a cabriole leg, it took on a more refined form.

Scroll-over arm. This term was used to describe a type of chair arm that was popular during the Queen Anne and early Georgian periods. The

A segmental pediment

wooden arm of the chair scrolled over and then went down to the seat in a concave sweep. The design recalls a shepherd's crook, and has also come to be known by that name.

Secretaire, secretary. A general term that covers bureau, escritoire, and scrutoire. It can therefore only be defined as a fall-front desk, frequently with a superstructure.

Segmental arch or **pediment.** The curve of an arch, pediment, or opening which is a segment of the circumference of a circle. The segment is generally fractional and of a very low rise, and in the case of the arch has been described from a point well below the springing line.

Sehna knot. Used for carpets (qv). It entails winding the pile thread around one of two adjacent warp threads and tying it around the other. The term comes from Sehna in Persia, but the knot was used all over central Asia.

Secretary by Job Townsend

Semainier (French, *semaine* 'week'). A tall chest of drawers made in France during the reigns of Louis XV and Louis XVI. It had seven drawers, perhaps intended to hold a separate supply of linen for each day of the week.

Semi-circular or **round-headed arch.** A simple arch described from the centre on the springing line. It was the first type of arch to gain universal currency, being adopted by the Romans, who used it to wonderful advantage both structurally and decoratively, for example in their aqueducts.

Semper, Gottfried (1803–79). German architect, born in Hamburg and educated at Göttingen. He paid prolonged visits to Greece, Rome, Paris, and London. During his stay in London (1851–5) he advised on the Great Exhibition of 1851 and the proposed Victoria and Albert Museum. Like most nineteenth-century architects, Semper made eclectic use of historical styles,

The Opera House at Dresden designed by Gottfried Semper, 1871–8

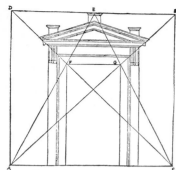

Doorway by Serlio, 1537

preferring the less severe forms of Gothic and Renaissance for his important public works. Most of these were in Dresden, where Semper held the chair of architecture at the Academy (1835–49). They include the Opera House (1837–41) and the Picture Gallery, which formed part of the Zwinger (begun 1847). Semper's book *Der Stil* (1860–3) was an important contribution to design theory.

Serliana. The tripartite window, also called a Venetian or Palladian window, that is illustrated in Serlio's *Architettura* (1537). It became one of the most characteristic features of Palladianism, and is described under Palladian window.

Serlio, Sebastiano (1475–1554). Italian architect and writer. Serlio was born in Bologna, originally trained in that city as an artist, and undertook important commissions which led him to Rome. In middle age he was forced by the Sack of Rome to leave, and went to Venice. *L'Architettura,* the result of extensive travel and examination

Serpentine fronted commode

of ancient buildings, was published in parts between 1537 and 1551. English and French editions were not published until almost a century later, although the book had a profound influence upon the designs of European architects throughout the sixteenth and into the early seventeenth century. Serlio practised as an architect during his sojourn in Venice between 1527 and 1540. He assisted Sansovino in the design of S Francesco della Vigna and designed the ceiling of the library in St Mark's. In 1541 he was invited by François I to work in France, and worked at Fontainebleau until his death. The design of the Hôtel d'Este is reliably attributed to him, but other attributions are less certain. His continuing fame rests upon his authorship of *L'Architettura,* the first major architectural work to be concerned with the practical rather than the theoretical and philosophical aspects of architecture, and the first to classify the five orders.

Serpentine front. The curved front on cabinets, commodes, sideboards, and other pieces, consisting of a convex curve flanked by two concave curves. It was introduced in the mid-eighteenth century and remained popular until the end of the century.

Settee. The words 'sofa' and 'settee' are almost interchangeable. Neither was used before 1700; seats now called settees that were made during the seventeenth century were probably known as couches.

Both sofas and settees provide seating for two or more people. 'Sofa' is usually reserved for the larger and more heavily padded versions, most of which date from 1750 and after.

The earliest settees resemble upholstered settles, and belong to the Jacobean period. However, it was not until the second half of the seventeenth century that there was a continuous development in design.

The seat, back, and arms were usually upholstered in leather, fabric, or needlework; a notable variant has only an upholstered seat, the arms being open un-padded rails and the back a row of carved chair-backs. One or two settees were frequently made *en suite* with a set of chairs and stools.

Settle. A form of seating introduced in the Middle Ages and surviving into the nineteenth

Hepplewhite mahogany settee, c 1780

century as cottage furniture. It was a long bench similar to a chest (the seat lifted to reveal a locker) with a solid back, and arms at either end. Some early versions were in fixed positions, but the majority of surviving examples are movable. They are often depicted in contemporary paintings of interiors. One type, the settle-table, has a back that can be pivoted into a horizontal position to form a table top. In the late seventeenth century the backs of settles were generally lower, and the locker was replaced by four to eight legs. From the early eighteenth century, settles were only found in the homes of the poorer classes, and their decoration was often old-fashioned.

During recent years, furniture designers have adapted the high protective back of the traditional settle for linked armchairs; these form a continuous settle-type seating, well-suited to the needs

of hospital and airport waiting-rooms.

Severy. The bay of a vault; ie the compartment between two transverse arches.

Sewing table. See **Work table.**

Sexpartite vault. A vault of six compartments, formed by the intersection of two diagonal ribs with a transverse rib.

Seymour, John (1738–1818). An American cabinetmaker who first settled in Portland, Maine, in 1785, moving to Boston in 1794. He worked with his son Thomas, and it is impossible to distinguish between their pieces. Seymour furniture was well made, with fine dovetailing, mainly in the Sheraton style. Most pieces were of patterned satinwood and bird's-eye maple veneers. Many had inlaid tam-

A sideboard made by Thomas Seymour of Boston, 1808-10

Chair and locker-desk from the Shaker Community in New Lebanon

bour shutters, ivory key escutcheons, and greenish blue interiors. Only four labelled items are extant, but several hundred others are attributed to father and son.

Sgraffito. See **Graffito; Slipware.**

Shaft. The part of the trunk of a column between the base and the capital.

Shaft-ring. A moulded ring or annulet around the shaft of a column, or around a circular pier.

Shaker furniture. The austere forms of furniture made by the United Society of Believers in the Second Appearing, more generally known as Shakers or Shaking Quakers. The sect was founded in Bolton and Manchester in England. A party of eight Shakers emigrated to America in 1774, and established their first settlement at Niskeyuna, near Albany, New York. Their beliefs favoured co-operation and the suppression of personal tastes. Their houses and furniture were therefore of the utmost simplicity and uniformity, and have received attention from twentieth-century scholars as early expressions of the principle of fitness-for-purpose. They were craftsmen and masterly workers of wood, and during recent years the collection of Shaker furniture has become something of a cult in the USA. Examples have been assembled in New Lebanon, where a few members of the declining colony continue to live.

Sharawaggi, sharadwadgi, sharawadgi. A term applied to carefully considered irregularity in design and decoration. Although the etymology of the term is obscure, as early as 1685 Sir William Temple attributed it to the Chinese in his *Upon the Gardens of Epicurus*. 'Their greatest reach of imagination is employed in contriving figures, where the beauty shall be great, and strike the eye, but without any order or disposition of parts that shall be commonly or easily observed: and though we have hardly any notion of this sort of beauty, yet they have a particular word to express it, and, where they find it hit their eye at first sight, they say the *sharawadgi* is fine, or is admirable, or any such expression of esteem.' Horace Walpole also used the term in a letter of 1750, referring to his fondness for 'the sharawaggi, or Chinese want of symmetry, in buildings, as in grounds or gardens.'

The word fell into disuse during the Victorian era, but was revived in the 1940s by Sir Hugh Casson and other architectural writers as a lively alternative to the Picturesque (qv) in particular reference to town-planning.

Miles Hadfield, in his *Gardening in Britain* (1960), puts forward a convincing argument that sharadwadgi is not a Chinese word but derives from the Japanese.

Shaving chair (also known as a Barber's chair). A high-backed, three-cornered form of chair, known in more rudimentary forms in earlier times, which acquired more sophisticated forms in the eighteenth century. The high back provided a head-rest for the tonsorial operation.

Shaw, Richard Norman (1831–1912). Scottish architect. Shaw was born in Edinburgh, but his family moved from Scotland to London when Shaw was in his

A Shaker cupboard and chest of drawers

Sharawaggi at the garden at Nuneham Park, Oxfordshire

Garden front at Queen's Gate, London, designed by Norman Shaw

New Scotland Yard, Whitehall, London, by Norman Shaw

teens. He was apprenticed to a London architect, and later entered the office of William Burn, where he worked for some years. In 1854 he won the gold medal and travelling scholarship of the Royal Academy. He joined the practice of G E Street (qv) as chief assistant in 1858, and in the same year published his *Architectural Studies from the Continent*.

In 1862 Shaw started in private practice with William Eden Nesfield (1835–88). Most of the time they worked separately, but it seems likely that Nesfield played a considerable part in developing the style that was to make Shaw internationally famous, a style derived from seventeenth-century Anglo-Dutch domestic buildings in brick. Shaw and Nesfield jointly designed Holy Trinity Church, Bingley, Yorkshire (1867), but after building Leys Wood, Sussex, in 1868, they dissolved their partnership. Shaw's energy and enterprise enabled him to build up one of the largest practices in Europe, including churches, commercial buildings, theatres, hotels, offices, mansions, apartments, and houses. Among the more important of these buildings were Lowther Lodge, Kensington (1873), now the Royal Geographical Society; Swan House, Chelsea (1876); Bryanston, Dorset (1890); the Gaiety Theatre (1902); and Piccadilly Hotel (1905). Shaw is now chiefly known for his work at Bedford Park (1880), and for various Kensington houses which owed their charm to mid-seventeenth-century Dutch prototypes. Shaw's last commis-

sion was the rebuilding of Nash's Regent Street Quadrant, London, but here the heaviness of his treatment made later modifications (by Sir Reginald Blomfield) inevitable.

Shearer, Thomas. Cabinet-maker and designer. Almost nothing is known of him apart from what can be deduced from the engraved plates of his *Cabinet Maker's London Book of Prices* (1788). Shearer executed the majority of these engravings, though Hepplewhite also contributed. As its title indicates, the book was simply a catalogue of prices for the use of cabinet-makers. A revised edition of this was published later in the same year as *Shearer's Designs for Household Furniture*.

Shearer's drawings are distinctive and well executed. The most notable was his etching of a sideboard, which is the earliest known design for a sideboard with pedestals all in one piece. Sheraton compared Shearer's guide favourably with Hepplewhite's, though Shearer's furniture was only slightly more advanced; his place as a designer is midway between Hepplewhite and Sheraton.

Sheffield plate. Fine sheets of silver fused over a copper core. This made possible the cheap production of plate to meet growing demand in the late eighteenth century. Discovered by Thomas Bolsover in 1743, Sheffield plate was widely manufactured by the 1770s. With technical improvements (including a whiter central alloy) it remained in vogue well into the

nineteenth century. It tended to be superseded by electroplating.

Shell-work. A form of ornamentation much practised by amateurs. Small shells, sometimes already coloured, were fixed in decorative arrangements on to mirror frames, small caskets, boxes, and other objects. Paper filigree work was occasionally combined with the shell pattern. This type of decoration was first employed in the late seventeenth century.

Shell structures. Architectural term for constructions based upon the eggshell principle, ie with a thin rigid curved surface for roofing. Shell structures were developed in the early 1920s by Bauersfeld and Dischinger, who demonstrated its theoretical and practical advantages. Most examples of the 1920s were of dome or barrel shells such as Freyssinet's Market Hall at Rheims (1928–9). The hyperbolic paraboloid form was used as early as 1934 and became very popular during the 1940s. Shell structures are of primary importance for buildings with large areas that can be covered by a single span, buildings such as Nervi

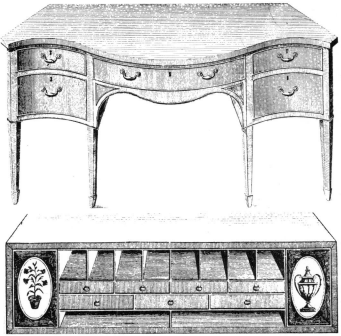

Designs for a sideboard and writing compartments by Shearer, 1788

The interior of the shell structure roof over the Exhibition Hall, Turin, by Nervi, 1948-9

Knifecase by Sheraton

Fellows' flats at Churchill College, Cambridge, by Richard Sheppard, Robson and Partners

and Vitellozzi's Palazzetto dello Sport (1956–7), and Eero Saarinen's TWA reception at Kennedy Airport, New York.

Sheppard, Richard (*b* 1910). British architect. Sheppard trained at the Architectural Association in London, and set up in private practice in 1938. The firm became Richard Sheppard, Robson, and Partners. Much of the work of the partnership has been concerned with university building. Churchill College, Cambridge (won in competition in 1959), with its informal grouping of small courts, is probably the best known. The firm was also responsible for designing the halls of residence at Imperial College, London, for Brunel University, Uxbridge, and for Digby Hall, Leicestershire.

Sheraton, Thomas (1751–1806). British furniture designer and maker. Sheraton was born in humble circumstances in Stockton-on-Tees, Durham, and was trained as a journeyman-cabinetmaker, a craft he was to forsake for authorship and drawing. He seems to have settled in London when he was about 40, and made no great mark, living with his family in a 'half-shop, half-dwelling house' in Soho. His trade card records that he taught 'Perspective, Architecture and Ornaments, makes Designs for Cabinet makers, and sells all kinds of Drawing Books.' Despite the later fame of his *Cabinet Maker and Upholsterer's Drawing Book*, which he published in four parts between 1791 and 1794,

he seems to have gained no substantial rewards for his work, although a third edition appeared in 1802. The following year he published *The Cabinet Dictionary*, containing an explanation of all the terms used in the 'Cabinet, Chair and Upholstery Branches, with Directions for Varnishing, Polishing and Gilding.' Two years later he began an ambitious scheme for an encyclopaedia for cabinet-makers, upholsterers, and 'general artists.' Only one part was published, probably because of Sheraton's financial difficulties and declining health. He died the following year. With his contemporaries Chippendale and Hepplewhite, Sheraton undoubtedly did much to raise the design and quality of English cabinet-making. Although many of his designs exhibit a certain austerity, he was also capable of producing some highly esoteric and exotic pieces.

Shevret or **chevret**. A term used by Gillow (qv) to describe

A design by Thomas Sheraton for a Pembroke table, 1803

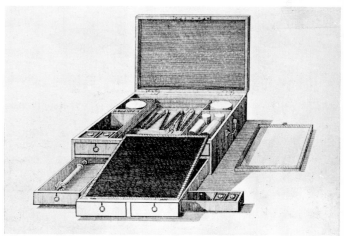

A design for a lady's travelling box by Sheraton, 1792

A shield back chair

a type of small writing desk. It had a shelf above a superstructure of drawers or pigeon holes, and stood on tapered legs. It was made in the late eighteenth century, usually of mahogany or satinwood.

Shield back. Chair and settee backs shaped like shields were popular in the second half of the eighteenth century. Although invariably associated with Hepplewhite, who illustrated them in his *Cabinet Maker and Upholsterer's Guide* (1788), they are known to have been made before the publication of his book.

The back splats within the shield frame take a variety of forms: swags, lancet, Prince of Wales feathers; and in some instances the whole back is caned.

Shingles. Timber tiles, usually made from western cedarwood; used for covering roofs, outside walls, and sometimes church spires. Shingles have been widely used in domestic building in the United States, and are still commonly used today on the roofs of houses of traditional design.

Shingle style. Architectural style, the alternative (American) term for the Domestic revival of the 1870s and 1880s in the United States. It derived from H H Richardson's designs for William Watts Sherman's house in Newport, USA (1874), in which decoratively-shaped shingles were used in walls and roofs. The building was greatly influenced by the designs of Norman Shaw and Nesfield. The Sherman house initiated a widespread use of shingles as a wall-covering and established a characteristic style of American domestic architecture. The shingle style is seen at its best in Stoughton House in Cambridge, Massachusetts (1882–3), designed by Richardson, and the W G Low house, Bristol, Rhode Island (1887), designed by McKim, Mead, & White. The Low house was a precursor of the 'ranch house' (qv).

Shore. A timber post used in supporting or shoring the wall or floor of a building likely to collapse or needing support during building operations. There are three types of shoring, which are frequently employed in one building: (*a*) a 'dead' or vertical shore, which supports a floor; (*b*) a 'raking' shore, a massive sloping post (or series of posts) set against a wall in urgent and substantial need of support; (*c*) a 'flying' shore, a post placed horizontally between and against the upper walls of two buildings on either side of a space left by a demolished building. The strain imposed upon these horizontal or flying shores is relieved by sloping or 'raking' shores.

Shouldered arch. A relatively uncommon arch in which two shoulders, one at the top of

A side table of carved and gilded wood, c 1795

either impost, project into the open space.

Shouldered architrave. See **Architrave.**

Shutter. A hinged wooden or metal screen, hung inside or outside a window, over which they can be closed. They have long been used in hot climates to regulate the amount of light and heat entering the interior. In temperate regions they provide security and privacy. Louvre shutters (qv) are fitted with slanting slats.

Sideboard. A piece of dining-room furniture, developed towards the end of the eighteenth century. In the Middle Ages, court cupboards (qv) had probably been used; later, side tables provided space for the display of plate and tableware.

The standard form of sideboard was established through the designs of Shearer, Hepplewhite, and Sheraton. It had a shallow central drawer and deeper drawers or cupboards on either side. The storage space became even larger in the nineteenth century, sometimes incorporating pedestal cupboards. However, the standard late eighteenth-century design usually had one drawer fitted as a cellaret, lead-lined and compartmented. This design was introduced to America c 1785.

Sideboard table. The term introduced in the mid-eighteenth century for side tables used in dining-rooms. The word is sometimes interchangeable with 'sideboard.' It is a large side table, often with a marble top and a decorative frieze.

Adam was probably responsible for the very impressive arrangement of a sideboard table flanked by two pedestals carrying urns. In his designs for Kenwood, the group is shown with a sarcophagus (qv) for wine placed in the centre of the area beneath the table.

Shingle style house in New England

An elaborate sideboard from Sheraton's 'Encyclopedia', 1804

A modern sideboard in teak designed by Ronald Carter, 1965

Side chair or **small chair.** The name given to a single chair without arms, eg the farthingale chair (qv).

Side table. A fifteenth-century development of the chest. In many medieval households the chest was used as a table as well as for storage, and the earliest side tables were made with cupboards.

During the late seventeenth century and eighteenth century, side tables were elaborate and impressive, conspicuously positioned against a wall. They usually have one unornamented side or, in the case of console and pier tables, a very pronounced frontal view. A console table is a side table with consoles instead of legs, and a pier table one designed especially to be positioned at the base of a pier (ie flanked by windows or alcoves). Ornate versions are rare in America. See also **Sideboard table.**

Silesian stem. Glass stem, known as a moulded pedestal or shouldered stem. It was moulded, not blown, and is an inverted pedestal, usually semi-hollow or with a tear. Although called 'Silesian', it may have originated in Hanover, and became popular after George I's accession in 1714. It was fashionable for drinking glasses from c 1715 to c 1730, and remained popular for sweetmeats and salvers until c 1765. Early versions had four-sided stems with sloping shoulders, but these were soon superseded by six- and eight-sided stems, while diamond-shaped bosses began to appear on the shoulders.

Silver, decorative techniques. There are numerous methods of decorating plate. In the medieval period it was common to inset precious stones and/or overlay the silver with a fine layer of mercurial gilding. Plate thus decorated is described as silver gilt; if only partly gilded, it is parcel gilt. Gilding remained common until the sixteenth century, but declined from the early seventeenth, being used only for lavish ceremonial pieces. Casting was common from an early date. Elaborate details such as handles, finials, and stems would be cast separately and soldered on to the body of a piece. Casting probably reached its peak in the Rococo period, when much high relief ornament was made by this method.

Embossing is a term for decoration punched into relief from the back or inside of a piece of silver. This method involves no loss of silver, and in fact strengthens thin-gauge metal. Embossing may be heightened and given additional detailing by hammering along the surface with a fine hammer. This is known as *repoussé chasing.* Another delicate use of this technique, called *flat chasing,* closely resembles engraving, which it tended to supersede during the eighteenth century.

In *engraving,* the ornament consists of incised work, cut with a sharp tool into the body of a piece. Used in conjunction with embossing in earlier times, engraving was at its finest during the late seventeenth and early eighteenth centuries, when superb coats of arms within delicate frames were often the only form of decoration on simple plate. In the late eighteenth century, bright-cut engraving developed, executed with a tool which burnished as it cut, giving the plate a sparkling brilliance.

Cut-card work. A technique superbly executed by Huguenot silversmiths (qv). A silver pattern, generally pierced into a filigree design with a hammer and chisel, was soldered on to a piece of silver to add delicate relief decoration. It was used in the seventeenth century to disguise the clumsy join of spout or handle and body, but during the eighteenth century it was carried out in an elaborate Rococo style, and was often used over the whole piece.

Piercing, developed in the seventeenth century on the tops of sugar-casters, became extremely intricate in the Rococo period, then simpler again as a result of Neo-classical influences. By this time the saw had replaced the hammer and chisel, making this technique quicker and easier. It became very popular for bread-baskets, épergnes, and salt-cellars, lined with transparent or dark blue glass.

During the late eighteenth century many of the standard methods were developed to aid the silversmith. Machines for stamping patterns appeared, and etching replaced the more laborious engraving technique. In Victorian times, these inventions led to the mass production of silver, and many of the old-fashioned skills and methods of decoration were all but lost.

In the last decade texturing has been revived, and has become a major method of decoration.

Silver gilt embossed basin, marked FT, 1618-19

Pierced work on sugar caster by Simon Pantin, 1716

It has been used sporadically over the centuries, but never to such advantage or to such an extent as the present day.

Silver gilt. See **Silver, decorative techniques.**

Silvering. The application of silver powder or leaf to furniture and small objects, a process similar to gilding. It was introduced in the eighteenth century. It never won great popularity because of its unsatisfactory finish. Blemishes – and especially discoloration – were avoidable

Glass with Silesian stem

Sugar tongs with bright cut engraving, Hester Bateman, 1787

Lever House, New York, by Skidmore, Owings and Merrill, 1951-2

only by the use of varnish; and this produced a yellow-goldish hue, defeating the whole object of the process.

Silvering is also the term for the foil and mercury backing of mirror glass.

Silverwood. A name that was coined in the eighteenth century; it referred to a particular type of stained sycamore. See **Harewood.**

Single-framed roof. A roof made entirely of transverse members tied together by tie beams, an upper floor frame, or by boards nailed across horizontally. All longitudinal trusses, such as ridges and purlins, are omitted.

Skidmore, Owings and Merrill. The American architect Louis Skidmore (1897–1962) was trained at the Massachusetts Institute of Technology. In 1924 he joined the Boston architects Maginnis and Walsh, remaining with them for two years before leaving to study in Europe. He returned to the USA in 1928 and began working with Nathaniel Owings (b 1903) in the early 1930s. In 1936 they founded their own architectural firm in Chicago, opening a New York office in the following year. In 1939 the partnership was joined by engineer John O Merrill (b 1896), and the firm was established in Chicago as Skidmore, Owings, and Merrill. It was to become one of the largest and most influential practices in the USA, with offices in San Francisco, Portland, Oregon, and Oak Ridge, each with its own design projects. The firm's first major commission was to build the city of Oak Ridge in Tennessee for the Manhattan Project. In the post-war years the firm has been closely linked with other US government projects, such as the US Air Force Academy at Colorado Springs, and with major industrial developments ranging from the Lake Meadows housing scheme for New York Life Insurance Company to Lever House in New York (1952). This became virtually a prototype for the highrise, curtain-walled block, based on a modest three- or four-storey podium, and, where possible, a public patio-garden. Critics have sought to show that much of the firm's work derives from Mies van der Rohe. But although his influence is apparent in its curtain buildings, the firm has consistently designed on a strictly logical, anonymous, technological basis. The results have been as spare and functional as any designs in the modern world.

Some recent buildings are the ALCOA offices at the Golden Gate Center, San Francisco (1968); the campus for the University of Illinois; the Brunswick Corporation Offices, Chicago; and, in collaboration with Yorke, Rosenberg, and Mardell, the Boots head offices in Nottingham, England.

Skylight. A framed window inserted into a sloping roof; much used in artist's studios; and more recently in the roofs of farm buildings and factories. Until fairly recently, skylights were glazed, but they are now increasingly constructed of plastic, available in corrugated form for more convenient insertion into sheet roofing.

Skyscraper. The term 'skyscraper' was applied to a windjammer's sky-sail in the eighteenth century, and to a tall horse or man in the nineteenth century. According to a letter in the *Morning Post* (26 January, 1935), the first building it was applied to was Queen Anne's

US Air Force Chapel by Skidmore, Owings and Merrill, 1956-62

Skyscraper: the 11-storey Tower Building, Broadway, 1888

A carved and giltwood sleeping chair, late 17th century

The Royal College of Physicians in London designed by Sir Robert Smirke, 1824-7

Mansions near St James's Park, London, in the early 1880s, well before the American urban skyline had been changed by high-rise buildings. But H L Mencken, the American lexicographer, dismisses this as a '*nonce-use.*' The American use of the term seems to date from a reference in the Boston *Journal* (1891).

The skyscraper succeeded the so-called 'cloud-scraper' of Chicago, occasioned by the rebuilding of much of that city after the great fire in 1871. Rising land values, steel frame construction, and technological advances in the design of the elevator or lift, encouraged Chicago architects to experiment with higher and higher buildings. The Leiter Building (1889) was the first example of what Lewis Mumford terms building by means of 'the iron cage and curtain wall', and was soon followed by the buildings designed by Louis Sullivan (qv) and other Chicago architects.

The first skyscraper in New York was the Flatiron building (1902) by D H Burnham and J W Root.

Slat-back chair. The typical

A Staffordshire slipware charger, by R Simpson, c 1700

seventeenth-century American slat-back chair was a wooden armchair with turned uprights, the back two terminating in bobbin finials. It had three wide slats, crested in outline. During the following century, with the greater refinement of furniture-making, the slats decreased in size and increased in number. Chippendale and Sheraton provided models for many variations, and seat rails and stretchers varied regionally.

Slatehanging. A wall cladding of slates hung vertically in overlapping rows.

Sleeping chair. A rare early English chair that takes its name from an armchair at Ham House in Surrey, described in the inventory of 1679 as a 'sleeping chayre.' It has a padded seat and armrail, and a high upholstered winged back that is adjusted by means of a quadrant stay (qv). Similar reclining chairs are usually without arms.

Sleigh bed. An American version of the elegant French Empire bed, with a high scrolled headboard and a similarly scrolled, slightly lower foot board.

Slider. An unobtrusive sliding shelf that was fitted into the carcase of a piece of furniture beneath the top drawer; eighteenth and nineteenth century. Coasters (qv) and lopers (qv) have also been called sliders.

Sling chair. Modern American

type of chair, with a metal rod frame and leather sling. It was designed by Bonet, Hurchan, and Ferrari-Hardoy in 1938.

Slip cover. See **Loose cover.**

Slipper chair. The general name for a short-legged American upholstered chair, with a seat about two-thirds the normal height. It was made with or without arms, and even upon rockers. The back was usually oval, a shape exploited by John Henry Belter (qv) in his versions of the chair, with their heavily carved backs full of foliage and Rococo carving.

Slip seat. A loose-framed seat that can be fitted into the main seat frame of a chair. These seats are usually upholstered, but are occasionally caned.

Slipware. Slip is a mixture of clay and water mixed to the consistency of cream; slipware is earthenware decorated with slip. Although slip decoration was used in Roman and medieval times, it was not fully exploited until the seventeenth and eighteenth centuries.

Slip decoration was carried out by washing the body of the ware with slip of another colour, and then applying a fresh, differently coloured slip to the surface. This was poured from an enclosed vessel with a spout made of a quill; the vessel had a small hole in the top which the potter controlled with his thumb, allowing the slip to trail out. A steady hand and accurate eye were

essential. The slip could be applied in lines and then combed through with a metal comb, or stroked into patterns with a feather. Or a slip coating could be incised to show the different colour of the body beneath, a technique known as sgraffito decoration. The decorated ware was then dipped in a lead glaze and fired again. Redware decorated with sgraffito slip decoration was made in considerable quantities by American potters from the seventeenth century. It was particularly favoured by the German settlers in Pennsylvania.

Slipware was made in many districts in England, notably at Wrotham in Kent, and in Staffordshire and Devonshire. Most of the seventeenth-century slipware found in and around London, however, was made at Harlow in Essex.

The techniques described are still practised by studio potters all over the world.

Smirke, Sir Robert (1781–1867). British architect. Smirke, the son of a Royal Academician, began his architectural training in the office of Sir John Soane, but the two men did not get on, and Smirke soon left. He entered the Royal Academy Schools in 1796, gaining the gold medal in 1799, on the completion of his studies. He travelled widely on the Continent between 1801 and 1805, before setting up in practice in 1806, when he published his *Specimens of Continental Architecture*. He was uncommonly successful, within a year gaining the commission to design Lowther Castle for the Earl of Lonsdale.

Over the next 40 years Smirke was to become one of the most successful nineteenth-century architects, thanks to his technical knowledge, reliability, and skills as a structural designer. He was appointed architect to the Board of Trade at the age of 26, and soon acquired several other official appointments, including the surveyorship to the Inner Temple. He was regarded as 'the best constructor of his day.' He designed his façades in a dignified Neo-classical (mainly Greek) style that was not particularly original; but he was something of an innovator in his extensive use of concrete and cast-iron in construction. His buildings included the Royal College of Physicians, Trafalgar Square (1824–7), the Oxford and Cambridge Club, Pall Mall (1835–8), Covent Garden (1809–10), the British Museum (1823–47), King's College, Strand (1830–1), and the Ophthalmic Hospital, Moorfield's.

Smithson, Alison (*b* 1928) and Peter (*b* 1923). British architects, whose secondary school at Hunstanton (1953) represented a reaction against the Neo-pic-turesque architecture of the immediate post-war years. To architects of the Smithsons' generation, the feeble planning of the New Towns was as much the legacy of Neo-picturesque theory as was anarchic sub-topia; in their view, appearance should be strictly determined by requirements. This uncompromising position was emphasized at Hunstanton by the choice of a Miesian idiom: a geometric two-storey grid of black-painted steel girders with plate-glass infill. Its symmetrical plan and elevation was consciously anti-picturesque. Inside, a virtue was made of the technology: the exposed plumbing of the washbasins stood out against a plate-glass wall.

The Smithsons' Berlin Hauptstadt plan (1958) exhibited the qualities they believed most necessary in the 1950s, mobility and communication. The plan was divided hierarchically into roads for huge numbers of modern cars, to provide a fast exit from the city, and into streets whose role was conceived largely in social terms. The two types of communication were expressed by elevating the one (streets) above the other (motorways). The houses themselves were first of all to be suited to their purpose; then they must be fitted into the street scheme. This is the common feature in the Smithsons' schemes for working-class housing at Golden Lane in the East End of London (1952) and for the offices of the *Economist* in the West End (1964). Both the housing development and the office block set out to answer the problem as set; and both are fitted into a scheme of pedestrian communication – a 'street-deck' at Golden Lane, and an open piazza outside the *Economist* building.

These considerations aside, the house could be standardized: 'things of the same order should be alike as leaves', according to the Smithsons. Their House of the Future at the 1965 Ideal Homes Exhibition was compact and easy to reproduce, like the elements of a caravan. It made the fullest possible use of domestic technology and was entirely geared to human needs.

The Smithsons' socially-orientated doctrine has had the label 'Brutalist' attached to it, somewhat misleadingly. Whatever the origins of this word, it has now come to characterize the appearance of the more plastically conceived buildings of the 1960s, with their large, uncon-cealed rough concrete members. The Smithsons, however, have propagated a procedure, not a style.

Smoker's bow. The American name for a nineteenth-century Windsor chair with a low horizontal bow back comprising arms and yoke rail. It was taller in the central section forming the back of the chair, the seat was shaped, and members were turned. The design was a simplified version of the eighteenth-century bow back Windsor chair.

Smythson, Robert (1535–1614). English mason-architect, the best known of a family of masons who became involved in architectural design in the late sixteenth century. Smythson, with his group of masons, was employed by Sir John Thynne in the building of Longleat in Wiltshire between 1568 and 1580, being concerned in the third and fourth (final) versions of the house. In 1576 he began work for Sir Matthew Arundell on Wardour Castle, also in Wiltshire, and also seems responsible for the design of Wollaton near Nottingham for Sir Francis Willoughby. Smythson was also connected with the

The Economist Building, London, by Alison and Peter Smithson, 1964

Hardwick Hall, Derbyshire, by Robert Smythson, 1590–7

Sir John Soane

design of other notable Elizabethan houses, including Hardwick Hall, Derbyshire (1590–7), Burton Agnes, Yorkshire (1601–10), and Pontefract Old Hall (*c* 1591). Smythson's son John (*d* 1634) and grandson (*d* 1648) continued the tradition, working

Holy Trinity Church, Marylebone, London, by Soane, 1824-5

as architect-surveyors on a number of great houses in the Midlands.

Snake foot. The American name for an elongated club foot.

Snakewood. *Piratinera guiranensis.* The vibrant red markings on the heart of this South American wood are responsible for its peculiar name. It is a hard and decorative wood occasionally used for inlay work in the eighteenth century, and for veneer work in the later eighteenth and early nineteenth centuries.

Snap table or **tilt top table.** The terms used for an eighteenth-century tripod table with a hinged lid. The table top could be tilted and fixed in a vertical position, so that it took up less room when it was not in use. Tilt top is used mainly in the United States.

Soane, Sir John (1753–1837). British architect. Soane, born Soan, was the son of a bricklayer of Goring-on-Thames. He early decided to be an architect, and in 1768 entered the drawing office of George Dance the Younger. Soane attended the Royal Academy Schools, winning the silver medal in 1772, in which year he moved from Dance's office to Henry Holland's. Four years later he won the gold medal of the Royal Academy, and the following year the travelling studentship. The impact of his sojourn in Italy was a lifelong influence on his thoughts and practice. While in Rome he met the rich and eccentric dilettante, Frederick Hervey, Bishop of Derry, who dazzled him with promises of commissions that were never honoured. After further disappointments – and Soane was a man given to brooding over setbacks, real or imagined – he began to build up a modest architectural practice in East Anglia, later documented in his *Plans of Buildings* (1788). He married in 1784, unaccountably adding the 'e' to Soan, presumably to give his name some imagined social distinction. Finally Soane was given the surveyorship of the Bank of England, the most important commission of his life, thanks to the patronage of William Pitt. This commission quickly made him one of the leading British architects, his practice ultimately rivalling James Wyatt's. The next two decades following this were the most fruitful and happy

The Bank Stock Office by Sir John Soane, 1792

of Soane's long life. As well as much official work, he carried out important private commissions, notably Tyringham Hall, Buckinghamshire (1793–1800). Between 1800 and 1803 he built Pitzhanger Place at Ealing (now the Ealing Public Library) as his own country house, and it was here that he began to assemble the collections which were to become the nucleus of the museum, now housed in Soane's London House at No 13, Lincoln's Inn Fields.

The later years of Soane's life were clouded by family and professional difficulties. But his architectural theorizing and innovations continued unabated, and he began those spatial and structural experiments which have caused latter-day writers to term him 'the first of the modernists.' His building at the Bank of England (1788–1833), the Dulwich Art Gallery (1812–

14), and his own house embodied the results of his architectural insights. He indicated a way to escape from the dominance of the classical orders and of Gothic, then inseparable elements in the training of architects. His preoccupation with shallow domes, unusual lighting effects, and spatial adventures within constricted areas, have earned him the praise of almost all twentieth-century critics and historians.

Social table. See **Wine table.**

Sofa. A term of Arabic derivation, applied to an upholstered seat accommodating two or more persons and with upholstered arms. The sofa was introduced in the middle of the eighteenth century, supplementing the more formal, less comfortable settee. Chippendale showed versions of the sofa in his *Director* of 1762.

A modern sofa upholstered in a floral print

A mahogany sofa table, c 1820

Sofa table. A form of table introduced towards the end of the eighteenth century, to take a useful place before the sofa, as Sheraton put it.

The sofa table was a form of Pembroke table (qv), with two extending flaps supported by brackets. But whereas the Pembroke had four tapering legs, the sofa table was supported in a variety of ways, including by X-shaped or lyre supports. The table had one or two shallow drawers in the frieze, and occasionally a chess board concealed by a sliding panel, or a rising desk for writing or reading.

Soffit. The underside of a projecting plane or surface. The term is most frequently applied to overhanging eaves, but can also be used of the undersides of balconies and canopies.

Solar (Latin, *solarium* 'a sunny part of the house'). In a late medieval household, the private withdrawing-room reserved for the owner's family.

Soldier course. The top-most course of bricks in which the stretchers are laid upright like soldiers.

Sopraporte. See **Overdoor.**

Soufflot, Jacques Germain (1713–80). French architect who designed the great Neo-classical church of Ste Geneviève, known since the Revolution as the Panthéon (the shrine for national heroes). Two other buildings in the same square were by Soufflot, the Ecole de Droit (1771), and the local *mairie*, which was erected in the nineteenth century. He designed only a few other buildings.

Soufflot gained his knowledge of classical architecture in several years of study at Rome. Ste Geneviève was none the less designed with two Baroque towers which were removed by Quatremère de Quincy in 1791, when the edifice became the Panthéon, a sober symbol of Revolutionary France.

Space-frame. A revolutionary constructional concept, most frequently associated with the geodesic domes of Buckminster Fuller (qv). It is based on the interrelation and mutual stress of members working as an entity to resist outside pressures. There is one basic geometric unit, the form that distinguishes one system from another, and it is repeated as many times as is necessary to achieve the required size. The use of the mutual tension principle makes the advantages of traditional building materials irrelevant, and means that materials such as plastic can be used. Space-frames, supported only on their circumference, can cover large areas.

Spade foot. See **Therm foot.**

Planked soffit to a balcony

The Pantheon in Paris designed by Soufflot

A helicopter lifting a Fuller geodesic dome

The south door of Coventry Cathedral designed by Sir Basil Spence

Sir Basil Spence's own weekend cottage in Hampshire

Span. In architecture, the horizontal distance between two supporting components, eg abutments supporting an arch, or walls carrying a roof. The measurement of the span is sometimes reckoned from the centre of each support.

Spandrel. The triangular area that lies between the outer curves of two adjacent arches and the string course above or the area bounded by the extrados of a single arch and lines drawn horizontally from the apex and vertically from the springing. The surfaces of spandrels are often decorated.

Spanish chair. A Victorian easy chair with a continuous upholstered seat and back. It had short, stubby turned legs, was deeply buttoned, and had no arms.

Spanish foot. A foot found on legged rather than cabinet furniture, dating from the end of the seventeenth century. It is grooved, and terminates with a slightly depressed inward scroll,

Sir Basil Spence

so that the profile is not unlike a club foot. Also known as paintbrush foot (qv).

Sparver. The name by which bed hangings or curtains were known from the fifteenth to the early seventeenth century. Occasionally the word sparver bed was used to describe a bed with a tent-shaped or slightly domed canopy.

Spence, Sir Basil (*b* 1907). British architect, once a pupil of Lutyens, whose position as a modern architect acceptable to public bodies Spence has to some extent inherited.

In 1950 he won the competition for Coventry Cathedral with an apparently rationalist scheme (a basilica) which none the less achieves very dramatic effects. Its completion in 1962 won him a knighthood.

In 1947 Spence established a practice in London as an architect of public buildings, including a section of the 1951 Festival of Britain. (He had gained some experience of this type of work in the 1938 Empire Exhibition at Glasgow and later increased it by designing the British Pavilion at Expo 67 in Montreal, Canada.) Since 1951 his firm has been one of the important practices for public buildings in Great Britain, specializing particularly in universities and civic centres. The universities include Sussex, begun from scratch in 1959; Southampton, expanded since 1956; and additional blocks to existing universities, notably at Queen's College, Cambridge, in 1960. Of the civic centres, Hampstead, London, phase I was completed in 1964; Sunderland was completed in 1970; and Kensington and Chelsea, London, begun in 1971.

This major architect has been able to use the idiomatic vocabulary of 'Brutalism' (the exposed concrete and broken-up brickwork masses of the Household Cavalry Barracks, London, 1970) to create a formidably monumental style (British Embassy, Rome, 1970) reminiscent of the Neo-Baroque, popular around 1900.

Spice cabinet. In eighteenth-century America, highly prized spices were kept in special cabinets with many drawers. Such cabinets are between 2 and 4 ft high.

Spindle. A turned member used in eighteenth- and nineteenth-century chair-making. It is straight or slightly swelling, reminiscent of the spindle used in spinning. Chairs with rush seats often carried a row of spindles in the back.

Spire. A slender pointed structure on the top of a building. It originated in the steep tower roofs of medieval French and German secular buildings, and then became an important element in ecclesiastical architecture – perhaps because of the visual symbolism, the spire pointing towards heaven. It is believed that every church tower built between the thirteenth and sixteenth centuries was intended to have a spire. Spires were made of stone, or of wood covered with lead or shingles. Many were built to a great height.

Spirelet. See **Flèche.**

Splat. The central vertical part of the chair back, between the uprights. Treatment of this feature has varied greatly from period to period. During the early

eighteenth century there was great emphasis on the outline of the splat, giving rise to fiddle and baluster chair backs. By mid-century these had been replaced by pierced splat designs such as the wheatsheaf back (qv).

Splay. Generally used to describe a surface that forms an oblique angle with another surface. More particularly it refers to sloping jambs on doors and windows.

In furniture, 'splayed' refers to the spreading or curving of the leg or foot rather than the particular junction of two surfaces.

Split turning. A general term, covering split balusters, bobbins, and spindles. In each case the turned ornament is split either centrally or segmentally, and applied to the flat surfaces of case furniture, chairs, and chimney-pieces. Used in the late sixteenth and the seventeenth century.

Spode. A factory founded by Josiah Spode (1733–97) in 1770. It made a great deal of underglaze blue transfer-printed ware,

American Chippendale back splat

A Copeland vase

in numerous designs and of superb quality. Many of the designs were based on Chinese, Indian, or classical patterns; others were based on floral motifs.

Josiah Spode also made porcelain of a fine quality, adding calcined bones to the body of the clay. This was the forerunner of present-day 'bone china.'

When Josiah Spode I died, his son, Josiah Spode II, took over the factory. He was greatly influenced by his father's friend William Copeland, at whose London warehouse he had received part of his training. He took Copeland into partnership and left him to manage the London side of the business. In 1820 William Taylor Copeland (William's son) joined the firm,

which became Spode, Copeland, and Son. William Copeland died in 1826, and Josiah Spode II in 1827. The younger Copeland took Thomas Garrett into partnership in 1833.

Throughout the nineteenth century much elaborately decorated tableware of a superb quality was produced, and the firm also made vases and other decorative pieces. From about 1800 most of the wares were marked.

Until 1966 the Copeland family owned the firm, which still continues to make fine pottery and porcelain.

Spool turning. Used on mass-produced furniture made in America in the mid-nineteenth century. Pine, stained to pass for mahogany, was most commonly used, but better-quality furniture was of walnut, maple, or cherry. This turning resembled a string of beads, and was derived from the earlier bobbin turning (qv).

Spoon back. A descriptive term that refers to:

(1) The very plain, elegant, early nineteenth-century chair with a low seat and splayed legs. Its plain back curves downwards onto the two front corners of the seat, forming the arms of the chair.

(2) Victorian chair backs with a spoon-shaped contour.

(3) The alternative name for a bended back chair (qv) of the Queen Anne period. 'Spoonback' is an alternative name used in America, and quite commonly in England.

Springing line. The point at which an arch curves away from

the impost. The lowest voussoir (qv) laid at the springing line is called the springer.

Sprocket. One of a series of short rafters, each of which is fastened to the foot of a roof rafter. It is of flatter pitch than the large rafter, thereby raising the level of the eaves and giving them an outward curve.

Squinch. An arch or system of concentric arches placed obliquely across the angle of two walls, thus performing the functions of a pendentive (qv). The particular virtue of squinches is that they enable a square-planned building to carry a polygonal or circular superstructure.

Staffordshire pottery. The English pottery industry, with its world-wide exports, is based in Staffordshire. This great industry had its humble beginnings in the early seventeenth century. In north Staffordshire there were rich deposits of clay and coal with which to fire pottery, and lead from which the glaze was made.

The earliest Staffordshire pottery was crude and strictly utilitarian, including such things as butter pots and tobacco pipes.

By the mid-seventeenth century, many potters in this area were making slip-decorated earthenware with considerable skill. They worked in small primitive thatched buildings, each with its own kiln nearby. In the eighteenth century, salt-glazed stoneware (qv) superseded slipware.

It was not until the mid-eighteenth century that the industry was properly organized. This was the achievement of Josiah Wedgwood (qv), who in addition to his great creative work, organized the improvement of the roads and instigated the development of a canal system to transport Staffordshire pottery. He also introduced many new processes for refining and improving the clays, and instituted the first modern factory system in the industry.

By the time of Wedgwood's death in 1795, the Staffordshire Five Towns were well established as the centre of pottery-making in England. Throughout the nineteenth century the demand for pottery and porcelain increased and the industry flourished. Staffordshire is still the heart of the industry, though modern techniques have transformed the whole aspect of the area. With the introduction of

The Adam staircase at the Courtauld Institute, London

gas, oil, and electrically fired kilns, the old coal-fired bottle kilns became obsolete.

Staining. The art of staining has been practised extensively by cabinetmakers, and counterfeit walnut and mahogany furniture began to be made not long after the appearance of the genuine pieces. In *Sylva* (1664), John Evelyn describes several of the more common techniques. But marquetry work in particular did need staining, and Sheraton noted in his *Cabinet Dictionary* (1803) that staining was of particular use for inlay, on which 'at present red and black stains are those in general use.'

Stair(s). Single and multiple steps employed for ascent to and descent from one level to another. A series of steps set within an encompassing framework is termed a staircase. The parts of a stair are known as the tread and the riser, which are set into an angled frame or skirting consisting of the wall string and the outer string. The string is braced

Staffordshire figure of a lion

Modern spiral staircase

The state bed at Kedleston in Derbyshire, 18th century

and supported by a post or newel which is set into the floor or landing.

Stamping. The decorative rosettes, circles, and patterns that were stamped out as the background ornament for gouge work (qv) or sunk carving (qv).

Standing tray. An occasional table, dumb waiter (qv) for tea, or, when used in the dining-room, a butler's tray or table (qv). Standing trays are usually rectangular, and are supported by a four-legged stand or by an X-shaped support, a design that became popular *c* 1750.

Standish. The original term for an inkstand.

Stands. Free-standing supports for cabinets, chests, flowers, candles, trays, and basins.

Starling. A breakwater or pointed projection on the pier

of a bridge, protecting it from the impact of the water.

State. A canopy over an imposing chair; hence the term state chair. In his *New Atlantis* (1626), Bacon writes, 'over the chair is a state made round or oval.'

State bed. A tall, imposing, and heavily ornamented bed made from the Restoration period to the mid-eighteenth century. No woodwork was exposed, for the whole, including the bedposts, was covered or draped with rich fabric. Finials decorated each corner of the tester (qv); they were often vase-shaped, with sumptuous ostrich plumes.

Stave church. A medieval Norwegian church strongly reminiscent of an oriental pagoda. About five or six hundred of these wooden churches were probably built from the eleventh

to the thirteenth century, though not more than 22 survive. They were built in the more remote regions, and look curiously pagan, with pagoda outlines and a great deal of carving and painting. The highest part of the building is the central hall, around which there are usually two lean-to aisles.

Steeple. A tall tower attached to a church or public building, and frequently containing bells. The term comprehends the tower and its spire, lantern, or other superstructure.

Stellar vault (Latin, *stella* 'star'). A Gothic vault in which the liernes (qv), tiercerons (qv), and main ribs create a star-shaped pattern.

Stepped curve. A serpentine curve that is concave as it rises to a narrow flat step, and convex after leaving it.

Steuben glass. This takes its name from Steuben County, New York. Here, in 1903, an Englishman from Stourbridge, Frederick Carder, established a glasshouse at Corning. Like Tiffany, Carder was a devotee of Art Nouveau; one of his products was an iridescent glass that he called Aurene. In 1918 the Steuben works were acquired by the Corning Glass Company, but most of the ware produced was undistinguished until 1933, when Arthur Amory Houghton, Jr took the unusual step of appointing an architect, John Monteith Gates, as chief designer, and the sculptor Sidney Waugh as his associate. Their early designs were deliberately simplified to exploit the crystal's brilliant qualities, and were in complete contrast to the work produced in the 1920s. As they became more familiar with the medium they realized the possibilities of using the crystal as an art form. Naturally round forms could be cut to asymmetrical shapes, and wall thicknesses could be varied to give the glass a sculptural quality. Copper wheel-engraving was increasingly used, and Waugh's early designs for mythological, historical, and literary subjects were so enthusiastically received that Steuben began commissioning designs from leading artists and sculptors. Among the most distinguished of the very many have been Henri Matisse, Salvador Dali, Aristide Maillol, Eric Gill, Duncan Grant, Grant Wood, Sir Jacob Epstein, Sir Matthew Smith, Graham Sutherland,

A Steuben plate of an Arctic tern by Sidney Waugh

Laurence Whistler, and John Piper.

Stickback furniture. A general term occasionally used to describe chairs with small members or spindles in their backs.

Stiff leaf. The curly, drooping, stylized foliage that was sculpted on column capitals of the Early English period.

Stile or **side post.** The outside vertical post in the framework of panelled construction.

Stilted arch. An arch raised up on piers – as if on stilts – so that the springing line is above the impost level.

Stippled background. The term used when the background of sunk carving (qv) is covered with fine dots that have been pricked out, creating a stippled effect. Employed in the sixteenth and seventeenth centuries.

Stirling, James (*b* 1926). Scottish architect, born in Glasgow. His family moved to Liverpool, where he studied at the University School of Architecture. He went to the USA on an exchange scholarship, and then in 1949 became a student at the Associa-

James Stirling

New Residence, St Andrews University, Scotland, by Stirling

General Motors Building by Stone

on for Town Planning and Regional Research in London. He was an architectural assistant, and then senior assistant in various London practices, before setting up in private practice with James Gowan in 1956.

For some years Stirling and Gowan specialized in designing flats and houses, but between 1959 and 1963 the partnership gained an international reputation through their design for the Leicester University Engineering Building. In 1964 the partners set up individual practices. Stirling has since been responsible for the design of the Cambridge University History Building (1964–7), and buildings at St Andrews University and Queen's College, Oxford. He also engaged in a large urban project for Mid-town, West Side, New York.

He has been visiting professor at Yale University, and his designs were exhibited at the Museum of Modern Art, New York, in 1969.

Stone, Edward D (*b* 1902). American architect. Stone's work exemplifies one of the ways in which American architecture departed from the Miesian idiom in the 1950s. For Stone the route led towards elegance and prettiness. His US Embassy in New Delhi (1957–9) was designed as part of a large Federal programme of embassy-building. The elevation, viewed (like the Taj Mahal) across pools and fountains, bears a distant resemblance to Schinkel's Altes Museum in Berlin (1824–8). But whereas Schinkel's museum colonnade is massive and im-

posing, Stone's is brittle and spiky; and while Schinkel's colonnade is severely backed by a wall, Stone's is backed by a delicate pierced screen that is ineffably decorative. For the 1958 Brussels Exposition, Stone designed the US Pavilion with an elevation similar to that of the Delhi Embassy, but on a circular plan. Here, however, the charge of inappropriateness to its (fairground) surroundings cannot be maintained. After these works, Stone's National Geographic Society Building in Washington DC (1962) comes as a surprise. While retaining the formal scheme of his earlier work, it has a simple dignity that suggests a Sullivan building (particularly the Wainwright Building), albeit a Sullivan stripped of all ornament. Among Stone's later works are the Gallery of Modern Art (and now the New York Cultural Center), finished in 1964; the General Motors Building (1971), occupying an entire block on Fifth Avenue, between 58th and 59th Streets in New York City (in association with Emery Roth and Sons); and the John F Kennedy Center for the Performing Arts in Washington DC (1971).

Stoneware (French *grès*). A dense, red or grey, opaque and impervious ware; in hardness it is midway between earthenware and porcelain (qqv). It is made either from a mixture of clay with flint and sand, or from an extremely siliceous clay. It is fired at a very high temperature of about 1,200 degrees centigrade. Some of the best stoneware was made in Germany, notably at Cologne. Production began in the fourteenth century, and with the development of more artistic forms during the sixteenth century it was exported widely. English manufacture began in the following century, and

the best-known ware was made by John Dwight at Fulham, the Elers brothers, and Josiah Wedgwood.

Stool. A seat without arms or legs. Late medieval stools were of plank construction, and resembled miniature benches with shaped underframing; they were known as board or slab-ended stools. They were replaced by the standard joint stool (qv) which for a century after *c* 1600 was made up into sets upholstered *en suite* with chairs and footstools. Strict rules of etiquette governed their use. From the late seventeenth to the mid-eighteenth century, when the manufacture of stools declined, their development parallels that of chairs, although the legs and stretchers of stools, unlike those

Edward Stone

North Carolina Capitol at Raleigh by Edward Stone

Fulham stoneware jug

A Louis XV beechwood stool

Redland Court, Bristol, by Strahan, c 1735

of chairs, are the same back and front. The long window stools with scrolled ends, favoured by Adam and his contemporaries, are most elegant and played an important part in the formal arrangement of furnishings.

Storr, Paul (1771–1844). The leading silversmith of the Regency period, and one of the most important figures in the history of English silver. He trained under Andrew Fogelberg and from 1792 worked on his own, though he frequently carried out work for Rundell, Bridge, and Rundell (qv). He became a partner in their firm in 1811, but broke away in 1819. He retired in 1839.

Storr made silver in the popular heavy Neo-classical taste, and also in the revived Rococo style. He could work on a monumental scale, and produced many large ceremonial trophies after the Napoleonic wars. He often employed casting to achieve sculptural effects. The Prince Regent was his chief patron, and many members of the English aristocracy bought his work, with the result that he is well represented in public and private British collections.

Cream jug by Paul Storr

Strahan, John (*d* 1740). British architect. Research has so far failed to reveal any details of Strahan's early years, although it has been surmised that he was a Scottish carpenter-builder. He appeared in Bristol in 1725, offering his services as 'land surveyor and Architect', much to the annoyance of John Wood (qv), who regarded building in Bath as his exclusive domain. Strahan soon obtained the patronage of influential citizens, including one John Hobbs, who employed him on development schemes. Strahan's first major work was to lay out parts of Bath, including Kingsmead and Beaufort Square, but his most memorable building is Redland Court (*c* 1735) in Bristol. Frampton Court (1731–3), near Bristol, and the Barber-Surgeon's Hall in Bristol, are also attributed to him.

Strainer arch. An arch that is usually found spanning a nave or aisles to counter unevenly distributed pressure.

Strapwork. An extremely popular form of ornament that is a characteristic of Elizabethan and Jacobean decoration. It originated in the Netherlands in the early sixteenth century, whence it was imported to England, largely through pattern-books.

Strapwork resembles leather straps that criss-cross and interlace in geometric and arabesque forms; it was used as pure decoration, or sometimes to enclose devices. It was widely employed as low-relief ornament, and occurs upon furniture, chimney-pieces, and screens. It was especially effective in plasterwork.

Straw work or **straw marquetry.** A decoration made up of cut and tinted straws that were arranged into patterns or scenes upon the specially prepared surfaces of furniture, boxes, panels, etc. Though most examples were rather simple in design, some intricate and pretty effects were achieved, notably in the late eighteenth century in France.

Street, George Edmund (1824–81). British architect. Street was one of the most important and influential of Victorian ecclesiastical architects. In 1848 he set up a practice in Wantage, Berkshire, moving to Oxford few years later to supervise hi work for the Oxford diocese and then going to London. Hi extensive travels on the Conti nent resulted in two importan books, *Brick and Marble Archi tecture in Italy* (1855) and th *Account of Gothic Architecture i Spain* (1865). His practice as church architect was extremel successful, his High Churc beliefs and passion for Gothi recommending him to man ecclesiastical authorities. Amon his most important churches wer

The Royal Courts of Justice, London, by Street, 1868-81

St Paul's American Church, Rome, by Street, 1873

St James-the-Less, Westminster (1859–61), All Saints, Clifton, Bristol (1868), All Saints, Bolton (1870), St John the Divine, Kennington, London (1870–4). He also designed the Courts of Justice in the Strand, London (1868–81).

Stretcher. The side face of a brick; when employed continuously, such brickwork is termed

a stretcher course. The more usual procedure for a nine-inch wall is to lay header-and-stretcher courses, ie with head and side faces laid alternately.

In cabinetmaking and joinery the term stretcher (also known as a barr) is applied to the horizontal members which join and brace the legs of tables, stools, chairs etc. Although the stretcher was initially used to strengthen furniture, it gradually became a decorative feature of furniture. It fell into disfavour towards the end of the eighteenth century. Chippendale calls the stretcher a 'stretching rail.'

Strickland, William (1788–1854). American architect, practising mainly in Philadelphia at a time when it was the cultural capital of the USA. He was a pupil of Latrobe, and an engineer as well as an architect. Like C R Cockerell in England, he succeeded in transcending the merely historically accurate work of his contemporaries, creating a suave personal style grounded on a mastery of the Greek vocabulary. His Philadelphia Merchants' Exchange (1832–4) is in this respect an advance on his Philadelphia Branch Bank of the United States (1819–24). The state capitol which he built for Tennessee at Nashville (1845–9) is probably the most diffuse as well as the most elegantly detailed of the temple-like state capitols built in the wake of Jefferson's Richmond Capitol.

Striges. The channels of a fluted column or pilaster. As an enrichment to an interior decorative scheme, the lower parts of the striges were sometimes filled with a cable moulding (qv).

String. One of the side members of a staircase, encasing and supporting the treads and risers.

Belmont, Nashville, Tennessee, by William Strickland, 1850

The inner string is set against the wall, the outer string is supported at the base of the staircase by the newel post.

String course. The term applied to a course of brickwork, or to a projecting band on the façade of a building.

Stringing. In furniture decoration, a very narrow linear inlay of contrasting colour, sometimes employed as a framework to a marquetry panel. The strings are made of metal (brass was especially popular in the Regency period), and of woods such as satinwood, holly, purplewood, and ebony.

Struck moulding or the corrupted **Stuck** refers to a moulding that has been carved directly on the member rather than applied or planted. Stuck is also misleadingly used to describe a planted moulding.

Strut. In framed roof construction, a member lending support to the principal rafter, either diagonally, resting on the king post, or upright, resting on the hammer beam.

Stuart. A furniture term used for the years 1603–88, when England was ruled by the Stuart kings (excepting for the Commonwealth period, 1649–60). Since the period lacked stylistic cohesion, the term is not very useful. See **Carolean** and **William and Mary.**

Stucco. Strictly speaking, this term covers all forms of plastering, whether for an internal cornice, a fresco base, or an outside wall covering. The last is the most popular use now, while internal work is called plasterwork (qv).

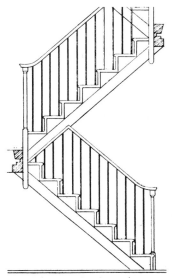

Diagram showing strings

Stucco work on wall and ceiling

Stretchers shown on a sofa table and two chairs

A stumpwork picture of David and Bathsheba, 1656

New York Guaranty Building, Buffalo, by Sullivan, 1894-5

Stump foot. A term occasionally used to describe a furniture leg that descends directly to the ground, without a carved or turned foot.

Stumpwork. English relief work embroidery of the seventeenth century; it probably derived from the earlier raised ecclesiastical work. It belongs mainly to the years 1640 to 1660, and was practised by young girls – a fact which no doubt accounts for much of its charmingly naïve character.

Stumpwork is always figurative, and though Old Testament and mythological stories are perhaps the most common subjects, others such as the seasons and elements, or the king and queen gorgeously arrayed, are quite frequently found. Despite the faded quality of much surviving stumpwork, and the tears in it, enough remains to show that it was colourful and rich. The background was invariably of heavy white satin, and the stitches were of coloured silks; spangles, and tiny seed pearls were used for additional decoration. The raised section of the design was built up with fabric, tow, horse-hair, cotton wool, or similar stuffs, and the figures were made of carved box wood, with hands and heads of composition. The background motifs dotted between the figures were usually of uniform size, whether they were butterflies, smiling lions and unicorns, or castles with mica windows. Much of the surviving work is on small caskets completely covered in stumpwork panels, but stumpwork mirror frames, small embroidery pictures, and bookbindings also exist.

Stylobate. In temple designs of classical architecture, the columns stand upon a base of three steps, the crepidoma; the top step is the stylobate. The term is also used loosely for the whole columnar substructure.

Subtopia (from *suburb* and *utopia*). Coined by Ian Nairn in his book *Outrage* (1955), subtopia defines the man-made world of low-density mess, 'a mean and middle state, neither town nor country, an even spread of abandoned aerodromes and fake rusticity, wire fences, traffic roundabouts, gratuitous notice-boards, car parks, and Things in Fields.'

Sullivan, Louis Henry (1856–1924). American architect, born in Boston. Sullivan received his early training in architectural design at the Massachusetts Institute of Technology, leaving to work in a Philadelphia architect's office. In 1874 he went to Paris and studied briefly at the Ecole des Beaux Arts, returning to Chicago the following year. There he became chief draughtsman in Dankmar Adler's practice, becoming a partner in the firm in 1881.

Sullivan's highly original, individual style began to emerge in his design for the hotel-office-opera-house complex of the Auditorium Building (now Roosevelt College), Chicago (1886–9). This demonstrated his determination to break free from traditional styles, whether Renaissance or Gothic, and to evolve a style that was both functional and indigenous. But the decoration he applied to his early buildings was far too elaborate for later taste, and he only gradually learned to eschew ornamental self-indulgence.

During the 1890s Sullivan designed the skyscrapers and other buildings which have so notable a place in the history of modern architecture. The first was the Wainwright Building in St Louis (1890–1), in which Sullivan essayed a skyscraper construction. Other important works of the 1890s were the Transportation Building at the Chicago World's Fair (1893) and the Guaranty Building, Buffalo (1894–5). Sullivan also designed banks, warehouses, and commercial buildings in Chicago, St Louis, and smaller towns throughout the Middle West. The Adler-Sullivan partnership ended in 1895, but Sullivan continued in practice. He was responsible for the elevations of several buildings which were planned by other architects, including the Chicago department store for Carson Pine C Scott (1899–1904) and the Gage Building (1898–9).

Summer bed. 'Summer Bed in Two Compartments . . . These

Louis Sullivan

Summer bed in two compartments by Sheraton

beds are intended for a nobleman or gentleman and his lady to sleep in separately in hot weather.' (*The Cabinet Maker*, 1802.) This was a design of Sheraton's for two single four-posted beds, separated by a single cornice across the testers.

Sunburst. A semi-circular decoration that was carved on American tallboys and bureaux of the mid-eighteenth century. The design itself is of formalized sunrays, and is not unlike a stylized version of the scallop motif.

Sunderland pottery. Although some rather crude brown and white earthenware was made near Sunderland as early as 1720, it was not until 1762, when the Malings started a pottery at North Hylton, that the area became important. Much of the ware was shipped to London and found its way to western Europe and America.

Sunderland pottery was of many different types, from coarse brown kitchenware to cream-coloured earthenware; a great deal of lustre-decorated ware was produced in copper, silver, and pink (gold lustre). Many of the pink-lustre pieces were decorated with black transfer-printed designs. The Sunderland potters catered mainly for people with moderate incomes, and a great deal of the ware was aimed at the 'gift' trade. Many pieces were decorated with ships or nautical scenes, and verses designed to appeal to the many seafarers who put into the port.

The most famous Sunderland decoration was a transfer engraving of the Iron Bridge over the River Wear, opened in 1796.

A quantity of blue printed tableware was also produced. By the end of the nineteenth century, the importance of the Sunderland pottery industry had diminished.

Sunk carving. A primitive form of carved ornament in which the background is removed from around the design.

Sunk panel. A panel on a wall or door, set back from the stiles and rails. For recessed ceiling panels, see the entries on lacunaria and coffer.

Sunderland jug, c 1796

Suprematism. The Russian artist Kasimir Malevich (1878–1935) coined this term in Moscow in 1915 to define 'the supremacy of pure feeling or perception in pictorial art. From the Suprematist point of view, exterior appearances offer no interest; only sensibility is essential, independent of the mood in which it exists.' Suprematism is thus an abstract art practised by artists who prefer the sense of an object to the object itself. Malevich taught at the Moscow Academy of Fine Arts, and his 'architectonic' compositions influenced many Russian architects.

Surbase. A moulding or group of mouldings running along the top of a basement storey exterior, or above the wainscot or dado of an interior.

Swag. A festoon of fruit or floral motifs carved to hang within a panel. Swags were a decorative feature of Renaissance and eighteenth-century interiors. They were most frequently used as decorations above chimney-pieces.

Swag drapery was imitation material hung above windows instead of a pelmet.

Swan-neck. A form of broken pediment which incorporates two opposed S-shaped curves or scrolls. It was used as a decorative element over the cornices of wardrobes, bookcases, or door-cases. Chippendale shows an elegant version in the third (1762) edition of his *Cabinet Maker's Director*.

Swansea. See Nantgarw.

Swedish glass. Most of the glass made in Sweden up to the eighteenth century followed German and Bohemian fashions. In the nineteenth century, cut decoration was fashionable on wine glasses and decanters. However, it was not until the early twentieth century, when the reorganized Swedish Society of Arts and Crafts vigorously promoted design experiment, that Swedish glass became world-famous.

One of the pioneer factories was Orrefors, which was established in 1726 as an ironworks, and began making window and bottle glass in 1898. In 1913 it was bought by Consul Johan Ekman, who, with the help of the Society of Arts and Crafts, set about raising the quality and aesthetic standards of the glass. Ekman began to employ the designer Simon Gate in 1916,

Swan-necked pediment

and Edward Hald (qv) in 1917. Together they developed a multi-coloured glass known as *Graal*, which consisted of several layers of coloured glass that were overlaid at the furnace mouth. In the 1930s, air bubbles were used to give an added dimension to this type of glass, and it became known as *Ariel*. Table glass also developed a new character. Gilding and excess cutting were avoided, and from as early as 1916 plain or tinted glass was produced. Its beauty of design is still one of the hallmarks of Swedish tableware.

Sycamore. *Acer pseudoplatanus.* There are American and English varieties of this wood. The American, because of a tendency to warp, was generally confined to use in interiors. Commonly known as buttonwood or fiddle-backed sycamore, it is a ruddy wood that is now more regularly referred to as American plane.

The English variety is similar to maplewood. It is white, ageing to pale yellow, and is marked with numerous flakes in the grain. This fine-grained, glossy wood was used for flowered marquetry in the late seventeenth century. It was also used in the late eighteenth century for furniture, and was often stained for turned work. When dyed grey, it was known as harewood (qv).

Swedish glass by Boda

Ancient bronze table found at Chiusi

Uppark in Sussex attributed to William Talman, c 1690

Table (Latin, *tabula* 'a board'). This basic piece of furniture was used by the ancient Egyptians, Greeks, and Romans, and examples of four-legged and pedestal tables are still extant.

However, the modern table, as its derivation suggests, developed directly from the medieval board and trestle table. This in turn became a fixed dining and general-purpose piece until the end of the sixteenth century, when the first specialized pieces were made, eg games tables. See separate entries for the various kinds of table.

Tabouret. A low upholstered seat for one person. The word was used in both the seventeenth and eighteenth centuries for the stools used at court, which were the subject of rigorous rules of etiquette.

Tallboy. Basically a chest-on-chest with eight drawers, two small ones at the top and six wide ones below. It became extremely popular in the last years of the seventeenth century, when most pieces were faced in walnut veneer on an oak or pine carcase. This handsome, compact form of storage remained in favour throughout the eighteenth century, with mahogany gradually supplanting walnut. In North America, where it was (and is) very popular, the tallboy is usually known as a highboy (qv). The American form was often more richly decorated, with broken and swan-neck pediments and a dentil cornice.

Talman, William (1650–1719). British architect. All that is known of Talman's early life, education, and training is that he was the son of a small landowner in Wiltshire. He seems to

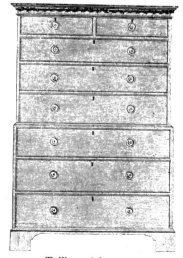

Tallboy 18th century

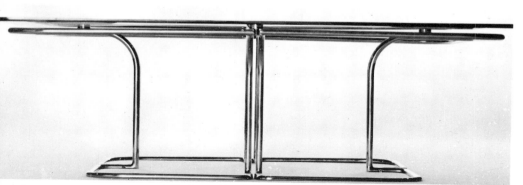

Modern table of glass on a metal frame

Tiles. *Patterned tiles on the exterior of the Topkapi Palace, the residence of the former Ottoman Emperors in Istanbul*

An engraving of Chatsworth, Derbyshire, designed by Talman, 1687-96

The Sports Hall in Tokyo designed by Tange, 1961-4

have set up as an architect at an early age. The building of Thoresby Hall, for which Talman was the architect, is generally dated as taking place in 1671, when he was barely 21. Talman gained several other important commissions for houses, including the rebuilding of the south and east fronts of Chatsworth for the 1st Duke of Devonshire (1687–96); Swallowfield in Berkshire (1689–91); Uppark in Sussex (c 1690); Dyrham (1698–1700); and Kineton, Yorkshire (1699–1701). In 1689 he was appointed comptroller of the king's works, but three years later, on the death of William III, Sir John Vanbrugh was given the appointment.

Talman was plainly a man of some substance, acquiring the manor of Felmingham in Norfolk in 1718, and leaving his son money and property. Although Talman's achievement was considerable, his reputation has been overshadowed by those of Wren and Vanbrugh. His abilities must have been recognized by his patrician contemporaries, for notable commissions came his way despite his litigious disposition and what seems to have been a far-from-agreeable personality. Talman was also an outstanding collector of prints and drawings, and supported his eldest son John (1677–1726) during his long stay in Italy: John Talman returned from Italy

in 1715 to become the first director of the Society of Antiquaries.

Tambour. A shuttered form of covering used in cabinet-making. It occurs most frequently as a pull-down curving lid for a roll-top desk, but is also found in a vertical form for cabinet and cupboard doors, particularly the doors of bedside cabinets, and pot cupboards. The shuttering, normally made of thin strips of flat or moulded wood on a stiff canvas backing, presents a decorative reeded appearance when closed. According to Sheraton, it should only ' be employed 'when no great strength or security is requisite.'

Tange, Kenzo (b 1913). Japanese architect. Tange was born in Imabari, and after attending Hiroshima High School, studied architecture and engineering at Tokyo University. He graduated in 1938, first joined Kunio Mayekawa's practice, then the Japanese Werkbund, and then took a postgraduate course in the university. Tange's first design to be constructed was a temporary pavilion at Kobe Trade Fair in 1950. From that time onwards his work was increasingly in demand, and he has designed some of the most influential buildings in Japan. His series of city and town halls is remarkable, including the complex of the Tokyo City Hall

A tambour desk by John Seymour of Boston, Massachusetts

Tokyo Cathedral designed by Tange, 1962-4

Kurayoshi City Hall designed by Tange, 1955-6

An armchair in tapestry

(1952–7), and town halls at Shimizu (1954), Imabari (1957), and Kurashiki (1960). He has also been responsible for several other important public buildings, including the Peace Centre, Hiroshima (1955–6), which includes an unusually imaginative children's library; Tokyo Cathedral (1962–4); and Sports Stadia for the 1964 Tokyo Olympic Games.

Tange has been greatly influenced by Le Corbusier, especially in his technical proficiency and imaginative skill in the use of concrete, but has increasingly concerned himself with adapting Japanese forms to modern conditions. The social context of his commissions is important to Tange, as is evident in such different buildings as the Peace Centre children's library and the town halls, which are integrated into a communal environment, and not isolated, intimidating, official structures. Tange is not only one of Japan's foremost architects, with a growing influence on Western designers; he exercizes a profound influence upon the younger generation in his position as professor of architecture at Tokyo University,

where he lectures to engineering as well as architectural students. In this position he has advocated the development of a specifically Japanese style within or against the pervasive International style. Tange has also published essays on regional planning and urban architecture.

Tapered leg. Although often applied to any chair or chest leg which tapers from the jointure to the foot, in cabinetmaking and chairmaking the term is normally reserved for a leg of square section. This form was introduced in the second half of the eighteenth century, mainly for armchairs, dining-chairs, tables, and sideboards. It was only occasionally used for the legs of commodes.

Tapestry (Latin, *tapetum* 'carpet'). A term first applied to a wall-covering, and later (less accurately) to carpets and furniture coverings woven on a loom using multi-coloured threads. An outline of the cartoon or design to be copied is traced in black crayon upon the taut threads before weaving begins. The process is extremely in-

volved and painstaking.

The craft is of ancient origin and remnants of tapestries dating from the Greek and Roman periods have been discovered in Egypt. In more recent times the craft of weaving has been most skilfully practised in France. Francis I (1494–1547) is usually credited with the introduction of tapestry weaving on a large scale, establishing a factory at Fontainebleau with Flemish workmen. However, the oldest examples of French tapestry work are earlier: scenes from the Book of Revelation were woven in Paris in the fourteenth century for the cathedral at Angers. Henry IV (1553–1610) continued royal patronage of the craft, and the famous Gobelins factory (qv) was established in 1630, under Louis XIII. A high-warp loom was used for the reproduction of paintings and cartoons of leading artists.

Tassel. A highly decorative object, made of cut and banded cords, normally silk. These are gathered around a wooden sphere covered with a material of the same colour as the cords. Tassels are normally used in conjunction

Tapestry pole screen, c 1770

The Administration Building of Tokyo City Hall designed by Tange, 1952-7

Tassels on a chair

Sir Robert Taylor

Gorhambury, Hertfordshire, by Sir Robert Taylor, 1770-90

A modern tea table

Two views of Ely House, London, by Taylor

with draped canopies or pelmets. They were extremely popular in late-Victorian and Edwardian decorative schemes, and have never completely ceased to be used.

Tavern table. The American name for a small oblong table of plain country make, with carved support at either end and a stretcher in between. They are mainly of seventeenth- and eighteenth-century origin, and are popularly associated with inns.

Taylor, Sir Robert (1714–88). British sculptor and architect. Taylor was the son of a master-mason and was himself trained as a mason and sculptor. His father sent him to study in Rome, but died bankrupt while his son was abroad.

Taylor returned and set up as a sculptor, rapidly gaining a considerable reputation. Examples of his monumental work were erected in Westminster Abbey, and he carved the pediment for the Mansion House. But realizing his limitations as a sculptor compared with his great contemporaries (Roubiliac, Rysbrack, and Scheemakers), he turned to architecture.

Within a few years, by a combination of skill, energy, and efficiency, Taylor built up a wideranging practice, sharing with Paine (qv) the most lucrative commissions of the day. He specialized in building houses for the prosperous mercantile class, with whom he was in particularly close contact after his appointment in 1765 to the surveyorship of the Bank of England. He succeeded Sir William Chambers as architect of the king's works in 1769, and became master-carpenter in 1777. He became Sheriff of London, and was knighted in 1782.

Taylor's originality as an architect was for long overshadowed by his technical skills. In recent years there has been wide appreciation of his thoughtful and fresh adaptation of the Palladian villa to the requirements of the merchant class. Taylor's main claim to fame rests on country houses such as Harleyford Manor, Buckinghamshire (1755); Asgill House, Richmond (1757–8); and Purbrook, Hampshire. His public buildings include the Bank of England (1766–83) and Stone Buildings, Lincoln's Inn (1774–80).

Tazza. Italian word for 'cup.' In England the term was introduced in Tudor times to describe a wide shallow bowl on a high stem, usually executed in silver.

Tea caddy, tea chest. A container for tea. The term derived from a Malayan word, *kati,* designating a measure of tea rather more than a pound in weight. As tea-drinking became popular in eighteenth-century England, numerous decorative versions of the tea caddy were produced. The object itself was long known as a 'tea chest' and is so called by Chippendale in the 1762 edition of his *Director.*

Cabinetmakers and metalworkers lavished a good deal of attention on tea caddies, which were made in a variety of sizes and a miscellany of materials, ranging from pewter and silver to rosewood and tortoise-shell. Larger metal versions developed into the tea canister, a circular container decoratively painted. The traditional tea caddy – presumably known as such in the early nineteenth century, for Sheraton refers to 'caddy' in his *Cabinet Dictionary* of 1803 – is now a collector's item. It is basically a miniature casket, usually with two metal containers for the two blends of tea, green and black, or for tea and sugar.

Teague, Walter Dorwin (1883–1960). American designer. The son of a minister, Walter Teague was born in Decatur, Indiana. He studied for four years at the Art Students' League in New York, and then embarked upon a career that was to make him one of the best known American designers. He began by working in advertising and book illustrating. In 1929 he set up his own industrial design practice, becoming consultant to Eastman Kodak and Boeing Airplane, and later worked for such firms as US Steel, Du Pont, and Cadillac. The Society of Industrial Designers elected him their

Tea caddies in fruitwood, tortoise-shell and satinwood c 1780

Thomas Telford

The aqueduct across the River Dee at Pont-y-cysylte designed by Thomas Telford

first president, and in 1951 he was made an honorary RDI by the British Royal Society of Arts. He was author of *Design This Day* (America, 1940; England, 1946).

Teak. *Tectena grandis.* An extremely hard, golden-brown Oriental wood. It was employed extensively for nautical furniture such as chairs and chests, as well as for joinery. Much contemporary furniture, particularly from America and Scandinavia, is made of teak.

Teapoy. A tea caddy on a stand. 'Teapoy' is an Anglo-Indian word; the Hindi original is associated with a three-footed object rather than with tea, but the sound of the first syllable led to its taking on its present main meaning. Many teapoys are extremely decorative; they are made of wood, or sometimes papier maché, and inlaid or painted with floral motifs.

Tea table. A term reserved by eighteenth-century cabinet-makers for tables with tops edged by fretwork galleries to prevent tea services from slipping off. These tables were also known as china tables.

Telamones. Figures of men used to support an entablature instead of columns.

Telford, Thomas (1757–1834). Scottish civil engineer. Telford was born at Eskdale in Dumfriesshire, Scotland, the son of a shepherd. He was apprenticed to a local stonemason, and after serving his time, moved to Edinburgh where he worked on

various buildings in the fast-rising New Town. Then in London he worked on Somerset House before being appointed foreman in charge of the building of the commissioner's house in Portsmouth Dockyard (1784–5), designed by Samuel Wyatt.

In 1787 Telford was summoned to Shrewsbury by Sir William Pulteney, his first patron, to supervise the rebuilding of Shrewsbury Castle. Soon afterwards he was appointed surveyor of public works for Shropshire, and in this capacity designed St Mary's Church, Bridgnorth, and began to build the canals and bridges that were to make him famous.

Telford was the first engineer to use cast-iron extensively in building bridges and aqueducts. He built his first bridge across the River Severn at Buildwas (1795–6), demolished in 1905, and this was followed by Bewdley Bridge (in stone), the cast-iron Mythe Bridge at Tewkesbury (1823), and the Conway Bridge (1822–6). Telford also designed many small iron bridges based on standardized cast-iron forms. His fame became such that he was commissioned to design a project for a 600 ft single span cast-iron London Bridge; the design was accepted but the bridge was not built. Telford's most remarkable achievements were his canals and aqueducts, feats of engineering on a large scale. The Ellesmere Canal (1795 –1803), a 100-mile network of waterways linking the Rivers Dee, Mersey, and Severn, incorporated two immense aqueducts at Chirk and at Llangollen.

In 1801 Telford carried out a survey of the Highlands for the

government. During the next 30 years he planned over 900 miles of roadways, and numerous harbours and bridges, bringing transport facilities to hitherto remote areas. His greatest achievement in his native land was undoubtedly the Caledonian Canal, although he also planned the first adequate water supply for Edinburgh. He was consulted by foreign governments, designing the Göta Canal for the Swedish Government and the 100-mile Warsaw-Briesc road for the Russian Government. He also prepared projects for bridges in France, Germany, and Italy.

In 1820 Telford became the first president of the Institution of Civil Engineers. Among his most notable later works was St Katherine's Dock at Wapping

(1826–8), where clearance and excavation projects preceded the building of the dock, which was carried out at a speed that Telford deprecated but controlled.

Tempietto (Italian, from *tempio* 'a temple'). A small temple-like structure, usually upon a circular base. The finest example is surely Bramante's Tempietto, built in 1502 in the cloister of S Pietro in Montorio, Rome. It is a majestic and solemn chapel, built upon the reputed site of St Peter's martyrdom and perhaps approaching the spirit of classical antiquity more than any other Renaissance building.

Template. A block of stone inserted at a strategic point in

St Katherine's Dock, Wapping, London, by Thomas Telford, 1826-8

An ancient Greek doric temple at Aegina

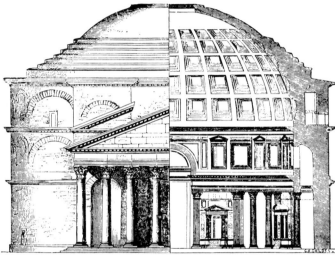

Half elevation and half section of the Pantheon at Rome

The Maison Carrée at Nîmes, 16 BC

an otherwise rather insubstantial wall (eg of rubble or brickwork); thus placed it bears and distributes the massed weight of a superstructure or the applied thrust of a girder. The term is frequently confused with **Templet,** which is the correct term for any shaped piece of metal, wood, cardboard, or plastic, cut to a required pattern and used as a guide for wood- and metalwork, stonemasonry, patchwork, etc. A templet is invaluable when repeat motifs are required.

Temple. Buildings exclusively reserved for the worship of a god or gods are a feature of many religions. The term 'temple' describes Greco-Roman places of worship (Latin *templum*), and also religious buildings without widely received special names. Anything that is not a church, cathedral, synagogue, or mosque tends to be called a temple. Exceptions to this usage are Solomon's Temple, the Temple Church, and City Temple in London, and the Mormon use of the term for their churches. The wider usage covers the gigantic temples of ancient Egypt, built over many years by slave labour, the rock-cut Hindu and Buddhist temples of India, and the smaller and more intimate temples of ancient Greece and Rome. Roman temples with their domed roofs and colonnaded entrances, eventually became the prototypes for the Palladian villa.

Tenia. The continuous band

'The Temple of the Four Winds' at Castle Howard, 18th century

or fillet at the top of a Doric architrave (qv).

Tenon. In joinery, the tenon is a short projection at the end of a member; it fits into the mortise – a corresponding cavity in another member – to form a mortise and tenon joint.

Tern foot. An ornate triple-scrolled foot, found on mid-eighteenth-century furniture of Chippendale design.

Terrace. A flat grass or paved area alongside a building, usually at a higher level than its immediate surroundings. Its chief function is to provide an area out of doors for relaxation.

Terra cotta (Italian, 'baked earth'). A hard baked clay

A terrace at the back of a town house

A terra-cotta urn

ranging in colour from a pale buff to the familiar deep brick red and brown. The ancient Greeks and Etruscans used terracotta for a variety of purposes, from architectural ornament to household utensils.

Notable instances of its decorative use are the relief plaques executed in the Italian Renaissance period by the Della Robbia family; the pieces were tinenamelled in bright blue, white, and yellow and green. Another interesting use of terracotta was on the Queen Anne style houses of the 1870s and 1880s, which were decorated with unglazed low-relief plaques of lilies and sunflowers.

In America, Louis Sullivan, James Renwich, and others promoted the use of terracotta for moulded ornament.

Terragni, Guiseppe (1904–42). Italian architect. Terragni studied architecture in Milan, graduating in 1926. He was soon caught up in the violent aesthetic controversies which then raged in Italy, and became a member of an influential Milanese group of artists, designers, and architects who opposed the artistic theories of Futurism with its rejection of the past. This group, of which Terragni is generally regarded as the most talented member, established the basis of Italian Rationalism. While still only 25, Terragni became one of Italy's leading architects with his design for an apartment house at Como, followed by an apartment house at Corso Sempione (1935). But his most important and memorable commission was for the Casa del Fascio, also at Como (1936). This building, with its assured and logical symmetry, and its juxtaposition of solids and voids producing a dramatic interplay of light and shadow, gives him an assured place in the history of modern architecture. His achievements span little more than a decade. After active army service on the Greek and Russian fronts he was invalided out of the army, and died at Como in 1942.

Tester. The canopy over a bed. During the fifteenth century the tester was suspended from the ceiling, but it later became fixed, supported by either the vertical celure (qv) or the bedposts. The word has been used for the vertical headboard, and very occasionally for the posts and the whole superstructure.

Tête-a-tête seat. An S-shaped seat for two people. It enabled a couple to sit together and yet face each other. These curious seats were made in England and America during the nineteenth century.

Tetrastyle. Describes a portico with four columns along the front.

Above: The underside of a tester of a state bed, 1695
Below: 16th century tester

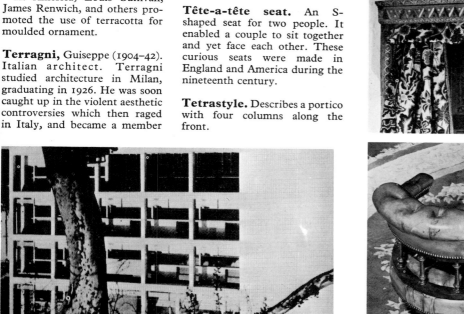

The Casa del Fascio in Como by Terragni, 1936

A Victorian style tête-a-tête seat

Thatched roofs on cottages at Buckland on Dartmoor, Devonshire

Tiffany Favrile vase

Thatch. Thatched roofs are still part of the rural scene in some parts of Britain and Europe, despite the fact that the craft of thatching has been declining steadily. The most durable work, lasting with repairs 60 to 70 years, is carried out with reeds, but most thatching is of straw, with a life-span of not more than 20 years. The principal disadvantage, the fire risk, has been lessened by the use of a fire-resistant solution instead of water for the initial soaking.

Therm or **spade foot.** A short tapered foot of square section that was used in the late eighteenth century. The top projected slightly beyond the width of the leg.

Three-centred arch. An arch constructed from three centres. The two side arcs are described from points on the springing line, while the third centre is below.

Thrown chair. A simple chair made from turned members.

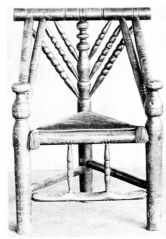

A thrown chair, mid-17th century

Thrust. The lateral force that an arch or part of a building exerts against its abutment or support.

Thuya. *Tetraclinus articulata.* Not to be confused with the variety of cedar called thuja. Thuya is an African wood, used by the ancient Romans for veneering, and again during the eighteenth century for figured veneers. It is an attractive brown, with peculiar markings.

Tie-beam. The bottom horizontal member of a framed roof, spanning the width and tying together the principal rafters.

Tierceron. In Gothic vaulting the tierceron or intermediate rib springs from the wall supports between the transverse and diagonal ribs.

Tiffany, Louis Comfort (1848–1933). American glass designer, interior decorator, and jeweller. Tiffany was born in New York; his father was Charles L Tiffany, founder of Tiffany, Young, and Ellis, who became the most famous jewellers and silversmiths in America. Louis Tiffany preferred the idea of being a painter to joining the family firm. He studied under George Innes, and then in 1868 went to Paris to study with Leon Bailly. On his painting travels around Europe and the Near East, he also studied medieval French stained glass windows, and Islamic objets d'art, of which he became a collector. He almost certainly met his compatriot Whistler and, like Whistler, was impressed by Japanese art and oriental motifs, such as peacock feathers. He probably also knew William Morris, whose activities included the revival of stained glass as an art form.

In 1875, in Brooklyn, Tiffany began to study the making of window glass, and began experimenting with colour and texture. In 1878 he formed the Louis C Tiffany and Associated Artists arranging for the collaboration of furniture stores, glassworks, textile and tile manufacturers, etc, in his interior decorating schemes. He soon won a tremendous reputation for his originality, and for what have been termed his 'harmonized' details. He received prestigious commissions, eg to decorate the White House for President Arthur, and exercized such a great influence on contemporary decorative trends that 'Tiffany-type' windows even appeared in elevated railway waiting-rooms.

From 1885, when Tiffany renamed the company his Tiffany Glass Co, he began to concentrate on producing glass objets d'art. He called his glass *Favrile*, and perfected a technique in which layers of coloured glass flowed transparently or opaquely over one another, creating abstract effects in the play of line and colour. He used twenty-dollar gold pieces to achieve a golden corroded surface on classic Roman and Near Eastern forms, which look like ancient glass that has been buried for centuries, and also used gold to produce swirling rings, flowers, and exotic blue-green peacock feathers with a satin-smooth iridescence. Many of the vases themselves were made in an elongated flower form.

As electricity became more popular, Tiffany designed lamps whose bronze bases displayed his interest in sculpture. At the Turin Exhibition of 1902 he won the grand prize for his lily cluster lamp; this and his wistaria lamp were among his most successful models. In recent years they have come back into fashion, and fetch very high prices at auction.

After the death of his father in 1902, Tiffany designed much of the jewellery and enamels for the family firm. His work represents the most important American contribution to Art Nouveau.

Tile (from Latin *tegula*). A thin piece of baked clay, flat or moulded into shape, that is commonly used as a cladding for roofs, walls, and floors.

The earliest Greek and Roman roof tiles were of two kinds: a flat tile (*tegula*) with two opposite raised edges, and a convex or pointed tile (*imbrex*). The flat tiles were laid end to end, and the convex tiles were placed over them at the joints. A decor-

Tiffany Wisteria lamp

Tile decoration in the Topkapi Palace in Istanbul

Portuguese tiles in the garden of the Palace at Queluz

ative upright, the antefix, was placed at the lower end of each ridge. This method provided an extremely effective covering; a similar method was employed in the Far East, where concave tiles with cylindrical covering tiles were used.

Two tile systems from antiquity are still in use. One consists of ordinary flat overlapping tiles, the other is a system of interlocking S-shaped pantiles, which are still extensively used in Mediterranean countries. Flat roof tiles, known as plain tiles, are occasionally hung vertically on battens on the face of a building. Tile-hanging is a regional characteristic and is usually employed only on the upper storey.

Tiles have been in use as floor and wall coverings since ancient times; the famous friezes of lions and archers on the palace of Artaxerxes II at Susa date from the early fourth century BC. Other spectacular uses of tiles were made in Persia, where mosques and palaces were tiled both inside and out, and at the Alhambra in Granada, Spain. In northern Europe the rich and ornately patterned tiles of St Denis, Paris, dating from the early twelfth century, were imitated in many French Gothic churches.

During the period of the Renaissance, both Italy and Spain produced large numbers of painted maiolica (qv) tiles, which were exported throughout western Europe.

The Delft tiles of the seventeenth century enjoyed enormous popularity, mainly for use on stoves and fireplaces, and were even exported to America.

Today decorative and plain tiles for kitchens and bathrooms are in universal use.

Tile hanging. The practice of hanging tiles vertically on the side of a building to keep out the rain. The pattern made by the tiles, particularly if their lower edges are shaped, creates an attractive variant on the usual smooth façade. The practice is usually confined to the uppermost part of the wall. Alternative terms are vertical tiling and slat hanging.

Tiles lining the walls and floor of a shower-room

The timber framed Lord Leicester's Hospital in Warwick

The timber-framed Schiefes Haus (crooked house) in Ulm, Germany

Tilting chest. A type of medieval chest probably belonging to the fourteenth and early fifteenth centuries. It had realistic representations of a tournament or tilting match carved upon the front.

Tilt-top table. See **Snap table.**

Timber-framed. A common form of building in which walls are constructed from a skeleton of timber, the spaces between timbers being filled up with some other material. In medieval and Tudor times the infilling was of brick, plaster, or wattle and daub. The half-timbering (qv) of Tudor cottages is extremely pleasing; its imitation ('pseudo-Tudor') less so.

Timber-framing has again become a popular method of construction, especially in Scandinavia, North America, and England (where it is widely used for industrialized building). Nowadays the framework is clad on the outside with timber, brick, tiles, or asbestos, and the inside with plasterboard.

Toby jug. See **Wood,** Ralph.

Toile de Jouy. An attractive fabric with printed scenes, manufactured at Jouy in France. In 1760 Christoph Philippe Oberkampf, a dyer and cloth printer from Germany, established a factory at Jouy, near Versailles. He employed designers such as J-B Huet and J Pillement to provide the patterns, and the enterprise was an immediate success. The first linen and cotton were all printed in single colours from wooden blocks; but with the introduction of metal plates a decade later, several colours could be produced on each design. Typical Toile de Jouy is printed in a single colour showing pastoral scenes upon a light background.

Toilet mirror. The earliest surviving examples of toilet mirrors date from the Restoration period. They are small, with wide borders decorated with stumpwork, and were either hung on a wall or supported by a hinged strut.

The mirrors made in 1700–10 were elaborately fitted with bases like bureaux, and were usually placed upon plain tables. The more familiar version, pivoting between two uprights and set on a box stand, was like a miniature cheval mirror (qv); it was produced from the early eighteenth century. The advent of the fitted dressing-table meant that elaborate bases were no longer necessary, and so single drawers became the rule; in some instances even these were omitted.

The dressing-table and the cheval mirror, with its larger area of glass, were largely responsible for the declining manufacture of toilet mirrors.

Tôleware. Enamelled or lacquered metalware, usually decorated with gilt designs. From the eighteenth century onwards, this was particularly popular in America for lamps, boxes, trays, and other accessories.

Topiary. The art of pruning or clipping shrubs into fantastic and fanciful shapes. Yew, box, and holly are the most common, and the trees are usually planted in formal arrangements. Some of the best examples have survived for many centuries, as is the case with the finest topiary garden in England, at Levens in

15th century house

French toile de Jouy, printed cotton, c 1790

George I japanned toilet mirror

Topiary in an English garden

The Zarzuela Racecourse Grandstand at Madrid by Torroja, 1935

Italian torchères, late 17th century

American candlestand, c 1805

Westmorland. The word topiary comes from the Greek *topos*, a place; *topiarius* became 'the man in charge of the place' – in fact, the gardener.

Torchère or **candlestand.** A tall stand that carried a candlestick or lamp. Torchères were frequently made in pairs, and were used to supplement the lighting of a room. They were in general use throughout the eighteenth century, ceasing to be made when improvements in lighting rendered them superfluous.

The early candlestand, a tripod with a circular or octagonal top and scrolled feet, was sometimes made *en suite* with a lookingglass and side table. The design remained standard until affected by Rococo and Neo-classical influences in the second half of the century. The shaft was broken up by scrolls, and then dispensed with altogether in favour of designs such as those of Robert Adam, containing slender uprights. There are numerous designs in contemporary pattern-books.

Torroja, Eduardo (1899–1961). Spanish architect. After studying civil engineering in Madrid, Torroja became increasingly interested in the fusion of architecture and engineering. He was unusually well-equipped to give practical form to his beliefs, and from 1930 onwards designed many remarkable structures, including bridges, halls, aqueducts, and churches. His first considerable commission was for the Tempul Bridge, which was followed by the ribless-roofed Market Hall at Algeciras (1933). Among the most spectacular of his buildings is the grandstand at the Zarzuela race track near Madrid (1935), with its emphatically fluted and cantilevered roof. This was followed by a reservoir for Madrid (1936) with a domed water tower. The 623 ft span of the railway bridge that Torroja designed to cross the Esla river (1940), was at the time the longest in the world.

However diverse the projects, each of Torroja's solutions to difficult structural problems was also a work of high architectural merit. These qualities appear in churches he designed towards the end of his life at Xerraló, Sant Esperé, and Pont de Suert in Spain, and in the Táchira Club at Caracas (1957). Torroja explained his attitude towards building in his *Philosophy of Structures* (1958), in which he argues that the imagination of the designer must control the structural formulae rather than vice versa.

The canopy of the Zarzuela Grandstand, Madrid

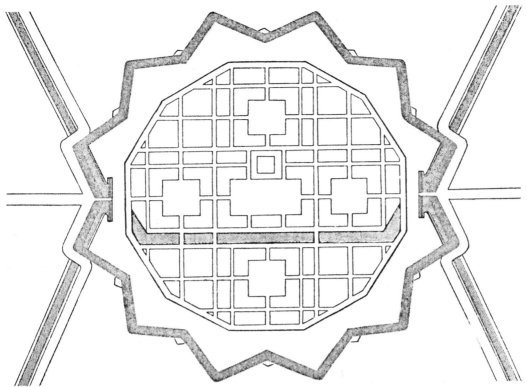

Vincenzo Scamozzi's plan of an ideal city, 1615

Tortoise-shell. The semi-transparent, mottled, or cloudy shell of certain tortoises, especially the hawk's-bill. The shell was flattened and made into sheets so that it could be used for inlay and the veneering of furniture and small articles such as boxes.

Torus. In architecture, a large convex moulding, usually semicircular in profile.

Town-planning. Since the beginning of the Industrial Revolution, the problem of creating an efficient, healthy, happy urban environment has vexed architects and technologists. It has now been elevated to a semi-scientific level, with university chairs, international associations, and multi-language publications devoted to the subject. But although professional town-planners proliferate, town-planning in any coherent sense seems no more satisfactory than it has ever been.

In its earliest stages, town-planning largely turned upon the need for defence. Walled cities required barracks, storehouses, streets, assembly points, etc. Some kind of grid system became an almost inevitable formula, modified by topographical considerations.

Once there was no need for urban defence, towns grew apace without effective control. Many theorists – from Vitruvius to Leonardo da Vinci – evolved plans for an ideal city, but none was realized in practice. The need for factories, shops, and above all housing, resulted in piecemeal unplanned developments which invariably burst the city's boundaries. Attempts at logical town-planning were nullified by personal greed and communal apathy, as is demonstrated by the rejection of the rational plans submitted by Evelyn, Wren, and others after the Great Fire of London in 1666.

Other towns were more fortunate. Rome was improved by successive popes, and in Paris the efforts made by Henry IV were renewed by Louis XIII and Louis XIV (and later, less happily, by Napoleon).

During the eighteenth century several cities were planned: Mannheim in Germany; Nancy in France; a large part of Edinburgh; and Washington in America. Elsewhere a few enlightened landowners made praiseworthy but essentially modest and personal contributions.

The increased pace of the Industrial Revolution, the breakdown of an established architectural tradition, and the greed and hypocrisy of landowners, developers, speculators, and builders, created appalling conditions in London and other industrialized cities. The planning of fashionable spas and the inspired developments by Nash in London were exceptions. Furthermore, the last years of the nineteenth century saw the first industrial towns laid out, and in Letchworth (1903) the first Garden City followed close behind.

Meanwhile, in the nineteenth century, as the cities expanded, they absorbed outlying villages and towns. In order to escape this concentration of buildings and people, those who could afford it moved out of the city, setting up suburban developments which were in turn engulfed by urban sprawl. Thus grew the great cities – London, Paris, Berlin, New York, Tokyo – creating vast new problems of overcrowding.

Such problems eventually reached a pitch at which at least some publicists, politicians, and civic authorities were roused to action. Yet it was left to private enterprise in the wealthier nations, and to the smaller, less urbanized states, to institute legislation for town-planning. Italy and Sweden were among the first of the latter in the 1860s.

Today the relationship between planners and public is not yet as harmonious as might be wished. Some of the difficulty undoubtedly stems from insufficient knowledge of what people really want and need, and New Towns still find only reluctant residents. Another major difficulty is the apathy of the public at large towards the quality of their environment; while sectional interests bedevil most decisions.

Townsend-Goddard. Two American families of cabinet-makers, united through marriage. Twenty members of these families, spanning three generations, made furniture in styles ranging from Queen Anne to Empire. John Goddard (1723–

A block fronted chest of drawers by John Townsend, 1765

Early English tracery

Tracery by Batty Langley, 1742

Transfer printing on a Liverpool jug, c 1790, and Copeland and Garrett plate, c 1833-47

86), along with Job Townsend (1699–1765) and John Townsend (1732–1809), developed the Newport block-front style. The front of this furniture is divided vertically into three panels, the centre panel being concave, and the panels on either side convex. A shell motif, carved in relief or intaglio, is placed at the top of each panel.

Trabeated architecture (Latin, *trabs* 'a beam'). The principle of construction by post and lintel rather than the arch (arcuated architecture). Greek architecture is trabeated; Roman and Gothic are arcuated.

Tracery. The ornamental pattern within the head or upper part of a Gothic window or doorway. The term was also applied to similar decorative treatment of the upper part of the doors in eighteenth-century cabinetmakers' designs for bookcases, chairbacks, and other furniture. The decorative motif is established by piercing or application.

A Trafalgar chair

The basic tracery designs of Gothic windows were often still further decorated by the introduction of cusps (qv), and the addition of trefoil (three-lobed leaf), quatrefoil, and cinquefoil designs.

Trafalgar chair. After Nelson's victory at the Battle of Trafalgar (1805) a number of cabinetmakers sought to increase sales by incorporating nautical motifs in their designs. Sabre-legged chairs are often called Trafalgar chairs, and Sheraton published a design for a Nelson chair which is also sometimes known as a Trafalgar chair.

Transept. The transverse arms that cross some churches between the nave and choir. Similar arms farther east, or at the west end, are also called transepts.

Transfer printing. This ceramic technique was invented by Sadler and Green of Liverpool *c* 1752. The designs were drawn, and then engraved on to a copper plate; the plate was inked, the surplus ink wiped off, and a thin tissue paper placed over the plate, which was then put through a press. The ink still in the engraved part of the design was transferred to the paper, which was then pressed on to the ceramic surface to be decorated. The transfer paper was brushed thoroughly and then soaked off, leaving the design on the ceramic surface, which was then glazed and fired. Sometimes the transfer designs were put on over the top of the glaze.

Sadler and Green used this procedure first to decorate tiles, which they produced in large numbers, but soon the Wedgwood firm was sending them shiploads of cream-coloured earthenware to be transfer-

printed. Wedgwood's then took to doing the transfer printing themselves, and soon afterwards dozens of potters were using the process.

The original Sadler and Green tiles are usually printed in black, or occasionally a brick red or a manganese purple. The early Wedgwood transfer decorations were black and occasionally red. Josiah Spode, who had seen a form of blue underglaze transfer printing at the Caughley porcelain works, introduced it into Staffordshire. Soon the blue designs were made by dozens of potters, and Minton introduced the famous Willow pattern, which was copied over and over again, especially in France and Germany, and later in America.

Transfer printing on tableware was also carried out at the Leeds Pottery, and at Swansea and Stockton-on-Tees. Besides blue and black, a pinky red, green, and brown were also popular. Transfer printing of a rather cruder variety was done at Newcastle-upon-Tyne and Sunderland. Here the technique was often used with pink lustre, and thousands of jugs must have been made with an engraved design showing the new iron bridge over the River Wear.

Transfer printing using the original techniques has been practised ever since its invention. However, a new technique has been developed during the last few years. In this, the Murray-Curvex process, a gelatine mould picks up the design from the inked plate and transfers it straight on to the ceramic surface, obviating the need for transfer papers. There is a slight loss of quality but the process cuts out so many of the stages essential in the old technique, that it seems here to stay. So far,

however, it can only be used on flat ware.

Transom. The horizontal mullion or cross-bar dividing a window into glazed sections or rows of lights. Thus a single transom will establish two lights, two transoms three, and so on.

Transverse arch or **rib.** An arch that spans a vault, giving it support and separating each bay.

Travertine. A creamy-toned limestone which has been quarried since Roman times in Italy. It has been so widely

Transoms on the windows of a Renaissance house

Trefoil

A group of typical small treen objects

utilized because of its ready and longlasting response to polishing. During recent years travertine has been employed for coffee-table tops by interior designers.

Tray. A single flat piece of wood, metal, or some other material with a raised edge or side. It was made in a variety of shapes, and was normally used to carry a teapot and china. The tray-top table is a small table with a raised edge or gallery; this can be straight, but it is often scalloped. The tray itself may be either fixed or movable. In cabinetmaking, a tray is a shallow sliding drawer in a cabinet, acting as a receptacle for knives, spoons, and forks, or for toilet accessories. Sheraton uses the term in his *Cabinet Dictionary* (1803).

Tread. The horizontal plane or upper part of a step, above the vertical risers.

18th century tray

Treen. A term applied to relatively small wooden objects, mostly turned by cabinetmakers and carpenters. There is a sixteenth-century reference to treen chalices by John Jewel, Bishop of Salisbury. However, treen ware was usually more domestic; including a wide range of kitchen objects such as pastry rollers, ladles, spoons, etc. More decorative treen ware included children's toys, caskets, jars, wig stands, tumblers, and cups.

Tree of life. An ancient Eastern motif, perhaps originating with the Assyrians. It is a large spreading tree, the boughs laden with fruit, flowers, and birds, and is often represented growing from a vase fed by the water of life. The symbol has been adopted in several cultures, and can, for example, be found in Gothic window tracery, crewelwork embroidery, and fracturs (qv).

Trefoil (Latin, *trifolium* 'three-leaved'). A motif frequently used in Gothic architecture. It was introduced as a three-lobed opening in tracery; or as a three-lobed carving set in relief and used singly or in repeat patterns. In eighteenth-century gothick architecture and cabinetmaking

the trefoil was again widely used. In the early nineteenth century it appeared as a motif inlaid in brass in the friezes of bookcases and writing-tables.

Trellis, trellis work, treillage. A latticed design made by thin flat bars or slats, normally in timber, which are overlaid to form square or diamond-shaped patterns. Such designs are used on the outer walls of houses for training roses and other climbing flowers. This lattice form is usually known as treillage.

Trellis work is used as a decorative element in porches and for the supports to balconies. In cabinetmaking the term is used of fretwork galleries on table tops, the supports for tables, and chairbacks in the *chinoiserie* manner.

Trencher salt. A low container for salt on a moulded base. It was used in Tudor times alongside the standing or ceremonial salt, and its simple shape

Trellis cladding to a house and a decorative obelisk

Trellis trompe-l'oeil on a garden wall

A modern trestle table of glass on metal stands

The Early English triforium at Lincoln Cathedral

survived into the eighteenth century.

Trestle table. A medieval form of dining-table consisting of a heavy plain board, usually of oak or elm, placed on stout cross-shaped supports known as trestles. Such tables could be dismantled by the servants after the meal, and remained in general use until the early sixteenth century.

During recent years the trestle table has been revived, thanks to designers who have experimented with glass and plastic tops supported by trestles in a variety of materials, from ebonized wood to chrome, steel, and brass.

Tribune. See **Gallery.**

A tripod table

Tridarn. The Welsh name for a particular variety of cupboard or press that was made in the late seventeenth and eighteenth centuries. It was in three stages: a two-door cupboard at the bottom, a row of three low, recessed cupboards in the middle, and at the top an open shelf for the display of plate.

Triforium. Sometimes known as a blind storey in contrast to the clerestory (qv) or clear storey. The triforium was usually a series of arches spanning an enclosed (and therefore darker) space beneath a roof.

Triglyph (Greek, *trigluphos* 'thrice grooved'). In a Doric frieze, the triglyph blocks alternate with the metopes (qv), one triglyph usually being centred over each column with one or two between. Each of the blocks carries three vertical grooves.

Tripod table. A small table which became popular during the early eighteenth century, mainly for serving tea. The term derived from the three legs supporting a central pillar or pedestal; an alternative name was 'pillar-and-claw table.' The table-top was rectangular, oval, or circular, and was often decorated with a gallery.

Triptych. A three-panelled carving or painting, usually an altarpiece. Triptychs were invariably made for private patrons. The two side panels could be folded over the central panel, in which position they often displayed the owner's coat of arms.

Triumphal arch. The Romans invented this type of monument, of which over 150 still exist. They were not necessarily triumphal, being erected in honour of private citizens and rulers as well as military victories; but they have since become identified with war and conquest. Of modern arches, the Washington Arch, the Arc de Triomphe, and the Brandenburger Tor are the best known.

Trivet. A small, three-legged stand of brass or iron. It stood in front of a hearth, and was used for keeping a tea-kettle or open dish warm.

Trompe-l'oeil (French, 'deceive the eye'). A visual deception most frequently associated with painting, but common also in architecture and decoration.

The basic technique is extremely ancient, appearing in

The Arch of Tiberius at Orange, c *30* BC

Trompe-l'oeil painting by Sir James Thornhill at Greenwich, London

Trompe-l'oeil brick work on the garden wall of a town house

Roman wall-paintings from 100 BC. At the Villa of Livia at Primaporte, dating from *c* 20 BC, an entire wall is painted to simulate the view of an idyllic secluded garden. In the House of the Vettii at Pompeii, a complete wall is painted to appear like marble panels framing paintings, while non-existent windows open on to elaborate architectural sets.

Paolo Veronese used the tech-

Trompe-l'oeil picture frames

nique at the Villa Maser, Vicenza (*c* 1561), in frescoes broken by 'openings' showing the sky and countryside. A woman, her children, and a nurse look over a parapet into the room, and a page and children appear through half-open doors.

Illusionism was particularly favoured in the Baroque age, when innumerable church ceilings appeared to open to the heavens, and clouds, putti, and heavenly beings mingled in the empyrean, the real architecture fusing with painted architectural motifs and figures. The Roman churches of Gesù and S Ignazio are excellent examples.

Architectural trompe-l'oeil is deception achieved by perspective foreshortening and an actual realignment of components to give a false impression of an object's real dimensions. Examples can be seen during the Renaissance period. At Palladio's and Scamozzi's Teatro Olimpico, Vicenza (1579–84), the elaborate set is constructed to give the appearance of streets leading to the back of the stage; in Bernini's Scala Regia at the Vatican (1663–6), cunning placing of columns makes the stairway appear longer and more impressive than a more conventional treatment could achieve. This method of perspective foreshortening can also be used to great effect in gardens.

Occasionally illusionistic painting consists of straight-forward mock architectural motifs such as rows of pilasters or an aedicule. James Thornhill's Painted Hall at Greenwich (1717) is one such case. The technique was practised throughout the nineteenth century, and towards the end of the century enjoyed a particular vogue in America.

Trompe-l'oeil remains popular today for special decorative effects, the photographic lens occasionally replacing the artist's brush.

Trophy (Greek *tropaion*, from *trope* 'rout'). The origins of this splendid wall decoration were victory memorials, consisting of captured arms and standards, that were erected on the battle-fields of ancient Greece. The asymmetry and pictorial variety of the arrangement recommended the motif to designers of the seventeenth and first half of the eighteenth century; it occurred most frequently as a sculptural decoration, although examples in grisaille were also extremely effective.

Troubadour style. French Gothic revival furniture of the 1830s.

Truckle or **trundle bed.** A low bed on wheels that could be rolled beneath an ordinary bed

during the daytime. It was chiefly used by servants who slept in their masters' bedrooms, and by children. They were made from the late fifteenth to mid-eighteenth century in England, and until the early nineteenth century in the United States.

Trussing bed. A medieval and Tudor bedstead that could be dismantled and packed into bags for travelling and military campaigns. The actual structure is unknown, but it is clear from inventories that the framework had become more elaborate by Tudor times.

Trussing coffer. A late medieval travelling chest covered in leather, nail-studded, and banded with iron.

Tubbs, Ralph (*b* 1912). British architect. After training at the Architectural Association School in London, Tubbs became secretary of the MARS (Modern Architectural Research) Group while establishing himself as an independent architect. His wider reputation was initially based upon a remarkable structure, The Dome of Discovery, which he designed for the Festival of Britain on the South Bank in 1951. This structure, 365 ft diameter, was at that time the largest dome in the world. This project was followed by a num-

Traditional and modern Danish versions of the tub chair

Tudor flower

ber of other buildings, all having unusual distinction in their elevations, imaginative planning, and care in detailing. Tubbs's design for the Indian Students' Building in London became something of a model for university hostel buildings. The Baden-Powell Memorial Building in South Kensington, London, also demonstrated his considerable abilities. Tubbs has designed many industrial and residential projects and has been actively involved in New Town developments at Basildon and Harlow. He has published *Living in Cities* (1942) and *The Englishman Builds* (1945).

Tub chair. Small, upholstered easy chairs with shaped spoon backs. Sheraton illustrates one in *The Cabinet Dictionary* (1803), and says that it is 'a tub easy chair, stuffed all over, and is intended for sick persons, being both easy and warm.' Whatever its original purpose, this piece achieved its greatest popularity as a lady's chair in the Victorian era; it appears in many pictures of mid-nineteenth-century interiors. It fell into disfavour after the end of the century, and did not begin to regain its popularity until recent times, when Scandinavian designers began to use the concave back shape of the chair as the basis for a streamlined version.

Tucker. American ceramic company. In 1825–6, William Ellis Tucker established a kiln in Philadelphia; one of the earliest in the history of American porcelain. From 1828 the ware was marked 'Tucker and Hulme, Philadelphia', sometimes with the addition of 'China Manufacturer.' William Tucker died in 1832, but the firm continued under Thomas Tucker and his partner Judge Joseph Hemphill. The next few years (1833–6) are known as the Hemphill period. The factory was fairly successful in imitating Sèvres porcelain, importing workmen for that purpose. The ware was richly decorated with portraits of the famous, monograms, and coats of arms, all carried out in enamel painting with much gilding.

Tudor. England's Tudor monarchs reigned from 1485, when Henry VII came to the throne, to 1603, when Elizabeth I died and the ill-starred Stuart dynasty began. This period thus opens with the late medieval style prevailing in furniture, and the Perpendicular style in architecture; and in its course the medieval only slowly gave way to the Renaissance. One of the finest examples of Perpendicular, Henry VII's chapel in Westminster Abbey, was built in the early Tudor period, and the style persisted in Hardwick Hall, Derbyshire (1590–7), one of the late Elizabethan glories, erected only a few years before the first true Renaissance building, the Queen's House at Greenwich (1618). 'Tudor' is therefore rather unsatisfactory as a stylistic term and is most commonly used with reference to the earlier medieval part, up to about the death of Queen Mary in 1558.

Tudor arch. The term for the late medieval depressed pointed arch. It is usually four-centred, one pair of centres being on the springing line and the other below it.

Tudor flower. A late Gothic architectural decoration (early sixteenth century). The motif is a trefoil pointed flower that probably derived from the cusps in foliated arches and tracery. It is also known as brattishing (qv).

Tulipwood. *Genus dalbergia.* A hard striped wood, native to Brazil. Tulipwood, of a pale brown to pink shading, is called Pinkwood in the USA and bois de rose in France, where it was used extensively for Louis XV furniture. The wood is particularly suited for veneer work and in the eighteenth century was particularly used for banding on furniture.

Tunbridge ware. A wood mosaic in which small pieces of different woods, some artificially

The interior of the Dome of Discovery by Tubbs at the Festival of Britain, 1951

Tunbridge work on a work table

Geometrically patterned Turkish carpets from Kulah (above) and Ladik (below)

A Turner earthenware tureen and cover in blue, late 18th century

coloured, were laid in patterns representing foliage, landscape, and other motifs. This technique, mainly used for trays, tea caddies, and boxes, was practised in Tunbridge Wells from the mid-seventeenth to the early nineteenth century.

Turcoman or **Turkoman.** This term describes rugs made by the nomadic tribes that wandered through Turkestan, the area to the west of Persia and Afghanistan, and to the east of China. Persian and Afghan influences were particularly strong. The rugs are relatively familiar to Western eyes, having been exported since the eighteenth century. They are characterized by a repeated motif of an octagonal gule or medallion. These figures, popularly known as elephant feet, comprehend a variety of forms from diamonds to elongated and regular octagons. The rugs are knotted with the Sehna knot (qv), and the main colours are a rich reddish brown, Turcoman red, black, and dark blue. The various Turcoman carpets include Saryk, Salor, Yomud, Baluchistan, Esari, Afghan, and Beshire; the very finest are the Bokharas (qv) made by the Tekkes.

Turkish carpets. These first arrived in western Europe in the sixteenth century, usually via the port of Smyrna. They are the rich-looking carpets draped over tables in the indoor scenes of Holbein and Vermeer, and in Italian paintings. Today, too, good antique Turkish carpets are really too valuable (and often too frail) to put on the floor, and most are used as wall-hangings.

Almost all Turkish carpets are knotted with the Ghiordes knot. The pile is often longer than in Persian carpets, the colours fewer. Patterns are bold and tend to be geometric. Typical are stylized flowers such as the Rhodian lily, the pomegranate, and the hyacinth, the only living forms represented. In the mihrab mosque pattern on prayer rugs there is a lamp or ewer suspended from an arch. On the Ghiordes the arch is steep but gently stepped.

The Ghiordes, with their attractive arabesques, floral designs, borders, and stripes, are the best Turkish carpets, and are considered the equals of the finest Persian carpets. Other carpets made in Asia Minor are the Ladik, Kulah, Oushak, Melez, Bergama, and Kir Shehr.

Turkoman. See **Turcoman.**

Turner, John (b 1738). British potter, apprenticed in 1753 to Daniel Bird, who was killed later that year. Turner went into

Ironstone jug by W Turner

Turned members on a chair

partnership with a man called Banks, and began making white salt-glazed stoneware at Stoke-on-Trent, on the site of the present Copeland factory. In 1762 he moved to Lane End. His son William followed him into the business, and the Turner factory made all kinds of pottery, including agate ware, salt-glazed stoneware, black basalt and jasper ware, can ware, a fine, hard, white stoneware, cream-coloured earthenware, and pearlware. The quality of the pottery (marked TURNER, impressed) was almost as good as Josiah Wedgwood's, though it never achieved the same popularity. The Turners exported ware to Holland, where

Medieval church turrets c 1150 (left) and c 1450 (right)

it was appreciated because it was stronger and more heat-resistant than Delftware. They also exported much pottery to France: because of the French Revolution they were unable to collect the large sums of money owed to them, and in 1806 went bankrupt. The factory itself was sold in 1829, when Spode and Adam bought up many of the Turner moulds.

Turning. Wooden legs, posts, and other elements in chairs and cabinets, shaped by tools applied to the timber as it rotates in a lathe.

Turnip foot. An American term for a spherical foot used on cabinet furniture. It is rather similar to a bunfoot, with a slight ringed moulding and a narrower neck.

Turret. A form of tower. The term is usually reserved for small towers, often at the angle of a building, that have been given a fortified appearance, with crenellations, arrow-slits, etc. The term is also applied to church towers.

Tuscan order. An essentially Italian order, dating in developed form from the second century BC. It has been variously described as a derivative from Etruscan architecture and from the Greek Doric order (qv). The

Tuscan column and capital were established by the fourth century, consisting of a smooth, tapering column on a circular base or plinth, with abacus and echinus above the necking. At this stage a projecting cornice was the only form of entablature, but this was later replaced by an Ionic archi-

Tympanum, 18th century

trave and unadorned frieze, and a Doric cornice with bed moulds and dentils. An example of second-century BC Tuscan is the south temple at the Foro Olitorio, Rome.

The Tuscan order was prescribed by Renaissance writers for architectural works such as town gates and country houses, in which an impression of strength and simplicity was required. It was elaborated during this period in order to distinguish it from the Doric; Bernini's colonnade at St Peter's, Rome, is probably the most famous example.

Tympanum. The area within a pediment on classical buildings, or within an arch over an entrance. It is often enriched by carving. The term is also applied to the face of a plinth or pedestal, and in medieval church architecture to the screen set between the chancel and rood screen.

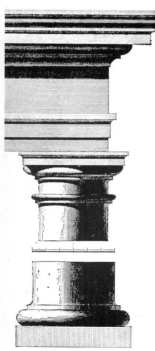
Tuscan Order

Sculpture in the tympanum of a portal at Notre Dame, Paris

The medieval undercroft at Burton Agnes Hall, Yorkshire

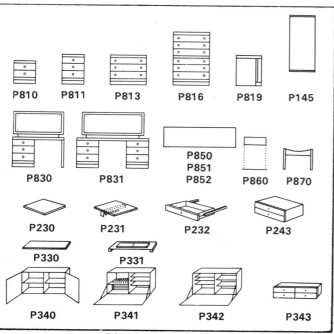

Diagram of unit furniture

P810 P811 P813 P816 P819 P145

P830 P831 P850 P851 P852 P860 P870

P230 P231 P232 P243

P330 P331

P340 P341 P342 P343

Undercroft. The vaulted substructure of a cellar, basement, semi-basement. In medieval times such a room was often used as a refectory or dormitory in monastic buildings.

Underframe, underframing. Terms applied to the support from below needed by chairs, table-tops, and cabinets. Underframes have been made in various shapes, from the X-shaped framing used to brace and support medieval seats and trestle-tables to the elaborate carved underframes of lacquer cabinets and display stands. The underframing of seats and tables, which was plain and basic until late medieval times, later gave joiners and carvers opportunities to demonstrate their craftsmanship and virtuosity. In much modern furniture a return has been made to the simplest forms of underframing.

Unit furniture. Ranges of furniture consisting of related standard units, easily assembled and added to; eg bookcases in horizontal units that could be multiplied at need. Unit furniture first became popular in the early 1930s, when a well-designed range by Serge Chermayeff was marketed. It became something of a necessity during World War II as part of the Utility furniture scheme (qv), which restricted furniture design and manufacture to basic requirements. In the post-war period, unit furniture ranges were introduced by leading manufacturers as part of a general programme of rationalization in the industry.

Unwin, Sir Raymond (1863–1940). British architect and town-planner. Unwin was born in Rotherham in Yorkshire, and was trained as an engineer. He

Multi-X-shaped underframe for a seat, 16th century

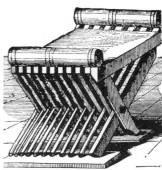

Underframe in chrome steel for a stool, by Ciancimino

Raymond Unwin

Urn. *A stone urn by the pool of Latona in the gardens of Versailles laid out by Le Nôtre*

Quadrangle from Unwin's 'Cottage Plans and Common Sense'

Trinity Church, by Upjohn

government service, and eventually became chief architect and town-planner at the Ministry of Health.

All Unwin's work displays an unusual grasp of the human needs that must be met in town-planning. His knowledge of Oxford taught him the importance of devices such as inward-looking quadrangles and squares in promoting human association and co-operation. An Oxford college, he asserted, was simply a collection of small tenements built in squares with some central common buildings.

Upholsterer, upholstery.
The craftsman and craft concerned with stuffing padded chairs and sofas; the term derives from the medieval upholders and upholsters, who made mattresses and hangings. The term 'upholstery' is applied to all forms of padding or covering, whether of seating or bedding.

Upjohn, Richard (1802–78). Anglo-American architect. Upjohn was born in Shaftesbury, Dorset, was apprenticed at an early age to a local cabinetmaker, and set up on his own in his early twenties. In 1829, however, he emigrated to America, and in 1834, after working in Massachusetts as a

later set up partnership with Barry Parker, an architect, in Buxton in Derbyshire. An early interest in social questions encouraged him to study town-planning, and he and Barry Parker won a competition for the planning of the first English Garden City (qv) at Letchworth in Hertfordshire.

The Unwin-Parker plan was based on what has since become known as the neighbourhood

principle, with the railway station at the town centre and a village-like development of small houses and cottages around a radial road system. The publicity attending the development of Letchworth brought the partners a commission to build another model village, at Earswick near York. This was followed by an invitation to design the now-famous Hampstead Garden Suburb. Unwin was later co-opted into

cabinetmaker, he entered the drawing office of the then-elderly leading Boston architect Charles Bullfinch (1736–1844), architect of the State House in Boston. Due, no doubt, to his early training, Upjohn quickly made his mark in the office as Bullfinch's assistant, and by 1835 was designing houses on his own account. At that time he was prepared to design in Gothic or Neo-classic style, but the designing of Trinity Church in New York (1844–6), followed by St. Thomas's Church, also in New York, established Upjohn as the undisputed leader of ecclesiastical

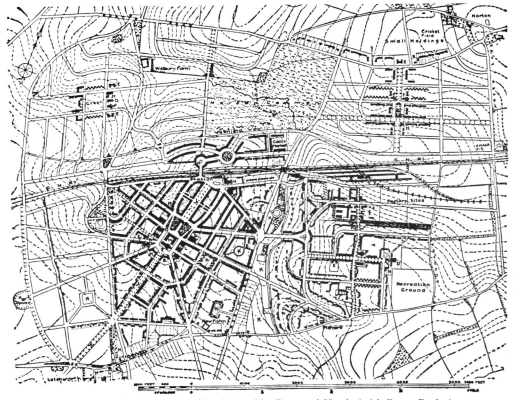

The plan for Letchworth Garden City designed by Raymond Unwin (with Barry Parker), 1903

City Hall, Utica: Upjohn

Urns in a garden designed by William Kent

architects and of the Gothic revival in America, although he continued to use a Neo-classic of Italianate derivation in his designs for houses and other buildings, notably his design for the City Hall, Utica, New York State (1852–3). His early training as a worker in timber enabled him to design various wooden village churches in Massachusetts with uncommon imagination and authority.

Urn. Originally a memorial vessel made to contain the ashes of the dead, but later widely adapted as decorative shape in architecture, cabinetmaking, and garden design. In stone it was

used as a finial for the façades of buildings, in wood as a container for knives, and in bronze and other metals as a decorative element on chimney-pieces. It was also made in stone or terra cotta as a pivotal or focal point in formal garden design.

Utility furniture. Furniture made in Britain during World War II, which was designed to rigid standards of maximum economy in the use of materials and labour. The scheme was set up by the Board of Trade in June 1942, under the direction of Sir Charles Tennyson. Although utility furniture was widely criticized for the starkness and austerity of its design, it had a lasting and beneficial effect on post-war British furniture design.

Utzon, Jørn (b 1918). Danish architect. Utzon was trained at the architectural school of the Copenhagen Academy of Arts, continued his training in Stockholm, and spent some months in Alvar Aalto's drawing office in Helsinki. Utzon is chiefly known as the designer of Sydney Opera House, the commission for which he won in an international competition (1956). He had previously made a reputation in Denmark as the most original of the younger school of architects, designing a number of private houses and a housing estate at Elineberg (with E and H Andersson). The Opera House, basically a series of shells on a vast platform on the marine frontage of the city, houses other

Jørn Utzon

functions besides the Opera, including an experimental theatre and a concert hall. The structure was evolved in association with Ove Arup.

Unfortunately rising costs involved in the complex shell structure design gave rise to serious controversies in Australia, and the architect was for a time virtually dissociated from the work in progress.

In Denmark, Utzon has been responsible for a number of major buildings, including the Højstrup Workers' High School, housing estates in Zeeland, and various projects in Copenhagen. He has also designed furniture.

Sydney Opera House on Bennelong Point, Sydney Harbour, by Utzon

Swagged terra-cotta urn

Utzon's own weekend house at Hellebak, Denmark

A valance from a state bed, late 17th century

A valance as a decorative frill on a tester

Sir John Vanburgh by Kneller

Vallance or **valance.** A term applied to almost any form of gathered or pleated covering which is attached horizontally to chair bases, pelmet boxes, testers, etc. The term is also used to describe a skirting or dado.

Valley. The internal angle at the intersection of two sloping roofs.

Vanbrugh, Sir John (1664–1720). British architect and dramatist. Vanbrugh is the most colourful, engaging, and meteoric figure in the history of English architecture. He was the son of Giles Vanbrugh (Van Brugg), a Dutch merchant who had come to England to escape Catholic persecution in the Netherlands. Little is known of Vanbrugh's early life, except that he was one of 19 children and grew up in Chester, whence his parents removed from London – possibly to escape the plague – when he was three years old. At the age of 22 he obtained a commission

The Great Hall, Blenheim Palace, Oxfordshire, by Vanburgh, 1702-20

Vanburgh. *The central hall at Castle Howard in Yorkshire designed by Sir John Vanburgh, 1699-1726*

The façade of Blenheim Palace in Oxfordshire designed by Sir John Vanburgh, 1706-20

Van de Velde by Kirchner

in a foot regiment, which he soon resigned. He was arrested in Calais for being without a passport, and spent the next eighteen months in French prisons, ending up in the Bastille. After his release he was commissioned into the marines, and while still a serving officer, began to write plays. He was successful as a playwright in his own day, and remains a figure of considerable importance in Restoration drama.

In 1698 Vanbrugh resigned his commission and in 1699, apparently without any previous technical training or experience, was asked by the Earl of Carlisle to prepare designs for Castle Howard in Yorkshire. These designs, combined with the continued patronage of Lord Carlisle, introduced Vanbrugh into

the quite lucrative world of official architecture. In 1702 he was appointed comptroller of the king's works, replacing Talman (qv) in this position as he had replaced him at Castle Howard.

Vanbrugh held this sinecure for a decade, later adding the surveyorship of Greenwich Hospital.

Vanbrugh's greatest commission was to build a house at Woodstock in Oxfordshire for the Duke of Marlborough; this was to be an expression of national gratitude for the duke's great victories over the French. The result was Blenheim Palace, a monumental work that Vanbrugh was never allowed to see in its completed form: he quarrelled violently with the duchess, who refused to allow him beyond the gates.

Despite the association of his name with a group of great buildings – Castle Howard, Blenheim, Seaton Delaval, Eastbury, and Greenwich Hospital – Vanbrugh's practice extended to many kinds of designs, including smaller houses at Greenwich, garden buildings at Stowe, and the restoration of castle buildings such as Kimbolton in Huntingdonshire and Lumley in Durham. His architectural style is unique, not only in England but in Europe. It owed little to Palladian precedents, then beginning to attract attention of the Whig aristocracy, but gained its effect from Vanbrugh's preoccupation with 'movement.' This quality is present in all the elements in his designs, from their massive centrepieces to their theatrical skylines, from

their depth, recession, and shadow to the way in which subsidiary buildings are related to the central block.

In all his buildings Vanbrugh was assisted by the redoubtable and scholarly Nicholas Hawksmoor (qv), with whom he seems to have established a relationship of unusual mutual trust.

Van de Velde, Henry (1863–1957). Belgian architect, pioneer designer, teacher, and advocate of the modern movement in art and architecture. In 1881 he studied painting at the Académie des Beaux Arts in Antwerp. In 1889, after further studies, he became a member of the Belgian avant-garde group, Les XX, and came into contact with William Morris and the English Arts and Crafts Movement. He was now launched on a career as a modernist designer and apostle of Art Nouveau.

Van de Velde's first venture into architecture was in 1895, when he built his own house at Uccle in Brussels, and designed all the furnishings down to the hardware and cutlery. In the following year a Paris dealer, Siegfried Bing, commissioned him to design four complete rooms for Bing's gallery, Maison de l'Art Nouveau. These were a tremendous success at the Dresden Exhibition of Applied Arts in 1897, and after this Van de Velde's career was centred in Germany, although he did undertake decorating commissions in Paris. In 1900 he designed the interior of the Folkwang Museum (now the Karl-Ernst-Osthaus Museum), Hagen, and in 1902 he was appointed artistic adviser to the Grand Duke of Saxe-Weimar. As such he organized the founding and building of the Weimar School of Arts and Crafts, later to become the famous Bauhaus (qv). Here Van de Velde revolutionized the teaching of design and crafts,

The façade of Castle Howard in Yorkshire designed by Sir John Vanburgh, 1699-1726

Wrought-iron weather vane

Norman groined vault at Sherbourne Castle and rib vaults at Gloucester Cathedral crypt, c 1100

Early English rib and panel vaults at Westminster Abbey, 1260, and Salisbury Cathedral, 1240

and created an area of contact for artist-designer, craftsman, and industrialist. Among the buildings for which he was responsible during this period was the renowned Werkbund Theatre at Cologne (1914), now demolished.

During World War I, Van de Velde moved to Switzerland, where he was commissioned by the Kröller-Müller family to design a museum which was eventually built in Otterlo, Holland (1937–54). In 1925 he returned to his native Belgium, becoming professor of architecture at the University of Ghent (1926–36). His abilities as a teacher were given wider scope at the Institut des Arts Décoratifs de la Cambre, of which he was the founder and, until 1935, first principal. He designed the Belgian pavilions at the Paris Exposition Internationale (1937) and the New York World's Fair (1939–40).

Vane. A plate or strip of metal that turns on a vertical spindle or pivot, showing the direction of the wind. Vanes were fixed on the higher parts of buildings such as fortified towers, church spires, and stable turrets. They were usually given a decorative form, the most common being that of a cock; hence 'weather cock.' Flags and heraldic devices were also popular.

Varnish. Two types of varnish were used on furniture before the introduction of French Polish (qv) in the early nineteenth century. The first was oil-based; the second and later, introduced in the second half of the seventeenth century, was spirit based. The spirit varnish, shellac, or linseed, dissolved in spirits of wine, was applied in thin layers to the surface; good-quality furniture was given ten or more coats. The spirit in each coating evaporated, leaving a residue of lac that could be polished to a high shine.

Vase. The formal and decorative possibilities of the vase have ensured its enduring importance in design and decoration. It has been interpreted and reinterpreted in a wide variety of forms and materials, and was widely and variously used as a decorative device by eighteenth-century cabinetmakers.

Vault (French *voute*; Latin *volvere* 'to turn'). An arched structure which is either self-supporting or supports a building above the vaulting. The elements of vaulting were known to the ancient Babylonians *c* 4000 BC, but the techniques were improved beyond recognition by Roman builders. The greatest advances in vaulting, both technically and aesthetically, were made by the builders of Romanesque and Gothic cathedrals in western Europe. The barrel vault (qv) was the method most favoured by the Romans, who developed intricate forms of

Perpendicular fan vaulting at Gloucester Cathedral

Queen Anne Vauxhall glass

intersecting barrel vaulting; but this had its weaknesses, particularly in spanning large areas. The problem was partly solved by the introduction of the Romanesque ribbed vault, but it was the development of the pointed arch and the Gothic ribbed vault that made possible the dazzling spatial effects seen in Gothic cathedrals. The builders of the Gothic period became increasingly accomplished and experimental in their use of intricate forms of vaulting, aided by the introduction of subsidiary ribs. This led to the complex virtuosity of fan-vaulting (qv). See also the articles on groined, ribbed, and quadripartite vaulting.

Vaulting shaft. The column or shaft from which the vaulting ribs spring. It may rise up from the ground or be a short column high up on a corbel.

Vauxhall bevel. A traditional bevel for mirrors and glass, said to have originated at the Vauxhall glasshouse (see **English glass**). It is a very shallow, broad bevel of seven and a half degrees or less.

Velvet (French *velour*). A fabric usually made of silk, with a close pile surface. It probably originated in the Orient, and is made by the introduction of extra warp threads, which are later cut to give the tufted surface of cut velvet. Where the loops of warp threads are left uncut, the velvet is called *épinglé* or *frisé*. Until the seventeenth century it was used for clothing, hangings, and ecclesiastical vestments. Then it began to be increasingly used for upholstery, at first used for cushions and the hangings of some state beds.

Veneer. A thin slice of decoratively grained wood that is glued to the furniture frame, the carcase itself being of a strong but less attractive and less expensive wood. Veneering is a very ancient technique that was rediscovered in the late seventeenth century, when ebony was introduced to France. This wood is especially hard, and necessitated a layered treatment, giving rise to the term *ébénisterie*. The wood for veneering is cut so that the maximum number of decoratively figured sheets is obtained. These were cut by a saw, and varied in thickness from $\frac{1}{16}$ to $\frac{1}{8}$ of an inch; nowadays, with machine cutting, most are $\frac{1}{16}$ of an inch. The most highly prized figures are obtained by special cutting or as a result of irregularities in the wood such as burrs. See, for example, **Oystering** and **Quartering**.

Venetian glass. The revival of fine glassmaking in western Europe occurred in Venice. There are records of glassmaking in the city from the end of the tenth century, and the glasshouses were moved to the island of Murano in 1292, as a fire precaution and as a way of maintaining rigid state control of the industry. But little is known of the glass itself until the fifteenth century. As traders between East and West, the Venetians must have assimilated and adapted the more sophisticated styles of the Near East, and they also benefited from an influx of skilled glass craftsmen after the sacking of Damascus by Tamerlane in 1400 and the capture of Byzantium by the Turks in 1453. The most striking thing about fifteenth-century Venetian glass is the use of painted enamel and gilt decoration, usually on brilliant blue, green, or purple backgrounds.

In the sixteenth century Venetian glass reached its zenith. The enamel decoration developed a jewel-like quality, and the clear *cristallo* glass was blown increasingly thinly into new and elaborate shapes like the 'nefs' or boat-shaped ewers. There was a new emphasis on stems, which developed from the pedestal into elongated hollow forms, and gradually into fantastic serpentine and winged forms. The Venetians also made ice or crackle glass (qv) and *calcedonio* or *smelz*, a marbled glass which resembled semi-precious stones. But their greatest achievement was *vetro-di-trina* or lace glass, in which (usually) white glass threads were embedded in clear glass.

Venetian glass was in such demand throughout western Europe that sixteenth-century courts vied with one another in bribing Italian glassworkers to

Modern Venetian chandelier

Vases by Venini

abscond and pass on their skill and knowledge. This made it possible for most countries to produce their own glass 'à la façon de Venise.' Until the seventeenth century, when national styles began to develop, *façon de Venise* ware is often indistinguishable from ware actually produced in Venice.

In the seventeenth and eighteenth centuries, Venice became famous for mirror plate, set in extravagant frames decorated with a profusion of coloured flowers and foliage, and for great Baroque chandeliers. Opaque white glass was also produced in deliberate imitation of porcelain.

However, most Venetian blown tableware deteriorated in quality and design. As rival industries flourished in other countries, Venice's export trade declined, particularly after the late seventeenth-century discovery of lead glass in England, which was far more suitable than the brittle Venetian glass for the fashionable wheel-engraved and cut decoration.

In the second half of the nineteenth century many of the early techniques and Renaissance styles were successfully revived by an Italian lawyer, Dr Antonio Salviati.

Venetian Murano goblet, c 1500

Goblet, early 18th century

A veranda on an Australian house, 19th century

In the 1920s two glasshouses, run by Paulo Venini and Ercole Barovier, broke away from the old traditions, using splashed and mottled surfaces and new forms. Both have done much to encourage good glass design, both in Italy and elsewhere.

Venetian window. Another name for a Palladian window (qv).

Verandah. Open gallery or balcony extending down the side of a building. It is usually roofed, and provides protection from rain and sun.

Vermiculation (Latin *vermi-culus*, from *vermus* 'worm'). Channels in masonry that resemble the tracks of worms in wood.

Vernis Martin. A technique named after the Martin brothers, highly skilled French craftsmen who perfected a remarkably brilliant lacquer finish that was applied to furniture, carriages, and various small objects. The lacquers were translucent, the most highly prized being a green flecked with gold. The Martins were granted a monopoly in 1730, and by mid-century were in control of at least three lacquer factories. The family began as coach painters, but Robert Martin (1706–65), the most famous of four brothers, was the greatest *vernisseur* of his time.

Verre églomisé. A technique of decorating glass by drawing and painting on the underside and then backing it with a metal foil of gold or silver. It was perfected in about the third century BC in Alexandria, where incised gold leaf was sandwiched between two tightly fitting pieces of glass. The name is derived from Jean-Baptiste Glomy (d 1786), a Parisian art dealer and collector whose framed prints were decorated and backed on the underside of the glass.

Verre églomisé decoration was used in England on looking-glasses in the late seventeenth and early eighteenth centuries, and in the Regency period. American furniture of the Federal period, Salem secretaries, clocks, and looking-glasses sometimes incorporate panels of *verre églomisé*.

Verzelini, Giacomo or Jacob (1522–1606). Glass manufacturer. Verzelini was a Venetian who arrived in England via Antwerp in 1571. The following year he took control of the glassworks of Jean Carré at Crutched Friars, Aldgate. In 1575 he was granted the sole right of manufacturing glasses in the Venetian style, and his business was further protected by a ban on the import of Venetian glass. Verzelini made full use of this privileged position, and his career became the turning-point in the history of English glassmaking.

There are eight known surviving Verzelini goblets, all of which are decorated with diamond-point engravings of trees, foliage, hounds, unicorns, and stags. They are all inscribed, and one dated 1577 is the earliest dated specimen of any English glass. The engraving may have been the work of Anthony de Lysle.

Verzelini retired in 1592, when his business was taken over by Sir Jerome Bowes.

Vestry. A room either attached to or within the main fabric of the church. It is the robing room for choir and clergy, and vestments and sacred vessels are kept there.

Viaduct. An elevated road or railway carried over a valley or another road. In its most common form it consists of a series of stone arches or a concrete structure.

Victorian. The term usually applied to mid- and late-nine-

Vermiculated rustication

teenth-century design in the English-speaking countries. It was a period of revolutionary changes in the human environment, and one in which architectural ideas inherited from the eighteenth century interacted with ideas evolved to meet a completely new situation.

The most enduring of the eighteenth-century ideas was Rationalism, which acted as a basic theoretical criterion during the tempestuous controversies of the mid-century. Whatever the style to be adopted, it was held that form must follow function:

A Louis XV bombé commode in Vernis Martin

Verzelini glass dated 1581

Harrington House, Kensington, London, by C J Richardson, 1854

Heal's in Tottenham Court Road, London, by J Morant Lockyer, 1854

in a church, the chancel must be long or short according to the relative importance of clergy or congregation; in a railway station, the form of the whole must be determined by the train sheds as in Lewis Cubitt's King's Cross (1854), and thus indirectly by the trains. Whether hallowed by antiquity or not, the materials used must be those most appropriate for the job – iron and glass for Paxton's Crystal Palace, unstained oak for William Morris's furniture. As with the flying buttresses of a Gothic cathedral, structure must be honestly expressed, so that the interior could be read from the exterior; the French theorist Eugène Viollet-le-Duc even maintained that Gothic architecture owed its appearance less to any conscious formal intention than to the character of the structure. This ruthless exposure imparted a rough, broken-up appearance even to monumental public buildings like G E Street's Law Courts (1818–84), which provided a welcome contrast to the Beaux Arts slickness of its Continental counterparts.

However, the wide range of stylistic alternatives that had been uncovered by historical research undermined any sense of absolute standards. Instead there was a choice of historical styles (not just Gothic or Classical), an absurd state of affairs which was shown up by the controversies as to whether the British Foreign Office should be a Gothic or a Renaissance building. From this chaos emerged a different type of absolutism, the idea of art as cultural superstructure, propagated by A W N Pugin. Pugin maintained that contemporary architecture was squalid because it emanated from a squalid society. His Scarisbrick Hall, Lancashire (1837), was designed as if for a fourteenth-century tenant, eschewing the use of iron exactly as contemporary furniture-makers eschewed nails in favour of wooden pegs.

By contrast, John Ruskin argued that squalid building would produce a squalid society, and that form should above all be uplifting. To this end he advocated the use of colour in building (as in Butterfield's All Saints, Margaret Street, 1849), and individual craftsmanship for ornament (as in the O'Shea brothers' sculpture on the Oxford University Museum, 1855). This was in effect a picturesque

Victorian Commercial Gothic in Corporation Street, Birmingham

A papier-mâché sofa inlaid with mother-of-pearl and painted, c 1850

Easy chair by George Jack

A George III mahogany bombé commode by William Vile and John Cobb

aesthetic whose ultimate sanction was visual pleasure, and Ruskin's views form a link between this eighteenth-century inheritance and the idea of art for art's sake.

Thus in the latter part of the century the desire to be artistic overrode all other considerations, breeding a scorn for historical correctness and a cult of originality. At first this meant an eighteenth-century revival–Norman Shaw's 'Wren' or 'Queen Anne' houses, 'Adam' interiors in pastel shades, and the delicate 'art' furniture of Godwin and Gimson. Later Japanese influence· led to a certain exoticism liberally mixed with eighteenth-century motifs. Voysey's conscious simplicities were followed by the mannered style of Charles Rennie Mackintosh, who drew the attention of Art Nouveau architects on the Continent to the extraordinary vitality of Victorian architecture.

Vile, William (d 1767). British Rococo cabinetmaker and upholsterer, who was in partnership with John Cobb from about 1750 to 1765. Vile appears to be the senior member of the firm, the name of which appears in the royal accounts only during the period of the partnership. He worked for George III both before and after George's accession to the throne.

Records show that Vile supplied furniture to Strawberry Hill, Middlesex, Longford Castle, Wiltshire, and Came House, Dorset. A great deal of superb Rococo furniture has been identified as Vile's, establishing him as one of the leading cabinetmakers of the period. There are pieces of his work in the royal collections, such as the jewel cabinet and secrétaire he made for Queen Charlotte. Their imposing design, and the magnificent quality of the detail, put them among the finest pieces of furniture made in England.

Villa. According to Pliny, who is the main authority on the subject, there were two types of Roman villa: the *villa urbano*, a rambling country seat complete with subsidiary buildings and grounds, and a *villa rustica*, which was essentially an extended farmhouse. The six-

Clock to commemorate Queen Victoria becoming First Empress of India

The Villa Cornaro on the Veneto, designed by Palladio, 1560-70

The Palladian Villa Cordellina at Monticchio Maggiore in Italy

teenth-century Barbarini villa at Castle Gandolfo probably resembles a Roman *villa urbano* fairly closely. Hadrian's villa is the best known and probably the largest of ancient villas; it was built by the Emperor Hadrian (AD 120–4) about AD 123, just outside Rome. It is a vast building complex and incorporates reproductions of buildings that Hadrian had admired on his travels.

During the Italian Renaissance villas were again built as summer residences. A number were built near towns, eg the Villa Medici (1540) near Fiesole, outside Florence, and the Villa Doria Colonna (now Pamphili, and now actually in Rome); others, such as the Villa d'Este (1549) in the Roman Campagna, were farther afield.

In early eighteenth-century England, several Palladian villas were built in the Thames valley, for members of the aristocracy. The use of the term in England became debased, and by the

nineteenth century both the British and the Americans were employing it to describe a detached or semi-detached suburban house.

Villanueva, Carlos Raúl (*b* 1900). Venezuelan architect, born in Croydon, England. Villanueva went to France to be educated, first at a lycée and then at the Ecole des Beaux Arts, where he studied architecture.

He is one of the small group of architects who have brought South American architecture into the twentieth century. The University City of Carácas is one of his best known works. The individual faculties, library, and auditorium all have separate buildings, and the facility with which Villanueva incorporated mobiles by Alexander Calder, sculptures by Arp, and murals and windows by Fernand Léger have made it an impressively coherent scheme. Villanueva also became very involved in high-density housing schemes in

Carácas (Dos de Diciembre, El Paraiso, El Silencio, Maracaibo), where the population is expanding very rapidly. Other notable works are the Olympic Stadium (1950–1), and an office building, Fundación La Salle.

Viollet-Le-Duc, Eugène-Emanuel (1814–79). French restorer, architect, and theorist. Wealthy, well-educated, agnostic, and progressive, Viollet was greatly influenced by Prosper Mérimée, the author of *Carmen*, who was an official inspector of monuments. Before and during his appointments in 1853 as *Inspector Général des Edifices Diocesans*, Viollet restored and remodelled a great number of medieval buildings: Vézeley, the Ste Chapelle, and Notre Dame are the most famous. Much of his work would be unaccepted today, for he went far beyond the available evidence about the previous state of the buildings, 're-creating' them without hesitation.

Viollet admired the rationalism of Gothic architecture, and by applying the same principles to contemporary metal construction found much to his praise in the engineering feats of the nineteenth century. His writings, *Dictionaire raisonné de l'architecture française* (1854–68) and *Entretiens sur l'architecture* (1863, 1872), were extremely influential and of greater weight than his own architectural designs, which entirely failed to live up to his ideas.

Vitrine. A case in which decorative objects can be put on display. It could be in cabinet form with glazed doors and shelves, as in eighteenth-century French work; or it could be a shallow case on a stand, with glazed sides and top.

Vitruvian opening. A door or window which narrows towards the top. It was advocated by Vitruvius in Book IV of *De Architectura*.

Vitruvian scroll

Vitruvian scroll. Convoluted running pattern named after Vitruvius. It can be seen at Pompeii, where it is undulating, fanciful, and varied. In early Georgian work it resembles waves. Also known as wave scroll and running dog.

Vitruvius, Pollio Marcus (first century BC). A Roman architect and engineer, who is mainly remembered for his theoretical treatise *De Architectura* (27–23 BC). Vitruvius was a contemporary of Cicero, and was reputedly of rather humble origin. His extensive studies of architectural works provided the basis for *De Architectura*, which is in ten books and deals with all aspects of architecture, including the

The medieval city walls of Carcassonne in Southern France restored by Viollet-le-Duc

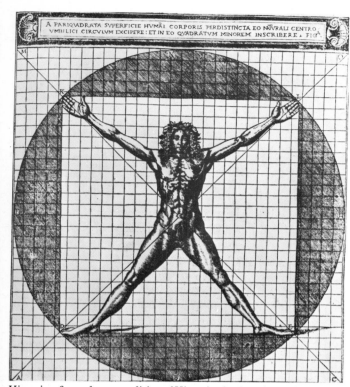

Vitruvian figure from an edition of Vitruvius by Cesariano, Como, 1521

The Orchard House at Chorley Wood, Hertfordshire, by Voysey

training of the architects, the solution of technical problems, and the use of various materials. The data was doubtless derived from personal experience, for Vitruvius is himself reputed to have been a notable engineer, in *De aquaeductu urbis Romae*, Frontinus notes Vitruvius's appointment as engineer to the public water system of the city of Rome.

The influence of *De Architectura* has always been extensive. The monasteries of the Middle Ages used it as an unquestionable source book of ancient architecture, and it was 'rediscovered' during the Renaissance. The *De re aedificatoria* of Alberti was inspired by *De Architectura* and

it influenced the buildings and theories of Bramante, Raphael, Peruzzi, Palladio, Serlio, and Vignola. It retains much of its importance as the one direct, extensive, and authoritative commentary upon the architecture of ancient Greece and Rome.

Voider or **Voyder.** A large medieval dish or tray, upon which scraps of food or dirty plates were placed to be cleared away after a meal. The word subsequently came to mean a large tray, and it was in this sense that Chippendale and Ince and Mayhew used it, although 'tray' was a current term. 'Voider' became obsolete in the early nineteenth century.

Volute. The spiral-shaped ornamental flourish which terminated the capital of the Ionic order. It is also used for lesser architectural features in the Corinthian and Composite orders.

Voussoir. One of the series of wedge-shaped blocks used to form an arch or vault.

Voysey, Charles Francis Annesley (1857–1941). British architect, industrial designer, and writer. Voysey was born at Hessle, near Kingston-upon-Hull in Yorkshire, where his father was a clergyman. He was educated at Dulwich College,

and then joined John Pollard Sedden, with whom he continued to work as an assistant before setting up independent practice in 1881. He early became interested in the modern movement, and a house which he designed in 1888 at Bedford Park, Turnham Green, although influenced by the earlier work of A H Mackmurdo, marked an emphatic break with the Queen Anne revivalism of Norman Shaw (qv). This somewhat assertive building was followed by rather more restrained works which, although touched by certain original features, placed his houses in the long tradition of English country-house architecture. The main distinction of these designs lay in their sound proportions, the way in which they were characterized by high-pitched roofs, plain unfussy façades, emphatic bay windows, and practical interiors. Voysey's manner was widely copied – and debased – by hundreds of speculative builders, during the years between the wars.

Voysey also became deeply involved with the design of furniture textiles, wallpapers, and the fittings of the houses he built. Here, too, he showed no revolutionary impulse to redesign such items from scratch: instead he

sought to bring to them something of the rationalism which he had already practised in architecture. His designs are never assertive: in many ways they express in Art Nouveau terms a desire to forego Victorian overdecoration and a return to the simplicity of eighteenth-century models. Voysey outlined his philosophy of art and industry in the book he published, entitled *Individuality and Reason as a Basis of Art.* He lived to see a growing acceptance of the theories he had preached and practised, although he designed little during his last 20 years.

Vries, Hans Vredeman de (1527–1604). Flemish painter, engraver, designer, and architect. His pattern-books, *Architectura* (1565) and *Compartimenta* (1566), were circulated throughout northern Europe and exercised an immense influence. They publicised Renaissance buildings such as the Antwerp Town Hall (1561–5), by Cornelis Floris, and a Mannerist style of decoration that found favour in England. The decoration consisted mainly of strapwork (qv) and over-ornate concoctions burdened with heavy allegorical figures.

Charles Annesley Voysey

A typical interior designed by Voysey

Otto Wagner

Wagner, Otto. (1841–1918). Austrian architect. Wagner was born in Penzing, a suburb of Vienna. He studied at the technical college in the city, and then spent a brief period at the Berlin Academy in 1860. On his return to Vienna he studied architecture at the Academy, where he was later appointed professor of architecture. It was at his inaugural lecture there, in 1894, that he put forward the influential news that he later published as *Moderne Architektur*.

Wagner saw that nineteenth-century eclecticism, to which he himself had subscribed, must give way to a general recognition that 'the only point of departure for our artistic activity can be modern life.' This meant that 'nothing that is not practical can be beautiful.' Wagner then predicted the emergence of a new functional style with horizontal lines and flat roofs.

Wagner's previous work was itself in the nineteenth century eclectic spirit; he described it as 'free Renaissance.' His planning, however, was far more functional than that of most of his contemporaries. He won a city planning competition in 1892, and the authorities awarded him a commission to plan the Stadtbahn, the proposed underground railway system.

In 1899 Wagner became a member of the Vienna Sezession, designing interiors, furniture, and craft objects. Then came his Post Office Savings Bank in Vienna (1904–6). Compared with his early works in a variety of Renaissance idioms, this was a herald of the new era. It is planned logically and clearly around a large central-domed hall with a glass barrel-vault. The integration of glass and steel into the structure is remarkable; there is a clear streamlined design inside, and on the façade smooth marble is punctuated by aluminium bolts, making a strong textured contrast to the simple, regular fenestration. Wagner profoundly influenced the whole Viennese school, and in particular influenced Olbrich, Loos, and Hoffmann.

Wagon roof. A method of roof construction that resembles the inside of a canvas-covered wagon. It is formed with closely set arched braces, which are sometimes panelled or plastered, and without the tie-beams of more usual construction. Known also as a cradle roof.

Wag-on-the-wall. The American term for a weight-driven clock that was hung uncased upon the wall.

Wagon vault. Another name for a tunnel vault (qv).

Wainscot. A term often applied to the complete panelling or dado of a room. It is more accurately reserved for the wooden covering or lining of interior walls which was used before more sophisticated forms of panelling were introduced.

Wainscot bedstead and chair. From the years 1500 to 1800, furniture was commonly described as 'wainscot' when its construction was particularly solid. For example, beds with wooden panels for head and foot boards, and chairs with panelled backs, came to be known as wainscot bedsteads and wainscot chairs. Wainscot bedsteads are also called boarded bedsteads.

Wall arcade. See **Blind arcade.**

Wall light. See **Sconce.**

Wallpaper. Originally a cheap substitute for tapestry, panelling, etc, wallpaper seems to have been used occasionally in the fifteenth century. The earliest known wallpaper in England was an Italian-inspired woodcut design, printed on the reverse side of a proclamation issued by Henry VIII. It was discovered in 1911 at Christ's College, Cambridge, and is reputedly the work of Hugo Goes, a York printer.

However, wallpapers only came into general use in Europe in the late seventeenth century. John Houghton, in his *Collection for Improvement of Husbandry & Trade* (1699), states 'Of paper there are divers sorts, finer and coarser, as also brown and blue paper, with divers designs that are printed for the hanging of rooms; truly they are very pretty, and make houses of the more ordinary people look neat.'

Flock wallpaper was also a seventeenth-century innovation.

16th-century wallpaper

Modern wallpaper

Wright. *The Kaufmann House at Bear Run, Pennsylvania, designed in 1936 by Frank Lloyd Wright and known as Falling Water*

A Pennsylvania Dutch wardrobe, dated 1779

A modern Italian wardrobe in plexiglass

This process involved scattering powdered wool over a printed canvas or paper covered with a slow-drying adhesive.

By the eighteenth century, wallpaper design had attracted the attention of, artists and of connoisseurs such as Horace Walpole, the walls of whose Gothick villa at Strawberry Hill were elegantly papered.

The Industrial Revolution had a major impact on the manufacture of wallpaper. The breakthrough in mechanical production is usually credited to a firm of calico printers, Potters of Darwen in Lancashire. One of their calico-printing machines was adapted by a foreman, Walmsley Preston, and patented in 1839. Thereafter, production increased phenomenally, bringing cheap wallpaper into most homes.

Wallpaper design has often attracted the attention of artists, from the wood-block engravers of the seventeenth century to Victorian artists such as William Morris and C F A Voysey. In more recent times, many famous artists have occasionally been employed to design wallpaper.

Wall plate. In a roof truss this is the lowest longitudinal member, lying along the top of the wall at eaves level to receive the lower ends of the rafters.

Walnut. *Juglans regia.* Thanks to its richly coloured grain and ease of carving, walnut was widely used for furniture from the early sixteenth to the beginning of the eighteenth century. It was most popular during the reign of Queen Anne, when it

was used for the cabriole legs of chests and chairs.

Wardian case. A glazed dome named after its early nineteenth-century inventor, one Nathaniel Ward, and widely used during the Victorian and Edwardian eras for the indoor cultivation of ferns and other plants. The case was usually placed within a window or on a stand.

Wardrobe. A term which has changed its meaning over the centuries. The Chaucerian definition of a wardrobe was a privy; the medieval meaning was a closet reserved for clothes. It received its current meaning in the eighteenth century: Chippendale called it a 'cloaths press', but Hepplewhite used the term wardrobe. The heyday of the wardrobe was the Victorian era, when middle-class houses had rooms large enough to accommodate these specially built combination cupboards and chests of drawers.

Ware, Isaac (*d* 1766). British architect and writer. Ware's origins are unclear, although he

Design for a wardian case, 1877

An engraving from Ware's 'Complete Body of Architecture', 1756

was reputedly taken up by Burlington as an impecunious youth, educated, and sent to Italy at the earl's expense. He certainly became one of the coterie around Burlington, to whom Ware's translation of Palladio's *Quattro Libri dell' Architettura* was dedicated (1738). Ware was appointed to various official posts, and was evidently an able draughtsman, since he was responsible for the preparation of plans and elevations for Kent's designs for the Horse Guards in Whitehall. His own architectural commissions included a number of important country houses, including Clifton Hill House, Bristol (1746–50), Chesterfield House in London for the 4th Earl of Chesterfield (1748–9), and Wrotham Park, Middlesex, for Admiral Byng (1754).

But Ware's reputation rests on his writings. His compilation, *The Complete Body of Architecture* (1735), went into several editions and became one of the most influential of all eighteenth-century architectural pattern books, illustrating the pure Palladian canon. Ware also translated, wrote, or engraved plates for several other books, including Sirrigatti's *Practice of Perspective* (1756) and Ripley's *Houghton House* (1735).

Wash-hand stand, wash-hand table, wash stand; washing stand. These more or less interchangeable terms derive from the use of a basin on a rudimentary stand or table, later elaborated by the addition of a chest to accommodate a ewer and other toilet requirements. The wash-hand table was a solid piece of furniture with built-in basin, hinged mirror, and chest of drawers. It was the forerunner of the nineteenth-century wash-hand stand, a large elaborate affair typical of Victorian taste. Wash, or washing stand are alternative names for basin stand (qv).

Interior of the Natural History Museum, London, by Waterhouse, 1868

Water bed. See **Plastic furniture.**

Waterhouse, Alfred (1830–1905). British architect. Waterhouse was born in Liverpool. He was a pupil of Richard Lane in Manchester, and began to practise there in 1853. His first major commission was the Assize Court, won in competition in 1859, and soon followed by the Town Hall (1869–77). Both buildings were in the Gothic style, but in others he did not adhere rigidly to it. Caius College, Cambridge (1868), for example, is Gothic with an admixture of classical detail; while the Natural History Museum, London (1868), is more Romanesque, with extensive use of terracotta. Waterhouse's other works include Balliol College, Oxford (1867); Pembroke College, Cambridge (1871); University Colleges at Manchester, Liverpool, and Leeds; University College Hospital and the Prudential Assurance, both in London; the Metropole Hotel, Brighton, and Eaton Hall, Chester (1870).

Water leaf. One of a series of broad unveined leaves encircling

the capital of a late twelfth-century column. The motif was based on the water-lily leaf; it tapers up towards the angle of the abacus and turns in at the top.

Wattle and daub. Infilling for timber-framed buildings (qv), consisting of interlacing twigs or

split staves (wattles) which were daubed with clay or mud.

Wave scroll. See **Vitruvian scroll.**

Weatherboarding. A protective covering for outside walls, made up of a series of overlapping horizontal boards.

Weathering. An inclined course or slope on the face of a wall which throws off rainwater, thus preventing it from lodging in the fabric.

Web. The infilling between the ribs of a vault. Also known as a cell.

Webb, Sir Aston (1849–1930). British architect. Webb was born in London, where he studied under Banks and Barry. In 1873 he set up his own office, and was so successful that by the end of the century he had the leading practice in the design of public buildings. The most important are the Victoria and Albert Museum (1891), and the Imperial College of Science (1900–

Victorian wash stand

Norman water leaf capital

Weatherboarding on Ashley Home at Deerfield, Massachusetts

The Admiralty Arch in London designed by Sir Aston Webb, 1911

6), Kensington, London; the Metropolitan Life Assurance, Moorgate, London (1890–3), and Christ's Hospital, Horsham (1894 –1904), both with Ingress Bell; the Victoria Memorial, Admiralty Arch (1911), and the façade of Buckingham Palace (1913), all in London; Birmingham University (1906–9) and Law Courts (with Bell, 1886–91); and the Royal Naval College, Dartmouth (1899–1904).

Webb, John (1611–72). British architect. Webb was educated at Merchant Taylors' School, and then became a pupil of Inigo Jones (whose niece he later married). In this privileged position he acquired a considerable knowledge of the published works of Serlio, Palladio, and other Italian Renaissance architects. On the outbreak of the Civil War, Jones left Webb in London in charge of the royal works. Webb supplied the Royalists with information about the metropolitan fortifications, but was discovered and imprisoned. On Jones's return to practice, Webb once again became his assistant. After Jones's

death in 1652, Webb was passed over for surveyor of the works in favour of John Denham. However, he was commissioned to design the King Charles block at Greenwich Palace, and also superintended works at Woolwich Dockyard. Yet after Denham's death in 1669, Webb was again passed over in favour of Wren. As an architect, Webb has inevitably been overshadowed by Inigo Jones and Wren, but his work is a link between the two in the evolution of English Renaissance architecture. He was Jones's devoted pupil, assistant, and colleague, and many plans and drawings long attributed to Jones were later shown to have been the work of Webb.

Webb, Philip (1831–1915). British architect, one of the most important figures of the Domestic revival in England. Although Norman Shaw (qv) received contemporary acclaim, it was Webb whose work and ideas had the more enduring influence.

Webb studied under the ecclesiastical architect G E Street, in whose offices he met William Morris (qv). Webb and Morris formed a lasting association, and Webb designed furniture and glass for Morris's firm. For Morris himself he designed the famous Red House (1859) at Bexley Heath, just outside London. It was his first work and was destined to be his most important; a sturdy and unpretentious house incorporating a miscellany of features that answered Webb's purpose irrespective of their historical context. Steeply pitched roofs, pointed arches, Queen Anne sash windows, and a late medieval asymmetry are all found.

Philip Webb

Webb also designed the first 'studio houses', with large welllit studios, for the artists Val Prinsep and G B Boyce. His other major works were 1 Palace Green and 19 Lincoln's Inn Fields, both in London, Smeaton Manor, Yorkshire (1878), Trevor Hall, Hertfordshire (1868–70, now destroyed), Arisaig, Inverness-shire (1863), and Conyhurst, Surrey (1885).

Web foot. A variation of the conventional design, the claw and ball foot.

Wedgwood, Josiah (1730–95). British potter, born in Staffordshire. Wedgwood's family had long been established as potters. His father died when he was nine, and he immediately went to work with his elder brother Thomas, to whom he was later apprenticed. Ten years later he was working with Thomas Whieldon, one of the most

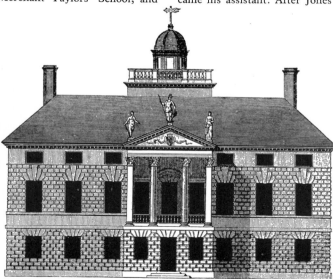

An engraving of Amesbury House, Wiltshire, by John Webb

The Red House at Bexley Heath by Philip Webb, 1859

Josiah Wedgwood

notable potters of the time, and five years after that he set up on his own in premises in Burslem.

When he was working with Whieldon, Wedgwood had developed a particularly beautiful green glaze, which he used in the production of his cauliflower ware. He was encouraged by Whieldon to make experiments with different bodies and glazes.

Whereas Whieldon specialized in mottled ware, which concealed imperfections in the body of the ware, Wedgwood tried to develop a clay body that could stand on its own without the addition of coloured glazes. By 1763 he had perfected a cream-coloured earthenware so effective that it superseded salt-glazed stoneware and the tortoiseshell Whieldon ware. Wedgwood made a tea-service in this cream-coloured earthenware for Queen Charlotte, which so pleased her that she appointed him 'Potter to the Queen' and allowed him to call the ware 'Queensware.'

This Queensware was made in elegant classical shapes, for Wedgwood was influenced by

Wedgwood vase, 1775

the Neo-classical movement rather than the craze for *chinoiserie*. Some of the Queensware was left quite undecorated, some was sent to Liverpool to be decorated by transfer printing, and some was hand-painted with charming little floral borders or simple geometric designs.

In 1767 Wedgwood went into partnership with Thomas Bentley, who acted as business manager for him until his death in 1780. In 1769 Wedgwood and Bentley opened the big model factory which they called Etruria, at Stoke-on-Trent. This was where the decorative ware was produced.

Wedgwood was a tireless experimenter, and in addition to the cream-coloured earthenware he also made black basalt or Egyptian black ware, a fine hard black stoneware, and the Jasper ware for which he is probably most famous. This Jasper ware was a dense hard stoneware with a blue, green, yellow, black, or lilac body; it was decorated with friezes of classical figures in white relief against the coloured background. In fact, the word 'Wedgwood' to many people conjures up blue-and-white Jasper ware.

Wedgwood also made vases in imitation of agate or porphyry, and he introduced a new body which he called 'pearl white', which was whiter and colder than the cream-ware. He also experimented with ceramics for industrial purposes.

In addition to all his experiments with pottery, he reorganized and to a large extent mechanized the ceramic industry, introducing steam power. He also improved Staffordshire communications, organizing better roads and the building of canals. He died in 1795 and was succeeded by his third son, Josiah Wedgwood II.

The firm continues under the direction of a descendant of the original founder.

Wegner, Hans (*b* 1914). Danish furniture designer, best known for his light wooden chairs, which are a synthesis of traditional form and modern functionalism. Wegner trained at the Copenhagen School of Arts and Crafts, later returning to teach there (1946–53). In 1943 he established his own drawing office at Gentofte. He produced a wide selection of designs, ranging over light fittings to furniture, and silver-ware and wallpaper.

Wegner has had one-man exhibitions in Europe and America, has been represented

Wedgwood bowl with bas relief by John Flaxman, 1775

at many international events, and has won many design awards.

Welch, Robert Radford (*b* 1929). British industrial designer and silversmith. Welch studied at Malvern School of Art, Birmingham College of Art, and the Royal College of Art, where he specialized in stainless steel design. He was appointed consultant designer to the Old Hall Tableware Company in 1955, and in the same year established a silversmithing workshop and design practice in an eighteenth-century silk mill at Chipping Campden.

Since then Welch has undertaken many important silver commissions, eg for the Royal Society of Arts, Birmingham University, and Churchill College, Cambridge. He designed a collection of silver for Heal's, and a pair of candelabra for the Goldsmiths' Company (1970).

Robert Welch's design practice covers a wide variety of products from stainless steel cutlery to clocks.

He has received a number of Design Centre awards, and his work has been acquired by various international museums, including the Museum of Modern Art, New York.

Chair by Hans Wegner, 1950

Wellington chest. A narrow form of chest of drawers with six or more fairly shallow drawers, sometimes graduated in depth. The name has no particular relevance to the Iron Duke, probably signifying the period of its first appearance. The chest was usually of plain design and made in mahogany. Exotic woods such as amboyna and bird's-eye maple were also often used, particularly for chests which also incorporated a writing slide. Wellington chests were usually

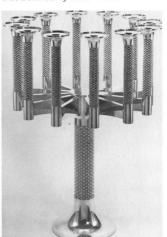

Two silver candelabra designed by Robert Welch

A Welsh dresser made of pine, 19th century

A Wellington chest, c 1840

A Regency whatnot

spent some time as cultural attaché at the German Embassy in London, where he became deeply impressed by the teachings of William Morris. On his return to Berlin he published *Das englische Haus* (1905) and set up the Werkbund. The Werkbund's aims were supported by many architects, artists, and craftsmen, and bitterly opposed by many industrialists. Some, however, realized the commercial advantage of good design, and employed avantgarde architects and designers, the most significant example being the appointment of Peter Behrens (qv) as consultant to AEG.

The decisive difference between the Deutscher Werkbund and the British movement was that the Werkbund made a more or less successful attempt to come to terms with machine production. Some members of the German movement, notably Henri van de Velde, held out against mass production and standardization, but an exhibition of industrial art held at Cologne in 1914 demonstrated that the influence of architects and designers upon the machine was becoming increasingly effective. The exhibition showed also some of the earliest buildings designed by architects who were later to become leaders of the modern movement, including Gropius and Taut.

In 1927 the Werkbund sponsored an exhibition at Stuttgart, directed by Mies van der Rohe, for which many of the leading modern architects designed buildings, mainly houses and apartment blocks. It aroused considerable international interest, and was followed by an important Werkbund contribution to the Paris Exhibition of 1930, under the direction of Gropius.

Muthesius died in 1927, the year of the Stuttgart exhibition. The Werkbund was 'reorganized' – ie in effect dissolved – by the Nazis, but was revived during the post-war years.

Whatnot. A curious term applied to a tiered display unit. In this, three or four open shelves, and occasionally a drawer, are ranged between four slender supporting columns or posts, usually turned, which terminate in decorative finials. The whatnot seems to have been an innovation in late-Georgian interiors, but its heyday was the Victorian era, and most cabinet-makers made their own official versions of the form. Early

provided with side slats, sometimes carved in the form of pilasters, which were hinged to fold flat against the drawers and lock. Some Wellington chests were adapted for collectors with up to two dozen drawers.

Welsh dresser. An open-shelved dresser with drawers and cupboards in the lower part. Despite its name, this basic form of kitchen furniture was also made in several parts of England, during the late seventeenth and early eighteenth centuries. Another variety, with a low pot board instead of an enclosed cupboard, was made until the nineteenth century. The Welsh dresser is usually made of pine, which is left unpolished and unpainted, but current examples are made in oak and polished.

Werkbund, Deutscher. A German equivalent to the Arts and Crafts Movement (qv) founded in 1907 by the architect Hermann Muthesius. Muthesius

whatnots were sometimes made of exotic woods and given highly decorative shapes, but Victorian versions were over-elaborate and little more than open display stands for domestic *bijouterie*.

Wheat-ear. A carved, painted, or inlaid motif commonly associated with Hepplewhite. The wheat-ear is typical of late eighteenth-century decoration. It is most commonly found on chair backs.

Wheatsheaf back. The back splat of a chair, pierced and waisted to represent a wheatsheaf. A mid-eighteenth-century device that was readopted by the Victorians.

Wheelback. This usually refers to a Windsor chair with a small

American wheat-ear decoration on a looking-glass, 1790-1800

Tortoise-shell Whieldon, c 1750

others topple and fall around him.

Whieldon ware. Thomas Whieldon is known to have made agate-ware knife handles for the Sheffield cutlers some time before 1740. Later he experimented in the use of coloured glazes, which he used in various ways in imitation of tortoiseshell. The colours were brown, green, yellow, blue, and grey, all oxide colours. Most Whieldon ware is basically brownish or greenish, with the other colours added as large occasional blotches. Whieldon made tableware, and also rather primitively modelled figures which were glazed with the same tortoiseshell technique. He was considered one of the best potters of his day, and many of his apprentices, including Josiah Spode, became well known. In 1754 he took Josiah Wedgwood into partnership, but in 1759 they parted, and Wedgwood went on to develop cream-coloured earthenware. Whieldon continued to make his tortoiseshell ware until he retired in 1780. It was much imitated by other potters, and the name Whieldon can only be safely applied as a generic term.

White, Standford (1853–1906). American architect, and partner in the firm of McKim, Mead, and White (qv) from 1879. In the

carved wheel in the back splat. An older, late eighteenth-century chair back is also called a wheelback, with more justice, since it is circular and has slender spokes radiating from the centre.

Wheel of fortune. A medieval emblem of mutability. It shows a crowned figure sitting on the highest point of a wheel while

Madison Square Church, New York, by McKim, Mead, and White

Modern wicker chairs in a conservatory

1880s at least, his contribution to the firm seems to have been that of a draughtsman supplying the 'artistic' elements, ie very pretty designs.

White's sources were similar to those of many contemporary English designers. Indeed, his previous work (for H H Richardson, in whose office he succeeded Charles McKim from 1872 to 1878) had been directly inspired by Norman Shaw. His contribution to Richardson's Sherman House, Newport, Rhode Island (1874), probably included the horizontal window bands, the window walls, the half-timbered gables with painted plaster decoration, and the shingles cut to suggest Sussex tile-hanging.

Further sources of design were suggested by a trip down the New England coast sketching early colonial houses, which White made in company with McKim and Mead (1877). The results were comparable to the Queen Anne revival in England. After leaving Richardson in 1878, White made a sketching trip by himself to France. This visit was probably responsible for the round towers which appear in many of the shingle style houses produced by the new partnership.

Above all, White seems to have taken an interest in Japanese-type ornament, as did Shaw's partner Nesfield in England. This appeared as early as 1874 in the library of the Sherman House, and later in the dining-room White added to Upjohn's Kingscote. It was used with still greater originality in the dining-room of the Isaac Bell house at Newport, Rhode Island, built by the firm in 1881–2. In their H Victor Newcomb house, Elberon, New Jersey (1880–1), the hall is defined by friezes which

become grilles over the subsidiary spaces; if this was White's contribution, it represents an excursion into Japanese-inspired architecture. It was followed in 1881 by the Japanese-inspired carpentry of the verandah of the Chris McCormick House at Richfield Springs, New York.

Whorl or **French scroll foot.** An elegant mid-eighteenth-century foot carved as an upturned scroll.

Wicker chair. The name given to nineteenth-century basket chairs that were especially popular in the garden; one long-seated version was called a croquet chair. If enclosed, the backs and bases were of an openwork design; loose cushions were used for greater comfort.

Whorl foot, mid-18th century

The National Gallery in Trafalgar Square, London, designed by William Wilkins, 1834-8

William and Mary armchair, 1685

Wickerwork (alternatively **basketwork**). A method of chair construction known since ancient times: twigs, rushes, and/or reeds were plaited to make a rough kind of seat, but one often a good deal more comfortable than the wooden chairs available. There were wickerwork chairs in Roman Britain. In the sixteenth and seventeenth centuries they seem to have been in fairly general use, but the heyday of the basket chair was in the Victorian era.

Wilkins, William (1778–1839). British architect and historian. Wilkins was the son of a Norwich architect and theatre-owner. He was educated at Norwich Grammar School and Caius College, Cambridge, and then travelled widely in Greece and Italy. On his return to England after four years abroad, he set up as an architect in Cambridge. Thanks to his many academic contacts and a fellowship at Caius, he quickly established a very successful practice. Thomas Hope was among his friends, and their joint advocacy of a revival of the

William and Mary walnut stool

ancient Greek orders led to the acceptance of Wilkins's designs for Downing College. This commission established him as one of the leading exponents of the Greek revival. Wilkins's most notable buildings in London were University College, London (1827–8), St George's Hospital (1828–9), and the National Gallery (1834–8), in which columns from Carlton House were used. He also designed a number of collegiate and scholastic buildings in Cambridge; rebuilt the Theatre Royal at Norwich, and was concerned with other East Anglican theatres in a managerial or architectural capacity. He wrote a number of books, notably *Antiquities of Magna Graecia* (1807) and a translation of *The Civil Architecture of Vitruvius* (1812).

Willard, Simon. See **Banjo clock.**

William and Mary. English furniture of the reign of William and Mary (1689–1702) was strongly influenced by Dutch taste (William was Dutch), which was more sober and less exuberant than that of Restoration England. The Frenchman Daniel Marot (qv) designed quieter versions of Louis XIV style furniture, and he and other immigrant Huguenots injected new Continental ideas into the trade, and did much to improve craftsmanship.

Most William and Mary furniture was of walnut, and oystering and burr markings were frequently used. (Walnut furniture *par excellence* belongs to the

reign of Queen Anne.) The great demand for writing furniture, card- and tea-tables, chests, and cabinets with numerous drawers for collections, stemmed from the growing wealth and leisure of the upper and middle classes.

American William and Mary is similar in only the broadest sense, for the term embraces Restoration as well as William and Mary, covering the period from 1675 to 1720. It witnessed the introduction of the highboy, the slope-front desk, the wing chair, the gate-leg table, and even the secretary bookcase, a comparatively rare piece in America.

Willow. *Salix.* In his third edition of *Sylva*, published in 1679, John Evelyn recommends the use of the many varieties of willow for 'Boxes such as apothecaries, and goldsmiths use', and the osiers or willow saplings for 'all wicker, and Twiggie works', particularly for the construction of chairs. Willow is a resilient though soft wood, first popularly used during the seventeenth and eighteenth centuries for decorative work. When dyed black it resembles ebony.

Willow pattern. A mock-Chinese design evolved during the eighteenth-century vogue for *chinoiserie* decoration on china. Its first use is generally attributed to Thomas Minton c 1780. It was very popular and was soon plagiarized by many designers working in other potteries.

Wilton carpets. Carpets have been made at Wilton in Wilt-

shire since the 1740s, when the 9th Earl of Pembroke introduced looms to manufacture moquette (qv) or 'Brussels carpet' similar to those being produced at Kidderminster. The cutting of the loops of the moquette pile probably first occurred at Wilton, and in any event took its name from there. In Wilton carpets the number of colours is normally restricted to five or six, but additional colours can be added to individual frames. In 1835 Axminster looms were introduced and production of knotted pile carpets began.

Window. A term that apparently derives from old Norse *vindauga*, wind eye. Until post-medieval times, glass was rarely available for domestic building, and window openings were small on all but the most important secular and ecclesiastical buildings. In England, for example, glazed windows were widely used in ordinary houses only in Tudor times. Such windows were divided into small glazed sections by the use of mullions and transoms in dwellings, and by the

Swansea willow pattern plate

*An English Windsor writing chair (left) and an
American chair of oak, pine and maple, c 1750-75*

use of tracery in ecclesiastical buildings. All such windows were fixed. Then basement windows, hinged or hung at one side to open outwards, were gradually introduced. With the introduction of the sash, or double-hung sliding window, towards the end of the seventeenth century windows could be opened vertically, the two half-section frames sliding past each other.

The form of windows has varied greatly with changes in architectural style, from the pointed leaded window of early Gothic to the standardized rectangular twelve-pane window of the Georgian era.

The building terms normally employed in window-making are 'head' for the top, 'sill' for the base, and 'jambs' for the sides.

Window stool. A long stool with scrolled ends. Most window stools are very elegant pieces, usually backless and upholstered end to end. They belong to the second half of the eighteenth century and are also known as French stools (qv). See **Stool.**

Windsor chair. A form of chair long popular in Britain and the United States, and produced in innumerable local and national variations. Basically the chair was made in two forms. In the hoop-back form, sticks or turned spindles were set into sockets in a hoop-shaped frame, and also into a solid wooden seat. The turned legs were also set into sockets on the underside of the seat and strengthened by simple stretchers. The comb-backed form had a back shaped like a curved comb or yoke into which the spindles were socketed. Both forms of chairs were widely known as 'stick back chairs.'

The origin of the term 'Windsor chair' was long associated with the legend that George III had favoured such a chair, made in the locality of Windsor Castle. Recent research has shown that they were, in fact, so known in the early years of the eighteenth century, well before the king was born. The place most associated with the production of the chair was High Wycombe, where they are still produced. The wood employed is mainly beech, although yew and elm are used for seats, and ash for the hooped frame.

The Windsor chair was very popular in the eighteenth and nineteenth centuries, and quantities were exported to the American colonies. It soon began to be made there in various forms of comb back and under a variety of labels, from Philadelphia Windsor to New England comb back.

In the quest for novelty, changes were made in the backs of the chair. For example, a central splat was introduced which strengthened the structure and also provided a surface for decorative piercings. Another version had a back in a circular or wheel shape, with sticks or spokes radiating from a central hub solid or pierced. Hence the term wheel-back chair.

The Windsor was also made as a rocking-chair; and Thomas Jefferson is thought to have written the first draft of the Declaration of Independence (1776) seated in a writing-chair version of the Windsor which he had designed himself.

Wine cooler or **cistern.** In his *Cabinet Dictionary* (1803), Sheraton groups together cellarets, coolers, and cisterns.

However, it is generally held that the cellaret is primarily a container and should be distinguished from the wine cooler or cistern, which is a watertight receptacle, generally oval, in which ice can be used to cool bottles.

Simple tubs filled with cold water are known to have been used in the fifteenth century, but most good examples of wine coolers date from the late seventeenth century to the Regency. The earliest of these were beautifully wrought examples with elaborate handles, made of silver and other metals. They were followed by wooden lead-lined coolers, which were first made c 1730. Wine coolers were luxury items and followed changes of style in other fields; early coolers were set on cabriole legs, Regency coolers on pillar and claw pedestals when they were not shaped like sarcophagi. These late examples often carried a tap to let out the water. On occasion the water in wine coolers was also used to wash the glasses.

Wine table. A general term that came into use in the late eighteenth century; it described a variety of tables made especially for after-dinner drinking. One type was a pedestal of normal height, with a notched circumference to hold the glasses downwards and a raised central area that was perforated for decanters and larger goblets. This particular design probably evolved for the convenience of

Wine cooler by Matthew Boulton

servants rather than that of guests. Another type was a large, horseshoe-shaped table designed to be placed in front of the fire. This had movable coasters running either on a pivoting brass rod or in a well on the inside curve of the horseshoe. Some of the smaller examples of horseshoe and tripod wine tables were known as social tables.

Wine waiter. A rare eighteenth-century wagon on casters that was used to circulate bottles around a dining-room. It resembled a stool in size and basic framework, but had open partitions and a central handle instead of a seat.

Wing chair. A form of easy chair which became popular during the later seventeenth century. The wings or lugs were added to the upper sides of the chairs to give protection against

Wing chairs in a library

Wine carafes designed by Tapio Wirkkala

A model of the Circus at Bath and its surrounding area

draughts. The wing chair was later known as a grandfather chair and is still popular as a club armchair. See **Saddle-cheek.**

Wing wardrobe. The term applied during the late eighteenth and the nineteenth century to a large wardrobe in which two narrow cupboards are set on either side of a larger projecting hanging section. The side sections were normally joined to the main section, but were occasionally separate. Such wardrobes were usually made of mahogany, but sometimes in amboyna or maplewood.

Wirkkala, Tapio (b 1915). Finnish industrial designer best known for his work in glass, silver, and wood, although he has also designed light fittings, postage stamps, and bank notes. He was trained at the College of Industrial Art in Helsinki, where he was later director (1951–5).

The pre-eminence of Finnish design in the 1950s owes a good deal to Wirkkala. His work has won international acclaim; he has been awarded the Grand Prix seven times at the Milan Triennale

Wood, Enoch (1759–1840). British potter. He was apprenticed to Humphrey Palmer of Hanley, after which he worked with his cousin Ralph Wood the Younger (qv), making enamel coloured figures and Toby jugs. About 1790 he went into partnership with James Caldwell, the firm using the mark WOOD & CALDWELL. In 1819 Wood bought out Caldwell and took his sons into business, the firm then becoming known as Enoch Wood and Sons.

Wood was an accomplished modeller: a plaque still exists of the Wood arms in relief, which he made at the age of 11. He made many pottery portrait figures which he painted with

enamel colours: Shakespeare, Milton, Handel, John Wesley (modelled from life), etc. His firm built up a big export trade to America, largely based on blue transfer-printed earthenware of good quality. Many of the designs were of American scenes. The firm also made black basalts, jasperware, and cream-coloured earthenware.

Wood, John (1704–54). British architect, town-planner, and writer. Wood was born in Bath, the son of a builder. He was probably trained in that craft, for he undertook exceptional building operations while still in his early twenties. Yet little is known of his early life, although he is thought to have arrived in London when he was about 20. There he certainly worked as a builder and surveyor in the development of the Marylebone estates of the Earl of Oxford. He was also employed in Yorkshire, notably in Bramham Park, where

he was responsible for the original layout of the grounds.

During these years Wood began to formulate his ideas for the great Bath project that he was later to term his 'Improvement of the City of Bath.' It was of great imaginative scope, including schemes for mansions and smaller houses, an impressive civic centre, and a navigation scheme for the Avon. Wood's organizing and administrative skills were also remarkable for he had to obtain authorization for his developments from the owners of the Bath lands, while continuing his building works in the north of England.

From 1727 Wood began to concentrate all his energies on his Bath improvements, a decision virtually forced upon him by the pusillanimous withdrawal of his patrons and the opposition of the Bath Corporation to rebuilding the old town. Wood then undertook the building of Queen Square at his own risk

Shakespeare by Enoch Wood

Northern segment of the Bath Circus designed by John Wood the Elder

(completed in 1736). This was followed by the Circus and the partly-finished Forum, developments that represented the fulfilment of one of Wood's earliest dreams.

The fame and success of the Bath project brought Wood further commissions. He was invited to design public buildings in Bristol and Liverpool, and he also designed and built Prior Park, a substantial private mansion on the outskirts of Bath, for Ralph Allen.

Apart from his activities as architect, planner, and builder, Wood also found time to write a number of eccentric historical works. He also wrote, more soberly, about his own approach to building in *An Essay towards a Description of Bath* (1742).

Wood's architectural preeminence in the city of Bath was taken over by his younger son, also John Wood (qv).

Wood, John (1728–81). British architect, town-planner, builder, and writer. Wood, frequently known as John Wood the Younger, was trained as assistant to his father (John Wood the Elder, qv), who seems to have had uncommon paternal confidence in his offspring. In 1749, when Wood the Younger was only 21, his father left him in charge of the building of the New Exchange at Liverpool.

After his father's death, Wood continued with the project for improving Bath, completing the Circus, and adding the Royal Crescent. He was a designer of rare range and versatility, characteristics exhibited in his designs for the palatial New Assembly Rooms and the more modest Hot Bath. Wood also designed buildings outside Bath, notably Buckland House in Berkshire

Shepherd and shepherdess by Ralph Wood, c 1775

and Tregenna Castle in Cornwall. He published *A Series of Plans for Cottages or Habitations of the Labourer* (1781).

Wood, Ralph (1715–72), and his son Ralph (1748–95). British potters. The Woods were the most important mid-eighteenth-century English makers of earthenware figures and Toby jugs. Ralph Wood the elder probably began making figures in the 1750s. They were moulded in cream-coloured earthenware, and though the Woods used the oxide-stained glazes that Whieldon (qv) had developed, they contrived to keep the colours separate by painting them on carefully with a brush instead of allowing the colours to mingle together. Some figures were uncoloured, being covered with a colourless lead glaze. The Woods were the first of the English figure-makers to mark their ware with impressed names, R WOOD for the father and RA WOOD for the son.

The figures vary in subject and complexity; some are beautifully modelled equestrian figures of such different characters as St George, William III, and Hudibras; others are contemporary figures like Alderman Sir William Beckford, twice lord mayor of London. There were satirical groups such as The Vicar and Moses, a number of classical and allegorical figures, and many charming rustic characters and models of animals. The introduction of the popular Toby jug is attributed to the elder Wood, and many variations were produced. The Woods' figures are simply and economically modelled, and the beautiful colour of the glazes was never surpassed.

Wood ware, wooden ware. Alternative and more colloquial terms for treen (qv).

Worcester porcelain. The Worcester Royal Porcelain factory (once a glassmaking factory owned by William Lowdin) originated in Bristol c 1748, and moved to Worcester in 1752.

The main ingredient of the Worcester soft-paste porcelain body was soap-rock, which had been discovered in Cornwall, probably by William Cookworthy. The porcelain made from this material was of a very good quality, and soap-rock continued to be used until c 1823, when it was superseded by bone china.

The early Bristol porcelain was covered with a bluish glaze and

Worcester cup and saucer, c 1780

decorated with oriental designs in blue, and occasionally polychrome. In 1751 Dr John Wall, Richard and Joseph Holdship, and William Davis were among the signatories in a partnership agreement. John Wall eventually (1772) became head of the factory. After a number of changes, in 1862 the firm became the Worcester Royal Porcelain Company.

In 1757 Robert Hancock went to work at Worcester. He had been employed at the Battersea enamel works where transfer printing had been perfected, and brought the secret of the technique with him. He stayed with the firm until 1774. By 1760 the factory was producing the earliest outline transfer prints to be coloured in by hand.

The earliest Worcester porcelain was either oriental in character or inspired by the work of contemporary silversmiths. A particularly beautiful scale-blue pattern was much used, and porcelain decorated with armorial bearings was also made. The Sèvres factory had a marked influence in the 1770–80 period, when pieces were elaborately gilded. Pretty fluted shapes decorated with gilt or coloured flowers were very popular.

The Worcester glaze was of a greenish hue, and it never crazed (qv).

The crescent mark of the Worcester factory, in underglaze blue or overglaze enamel, was a common factory mark. A swash capital W was also used in underglaze blue. Pseudo-Chinese seal marks, again in blue, are found on the orientally inspired pieces, and the crossed swords of Meissen were 'borrowed'. Some pieces were marked with an anchor and a capital H (which was the rebus mark for Hold-

ship), and the pieces by Robert Hancock were marked with his initials, RH.

Work table. Known also as a sewing or pouch table and widely produced in the late eighteenth and early nineteenth centuries. It is a small, elegant table of mahogany or satinwood, with fitted drawers, compartments for reels and bobbins, and usually a suspended silk bag in which light sewing could be kept. There was frequently a screen at the back to shield the needlewoman from the fire. Most work tables have four tapered legs, but some nineteenth-century examples are on a pedestal base. A rare variant has a folding top that sometimes incorporated a veneered or inlaid games board.

Wormley, Edward (b 1907). American designer and interior decorator, a winner of the Elsie de Wolfe Award. He studied at the Art Institute of Chicago (1926–7) and then went to work

American work table by Duncan Phyfe

Sir Christopher Wren from a painting by Sir Godfrey Kneller, 1711

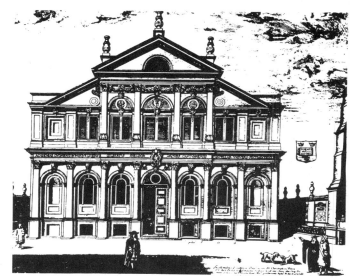

The Sheldonian Theatre, Oxford, by Sir Christopher Wren, 1664-9

The Chapel, Pembroke College, Cambridge, by Wren, 1663-5

in the design studio of Marshall Field in Chicago. In 1931 he joined the Dunbar Furniture Corporation, where he became director of design.

Wreathed column. A column with a spiral shaft. It was used in the late Roman Empire, and revived in the Baroque era. The most famous examples are on Bernini's *Baldacchino* at St Peter's, Rome, where the spiral is relieved by small flowers and bees, symbols of the Barbarini family.

Wren, Christopher (1632–1723). British architect. Wren was the son of the rector at East Knoyle in Wiltshire. He was educated at Westminster School and Wadham College, Oxford, where he became interested in scientific studies (at first anatomy, and later astronomy); he also showed uncommon skill and invention in constructing scientific models, qualities that were to stand him in good stead when he became an architect.

In 1653 Wren became a fellow of All Souls, and in 1657 was appointed professor of astronomy at Gresham College, London. He returned to Oxford in 1661 as Savilian professor of astronomy. He was offered the post of surveyor-general of the royal works and asked to supervise the fortifications of Tangier (then a British possession); but he declined on grounds of ill-health. He did, however, accept an appointment to sit on the Commission for repairing St Paul's, then in a sad state of decay. This gradual transition from scientific inquiry to architecture was not particularly remarkable in an age when all men of taste were expected to have a practical acquaintance with the subject.

Wren's architectural career proper began under family patronage. His uncle, the Bishop of Ely, commissioned him to design a new chapel for Pembroke College, Cambridge. The competence and assurance of the design led to his being asked to undertake that of the Sheldonian Theatre at Oxford. Borrowing his decorative theme from ancient Rome, but incorporating his own structural ingenuities in the design of the roof – aided by advice from the professor of geometry – Wren created a building that assured his architectural future. He was then asked to prepare designs for a new building for Trinity College, Oxford. In 1665 Wren made his solitary excursion abroad in order to survey 'the most esteemed Fabricks of Paris', a journey which has led to a good deal of French influence being read into his works by foreign critics.

Soon after Wren's return, the Great Fire of London made the rebuilding of the City of London – including St Paul's – a matter of urgency. Within a remarkably short time, Wren presented the king with plans for a logical replanning and rebuilding of the City. However, this would have necessitated the agreement of a multitude of land- and house-owners. The exigencies of the situation caused reconstruction to begin on the old haphazard lines, and Wren's imaginative plan remained on paper.

His appointment as one of the six commissioners responsible for the rebuilding of the 52 London churches led to happier results.

The north façade and crossing of St Paul's Cathedral, by Wren

In this project Wren displayed a combination of inventiveness, and versatility, planning ability, and structural ingenuity that is unsurpassed in the history of English architecture. Among the churches designed by Wren himself were St Stephen Walbrook, probably the greatest of all; St Clement Danes; St James's, Piccadilly; St Dunstan-in-the-East; St Bride's; St Mary-le-Bow; and St Vedast. Meanwhile. coincident with the design of the City churches, Wren was involved in the long drawn-out task of redesigning St Paul's Cathedral, as much an exercise in diplomacy as architecture. The first or Great Model (1673) was liked by Wren's intellectual peers but found little favour among the ecclesiastical hierarchy. This was followed by the Warrant Design (1675), which redressed the traditional cathedral plan within a classical form, although the original design was considerably amended as the building progressed.

In 1669 Charles II appointed Wren surveyor-general of the king's works. This was no sinecure, but a job involving much designing and administrative work, and impelled Wren to relinquish his Oxford professorship four years later.

During the next two decades he was given further appointments, taking over the comptrollership at Windsor and the surveyorship of the royal palace at Greenwich following the decision that it should become the Naval Hospital. He also designed the Military Hospital at Chelsea, and was deeply involved in the repair of Westminster Abbey. Thanks to his great reputation, Wren retained these appointments, despite his Tory connections, even after the Whigs came to power in 1668. In 1718, when he was 86, he was supplanted as surveyor-general by William Benson, but retained his surveyorships of St Paul's and Westminster Abbey.

Despite his comparatively late start as an architect, Wren's long life and unfailing creativity has left a considerable body of work which can be authoritatively attributed to him. There are, besides, a huge number of buildings by his imitators which are falsely attributed to him. Primarily, of course, his fame rests on St Paul's, but his City churches, collegiate buildings at both Oxford and **Cambridge**, public buildings, and **a number** of private houses would **in any case** place him at the very forefront of British architects.

527

Frank Lloyd Wright

Winslow House, River Forest, Illinois, by Frank Lloyd Wright, 1893

Wright, Frank Lloyd (1867–1959). American architect. Wright's education was somewhat irregular. As a child he was greatly influenced by his mother, whose passion for Froebel's teaching methods, with their emphasis on model-making with block units, was possibly decisive. Then after his father had abandoned his wife and family, Wright spent much of his boyhood on an uncle's farm at Madison in Wisconsin, an experience which gave him a lasting love of the countryside and rural values. A job as apprentice, and later supervisor, for a local builder enabled Wright to study engineering at Wisconsin University in his spare time.

When he was 18, Wright left Madison for Chicago, and took a job in the drawing office of Lyman Silsbee, a designer of conventional but pleasant houses for the city's businessmen. In 1887 he entered the firm of Adler and Sullivan, which had recently been commissioned to design the new Chicago Auditorium.

After an unhappy start in the drawing office, Wright's talent and his growing involvement with the Auditorium building gained him a private office adjacent to that of Louis Sullivan.

He went on to supervise the transportation building for the World's Fair Exhibition in 1893, and also undertook most of the designs for houses that came into the office. In this latter capacity he began to show the highly individual characteristics that were to make him internationally famous. In Charnley House (1891), a three-storey design of Neo-classical symmetry, conventional architectural adornment was almost wholly absent, although he did introduce Art Nouveau motifs derived from Sullivan's taste for them, a decorative touch Wright was to indulge throughout his career. The success of Wright's designs for houses brought him an increasing number of commissions, which he undertook outside the Sullivan practice. The discovery of these extra-mural commissions caused a lasting rift between Sullivan and Wright, who thereupon set up on his own.

One of his first commissions was the now-famous Winslow House in River Forest, a suburb of Chicago. The horizontal emphasis so successfully achieved in what was nominally a conventional two-storey house, and the subtle spatial and textural means whereby that emphasis was maintained in exterior and interior, led Wright towards designs for a group of houses in which horizontality was the overriding theme. These so-called Prairie Houses – most of which were built on Chicago suburban sites – remain among his most revolutionary and enduring

achievements; the 'Prairie' label derives from their subtle and sophisticated echoes of the low-built, earth-tied, rugged, and seemingly rambling ranch houses. They were essentially American houses, owing nothing to European prototypes. Even the Win-

The Unity Church, Oak Park, Illinois, by Wright, 1906

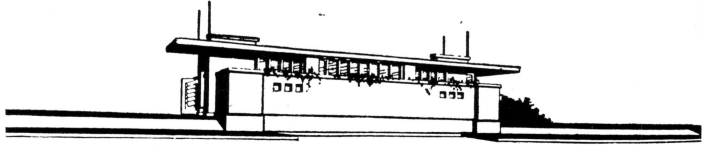

Project for the Yahara Boat Club, Madison, Wisconsin, by Frank Lloyd Wright, 1902

slow House seems a four-square structure compared with the Martin House, Buffalo, New York (1904), or Robie House, Chicago (1909). The exteriors were dominated by vast low-pitched roof planes, with deep soffits, set above massive, low-set frames with extensive terraces linking house and landscape. Their interiors were interdependent spaces, flowing one into another, far removed from the conventional assembly of cubic boxes. The Prairie Houses have now influenced American domestic architecture for over half a century, and thousands of imitations and adaptations are built annually. Wright's success was reflected in an increasing number of non-domestic commissions. Some, such as a project for the Yahara Boat Club, Madison, remained drawing-board exercises, but others were built, and added to Wright's international reputation, eg the Larkin Building at Buffalo, New York, the first air-conditioned office-block, and the Unity Church, Oak Park, Illinois. Partly for reasons connected with his stormy private life, Wright spent two years in Europe; he returned to the USA to start the first building of his own home, Taliesin East, which was greatly influenced by his interest in traditional Japanese architecture.

Wright's return to the USA brought him further commissions, notably the Midway Garden restaurant in Chicago (1914), although he returned to Japan to design and supervise the building of the Imperial Hotel in Tokyo (1916), which incorporated many technical innovations to counteract the silt-like soil of the foundations and the possibility of earthquake shock. The project required Wright's residence in Japan until 1921. In 1923 the hotel withstood severe earthquake shocks when much of Tokyo was destroyed, an event which has become an architectural legend.

For some years after this, Wright seemed to be marking time. His continuing preoccupation with what he termed 'organic Architecture', and his use of surface decoration, set him apart from the exponents of the austere International style (qv). His championship of the organic architecture and designation of the International style was one of many controversies in which he engaged.

Wright's interest in designing houses never diminished. His Kaufmann house, 'Falling Water' at Bear Run, Pennsylvania, de-

The interior of the Honeycomb House designed by Frank Lloyd Wright

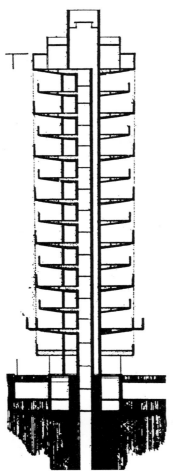

Johnson Tower structure

The S C Johnson Building in Racine, Wisconsin, by Wright, 1950

A house in Arizona designed by Frank Lloyd Wright, 1959

A George III writing chair

signed in 1936, was perhaps the most beautiful of all his houses, with a group of rooms and balconies dramatically cantilevered over a waterfall.

Wright came rather later than his great contemporaries to the design of skyscrapers, despite his early experience with Sullivan; it was not until after World War II that he was given his first commissions for tower buildings. In these he once again demonstrated his extraordinary flair as a designer and technical innovator. The first was his building for a laboratory tower (1950) for the S C Johnson Wax Company at Racine, Wisconsin. This was the final unit in an industrial complex on which Wright had been working since 1930; its now well-known structural principles – floors, based on mushroom-shaped supports – were questioned at the time but in the event proved wholly successful.

Wright's inventiveness showed no signs of diminishing in old age, rather the reverse. Projects and ideas flowed from his pen. Many were of astounding imaginative scope (such as his scheme for a mile-high dwelling tower-cum-town, and were backed by new technological skills which Wright seemed to master with rare ease. While he was supervising new campus buildings for the Florida Southern College at Lakeland, which occupied much of his energies as a designer during the last 20 years of his life, he was also making influential experiments in building with what he termed 'desert concrete.' This involved using huge blocks of natural stone, which were abundantly available in the desert areas of Arizona, to build a new range of houses almost as influential as Prairie Houses. Such activities were all part of Wright's passion for organic architecture. At the same time, his lifelong interest in the basic geometric forms were demonstrated in one of his last

executed designs, for the Guggenheim Museum (1956–9).

Throughout his long life Wright was a ferocious controversialist. His contempt for contemporary building technique and conventional *mores*, inevitably aroused the enmity of more conventional architects and other citizens. Yet youthful architects and designers responded enthusiastically to his teachings and flocked to his seminary-workshops at 'Taliesin West' near Phoenix in Arizona. He remains by far the greatest of all American architects.

Writing-chair. An early eighteenth-century armchair with three cabriole legs in front and a fourth behind, though this is sometimes just a straight support. The top rail has a serpentine curve and usually rests upon three carved or moulded supports and two baluster-shaped splats. There is no evidence to support the idea that this type of chair was intended specifically for writing. It is also known as a corner chair.

Writing-desk or **writing-table.** Writing-tables became popular in the mid-eighteenth century and enjoyed great popularity over the next half-century – an age when letter-writing and journal-keeping were middle- and upper-class pastimes. Chippendale showed designs for writing-tables in his *Director* (1762 edition), but the most inventive and ingenious designs were introduced by Thomas Shearer in his *Cabinet Maker's London Book of Prices and Designs of Cabinet Work* (1788; 2nd edition 1793). These designs ranged from a cylinder-fall writing-table, 'three foot long, one drawer in front, cockheaded, three small drawers, three sham ditto and six letter holes inside', on plain tapered legs, to a rising-top writing-table, and from a 'kidney writing-table' to a lady's writing fire screen.

Writing fire screen. A combined writing-table and screen

The Guggenheim Museum, New York, by Wright, 1959

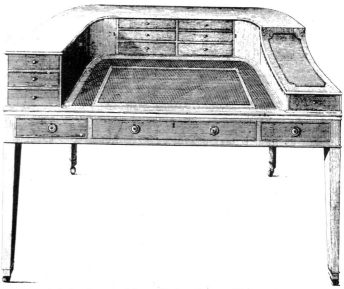

A design for a writing table by Thomas Shearer, 1793

Wrought-iron hinge work on a door in a 12th century Abbey

which enabled the writer to sit before the fire without discomfort. The tall carcase acted as a screen, but was raised on legs so that the writer could warm his feet. He worked at a full-front desk fitted with drawers and compartments; below was a cupboard.

Wrought-ironwork. The smelting and working of iron, one of the more ancient of mankind's crafts, seems to have been carried out in central Europe and the Near East over 3,000 years ago.

Early examples of wrought-ironwork are rare, for the metal, despite its strength, oxidises fairly quickly, rusts, and disappears. Its strength led to its use for innumerable utilitarian articles, but in those early times its intractability precluded sophisticated decorative work.

Among the earliest examples of decorative ironwork are the hinges of doors on ecclesiastical buildings, which have survived thanks to protective coverings of

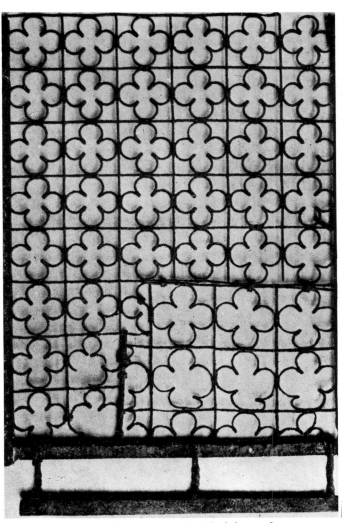

A section of a gate at Chichester Cathedral, late 15th century

The wrought-iron 'fish' gate at Kinross House in Scotland

paint or gilding.

With increasing technical skills, the work of the ironsmith became more intricate, complex, and cursive, so that quite early church grilles are beautifully if naïvely decorated. These examples were forged with the hammer while the metal was at white or red heat; but during the fourteenth century, smiths began to work the metal cold, and additional tools such as the saw and file became part of the

Balcony railings, 18th century

A low wrought-iron gate in Baroque style

Wrought-iron gate at Cliveden

A wrought-iron fanlight designed by Robert Adam

Design for stairway rotunda for Drury Lane Theatre by B D Wyatt

craftsman's armoury. Most of this work was in the Gothic manner, well suited to the techniques of the ironsmith. Superb ironwork was produced in Europe from Renaissance times, but there was little English work of significance until the arrival of the Huguenot smith Jean Tijou in the late seventeenth century. During the nineteenth century the craft of wrought-ironwork was virtually extinguished by the production of cheap cast-iron decorative units for balconies and balustrades.

Wyatt family. The members of this family were influential in English, Welsh, and Irish building for almost a century. Their geographical range was as wide as their aesthetic range, extending from Government House in Calcutta (built in 1805 to the designs of Charles Wyatt, 1759–1819, nephew of James Wyatt) to the Marine Baths in Penrhyn in Wales (designed by Benjamin Wyatt, 1745–1818, brother of James); from Castle Coole at Fermanagh in Ireland (built between 1790 and 1797 to the design of James Wyatt, qv) to the restoration of Windsor Castle by

Jeffry Wyatt (later Sir Jeffry Wyatville, qv).

The progenitor of this extraordinary family was Benjamin Wyatt (1709–72), who combined building and architecture in his native county of Staffordshire. He had seven sons, five of whom became architects. The most notable being James Wyatt.

Benjamin Dean Wyatt (1775–1850) was the eldest son and pupil of James Wyatt, but after leaving Oxford under a cloud, went to India as writer in the East India Company. After his return to England he set up as an architect and succeeded in securing the commission to design Drury Lane Theatre (to the expressed distress of his father who wanted the commission for a younger son). Benjamin Wyatt succeeded his father as surveyor of Westminster Abbey.

James Wyatt (1746–1813) was the sixth son of Benjamin Wyatt. At the age of 16 he was sent to Italy, where he remained for six years, studying architecture in Venice and Rome.

While still in his early twenties, he was given the commission to design the Pantheon in Oxford Street, a projected winter version

of the popular Ranelagh pleasure gardens. Although the commission had been obtained through family influence, the quality of the Pantheon was immediately acknowledged, and established Wyatt as both a professional and a social success.

When he was 30 Wyatt succeeded to the surveyorship of Westminster Abbey; he later was appointed surveyor of the ordnance. Following the death of Chambers in 1796, he was appointed surveyor-general and comptroller of the works. These official positions, combined with his very considerable private practice, made him the leading architect of the time, despite the fact that his working methods were often obviously negligent.

Wyatt's practice included work on several Oxford collegiate buildings, many churches, and an enormous number of country houses, on which his reputation is mainly based. He also built the

extraordinary Fonthill Abbey (begun in 1796), with a 225 ft tower that collapsed in 1825, for the writer William Beckford. Wyatt established no highly original manner; his work was characterized by a resilient eclecticism, drawing on the architectural manner of Sir William Chambers, and the decorative manner of Robert Adam, who was moved to protest at Wyatt's plagiarisms. His most positive architectural achievement was his curiously successful exploitation of a decorative if somewhat unscholarly Gothic. He invested the more obvious motifs and devices of the style with a freshness and lightness which aroused the ire of antiquaries, but undoubtedly satisfied his clients. Most of his country houses have a charm frequently lacking in the more sober classical and the more earnest Gothic work. His remodelling of Sandleford Priory, Berkshire (1780–1) and Wycombe

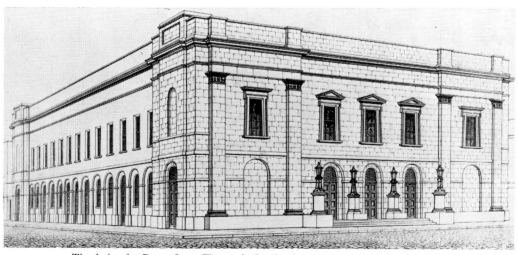

The design for Drury Lane Theatre in London by Benjamin Dean Wyatt, 1811-12

James Wyatt

The designs for the exterior and interior of the Pantheon in Oxford Street, London, designed by James Wyatt

Abbey, Buckinghamshire (1804), are typical of his manner.

Samuel Wyatt (1737–1807) was the third son of Benjamin Wyatt. Although never as famous as his brother James, he did acquire a very considerable and varied practice. He built several country houses, some of such distinction that they have been attributed to James Wyatt repeatedly; the façade of the Theatre Royal, Birmingham (1780); and Trinity House, London (1793–5). He also, in the manner of the time, went in for speculative building enterprises, in which he was joined by his brothers James and George.

His reputation was sufficiently high for him to succeed Robert Adam as clerk of the works at Chelsea Hospital (1792).

Wyatville, Sir Jeffry (1766–1840). British architect. Wyatville was born Wyatt, the son of an unsuccessful brother of the architect James Wyatt (qv). He served lengthy apprenticeships with each of his two uncles, first Samuel, then James, and only set up in independent practice when in his thirties. He was quickly successful, and soon established profitable building and designing contracts in London, particularly in Pimlico. At first he designed in the classical manner, but he soon began to specialize in the Gothic style for domestic and collegiate buildings. This brought him to the notice of George IV, who gave him the most important commission of his career: the series of alterations and renovations that he carried out at Windsor Castle between 1820 and 1840. This included remodelling the Upper Ward and raising the height of the Round Tower.

For this work he was authorized by the king to call himself Wyatville (in order, it is said, to distinguish him from James Wyatt, who had previously worked at Windsor) and was knighted in 1828. Wyatville also conducted a highly successful practice, mainly concerned with churches and country mansions. He completed Ashridge in Hertfordshire after James Wyatt's death, and was responsible for Dinton House, near Salisbury (1813–16), Lypiat Park in Gloucestershire (1809), and Bradby Hall (1813–15), all notably Gothic in architectural style.

Fonthill Abbey in Wiltshire designed by James Wyatt, 1786

George IV's Gateway at Windsor, redesigned by Wyatville, 1824–37

Sheffield Place, Sussex, enlarged and gothicized by James Wyatt

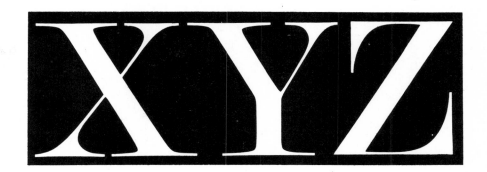

X-frame, X-shape chair, X-shape frame, X-stool; X-stretcher; X-table. In furniture a basic frame consisting of the crossed strokes of the letter X. The simplest X-form is to be seen in the legs of folding stools, of which examples with leather seats are extant from ancient Egypt.

An early reproduction from a *Book of Hours* shows a monastic scribe seated on a more elaborate form of X-framed chair. Here the crossed members have become virtually two opposed semicircles, one used as base and legs, the upper underpinning the seat.

The early velvet-covered seventeenth-century chair has a double X-frame, front and back. A similar but simpler form is also used in the construction of modern metal chairs. The X-form also has been used in a horizontal form for the strengthening and bracing of chair legs; it was widely employed during the seventeenth century for walnut chairs.

The X-form was further popularized by Thomas Hope's revival of ancient Egyptian forms. Stools based on his designs became almost standard for use at ladies' dressing-tables, and continue to be popular.

Yamasaki, Minoru (*b* 1912). American architect. Yamasaki was born in Seattle, where he was educated before studying architecture at Washington and New York. He worked for leading New York architectural firms and the Raymond Loewy industrial design organization, then moved to Detroit and became chief designer for Smith, Hinchman, and Grylls. In 1949, with two associates from the firm, Joseph Leinweber and Hellmuth, Yamasaki set up in independent practice to design a large housing

X-frame chair in a French illumination, 1400

X-frame chair in a room designed by Hope, c 1800

X-shaped stool, c 1807

Ancient bronze table

Upholstered chair, c 1640

Chair by Hope, c 1807

Minoru Yamasaki

Zimmermann. *The interior of Die Wies church in Upper Bavaria designed by Dominikus Zimmermann, 1745-54*

The Northwestern National Life Insurance Company, Minneapolis, Minnesota, by Yamasaki

World Trade centre in New York; project by Yamasaki, 1963

project in St Louis, Missouri. The firm gained international notice with its designs for the St Louis airport (1935–55), one of the first thin shell concrete structures in the United States. Its three pairs of soaring, 120 ft span barrel vaults spring from small point supports. With its dramatic roofing and glazed ends and sides, the building is one of the first to break away from the rectilinear International style. Later, based in Detroit, Yamasaki was responsible for several buildings in the city which aroused international interest, notably those for the American Concrete Institute (1958) and the Reynolds Metals Office (1959). He also designed the US pavilion at the New Delhi Fair (1960) and the Century 21 Exposition at Seattle (1962).

Yamasaki has consistently shown himself to be one of the most eclectic and sensitive architects in the USA, evolving designs sympathetic to the *genius loci* of other lands and other cultures. This is well shown in his design for the Dhahran Air Terminal in Saudi Arabia.

Yew. *Taxus.* Because of its close-grained toughness, yew has been used in furniture-making for many centuries, while its response to a high polish made it a favourite wood for inlay and veneered effects from the seventeenth century onwards. In the Regency period, yew was used along with maple-wood and amboyna. In recent years it has been widely used in the manufacture of reproduction furniture.

Yoke-back chair. American term for eighteenth-century

F R S Yorke

chairs in which the curving top rail resembles an ox yoke.

Yorke, Francis Reginald Stevens (1906–62). British architect. Yorke was born at Stratford-

A modern military couch in yew wood

A house at Iver, Buckinghamshire, by Yorke, 1936

A project for a shopping centre in a modern city, by F R S Yorke and Marcel Breuer, 1936

Adrian D Zakharov

on-Avon in Warwickshire, was educated at Chipping Campden Grammar School, and received his architectural training at the Birmingham School of Architecture. He was one of the first British architects to be influenced by Continental theories of modern architecture; and was a founder-member of MARS (the Modern Architectural Research Group).

From 1935 to 1938 Yorke was in partnership with Marcel Breuer, whose Bauhaus background increased Yorke's interest in modern design and helped to make him a pioneer of the International style in Britain.

After World War II, Yorke went into partnership with

Eugene Rosenberg and Cyril Mardall. The firm was one of the first to be commissioned to design a post-war school: the Barclay Secondary School at Stevenage in Hertfordshire. As a result of this commission, Yorke, Rosenberg and Mardall was established as one of the leading modern architectural firms in Britain.

Yorke was a patron as well as an architect, seeking out the work of living artists and encouraging clients to commission such work. At Stevenage he persuaded the local education authorities to accept the now-famous Henry Moore *Family Group*.

Yorke's last work was the London offices of his firm; built

in 1961, for which he was awarded the RIBA bronze medal in 1962.

Yorkshire chair. A form of chair made during the seventeenth century, usually of oak and with a carved back panel or wainscot. It is unlikely that this form of chair originated in Yorkshire; the term probably derives from its prevalence in that county.

Yorkshire dresser. A type of oak or deal dresser which differs only slightly from the Welsh dresser (ie with cupboards below and open shelves above). It is sometimes claimed that the Yorkshire dresser has a lower back.

Zakharov, Adrian Dmitrievich (1761–1811). Russian architect. Zakharov was born in St Petersburg and trained there at the Academy of Arts, graduating with the Grand Gold Medal at the age of 21. He continued his architectural studies for four years in Paris under the French architect Jean François Chalgrin (1739–1811), and then travelled in Italy. He returned to St Petersburg in 1787 to teach at the Academy of Arts.

Zakharov designed bridges over the Neva, the extension of the Academy of Sciences in St Petersburg, the church of St Andrew at Kronstadt, and the Gatchina monastery. In 1805 he was appointed chief architect to the Admiralty, and authorized to prepare designs for what is now the great Admiralty building

in Leningrad, begun in 1806 and not completed until after the architect's death. This immense building, over a quarter of a mile in length, is dominated by a central section comprising a great entrance crowned with a spire. The side elevations, in the shape of pavilions, are pierced by round-headed gateways. Zakharov had a pre-eminent position amongst Russian Neo-classical architects, and is regarded by some authorities as the greatest Russian architect.

The Admiralty at Leningrad by Zakharov, 1806-23

A side pavilion of the Admiralty, Leningrad, by Zakharov, 1806-23

An English zebrawood secrétaire, 19th century

Zebra-wood. A highly decorative South American wood, golden in colour and streaked with variegated shades of darker brown. It was popularly employed as a veneer during the late eighteenth century, chiefly in the form of cross-bandings. Zebrawood is used for complete surfaces in contemporary furniture work.

Ziggurat or **Zikkurat.** A temple tower in the form of a stepped pyramid. Ziggurats were built of brick and erected in most of the important cities of Mesopotamia *c* 2200–500 BC. 25 have now been located, of which Ur is the best preserved.

Zimmermann, Dominikus (1685–1766). South German architect especially famous for the Rococo pilgrimage churches of Steinhausen (1728–31) and Die Wies (1745–54).

Zimmermann's training and early work was as a stuccoist and master-mason, and only around 1718 did he begin executing his own architectural designs. Most of these are ecclesiastical: Zimmermann's contribution to church design lay in that he made use of the oval plan, most clearly demonstrated in the major churches already mentioned. His designing and decoration of these was assisted by his brother, Johann Baptist Zimmermann, also a stuccoist and fresco painter of considerable reputation.

The interior of Die Wies has a wonderful, delicately-coloured plasterwork; the streaming light at cornice level and above produces an impression of soaring lightness and airiness. The particular brand of Rococo that the Zimmermanns produced at Die Wies uses Germanic naturalistic motifs and fuses the French sense of light and movement with the heavier and more fluid Bavarian taste. The result is an original contribution to the late Baroque and Rococo architecture of southern Germany.

Zoophorus (Greek, 'bearing figures of animals'). A frieze decorated with representations of animals.

Zucchi, Antonio (1726–95). Italian decorative painter. Zucchi was born in Venice and

A drawing room decorated by Zucchi to designs by Adam, 1722-54

instructed in the rudiments of perspective and architectural draughtsmanship by his uncle, Carlo Zucchi. He probably met Robert Adam, who visited Italy between 1754 and 1758, and later encouraged Zucchi to come to England. In London he married Angelica Kauffman (qv).

Although the marriage was scarcely a connubial success, the husband-and-wife team carried out a considerable number of commissions, usually under Adam's close direction, at Osterley, Kenwood, Harewood, Kedleston, the Adelphi, and elsewhere.

The church of S Maria at Steinbach, Bavaria, by D Zimmermann, 1746

Die Wies in Upper Bavaria by Zimmermann, 1745-54

Ziggurat. *A 17th century engraving of the Tower of Babel, an ancient ziggurat*

ACKNOWLEDGEMENTS

The HOUSE & GARDEN DICTIONARY OF DESIGN & DECORATION originated as a series by Robert Harling, Editor of House & Garden, which was published in the magazine over a number of years. It has proved impracticable to credit each illustration separately but the following list of organizations and individuals acknowledges our debt. Special thanks are due to the Victoria & Albert Museum, The National Monuments Record, Christies, Sothebys and Spinks.

Adams, Holden and Pearson; Alcan Industries; Inga Aistrup; Wayne Andrews; Australian News & Information; Austrian State Tourist Office; Baccarat Crystal; Ralph Bailey; Aldo Ballo; Bayon Bend Collection, Houston; Bazzechi Foto; Johan Berge, Oslo; Mrs P Bicknell; Tet Borsig; Jacques Boucher; Jacques Boulas; P Bressano; Margot Monica Brill; British Museum; British Travel & Holiday Association; Brooklyn Museum; Brown; Bullock and Turner Ltd; Buttermarket Studio; Californians Inc; Mr Mehdi, The Carpet Centre; Cement and Concrete Association; Central Photographic Service Ltd; Samuel Chamberlain; Chomon; City Museums, Stoke on Trent; Walter Civardi, Henry Clarke; B C Clayton; Peter Coats; Joe C Colombo; A C Cooper; Columbus Gallery of Fine Arts, Ohio; Commissariat Général au Tourisme, Paris; Council of Industrial Design; Courtauld Institute of Art; F H Crossley; Cuming Wright-Watson Associates Limited; Currier Gallery of Art, Manchester, New Hants; Danish Tourist Board; Daimler Benz; Wyatt Davis; Demmeler; Anthony Denney; Delamosne; André de Dienes; Frank Donaldson; Essex Institute, Salem, Massachusetts; Bruno Falchi & Liderno Salvador; Fasani; Feher; H Felton; Agneta Fischer; J Fitzpatrick; Ph de Flangergues; Felix Fonteyn; Henry Ford Museum; Raymond Fortt Studios; Hans Frank; French Government Tourist Office; Frick Collection; Ewing Galloway; Alexandre Georges; Kurt Gerlach; German National Tourist Bureau; Ghedina; John Walter Gillies; Ginsburg & Levy Inc; Golderstat; Worshipful Company of Goldsmiths; Goodhart-Rendel; Annette Green; Yves Guillement; Fritz Hansens; Dudley Harris; Harrison; Ray Harw; Hedrich-Blessing Studio; Hennell; Richard Hill; Christopher Holme; Jesper Høm; The Government of India Tourist Office; Italian Cultural Institute; Italian State Tourist Bureau; Irish Georgian Society; Marcus Johnston; Keystone View Co; Balthazar Korab; Landesbildstelle; Edward Leigh; London Daily Express; Nick Malan Studios; John Maltby Ltd; Mann Brothers; Mansell Collection; Eric de Maré; Marler; Richard Merrill Photo; Metropolitan Museum of Art; Gebr Metz, Tübingen; Millar & Harris; Minneapolis Institute of Art; Molzahn–Altheim; Douglas C Morris & Co; Morse Foundation, Minneapolis Institute of Art; Eric H Muller; Museum of Art, Rhode Island; Museum of the City of New York; Museum of Fine Arts, Boston; Gordon McLeish; National Gallery of Art, Washington; National Maritime Museum; National Portrait Gallery; National Park Service US; National Trust; National Trust for Scotland; New Mexico State Tourist Bureau; Sydney W Newbury; Norwegian National Tourist Office; Novosti Press Agency; Homer Page; Norman Parkinson; Peter Parkinson; Pennsylvania State Department of Commerce, Harrisburg, Pennsylvania; K Helmer Peterson; Philadelphia Museum of Art; Phillips Son & Neale; Pierpoint Morgan Library; Pilgrim Society, Plymouth, Massachusetts; Pilkington Bros, Ltd; Henry Francis Du Pont; Presse–und Informationsamt der Bundesregierung; Radio Times Hulton Picture Library; Renner, Frankfurt; Hans Retzlaff; Andrew Rhodes; Rieger; Willy Ronis; John Rose and John Dyble; Jean Roublier; Derek Rowe Ltd; Royal Institute of British Architects; Royal Pavilion Art Gallery and Museums, Brighton; Satour; The Scalamandre Museum of Textiles; J Scheerboom; Gottscho-Schleisner; The Shaker Museum; Julius Shulman; Martin Simmonds; Sleepy Hollow Restorations; Sperryn's Ltd; Edwin Smith; Percy Smith; Smithsonian Institute; Henk Snoek; Ezra Stoller Associates; Freddie Squires Ltd; Staatsbibliotek Berlin; Standard Oil Co; Steuben Glass; Bert Stern; Strüwing; Studio Bersani; Peter Suschitzky; H N Taunt; Taylor's; Sven Thony; Ralph R Thompson; The Times; Charles Gordian Troeller; Turkish Tourist Information Office; United States Information Service; United States Travel Service; J A Viguier; Wallace Collection; Josiah Wedgwood & Sons Ltd; Colin Westwood; Michael Wickham; Ray Williams; Thomas L Williams, Colonial Williamsburg; J Wingrove; Winterthur Museum; G B Wood; Geoffrey N Wright.